HOUSE OF LORDS

Select Committee on the Barnett Formula

1st Report of Session 2008–09

The Barnett Formula

Report with Evidence

Ordered to be printed 9 July 2009 and published 17 July 2009

Published by the Authority of the House of Lords

London: The Stationery Office Limited
£13.50

HL Paper 139

The Barnett Formula Committee

The Select Committee on the Barnett Formula was appointed by the House of Lords on 10 December 2008 with the orders of reference "To examine the purpose, methodology and application of the Barnett Formula as a means of determining funding for the Devolved Administrations of the United Kingdom, to assess the effectiveness of the calculation mechanism to meet its purpose and to consider alternative mechanisms.

These orders of reference *exclude* consideration of three main areas:

- The overall system of funding the Devolved Administrations – in particular the question of whether greater tax-raising powers should be accorded to the devolved administrations;
- Other political aspects of the devolution settlements; and
- The distribution of funds within the different regions of the United Kingdom".

Membership

Lord Forsyth of Drumlean
Baroness Hollis of Heigham
Lord Lang of Monkton
Lord Lawson of Blaby
Earl of Mar and Kellie
Lord Moser
Lord Richard (Chairman)
Lord Rooker
Lord Rowe-Beddoe
Lord Sewel
Lord Smith of Clifton
Lord Trimble

Mr Alan Trench, Research Fellow in the School of Law at the University of Edinburgh and Mr Peter Kenway, Director of the New Policy Institute, were appointed as Specialist Advisers for the inquiry.

Information about the Committee and Publications

Information about the Select Committee on the Barnett Formula can be found on the internet at http://www.parliament.uk/hlbarnettformula. Committee publications, including reports, press notices, transcripts of evidence and government responses to reports, can be found at the same address.

Committee reports are published by The Stationery Office by Order of the House.

General Information.

General Information about the House of Lords and its Committees, including guidance to witnesses, details of current inquiries and forthcoming meetings is on the internet at: http://www.parliament.uk/about_lords/about_lords.cfm

Contacts for the Barnett Formula Committee

All correspondence should be addressed to:
The Clerk of the Ad Hoc Committee, Committee Office, House of Lords, London SW1A 0PW

The telephone number for general enquiries is 020 7219 4878.

CONTENTS

NOTE: Reference in the text of the report are as follows:
(Q) refers to a question in oral evidence
(p) refers to a page of written evidence

SUMMARY

The Barnett Formula is the mechanism used by the United Kingdom Government to allocate more than half of total public expenditure in Scotland, Wales and Northern Ireland.

The Formula has been used for the last thirty years to determine the annual increase in allocation (the increment). Each year these increments are added on to the previous year's allocation (the baseline) to create what is now a significant block grant of funds. The Formula accounted for almost £49 billion of public spending in 2007-08. Despite the political changes within the United Kingdom the Formula has continued to be used. The Formula has been neither reviewed nor revised during the last thirty years.

There is both increasing debate on the future funding of the devolved administrations and increasing scepticism about the fairness of the Barnett Formula which may be exacerbated by any deterioration in the public finances.

We have concluded that the Barnett Formula should no longer be used to determine annual increases in the block grant for the United Kingdom's devolved administrations.

Although the annual increment in funds is made on the basis of recent population figures, the baseline—accumulated over the last thirty years—does not reflect today's population in the devolved administrations. The Barnett Formula also takes no account of the relative needs of any of the devolved administrations.

A new system which allocates resources to the devolved administrations based on an explicit assessment of their relative needs should be introduced. Those devolved administrations which have greater needs should receive more funding, per head of population, than those with lesser needs. Such a system must above all be simple, clear and comprehensible. It must also be dynamic: able to be kept up to date in order to respond to changing needs across the United Kingdom.

The precise details of a new system are not defined in this report. Rather we set out broadly how a new system might be determined. However we are satisfied that an alternative to the Barnett Formula that meets the criteria we have set out can be achieved. The process of reviewing the grant allocation and the range of functions needed to make the new system work should be carried out by a new independent expert body perhaps called the United Kingdom Funding Commission.

The Commission should begin its work by determining a new baseline based on up to date population figures and an assessment of relative needs. Relative needs should be decided by using a small number of need indicators. The Commission should then conduct a periodic assessment to review the allocation. Some factors affecting the grant allocation should be adjusted automatically and annually as new statistics are published. In addition a periodic review of the baseline should be carried out by the Commission.

There will need to be a transition period to bring the baselines and the levels of funding under the new system into full effect. The transition to the new system could be asymmetric, reflecting both the nature of the United Kingdom's devolved administrations and the differing levels of funds devolved to them. We anticipate that the level of increased grants due under the new system could be reached within three years and that where grant is to be reduced it could be phased over a longer period, preferably not exceeding seven years, depending on the degree of change.

This inquiry was designed to examine the operation of the Barnett Formula; whether it should be replaced and, if so, by what. We have concluded that it is now time for the Formula to be changed. This report demonstrates that a formula based on relative need is a practical possibility.

CONCLUSIONS AND RECOMMENDATIONS

The advantages of the Barnett Formula—simplicity, stability and the absence of ring-fencing—are important and should be maintained whatever the future method of allocating funds to the devolved administrations (para 51).

The changing populations of the devolved administrations and the failure of the Formula to take account of population changes over time within the baseline create a significant problem for the Barnett Formula today. In our view, the resulting per capita allocations are arbitrary and unfair. In essence the baseline of the grant provides funds for a level of population that has changed (para 56).

On every funding decision the Treasury is judge in its own cause, including whether to bypass or include any expenditure within the application of the Barnett Formula. We recommend that before decisions are made on whether the system is bypassed or creates a consequential payment there is a clear process and open consultation with the devolved administrations (para 60).

Although we acknowledge that the data on public spending have improved since 1999, we continue to be concerned that clear, thorough and readily accessible data on public spending across the United Kingdom are not yet being provided (para 62).

We recommend that the Treasury publish their statistics of the workings of the Barnett Formula, or its successor, in a single, coherent and consistent publication. This annual publication should contain all material data on devolved finance, showing the allocations of grant to the devolved administrations, changes from previous years and explanations for any changes made. We recommend that the statistics be monitored by the UK Statistics Authority (para 63).

The role of the Commonwealth Grants Commission (CGC) in Australia offers a useful institutional model of an independent body that has responsibility for making recommendations about the allocation of finance (para 72).

An independent body, similar to the CGC, should be established in the United Kingdom. It should be the role of such a body to recommend the allocation of public monies based on population and through a new needs-based formula. Within the new framework the Treasury will need to retain its authority over the overall level of the block grant but not the proportionate allocation of the grant between the devolved administrations. This independent body might perhaps be called the United Kingdom Funding Commission. This Commission would carry out an assessment of relative need, undertake periodic reviews, and collect and publish information on an annual basis about the allocation of finance to the devolved administrations (para 73).

The Commission should be advisory in nature rather than have the power to make substantive allocations of funds on its own account. Its advice should, however, be published (para 74).

The remit of the Commission should be to determine the relative needs of each devolved administration on a regular basis, perhaps every five years. The Commission should also advise on the relative proportions of public spending for the devolved administrations, compared with spending within

England, during a transitional period and recommend annual increments based on the latest population figures (para 75).

The Commission should be appointed by the United Kingdom Government as a non-departmental public body. It should be politically neutral and independent. It should be composed of a small number of members with sufficient expertise to ensure the dispassionate and authoritative nature of its work (para 76).

We recommend that future grants be payable directly from the United Kingdom Government to the consolidated fund of each devolved administration (para 78).

We find the argument that devolution funding should be based on relative need to be a compelling one. Public spending per head of population should be allocated across the United Kingdom on the basis of relative need, so that those parts of the United Kingdom which have a greater need receive more public funds to help them pay for the additional levels of public services they require as a result. Those levels of need—and which parts of the United Kingdom need them—may well change over time. Historically, they have certainly done so (para 81).

The new system should be based on the following principles:

- It should consider both the baseline and any increment in funds;

- It should be fair and seen to be fair;

- It should be comprehensible;

- It should respect territorial autonomy; and

- It should be stable and predictable (para 88).

Any needs assessment should take these aspects into account:

- The age structure of the population;

- Low income;

- Ill-health and disability; and

- Economic weakness (para 94).

While we are not in a position to reach a conclusion about precise relative needs in the four countries and regions, on the basis of our initial analysis, we believe that Scotland now has markedly lower overall need than Wales and Northern Ireland in comparison to England. The current allocation of spending does not properly reflect this basic pattern across the devolved administrations (para 101).

We recommend that an alternative system on the broad lines suggested above be created to establish a new baseline grant for the devolved administrations and to review needs on a regular basis so that allocations of funds to the devolved administrations reflect the changing patterns of relative need (para 102).

The task envisaged for the Commission is to select indicators of the type illustrated above and to combine them in the way suggested. It is a feature of this approach that there can be choice about which, and how many, of the indicators are used for the ultimate formula. All of them will be brought into the analysis (para 106).

We recognise the need for a carefully-handled transition to implement the new arrangements. We anticipate a transitional period of between three and five years, preferably no more than seven, before the new arrangements are brought wholly into effect. Smoothing mechanisms would need to be put in place to manage the change from present levels of funding to those that the new arrangements would supply (para 110).

Both the length of the transition period before the new system is brought wholly into effect and the pace at which the actual levels of grant per head converge with the needs-based levels are issues upon which the new Commission should advise the United Kingdom Government (para 110).

The new arrangements we propose will need to be embodied in statute, at least in general outline. The legislation should contain provisions to ensure that the quinquennial reviews indeed take place (para 112).

The Barnett Formula

CHAPTER 1: BACKGROUND TO THE INQUIRY

1. The Committee was appointed by the House: "to examine the purpose, methodology and application of the Barnett Formula as a means of determining funding for the devolved administrations of the United Kingdom, to assess the effectiveness of the calculation mechanism to meet its purpose and to consider alternative mechanisms". [1]

2. Our orders of reference were intended to exclude consideration of three areas:

    *   the overall system of funding the devolved administrations—in particular the question of whether greater tax-raising powers should be accorded to the devolved administrations;

    *   other political aspects of the devolution settlements; and

    *   the distribution of funds within the different regions of the United Kingdom. [2]

3. The scope of this inquiry is therefore tightly focused on the methodology and practical application of the Barnett Formula. It focuses on the funding provided by the United Kingdom Government to the devolved administrations. The inquiry does not consider the policy and funding decisions of each devolved administration. Under devolution legislation[3] it is for each devolved administration to decide the funding policy for its activities. From the outset we accepted the principle of the provision of a block grant from Westminster to fund the devolved administrations so that each administration would be free to allocate resources in line with its own policies.

4. The Formula has been criticised for many years. In 2002 the House of Lords Constitution Committee acknowledged that "there are serious difficulties presented by the long-term continuation of the Barnett Formula. We do not think that it will be a sustainable basis for allocating funds to the devolved administrations in the long term".[4] Criticisms of the Formula have increased over time as public services across the United Kingdom have diverged as a result of the policy decisions of the individual devolved administrations (for example university fees or medical prescription charges) which are not replicated throughout the United Kingdom but which are a consequence of devolution. Differences in public service provision have given rise to debate about the equity of the funding allocations made through the application of the Barnett Formula.

5. The current financial climate is also likely to lead to increased pressure on public spending, including that distributed through the Barnett Formula.[5] We are aware that any mechanism which distributes public money will

---

[1] The members of the Committee were appointed by the House on 10 December 2008.

[2] Liaison Committee, 2nd Report, 2007–08, HL Paper 142 p3.

[3] Government of Wales Act 1998; Scotland Act 1998; Northern Ireland Act 1998; Government of Wales Act 2006.

[4] House of Lords Select Committee on the Constitution: Devolution: Inter-Institutional Relations in the United Kingdom HL 28, 2002–03 para 103.

[5] This was acknowledged by the Finance Committee of the Scottish Parliament on 9 June 2009.

attract some criticism and that recipients of public funding rarely consider their allocation to be adequate. However, the spending decisions and the subsequent policies of each administration are beyond the remit of this inquiry. They are a matter for each administration, not for us.

6. In conducting this inquiry we assumed that a mechanism for distributing financial resources from the United Kingdom Government to the devolved administrations was necessary. The questions we asked ourselves therefore were:

    • Why was the Barnett Formula created?

    • What were its original purposes and have they been achieved?

    • Are the original purposes of the Formula still valid?

    • If it were to be replaced what mechanism should be adopted as an alternative?

7. When we began our inquiry in December 2008 several other commissions and committees were investigating issues associated with the Barnett Formula. Our inquiry was conducted in parallel with the following:

    • the House of Commons Justice Committee's inquiry into devolution;[6]

    • the Calman Commission review of the devolution settlement, including the financial powers of the Scottish Parliament;[7]

    • the Welsh Assembly Government's Independent Commission for Funding and Finance for Wales chaired by Mr Gerry Holtham[8]; and

    • the First Minister of Scotland's "National Conversation" to consider the constitutional future of Scotland including financial arrangements.[9]

8. This report sets out broadly how a new system might be determined.

9. The membership and interests of the Committee are set out in Appendix 1 and those who submitted written and oral evidence are listed in Appendix 2. Our Call for Evidence, which was issued on 2 February 2009, is reprinted in Appendix 3. In response we received 41 submissions of written evidence, and we subsequently took oral evidence, in London, Edinburgh, Cardiff and Belfast, from 46 persons or organisations. We would like to thank all those who have assisted us in this way: without their help our inquiry could not have been carried out.

10. Finally, we are very grateful to our Specialist Advisers, Mr Alan Trench of Edinburgh University and Dr Peter Kenway, for their expertise and guidance. We stress, however, that the conclusions we draw and the recommendations we make are ours alone.

---

6 House of Commons Justice Committee, 5th Report 2008–09 HC 529. In addition the Barnett Formula was considered by the House of Commons Treasury Select Committee HC 341 1997–8 and the House of Lords Select Committee on the Constitution: *Devolution: Inter-Institutional Relations in the United Kingdom* HL 28, 2002–03.

7 Commission on Scottish Devolution *Serving Scotland Better: Scotland and the United Kingdom in the 21st Century; Final Report;* June 2009.

8 Independent Commission on Funding and Finance for Wales: *Funding devolved government in Wales: Barnett & beyond,* First Report to the Welsh Assembly Government, July 2009.

9 Scottish Executive *Choosing Scotland's Future: A National Conversation,* 2007; Scottish Government *Fiscal Autonomy in Scotland: The case for changes and options for reform,* 2009.

CHAPTER 2: UK PUBLIC SPENDING AND THE BARNETT FORMULA

The territorial distribution of public spending in the United Kingdom

11. The Barnett Formula is the mechanism used by the United Kingdom Government to allocate just over half of total public expenditure in Scotland, Wales and Northern Ireland. Public spending, considered on a per capita basis, is unevenly distributed across the four parts of the United Kingdom. Some forms of spending—on defence and foreign affairs in particular—cannot be accounted for on a territorial basis and are treated in public statistics as national. Several areas of public spending are territorially identifiable but remain the responsibility of the United Kingdom Government; the most important of these is social security, which is paid according to the status of individual claimants irrespective of their geographical location. The amounts involved, and the relationship they bear to the total amounts of identifiable public expenditure,[10] are shown in Table 1.

TABLE 1

UK Public Spending and the Importance of the Barnett Formula, 2007–2008

	£ million	As percentage of total identifiable UK public spending	As percentage of total identifiable public spending in appropriate territory
Total Managed Expenditure UK Government spending	582,676		
Total (territorially) UK identifiable public spending	467,981		
Total territorially identifiable public spending in Scotland	46,409	9.92	
Of which spending by the Scottish Executive and local authorities[11]	32,314		69.63
Of which DEL[12] spending (subject to the Barnett formula) [13]	26,946		58.01

---

10 "Identifiable Expenditure" is defined within the Public Expenditure Statistical Analysis as "expenditure that can be recognised as having been incurred for the benefit of individuals, enterprises or communities within particular regions. Examples are most health, education and transport services, and spending on social security and on pensions."

11 Local authority spending, and that of local government public corporations, is included with the devolved administrations' spending as local government is under the control of the devolved administrations.

12 See para 13.

13 Includes Capital and Resource DEL allocations. From Scotland Office *Annual Report 2009*, Annex 1.

Total territorially identifiable public spending in Wales	25,309	5.41	
Of which spending by the Welsh Assembly Government and local authorities	16,147		63.80
Of which DEL spending (subject to the Barnett formula)[14]	13,538		53.49
Total territorially identifiable public spending in Northern Ireland	16,863	3.60	
Of which spending by the Northern Ireland Executive and local authorities	14,495[15]		85.96
Of which DEL spending (subject to the Barnett formula)[16]	8,492		50.36
Total spending by devolved administrations (sum of lines 4, 7 and 10)	62,956	13.45	
Total spending subject to the Barnett formula (sum of lines 5, 8 and 11)	48,976	10.47	

All data for 2006–7, taken from Public Expenditure Statistical Analyses 2009 Cm 7630 (London: HM Treasury, 2009), tables 1.1, 1.12, 9.1 and 9.21 and the Scotland Office Annual Report 2009 Cm 7401 and Wales Office Annual Report 2009 Cm 7603.

12.   The Barnett Formula's importance (baseline and increment) is shown by Table 1. In 2007-08 the Formula accounted for almost £49 billion of public spending, which was more than half of total public spending in Scotland, Wales and Northern Ireland and ten per cent of total territorially identifiable public spending in the United Kingdom.

13.   The devolved administrations' budgets consist of the Departmental Expenditure Limit (DEL) and Annually Managed Expenditure (AME). Since the 1998 Comprehensive Spending Review, the spending of all UK spending departments (Whitehall departments and the devolved administrations) is divided between the DEL and AME budgets. DEL public expenditure is that which can be planned and controlled on a three year basis through spending reviews. This applies to the cost of providing services which can be reasonably predicted, for example, education, health or transport. AME expenditure is public expenditure which varies according to external circumstances and which cannot reasonably be subject to firm multi-year limits, such as unemployment benefit.[17] The Formula only applies to funding allocated under the DEL budget.

---

[14] Includes Capital and Resource DEL allocations. From Wales Office *Annual Report 2009*, Annex 7.

[15] Includes social security spending, which is a responsibility of the Northern Ireland Executive but subject to requirements to ensure parity with Great Britain. This is AME spending and not part of the Northern Ireland Executive's DEL.

[16] Includes Capital and Resource DEL allocations.

[17] For the devolved administrations AME has applied to three major areas of spending: agricultural subsidies paid under the Common Agricultural Policy, payments for certain pensions (teaching and NHS pensions in particular) and for housing benefit and council tax benefit. AME expenditure is reviewed twice a year, and is not subject to the Barnett Formula.

14. An important element of total identifiable public expenditure *not* subject to the Barnett Formula is social security spending. Table 2 shows the differences if social security spending is removed from total identifiable public expenditure; it indicates a closer estimation of the effect that the Barnett Formula has on spending. Table 3 reduces these figures to indices expressed as per capita expenditure across the regions of the United Kingdom.

TABLE 2[18]

The importance of social security spending in Scotland, Wales and Northern Ireland 2006–07

	£ million
Scottish Executive and local authorities	30,077
Social Security	12,148
Other non-devolved expenditure	1,493
Total identifiable expenditure in Scotland	**43,718**
Welsh Assembly Government and local authorities	15,229
Social Security	7,471
Other non-devolved expenditure	1,537
Total identifiable expenditure on Wales	**24,237**
Northern Ireland Executive and local authorities	13,253
Social Security	5,072[19]
Other non-devolved expenditure	1,492
Total identifiable expenditure on Northern Ireland	**15,658**

Figures, taken from PESA 2008 Table 9.17. Figures may not add up due to rounding. This table includes both AME and DEL expenditure.

TABLE 3

Index of per capita public expenditure, including and excluding social security

UK = 100

2006-07	England	Wales	Scotland	N. Ireland
Total identifiable public expenditure	97	112	117	123
Total identifiable public expenditure less social security payments[20]	96	112	122	125

[18] Source: *Public Expenditure Statistical Analysis 2008*, tables 10.1 to 10.4 and appendix table F1. ESA expenditure. What has been excluded under the heading of 'social security payments' is all spending in tables 10.1 to 10.4 under the category of 'social protection' except for that described as 'personal social services.'

[19] Includes social protection funding administered by the Northern Ireland Executive, subject to requirements to ensure parity with Great Britain.

15.   Table 4 shows the territorial distribution of public spending between 2001 and 2008 on a per capita basis. There are problems with the accuracy of the historical statistics; the poor quality of data for earlier years means that we have not been able to assess the change in public spending over a longer period. But the table shows changes even since 2001. The change in Scotland's per capita allocation in 2004–5 may have been due to convergence but it is more likely to be the result of the revision of population figures for the increment in the 2004 Spending Review, which took effect from 2004–5.

TABLE 4

Index of changes in the territorial distribution of overall per capita public spending, 2001–02 to 2008–09

(UK = 100)

	England	Wales	Scotland	NI
2001–02	96	112	119	132
2002–03	96	113	118	133
2003–04	97	113	117	126
2004–05	97	111	114	126
2005–06	97	111	117	124
2006–07	97	112	118	123
2007–08	97	111	118	125
2008–09 (plans)	97	111	116	122

Sources: for 2001–02 and 2002–03, PESA 2005, table 8.2; for 2003–04 and subsequent years, PESA 2009, table 9.2.

All data for 2006–7, taken from Public Expenditure Statistical Analyses 2008 HC 289 (London: HM Treasury, 2008), tables 1.12 and 9.17 and the Scotland Office Annual Report 2008 Cm 7403 and Wales Office Annual Report 2008 Cm 7404.

How the Barnett formula works

16.   The annual allocation of funding made under the Barnett Formula (the block grant) is comprised of the baseline plus the annual incremental change. The baseline each year is made up of the total block grant (baseline plus increment) from the previous year. We use the term the "Barnett Formula" to refer to the Formula used to determine the increment and the mechanism for deciding the total allocation of block grant. Where necessary we specify whether we are referring to the incremental Formula (increment) only or the method of determining the total block grant (baseline and increment).

17.   The baseline in any particular year is made up of the baseline in the previous year plus the previous year's increment, thus everything in the past is taken as given. The original baseline when the Formula was first applied now represents barely one tenth of the total expenditure but there are a culminating series of new baselines, which become increasingly out of date, leading to further anomalies. Together, these account for the vast bulk of the block grant.

---

[20] Precisely: including only personal 'social services' from within the category of 'social protection'

18.   Each year, once they receive the grant, the devolved administrations allocate it in order to suit local priorities. For example if a consequential payment[21] is triggered by an increase in English health spending that does not mean that it has to be spent on health elsewhere; it can be allocated as the devolved administration sees fit. In practice, however, most expenditure in the devolved administrations does tend to follow the pattern established for England.

19.   Since 1999, the details of how the Formula works have been published by the Treasury, in its document *Funding the Scottish Parliament, National Assembly for Wales and Northern Ireland Assembly: Statement of Funding Policy*. This document has been revised and reissued following each Spending Review and Comprehensive Spending Review.

BOX 1

How the Barnett Formula works

The Barnett Formula applies only to some types of expenditure: large expenditure areas, such as welfare payments, are outside the formula's remit. There are three elements to the formula:

(i)   the change in planned spending in departments in England;

(ii)   the extent to which the relevant English departmental programme is comparable with the services carried out by each devolved administration (see para 22); and

(iii)   the population proportion in each devolved administration of the United Kingdom, in relation to the appropriate one for the United Kingdom Government's programmes. (In many cases, this is for England, but for Home Office and legal department matters, the comparison is with England and Wales, and in some cases for Northern Ireland the comparator is with Great Britain) (see paras 54–56).

For the financial year 2007–08, these proportions were:

	Scotland	Wales	Northern Ireland
England	10. 08	5.84	3.43
England and Wales	9.52		3.24
Great Britain			2.96

(The population proportions used in the 2007 Comprehensive Spending Review, covering the years 2008–09 to 2010–11, are those from the mid-year of 2007 and are set out in the latest edition of the *Statement of Funding Policy*.)

The formula simply multiplies (i) x (ii) x (iii). The increase in funding payable to the devolved administration is therefore the increase for England, multiplied by the extent to which a programme is comparable, multiplied by the population of the devolved region as a proportion of the English population.

Sources: HM Treasury, Funding the Scottish Parliament, National Assembly for Wales and Northern Ireland Assembly: A Statement of Funding Policy Fifth Edition (London: HM Treasury, October 2007), pp.10–11. House of Commons Library, The Barnett Formula (Research Paper 01/108, 30 November 2001).

---

21   See paras 20–21.

20. The increases in grant allocated to Scotland, Wales and Northern Ireland are calculated on the basis of a population share (a per capita share) of the changes made for England. We discuss the details of this, and how it has changed over time, in Chapters 3 and 4 below. If Scotland's population is 10 per cent of that of England (which roughly it is), the Formula adds to the Scottish block grant 10 per cent of the changes made in spending for England. If health spending goes up by £2 billion in England, Scotland gets a 10 per cent share, or £200 million. The converse would apply if spending were to go down in England—it would trigger proportionate reductions in spending allocated to Scotland, Wales and Northern Ireland. These payments are known as 'consequential' payments.

21. A 'consequential' payment is triggered by a decision made by the United Kingdom Government about spending in England. Therefore the overall structure of public spending continues to reflect decisions about priorities in England. The Formula takes the additional amounts allocated for spending on 'comparable functions' in England each year and multiplies it by the relevant population proportion. This makes up the increment for that year. That increment is added to the block grant from the previous year to make up the new totally block grant. In turn, that figure forms the baseline for the following year.

22. The list of 'comparable functions' is set out in the *Statement of Funding Policy* (Schedule C) and is based on the allocation of functions for England within United Kingdom Government departments. Each department has a list of sub-programmes; a percentage is set for any 'consequential' payment for each of the devolved administrations depending on whether the sub-programme is devolved or not. For example, at the Department for Transport the Rail Network Grant is 100 per cent devolved in Scotland and Northern Ireland but set at 0 per cent for Wales because this is not devolved. Each individual percentage is used to calculate an overall percentage for each department, according to how much of its functions are devolved to each administration. Those overall percentages vary: for Transport, they are 91.5 per cent for Scotland, 68.3 per cent for Wales and 94.0 per cent for Northern Ireland. Any change in the budget of the department triggers 'consequentials' in those ratios, multiplied by the appropriate population percentage. So if the Department for Transport were allocated an extra £100 million, Scotland would get 91.5 per cent of its per capita share of that money, Wales 68.3 per cent and Northern Ireland 94.0 per cent.

CHAPTER 3: THE DEVELOPMENT OF FORMULA FROM 1978–1997

The original purpose of the Formula

23. A formula was first used to calculate funding for services in Scotland and Ireland compared with England and Wales in 1888. The 'Goschen Formula', named after the then Chancellor of the Exchequer, allocated funds based on population in the proportion 80:11:9 to England and Wales, Scotland and Ireland respectively (p 301). After World War II successive Scottish Secretaries of State negotiated additional allocations for their territorial departments by arguing special needs, such as sparsity of population in the remote areas and density and poor housing in the central belt. The current Secretary of State for Northern Ireland, Shaun Woodward MP, suggested: "certainly what was there before 1979 was tortuous, unfair, involved line by line negotiation, was pretty opaque and did not much work" (Q 893).

24. The introduction of what became known as the Barnett Formula was part of a wider attempt to constrain public spending in what were difficult times, for the economy in general and for public spending in particular (Q 7). It coincided with the introduction of cash limits for public spending by Denis Healey MP, then Chancellor of the Exchequer, following the 1976 loan from the International Monetary Fund. The creator of the Formula, Joel Barnett MP, intended to find a way of apportioning changes in public spending to the territorial departments by allocating proportional shares to the Scottish and Welsh Offices and Northern Ireland departments when there were changes in spending on 'comparable functions' for England. Those proportional shares were based on the relative populations of the regions and countries of the United Kingdom in the late 1970s (Q 11).

25. In essence, Barnett was an update of Goschen, but with the distinguishing feature that, instead of quantifying the annual per capita spending increase as a percentage of the Scottish baseline it was granted instead as a cash figure per capita, derived from the percentage increase granted to the (lower) English baseline. In other words, if England received say, a 4 per cent increase per capita which amounted to £1,000, Scotland would receive £1,000 per capita although that would be less than 4 per cent of the (higher) Scottish baseline. This new arrangement injected into the process the concept of gradual convergence.[22]

26. The Barnett Formula began to operate in Scotland and Northern Ireland in 1979 and in Wales in 1980. The Secretaries of State continued to be free to allocate money to their chosen spending priorities in Scotland, Wales and Northern Ireland (p 204).

27. The purpose of the new Formula was to respond to pressure from ministers in other departments to rein in the excessive, as they saw it, share of resources going to territorial departments, in particular to Scotland, at a time of cash limits and in dire economic circumstances nationally. Although intended to be temporary, until a formula that paid more attention to

[22] See paras 33–34.

relative need could be devised and agreed, Barnett brought a welcome measure of certainty and stability. However, since the Formula did not cover all public spending in Scotland, Wales and Northern Ireland, the territorial Secretaries of State remained able to negotiate special deals outside the Formula.

The Formula before devolution

The 1979 and 1993 Needs Assessment Studies

28. The decision to introduce the Formula took place at a time when devolution to elected assemblies in Scotland and Wales was being contemplated by the Government, and the question of their funding had yet to be resolved. The Government planned to fund the devolved administrations on the basis of their relative spending needs, and details were to be discussed with the devolved bodies when they came into being.[23] At the time the Formula was introduced, a needs assessment study was underway in the Treasury to assess the relative needs of Scotland and Wales for the six main policy areas which were to be devolved.[24] Following referendums in March 1979 the project to create devolved assemblies was halted and the Needs Assessment Study was never pursued.[25]

29. Although the Formula (including the baseline) was not reviewed during this period, funding was nonetheless a recurrent topic of debate between the Scottish and Welsh Offices and the Treasury. The Treasury periodically sought a review of Scotland's relative needs in order to counter bids from Scotland for increased spending; it was for the Scottish Secretaries to resist such calls. Twice this reached the stage of an interdepartmental discussion: in 1986 a report was prepared by the Cabinet Office on 'corrective action' which might be undertaken; and in 1993 a new needs assessment was carried out by the Treasury updating the 1979 exercise but its results were never published.[26] The most recent needs assessment is therefore fifteen years out of date.

30. Had the Needs Assessment Studies been brought into effect, they would have changed significantly the levels of spending across the United Kingdom. Table 5 below illustrates the impact they would have had both for the 1970s and the 1990s:

[23] Devolution: Financing the Devolved Services Cm 6890 (London: HM Stationery Office, July 1977); p 66.

[24] HM Treasury Needs Assessment Study—Report (London: The Treasury, December 1979). The service areas were Health and personal social services, Education and libraries (excluding universities), Housing, Other environmental services, Road and transport (excluding railways), and Law, order and protective services (excluding police).

[25] HM Treasury Needs Assessment Study—Report, December 1979.

[26] The Unwin Report 1986, was disclosed by HMT, but not published, following a request made under the Freedom of Information Act, Sir Brian Unwin QQ 509–10. The 1994 Needs Assessment was not published and was only made available to us by HM Treasury in June 2009.

TABLE 5

United Kingdom Government Needs Assessments 1979 and 1993 and actual levels of spending (in index terms)

	Per capita spending on 'devolved services' in 1976–7	Per capita spending on 'devolved services' recommended in 1979 Needs Assessment study	Per capita spending on 'devolved services' in 1993–4, according to 1993 Treasury Needs Assessments	Per capita spending on 'devolved services' recommended in 1993 Treasury Needs Assessments
England	100	100	100	100
Scotland	122	116	133	115
Wales	106	109	122	112
Northern Ireland	135	131	127	122

Sources: HM Treasury Needs Assessment Study—Report (London: HM Treasury, December 1979), pp. 6; HM Treasury Assessment of Relative needs—Scotland, (September 1993), chapter 4; HM Treasury Assessment of Relative needs—Wales, (September 1993), chapter 4; and HM Treasury Assessment of Relative needs—Northern Ireland, (September 1993), chapter 4.

31.   In both cases, this would have meant a reduction in Northern Ireland and in Scotland relative to spending in England and an increase in spending in Wales in 1979 but not in 1993.

The future of the Formula

32.   Lord Barnett made clear to us that the Formula was not designed as a permanent solution: "I thought it might last a year or two before a government would decide to change it. It never occurred to me for one moment that it would last this long" (Q 2). The fact that the Formula was intended originally as a short-term expedient was echoed in other evidence (p 145, p205). Despite this, the Formula has proved remarkably durable, surviving both financial stringency and retrenchment in the 1970s and 1980s and considerable growth in public spending in more recent times.

Application of the Formula in practice up to 1997

Convergence 1978–1997

33.   It is a mathematical property of the Formula, all other things being equal, that spending subject to the Formula in Scotland, Wales or Northern Ireland would tend to converge on the English level, per head of population, over time (QQ 81–82, 86). Lord Barnett told us that he did not intend the mechanism to produce convergence and was not aware at the time that it should, or could, do so (Q 12). As it was not expected that the Formula would last long, the convergent aspects of the Formula were not material when it was first applied.

34. In fact there is little evidence that convergence actually took place during the period 1978–1997.[27] This appears to be the result of the fact that population changes were not adequately reflected year by year in the baseline.[28] The relative populations were not updated until the 1990s, despite significant changes—in particular, a decline in Scotland's share of the United Kingdom population from 9.3 per cent in 1976 to 8.7 per cent in 1995.[29]

'Formula bypass' up to 1997

35. The application of the Barnett Formula during this period did not remove all negotiations between the Treasury and the Scottish and Welsh Offices. There were extensive discussions which were vital in ensuring that the system was appropriately flexible to respond to the differing needs of Scotland, Wales and Northern Ireland. This worked well when all three administrations were part of a single United Kingdom Government before devolution, and for a while after the Scottish Parliament and Welsh Assembly were in operation, as it applied in the context of decisions taken within Governments (based at Westminster, in Edinburgh and Cardiff) with predominantly shared common agendas. However, in the process, it appears that Scotland and Northern Ireland were more successful than Wales in obtaining favourable treatment from the Treasury in allocations of public spending outwith the Formula. In that respect, Wales was the least generously treated (p 178). During this period the most significant formula bypasses were to cover public sector wage increases which, if met from within the block grant, would have had a disproportionate effect on the other elements of the territorial departments' spending programmes.

---

[27] See Chapter 3.

[28] See Chapter 5.

[29] Ibid.

CHAPTER 4: THE FORMULA SINCE 1997

Devolution

36.   When planning for devolution after the 1997 general election, the United Kingdom Government decided at an early stage to continue to use the Barnett Formula to allocate funding for the devolved administrations.[30] It was incorporated into the devolution white papers published early that summer.[31] The Formula was slightly adapted to cater for the fact that different administrations, accountable to separate elected bodies, were to be responsible for wide but differing ranges of public service provision.[32]

The application of the Formula in practice since 1997

37.   From 1997 the use of the Formula was increasingly formalised. In 1999 the methodology used was set out in the Treasury's document *Funding the Scottish Parliament, National Assembly for Wales and Northern Ireland Assembly: A Statement of Funding Policy*.[33] The basis on which it operated was explicitly stated and its application was therefore less flexible with little scope for negotiation within the published rules. But, by explicitly stating that the Treasury had unlimited discretion on any significant decision that remained to be taken, it reinforced the power of the Treasury.[34]

38.   Since 1997 the application of the Formula has been largely a technical, even arithmetical, exercise. This has been described as 'Pure' Barnett (QQ 246, 698). While there remain subjective decisions for the Government about whether particular matters attract 'consequential' payments for the devolved administrations (some of which are discussed in more detail below), the Formula is otherwise simple to apply. This was clearly set out in the Treasury's evidence to us (p 85).

39.   As well as being simple to operate, the Formula delivers stable funding to the devolved administrations. These virtues have been set out in evidence submitted to us, and are not to be underestimated (Q 415) (see paras 50–51). On the other hand, the present system of calculating the grant takes no account of the broader issues of spending need.

Handling disagreements about finance

40.   In place of the previous arrangements the *Statement of Funding Policy* sets out procedures for dealing with disputes for bilateral negotiations between the devolved administration concerned and the Treasury. In theory the main forum for resolving disputes is now the Joint Ministerial Committee (JMC), the body responsible for co-ordination between the United Kingdom Government and the devolved administrations. In its plenary form the members of the JMC are the Prime Minister and the devolved First Ministers, along with the Deputy First Ministers and the territorial

---

[30] A Trench (ed) Devolution and Power in the United Kingdom 2007 p 89.

[31] Scotland's Parliament 1997 Cm 3658; A Voice for Wales 1997 Cm 3718.

[32] Statement of Funding Policy 1999.

[33] Statement of Funding Policy has been subsequently reissued following each spending review or comprehensive spending review.

[34] Statement of Funding Policy para 3.199–3.202.

Secretaries of State. However, as in the past, ultimate responsibility for financial matters rests with Treasury Ministers and the United Kingdom Cabinet, not the JMC. As the Treasury told us, no disagreement relating to devolution finance has ever been referred to the JMC for resolution (QQ 476–478). In practice this leaves the Treasury with the last word when determining the financial allocations for the devolved administrations.[35]

41. Although, as a result of devolution whilst the role of the territorial Secretary of States has been much reduced in favour of the First Ministers from the devolved administrations, financial issues of primary importance are still determined within the United Kingdom Government (mainly by the Treasury). The Scottish Cabinet Secretary for Finance and Sustainable Communities, John Swinney MSP, expressed his concern that he was not responsible for approving the *Statement of Funding Policy* on behalf of his government, but that assent was signified by the Secretary of State for Scotland (QQ 166–8). Richard Pengelly, Public Spending Director, Department of Finance and Personnel, Northern Ireland Civil Service, agreed: "I cannot think of anything where there is active discussion with the Treasury, it is all Barnett-based and formulaic. The negotiation, as such, happens around the statement of funding policy and that is where the difficulties are as opposed to the quantum of any specific item of funding that flows through Barnett"(Q 653).

'Formula Bypass' since 1997

42. Notwithstanding the fact that the Formula has been applied more rigidly since 1999, there have been significant increases in funding for the devolved administrations outside the application of the Formula. For Northern Ireland, the Reform and Reinvestment Initiative was introduced in 2002, and provided for borrowing powers, a fund for capital investment in infrastructure, and a strategic investment board to manage infrastructure improvements. In addition, Northern Ireland benefited from additional funding from the Treasury to support European Union (EU) funding as well as under the 'PEACE 2' programme. Wales also secured additional funding to support use of EU Objective 1 monies (and subsequently Convergence Fund monies, as the successor to Objective 1). Such funds are transferred outside the scope of the Barnett Formula, so in that sense constitute 'Formula Bypass'.[36] Decisions about whether they should be granted or not have been taken by the United Kingdom Government to date, after representations by the devolved administrations but without, so far, involving the JMC formal machinery.[37] Another issue which may have to be similarly dealt with is the future funding of policing in Northern Ireland.

The powers of the Treasury

43. In recent years the powers of the Treasury to make decisions about financial matters have been exercised in relation to a number of controversial matters. When considering funding any project or event in the devolved administrations the Treasury has two options: they can decide that it should

---

[35] The role of the territorial finance ministers and the JMC are discussed the in Calman Commission report.

[36] See para 35.

[37] House of Lords Select Committee on the Constitution: *Devolution: Inter-Institutional Relations in the United Kingdom* HL 28, 2002–03, QQ 191–4, 1268–71.

be met from within the block grant provided by the Barnett Formula (baseline and increment) or the funding might be found from other United Kingdom Government sources.

44. When making spending decisions for a project or event in England the Treasury has to decide whether that expenditure is "UK-wide" or "England only". The decision to categorise spending in England as "England only" requires an exercise of judgment by the Treasury triggering a 'consequential' payment through the Barnett Formula to the devolved administrations. By contrast categorising expenditure as "UK-wide" does not trigger a 'consequential' payment. The following examples highlight a subjective application of the Formula by the Treasury—mainly on the categorisation of spending:

- The planned expenditure for the 2012 London Olympics, including spending on regeneration schemes in east London, has been classified as "UK-wide" rather than "England" only. This has the effect of preventing 'consequential' payments to the devolved administrations. If specific regeneration spending had been classed as such it would have triggered automatically 'consequential' payments for the devolved administrations. (QQ 165, 167, 653, 675, 679–82). There were extensive discussions about this between the devolved administrations and the United Kingdom Government and it was considered at Cabinet (QQ 924–5).

- By contrast, the Treasury eventually agreed to the classification of spending on Crossrail (which will overwhelmingly benefit London and the South East) as an "England" expenditure therefore triggering 'consequential' payments for the devolved administrations. This amounted to some £500 million for Scotland (QQ 469, 925–7). This appears to have been a decision taken to resolve a difficult political disagreement rather than the application of a consistent principle.

- The capital costs of a replacement Forth Road Bridge have been an issue of contention between the United Kingdom Government and Scottish Executive for some time. We were told by the Secretary of State for Scotland that part of the rationale for the decision about Crossrail was that this was of comparable importance to the Forth Bridge project (QQ 25–6). A resolution was said to be near in early April 2009, although to date no final decision has been announced (QQ 928–31).

45. The Treasury also makes unilateral decisions when there is a claim on the UK Contingency Reserve. Cases involving claims on the Reserve since 1999 have included outbreaks of Foot and Mouth Disease (devolved claims were permitted in 2001), the cost of policing the G8 summit at Gleneagles in 2005 (again, the Scottish claim was allowed), and the costs of implementing the Carter Review[38] in Scottish prisons. In the latter example the Treasury rejected Scotland's claim for a proportion of the share of the funds used to improve the prison estate in England and Wales (paid for from the Reserve) and the cost of improvements in Scottish prisons were funded from within the block grant (QQ 143, 470). The Chief Secretary to the Treasury, Liam Byrne MP, set out the criteria on which a bypass is determined: "the devolved administrations can bid to the reserve on an exceptional basis, but

---

[38] Securing the future: Proposals for the efficient and sustainable use of custody in England and Wales; Ministry of Justice, December 2007.

there are three tests, if you like: the spending does indeed have to be exceptional, it has to be unforeseen, and third, it cannot reasonably be 'absorbed' (I think is the word) within existing budgets" (Q 1013).

46. The Treasury determines the extent of any End-Year-Flexibility in relation to DEL budgets. During the 2007 Comprehensive Spending Review the Treasury agreed to release accumulated (and mainly Scottish) underspends; this accounted for the release in Scotland of approximately £900 million a month before the publication of the Spending Review.[39]

47. The Treasury also enforces the distinction between the levels of capital and current spending within the block grant; such levels were set as part of the 2007 Comprehensive Spending Review. This amounted to a form of hypothecation of devolved spending as it restricted the devolved administrations' freedom to determine their own allocations of spending. It was reinforced as part of the 'reprofiling' of public spending in the 2008 Pre Budget Review with the amounts required to be spent by the devolved administrations adjusted in accordance with the changes in the capital investment programme of the United Kingdom Government (p 318). Similarly a retrospective review of the baseline for the NHS in England in 2006–07 led to a reduction of the baseline of some £3 billion (apparently due to underspending on its capital budget triggering 'consequential' reductions in the baseline for the devolved administrations) (QQ 155–63, 677–8).

48. These examples illustrate the extent of the exercise of the Treasury's discretion within the current system. Some examples raise the question whether a particular item of United Kingdom spending entitles devolved administrations to 'consequential' funds (applying the rules); a number involve claims on the UK Contingency Reserve (exceptional cases outside the normal rules); while others involve decisions about the framing of the *Statement of Funding Policy* for the period of the next spending review (setting the rules). Leo O'Reilly, Permanent Secretary, Department of Finance and Personnel, Northern Ireland Civil Service, told us: "at times we have concerns as to the way the Treasury decide what is and is not falling within the scope of the Formula and what is and is not English expenditure as distinct from UK-wide expenditure. To some extent we are entirely dependent on the Treasury telling us what our comparable adjustments in expenditure are" (Q 649). These issues have been handled differently depending upon their treatment within the *Statement of Funding Policy*. Inevitably the effect of the Formula, as now applied, cannot be regarded as wholly predictable.[40]

---

[39] Scotland Office Press Release, 9 October 2007, 'Response to announcement of CSR and Pre Budget Report'.
[40] See Chapter 5.

CHAPTER 5: IS REFORM NECESSARY?

49.   There was general agreement among most of our witnesses that the Barnett Formula is no longer an appropriate mechanism to allocate funds to the devolved administrations. Only a minority of witnesses argued for the Formula to be retained. The Treasury told us that they considered the Barnett Formula to be effective and appropriate and they had no plans to consider any alternatives (QQ 413–423). The Chief Secretary to the Treasury described the Formula as "fair enough" (QQ 979, 982, 984, 988, 992–4). John Swinney MSP, Cabinet Secretary for Finance and Sustainable Growth in the Scottish Executive, argued for retaining the current Formula but only unless or until there was further reform of the devolution settlement to include fiscal autonomy (Q 226).[41] Professor Arthur Midwinter, in a submission to the Calman Commission, highlighted the importance of stability, predictability, political acceptability and simplicity.[42]

50.   The Barnett Formula has several important advantages: it is simple, stable and not pre-committed; allowing freedom of choice to the devolved authorities as to how the grant is spent. There have been improvements in the transparency of the Formula and its application, prompted in part by devolution in the late 1990s,[43] but the price of that has been reduced flexibility in funding the devolved administrations. We have found that the way in which the Formula has been administered in the past is opaque and subjective.[44]

51.   If the existing Formula is to be replaced or reformed, any alternative must represent an improvement on the current system. **The advantages of the Barnett Formula—simplicity, stability and the absence of ring-fencing—are important and should be maintained whatever the future method of allocating funds to the devolved administrations.**

52.   Although the advantages of the Formula are clear, the disadvantages call into question whether the Formula is an adequate mechanism to allocate funding to the devolved administrations. Whilst most witnesses conceded that the present system was relatively quick and easy for the Treasury to administer, only a minority thought that it could be justified in terms of fairness (Q 979).

The baseline

53.   The most serious criticism of the current basis of funding is that, whilst the core allocation (the baseline) has been built upon since the Formula was first applied, it has never been reviewed. "The Formula does not determine the overall sizes of budgets (these are based on past allocations and decisions) … any perceived inequity is due to the historical levels of funding since these are by their very nature 'locked-in' the system" (p 351). "Baseline expenditures to which 'consequential' increases were cumulatively added were based on expenditure patterns prior to 1978: indeed in the case of Scotland allocations were partly related to the Goschen formula established in the late nineteenth

---

[41]   We are prevented from considering fiscal autonomy by our orders of reference.

[42]   A Midwinter written submission to the Commission on Scottish Devolution 18 March 2009 pp 30–34 available at: http://www.commissiononscottishdevolution.org.uk/engage/submissions-received.php.

[43]   See Chapter 4.

[44]   See paras 57–63.

century" (Q 568, pp 134, 353). According to The Economic Research Institute of Northern Ireland, the core funding allocated through the Barnett Formula reflects and preserves "a myriad of past changes" (p 227). Therefore it cannot be said that the baseline reflects the needs of each devolved administration as they are today.

Population effects

54.   After many years during which the population statistics were not kept up to date, population statistics are now updated every three years with the reissue of the *Statement of Funding Policy*. But they are applied only to the annual increment of the Formula. The underlying baseline grant (the most significant proportion of the funds allocated through the application of the Barnett Formula) is not re-examined to take account of population changes. If the populations of the four countries and regions had followed similar paths over the years, this would not have mattered very much. But as Figure 1 shows, the populations have diverged. Over the period since 1981, the populations in Wales, England and Northern Ireland have grown by some six per cent, nine per cent and 14 per cent respectively. By contrast, the Scottish population, after a period of absolute decline, is now only back at its 1981 level.

FIGURE 1

Actual and projected populations 1971 to 2031, as a percentage of the 1981 level[45]

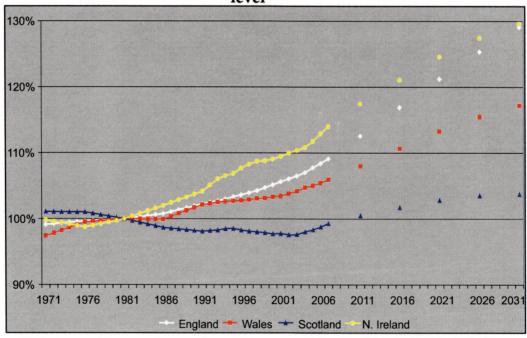

55.   What matters, as far as the Formula is concerned, is not whether populations grow or decline in absolute terms but how they change relative to one another. As well as showing that change of this sort has been going on for several decades, Figure 1 also shows (using projections made by the Government Actuary) that they are expected to continue to do so at least up until the 2030s. Whilst some changes took place to annual increments to reflect population statistics, the failure of the Barnett Formula to adjust the

---

[45] Source: ONS population trends dataset, table 1.2. In the interests of clarity, values for the years when official estimates were not produced (those years not ending in either a 1 or a 6) have been interpolated.

baseline to reflect this population effect is a serious weakness. Over the short time for which it was originally expected to operate, this would not have mattered. But left to run unchecked for decades, the absence of any correction mechanism has led a pattern of grant per head which is now arbitrary.

56. **The changing populations of the devolved administrations and the failure of the Formula to take account of population changes over time within the baseline create a significant problem for the Barnett Formula today. In our view, the resulting per capita allocations are arbitrary and unfair. In essence the baseline of the grant provides funds for a level of population that has changed.**

The administration of the present system

Opaque decision making

57. Treasury officials argued that their decisions on the categorisation of expenditure as "England" only or "UK-wide" spend were relatively clear because they simply flowed from legislation that specified which areas were devolved and which were reserved (Q 471). However the issue is not as simple as they suggest. Under the Scotland Act 1998, all matters are devolved save those expressly excepted or reserved to Westminster (set out in Schedules 4 and 5 to the Act). For Northern Ireland, all matters are similarly devolved save those excepted or reserved (though the lists of such matters are different there, and the meaning of 'excepted' and 'reserved' is also different under the Northern Ireland Act 1998). For Wales, under the Government of Wales Act 2006, only matters expressly devolved are within the competence of the Welsh Assembly Government and National Assembly for Wales. While, in substance, many matters are devolved in each case, there are important variations in both the topic devolved and the form in which they are devolved. While some functions—such as education and health care—are devolved in each case, policing and criminal justice are devolved in Scotland but not Wales (and have yet to be devolved to Northern Ireland). These variations mean that the system is inherently complex and asymmetric.

58. There was general agreement from all our witnesses, except the United Kingdom Government, that the application of the Formula is unclear. Some decisions, especially those relating to Formula by-pass, are taken within the Treasury with little or no consultation. Phil Jarrold of the Wales Council for Voluntary Action summed this up for us: "Our members are regularly confused, I think, by the way the Formula applies, or maybe does not apply, to individual announcements. Spending announcements are frequently silent on whether they apply to the devolved nations and whether or not there is any consequential. I do think that that lack of transparency creates problems for organisations that are trying to track these issues" (Q 624).[46]

59. Treasury Officials argued that the dispute resolution process set out in the *Statement of Funding Policy* was adequate to resolve any issues arising from Treasury decisions (QQ 476–78). However, they admitted that the dispute resolution process has never been used (Q 478). It remains untested. Moreover, the fact that the dispute resolution process has never been used is not to be taken as indicative of satisfaction across the United Kingdom with

---

[46] See para 43–48.

the decisions made by the Treasury on grant allocations, bypass and 'consequentials'. The Committee has heard considerable disquiet in the nations and regions over the decisions taken by the Treasury (paragraphs 42-48 above). Whilst devolution legislation provides a broad framework within which administrative decisions are taken, a published set of detailed criteria by which the Treasury make decisions on how to categorise expenditure would improve transparency.

60. **On every funding decision the Treasury is judge in its own cause, including whether to bypass or include any expenditure within the application of the Barnett Formula. We recommend that before decisions are made on whether the system is bypassed or create a 'consequential' there is a clear process and open consultation with the devolved administrations.**

Inadequate and inaccessible data

61. A further concern relates to the data available on the operation of the Formula. Despite its importance, the Treasury only publish limited data about devolved public spending, and the published official data appear in a number of places—in the *Statement of Funding Policy*, the *Public Expenditure Statistical Estimates*, and the annual reports of the Scotland and Wales Offices. Older published data do not distinguish clearly which level of government is responsible—United Kingdom or devolved—for particular spending in the breakdowns published in the *Public Expenditure Statistical Estimates*. There is no time series showing how expenditure has changed as a result of spending decisions made in previous years or spending reviews. It is difficult to establish comparable levels of spending in England for devolved functions as they are different in each part of the United Kingdom. At the start of our inquiry we asked the Treasury to provide data to show how the Formula has been applied to shape the grant allocations to the devolved administrations since 2003–04. We now publish this information in order to make sure that it is placed in the public domain (see pp 103–120). The Chief Secretary to the Treasury acknowledged that Treasury data could be improved and he suggested that the Committee had a role in making recommendations to that end (Q 1030).

62. **Although we acknowledge that the data on public spending have improved since 1999, we continue to be concerned that clear, thorough and readily accessible data on public spending across the United Kingdom are not yet being provided.**

63. Rather than having a multiplicity of official documents providing some data on devolved finance, **we recommend that the Treasury publish their statistics of the workings of the Barnett Formula, or its successor, in a single, coherent and consistent publication. This annual publication should contain all material data on devolved finance, showing the allocations of grant to the devolved administrations, changes from previous years and explanations for any changes made. We recommend that the statistics be monitored by the UK Statistics Authority.**

CHAPTER 6: ALTERNATIVE APPROACHES

What are the most useful comparators?

64. The Secretary of State for Northern Ireland, Shaun Woodward MP, suggested that if the Committee were to identify different approaches to delivering the block grant it would amount to a reinvention of the wheel (Q 878). We disagree. There is much to be learned from other similar exercises both in the United Kingdom and abroad. We are particularly interested in the United Kingdom-based examples which use both population figures and needs-based formulae to distribute public spending. Allocating public funds on the basis of population and an assessment of relative need is not a new concept. The most useful examples came from local government and health spending across the United Kingdom. The Committee was also interested by the formula used to determine how the Big Lottery Fund allocates its funds territorially. In addition we considered international examples, in particular those in Germany and Australia.

Local government and health spending methods

65. We were surprised at the similarity in the methods used by local government and health authorities to allocate spending based on relative need. Local government models are much more complex[47] than those used to allocate health spending but there are several common features:

- a bottom-up process which starts with the services (or sub-groups of services) provided by each authority;
- an initial allocation, reflecting population;
- adjustments to reflect heightened needs (for example, arising from deprivation);
- adjustments to reflect relative resources (for example, in the case of local government this reflects capacity to raise income from council tax);
- adjustments to reflect varying costs of service provision (for example, due to sparsity in rural areas as well as labour costs);
- a central allocation is provided to ensure authorities can provide services to the same standard (for the health service this is known as the 'health inequalities' formula); and
- 'damping' mechanisms are employed so that significant changes in the funding do not take place all at once.

66. Moreover the devolved administrations use similar formulae to allocate funds to the local authorities for which they are responsible. We see no reason why a similar type of formula based on need should not, in principle, be used to allocate funds to the devolved administrations.

The Big Lottery Fund

67. The Big Lottery Fund (BLF) distributes National Lottery funds for projects connected with health, education or the environment which are intended to

---

47 This is mainly due to the small size of the units involved.

transform communities, regions or the nation. Since 1995, the BLF has used a formula that takes into account levels of social deprivation as well as population (pp 290–1). This formula allocates funding with 77.5 per cent going to England, 11.5 per cent to Scotland, 6.5 per cent to Wales and 4.5 per cent to Northern Ireland.

68.   The BLF formula has the advantages of being comprehensible and simple. While it is not for us to comment on what the Lottery does, their formula, as it stands, is not proposed as a replacement to the Barnett Formula as the allocations between the countries are fixed and have not changed since they were first agreed. Any replacement to the Barnett Formula would need to be more flexible than that. At a more detailed level, a key component of the BLF formula, namely the number of social security claimants as a measure of deprivation, would not be appropriate either since this is outwith the block grant system.[48] The BLF formula shows that a policy based on need is feasible.

Comparative lessons from overseas

69.   We have looked with interest at the systems used to finance sub-state governments in other parts of the world. Many countries—such as Canada, Spain or Switzerland—have equalisation systems, but these operate in the context of a high degree of fiscal decentralisation and their concern is chiefly to provide a degree of parity in the ability of state or regional governments to provide public services given variations in the *tax-raising* capacity of the different parts of the country.[49] These systems do not address different levels of spending need, that which is required in the United Kingdom. The German system takes into account certain need factors, but only relating to population density and sparsity, and in the context of a complex system of horizontal (not vertical) distribution of revenues collected by the *Länder* themselves.[50]

70.   A number of witnesses drew our attention to the model of the Australian system (Q 102, 105, pp 162, 322, 342).

BOX 2

The Australian System

Australia has an advanced system of equalisation payments from the Commonwealth to the states, in which the Commonwealth Grants Commission (CGC) plays a pivotal role.

The Australian system is designed to cope with the substantial fiscal autonomy of the states and a high degree of vertical fiscal imbalance (that is, the federal government raising more money than needed for services it provides, and the states and territories being unable to raise enough money for the services they provide). While there are differences in fiscal capacity between the states and territories, these shift over time and with the exception of the Northern Territory are within a fairly limited range.

---

[48]   See Chapter 2.

[49]   See R. Boadway 'Canada', J. Lopez-Laborda, J. Martinez-Vazquez and C Monasterio 'Kingdom of Spain', and G. Kirchgassner 'Swiss Confederation' in A Shah (ed), *The Practice of Fiscal Federalism (Montreal and Kingston)* 2007; B Dafflon 'Federal-cantonal equalization in Switzerland: an overview of the reform process' *Public Finance and Management*, vol 4, No 4, Fall 2004

[50]   See L P Feld and J von Hagen 'Federal Republic of Germany' in Shah *The Practice of Fiscal Federalism (Montreal and Kingston)* 2007

The principle underpinning the system is that each state should be given the capacity to provide the average standard of state public services, assuming it does so at an average level of operational efficiency and makes an average effort to raise revenue from its own sources.

The Commission measures both the economic and social conditions in the states as they affect the relative costs of providing services and the relative capacity of states to raise their own revenue.[51]

The relativities calculated by the CGC are used to determine relative shares of the aggregate revenue of the Goods and Services Tax (a federal tax analogous to VAT), which are allocated to the states and territories to provide public services. This tax is therefore hypothecated to help fund 'state-type' services provided by the states and territories. The relativities are weighted so that about two-thirds of the amounts allocated are determined by fiscal factors (differences in taxing capacity between states and territories), and only about one-third relates to factors relating to the costs of providing services (both demand for services and variations in the costs of providing them).

The Commission is an advisory body to the federal (Commonwealth) government with terms of reference framed by the Commonwealth Treasurer, after consultation with the states and territories. Currently it has four members in addition to the Chairman. Three of the present members of the commission and the chairman have a background as civil servants working for state or federal governments (or both) and one is an academic. In practice, the 'advice' the Commission offers the Commonwealth government has always been accepted, promptly and without demur. Its impartiality is accepted by the states and territories, even when they have concerns about the implications of the system overall.

The calculations of state relativities are carried out annually, and there are periodic reviews of the overall methodology used by the Commission (approximately every 5 years).

In 2007–8 the CGC employed 45 staff (as full-time equivalents), in addition to the Commissioners. Its total running costs were about $AU7 million (about £3.4 million at the current exchange rate).

71. It is clear that the United Kingdom differs in fundamental respects from all other funding systems. In particular, the United Kingdom is characterised by historic constitutional asymmetries and by the limited fiscal powers of the devolved administrations. Consequently, with the exception of the Australian Commonwealth Grants Commission, such systems can offer relatively little to help with United Kingdom issues. What is needed is a British system to address specifically British issues.

An independent commission

72. We have drawn attention above to the lack of transparency of the operation of the system, and the dominant role of the Treasury. It is no longer appropriate for the Treasury to make decisions on the allocation of funding and to administer that system without external independent advice and audit. Though we do not believe that the Australian model for grant allocation would be right for the United Kingdom, we consider that **the role of the Commonwealth Grants Commission in Australia offers a useful**

---

[51] Commonwealth Grants Commission *Report on State Revenue Sharing Relativities 2009 Update*, section 1, paras 2–3.

institutional model of an independent body that has responsibility for making recommendations about the allocation of finance.

73. **An independent body, similar to the CGC, should be established in the United Kingdom. It should be the role of such a body to recommend the allocation of public monies based on population and through a new needs-based formula. Within the new framework the Treasury will need to retain its authority over the overall level of the block grant but not the proportionate allocation of the grant between the devolved administrations. This independent body might perhaps be called the United Kingdom Funding Commission. This Commission would carry out an assessment of relative need, undertake periodic reviews, and collect and publish information on an annual basis about the allocation of finance to the devolved administrations.**

74. The Australian CGC advises the Commonwealth Government. It does not make grant allocations itself. This has merit and should be applied in the UK-context. However, the expectation should be that recommendations on the allocations of funding made by an independent Commission will be accepted by the United Kingdom Government, as is the case with the UK Boundary Commission. One means to ensure this would be for its recommendations to be required by statute to be laid by the Government before the House of Commons for approval. While it would remain open to the Commons to reject such recommendations, it would also require considerable disquiet for a rejection to occur. It would remain for the United Kingdom Government to decide on whether there were exceptional circumstances which required the new system to be bypassed. **The Commission should be advisory in nature rather than have the power to make substantive allocations of funds on its own account. Its advice should, however, be published.**

75. **The remit of the Commission should be to determine the relative needs of each devolved administration on a regular basis, perhaps every five years. The Commission should also advise on the relative proportions of public spending for the devolved administrations, compared with spending within England, during a transitional period and recommend annual increments based on the latest population figures.**

76. The Commission should be comprised of specialists from appropriate professional backgrounds. They could come from within the United Kingdom or from outside. While they should have a variety of personal, professional and geographical backgrounds, they should not speak for any place, government or other interest. Their role would be to contribute independent expertise, not advocate interests. **The Commission should be appointed by the United Kingdom Government as a non-departmental public body. It should be politically neutral and independent. It should be composed of a small number of members with sufficient expertise to ensure the dispassionate and authoritative nature of its work.**

77. In addition, we consider that the Commission should undertake a number of other functions in relation to funding the devolved administrations. These include:

- collecting and supervising the publication of data on the funding allocated to the devolved administrations. Such data should be published annually in order to improve the accuracy and clarity of both the data and system;

- advising on whether identifiable spending by the United Kingdom Government in England is on England-only or UK-wide functions, so that questions whether 'consequential' adjustments arise in the devolved nations no longer fall simply to be decided by the Treasury; and

- undertaking periodic reviews of the working of the system over its previous terms, and any problems that have arisen with application of the new formula. This would, in particular, include the appropriateness or otherwise of specific factors of the formula for the distribution of funding.

78. Under these arrangements, it would no longer be appropriate for the Secretaries of State for Scotland, Wales or Northern Ireland to receive the grants and transmit them to the devolved administrations. **We recommend that future grants be payable directly from the United Kingdom Government to the consolidated fund of each devolved administration.**

CHAPTER 7: THE PRINCIPLES OF A NEW APPROACH

A needs based approach

79.   The Chairman, in summing up Lord Barnett's evidence, said: "you devised a mechanism which you hoped would last for a few years. You did not expect it to last for as long as it has lasted. You are not sure now whether it is based on the right criteria and you lean towards having, among other things, a needs-based assessment". Lord Barnett agreed (Q 77). The first assessment of relative needs across England, Scotland, Wales and Northern Ireland was conducted between 1976 and 1979. That study was confined to the main services which were to have been devolved under the Scotland and Wales Acts 1978.[52] The Government's White Paper of November 1975, Our Changing Democracy, stated that, although a neat formula could not be devised to produce fair shares for the devolved administrations from year to year "objective information on standards and needs would help the Scottish [and Welsh] administration[s], the Government and parliament to make their judgments".[53]

80.   The idea of an assessment of relative needs was developed in the July 1977 White Paper, Devolution: Financing the Devolved Services, which stated: "it is clearly desirable that discussion of the appropriate level of devolved expenditure should be informed to the greatest possible extent by objective data and a mutual understanding of needs and problems".[54]

81.   **We find the argument that devolution funding should be based on relative need to be a compelling one. Public spending per head of population should be allocated across the United Kingdom on the basis of relative need, so that those parts of the United Kingdom which have a greater need receive more public funds to help them pay for the additional levels of public services they require as a result. Those levels of need—and those parts of the United Kingdom which require them—may well change over time. Historically, they have certainly done so.**

Achieving substantive fairness

82.   The territorial Secretaries of State told us that the Formula was 'fair' (Q 878).The Chief Secretary to the Treasury said that he considered the Formula to be "fair enough" and "It does a pretty good job. There is a minefield of issues involved in moving away from it which produce new risks to good public administration" (QQ 979, 988, 993). On the other hand most witnesses thought that the allocation of public expenditure under the Barnett system produced results that were not fair or equitable, though the reasons for their opinions differed. Lord Barnett said of the Formula, "The latest figures ... show that in England the average public expenditure is some £1,600 per head less than in Scotland ... I do not think it is fair. It cannot be fair with this kind of gap" (QQ 4–6). This was a view shared by the TaxPayers' Alliance: "The Formula has failed to deliver the more equitable

---

[52] See Chapter 3.

[53] Cm 6348, paras 99, 100 and 222.

[54] Cm 6890, para 71.

and fair allocation of spending originally envisaged ... In an era of devolved government, such spending gaps are impossible to justify to English taxpayers. They ask why they should subsidise higher Scottish, Welsh and Irish spending" (p 353). Many witnesses argued that the Barnett system produced unfair and inequitable results because it took no account of need (pp 132–3, 222, 344).

83. At present the annual adjustments in funding are calculated by reference to population figures. We heard evidence that this fails to recognise the particular needs in Wales and Northern Ireland. The Northern Ireland Confederation for Health and Social Services pointed out that because it is purely based on population, the Formula "places Northern Ireland at a disadvantage trapping the region within an ongoing cycle of underinvestment" because it fails to recognise the higher levels of deprivation in Northern Ireland (p 222). Plaid Cymru argued that the Formula disadvantages Wales because it "takes no account of the disproportionate impact that [the relative economic decline for much of the twentieth century] has had on Wales compared with the rest of the UK" (p 130). It could also be argued that the Formula fails to take account of the increased relative economic prosperity Scotland enjoyed over much of the past two decades.

84. The Chief Secretary to the Treasury, when asked about the Calman Commission report, indicated to us that his concern was not with the principle of a needs-based distribution but its practice: "I think it should be justified by need. I would agree with that, but my concern would remain that we would still need to devise a way of moving towards that position" (Q 1001). He argued that it might not be possible to agree on a new formula—to achieve what he described as 'consent'—"I wonder whether you could come up ... with a UK-wide formula which was able to command the consent of political parties and politicians in different parts of the UK"(Q 984).

85. He also said that he was open to suggestions: "if there is an alternative which is better, which is capable of commanding political consent, which can be delivered with satisfactory transitional arrangements which do not disturb too much the predictability which good public servants need in their finances, then I am all ears!" (Q 988).

86. John Swinney MSP told us that it would be very difficult to undertake an assessment of relative need (Q 192) and that in any event such an assessment should not be undertaken because it could not be 'objective'. Others said that financial arrangements should only be changed as part of a much more comprehensive review of devolution as a whole (or indeed of the whole constitution and governmental structure of the United Kingdom) (Q 741). We reject these views.

87. The 1979 Needs Assessment drew the conclusion that a simplified method of assessing need produced a very similar outcome to the more comprehensive and time-consuming approach which was the main focus of the study. This supports the view that a small number of broad-brush, proxy indicators may be a viable way to assess the relative needs of the devolved administrations.

88. Any new system of allocating funds should retain the clarity of the Barnett Formula and the stability over time which it affords. But unlike Barnett, it should also be related explicitly to an assessment of need. To do that it should be based on the following principles:

- **The new system should consider both the baseline and any increment in funds.** The entire block grant for each devolved administration should be subject to regular review to ensure that it continues to be appropriate for the needs of each administration and fair in relation to the needs of the other administrations.

- **The new system should be fair and seen to be fair.** By relating resources to current relative needs the system should help distribute funding to those areas of particular need across the United Kingdom as a whole and avoid the anomalies which arise from the present arrangements. Consequently it should ensure a substantial degree of territorial justice—something that is not achieved presently.

- **The new system should be comprehensible.** Although the Formula is clear in its method of calculating the proportion of incremental changes in the block grant, the basis on which the baseline—and therefore the block grant as a whole—rests is not. The statistics on which each allocation is made and the details of the allocations themselves should be placed on record and published. There should also be an audit process to ensure that the system is being appropriately administered.

- **The new system should respect territorial autonomy.** The new system must leave the devolved administrations free to decide what to do with their block grant. There should be no ring-fencing. Neither should the new system attempt to duplicate the detailed assessments of local needs that the devolved administrations must themselves necessarily make.

- **The new system should be stable and predictable.** Each administration must be able to make budgetary decisions in advance and to plan their spending as they see fit. The new system needs to reconcile flexibility (so resources change when relative needs change), with consistency of funding over budgeting periods to enable planning for both financial matters and service provision by the devolved administrations.

A system for determining the baseline

89. Any assessment of need involves both technical expertise and judgement. Many of these judgements will actually be made by technical experts (for example, the choice of precisely which version of any particular measure to use). If such an assessment is to command respect, it must be conducted by a body that is seen to be impartial. This is vital since any needs assessment is bound to be confronted with conflicting interests, not just between England and the devolved administrations but among the devolved administrations themselves. Scrutiny can be expected from all quarters. It is for this reason among others that we recommend that the work be carried out by an independent Commission. An explanation of that conclusion was set out in Chapter 6. But while independence is essential, it is not on its own enough to meet the vital condition that the results of the assessment must be capable of being clearly explained to the public. That depends on the method for assessing relative need adopted.

90. On the basis of our earlier consideration of specific needs across the four countries, we believe that a method capable of providing comprehensible answers is feasible. Its key features should be:

- a top-down approach;[55]

- the use of only a small number of specific measures of need, restricted to national statistics and, ideally, measured by the number of people having that particular need; and

- combined into a single measure for each country using weights that are consistent with the actual level of UK public expenditure.

A top-down approach

91. Our argument in favour of a top-down approach, using a small number of aggregate statistics, is based on the following considerations:

- given the priority we accord to comprehensibility, a simple approach is a high priority. While it may reasonably be countered that the cost of simplicity is a certain rough justice, we would expect that cost to be lower at the national level than locally since differences *between* countries are much smaller than differences between localities *within* countries;

- we also favour a top-down approach because of the inherently top-down nature of the exercise itself. The opposite approach, that the formula should be built up from a detailed assessment of a full range of needs locality by locality, would mean trespassing on the domains of the devolved administrations; and

- finally, although we are not recommending the Big Lottery Fund formula should be adopted, its formula shows that such an approach is viable.

Selection of measures of specific aspects of need

92. The first step is to choose measures of particular aspects of need which are deemed to be important. We can illustrate our approach with a few underlying points:

- First, we want indicators that measure the number of people with particular need X as a proportion of the total population of the country in question. This approach has a number of features. As a principle, it reflects the view that needs are inherent to people and that any two people with the same need should be treated equally. In practical terms, once the particular needs indicators are agreed what is then required is to count the number of people with that need.

- Second, each of the measures of need chosen should be a national statistic. While there will always be room to challenge the choice of measures, we believe that the measures themselves should be beyond reproach. The creation of the UK Statistics Authority (UKSA) in 2008 strengthens the capacity of the United Kingdom to take decisions about sensitive matters such as these on sound evidence. A way should be found to involve the UKSA in the process of needs assessment, not just in a quality assurance role but also in the construction of new measures of need where necessary. For example, the absence of any housing measure reflects the lack of a UK-wide measure of housing need (quantity and/or quality) and likewise, the absence of any sparsity measure.

---

[55] That is, top-down rather than the bottom-up very lengthy approach used by HM Treasury in the 1979 Needs Assessment exercise.

- Third, the indicators should not be capable of being affected by the policy choices of the devolved administrations. It would be inappropriate to create incentives which could be seen to encourage the devolved administrations to make policy choices which might increase their need.

93.   Our starting point is that funding should reflect the size of population. If that were all there was to it, an allocation would be one in which the amount of grant per head was uniform.[56] But needs also vary according to other factors. Children have very different needs from pensioners; and we would expect that both groups would have a higher overall level of need per head than working-age adults. It will be up to the Commission to decide on the factors used to build up the specific needs assessments but we expect it to take account of the age profile of the population—which therefore serves to modify the starting point of a uniform allocation per head. We also envisage other factors that might affect the territorial distribution of need. As with children and pensioners, there are groups of people whose overall level of need could be expected to be above the average such as: those with low incomes; those with disabilities or suffering from ill-health; and those with needs that may arise from a country's economic weakness. Some of these needs are met to a greater or lesser extent by social security.

94.   However, these indicators matter only insofar as there are differences between the four countries and regions. Figure 2 shows a small selection of what we regard as some of the key measures of relative need. It suggests that there are indeed differences between the needs of the devolved administrations and England, in some cases to a considerable extent. We do not regard this selection as complete or definitive; other factors might be chosen with equal validity. However, we consider that any needs assessment should take these aspects into account, the four aspects shown here being represented by eight measures of relative need, as follows:

- The **age structure of the population** is represented by the number of a) children aged under 5; b) children aged 5 to 16; and c) adults aged over 65.

- **Low income** is represented by the number of children in poverty as conventionally defined (that is, belonging to households with an income below 60 per cent of the UK median; and per capita household income). This is a measure of a very different kind from all the others. It is expressed as an inverse so as to preserve the rule that a high number (low income per head) indicates high need and vice versa. Since poverty tends to be associated with other aspects of deprivation, child poverty may also be seen as a more general measure of need.[57]

- **Ill-health and disability** are represented by the mortality rate (the number of deaths in each country, standardised for the age profile of the population) and work-limiting disability (the number of people of working-age in each country with a work-limiting disability).

- **Economic weakness** is represented here by unemployment (the number of people of working-age in each country without a job and actively

---

[56] It should be stressed that this is not just a statement about the increment added to last year's grant (which is, under Barnett, allocated on a uniform per head basis) but about the grant as a whole, that is, the baseline amount inherited from last year plus this year's increment.

[57] Note that both these income measures include the offsetting effects of the transfer payments made via Social Security and tax credits.

seeking one). Along with work-limiting disability, this may be seen as capturing aspects of additional need among the working-age population.

FIGURE 2

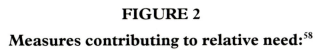

Measures contributing to relative need:[58]

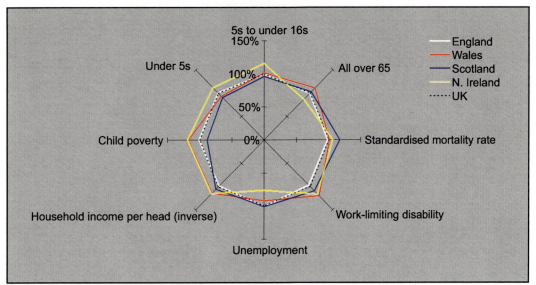

95.   Figure 2 shows each country's level of need for each measure relative to that of the United Kingdom. So for example, a value of 105 per cent indicates a level of need 5 per cent above that average. The further away from the centre a country is on any particular dimension, the higher its level of relative need on that measure. An appropriately coloured line then joins each country's eight points. All the measures used here come from official statistics for each of the four parts of the United Kingdom.

96.   The main points of note here are as follows:

   •   On most measures, the levels of relative need in England and Scotland are quite similar (that is, the blue and the white lines are usually quite close to one-another). England has slightly higher levels in matters to do with children and poverty and Scotland has much higher levels regarding disability and mortality.[59]

   •   With the main exception of mortality, need in Wales is usually higher than in Scotland (that is, the red line is usually outside the blue one).

   •   Reflecting its young population, need in Northern Ireland is high on the children measures and low on the pensioner measure. In this combination of highest need on some measures and lowest need on others, Northern Ireland is unique.

97.   This diagram does not produce a single overall estimate of relative need for each country because to do so requires that the individual measures be brought together in a weighted combination. On the other hand, provided that any two countries' lines in this diagram do not cross one-another too often, a robust conclusion can be drawn about which of the devolved administrations or England have the higher overall level of relative need

---

[58] A full description of the data used here, their sources and the numerical values, are contained in Appendix 5.

[59] One point to note is that the lower level of need on the dimension of child poverty in Scotland is a very recent phenomena dating only from the middle years of this decade.

irrespective of the precise weights chosen. On that basis, we could conclude that any well-based combination of the measures would show that England and Scotland have lower overall needs than Wales or Northern Ireland. But while overall need in England is almost certainly lower than that in Scotland, the relative positions of Wales and Northern Ireland could reasonably differ depending on precisely how the different measures end up being combined.

98.   Figure 3 is an extended version of Figure 2 that includes four extra measures. Two of these are possible alternatives to those shown in Figure 2 (to do with disability and employment) while two are additions or elaborations (to do with poverty and the age profile). Choosing different indicators obviously produces a slightly different picture. On this analysis there is some uncertainty about precisely how need in Northern Ireland relates to the others. The conclusion regarding England, Scotland and Wales remains undisturbed. This highlights the need to ensure that the choice of indicators is made by the independent Commission, as with the choice of weights that go with the chosen indicators.

FIGURE 3

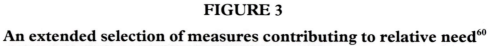

An extended selection of measures contributing to relative need[60]

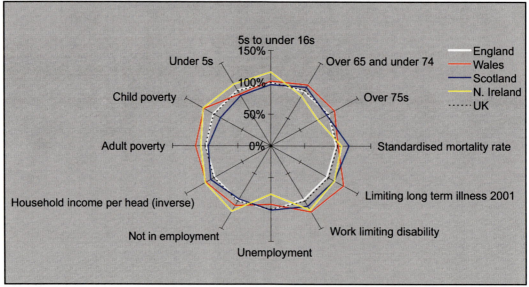

99.   Neither of our lists is definitive nor complete. The absence of any measure of housing need is the single most obvious gap, arising from the fact that there is no UK-wide standard (at least later than the 2001 Census) on which to base a measure. Another such gap is the lack of any measure of sparsity, which is usually seen as raising the cost (and therefore the need for resources) in remote areas. In acknowledging this last point, we would draw attention to the effect of sparsity in the latest resource allocation formula for the NHS in Scotland. This shows that while taking account of sparsity is vital for several remote areas (adding more than 15 per cent to the allocations for the Northern and Western Isles, and around 6 per cent to that for Highland), the overall resource effect is slight (between 1 per cent and 2 per cent for Scotland as a whole). This reflects the very small proportion of the total population actually living in such areas.[61]

---

[60] A full description of the data used here, their sources and the numerical values, are contained in Appendix 5.

[61] Source for the 2009/10 formula:
http://www.isdscotland.org/isd/servlet/FileBuffer?namedFile=2009–10 analysis—HB Summary.xls&pContentDispositionType=attachment

100. The order of relative need among the four devolved administrations and England shown here (with England and Scotland quite close to one another, and both clearly lower than Wales and Northern Ireland) in no way corresponds to the pattern followed by the current allocation of public expenditure per head which is shown in Table 4.

101. **While we are not in a position to reach a conclusion about precise relative needs in the four countries and regions, on the basis of our initial analysis, we believe that Scotland now has markedly lower overall need than Wales and Northern Ireland in comparison to England. The current allocation of spending does not properly reflect this basic pattern across the devolved administrations.**

102. **We recommend that an alternative system on the broad lines suggested above be created to establish a new baseline grant for the devolved administrations and to review needs on a regular basis so that allocations of funds to the devolved administrations reflect the changing patterns of relative need.**

Combining the specific measures into a single overall measure

103. Our examination of relative need in the devolved administrations has stopped short of taking the next step of combining the individual elements of need into a single overall measure for each country. To do this, weights are required to be attached to each individual measure of need, based on an analysis how much public expenditure each type of need gives rise to. In some cases, the public expenditure statistics provide the information required: for example, the division of educational spending between different age groups (under fives, other children, young working-age adults etc). In others, a crucial judgement has to be made as to what causes or drives cost: for example, although health spending per head can be broken down according to age, age may not be the critical factor driving spending. As for a need like child poverty, the question of how much spending (beyond social security benefits) this gives rise to (or ought to give rise to) is more uncertain.

104. Such a task is not for us to undertake. Clearly, the weights used to combine the specific measures of need into a single measure should yield results which in aggregate correspond to the actual level of public expenditure at the United Kingdom level. The aim is that the overall level or relative need in a country or region can be explained as the combination of (a) the number of people with various types of need (such as in the measures above) multiplied by (b) the United Kingdom average amount of public expenditure per head devoted to meeting that need at the moment.

105. In a sense, this is the precise opposite of the kind of approach (which has been suggested to us by some) that relative need should be measured by a single, simple proxy. If such a proxy were to be used (the inverse of household income per head seems the most suitable because it reflects the dampening effects of social security payments), it would lack any basis in how public expenditure is *actually* deployed to defend it.

106. **The task envisaged for the Commission is to select indicators of the type illustrated above and to combine them in the way suggested. It is a feature of this approach that there can be choice in which, and how many, of the indicators are used for the ultimate formula. All of them will be brought into the analysis.**

107. Within this overall approach, other issues will need addressing. One which we suspect may be quite important concerns capital expenditure and whether it should be treated equivalently to current expenditure. While a case can certainly be made to base current spending on current needs, capital may need to move more slowly—or indeed be adjusted for a period to reflect past over- or under-investment. Exactly how this might fit into the overall framework would need to be determined.

Annual increments and transition

108. Although we suggest that the baseline will require investigation and re-ordering on a needs-basis every five years, it will be for the Commission to determine changes made to the block grant on an annual basis. Two features of the current Formula should be retained for this annual up-rating. One is the degree of predictability over the aggregate grant which the devolved administrations currently enjoy. The other is the way that, by relating increases in each devolved administration to that in England, the Treasury is able to retain control over the aggregate increase in public expenditure.

109. The Chief Secretary to the Treasury told us that "there are big administrative and political risks associated with fundamentally restructuring some of these arrangements in a way which is contested. So given the complexities ... which I think would be involved in coming up with this formula, I think it would be inevitable that the dimensions, the mechanics of that formula, would be contested. I think the result of that would be quite complicated change arrangements" (Q 1004).

110. **We recognise the need for a carefully-handled transition to implement the new arrangements. We anticipate a transitional period of between three and five years, preferably no more than seven, before the new arrangements are brought wholly into effect. Smoothing mechanisms would need to be put in place to manage the change from present levels of funding to those that the new arrangements would supply.** If the pattern of grant per head related to need is indeed a long way removed from the current pattern, then these smoothing mechanisms will be a very important element of the new system. Since relative need can be expected to continue to evolve in the future (not least due to the continued divergence in population trends that is currently expected), these mechanisms will be a permanent part of the new system. It may be appropriate to manage the transition to reflect the needs of the devolved administrations so that those who are shown to need more funding should receive additional funds more quickly than those who are shown to need less funding to achieve their new level of block grant. An asymmetric answer may be appropriate when applied to an asymmetric problem. **Both the length of the transition period before the new system is brought wholly into effect and the pace at which the actual levels of grant per head converge with the needs-based levels are issues upon which the new Commission should advise the United Kingdom Government.**

Other matters

Review

111. A system of the sort we recommend would minimise the likelihood of any disputes between governments about grants or related matters. However, if

there were such a dispute, we regard the JMC as the appropriate forum for its resolution.

Status of the new arrangements

112. We acknowledge that there are other detailed administrative decisions which are for the new Commission to determine. **The new arrangements we propose will need to be embodied in statute, at least in general outline. That legislation should contain provisions to ensure that the quinquennial reviews indeed take place.**

APPENDIX 1: SELECT COMMITTEE ON THE BARNETT FORMULA

The Members of the Committee who conducted this inquiry were:

Lord Forsyth of Drumlean
Baroness Hollis of Heigham
Lord Lang of Monkton
Lord Lawson of Blaby
Earl of Mar and Kellie
Lord Moser
Lord Richard (Chairman)
Lord Rooker
Lord Rowe-Beddoe
Lord Sewel
Lord Smith of Clifton
Lord Trimble

Specialist Advisers:

Dr Peter Kenway
Mr Alan Trench

Declared Interests:

Lord Forsyth of Drumlean
Non-executive Director, J & J Denholm Ltd
Non-executive Director, Denholm Industrial Service (Holdings) Ltd
Senior Managing Director, Evercore Partners
Patron, Craighalbert Centre, Scottish Centre for Children with Motor Impairments
Director, Centre for Policy Studies
Member, Steering Committee International EB Research Appeal
Patron, CINI UK (registered charity No.1092674)

Baroness Hollis of Heigham
None

Lord Lang of Monkton
Non-executive Chairman, China Internet Ventures Ltd
Non-executive Director, Marsh & McLennan Companies Inc (insurance broking, investment, pensions, employee benefits etc)
Non-executive Chairman, SI Associates Ltd (management consultants)
Non-executive Director, Charlemagne Capital Ltd (fund management)
Non-executive Director of the Advisory Board of OJSC Sun Valley (a Ukranian company in which Waterford are major shareholders; unpaid as such but provided for within the fee received from Waterford)
Non-executive Director, SoyuzNefteGaz (Russian) (unpaid)
Consultant, National Strategies Inc (an American company) [non-political]
Consultant, The Waterford Group (a commercial not a political consultancy)
Member of the Council of The Rugbeian Society
Member of the Prime Minister's Advisory Committee on Business Appointments

Lord Lawson of Blaby
Chairman, Central Europe Trust Co Ltd (advisory)
Chairman, CET Capital Limited (private equity)
Chairman, Oxford Investment Partners
Shareholding in CET Capital Limited

Earl of Mar and Kellie
> *Member of the Scottish Independence Convention.*
> *Owns land in Clackmannanshire.*

Lord Moser
> *None*

Lord Richard (Chairman)
> *None*

Lord Rooker
> *None*

Lord Rowe-Beddoe
> *Chair of the Welsh Development Agency from 1993–2001*
> *Deputy Chair, UK Statistics Authority*
> *and other interests in Wales in the arts, Church and not for profit sectors.*

Lord Sewel
> *None*

Lord Smith of Clifton
> *None*

Lord Trimble
> *None*

A full list of Members' interests can be found in the Register of Lords Interests: http://www.publications.parliament.uk/pa/ld/ldreg.htm

Specialist Advisers

Dr Peter Kenway
> *Director of the New Policy Institute; an independent think tank founded in 1996. NPI undertakes a mixture of grant-funded and consultancy projects. NPI's principal grant-funded project is one of monitoring all aspects of poverty, deprivation and social exclusion, for the Joseph Rowntree Foundation. The output from this includes an annual UK report and biennial briefings for Scotland, Wales and Northern Ireland.*
> *Welsh Assembly Government's Child Poverty Expert Group*

Mr Alan Trench
> *Research Fellow in the Political Economy of Multi-Level Governance in the School of Law at the University of Edinburgh (funded by the Swiss Confederation, through the Embassy of Switzerland in London).*
> *Consultant to 'Unlock Democracy' for an educational website project*
> *Constitutional adviser to Tomorrow's Wales/Cymru Yfory (unpaid).*
> *Honorary senior research fellow, The Constitution Unit, Department of Political Science, University College London (unpaid).*
> *Contributor to the Constitution Unit's 'Devolution Monitoring Reports' for Scotland and Wales, on Intergovernmental Relations and related matters.*

APPENDIX 2: LIST OF WITNESSES

The following witnesses gave evidence. Those marked * gave oral and written evidence and those marked ** only gave oral evidence.

	Alliance Party of Northern Ireland
	Australian Commonwealth Grants Commission
**	Lord Barnett
	Madoc Batcup
**	Professor David Bell—University of Stirling
*	Dr Gillian Bristow—Cardiff School of City & Regional Planning
**	Mr Peter Bunting— Irish Congress of Trade Unions, Northern Ireland
	cebr ltd
*	Chartered Institute of Public Finance and Accountancy
	City of London
**	Mr John Corey—Northern Ireland Public Service Alliance
	COSLA
	David Hume Institute
*	Department of Finance and Personnel (Northern Ireland)
*	Department of Health
	East England Development Agency
*	Economic Research Institute of Northern Ireland
	Federal Trust for Education and Research
*	Professor James Foreman-Peck—Cardiff Business School
*	Mr Jim Gallagher—Ministry of Justice
*	Mr Paul Griffiths—Consultant to the Welsh Local Government Association
*	Dr Eurfyl ap Gwilym—Plaid Cymru
	Professor David Heald—University of Aberdeen Business School
*	Mr Victor Hewitt—Economic Research Institute of Northern Ireland
*	HM Treasury
	The Independent Experts Group to the Commission on Scottish Devolution
*	Professor David King—University of Stirling
	Local Government Association
	London Councils
**	Lord MacGregor of Pulham Market
**	Mr Seamus McAleavey—Northern Ireland Council for Voluntary Action
*	Mr Patrick McCartan—Northern Ireland Confederation of Health & Social Services
*	Professor Iain McLean—University of Oxford and IPPR North

Russell Mellet

★★ Mr David Moxham—Scottish TUC

★★ Rt. Hon Jim Murphy MP—Secretary of State for Scotland

★★ Rt. Hon Paul Murphy MP—Secretary of State for Wales

★ National Health Service

Northern Ireland Civil Service

★ Northern Ireland Confederation for Health and Social Services

★★ Mr John Osmond—Institute for Welsh Affairs

Parliament for Wales Campaign

★ Plaid Cymru

★ Mr Peter Price, Cymru Yfory—Tomorrow's Wales

Reform Scotland

★ Scottish Council for Voluntary Organisations

★ The Scottish Government (NHS Scotland)

★ Mr Ruchir Shah—Scottish Council for Voluntary Organisations

★ Professor John Simpson—Queen's University, Belfast

★★ Mr Michael Smyth—University of Ulster

Society of County Treasurers

Sustrans Cymru

★★ Professor Kim Swales—University of Strathclyde

★ Mr John Swinney MSP—Cabinet Secretary for Finance & Sustainable Growth, the Scottish Government

★★ Mr Geraint Talfan-Davies—Institute for Welsh Affairs

TaxPayers Alliance

★ Professor Colin Thain—University of Ulster

★★ Sir Brian Unwin

★ Wales Council for Voluntary Action

★ Welsh Local Government Association

★★ Rt. Hon Shaun Woodward—Secretary of State for Northern Ireland

APPENDIX 3: CALL FOR EVIDENCE

The House of Lords has established a Select Committee on the Barnett Formula. The Membership of the Committee is:

> The Terms of Reference for the inquiry are:
>
> *To examine the purpose, methodology and application of the Barnett Formula as a means of determining funding for the Devolved Administrations of the United Kingdom, to assess the effectiveness of the calculation mechanism to meet its purpose and to consider alternative mechanisms.*
>
> These orders of reference *exclude* consideration of three main areas:
>
> The overall system of funding the Devolved Administrations—in particular the question of whether greater tax-raising powers should be accorded to the devolved administrations;
>
> Other political aspects of the devolution settlements; and the distribution of funds within the different regions of the United Kingdom

The Committee would be pleased to have your views. The Committee in particular will explore the following key issues in detail and would welcome your views on any or all of the following questions. Please note that questions are not listed here in any particular order of importance.

Written evidence must arrive by no later than Monday 2 March.

Application of the Formula in practice

Are the present disparities in public expenditure per head of population between the countries of the UK a consequence of the Formula itself, the historic baseline or of other factors? To what extent are those disparities related to need?

What effect does the Barnett Formula have in terms of equity and fairness across the UK as a whole?

What effect does the Barnett Formula have on the aggregate control of public expenditure?

What measure of flexibility do the Devolved Administrations (DAs) presently enjoy in allocating funds, between various policy areas, between capital and current spending, and for accounting purposes? Is there any need for reform in this area?

Formula By-Pass and the Barnett Squeeze

Has convergence of levels of public spending in Scotland, Wales and Northern Ireland based on the English level of spending happened, and if not why?

To what extent did bypassing of the Formula occur before 1999? Has scope for such "Formula by-passes" changed? What have been the consequences of that change in scope?

Data Quality and Availability

Are sufficient data available to enable a clear understanding of how public spending is distributed across the UK, and to show the working of the Formula as set out in the Statement of Funding Policy?

What additional data, or ways of presenting data, would be necessary to undertake a new needs assessment, or otherwise to reform the Formula?

What additional data, or ways of presenting data, should be available to ensure that the Formula is transparent in its application?

What body should undertake the collection and publication of such data?

Need for reform/Alternatives to the existing Formula

Do the advantages of the Formula as presently constituted outweigh its disadvantages?

Should the Barnett Formula be (a) retained in its current form, (b) amended or (c) replaced entirely?

Should the Barnett Formula be replaced by a system more adequately reflecting relative needs, costs of services or a combination of both? If so, what factors should be considered as part of a needs assessment?

What practical and conceptual difficulties (particularly for defining 'need') would arise in carrying out a needs-based assessment? How can these difficulties be overcome?

Should a needs-based assessment seek to encompass a wide range of factors or be limited to a smaller number of indicators of 'need'?

Who should carry out a needs-based assessment, if one were to take place?

Decision making and dispute resolution

How effective, appropriate and fair are the processes and criteria by which HM Treasury determines matters relating to the Barnett Formula? In particular, is the way HM Treasury determines whether items of spending in England do or do not attract 'consequential' payments under the Formula, and claims by the DAs on the UK Reserve, appropriate and fair?

Are the existing procedures for resolving disputes between HM Treasury Ministers, territorial Secretaries of State and the Devolved Administrations about funding issues adequate?

How could dispute resolution procedures be improved?

For more information on the Committee, including Members' declared interests, please see:

http://www.parliament.uk/parliamentarycommittees/hlbarnettformula.cfm

APPENDIX 4: GLOSSARY

Annually Managed Expenditure (AME). Expenditure within Total Managed Expenditure (TME) that does not fall within Scotland's Departmental Expenditure Limit (DEL). Expenditure in AME is generally less predictable and controllable than expenditure in DEL and cannot reasonably be subject to firm multi-year limits.

Asymptotical. An asymptote is a straight line always approaching but never reaching a curve.

Barnett Formula. A non-statutory mechanism that is used to determine changes in the budgets of the Devolved Administrations in Scotland, Wales and Northern Ireland. Introduced in relation to Scotland in 1978 and extended to Wales and Northern Ireland in 1980 and 1981 respectively, it was named after Lord Barnett who was Chief Secretary to the Treasury at the time.

Barnett squeeze. A term used to describe one of the theoretical effects of the Barnett Formula, given its properties. Namely that, all other things being equal, the Formula would produce convergence in levels of funding per head. There is some debate about whether convergence has actually happened in practice.

Cash planning: A method of planning government expenditure entirely in cash. Under cash planning, expenditure plans for later years are expressed in expected outturn prices, and there is a strong presumption against compensation for unexpectedly high inflation. This can be compared to the earlier system of **Volume Planning** which expressed future years in terms of the prices of the current Survey year and which involved revaluing these plans each year in line with specific-price inflation.

Departmental Expenditure Limit (DEL). Expenditure within programmes which is not classified as Annually Managed Expenditure (AME). Expenditure in DEL is generally more predictable and controllable than expenditure in AME. DEL is therefore set on a multi-year basis.

Devolution is the process of transferring power from the centre to sub-national units. It can take three forms. *Administrative* devolution is the practice of transferring responsibilities from central government departments to territorial departments of the same government. *Executive* devolution is the process of transferring the prerogative powers from ministers of central government to ministers of devolved governments, usually under statutory authority. *Legislative* devolution describes the transfer of law-making powers from the centre to other legislatures. The devolution settlement in the United Kingdom is often described as being "asymmetrical", meaning there are fundamental differences between the arrangements in each country.

End-year flexibility (EYF). A mechanism to allow unspent provision in the Departmental Expenditure Limit in one year to be carried forward to the next.

European Structural Funds. The European Structural and Cohesion Funds are the European Union's main instruments for supporting social and economic restructuring across the EU. They account for over one third of the EU budget and are used to tackle regional disparities and support regional development through actions including developing infrastructure and telecommunications, developing human resources and supporting research and development.

Formula by-pass. A term used to describe the phenomenon of the UK Government providing funding to the Devolved Administrations without applying the Barnett Formula, in circumstances where the Formula would appear to be applicable.

Gross Value Added (GVA). Gross value added is the difference between output and intermediate consumption for any given sector/industry. That is, the difference between the value of goods and services produced, and the cost of raw materials and other inputs used in production.

Identifiable expenditure. The spending that can be identified as benefiting individual regions and countries in the UK. The Public Expenditure Statistical Analyses (PESA) take know out-turn spending data across all government departments and the devolved administrations and therefore across the whole UK and split this spending data into spending that can be identified as benefiting individual regions (identifiable expenditure) and that which cannot, because it benefits the UK as a whole, such as defence spending.

Horizontal fiscal equalisation (HFE). Transferring resources from rich areas to poor ones. In Australia, the Commonwealth Grants Commission, an independent statutory authority, oversees a horizontal fiscal equalisation regime.[62] See also **Horizontal fiscal imbalance (HFI)**

Horizontal fiscal imbalance (HFI). A situation in which governments at the same level have access to different levels of resources. Within each level of government, there are inevitably some jurisdictions that are richer than others, and it is this that results in differences in resources available to governments at the same level. See also **vertical fiscal imbalance**.[63]

Hypothecation means earmarking particular sources of finance to particular issues. Thus, hypothecated taxes are those earmarked to particular forms of spending. Hypothecation is designed to clarify the link between what the public pays and the services that it gets. Its advantages are that it can be a good way of ensuring revenue for popular programmes and overcoming public mistrust of the way politicians use tax revenue. Its disadvantages are that it introduces an element of inflexibility into spending and sometimes makes it hard to cut programmes once they are underway. Moreover, hypothecated taxes may prove to be less hypothecated than the public is led to believe. Officials can usually find ways to fudge the definition of the specific purpose for which a tax is hypothecated, letting government regain control over how the money is spent.

Northern Ireland Office. The Northern Ireland Office (NIO) was created in 1972. Its role is to support the Secretary of State for Northern Ireland in taking forward Government policy in Northern Ireland. In addition to supporting and fostering the political and democratic process in Northern Ireland, the Department has overall responsibility for upholding law, order and security including the provision of criminal justice services.

Scotland Office. A UK Government Department established on 1 July 1999. The Scotland Office replaced the old *Scottish* Office that existed before devolution and

[62] Mucatelli et al, *First Evidence from the Independent Expert Group to the Commission on Scottish Devolution* (Edinburgh: Heriot-Watt University, 2008), p 32, available at http://www.hw.ac.uk/reference/ieg-first-evidence.pdf (accessed 18 November 2008).

[63] Bird, R., International Studies Program Working Paper 0302, *Fiscal Flows, Fiscal Balance, Balance and Fiscal Sustainability* (Atlanta: GSU, 2003), online at http://ideas.repec.org/p/ays/ispwps/paper0302.html (accessed 19 November 2008).

had been a major government department led by the Secretary of State for Scotland. Now part of the Ministry of Justice, the Scotland Office is headed up by the Secretary of State for Scotland and has two key roles: to represent Scotland's interests at Westminster and to act as guardian to the Devolution Settlement.

The Treasury. Her Majesty's Treasury is the United Kingdom government department responsible for developing and executing the British government's public finance and economic policies.

Vertical fiscal imbalance (VFI). A situation in which some levels of government have relatively large tax revenues and relatively small expenditure responsibilities whilst other levels of government have relatively small tax revenues and relatively large expenditure responsibilities. In federal states, central (federal) governments often collect most taxes whilst state and local governments are often responsible for more expenditure than they can finance from their own sources of revenue. VFI is the difference between expenditures and own-source revenues at different levels of government.[64]

Volume planning: A method of planning public expenditure according to the volume of goods and services that the state will be providing—actual hospital beds, miles of roads and so on—rather than just the cash cost of such spending. **Compare Cash Planning.**

Wales Office. A UK Government Department established on 1 July 1999. The Wales Office replaced the old *Welsh* Office that existed before devolution and that had responsibility for a wide range of policy areas and a total annual budget of £7bn (1997–98). Now part of the Ministry of Justice, the Wales Office supports the Secretary of State for Wales in ensuring the smooth working of the devolution settlement in Wales. It is Wales' voice in Westminster and Westminster's voice in Wales.

---

[64] Bird, R., International Studies Program Working Paper 0302, *Fiscal Flows, Fiscal Balance, Balance and Fiscal Sustainability* (Atlanta: GSU, 2003), online at http://ideas.repec.org/p/ays/ispwps/paper0302.html (accessed 19 November 2008).

APPENDIX 5: DATA DEFINITIONS, VALUES AND SOURCES USED IN THE 'NEEDS DIAGRAMS'

The table below shows the definition, source and value for each of the needs measured shown in Figures 2 and 3. All figures are shown as a percentage of the UK average, with one exception (household income per head), all measures are calculated as the number of people with that need in any country as a proportion of that country's total population. [65]

Needs measure (2005 to 2007 average except where stated)	Data source	England	Wales	Scotland	N. Ireland
The number of under 5s	ONS: Population Trends dataset	101	94	91	112
The number aged 5 to under 16s	ONS: Population Trends dataset	100	102	96	116
The number aged over 65 and under 74	ONS: Population Trends dataset	99	111	106	91
The number of over 75s	ONS: Population Trends dataset	100	111	97	82
The number of deaths adjusted for the age profile of the population ('Standardised Mortality Rate')	NISRA: Annual Report 2007	98	101	117	106
The number of people with a limiting long-term illness (2001)	2001 Census	97	126	110	110
The number of working-age adults with a work-limiting disability	Labour Force Survey	97	120	109	116
The number of working-age adults who are unemployed	Labour Force Survey	101	92	101	76
The number of working-age adults not in employment	Labour Force Survey	99	108	96	119
Gross disposable household income per head (inverse)	ONS: Regional Gross Disposable Household Income April 2009	98	114	106	115
The number of adults in households with an income below 60% of the UK median income before housing costs have deducted ('Adult poverty')	DWP: Households Below Average Income 2009	99	115	95	107
The number of children in households with an income below 60% of the UK median income before housing costs have deducted ('Child poverty')	DWP: Households Below Average Income 2009	101	118	88	119

---

[65] So for example the measure of child poverty is not the same as the child poverty rate, which expresses the number of children in households with relative low income as a proportion of the total child population, rather than of the total population.

Minutes of Evidence

TAKEN BEFORE THE BARNETT FORMULA COMMITTEE

WEDNESDAY 28 JANUARY 2009

Present	Forsyth of Drumlean, L	Rooker, L
	Hollis of Heigham, B	Rowe-Beddoe, L
	Lang of Monkton, L	Sewel, L
	Lawson of Blaby, L	Smith of Clifton, L
	Mar and Kellie, E	Trimble, L
	Richard, L (Chairman)	

Examination of Witness

Witness: LORD BARNETT, a Member of the House, gave evidence.

Q1 *Chairman:* Lord Barnett, thank you very much for coming. Since you are the originator of the formula and it bears your name, it seemed appropriate to me that you should be the first witness that this Committee hears. Would you like to make an opening statement?

Lord Barnett: Thank you very much, Lord Chairman. I would be happy to do so. Can I make clear how it all began? It began of course when I was chief secretary in 1977–78. I changed the then method of increasing or decreasing expenditure annually, largely cutting public expenditure for most of my five years. The system I decided to use at that time to change was that any increase or decrease in the overall budget for public expenditure for the whole of the UK should be divided amongst the regions on a population basis which was roughly 85 per cent England, 10 per cent Scotland and 5 per cent Wales. Northern Ireland was taken as the same at 5 per cent but of course in Northern Ireland's case they got a lot more than that for a variety of reasons which will be fairly obvious. It was not then described as the Barnett Formula. Indeed, in a book I published in 1982 called *Inside the Treasury* there is no reference to the name Barnett Formula because it was not at that stage ever known as that. It only became known as the Barnett Formula when it was kept going, from a system I used in 1977–78, by the Thatcher government and then the Major government for 18 years. That is when it became known as the Barnett Formula. Nobody wanted to change it for fear of upsetting the electors in those areas. It did not have any particular effect on the 1997 election when it will be well known the then Conservative Government lost every seat in Scotland and in Wales. I would take some credit for that but I am not doing so this afternoon. It had no effect, I am sure. The latest figures for expenditure per head on average in the regions, which I am sure you will have seen, show that in England the average public expenditure is some £1,600 per head less than in Scotland. That is the planned expenditure for 2007–08 which is the latest figure published by the Treasury. The outturn may well be slightly different as it has been each year in the past. The latest figures will be out in April this year. They are not published until April in any year. These are the very latest figures. The reason I was worried about all this and why I pressed the Liaison Committee to allow there to be an *ad hoc* select committee was that I was worried that the figures would so upset people in England that they would demand a separation which would be, in my view, hugely damaging because I have no wish to see the UK split into three separate countries. I want to see the UK sustained and I thought it did not seem fair and therefore should be reviewed with a view to seeing whether changes were needed and what those changes should be. The terms of reference which I eventually agreed with the Liaison Committee, as you will have seen, are very tight. They exclude anything other than a review of the formula with a view to seeing whether it should continue and whether there should be any changes based on the need mechanism. How that need would be devised and defined would be a matter for this Committee to recommend. That basically is what has happened so far. I would now be very pleased to answer any questions that the Committee has for me.

Q2 *Chairman:* Can I perhaps go back to the origin of the mechanism that you introduced? When you introduced it, did you think that that was going to include the baseline grant to the devolved administrations or only changes in the overall amount?

Lord Barnett: I thought it might last a year or two before a government would decide to change it. It never occurred to me for one moment that it would last this long.

Q3 *Chairman:* Did you think it would deal with the block as well as changes to the block?

Lord Barnett: Within the total public expenditure of the areas concerned is included expenditure which is outside the formula, outside the system. For instance, all benefits—employment benefits, child benefits—are excluded from the formula but not excluded from the figures which are in this document. The figures in this document will include those. It is possible—indeed very likely—that in some parts—say, Scotland, Wales or Northern Ireland—some of the benefits are higher for all kinds of different reasons. Those are allocated on a need basis, on a benefit or entitlement basis. That would continue. The remainder of public expenditure is allocated under the system I used in 1997–78 and is still being used. The present government has continued it. The previous government under Tony Blair kept it going and it has been going now for some 30 years.

Q4 *Chairman:* Going back again to the position you were in when you introduced the mechanism, was it designed to produce a degree of automaticity in the way in which the Treasury expended its resources or was it designed to do something else?

Lord Barnett: I have seen the argument that there is automaticity, in that it would eventually be fairer based on population. I cannot recall having that in mind. When I used the system I asked my former private secretary at the time who, amazingly enough, is now the head of the new Statistics Commission—when I finished he went to Number 10—and he could not recall that I had ever put the idea to Cabinet. No doubt you can check that. When I devised the system, which I did not think would last, I never thought it would automatically lead to some fairer system as has been suggested. Indeed, if you look at the figures over the years, the gap between England and Scotland on average allocation has risen from 2002–03 when it was 1,100 to the current nearly 1,600. It never occurred to me for a moment that it would come together.

Q5 *Chairman:* You devised a mechanism which helped the Treasury to distribute money. You did not base it on need. It was a straight population index and you did not think it would last.

Lord Barnett: No.

Q6 *Chairman:* Do you think it has been successful?

Lord Barnett: Successive governments over 30 years have kept it going. I do not consider it is successful. I do not think it is fair. It cannot be fair with this kind of gap. It may well be that any investigation will show that there are other reasons for allocating more expenditure to particular regions, but that is a matter for this investigation and review. At the moment, all one can say is that the figures indicate a huge gap in the expenditure of the different regions. This is the argument I put on the floor of the House to the Liaison Committee to have this Committee set up. I got the support of a couple of Members of the Committee, for which I was grateful. We eventually persuaded the Liaison Committee to set up this Committee which I hope will be successful in making important recommendations which will be used by a government in due course.

Q7 *Lord Lang of Monkton:* Lord Barnett emphasised what he thought was the temporary nature of this formula. I have always understood that that was the case on the grounds that this was a deal put together under pressure by a chief secretary who had to try to cut expenditure under the pressures of the time and secretaries of state for territorial departments who had to defend in their territorial areas of responsibility the fact that they had protected spending. Would that be a fair summary of it?

Lord Barnett: Yes, I think it would. The job of chief secretary in those days was pretty difficult. I had to negotiate with all secretaries of state and they all wanted more money. It relieved me of a little pressure in the sense that, as you say, there was a round sum allocated to Scotland, Northern Ireland and Wales and they then decided on the allocation within their territories. I did not have to be involved in that.

Q8 *Lord Lang of Monkton:* We now know however that a needs assessment had been being carried out at roughly the same time in preparation for a Scottish Assembly which the government sought to legislate upon at that time, but the findings of that report have never been published and were not used as part of your negotiation at all. There was no needs assessment to try to rebase the figures?

Lord Barnett: Not to the best of my knowledge.

Q9 *Lord Lang of Monkton:* Why do you think that did not happen?

Lord Barnett: As you may know as a former secretary of state and a member of the Cabinet, making changes is something you try to avoid if you can. Nobody has wanted to change what has become a formula.

Q10 *Lord Lang of Monkton:* This was at the inception of the formula when you had the chance to—

Lord Barnett: It was not a formula at the inception. It was just a method of allocating public expenditure that I devised.

Q11 *Lord Lang of Monkton:* Would it be fair to say that the way in which you changed things was that, although it was a per capita grant, instead of making

it a percentage capita grant to Wales, Northern Ireland and Scotland, of the figures allocated in England, it was a cash figure per capita in that Scotland, Wales and Northern Ireland got the same cash figure as was allocated in England. Because their block base lines were higher, it was a smaller percentage increase and therefore gave the impression of creating convergence.
Lord Barnett: The percentage increase was purely based on approximate population, which was 10 per cent for Scotland, 5 per cent for Wales and 5 per cent for Northern Ireland and the rest England.

Q12 *Lord Lang of Monkton:* How were you contemplating achieving convergence?
Lord Barnett: I personally did not contemplate convergence. I do not know who did.

Q13 *Chairman:* As I understand it, you did not know that there was a needs assessment being prepared inside the Treasury at the time?
Lord Barnett: I am not clear what you mean.

Q14 *Chairman:* The Treasury was preparing a needs assessment at the time that you devised this mechanism.
Lord Barnett: If they were, it was not done by me personally. I was not doing any needs assessment.

Q15 *Chairman:* Why could not the mechanism have been based on the needs assessment?
Lord Barnett: The mechanism as it was devised was not based on needs. It was based on pure population.

Q16 *Baroness Hollis of Heigham:* There is this needs assessment study report which came out in December 1979 from the Treasury. You were aware of this?
Lord Barnett: I would be aware of it.

Q17 *Baroness Hollis of Heigham:* You chose not to use it or it was after the event or you thought it was too complex?
Lord Barnett: In December 1979 I had already left office.

Q18 *Lord Rooker:* It started in the autumn of 1976. It says, "It was agreed in the autumn of 1976 a study should be undertaken of the relative public expenditure needs in England, Scotland, Wales and Northern Ireland." That was when it was agreed, so during 1977 and 1978 and most of 1979, for three years, work was going on on this needs assessment.
Lord Barnett: Work goes on on all kinds of issues, certainly in the Treasury and I imagine in every other department. All that work did not result in any change in the method of allocating expenditure.

Q19 *Chairman:* Perhaps that is the point. What we are interested in is why not.
Lord Barnett: I cannot tell you why not now. It is 30 years ago. All I can tell you is it did not happen.

Q20 *Lord Forsyth of Drumlean:* Might I suggest a possible explanation? Given what you have said about your criticism of the Barnett Formula which most people take to be the base line plus the formula that gives the percentage share relative to population of the constituent countries that make up the United Kingdom, your criticism in your opening statement was about the level of the base line. You said that the amount being spent in Scotland was proportionately higher per head of population. That is a reflection on the base line. What is puzzling us is why, if you are concerned about that now, you were not concerned about it then and why the Barnett Formula did not just allocate the additional revenue relative to population; and why, given that in the Treasury at that time there was work being carried out on a needs based approach, which you also said in your opening remarks you wished to do, you have not gone for that. The explanation I have in my political head is that this was a time of great political difficulty with the nationalists on the rise and to introduce a formula which was based on needs that would have resulted in Scotland getting less would perhaps not be very appealing.
Lord Barnett: Basically, you are saying that politically major changes of such a description could have had great political consequences. Governments do not like making those kinds of changes. You are quite right.

Q21 *Chairman:* What I still do not quite understand is you did not know that the needs assessment was being carried out.
Lord Barnett: I would have some vague idea that some of my officials were looking at all kinds of things.

Q22 *Chairman:* Did you know they were looking at this?
Lord Barnett: I was not concerned with it, no.

Q23 *Chairman:* If you did not know about it, the political calculations which have just been put to you do not apply in the same way.
Lord Barnett: Certainly.

Q24 *Baroness Hollis of Heigham:* Another version of events might have been that the formula you devised was seen by you, as you suggested, in a relatively temporary way. This needs assessment might go on to displace it as and when consent had been gathered as a more permanent settlement.

Lord Barnett: They were very difficult times. I wanted to get out of the way the public expenditure allocation once a year. Any other matters I did not want to get involved in. I did not want to change anything else.

Q25 *Lord Lawson of Blaby:* May I try and inject a certain amount of clarification into this slightly confused picture? If I get it wrong, I very much hope that you will tell me. I am sure you will. First of all, as I understand it, you did not consider the long term consequences of the system because you did not consider it a system and you were not thinking about the long term. You were just dealing with the particular situation at the time. Is that right?
Lord Barnett: That is right. I just wanted to get through every day without too much trouble. That was what I was concerned with.

Q26 *Lord Lawson of Blaby:* No one would criticise you for that. The fact that some academics said that the Barnett Formula had mathematical properties which would ensure convergence was part of the thinking at the time. Not only is that completely wrong and not in your mind at all; also, is it not the case that the mathematical properties would suggest a minimal amount of convergence. The reason that there has been considerable divergence, which you pointed out in your original statement, is because population trends have diverged and this has not been taken into account.
Lord Barnett: In any population changes that have taken place over the years there have been slight adjustments. I recall when Alistair Darling was the Secretary of State for Scotland. There had been some small changes and he was asked: would he change the formula to the extent of those small changes? He made some moderate adjustments.

Q27 *Lord Lawson of Blaby:* You presented to us a stark picture of how a situation had arisen by the perpetuation of this system, which rightly or wrongly bears your name, that there had been now a great divergence which is unfair and, you suggested, dangerous because of ill feeling in England.
Lord Barnett: Yes.

Q28 *Lord Lawson of Blaby:* You have obviously looked into why this has happened. It seems to me to be the major reason but I may be wrong. Do you conclude that the main reason why it has happened is that the population of England has been increasing quite considerably; whereas the population of Scotland has been falling? There has not been anything remotely like an adequate adjustment for these different population trends and therefore the consequence is the consequence you spelled out for us in your opening statement.

Lord Barnett: Yes, I am sure that is the case. All one can say is those are the figures now.

Q29 *Lord Lawson of Blaby:* I am not blaming you for it.
Lord Barnett: You cannot blame me for the population change. I can be blamed for all kinds of things but not that. At the time, the mathematical calculations some had made, that it might eventually result in this, that or the other, frankly did not disturb me at all.

Q30 *Lord Lawson of Blaby:* You probably were not aware of them.
Lord Barnett: Yes.

Q31 *Lord Forsyth of Drumlean:* I wonder how you thought it would work. If the base line in Scotland, say, for health was 25 per cent higher per head than in England, under the formula, they would get the population increase of any increase in England, so they would get 10 per cent of whatever increase was agreed in England. If you take the health service for example, more than 70 per cent of the costs in the health service are pay. Pay is negotiated nationally. If the Scottish health service just got their population related increase, there would be a huge hole. Therefore, what needed to happen when there were various nationally agreed pay rises was that money had to be added over and above the formula. That is how the divergence came about.
Lord Barnett: That might well be the case. The fact is I never intended and thought—who knows what would have happened after an election?—or anticipated that it would last that long as a method of allocating expenditure. It was a purely simplistic method of allocating public expenditure.

Q32 *Lord Forsyth of Drumlean:* I think we have established that it was done as a deal to get you through and I understand that. I have been there myself. The government, of which you were a member at that time, had a policy which of course failed, but the intention was to set up a Scottish Assembly. It is widely believed that the Barnett Formula as it is described was the system that was going to be used to fund that Parliament. I wonder whether the work that was going on in the Treasury on a needs based assessment was the latest of plans to have a devolved assembly. Did you see it as a short term measure and, if you did, how were you proposing to fund the devolved assembly?
Lord Barnett: I did see it as a short term measure. I assumed that later there would be some kind of discussion on needs, of course, because needs were not discussed. You have to understand the circumstances of the time. To start discussing major

changes did not seem something that would be politically acceptable.

Q33 Lord Forsyth of Drumlean: I very much understand that.
Lord Barnett: There might have been wide belief of something going to happen. You may have been part of that wide belief. I was not.

Q34 Lord Forsyth of Drumlean: Not putting words into your mouth, if we were to conclude that the Barnett Formula system was a kind of interim measure to get you through some political difficulties and some public expenditure difficulties that occurred at that time but, for the devolved assembly which you were planning, you would probably have looked at something rather more permanent and more carefully thought through, based on needs, that is probably why the work was going on?
Lord Barnett: I am sure, but that was well before, as you know, the setting up of a devolved assembly for Scotland. The allocation of money to the Scottish Assembly and they way they would allocate it was not something at that time that was giving me a great deal of thought. There would be somebody thinking about it but I was not.
Lord Sewel: It is fairly clear from the publication of the needs assessment study that its whole history and genesis is leading up to devolution. It is related to devolution and what happens after the Scottish Assembly is set up. You can see how that silo thinking could absolutely persist while you are nicely handling your little formula to get you out of some scrapes and all this is going on in a room next door but the two never meet.
Lord Lawson of Blaby: The point which has emerged is that the needs assessment and the Barnett Formula or the Barnett arrangement are two separate things. The Barnett arrangement had nothing to do with devolution; whereas the needs assessment did look to that.

Q35 Baroness Hollis of Heigham: The question is why the needs displacement did not go on to displace the Barnett Formula in due course.
Lord Barnett: That came over the next 18 years which Lord Forsyth and Lord Lang were very directly involved in. They kept the formula going and turned it into a formula. I did not. In the book I published that was never referred to because I never devised it as a formula.

Q36 Lord Sewel: When you were applying the formula, was it your intention that that would determine the allocation of public expenditure to the Scottish Office or would it inform the allocation of public expenditure so that there would still be negotiations around the amount that the formula

produced; or was the formula going to be the be all and end all?
Lord Barnett: It should be clear—I hope it is—to the Committee that at that time the devolved assembly was certainly not in my mind.

Q37 Lord Sewel: I said "the Scottish Office".
Lord Barnett: Whatever the Scottish Office were discussing, they never told me and I was not terribly interested in what they were discussing.

Q38 Lord Sewel: I am not making myself clear. In allocating expenditure to the Scottish Office, the formula would come up with an amount.
Lord Barnett: Yes.

Q39 Lord Sewel: Did you see that amount as being the end of the matter or would you have discussions around the amount? Did the formula determine the allocation or did it help inform the allocation?
Lord Barnett: It determined it. They got 10% of whatever was the overall increase or decrease in expenditure.

Q40 Lord Sewel: In effect at some stages, at some times, you had to deal with the type of problem that Lord Forsyth has indicated where, if you had a large public sector wage settlement, you had to go outside the formula or else you would decimate everything that was in the formula.
Lord Barnett: Maybe Lord Forsyth as the Secretary of State for Scotland at that time went to the chief secretary and said he wanted more money. I am sure he did, as any good secretary of state would. Whether he got it or not is an entirely different matter and it has nothing to do with the formula.

Q41 Lord Sewel: Although it starts off determining it, what happens in the light of reality is that you have negotiations round it when the shoe starts pinching?
Lord Barnett: If the Secretary of State came to me after the allocation was made on the basis of the system that the Cabinet had accepted, I would very likely have told the Secretary of State what to do. There was no point in coming and discussing it with me. Indeed, lots of secretaries of state used to come and have discussions with me about more money. I usually gave them a gin and tonic and off they went. They did not get anything else.

Q42 Baroness Hollis of Heigham: If you had envisaged that your formula might well have been in place three to five years down the road and had you been in a position still as chief secretary, would you then have expected that the formula would not have been robust enough to carry the sort of pressures we have been talking about? In other words, is the difficulty in our discussion simply that you thought you were doing and intended to do a one, maximum two, year devise and thereafter people might or might not develop from that, start again, replace it or whatever?

Lord Barnett: That is precisely it. I never for one moment thought it would continue for very long. It did not seem to be done on a fair basis.

Q43 *Chairman:* In the last answer you gave, you talked about the formula or the mechanism—whatever you like to call it—applying to increases or decreases. Is that increases or decreases in the block as well as other expenditure?

Lord Barnett: Other expenditure would be based on needs or entitlement, benefits, unemployment benefits, child benefits. That would not be part of the formula. That would be quite separate, although it is included in the overall figures in this document.

Q44 *Chairman:* Your mechanism clearly was only concerned with the block because at that stage you did not have this problem of up and down expenditure.

Lord Barnett: Yes. It was quite separate from the expenditure that went in benefits.

Q45 *Lord Forsyth of Drumlean:* Lord Sewel's point is a very important one about this idea of whether it determined or informed. Would you accept, albeit you saw the formula as a temporary thing and you have been very kind in suggesting that Lord Lang and I did our bit in arguing our corner, that the thing depends very much on the old pre-devolution system where you have a secretary of state in Cabinet who can say when the chief secretary is being difficult with the Chancellor and you need to sort this out, and you have the opportunity for a continuing dialogue? If you do not have that opportunity for a continuing dialogue, is it not a weaker system for funding the devolved administration?

Lord Barnett: On the question of whether it is weaker or stronger, in some ways you have a better idea than me because you used it for longer than I did. I only used it for a year or two. Cabinet would have had an opportunity to say to you as secretary of state, "You should have more money or less money". You would presumably argue your corner in Cabinet, but under this system Cabinet looked at the total level of public expenditure and what was decided for the whole of the UK within it. Scotland, Wales and Northern Ireland got their share on a population basis, other than those on needs and entitlements.

Q46 *Baroness Hollis of Heigham:* Had this formula still been in place some three years down the road under your supervision, had there been the example just quoted of the NHS and had you agreed that in all decency the outcome had to be an increased resource

to Scotland, would you have gone back and expected to have adjusted your base line or would you have regarded that as continuing to be an area of negotiation which you would expect to crop up each and every year which might, each and every year, take up a larger and larger proportion of the total allocation going to Scotland?

Lord Barnett: You have to understand that if you change the base line with regard to Scotland in the total level of public expenditure that has been agreed by Cabinet, then somebody else is going to get less. That is why it would be so difficult to get it through Cabinet, to change the base line figure.

Q47 *Lord Lawson of Blaby:* There are two ways of looking at public expenditure. As I understand it, when the Labour Government first came in, they had a brick by brick approach, spending so much on this and so much on that. Then you had the total at the end of the day. Then times got a little more rigorous and you had to have instead the envelope approach, saying, "This is the envelope. Everything has to fit in the envelope." That was what I continued as Chancellor in the successive government. It is always the case, if you have the envelope approach, if you are going to give more for one, there is less for others. There is no way around that. This is not peculiar to the system of allocating funds to Scotland. It is a general feature of public expenditure control.

Lord Barnett: I am not clear what you are trying to make me say.

Lord Lawson of Blaby: Just say, "Yes".

Lord Sewel: Or, "Very wise".

Q48 *Earl of Mar and Kellie:* Can I bring you up to the operation of the Barnett Formula today and in particular I suppose in Scotland? All three of the devolved administrations have some other sources of revenue. They strike me as being council tax and business rates which have largely stayed the same. Also, there is the possibility of the Scottish variable rate of basic rate of income tax. Do you have any ideas as to why the Scottish variable rate has not been used?

Lord Barnett: You would have to ask the present leader of the government in Scotland. It is not a matter for me and it is not a matter for this Committee, I would have thought with great respect, under the very tight terms of reference that were eventually agreed.

Q49 *Earl of Mar and Kellie:* I might like to challenge you gently on that.

Lord Barnett: Do not challenge it with me, please. It is a matter for the Committee.

Q50 *Earl of Mar and Kellie:* We are still talking about a system which is basically a block grant system with possibilities of some small changes using the other means which were legislated for.
Lord Barnett: Are you talking about taxation?

Q51 *Earl of Mar and Kellie:* Yes.
Lord Barnett: Taxation is specifically excluded under the terms of reference of this Committee.

Q52 *Lord Lawson of Blaby:* Reading the summary that you gave us, Lord Chairman, of the terms of reference, we cannot consider whether greater tax raising power should be accorded or presumably whether less tax raising power should be granted but we can investigate how the current system operates.
Lord Barnett: It is not for me to interpret the terms of reference. That is for the Committee. As I read it, it says, "These terms of reference are intended to exclude consideration of the overall system of funding the devolved administrations." The Committee may want to change those terms of reference. I can only say that is what they are now and that is what I agreed with the Liaison Committee in the setting up of this Committee.

Q53 *Lord Forsyth of Drumlean:* I think Lord Mar and Kellie's question, which is a perfectly reasonable question, is nothing to do with taxation and how the Scottish Parliament might be funded or any of that. What he was getting at is, if you are just giving a population related share of the increase—we have examples like health and others—how do you deal with that gap? You can have the Secretary of State going along to see the Chancellor saying, "Houston, we have a problem" and doing a side deal outwith the formula. What Lord Mar and Kellie was suggesting is it is the tartan tax, the variable tax mechanism. Did you envisage something of that kind as being the least mechanism which would fill the gap? It is equivalent to the position of local government which gets revenue on a needs assessment basis, but they have the ability to levy a local rate or community charge or whatever it is in order to fill that gap. Was that in your mind?
Lord Barnett: No, it was not. I was talking simply about the allocation of public expenditure, nothing else.

Q54 *Lord Forsyth of Drumlean:* Lord Mar and Kellie's question is about this problem even with a needs based system. Is there a role for some kind of —?
Lord Barnett: Even with the existing system, it is still open to a secretary of state, as you would have done, to go to the Chief Secretary or the Chancellor and say, "I want more money."

Baroness Hollis of Heigham: Conventionally in other areas of finance—and this might have included House authorities that have funding raising powers and certainly local authorities—it is a double calculation. It is needs which include not just population obviously but sparsity, density and deprivation as the classic ones, and then the capacity of that community to meet its own needs by virtue of its own growth. You test that by proxies like have they increased school dinners, what is the taxable information we have going into the Treasury about the ability to pay and so forth; and therefore, the degree to which it is appropriate for other people from other areas to make good that deficit, that gap, if any or indeed whether the surplus gets to be redistributed. It is quite hard in some ways to envisage a needs based formula that I think we all feel would be more appropriate as a longer term basis for finance, I would guess, certainly from your remarks which I would share. On the other hand, we need to find the capacity of that community, territory or whatever to meet its own needs by taxing its own local people. I suppose that is the wider question. Is it appropriate to look at needs without also looking at resources? Your response has been that you do resources by getting the Secretary of State to argue for more money, but there is also the question of whether it would be appropriate, given that perception of how you approach public finance, to regard the capacity of the local community to raise money as being part of the consideration.

Q55 *Chairman:* We are straying a little outside the terms of reference.
Lord Barnett: Could I try to answer the question? The resources element in the whole of the devolution question is quite separate from this allocation of public expenditure. The resources element is something that was given when the assemblies were set up in Scotland in particular. That is quite separate from whether public expenditure allocation should be done under this system or any other system. That is now what this Committee, I assume, is going to look at. It is not for me to say how the Committee proceeds in this way. The resources element is not relevant.

Q56 *Lord Sewel:* We have to focus on the fact that what we are looking at is really how you apply a formula based allocation in the context of devolved government. Prior to devolution, you could get by if things got difficult because the Secretary of State would come knocking at your door and say, "We have trouble. We need a bit of a formula bypass here" and they would get it or they would not get it. That type of adjustment is virtually impossible under a devolved system so the formula becomes absolutely rigid. Is that an appropriate way of funding devolved governments?

Lord Barnett: That is a big, big question. It is not relevant, it seems to me, to the whole question of whether this method of allocating public expenditure is the right one. You may want to change the method of allocation.

Q57 *Lord Trimble:* In talking about alternatives so far, you have used the terms "fair" and "need". Do you regard a fair system as being a needs based system?

Lord Barnett: I would have thought it would be but of course it would need to be a flexible one. It need not be fixed in stone, but you would need to have a leading economist of some kind to devise or define how much of this total is including higher levels of unemployment, lower levels of unemployment, more children or whatever. When that is decided, then you would have to look at what would be a fair way of a needs basis. For example, it may well be in Scotland that, because of the large areas with small populations, you need to allocate more expenditure. It may be fairer that they get it. I am not saying that could not be the case.

Q58 *Lord Trimble:* This is where we have to work out what strategy to use. If you start to look at local, particular circumstances, does that not draw you on to doing a detailed examination of virtually every service to see what is the need with regard to education, how many children are there of particular ages, what expenditure or increased cost of delivering service will there be because of sparse populations, doing that the whole way in detail across the board; or could it be done by using some limited factors which would be proxies for need? For example, looking at GDP per head of the population in that particular region? Which route would you think of going down?

Lord Barnett: There could be a whole variety of ways of defining "need" for these purposes. I would have thought one element would need to be income per head for example in the various parts of the UK. That may mean that some parts like Scotland or Wales deserve to have a greater share of public expenditure. There would be some special cases of the kind Lord Forsyth mentioned that may need to be taken into account.

Q59 *Lord Trimble:* By saying "income per head", you are using something that I would think of as being a proxy, something that you are using as a substitute for indicating need, simply, and then you are adding to that possible special circumstances. Are you shying away from doing a detailed examination of every service in the way that this needs assessment published in 1979 does? I see a disadvantage of going

into a detailed examination because that might open up the block grant for detailed Treasury control.

Lord Barnett: The method of looking at it may well want to exclude going into that kind of detail. That would be for you, Lord Chairman, not for me. If you are going to look at this to try and see whether there is an alternative to the existing system, I do not see how you can avoid looking at various areas. The police, for example. In the past, Northern Ireland got more money for police, for obvious reasons, which would be included in these figures, which were quite separate from the formula. There may be other areas in different devolved areas of the UK deserving special needs and I do not see how you can avoid looking at that.

Q60 *Lord Smith of Clifton:* Looking at the way the system has evolved, what advantages do you think the existing system has? It must have some advantages because it has lasted for so long. What risks are associated with changing it?

Lord Barnett: The reason it has lasted so long is, as I have always said, because governments do not like making changes. For example, the present Prime Minister has said he does not want to change or review the formula. David Cameron, on his first visit to Scotland as leader, for some strange reason unknown to me and a bit of a mystery, assured the Scottish people that he was keeping the formula, since when he has, in an interview with *The Daily Mail*, made some rather different comments that he might just be interested, but not yet. The two major parties are opposed to review. That is why it has lasted so long. They are opposed to change. The question you asked me was what is the risk. The reason why I pressed that there should be a committee set up to review it is I believe a select committee of the House of Lords, an all party committee is better suited to this than the House of Commons because they would be much more partisan and party political, inevitably. The risk has always been that, if we do not make changes, the people of England will say, looking at these figures and with an astute leader in Scotland making the kind of changes, using the money in ways that are of interest to people in England but which they cannot have, as with a poll that was done in Berwick, do they want to be in Scotland or England? Obviously, if they are going to get an extra £1,600 a head, they would prefer to be in Scotland. If you ask the people of Manchester if they want to be called Scottish in order to get another 1,600, they would say yes as well. Obviously this is a real danger. That is the risk. If something is not done and an astute leader in Scotland uses the extra expenditure in ways that we cannot do in England, as with prescription charges and university fees, then the people of England will

get more and more upset and demand the very thing that they cannot get in Scotland, as I understand it.
Chairman: I like the idea of MacMancunians, I must say.

Q61 Lord Rowe-Beddoe: This afternoon has been most enlightening for me, to hear from your first hand experience and to put it all into historical context. I speak for myself and I might speak for a lot more people outside of this room. The misperception and misunderstanding of this formula are enormous. If you were to ask people in Wales, or certainly in Scotland, they would not have any understanding of what you have been saying today. It has been very refreshing from that viewpoint. We have talked about the formula and the fact that it was there on a "temporary" basis, as far as you were concerned. We are obviously discussing now perhaps a better way would be to address needs. If you were sat there with a white piece of paper in front of you today, how would you begin to define the needs requirements?
Lord Barnett: The straight answer to that is I would not because, to put it on a simple piece of paper, you would need to have discussions with all kinds of people. You certainly would need a senior and sensible economist—which is not necessarily the same thing—to examine the whole of the situation and see what he comes up with. I am assuming that this Committee would get such a person to help you come to a conclusion. That is what I would have done. I certainly would not have been able to sit down with a piece of paper and devise a system that would be acceptable to Cabinet or anybody else for that matter.

Q62 Lord Rowe-Beddoe: I was really asking you about how you would begin to identify the needs.
Lord Barnett: One would employ a senior economist to look at it in detail and come back to me with a report.

Q63 Lord Rowe-Beddoe: Do you think there are natural tensions between the efficiency and effectiveness of the spend? How do you think we can begin as a Committee to look at that?
Lord Barnett: There are always tensions amongst ministers in Cabinet. Tensions exist, I am afraid, and differences exist constantly, especially when it comes to expenditure. That is one of the problems I had for five years.

Q64 Lord Lang of Monkton: As chief secretary, looking at some of the policy decisions taken for example in the Scottish Parliament on student grants and care for the elderly, no doubt the devolved executive there would describe those as needs and they would want that to be fed into their needs assessment as something that should be

acknowledged, even though it does not exist on the same basis in England. Would you as Chief Secretary be sympathetic to that or would you say no?
Lord Barnett: These are political decisions that are being made.

Q65 Lord Lang of Monkton: I am asking you as a former Chief Secretary to say how you would react if you were in position now.
Lord Barnett: I would want to get the matter settled as quickly as possible. These were decisions ultimately that were outside my remit. Cabinet would have decided what should be the levels of public expenditure. I would not give them any more, so if they wanted to take money from one area and use it for another area, that would be a matter for them.

Q66 Lord Lang of Monkton: I am talking about the needs assessment though and how one acknowledges whether or not some items of expenditure do form a justifiable need in one part of the country but not another, even though the decision was taken on a political basis.
Lord Barnett: What is justifiable, as you know, is in the eyes of the beholder. Some people may say one area of expenditure is justifiable and some other minister would say another area is justifiable. Those are political decisions outside the whole area of devising how much expenditure should go to different parts of the country.

Q67 Lord Forsyth of Drumlean: Are you saying that, provided you have a system that is seen to be fair, whatever that is—you think it is probably on some kind of needs basis, either the simpler or more complex version—there is not a problem with the Scottish Parliament doing different things. The problem arises if the system of funding is not seen to be fair.
Lord Barnett: That is right. There is not a problem until they come to you and say they want some more money because they are doing this, that or the other. Once the allocation of expenditure is made and agreed, that is it. If I were chief secretary and they wanted to come to me before because they had made a political decision to do this, that or the other, I would say, "I am sorry."

Q68 Lord Lang of Monkton: You do not think that a needs assessment, once established, would need to be updated regularly to take account of ----?
Lord Barnett: I do not think you can avoid, in any political system, having problems every year with areas of expenditure because political views change from time to time in the decisions on how public expenditure should be allocated. That will always happen. I am not pretending that any new system would stop argument within Cabinet on the

allocation of expenditure. That would be one hell of a claim to make.

Q69 *Chairman:* Whether you use the word "formula", "mechanism" or whatever to describe the way in which you allocate the expenditure between the devolved administrations for the future, do you think that should be put on some statutory footing?
Lord Barnett: I do not think so. That would be too inflexible.

Q70 *Chairman:* You would have regular needs assessments?
Lord Barnett: In my view, it would be impossible to have such an inflexible statutory system. I do not see how you can do it.

Q71 *Baroness Hollis of Heigham:* On the question of whether the Barnett Formula allows the devolved administrations sufficient scope to shape their own policy agendas, what I gather you have been saying is that provided the allocation of funds en bloc is fair the internal discussion remains as that of a political policy judgment.
Lord Barnett: Of course.

Q72 *Baroness Hollis of Heigham:* Do you think that is where we are now?
Lord Barnett: We are there now except that the blocks of expenditure allocated do not seem fair.

Q73 *Lord Lawson of Blaby:* Is it not the case that the reason they do not seem fair is because the most important, single element of need is how many people there are who have to be provided for?
Lord Barnett: Yes.

Q74 *Lord Lawson of Blaby:* When you calculated this, you calculated it on the basis of the Scottish population, compared with the English population, compared with the Welsh population and compared with the Northern Irish population. What has happened since then—it is not your fault because you had no intention in this regard—is that the population trends have diverged and that has not, except to an absolutely minimal extent, been taken into account by your successors in the operation of the true system.
Lord Barnett: Yes.
Lord Lawson of Blaby: This element of population, although it is not the only issue in assessing what Scotland needs to have, is far and away the most

important and this has been totally neglected in practice.
Lord Lang of Monkton: In practice it has not, actually. There is a census and the figures are taken into account, but censuses are always slightly out of date.

Q75 *Baroness Hollis of Heigham:* Would Lord Barnett therefore be saying that it is precisely because the formula has produced unfair results that this has given an unfair headspace to the devolved administrations to make policy decisions which appear possibly very attractive, but which are not based on any realistic assessment of opportunity of choosing between alternatives as ways of trying to find out if they are add-ons, rather than policy alternatives within an agenda? We are not having to trade one against the other because the Barnett Formula has delivered additional headspace which allows for that honey pot funding?
Lord Barnett: At the moment from the bare figures it does look as if it has allocated additional money to Scotland for example, unless an investigation shows that those higher figures are perfectly reasonable, given the circumstances. In population terms, there may be a huge increase in the number of children. Maybe more and more families in Scotland will start having eight kids like we have been reading in the papers about some families. Maybe the population of children and therefore child benefit has grown enormously. I do not know. These are things that would have to be looked into.

Q76 *Earl of Mar and Kellie:* It is often said that the greater spend in Scotland is in fact the union dividend. Do you think that is right?
Lord Barnett: You can call it what you like. I am not giving it a title. It just happens that the figures show there is more money per head of population in Scotland at the moment than there is in England.

Q77 *Chairman:* Lord Barnett, on behalf of the Committee, can I thank you very much indeed. As the father of the formula, it is very good that we heard you first and, as I understand it, what you have been telling us can probably be summed up in two sentences. You devised a mechanism which you hoped would last for a few years. You did not expect it to last for as long as it has lasted. You are not sure now whether it is based on the right criteria and you lean towards having, among other things, a needs based assessment. Is that fair?
Lord Barnett: That is fair.
Chairman: Thank you very much indeed.

WEDNESDAY 4 FEBRUARY 2009

Present   Hollis of Heigham, B   Richard, L (Chairman)
                 Lang of Monkton, L   Rowe-Beddoe, L
                 Lawson of Blaby, L   Sewel, L
                 Mar and Kellie, E   Trimble, L
                 Moser, L

Examination of Witness

Witness: PROFESSOR IAIN MCLEAN, gave evidence.

Q78 Chairman: Thank you very much for coming; we are very grateful to you. You know broadly what the scope of this inquiry is. We have been asked to look at the Barnett Formula to see how it is working and to see whether there should be a different type of formula, both in terms of what the basis of the formula is about and the way in which it is done. I do not know whether you would like to make an opening statement or whether you would like us to launch questions at you.

Professor McLean: The only opening statement I would like to make is that, as you and your colleagues will know, I have written quite a lot about this subject, alone and with colleagues, so most of what I have to say is summarised in various publications which I believe you have had: most recently a pamphlet which I published with Guy Lodge and Katie Schmuecker of IPPR; before that a book, *The Fiscal Crisis of the United Kingdom* I would be astonished if it sold more than a handful of copies but gives my views and researches up to the date of publication: Thirdly, let me mention, as your clerks may already have told you, I am a member of the Independent Expert Group on Finance which is reporting to the Calman Commission and an exchange of emails among the members of that expert committee seems to be heading towards the view that the simplest thing is for the entire interim report or first evidence from that Committee to be submitted to you. That is not in my hands but in the hands of Anton Muscatelli, the chair.

Q79 Chairman: We have had that.

Professor McLean: In that case, because I have written so much, I do not want to make an opening statement but am happy to go straight to questions.

Q80 Chairman: Perhaps I can sum up by looking at the development of the formula as it seems to have developed in the 1970s. What do you see as the purpose of the Barnett Formula? What do you think the purpose of the Barnett Formula was when it was first introduced and has the purpose changed over time?

Professor McLean: My understanding from talking to civil servants involved in the early years and from listening to and reading the evidence of Lord Barnett himself, notably to the Treasury Committee some years ago, is that there were two purposes at the beginning: the first was to get precisely a single block of expenditure so that the Chief Secretary would not be arguing with the three territorial departments programme by programme; and the second was the convergence purpose of Barnett. As members likely know, at the same time as developing what we now know as the Barnett Formula the Treasury was working with the territorial departments on a needs assessment. I say "*with* the territorial departments" rather tentatively because it is now well established that some of the territorial departments were more resistant to this than others. That was intended to assess the relative need for expenditure on the services that would have been devolved under the Scotland and Wales Acts 1978 which, as members know, were never brought into operation. The Treasury calculations from this needs assessment were that Scotland and Northern Ireland were receiving relatively more expenditure than their relative need seemed to indicate and Wales was not; Wales was getting less. However, the second purpose of Barnett, as I understand it, was to bring about convergence until such time as the expenditure in each of the three territories was brought down to the level of their relative needs, whereupon, as Lord Barnett told the Commons Treasury Committee some years ago, he envisaged that a needs formula would replace it; instead, as members know, that has never happened and Barnett is still in place.

Q81 Lord Lawson of Blaby: What evidence do you have that convergence was the purpose? So far as I am aware, and I was only responsible for the Treasury for six and a half years, convergence was never a purpose and when Lord Barnett gave evidence to us he said that in his opinion that was not the purpose. What evidence do you have to contradict all that?

Professor McLean: I have two sources of evidence: one is the mathematics of the formula which bring about convergence and as the formula was devised in the Treasury, and the Treasury is populated by very clever people, I am sure that it was not an accident that its mathematical effect is to bring about convergence.

Q82 *Chairman:* It was to Lord Barnett. That is what he told us anyway. Clever people in the Treasury may have thought it was going to happen but I do not think he did.
Professor McLean: I can only repeat that it is the mathematical effect. The second source for my evidence is talking to successive officials in the devolved countries and regions' team and other public spending teams at the Treasury who have put on record that this was the purpose. I say two pieces of evidence but I should say a third, which is that the records of the needs assessment 1979 were released to me under a Freedom of Information request in 2005 and further records have been since put into the public domain of discussions between the Treasury and the territorial departments in 1984. These are my three pieces of evidence.

Q83 *Baroness Hollis of Heigham:* Are you confident that you are not aligning or running together what appears from Lord Barnett two completely parallel but unconnected pieces work, which is the work going into the needs assessment which you referred to which you had released and was available, in which there clearly was some consideration of needs resources and so on, and what went into Lord Barnett's Formula which was entirely temporary? As far as he was concerned he told us it was entirely and simply based on population without even any obvious way of adjusting for population pluses and minuses because he did not expect it to last for 12 months. As far as he was concerned he seemed to suggest to the Committee that convergence, if it happened, was an abstract appliquéd onto it by academics looking for elegance which was not there or intended. I wonder whether the evidence you are getting from your civil servants, from the devolved territories and so on, are related to the other piece of work which was the needs assessment which came out in December 1979 as opposed to the Barnett Formula itself. Again, Lord Barnett seemed to indicate to us very clearly that he knew virtually nothing about that piece of work which was going on and that the one, as far as he was concerned, did not inform the other.
Professor McLean: You are right that the needs assessment was an entirely separate exercise although done at the Treasury end by, as I understand, the same people in the Treasury, but the needs assessment gave a static picture of the relative needs as they were judged to stand at the time of the 1978 Acts. The convergence properties of the formula are dynamic. If you start from a constant base line and you add a population proportion to that base line each year then its effects are convergent. This is not the first time I have been put on the spot of trying to give a full

explanation which would involve a white board and showing you the differential equation system which lies at the root of it. I would imagine that is not what you want but I could submit it in written evidence subsequently.

Q84 *Lord Lang of Monkton:* I am surprised that Professor McLean has not been put on the spot before and memorised a simple answer. I do not profess to know precisely how convergence works but when I was at the Scottish Office the CFO, perceiving my mathematical shortcomings, made it easy for me. What she wanted pointed out was that Goschen had applied a per capita percentage increase to the block each year at the same percentage level as the increase in England but as the Scottish block was larger than the English expenditure base line divergence took place. The Barnett Formula allegedly, although I have had no confirmation of this from any other source other than the CFO of the Scottish Office at the time, changed from a percentage increase to a pounds and pence increase per head. In other words, if England got a 4 per cent increase, Scotland would get the cash product of that 4 per cent increase which, because of the higher Scottish base line, would produce a lower percentage increase figure thus creating vary gradual convergence.
Professor McLean: That is exactly correct and is clearer than what I have just said so thank you very much.

Q85 *Chairman:* There is one problem about your theory, if I may call it that, that convergence was at the heart of the Barnett Formula when people brought it up and that is by the time the report on needs was finished he had ceased to be in the government because the government had changed. We find no evidence at all to show that convergence was in Lord Barnett's mind nor anybody else's mind at the time it was done.
Professor McLean: Firstly, as to the name members are probably aware it was an entirely unofficial nickname conferred by David Heald, the public finance economist, after a Commons hearing in 1980. Secondly, you are quite right that Lord Barnett's accounts in the early days and going up to when he gave evidence to the Commons Committee some years ago concentrated on the first of the two rationales for Barnett. As he has frequently said, it made his life as Chief Secretary easier to be dealing with a single block rather than programme by programme amounts, but the convergence property is exactly the one which Lord Lang has just expressed more clearly than I have and that was inbuilt from the start.

Q86 *Lord Lawson of Blaby:* May I put it to you that the convergence property which you think the Treasury officials put in from the start is only of significance if the formula is going to be adhered to over a considerable number of years and that was not the intention at the time. Therefore, since it was not intended to last for a long period of time convergence was not a purpose of the formula.

Professor McLean: My understanding from Treasury officials and from the two lots of FOI releases of 1979 and 1984 was that convergence was indeed in the minds of Treasury officials from the start. I think that was also perceived by the officials of the devolved administration, certainly by those in Scotland. I have talked to civil servants in Northern Ireland also who have given me a similar story. They understood it as being intended from the outset as a convergent formula. I do not know what Lord Barnett said to you at the hearing last week but I have seen him say in other places that he understood that in so far as it was a convergent formula it would run until such time as it would be replaced by a needs assessment but of course he was out of government by the time that was said.

Q87 *Chairman:* Can I read to you, if I may, the last question that he answered when he came to us last week. I put to him "You devised a mechanism which you hoped would last for a few years. You did not expect it to last for as long as it has lasted. You are not sure now whether it is based on the right criteria and you lean towards having, among other things, a needs-based assessment. Is that fair?" and he said "That is fair." It seems to me fairly clear on the evidence we have seen that convergence was not part of the exercise.

Professor McLean: I do not follow the last bit because it seems to me that what he has said to you implies that he understands that it was intended to converge until such time as a needs formula replaced it.

Q88 *Baroness Hollis of Heigham:* It is exactly the opposite. There may have been an accidental and, in the Treasury's eyes, fortuitously happy consequence if this formula were to stay in place over time but it was never intended. It seems to me we are running together consequences and intentions here.

Professor McLean: On that matter I am with Lord Lang's CFO plus my interviews with Treasury officials. I believe it was entirely intended by Treasury officials to have a convergent effect.

Lord Lang of Monkton: Even as a short-term deal it had the merit of having a convergent component because it enabled the Chief Secretary, under considerable pressure to cut expenditure, to claim to Cabinet colleagues that he had a formula in place that would gradually create convergence and it gave the Secretary of State for Scotland, Bruce Millan, the

opportunity to say that he had protected for the long term expenditure levels in Scotland.

Chairman: I do not think we will wring any more out of this particular dishcloth.

Q89 *Lord Sewel:* Can we have a look at formula by-pass and its effect on the period up to devolution. How regular was formula by-pass? What was the cumulative effect of formula by-pass on the distribution of expenditure? Has the whole concept and idea of formula by-pass changed or indeed disappeared since the devolved settlements came into place?

Professor McLean: The easiest part of that question to answer is the last because the answer is one word: yes, as I understand it. The details of formula by-pass are very difficult and, if I may say so, somewhat embarrassing for me to attempt to assess from outside with at least three or four former players in the system on your side of the table. I understand that it went in several phases. The first phase ran until, I believe, financial year 1982–83. In that first period the public expenditure was planned on volume terms year to year and, therefore, there was in effect no convergence and the issue of formula by-pass did not arise. From then until 1992 it ran on a cash basis, as it has done ever since, and therefore the potential for convergence was there. It is said in the press, and I am not in a position to confirm or deny it, that there was in the later Conservative years, or the years up to 1992 at any rate, formula by-pass sometimes for pay settlements but I am repeating hearsay when I say that because I do not know. The next phase began in 1992 when Chief Secretary Portillo re-based the population bases which had drifted away in a way which was relatively favourable especially to Scotland, and it may have been relatively unfavourable to Northern Ireland whose relative population was increasing. My impression is that there has been considerably less formula by-pass since 1992 than there may have been before then. I can only say that to the academic community this is hearsay as we have no inside information on this.

Q90 *Lord Trimble:* When you say that there was no formula by-pass since devolution I defer to your knowledge of the position in Scotland and Wales, but I had the very distinct impression in my time there was formula by-pass.

Professor McLean: You are right and I cut my story off a little bit too early. Formula by-pass in more recent years has been in relation to EU programmes including the peace programme in Northern Ireland. My impression is since 1997 there have been relatively modest amounts of formula by-pass in Northern Ireland, modest in relation to public expenditure. There has been modest formula by-pass in Wales because the politics of that were the attempt by First

Minister Alun Michael not to concede that which led to his deposition by the National Assembly and therefore it was necessary to concede, from the Treasury's point of view, some formula by-pass in Wales. I believe there has been no formula by-pass in Scotland since 1997 because the Treasury, I believe, has held the line that any EU public expenditure which comes under Objective 1 is to be treated in Scotland as being within the block. That is my understanding although I would hope that you will take evidence from the Treasury on this point.

Q91 *Lord Trimble:* My impression on the matter is that with regard to the European programmes only the peace programme was genuinely additional in Northern Ireland and that was at the insistence of the European Union itself. Quite apart from that I think there was formula by-pass in some of the Comprehensive Spending Reviews although I cannot give you hard evidence on that.
Professor McLean: You, Lord Trimble, are better placed than I am to say. I am not aware of any formula by-pass since the present CSR regime began.

Q92 *Lord Sewel:* Let us assume that formula by-pass did take place in the period up to devolution and when it was used it was used predominantly to fund public sector wage settlements, nurses and schoolteachers, because if you did not then it had a disproportionate impact on the rest of Scottish expenditure. Post-devolution, as you say, it has not occurred. How do you think the devolved governments and the UK government would respond to the sorts of financial and political situations that caused formula by-pass in the first place?
Professor McLean: I think the response of the UK government, or at any rate of UK Treasury civil servants, is easy to say. They would say, "You have a block, you get on with it and it is your problem". The response of devolved administration ministers now I suppose would be if they had a complaint they would be invited to take it to the Joint Ministerial Committee. This mechanism which was set up at devolution and has been barely been used. It was, I think, never used during the period in which Wales and Scotland had labour-led governments and for a lot of the same period Northern Ireland was under direct rule. We can expect that we will see more of it in the next few years.

Q93 *Baroness Hollis of Heigham:* What I want to follow up is in your very interesting paper when you explain despite this why convergence did not occur. You gave a couple of reasons why you felt that convergence despite what you regard as the intent behind the original Barnett Formula nonetheless did not occur in Scotland. I was wondering whether you could enlarge on that.

Professor McLean: The first reason is the one that you have just mentioned in passing, which is that social security is outside the Barnett block entirely and until recently agriculture was. Therefore, as these are entitlement programmes, the spending on them is a straightforward function of the relative proportions of claimants in the four territories. The second reason I think is that the population re-basing introduced by Chief Secretary Portillo operates in arrears. If the relative population of Scotland is continuously declining then Scotland does well until the next re-basing at which point there is a step downward change which is painfully noticed in Scotland. If the population proportions continue to diverge, so that Scotland's relative and sometimes absolute population is declining, the effect is that expenditure per head does not converge as fast as the formula would have it do.

Q94 *Lord Lawson of Blaby:* May I ask a supplementary to that? What you have said about the failure to have a population adjustment when the trends of population in England and Scotland were in different directions is obviously of central importance. Was there not a greater mischief or a greater inequity than you have implied in the sense that although the population was adjusted in 1992 after more than ten years of the Barnett Formula there was no retrospective adjustment? In other words, if the expenditure per head had been increasing relatively in Scotland during that period because of the failure of the population adjustment and all that happened with the population adjustment, leaving aside the point you make correctly that adjustments are belated and there is always this catch up, the new base line in 1992 was inevitably a better base line from Scotland's point of view than the one in 1979?
Professor McLean: I am almost sure that is correct. People outside government are not in a position to confirm that because the relevant papers are not yet publicly available but I have a strong hunch that that is correct.

Q95 *Baroness Hollis of Heigham:* Could you help me on your first point, the growth in social security expenditure, of which you say the expenditure in Scotland is higher has served to protect Scotland from any effect of convergence by going from percentage to cash? Actually I do not think I really understand that because social security is cash but, secondly, all of the stats I have seen on what is happening to the pattern of social security expenditure, given that pension expenditure accounts for 40 per cent if not 50 per cent of social security expenditure and given the difference in mortality rates in Scotland, this seems to suggest to me that actually Scottish expenditure on social security while possibly increasing should not have been increasing at the same rate certainly as in England. I do not actually understand how this works. It may be that if I saw your stats I could have a go at them but from reading it again it actually puzzles me because it should have, at best, a neutral effect and possibly even, given what we know has been happening to social security expenditure in Scotland, added to the convergence effect not the other way around.

Professor McLean: I am afraid our stats do not help on this matter because throughout the IPPR report, which I think was the one you were looking at, we have excluded social security and agriculture for the reason I gave in an earlier answer. We do not have a table of social protection expenditure per head in the four countries or the 12 territories of the United Kingdom, however the Treasury does produce this every year in PESA. If it was helpful I could supply a note to the Committee attempting to answer the question about the per head trends in social protection expenditure.

Q96 *Baroness Hollis of Heigham:* The only reason I am pressing it is a large part of your argument as to why convergence was built into the formula has not happened is because of the way the social security stats have gone and you have excluded them from your workings and I find that counterintuitive or against what I would assume to be the case.

Professor McLean: We simply have no information from outside government. The only information that we have is the information which is provided in the PESA, about which I am willing to speak if members wish me to. I am afraid I cannot improve on my previous answer.

Q97 *Chairman:* If you could let us have a note on that.

Professor McLean: I will do my best.

Q98 *Lord Moser:* I have another supplementary on convergence. I have been trying to understand not so much what the original intentions were, you have discussed that with my colleagues, to what extent convergence was the intention or was not the intention, what I am interested in is are you surprised to what extent convergence has or has not worked out? To put it statistically, could you answer an examination question, not now, on just what was expected and what has actually happened? I still do not understand that.

Professor McLean: I hope that I never have to answer an examination question on that subject because the basic information which will be required to give a statistically acceptable answer to that question is missing, and that basic information is planned expenditure in England on the programmes which form the base line.

Q99 *Lord Moser:* When you say it is missing, which is what all the papers say, it is not actually missing but it is not being made available, is that not right? Surely the data exists on what was spent by whom for whom?

Professor McLean: The data is collected retrospectively in the PESA exercise. The planning data is considerably harder to come by for people outside government. The only public documents that people like me have are the annual PESA numbers and the statement of funding policy which comes out with each spending review. I am sorry, that made me forget the first part of your question if you would kindly ask it again.

Q100 *Lord Moser:* We do need to understand not just what the intelligence was but was has actually happened. Some papers say there has been much less convergence than was expected; some say it has worked out roughly what was expected. One answer is we do not really know because we do not have the data and then we do not have the data publicly but I am sure the data is available.

Professor McLean: On the data that is publicly available I would refer members who have it to figure 4.1 on page 16 of my IPPR pamphlet. That seems to show that on the basis that we are using, which is public expenditure excluding social protection and agriculture, and done with the retrospective out-turn data supplied by PESA, that in the period since financial year 2002 to 2003 there has been considerable convergence in Northern Ireland, some convergence in Wales (which is green for those looking at the diagram, Northern Ireland is the orange) and no trend in Scotland. If it helps, I could supply colour versions. I hope the clerks have a colour version. Northern Ireland is the descending line marked with diagonal crosses; Scotland is the up and down line marked with squares; and Wales is the gently descending line marked with triangles.

Q101 *Lord Lawson of Blaby:* You very modestly said you could not answer Lord Moser's question but it seems to me to a considerable extent you answered it earlier this afternoon. Convergence is convergence of spending per head of population. As you pointed out, this does not apply to Wales and Northern Ireland and that is why there has not been this difference but the population trends in Scotland and England have been very different. Population adjustment has been belated and always lagging, therefore it would be quite astonishing if there were convergence, in fact almost impossible.

Professor McLean: That could well be correct. I am at a loss because I do not have continuous population figures which one would need to have in order to test that hypothesis but I agree it is a very plausible hypothesis.

Q102 *Lord Lang of Monkton:* We have to move on to the alternative to the existing formula because we can talk about convergence all night. It was refreshing, if I may say so, to read an academic's paper that not only covered the issues but actually expressed views, sometimes sweeping and strongly expressed, and we would like to explore that with you. Before we go on to what the alternatives that you would favour for the existing formula might be, and that will no doubt emerge, I would like to ask you about your criteria you set down: equity, efficiency, accountability and procedural fairness. First of all, that seems to me to strike a very rigid formulaic approach which may be damaging to the ultimate outcome and difficult to sustain as it has to be regularly renewed. Secondly, they are rather subjective criteria and how would you define them, particularly equity and fairness?

Professor McLean: We did not intend equity and fairness to be two different things; we intended them to be synonyms. I think the best equity formula of which I am aware in this area is that used in Australia by the Commonwealth Grants Commission which I have quoted if not in the pamphlet then certainly in the book that I mentioned at the outset. I do not have their exact words on the tip of my tongue but it is to the effect that a similarly positioned citizen living in any of the States with an averagely efficient State government should have access to the same level of public services. That would be the Australian version of an equity criterion or a fairness criterion. Back at home both the NHS and the local government formula as used by what is now the DCLG and also by the Health Department to assign spending to units within England, local authorities and health trusts are intended to achieve something of that nature although I am not aware of an official statement of the equity formula. I think all ideas of equity and fairness are based on the idea of treating similarly situated citizens equally irrespective of the territory within the country that they live in.

Q103 *Lord Lang of Monkton:* Would the basis of that appraisal of equity and fairness be a needs-based assessment?

Professor McLean: It could be. It could be needs based or resources based or both needs and resources based. The first option would be to have some assessment of relative need, and I think since the 1970s there have been attempts to do that in the NHS within England, and then to fund for that relative need and so deliver more NHS funds per head to areas of poor health than to areas of good health. That would be a needs element. A resources element, which applies to a limited extent in the UK but much more in countries such as Canada, is to look at the tax base and tax-raising capacity of each sub-national government and to accept that some areas have a more robust tax base than others and to compensate those that have

a weak tax base. A needs and resources formula, which is what the Australians use, is to do both of those.

Q104 *Chairman:* Can I read to you the Australian Grants Commission criteria on page 31 of your pamphlet where you quoted "Its definition of equity is that 'each State should be given the capacity to provide the average standard of State-type public services assuming it does so at an average level of operational efficiency and makes an average effort to raise revenue from its own sources'."

Professor McLean: I should have put a post-it on that point before I came into the room.

Q105 *Lord Lang of Monkton:* Can I follow up the needs-based element first? How would you maintain that? Just as population ought to be counted regularly and readjusted into any formula presumably the kind of assessment that you are talking about would need to be regularly updated. How could that be done if it became really detailed or do you favour some kind of proxy?

Professor McLean: I probably favour some sort of proxy but it could be done, because it is done in Australia, at a fairly detailed level. The Australian operation is not a huge bureau. I visited it last July and it is a modest two-storey office block in Canberra. I believe the Grants Commission has a professional staff of about 50 in the Canberra office and they do not find it enormously burdensome to do a needs assessment. I think the dangers of an excessively fine attempt at needs assessment are shown by the English local government formula, which attempts to do needs at a very fine level and is lobbied by every interest in English local government such that whichever interest, in my cynical view, has the most effective lobby gets the most spending per head. In my view, as I said in the book and I have not changed my view, the English local government formula is a failed attempt at equity of the sort that I am describing. I would prefer a coarser version such as the Australian or an even coarser version where the presumption would be that a grant to each territory would be some sort of function of, for instance, relative GDP per head, or GVA per head, in that territory or, as other researchers have suggested, a function of social security expenditure per head in those territories.

Q106 *Baroness Hollis of Heigham:* My difficulty is I have always assumed that a fair distribution of public monies was to make up the shortfall for those who cannot reasonably meet their needs within their own resources given certain assumptions about average expenditure and so on and therefore you need to bring in sparsity, density GVA per head, as you just suggested, which will not actually do it seems to me.

What you cannot therefore do is have only one half of that equation which is just needs. It has to be matched by a capacity of a territory or even a region to meet its own needs within its own resources according to its wealth per head. Is this not going to be very difficult to establish any concept of equity, if you accept that, if all you can rely on is a distribution of central funding grant when there is no local capacity to raise the revenue to meet local resources?
Professor McLean: Yes, it is likely to be very difficult. It is not true that there is no local capacity.

Q107 *Baroness Hollis of Heigham:* It is local authorities obviously.
Professor McLean: In the case of distribution to local authorities there is local capacity in the shape of council tax and there used to be local capacity in the shape of business rates. If you wanted a more responsive needs-based system to be applied in England I believe it would be a good idea to re-localise business rates, although that is not the subject of this Committee and not what I am here to talk about. The devolved administrations have in effect the same tax base: council tax and business rates. Scotland only has the power to vary the standard rate of income tax by 3p in the pound up and down. I agree with you that these are extremely limited tax bases in proportion to the amount which is spent by the three territorial governments.

Q108 *Baroness Hollis of Heigham:* You accept, therefore, that you cannot have equity simply and solely on a needs-based formula because it cannot take account thereby of resource capacity.
Professor McLean: I agree with that.

Q109 *Chairman:* Can you produce a more equitable system, not a totally equitable one but a more equitable one?
Professor McLean: I would, as I have said a number of times in print, try to bring the UK as close as possible to the Australian model which seems to me to be the best one out there of a more equitable system.

Q110 *Lord Lawson of Blaby:* Why, in your opinion, has the Scottish ability to change, albeit modestly, the level of income tax never been used?
Professor McLean: In my opinion it has never been used because the Scottish government has never had to. It has found that funding under the block and formula arrangement has been sufficiently generous for it to spend what it has chosen to spend. As members will be well aware, there are some areas where policy has diverged, where the Scottish government is spending more generously on some provisions than is the UK government in relation to England. They have not used the tax power because

they have not needed to and politicians faced with re-election who do not need to tax, in my experience, do not tax.

Q111 *Lord Lawson of Blaby:* There is a perceived inequity, certainly this is why Lord Barnett has been agitating for some time for a change, that Scotland, in terms of expenditure per head, has been treated far too generously relative to England, indeed relative to the rest of the United Kingdom, and ideally he seeks a change to that. How much of that mischief, if it is a mischief, or that inequity, if it is an inequity, do you think would be remedied by having a clean-up of the base line in terms of spending per head of population and then use the Barnett Formula and the conventions that have developed alongside the Barnett Formula for by-pass from time to time as the annual adjustment for uplift, or it could be down-lift in some cases?
Professor McLean: I think that would likely achieve what one might want, however it is much easier to say "Clean up the base line" than to do it since I believe it would be impossible to clean up the base line without a comprehensive needs assessment. I know simply as a contemporary historian, but some people around the table will have more intimate knowledge than I do, that the needs assessment of 1979 was quite bloody, that the unilateral needs assessment conducted by HM Treasury in 1984 was also quite bloody because documents relating to it have recently been released, and I would foresee that any needs assessment of the sort Lord Lawson has just mentioned which would be required to clean up the base line would be very bloody indeed because what is a need is what philosophers call an essentially contested concept. Therefore, I think one would need new institutions which were not part of the UK government and not part of any of the devolved administrations in order to, as Lord Lawson put it, clean up the base line.

Q112 *Lord Lawson of Blaby:* Clearly we are getting to the heart of this. The problem is a very simple one and the solution is not all that difficult but the politics are bloody. That is in effect what you are saying and I would accept that. In the circumstances we are now thinking of in terms of if it is considered desirable to achieve this, however bloody it may be, do you feel that if you have a rough and ready assessment of need—I think this is what you are saying but I would like to get your clarification—this would be like an inverse GDP or social security spending per head, or whatever, and this would be somewhat less bloody and more practical than having a detailed needs assessment or do you think actually worse because people would feel since it was not a detailed needs assessment it had no real justification?

Professor McLean: The way I put it in my book was that either one of these admittedly rough and ready formulae might have the effect of bringing people to the table, that territory which was aggrieved by, as it might be, a Grants Commission or a Chief Secretary saying "In the next period your grant will be an inverse function of your GVA per head unless you can come up with a better idea" this would have the effect of persuading people to get into a serious discussion which I would imagine would involve the territorial administrations, the UK government and, as I said in my last answer, it would have to have some sort of neutral referee as to what the relative needs of the territories were.

Q113 *Lord Lawson of Blaby:* Finally on this question, have you, in the great amount of work you have done, spelt out and shown what precisely would be the practical consequences of moving from the existing system with a corrupt base line to a system with a cleaned-up base line? What would that actually mean on the ground? Have you done that? Secondly, how long a transition period would you recommend from getting to the present state of affairs to the state of affairs which you would like to see?
Professor McLean: The first exercise is very hard to do from outside government for the reasons that I gave earlier and I will not repeat myself. If one looked at the PESA numbers and the relative GVA numbers one might conclude that unless Scotland in particular can come up with some arguments which convince the neutral ring holder that its relative needs are indeed corresponding to its relative public spending per head, there would need to be a fairly long transition period. I am not in a position to say because I do not have access to the data but perhaps five or ten years.

Q114 *Earl of Mar and Kellie:* Clearly expenditure can be allocated according to need, efficiency or effectiveness. Am I right to think this is going to produce three separate answers and which would you regard as being the best?
Professor McLean: Again, taking those questions in reverse order, I think "best" is essentially a value judgment, a political judgment, and it has to be made by elected politicians and is not really for academics to say. Efficiency and effectiveness it is correct do, in some senses, pull in different directions to need. For instance, you could take as an example expenditure on supporting hi-tech industry. If a government decides to do that, it would make sense to spend the money where it was thought that it would create the most added value. That might in practice turn out to be in Cambridge rather than in Middlesborough because of the location of the people who would be best equipped to do the work. You could make a similar claim for many other programmes of public

expenditure. Effectiveness and need would, in those senses, diverge. By efficiency we mean efficiency at various levels. We mean tax efficiency in a narrow interpretation so that if sub-national governments have a certain power to tax they do not get involved in mutually destructive tax competition with one another for instance. We also mean it in a broader sense, and this is moving away from need to an idea of incentive compatible public finance, that sub-national governments should have an incentive to grow the economy on their patch in order to give themselves a more robust tax base. You were right that is in some tension with an entirely needs-based system.

Q115 *Earl of Mar and Kellie:* Do you think that this exercise should be primarily carried out by the devolved administrations or by the Treasury?
Professor McLean: The exercise of "watering", if that is the verb, their tax base is surely for the devolved administrations. They are the right people to see what they can grow on their patches in order to improve their tax base given the present taxation powers they have. I do not think it is a Treasury job because, given we have devolution, it is not for the Treasury to tell the Scots, the Welsh or the Northern Irish how they should grow their tax base. It could be for a neutral ring holder but essentially I would say it is for the devolved administrations.

Q116 *Baroness Hollis of Heigham:* Are you really saying that it is not a matter of concern to the Treasury whether a devolved administration may be raising taxes which the Treasury might think might trespass on the taxable basis of the UK as a whole?
Professor McLean: No, I was not saying that. My empirical experience is that the Treasury concern has been the opposite, namely that it has believed that the devolved administrations have not been making enough tax effort. I do not know whether Lord Trimble is in a position to confirm it but I know that for quite a number of years the Treasury was concerned that Northern Ireland administrations were not changing the domestic rates' burden on Northern Ireland households and Treasury officials thought that the Northern Ireland government could do more in that direction.
Lord Trimble: They did not just think it; they expressed it vigorously.

Q117 *Lord Rowe-Beddoe:* Assuming, from the content of this afternoon, that there will be a change, when who knows, you are on record as saying that you see the only alternative is a needs-based allocation formula. Forget how bloody that might be or not, as the case may be, maybe we have all got a little wiser in the intervening two decades. First of all, is that still your position or is there an alternative or a combination? If we seriously consider replacing this formula what can we be looking at?

Professor McLean: It is difficult to give a comprehensive answer to that question and stay within the terms of reference of this Committee because a comprehensive answer would have to reflect the degree of devolution which each of the three territories had and also whether England or, as it might be, the nine standard regions of England had some form of sub-national government. It is quite predictable that there will be pressures, perhaps to a different degree, in each of the three territories for more fiscal autonomy. If that happens then any statement that the only possible way to do it is a needs-based one is no longer correct. If I said that, I must have said it in the context of the arrangements that we have at present.

Q118 *Lord Rowe-Beddoe:* Why do we not stay with the political picture as we have it and ignore the fact we have nine English regions. We have three devolved administrations, they are what they, and one has tax raising power as it is. We are confronted with a situation which we have to actually try to see as it is today. There is one thing I wonder if you have a comment on. I have heard about resources, and you are talking about the local tax take, but what about the Treasury tax? Has anybody found out exactly what is the Treasury take from Scotland, what is the Treasury take for Northern Ireland and how does that relate to the present funding arrangements?

Professor McLean: The Treasury itself does not break down its tax receipts by territory but the Scottish government does, in relation to Scotland, in its annual publication GERS, Government Expenditure and Revenue in Scotland. Neither the Welsh nor the Northern Irish governments have yet done that. The GERS estimates are subject to considerable scope for argument because it is very difficult in the case of some taxes to determine where the tax take comes from, most obviously in the case of corporation tax. I think a more detailed answer on this would have to come from the civil servants who produce GERS but I would say that their publication is National Statistics and therefore it has to meet the required standards. On the expenditure side it interlocks with PESA and on the revenue side, which you asked about, the numbers interlock with those in the budget red book in the budget statement of the yield to each tax. A more detailed answer would have to come from one of the officials who are in this than from an outside academic.

Q119 *Baroness Hollis of Heigham:* Could I press you on that? I am trying to think back to the appendices and my memory fails me. The Layfield Report on local income tax had to do detailed work as to what this would raise by obviously much smaller units

which could then be subsequently aggregated by anybody for these purposes in order to see the disparity in the need for any equalisation grants and so on. That would be five years, or perhaps eight years, out of date but nonetheless those stats were there.

Professor McLean: If you mean Layfield, that was much longer than eight years ago.

Q120 *Baroness Hollis of Heigham:* NIT was based on an income tax as opposed to a property base. The whole of the Layfield Report was what happens if you substitute local income tax for rates.

Professor McLean: Do you mean Lyons? Again this is a question which is rather for the Treasury than for me. My understanding is that the Treasury certainly does calculations of what the yield of the Scottish variable rate would be. It has done some preparatory work, because the recent Lyons Committee on English local government considered the matter, on what would be involved in setting a local income tax rate for each of some rather large number of local authorities. I believe the Treasury view is that is an administrative nightmare but that is for the Treasury to say.

Q121 *Lord Rowe-Beddoe:* We have looked at needs, resources and needs and resources. Are there any other alternatives that you might consider?

Professor McLean: Given the asymmetrical devolution that we have in the UK, and assuming that neither a government of England nor governments of the nine regions of England come into existence in the near future, it is difficult to come up with a UK-wide system which is not one of those. A system of greater fiscal autonomy could work in a different way but I do not in the near future see, for instance, even Wales or Northern Ireland having the degree of fiscal autonomy for which the Scottish government is now pressing, which the Calman Commission may recommend although we do not know whether it will, therefore I would predict that we continue to have differential degrees of fiscal autonomy across the four territories for the foreseeable future.

Q122 *Lord Moser:* The question I want to ask relates to data. All the stuff I have read talks about two problems in terms of data gaps: one relates to gaps that would emerge if one went in the needs direction. That is quite a big issue and probably one should discuss that on another occasion because that relates to the whole needs question. I have no doubt myself that if one wanted to go in the direction of needs-based there is plenty of information. There are plenty of ways developed over the years for linking indicators, et cetera, but that is a big subject so I leave that to one side. What is much more serious is how little we seem to know about what we are actually talking about, namely the working of the formula. I distinguish between what is published and what is not published. I know a lot of stuff that is not published is available in the Treasury vaults. Surely this Committee ought to be fully aware and fully knowledgeable about the way public expenditure works between the four parts of the UK and to what extent different bits of expenditure relate to the Barnett Formula otherwise how can we monitor or analyse the working of the formula? What are your thoughts about what we should, come what may, try to get out of the masters of the Treasury?

Professor McLean: I will leave your first question aside as you invited me to and concentrate only on the second. The Treasury does now publish, and has done since the current spending review regime began in 1998, its statement of funding policy which will probably be familiar to all members of this Committee. That statement contains an appendix which breaks down to sub-programme level—I am hesitating because the jargon has changed as it used to be a SPROG but it is now something else—the extent to which each programme which is or is not devolved is devolved to each of the three territories. You can get an array of "100 per cents" and "0 per cents" at sub-programme level because a sub-programme either is or is not devolved. That then adds up to an overall percentage for each Whitehall department and the Barnett Formula is run off that. That is all public. If you were to use powers that you have and I do not to summon officials of the Treasury, I am not sure you would get much further on that front. It is not for me to say but what you might find helpful is to ask the Treasury representatives how they categorise any individual sub-programme, how they decide that the territorial extent of a certain sub-programme is England only or England and Wales or any of the possible combinations of the four nations of the UK. That is not revealed in the statement of funding policy. The procedure, by which the Treasury determines that each sub-programme is or is not devolved, so far as I know, is not public. It would have been easier if I had remembered to bring along a copy of the public funding policy but I think your advisers have one. It is appendix C.

Q123 *Lord Moser:* Are you saying that, from the point of view of this Committee analysing and monitoring what has happened to public expenditure through the Barnett Formula and not through the Barnett Formula because different things have devolved, we should have no difficulty? Are you saying that? I am surprised if you are. At the very first meeting of this Committee I said can we get data on this and the answer was we will see whether the Treasury would. Perhaps Lord Lawson will have all the data in his head.

Lord Lawson of Blaby: I do not have the data in my head but I am not sure this has a great deal to do with the real world. May I put a question to Professor McLean explaining where I am coming from? In the real world of politics and government nothing is going to be decided by precise formulae that are extremely detailed, that you then factor into a computer and the computer tell you what the answer is and everybody agrees. That is not how the real world works. What seems to me is more likely is it is helpful to have a formula and that formula is going to have some regard to need. In a way the main fashion in which need is factored into this whole arrangement is by the things that are outside it: social security and, as you pointed out, taxation, so that the prosperous territory pays more in taxation and requires less social security, a less prosperous territory gets more in social security and does not pay so much in taxation. That is the first cut, if you like, of need. For the public expenditure outside social security you do not need to be so worried about the detailed assessment of need. You want to have it on a population basis clearly because the purpose of public expenditure is to help people not territories, therefore you have to have accurate and up-to-date population. That is what we have not had so, therefore, that is clearly a need but beyond that the refinements are likely to be based on political judgment and negotiation. That was how it would appear to me and I would be grateful if you would comment.

Professor McLean: That is an entirely defensible point of view that a political party might take or a government might take and it is not for an academic to say yes or no. That would be an example of relatively coarse needs assessment where needs were driven by population. Of course arguments would be made by those who would benefit from them that aside from population certain things made it expensive to deliver public services, such as sparsity, conversely density, or ethnic diversity. I think I am right in saying that both sparsity and density have a weighting in the English local government formula and, therefore, the worst thing to be is an area of medium population density. Those arguments will be made in any forum by those who would prefer a finer assessment of needs than the one which you, Lord Lawson, have just suggested.

Q124 *Baroness Hollis of Heigham:* I am puzzling through some of the charts in your paper. What you actually show I think, if figure 5.5 represents an integration of needs and resources, on nearly all these tables London is doing better simply because London has more distribution away from the mean, in other words very, very minimal poor people so social security expenditure will come in high. Unless you have some sophisticated measure of reaching wealth, it has huge capacity and resource, the City of London et cetera, which is not being tapped and looped back in to meet that need particularly with the nationalisation of business rate in a sense. One of my difficulties is that given your very interesting tables here, unless one can actually get not just needs and resources but the distribution of both needs and resources to see the degree of scatter only then can one actually produce something. Your version of what counts as cost, like social security, would seem to be only a tiny fragment of what would be needed to do and would simply substitute one set of unfairness perhaps for another.

Professor McLean: The position of London, to which we draw attention in that figure and surrounding text, is exactly as you have described. It is the richest area of the UK by GVA per head but it also has, as we all know, extreme concentrations of poverty and so it has unusually high social protection expenditure. Exactly how much of an outlier London is depends on whether you talk about need before or after housing costs since London housing costs are very high. That is an open question which I have no expertise to pronounce on. It is also the case that if, let us say, London is a region but it had an equivalent degree of devolution to Scotland or that which Calman or the Scottish government's National Conversation might propose for Scotland, then we might see London having a more direct incentive than it does at present to solve its poverty and worklessness problems on its own patch, to make its tax base more robust and to use its own tax proceeds to deal with its own social problems. This is moving away to a world which we do not inhabit in which there are elected governments in all 12 regions.

Q125 *Baroness Hollis of Heigham:* There are more poor people in the richest regions than there are in the poorest regions. That is a social security stat.

Professor McLean: That is because the richest regions are the most populous.

Q126 *Baroness Hollis of Heigham:* That suggests, therefore, that the only reasonable way of expenditure is actually not through devolved expenditure but actually through UK expenditure, for example the social security system. It goes back to what you are interested in: people not territories. If that assumption is correct, given the problems of movement away from the mean, it is going to be very difficult on a territorial basis, simply because it is too broad, to come up with any needs assessment that would pick up all of these considerations.

Professor McLean: It would certainly be difficult to come up with a needs assessment that would pick up all these considerations but bear in mind that our figure 5.5, like all the other data in our pamphlet, is after excluding social protection and, therefore,

public expenditure in London, even on services not including social protection, is extremely high because the largest sub-service is health and the second largest is education. To an approximation this comes down to saying that NHS expenditure per head is very high in London and educational expenditure per head is very high in London.

Q127 *Lord Lang of Monkton:* I would like to ask Professor McLean about his hybrid model looking at his recommendation for an alternative to Barnett. He said "This combines the efficiency gains of greater fiscal autonomy with the equity of a needs-based grant" and then he talks about a combination of devolved and assigned taxes and a needs-based top-up block grant. I do not want to open all that up now but those of us who opposed devolution for many years did so because we were concerned that it would lead to the slippery slope and ultimately the possibility of the break up or fragmentation of the United Kingdom. I would add that coming to this Committee one sets that baggage aside and we are all genuinely keen to find a better system if there is a better system to be found. Certainly in my own case I would be concerned with any solution which took us further down that slippery slope. I want to know to what extent you have taken the broader picture into account in developing your own recommendations. It may be that you favour complete separation of Scotland, Wales and Northern Ireland but it may not.

Professor McLean: I am taking no position whatever on whether separation of Scotland, Wales and Northern Ireland is good or bad. I am taking devolution as it asymmetrically is, and it is clear, as I said a moment ago, from Calman and from the Scottish government's National Conversation that there is a mood in Scotland for more fiscal autonomy and that would have some good consequences irrespective of whether one is a unionist or a nationalist. Unionists and nationalists could agree, in the non-partisan spirit that you just referred to, that greater fiscal autonomy would have some good consequences for Scotland. The National Assembly for Wales's Commission on Public Finance and Funding has not, as far as I know, held any public hearings yet so it is difficult for me to second guess it. I would be surprised if its recommendations were in favour of as extensive fiscal autonomy as are likely to emanate from Calman or the Constitutional Convention. Northern Ireland I would guess to be intermediate between those two cases but I am not aware of any recent public statements on that. Lord Trimble may be able to advise us. Taking the asymmetrical devolution that we have and refusing to take a position on whether independence is good or bad because that is not the role of a political scientist, I would say it is likely that we will get some kind of hybrid anyhow and we will, in the foreseeable future, have a somewhat different funding system for Scotland to that which we have for Wales for instance. I do not know if that helps.

Q128 *Lord Moser:* I have a very quick follow-up on the statistical side. The reason why I am anxious that the Committee should be fully equipped to monitor the way the thing works is very straightforward. We are being asked whether there is an alternative method. There is an alternative method which is needs based which takes one in a totally different direction and I do not want to start on that now but I am still interested to understand what is wrong with the formula as such. When I started reading about it I thought it was a very straightforward operation but then as you start reading you come into convergence, then you come into squeeze, then you come into by-pass and it all goes rather mysterious. I simply think we should press the Treasury, now that we hear from you that most of the stuff is there, to see just how it has worked over the years on convergence, squeeze and on by-pass so we know what we are trying to improve. It is as simple as that.
Professor McLean: I have nothing to add to that.

Q129 *Lord Sewel:* Can I say that on page 35 of your IPPR paper there is an absolute gem as far as I am concerned. You say "It was said by Ron Davies that devolution is 'a process not an event'." I am enormously pleased to see that because some people, particularly Mr Henry McLeish, have been trying to pin that quote on Mr Donald Dewar and I never thought Mr Donald Dewar said it. I could never remember or find him saying it. If you have the precise reference I would be very grateful. On need, how would it work and what is an expenditure need and what is not? One of the reasons why expenditure in Scotland may be higher than expenditure in England is that in Scotland we have many, many more denominational schools. Is denominational education an expenditure need in itself or is it a policy choice?
Professor McLean: You have put your finger on a very painful point. Australians and also Canadians have had to argue that point over many years because there is no clear answer. I would be inclined to say that having separate denominational schools is a policy choice not a need but I know what will be said on the other side. I know that it will be said that the settlement in Scotland dates back to the Education Act 1918, that was the choice made a very long time ago and it is embedded. Similar things could be said about Northern Ireland. Those choices are so deeply embedded, it will be said, that they should be treated as needs. I incline to the view that separate educational systems are a choice not a need.

Q130 *Lord Sewel:* Around this table, from what I hear of the mutterings, the English take one view and the Scots take another view. I am not going to argue one case or the other but it does show the difficulty of even identifying what an expenditure need is.
Professor McLean: One could say at one extreme nobody would doubt that an indented coastline and a lot of your population on islands gives rise to a need.

Q131 *Lord Sewel:* You can make the choice of living there. The extreme argument is difficult.
Professor McLean: You could say that. In fairness, the government of Newfoundland, for instance, does tend to say that to its own outlying population. You could take a line so hard that even the existence of the Isle of Mull does not generate a need but that is a political argument I would rather not get into. It is very much in the day-to-day bargaining which goes on so much in the English, and I believe also in the Scottish, local government formula that rival parties will say that such and such is a need; indeed each lobby group will say whatever they happen to have a lot of is a need. That will be well known to some members of this Committee.

Q132 *Lord Sewel:* In your *Fair Shares* paper you say "While the Barnett formula itself is reasonably straightforward . . . what seems more arbitrary is the process by which the Treasury determines whether spending is subject to Barnett or not . . . the process through which such a clarification is made is unclear, and is not underpinned by any published criteria." What information should be published or other processes adopted to improve procedural transparency?
Professor McLean: This was what I was getting at in my earlier answer to Lord Moser. I would like to know on what basis some of the controversial calls are made. For instance, some of the ones to which attention has been drawn relate to transport expenditure. Is the Channel Tunnel rail link expenditure on behalf of England or London, the South East of England or the United Kingdom, or the Olympics expenditure and so on? In the jargon which has been used there is expenditure *for*, and expenditure *in*, a territory and those are not the same. Of course there is a judgment call in any of these controversial cases but once a block of expenditure, as it might be the Channel Tunnel, is called in one direction then it either has a Barnett consequential or it does not depending on which direction it is called. That is the process, as I said in my earlier answer to Lord Moser, that your Committee might find helpful to ask the Treasury about.

Q133 *Chairman:* Can I go back to Australia for a minute because that is a very interesting example of a way of doing it? I think you were telling us that the

Australians had a very crude but robust assessment of need which they apply to all the different territories. Here we have got an asymmetrical devolution but Australia does not. Does the fact of the asymmetry make it more difficult to do a similar exercise here and, if so, how and what can we do about it?

Professor McLean: I am not sure. I have heard the Chair of the Australian Grants Commission, who was recently in the UK giving evidence to Calman— and I think it would be possible for your clerks to get that evidence he addressed that very point. My recollection of what he said is they publish their assessments once a year and for 24 hours every one of the 8 territories rises up in revolt and says how terrible the Commonwealth Grants Commission is and then goes quiet for the next 364 days. His words were to that effect. He did that in a witness session to Calman. The fact that it is asymmetrical would make

some difference because at present there is no government of regions of England to which a block could be handed and which could be told to get on with it in the way that the three territorial administrations are told, but it would be possible to have a system in which you did your needs assessment, the resulting block grants were made to the three territories and the rest was what was available for the UK government to spend in England on the functional service in question.

Q134 *Chairman:* Thank you very much for giving us so much of your time, your experience and one hopes your wisdom which we will be delighted to consider in detail. It was very good of you to have come and it has been very useful. Thank you. Are you going to produce a piece of paper for us?

Professor McLean: I will attempt to and if I fail I will let your clerks know.

Supplementary memorandum by Professor Iain McLean

As I promised during my oral evidence, I have pleasure in sending you this supplementary note. Part A of this note has been agreed with my colleague on the (Muscatelli) Independent Expert Group reporting to the Calman Commission, Professor D N F Bell. The calculations in Part B were done by my coauthor Katie Schmuecker of ippr north.

A. THE BARNETT FORMULA AND CONVERGENCE

1. Three members of your Committee, all with experience of government, expressed opposing views as to whether the Formula was designed to converge towards equal public expenditure per head in all four nations of the UK; and whether, regardless of intention, it actually has led to convergence. I hope the following may help.

2. All researchers in the field[1] believe that the intention to bring about convergence (perhaps until "excess" spending per head in Scotland and maybe Northern Ireland had been brought down to the level implied by the 1979 Needs Assessment) was in the minds of some Treasury officials involved in the design and early implementation of the Formula. There is substantial oral evidence on this point, but little written evidence has surfaced.

3. However, the territorial departments in (at least) Scotland and Northern Ireland were very reluctant partners. The service-by-service details underlying the Needs Assessment were released to me in 2005 under a Freedom of Information request. They make it clear that the Scottish Office and HMT did not reach agreement as to the relative needs of Scotland.

4. The Treasury told me, in the letter accompanying that release, that there had been no subsequent "interdepartmental" needs assessment. However, a further FOI release at the insistence of the Information Commissioner in summer 2008 has shown that the Treasury conducted an in-house update of the Needs Assessment in 1984. Again, its conclusions were vigorously resisted by officials in the Scottish Office. It appears that pressure from the Secretary of State for Scotland led Treasury Ministers to agree to pursue the matter no further. That is my précis of the files released to the National Archives of Scotland at West Register House, Edinburgh, read in June 2008.[2]

---

[1] Eg, I. McLean, *the Fiscal Crisis of the United Kingdom* (Basingstoke: Palgrave 2005); D Bell and A Christie, "Funding devolution: the power of money" in A Trench ed, *Devolution and Power in the United Kingdom* (Manchester: Manchester University Press 2007), 73–85; J Mitchell, "Spectators and Audiences: The Politics of UK Territorial Finance", *Regional and Federal Studies,* Vol 13 (2003) Winter, 7–21; D Heald and A Macleod, "Revenue-raising by UK Devolved Administrations in the Context of an Expenditure-based Financing System", *Regional and Federal Studies,* Vol 13 (2003) Winter, 67–90.

[2] D Fraser, "Thatcher told her ministers to slash the Scottish budget", [*Glasgow*] *Herald* 06.06.2008, p 6; McLean *et al., Fair Shares . . .,* p 14; National Archives of Scotland, SOE6/1/1708–9, Sep–Oct 1984.

5. Therefore I believe that I was correct to state in evidence that, whatever may have been the intentions of Treasury Ministers (of both parties) over the period in question, it was the intention of Treasury officials to bring about some convergence to what the Needs Assessment had persuaded them were relative needs.

6. As to whether the Formula actually (regardless of intentions) brings about convergence, there are two relevant factors. One is whether public expenditure is planned on a volume or a cash basis; the other is the change in relative population among the four nations of the UK.

7. In a world of constant relative populations, the mathematics of the formula entail that whenever expenditure in England increases, the Barnett block grant to the three Devolved Administrations (DAs) increases by a smaller amount per head. Some experts have described this as a differential equation system, a label I used in my oral evidence. However, others disagree, and there is no need to argue the point in this note, since there are two large and opposing effects: the convergence effect of the Formula; and the declining relative population of Scotland. These come close to cancelling out, as will be shown below.

8. Public expenditure was planned on a volume basis from the inception of the Formula until 1982. Barnett consequentials (ie changes in the block grant to each DA) are a function of increases in corresponding planned expenditure in England. If expenditure per head in volume terms was constant, then block grant per head, in volume terms, would also remain constant.

9. Since 1982, with public expenditure planned on a cash basis, there has always been an annual cash (ie nominal) increase in planned expenditure in England. In a world of constant relative populations, this should have led to convergence towards equal cash per head to spend on devolved functions in each of the four nations of the UK. The convergence would not have been linear (the downward slope would gradually flatten out); but one would expect it to have been close to complete by now.

10. The above ignores changes in relative population. However the relative population of Scotland has been declining since the inception of the Formula (and indeed for longer than that, back into the days of the Goschen Proportion). Until 1992 population relativities for England: Scotland: Wales were fixed at 85:10:5, ratios which were over-generous to Scotland and insufficiently generous to Wales. In 1992 Chief Secretary Portillo first rebased the consequentials on up-to-date relative populations, but did not change the then-current baseline. Since then population relativities have been updated from time to time. The current practice is that the relativities are restated, from the latest available ONS population data, with each new edition of HMT's *Statement of Funding Policy,* which is available to members of your Committee. These relativities then apply for the period of the ensuing Comprehensive Spending Review (CSR).

11. Scotland therefore gets favourable treatment per head of population for two reasons: (a) the historic baseline was not adjusted for the relative populations of Scotland and England in 1992; (b) if its relative population is declining through the period of a CSR, as has been the case for each CSR since 1998, this is not reflected in Barnett consequentials during the lifetime of that CSR.

12. The graphs from McLean *et al, Fair Shares . . .* (ippr 2008), which were discussed during my oral evidence, show that since 2001–02 the convergence effect and the population effect for Scotland have roughly cancelled out, so that resources per head available to the Scottish Government to spend on devolved services are roughly constant. Because of deficiencies in earlier versions of HMT's PESA database (*Public Expenditure Statistical Analysis*), the numbers are not reliable for years before 2002–03.

B. The Effect of Social Protection Expenditure

13. Public expenditure may be grouped into three classes: non-identifiable; identifiable but not devolved; and identifiable and devolved.

14. Non-identifiable expenditure is to fund public goods such as national defence, foreign policy, UK debt interest, and the operation of central UK departments such as the Chancellor's departments. It is not apportioned to the population of the UK.

15. Some public expenditure is identifiable but not devolved. By far the largest component of this is what international statistical conventions group as "social protection". Until recently, agricultural support was also treated in the public expenditure system as if it were not devolved. This has recently changed, but for reasons of consistency over time the data in McLean *et al, Fair shares. . .,* on expenditure per head in the four nations of the UK excluded both of these functions of government. The purpose of this was to capture, as closely as the publicly available data permit, the "Barnett effect" of changes driven by the Formula on expenditure on devolved functions of government.

16. At my oral evidence session I was asked what would be the effect of adding social protection (and agriculture) back in to our data. This is done in the chart below. It is labelled "Figure 4.2 (Revised)" because it corresponds to Figure 4.2 in McLean *et al., Fair Shares*, with social protection and agriculture added back in.

17. On regional comparisons between public expenditure per head and GVA per head, our pamphlet already contained the data your Members requested. I apologise for failing to point that out to you at the time. The comparison with social protection and agriculture included is our Figure 5.2. The comparison with them excluded is our Figure 5.3. As your Members already have these charts I do not reproduce them again.

18. Comparing McLean *et al* Fig 4.2 with the attached Fig 4.2 (Revised), we observe:

18.1. Fig 4.2 (Revised) is somewhat more compressed. Regions with low relative spending (eg, Eastern and South East) and the region with highest relative spending (Northern Ireland) are closer to the UK average when social protection expenditure is included in the comparison than when it is excluded.

18.2. In Fig 4.2 (Revised), London does not overtake Northern Ireland, so it appears less of an anomaly than in McLean *et al.*, Fig 4.2.

18.3. However, the ranking of the nations and regions stays roughly the same. In particular, Scotland has notably higher public expenditure per head than Wales on both measures, although it has substantially higher GVA per head.

19. Comparing McLean *et al* Fig 5.2 (including social protection and agriculture) with our Fig 5.3 (excluding them) we observe:

19.1. London is a less extreme outlier when social protection is included than when it is excluded. But on both measures it is by far the region with the highest public expenditure per head in comparison to GVA per head.

19.2. The relative position of Scotland is essentially the same on both measures.

20. The two sets of data serve different purposes. The data with social protection stripped out arise from an attempt to isolate the "Barnett effect" for the three devolved administrations. The "Barnett consequentials" described in the *Statement of Funding Policy* cannot be measured directly; identifiable public spending per head excluding social protection is a proxy for measuring "Barnett consequentials". For the regions of England, the same data series is a proxy for the effects of the distribution formulae used for health and local government services. Health and local government expenditure is devolved to subnational authorities in England; social protection expenditure, essentially, is not.

21. The data with social protection included may be used to measure the performance of the United Kingdom as a social citizenship network, in which poor people and poor regions are protected from adverse shocks.

22. On both sets of data, Members may feel that the position of London (and perhaps Scotland) appears anomalous.

Iain McLean FBA
Official Fellow in Politics
Professor of Politics, Oxford University

13 March 2009

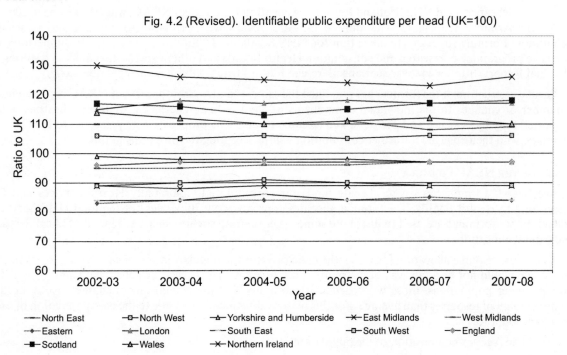

Fig. 4.2 (Revised). Identifiable public expenditure per head (UK=100)

FRIDAY 27 FEBRUARY 2009

Present	Forsyth of Drumlean, L	Rowe-Beddoe, L
	Richard, L (Chairman)	Sewel, L

Memorandum by the Scottish Government

INTRODUCTION

1. The 14 territorial Health Boards in Scotland are responsible for providing high quality healthcare services to the populations they serve. It is crucial that resources are distributed fairly across Scotland, taking account of the many factors that influence the need for healthcare in particular areas and the costs of supplying those services.

BACKGROUND

2. Prior to 1978, the funding for NHS Scotland was based on the distribution of NHS facilities across the country. Following the publication of the Scottish Health Authorities Revenue Equalisation (SHARE) report, the principle of using a weighted capitation formula to distribute funding according to the needs of the population and the costs of providing services to them was adopted. The SHARE formula ran for over 20 years until the National Review of Resource Allocation under Sir John Arbuthnott conducted their review. This review led to the establishment of the Arbuthnott formula which sought to provide fair shares to all Health Boards based on the guiding principle of the NHS that people should have equal access to services according to need.

3. The Arbuthnott formula assessed each Health Board's relative need for funding, using information about its population size, characteristics that influence the need for healthcare, and costs of delivery, in terms of hospital services, community services and GP Prescribing. The main drivers of the formula were:

— share of the Scottish population living in the Board area;

— age structure of the population and relative number of males and females;

— morbidity and life circumstances; and

— unavoidable excess costs of delivering healthcare in different geographical areas.

4. The publicly appointed NHS Scotland Resource Allocation Committee (NRAC) was established in 2005 to review the Arbuthnott formula. The aims of NRAC's review were primarily to improve and refine the Arbuthnott Formula for resource allocation for NHS Scotland. To fulfil this remit, NRAC undertook an extensive programme of research and consultation Health Boards and other experts/stakeholders resulting in the Final Report (http://www.nrac.scot.nhs.uk/research.htm) being published in September 2007.

5. The basic structure of the formula has remained the same as under Arbuthnott, but NRAC recommended a number of changes to the individual components of the formula. The bases for these adjustments are supported fully by evidence and peer reviewed research results. The proposals were presented to the Cabinet Secretary, who then engaged in further consultation before accepting the proposals in full.

BASICS OF THE NRAC FORMULA

6. The NRAC formula is used to allocate funds for Hospital and Community Health Services and GP prescribing to Health Boards. The formula allocates approximately 70 per cent of the total NHS Scotland budget. Other formulae are used to distribute some other funding streams such as General Medical Services and capital allocations.

7. As in most resource allocation formulae, the main driver is the population size of each area. However, this on its own would not be a fair way of distributing resources as there is clear evidence that some groups, for example older populations, those with particular morbidity and life circumstances characteristics, need a higher amount of resources than average. For this reason adjustments are made to the base population of each area to account for:

— The Age/sex composition of the population.

— The relative additional needs due to morbidity and life circumstances (MLC) and other factors.

— The relative unavoidable excess costs of providing services to different geographical areas.

8. The adjustments to the base population result in what is known as a weighted population. Calculations are initially carried out on the populations of small geographical areas and GP practices and then aggregated up to provide Health Board level shares. The small areas utilised within the formula are "data zones" which are key small-area statistical geographies in Scotland introduced by the Scottish Government for use in *Scottish Neighbourhood Statistics*. The use of this small area geography within the NRAC formula is seen as one of the key improvements on the previous formula, as it allows the characteristics, needs and costs of small areas to be better reflected in the formula.

9. Further details on the improvements to the formula which have been made as a result of the NRAC Review can be found at http://www.nrac.scot.nhs.uk/

Formula Structure: Hospital and Community Health Services (HCHS) and GP Prescribing

10. The four steps to creating a weighted population are:

— Take the base population of each Health Board at small area (data zone or GP practice) level by age and sex;

— Predict the expected resources required in each small area based on national average costs per head by age and sex (age/sex cost curves) to create an age-sex cost-weighted population index;

— Apply the Additional Needs (MLC) index to the above at each small area, and;

— Finally apply Unavoidable Excess Costs index to create the final overall index for each small area.

11. The small area indices are amalgamated to Health Board level, and applied to the population share to give the final output of the formula. This is then used to determine the target share of funding for each Health Board.

Applying the NRAC Formula in Practice

12. The NRAC formula does not determine the total amount of resources required to meet all the needs of a Health Board. The funds available to Scotland's 14 Health Boards are determined during the Spending Review process. The formula allocates this set amount on a basis that is fair and equitable, and reflects the relative need of each Health Board. It is then up to Boards to decide how to spend their allocation in a way that best meets the needs of their resident population.

13. The results of running the NRAC formula give "target shares" which are used only as a guide to the actual share of funds allocated to each of the 14 Health Boards. The budgets that the Health Boards receive are subject to a "parity" process which was introduced to ensure that the movement from the previous allocation formula (known as the SHARE formula), to the then "new" Arbuthnott Formula, did not result in any Health Board receiving a reduction in their funding while moving towards their new shares over a period of years.

14. In practice, this means that the revised formula will be phased in by way of "differential growth" whereby all Health Boards will receive a minimum resource uplift, with additional funding being allocated to those Health Boards who are below their NRAC share. Thus, each Health Board will receive a standard uplift each year to meet inflationary pressures whilst those Boards whose actual funding remains below their target level, as indicated by the NRAC formula, would receive an additional parity uplift from within the remaining resources available.

Further Information

15. More details on how the formula works and answers to frequently asked questions are contained in Annexes 1 and 2 to this note.

Health Analytical Services
Scottish Government Health Finance Directorate

February 2009

Annex 1

How the NRAC Formula works in Practice

Health Board target shares are calculated by adjusting the population of each Health Board area for three factors that are known to influence healthcare utilisation:

1. the age-sex profile of the population (age-sex cost weights),

2. the additional needs of the population due to Morbidity and Life Circumstances (MLC weights), and

3. the unavoidable excess costs of supplying services (excess cost weights).

The four main components within the formula (population, age-sex costs weights, MLC weights and excess cost weights) are generated for datazones (which are key small-area statistical geographies in Scotland introduced by the Scottish Government for use in *Scottish Neighbourhood Statistics*), intermediate datazone (IDZ) and GP practice level as appropriate.

1. POPULATION

Population is the primary component of the formula.

1.1 *Hospital and Community Health Services (HCHS)*

The population figures used within the formula are re-based General Register Office for Scotland (GROS) population projections. Re-based population projections are a simple adjustment made to the GROS population projections, by updating them using the latest mid-year population estimates (MYEs) that have been published since the Health Board level projections were published. For example, to re-base the 2004 based projection of 2008 using 2006 MYE the calculation is:

(2006 MYE) + [(2004-based projection of 2008)—(2004-based projection of 2006)].

This calculation takes account of any over or under-estimation of the projection in the years to 2006, and this adjustment is applied to the projection between 2004 and 2008.

1.2. *GP Prescribing*

The population figures used are based on the Community Health Index (CHI) population. The CHI population count is deflated at GP Practice level to match the re-based Scotland population projection used for HCHS (for more information see Technical Addendum B—Population—15 August 2007 document on the *NHSScotland Resource Allocation Committee* "NRAC" web site).

2. AGE-SEX

The formula adjusts for the age-sex profile of the population to take account of the effect of age differences on the cost of delivering different NHS services. On the whole, older people tend to consume greater resources and the costs can rise steeply with age.

Calculation of the age-sex cost weight starts with the age-sex breakdown for the population of each datazone. This gives a population structure for each area to which the national average cost per head of population (by age group) can be applied. These costs are specific to each of the care programmes (acute, care of the elderly, mental health and learning difficulties, maternity and community) analysed in the formula. The total "cost" associated with each care group within each age-sex band is obtained by multiplying the number of individuals by the national average cost per head appropriate for that age-sex group.

These "costs" are then totalled across all age-sex bands for each care programme. This total is then divided by the population of the datazone to get a datazone cost per head for the care programme across all ages and sexes. This is then compared to the Scottish average cost per head for the care programme to produce a care programme index (by datazone). This shows the amount by which the expected costs for the datazone are above or below the national average for each care programme.

All theses indices are combined using care programme weightings (obtained from the Scottish Health Service Costs Book—see table 1) to produce the final age-sex index (for more information see Technical Addendum C—age sex—19 September 2007 document on the *NHSScotland Resource Allocation Committee* "NRAC" web site).

Table 1

CARE PROGRAMME WEIGHTS (YEAR ENDED 31 MARCH 2006)

Acute	Care of the Elderly	Mental Health & learning Difficulties	Maternity	Community Travel-based	Community Clinic-based	Overall HCHS	GP Prescribing
49.4%	3.9%	12.7%	3.5%	10.1%	5.0%	84.6%	15.4%

3. ADDITIONAL NEEDS (MLC)—Due to Morbidity, Life Circumstances and Other Factors

In general, people who are less healthy and/or more deprived have a greater need for healthcare so this index directs relatively greater resources towards Boards with higher premature death rates and greater socioeconomic deprivation.

The factors that best explained the variation in need for each care programme were identified using statistical regression. For example, for the acute care programme the variables were identified as the mortality rate for under 75s and the limiting long-term illness rate. A combination of these two variables were used to calculate the MLC index for each IDZ. This represents the needs over and above those explained by the age-sex structure (for more information see Technical Addendum D—Morbidity and Life Circumstances—19 September 2007 document on the *NHSScotland Resource Allocation Committee* "NRAC" web site).

4. *Unavoidable Excess Costs of Supply*

This index takes account of the excess costs of supplying health services in different urban-rural areas and gives greater weights to remote and rural areas where hospitals and clinics serve smaller populations and where dispersed populations mean greater travelling distances for staff. There are four components of the unavoidable excess cost factor: hospital services, community clinic based services, community travel based services and GP prescribing.

The unavoidable excess cost index for hospital services is developed at datazone level based on the ratio of local to national average costs for the 10 Scottish Executive Urban-Rural Categories (SEURC) in which the datazone lies. The GP prescribing index is set to one for all areas as prescriptions are reimbursed at national fixed prices. The community care programme index has two elements; clinic based services and travel based services. Both community indices are calculated at datazone level and represent the excess costs of providing these services to residents of the datazone.

The overall unavoidable excess cost index for each datazone is obtained by combining all the hospital and community excess costs indices using care programmes weightings (table 1). (For more information see Technical Addendum E1, E2 & E3 on *NHSScotland Resource Allocation Committee* "NRAC" web site).

5. OVERALL INDICES

The indices for HCHS and GP Prescribing parts of the formula are calculated separately. These indices are then aggregated up to Health Board level for each care programme and each element of the formula. For example, the acute age-sex indices for every datazone in a Health Board are averaged (weighted by population) to give an acute age-sex index for that Health Board. Similarly, the additional needs indices are averaged using populations adjusted for age and sex as weights, and the calculations of the Health Board level excess costs indices use populations adjusted for age-sex and additional needs as weights.

With these small area "building blocks" the figures can be split in any number of ways eg to give Health Board level indices for individual factors (eg an additional needs index for Greater Glasgow & Clyde); an index for a particular care programme (eg distributions for maternity); or an index for a different geography eg CHP.

6. HEALTH BOARD SHARES

The small areas indices are amalgamated to Health Board level, and applied to the population share to give a final value that is used to inform the target share of funding for each Health Board. (for more information see NRAC—Final Report on *NHSScotland Resource Allocation Committee* "NRAC" web site).

Annex 2

FREQUENTLY ASKED QUESTIONS

This document provides background information on the basic principles applied to resource allocation in Scotland plus additional detail on the methodology adopted for the new NRAC formula due to be implemented in the calculation of the 2009–10 allocations.

1. Q: *How does the new NRAC Formula work?*

A: The Formula assesses each Health Board's relative need for funding, using information about its population size and characteristics that influence the need for healthcare in terms of hospital services, community services and GP prescribing. The main drivers of the Formula are:

  (i)   the share of the Scottish population living in the Health Board area;

  (ii) the age structure of the population and relative number of males and females;

  (iii) the additional needs due to morbidity and life circumstances (eg deprivation); and

  (iv) the unavoidable excess costs of delivering healthcare in remote and rural areas.

2. Q: *What is the underlying principle of the new NRAC Formula?*

A: The main objective of the NRAC Formula is to ensure equity among those receiving funds and provide a logical framework for decision making. Target shares are calculated for Health Boards on the basis of relative need for health care services within that population group, where use of services has been used as a proxy for need. Scotland uses an indirect approach to measure healthcare needs. The indirect approach relies on health service utilisation data to measure those needs based on (i) the demographic profile of the populations, taking into account the national average costs of providing services based on age and sex, and (ii) relative levels of deprivation, and its' estimated relationship on the greater use of services within each care programme. In addition to these two factors, the relative need for resources in each Health Boards is also influenced by the unavoidable additional costs of providing services in remote and rural areas. Also refer to Question 14.

3. Q: *What are the care programmes and diagnostic groups used in the new Formula?*

A: The table below sets out the care programmes and diagnostic groups that are utilised in the new NRAC formula being implemented from 2009–10.

Care Programme	Diagnostic Group(s)
Acute Services	Circulatory
	Cancer
	Respiratory
	Digestive system
	Injuries and poisoning
	Other
Care of the Elderly	None
Mental Health and Learning Disabilities	None
Maternity	None
Community[1]	None
GP Prescribing[2]	Circulatory
	Gastro-intestinal
	Infections
	Mental illness
	Musculoskeletal
	Other

[1] Practice Team Information data (PTI) and data from other sources are used as a proxy for all community services.
[2] Prescribing programme was disaggregated into the top five British National Formulary chapters

4. Q: *My Health Board provides healthcare services for 10 per cent of the Scottish population, yet may only have a target share of 9 per cent—why is this?*

A: Each Health Board's share of the population forms the basis of its allocation. However, this is then adjusted for factors that affect relative need for healthcare resources (age/sex, additional needs and unavoidable excess costs of delivering healthcare in different geographical areas). For example, elderly people tend to make more use of health care services and are more costly to treat. Therefore, a Board with a greater elderly population will require more health care resources than one with a relatively younger population base. Similarly, deprived people are recognised to have a greater need for healthcare than relatively affluent people and it is recognised that there are additional costs in providing services in remote and rural areas and so Boards with a larger deprived or rural population will require more healthcare resources than an affluent urban Board. The impact of these factors is combined to create an overall index of need for each Health Board, and this will determine the level of funding that a Board receives.

5. Q: *How do you estimate the population?*

A: For hospital and community health services (HCHS), the Formula uses re-based population projections. These are simple adjustments made to the GROS Health Board level population projections by updating them using population mid-year estimates (MYEs) that have been published since the Health Board level projections were published. It is a development of the method used in the formulae for allocating *Local Authority Grant Aided Expenditure* (GAE) in Scotland.

For GP prescribing the population source is the Community Health Index (CHI) which contains every person registered with a GP in Scotland (deflated to the same total population as the HCHS re-based projections).

6. Q: *Why is population calculated differently for hospital services and GP prescribing?*

A: For hospital services the population is based on the Health Board of Residence, however, for GP prescribing the population base is Health Board of Management. So for GP prescribing the relevant population is the number of patients on the lists of GP practices managed by each Health Board.

7. Q: *Why is it important to take into account the age/sex profile of the population?*

A: The Resource Allocation Formula uses this information to take account of the use of different specialities by each age/sex group (eg for maternity services), and also in calculating the costs of treating patients of different ages. It makes the Formula more "sensitive" to the healthcare requirements of the different population groups.

8. Q: *Why doesn't GP prescribing have an adjustment for remoteness?*

A: The GP prescribing element of the Formula covers the cost of prescribed drugs which are reimbursed at nationally fixed prices. Therefore, there is no need to build in a remoteness adjustment.

9. Q: *Does the Formula give enough emphasis to deprivation or remoteness?*

A: The weights attached to different elements in the Formula are based on the best available evidence at the time, depending on how each factor influences the need for healthcare. The weights were not chosen, but based on empirical analysis. The adjustment for morbidity and life circumstances therefore takes account of the need for services within diagnostic groups over and above the affect of the age and sex profile of the population. The adjustment for the unavoidable excess costs of supply then takes account of the additional costs of delivering services to meet the needs that are predicted by the age and sex and morbidity and life circumstances adjustments.

It should be remembered that the target shares for each Board are influenced not only by the different adjustments within the Formula but also by the profile of Boards. Most Boards are very variable, containing a mix of remote/urban areas and affluent/deprived areas, and this is taken account of when the results are presented at Board level.

10. Q: *How do you weight the different components of the Formula?*

A: The Formula has the following basic structure:

Population x age/sex x additional needs (MLC) x unavoidable excess costs

The aim of the modelling is to explain the current overall need for resources of each Health Board in terms of a percentage share.

An index is calculated for each element of the Formula and for each care programme in such a way that it compares each Board's position with the national average. For example, if the levels of additional needs (MLC) in a Board are higher than the national average its index will be more than one to reflect that its population will need more healthcare resources. By calculating each index in this way, the values can then be multiplied by the population share to determine how much more (or less) resource each Board requires compared with its basic population share due to age/sex, additional needs and unavoidable excess costs.

In order to determine the overall adjustment for each Board, each of the care programme formulae are weighted together by the national average expenditure on those care programmes.

11. Q: *How does the NRAC Formula take account of cross-boundary flows?*

A: The Formula allocates resources on the basis of Health Board of Residence and not by Health Board of Treatment. It is up to individual Boards to recover costs for patients treated from other Health Boards, and this has traditionally been done through Service Level Agreements (SLAs).

12. Q: *Are community hospitals covered in the hospitals section or the community services section?*

A: The costs of community hospitals are included under the appropriate care programme of the Formula eg acute, care of elderly, maternity etc depending on the activities that are carried out, rather than the location. They will not be included in the community section of the Formula as this only covers activity outside of hospital eg in the patients home.

13. Q: *How are temporary residents dealt with in the Formula?*

A: There are two aspects to healthcare provision for temporary residents—hospital admissions, and prescribing.

   (i) Hospital Admissions—Health Boards are able to claim back the costs of treating non-resident populations through the finance mechanisms that are in place. This applies to either residents in other Scottish Health Boards, or visitors from other countries—the latter is achieved through UNPAC (unplanned activity) provisions.

(ii) Prescribing—there is no capacity in the financial system to claim back the time spent with, or prescription costs of, visitors. Inter-board costs (or "cross-border flows" as they are known in Prescribing) are dealt with as part of the conversion of a Gross Ingredient Cost based formula modelled on Health Board of Management to a Net Ingredient Cost based allocation on Health Board of Residence in the finance system. For visitors, we therefore need to make an adjustment to the Formula—starting with the population base.

14. Q: *Why do the relative ("target") shares as calculated by the Formula differ from the actual shares that Health Boards receive in the final allocations?*

A: This issue relates to the movement towards parity. The policy of the Scottish Government Health Directorate is to phase in the target shares calculated by the NRAC Formula by way of "differential growth". Under this methodology, all Boards continue to enjoy real-terms growth in their allocations year-on-year, with those above parity (ie above their target share) receiving less growth than those below parity until the new distribution is achieved over time. In this way no Board receives a reduction in funding. This process is still ongoing.

15. Q: *The NRAC Formula does not provide us with sufficient resources to cover the healthcare needs of our population, yet it is supposed to be needs-based. Why is this?*

A: The Resource Allocation Formula does not determine the total amount of resources required to meet all the needs of a Health Board. The funds available to Scotland's 14 territorial Health Boards are determined by Ministers during the Spending Review process. The Formula suggests how to allocate this amount on a basis that is fair and equitable, and reflects the relative need of each Health Board. Health Boards to decide how to spend their allocation in a way that best meets the needs of its resident population.

Examination of Witness

Witness: MR JOHN SWINNEY, a Member of the Scottish Parliament, Cabinet Secretary for Finance and Sustainable Growth in the Scottish Government, examined.

Q135 *Chairman:* First of all, can I thank you very much for coming. As you know, this is an inquiry by a Committee set up by the House of Lords to look at the way in which the Barnett Formula operates. I hope you have seen our terms of reference?
Mr Swinney: I have, yes.

Q136 *Chairman:* Because it is a fairly restrictive set of mandates which we have actually been given by the House. There are things we can look at and things we cannot look at. Mainly what we are concerned with is the way in which the formula actually operates; whether it should be replaced now by a different formula on a different basis; and, indeed, how that might operate. What we cannot do is look at tax-raising powers and fiscal autonomy, which seems to figure up here at the moment, and, as I say, we are rather barred on that, so if you could perhaps bear that slightly in mind there are things that we cannot look at that we are not allowed to. Perhaps I could start by really asking a fairly basic question: in your view, what are the chief merits and demerits of the Barnett Formula, or the Barnett system if I can call it that, as the basis of funding UK devolved administrations, and particularly Scotland?
Mr Swinney: First of all, can I say that it is a pleasure to meet with the Committee and I look forward on behalf of the Government to giving a contribution towards the thinking of the Committee. I suspect that in respecting the parameters of the Committee's areas

of responsibility certainly my views about what is the alternative to the Barnett formula get us into the territory of replacing it with a system that gives greater financial responsibility to the Scottish Parliament through a system of fiscal autonomy. I am sure the Committee will have had sight of the documentation that the Government published during the course of this week, which essentially sets out a range of five options for structuring the finances of the Scottish Parliament, which we contribute to the debate, and obviously the Government's preference within that is that the Barnett Formula should be replaced by full fiscal responsibility for the Scottish Parliament. We have established and set out exactly how we think that should come about. In relation to your question, Chairman, essentially on the merits and demerits of the Barnett Formula, I suppose part of what has been one of the attributes that has been highlighted as a benefit of the Barnett Formula has been that it has brought an order to the distribution of resources within the United Kingdom between its constituent parts, in the sense there has been a formula there that has operated. I think that is an understandable conclusion, that there has been a distribution mechanism involved. As I think we find with all distribution mechanisms over finance, these things are never absolutely straightforward, they are never crystal clear, they are never completely scientific. They are essentially driven by judgments that are applied about the conditions and circumstances in which they are applied and also they are essentially subjective mechanisms. Some of the points of judgment that underpin the Barnett Formula are points that obviously are subject to great and intense debate, and have been so in the past, and I am sure will be so in the future.

Q137 *Chairman:* Can I just interrupt there. You said they are essentially subjective mechanisms. What do you mean by that?
Mr Swinney: Obviously it is a distribution formula. It is not scientific, it is not an absolute; it is a set judgments that has been arrived at as to what factors will be considered as being relevant for the distribution of resources. Judgments have been arrived at about which particular factors will be borne in mind and which particular proportions of comparability factors will be applied to certain circumstances in certain budget lines.

Q138 *Chairman:* Do you think the ones they are using at the moment are the correct ones?
Mr Swinney: They are the ones that are there. Obviously my perspective on the Barnett Formula is that it is a mechanism which distributes resources. I do not think it is a particularly robust mechanism for the purposes of what I want to see the Parliament being able to do, which is to exercise greater financial responsibility than it currently is able to exercise.

Q139 *Chairman:* Sorry to come back to it again, but given our terms of reference, the one thing that we cannot consider is how Scotland might pay for itself in the event of independence and therefore fiscal autonomy. What we have to look at is the way in which the Barnett Formula operates. I am not sure I fully understand even now what you meant by it is essentially a subjective mechanism. It seems to me the mechanism is there, it is a formula.
Mr Swinney: Two points on that, Chairman. Firstly, I would make the point that I think it is difficult to look at the question of the Barnett Formula without thinking of how it fits into the wider questions about the financing of the Scottish Parliament and the funding of the arrangements for devolution because, quite clearly, the debate that is underway in Scotland, and has been for some considerable time, is as to whether the existing financial arrangements are appropriate. I accept that the Committee is looking at a defined area of activity about the composition of the Barnett Formula, and the simple point that I advance to the Committee is that I do not think that is the ideal way for financing the Scottish Parliament and for delivering the financial flexibility that certainly the Scottish Government takes to be the case. When I say that there is essentially an element of subjectivity to the Barnett Formula, if we look at the various areas of comparability within the Barnett

Formula, there are judgments applying as to whether or not particular budget lines will carry full comparability for consideration within the Barnett Formula. That is ultimately a subjective judgment that is arrived at.

Q140 *Chairman:* By whom?
Mr Swinney: By the Treasury.

Q141 *Chairman:* In other words you are talking about the consequentials?
Mr Swinney: Yes.

Q142 *Chairman:* So that is the element of subjectivity you are talking about?
Mr Swinney: Of course, yes.

Q143 *Chairman:* Otherwise it is not a particularly subjective mechanism?
Mr Swinney: Other than the fact that there will be judgments applying about the population mechanism for example. You can ask why is it population; why is it not density of population, or all sorts of other indicators that one could consider. If I look at the distribution formula that we deploy within the Scottish Government in relation to Health Service expenditure in Scotland, or I look at the distribution formula we apply for local authority expenditure, it is a multiplicity of different indicators that we utilise for the distribution of resources. Population base is at the heart of the Barnett Formula, but there will also be other judgments. In our experience, I think one of the other deficiencies of the Barnett Formula is the fact that there is the ability for the formula to be essentially the product of subjective judgment about how it should be applied. I give the Committee an example of that. Just after we came to office in 2007 we went through a Spending Review with the United Kingdom Government. It was announced by the Chancellor somewhere round about the first or second week in October, and in about December 2007 the then Justice Secretary accepted a report from Lord Carter about prisons in England. The conclusion of that was that there needed to be an extra £1.2 billion expended in the English prison estate because of the fact that there was over-crowding and there was a need for investment in the prisons estate. The UK Government took the view that this was essentially a piece of emergency expenditure and that it would be funded out of the contingency, and therefore there were no Barnett consequentials because it was funded out of the contingency. The only reason it was an emergency was that it happened in December 2007 and not during the summer of 2007 when the Carter Review reported. If the Carter Review had reported in the summer and this had been part of the calculation underpinning the formulation of the

Comprehensive Spending Review, and £1.2 billion had been allocated to the English Prison Service to deal with the overcrowding and investment required, we would have had £120 million-worth of consequentials which we could have deployed on whatever we fancied. However, as it happened, we were using resources out of the Comprehensive Spending Review in any case to address the fact that we have virtually the same problems of prison overcrowding that exist in England and Wales. That is another perspective on subjectivity—that essentially the Barnett Formula can be bypassed and other devices for distribution of public expenditure can be found which ensure that some of what we might expect coming under the Barnett Formula is not what we actually realise.

Q144 *Lord Forsyth of Drumlean:* The bypass issue is important but surely it works both ways and is a bit of a red herring? I am just trying to understand what you are saying here. Are you saying that you would prefer to have a needs-based rather than a population-based means of assessing what the resources should be for Scotland?

Mr Swinney: Two points, Lord Forsyth. The first is that I do not understand how the bypass issue is a disregard. If the Barnett Formula is to be a robust and reliable mechanism of distributing public funds, then we have to have the confidence that it is going to be applied effectively and fairly and squarely in all circumstances. I am citing to the Committee that there are ways of bypassing the Barnett Formula which therefore undermine its credibility.

Q145 *Lord Forsyth of Drumlean:* Yes, but to give you an example in the other way, if we take the Health Service, where the baseline in Scotland is about 22 per cent higher than in England, and where more than three-quarters of the expenditure goes on pay, and where pay is subject to national agreements, if there is a huge increase in pay in the Health Service the formula consequences for Scotland will be grossly inadequate in terms of actually meeting the cost of that pay bill because you have a higher baseline and you have more people in the Health Service. Certainly in my day the formula was bypassed and we would get an extra very considerable slug of expenditure in order to compensate us for the fact that the baseline was higher. You are saying for example where the contingency fund is being used, where you have lost out and where the contingency fund is not there, but if you look at the main thrust of Barnett, there is nothing subjective about it, you get the proportion that relates to the population formula on top of the baseline, and then you have the ability to vire between different budgets. When you were talking about you wanted to have something that took account of population density and so on, that is

an argument for having a formula which is based on some kind of needs assessment like the local authority grant formula. Is that what you are advocating?

Mr Swinney: No, I am not. What I am advocating falls into my first answer to the Chairman, that the Scottish Government takes the view that the Barnett Formula is a product of the existing devolved arrangements and our preference is to move to a system of financing the Parliament which allows us to exercise greater financial responsibility for the revenue that is raised in Scotland and distributed in Scotland.

Q146 *Lord Forsyth of Drumlean:* I understand that but we are where we are and we have a system now, but we are looking at how that system could be made fairer. You made the point that you thought in the case of the prisons issue that it was not fair because you did not get the formula consequences and that it should not be subjective. That seems to me something of an own goal when it comes to something like for example the Health Service, if there was a big increase in pay or other matters. Is this not rather thin ice?

Mr Swinney: I do not follow the logic of the argument, Lord Forsyth, about how we somehow get compensated for an increase in health expenditure, because essentially what we get is the population share of the change in English public expenditure across programmes. That is a population share of the change in the public expenditure that is deployed in England and that is the basis of the mechanism. I do not see where there is anything additional that we get beyond that.

Q147 *Lord Sewel:* Could we explore this one because it is an interesting one. If you start off with Health Service expenditure per head of the population in Scotland being higher than Health Service expenditure per head of population in the rest of the United Kingdom, and the vast majority of that expenditure being accounted for by staff costs, then if there is a wage settlement effectively at a UK level, and that goes up by, say, 10 per cent, and if you apply the Barnett Formula figures to the Scottish share, you will get a figure which does not enable you to have a 10 per cent increase in wage costs in Scotland.

Mr Swinney: I accept that point, Lord Sewel.

Q148 *Lord Sewel:* That is the point.

Mr Swinney: That point contradicts Lord Forsyth.

Chairman: It does not contradict it.

Q149 *Lord Forsyth of Drumlean:* It is the point I am making.

Mr Swinney: Let me explain what happens in relation to health expenditure. We have a baseline in Scotland, there is a baseline in England, and when there is a certain level of increase in health expenditure in England, essentially we get a population share of that increase and that flows into the Scottish block. There is no additional element taken into account as to whether or not that is adequate for a pay settlement based on the number of Health Service workers we happen to have, that is a cash sum. If there is a nationally negotiated health deal which is essentially able to be afforded in England but is more challenging in Scotland, we have to find the resources to fund that by viring, as Lord Forsyth correctly says, between the different elements of the public expenditure we have at our disposal.

Q150 *Chairman:* That is exactly where you would want the Barnett Formula to be bypassed, would it not? You do not get enough money to do what they are doing in England, the consequentials are not enough so presumably you then try ad bypass the strict operation of the Barnett Formula and go and negotiate with the Treasury.
Mr Swinney: It may have been different when Lord Forsyth was a minister in the Scottish Office, but I can assure the Committee now that there is a strict application of the Barnett Formula, so it is a population share increase.

Q151 *Lord Sewel:* What we are asking is whether that is an aspect of the formula that you are dissatisfied with now, the fact that bypassing does not take place to enable the sort of accommodation that Lord Forsyth indicated being applied?
Mr Swinney: I think that justifies the argument that the Scottish Government makes that we need to have a different mechanism in place that allows us as a government to exercise a greater degree of financial responsibility by having greater control over our resources. That is why we argue as we do in our paper for fiscal independence.

Q152 *Lord Forsyth of Drumlean:* I am trying to help you here because when I was Secretary of State—and bear in mind we have had a period of unprecedented growth in public expenditure with lots of money sloshing around, but that is going to change—if there was a big pay increase in the Health Service, I would go along to see the Chief Secretary and say, "Look, there is no way that the formula consequences of the health budget increase in order to meet a pay increase is going to enable us to meet the pay bill in Scotland." The Chief Secretary would say, "You can vire from other budgets," and I would say, "Things are very tight, there is no scope to do that, so we need to have a sum over and above that which relates to the population because our baseline is higher," and the Chief Secretary would say, "Your baseline is higher because of what was agreed in 1979 and you need to demonstrate need," and we would then talk about

morbidity and mortality and the particular problems of the Health Service in Scotland, and we would have a very long argument, and in the end we would get the money. That meant that it was a workable situation. Where you are now, as I understand it, there is no mechanism whereby you can get that bypass and therefore the effect of the Barnett Formula as it is operating is to squeeze expenditure, and when you make an argument like you have just made on prisons and on the big stuff like health, it seems to me that is going to result in a squeeze on the Scottish budget which does not actually take account of need, which is why I thought you might be arguing that it would be better to have some kind of needs-based assessment rather than a population-based assessment, which would then look at the health budget in the context of the fact that Scotland has particular problems in health. That is where I am coming from.
Mr Swinney: I take a different view. I think we both accept that there are problems with the formula, which is why the Government in Scotland takes the view that we need to have a different system of funding of the Scottish Parliament, which is to have greater financial responsibility and control over both the ability to raise taxation and to control public expenditure. That is the rationale behind our argument. You have talked quite a bit about the baselines—

Q153 *Chairman:* I am sorry to interrupt again but I understand the argument which says we are not overly interested in Barnett because we want fiscal autonomy but, on the other hand, there is bound to be an interim period within which the Barnett Formula continues to operate even if on the most optimistic view you get fiscal autonomy. What do you want to do in the interim? Do you want to go on with the present system as it is or do you want to change it?
Mr Swinney: I do want to change it; I want to move to a system of fiscal autonomy. That is where the dynamic of the debate is going from the Government's perspective.

Q154 *Chairman:* But what happens in the interim? Do you go on operating Barnett as it is?
Mr Swinney: I want to advance the argument why we need to move towards a system of fiscal autonomy because I think the Barnett Formula and the existing financial arrangements do not serve us well.

Q155 *Chairman:* Tell us about that.
Mr Swinney: Let me give you another example. You have talked about baselines, and again as we prepared for the Spending Review last year the United Kingdom Government took a decision that, because of the performance of health expenditure in England, they would reduce the baseline of the

Department of Health in England by about £3 billion, and they consequentially visited that change of baseline on the Scottish Government, so essentially we had our baseline health component of what was calculated in the implications of the Barnett Formula reduced by about £300 million a month before the publication of the Spending Review. That in my experience was quite unprecedented

Q156 *Lord Forsyth of Drumlean:* How much had it gone up by year-on-year?
Mr Swinney: It would have gone up by the Barnett consequences of the increase in public expenditure in England.

Q157 *Lord Forsyth of Drumlean:* Which was?
Mr Swinney: In some years it would—

Q158 *Lord Forsyth of Drumlean:* No, in the year where you say there was this £300 million reduction?
Mr Swinney: The overall Scottish Government grant increased by 0.5 per cent above inflation.

Q159 *Lord Forsyth of Drumlean:* The health budget in England went up, it did not go down. There may have been an adjustment but I am just asking what was the net increase?
Mr Swinney: The point I am making is that the baseline was reduced in England by £3 billion and therefore the increase was applied to that reduced baseline. I cannot give you the specific number of what the percentage increase was in the English Department of Health expenditure at that particular time.

Q160 *Lord Forsyth of Drumlean:* You are saying the net baseline for England was reduced, there was a cut?
Mr Swinney: Correct.

Q161 *Lord Forsyth of Drumlean:* In health expenditure?
Mr Swinney: There was a cut in the baseline, a cut of £3 billion less than was expected to come into the baseline in 2008–09.

Q162 *Lord Forsyth of Drumlean:* That is not the same thing as a cut in expenditure. The overall amount went up. What you may have been anticipating went down but you still got an increase, just for the sake of clarity.
Mr Swinney: The overall increase above inflation in the Scottish Government's budget in that year was half a per cent.

Q163 *Chairman:* On health you got an increase, not as much as you expected but you got an increase?

Mr Swinney: I am saying that we got an increase of half a per cent above inflation, but one of the decisions that was arrived at was a reduction in the comparative baseline that the Scottish Government took because of a reduction in the expected baseline of the budget in the Department of Health in England.
Lord Forsyth of Drumlean: There was still an increase in the baseline, just in case people thought there had been a cut.

Q164 *Lord Rowe-Beddoe:* Mr Swinney, from this discussion, am I right to infer that what Lord Forsyth described as past practice with Secretaries of State for Wales and Scotland negotiating with Chief Secretaries and so on has stopped in recent years?
Mr Swinney: I only have 20 months of experience of all of this so I cannot really speak in detail before May 2007, but what I would say is that we now have, for example, in place—and I assume this is a different set of rules to the ones that existed prior to devolution—a Statement of Funding Policy which is a product of the establishment of the Scottish Parliament and the other devolved administrations. That effectively polices the financial relationship between the Scottish Government and the United Kingdom Government. When I came to office, the Treasury were reviewing the Statement of Funding Policy and essentially took that discussion forward with the Finance Ministers of the devolved administrations of Scotland, Wales and Northern Ireland. When we come to the conclusion of that process, the Statement of Funding Policy is not actually signed off by the Chief Secretary and myself in a mutual agreement. It is signed off between the Chief Secretary and the Secretary of State for Scotland, so I get consulted about it but I do not have to sign it off and I do not have to reach an agreement about the Statement of Funding Policy. I think it would be a much healthier situation if I did have the opportunity to sign off that Statement of Funding Policy and agree the basis of the rules upon which the funding arrangements were to be had. I think that would be by far a healthier process. In terms of the other discussions, of course on a day-to-day basis, my officials are in regular communication with the Treasury on a whole variety of different questions and, periodically, I will be in touch with the Treasury ministers in different ways and on different subjects. We will do that either by correspondence or we will do it by face-to-face meetings. In case of the run-up to the Spending Review, for example, it is fair to say that we had to kick start the process of a quadrilateral meeting between the finance ministers of Scotland, Wales and Northern Ireland and the Chief Secretary, if my memory serves me right, probably in July 2007, and subsequent to that I had two face-to-face meetings with the Chief Secretary prior to the

publication of the Spending Review to essentially advance some of the arguments and issues about which we were concerned.

Q165 *Lord Forsyth of Drumlean:* What sort of issues were these?

Mr Swinney: They would be about a number of things, the scale of the resources available, some of the elements of the Statement of Funding Policy, some of the issues that were proposed to be changed in that, and some of the questions such as judgments that were arrived at about individual financial decisions where for example the devolved administrations expressed their concerns about the fact that in relation to the regeneration aspects of the London Olympics funding it was proposed there would be no consequentials, whereas if it was regeneration activity in the east end of London we would expect to have consequentials from that factor, so a mixture of essentially procedural questions, headline financial numbers, and specific issues of concern.

Q166 *Lord Rowe-Beddoe:* So under current practice then, it would still be the territorial Secretary of State who would be the interface, if you like, on your behalf with the Treasury with regard to additional funding?

Mr Swinney: No.

Q167 *Lord Rowe-Beddoe:* No?

Mr Swinney: No, the Secretary of State for Scotland has the responsibility to sign off the Statement of Funding Policy. The Secretary of State for Scotland essentially receives the resources—that is not quite the right way to characterise it. The Secretary of State for Scotland has the first call on the contents of the Scottish Consolidated Fund to fund the offices of the Scotland Office and then the resources are controlled by the Scottish Government as part of the Scottish Consolidated Fund, but if there were to be a discussion about the size of the budget and any relevant financial issues, we would conduct those discussions directly with the Treasury. My frustration in relation to the Statement of Funding Policy is that I might have concerns about it, I might argue about it, I might want to have alterations to the Statement of Funding Policy, but ultimately the Chief Secretary has no obligation to secure my agreement to the Statement of Funding Policy. I think that is a weakness in the system because essentially I am the person who has the responsibility for controlling the absolutely enormous proportion of the Scottish Consolidated Fund, but I do not have access to securing the agreement of the procedures that underpin the interaction upon those questions.

Q168 *Lord Forsyth of Drumlean:* May I just pursue this issue of the administrative arrangements surrounding the working of the formula to which Lord Rowe-Beddoe has just alluded. Perhaps I was too interventionalist, but I find it extremely difficult to understand how it is possible to run the Scottish budget if you are just getting the population consequences under the crude Barnett Formula and there is not a dialogue about all kinds of issues. We have mentioned health for example—and I think you might have stopped council house sales—but the treatment of capital and all kinds of issues would come up where the formula as it operates would be fair or unfair. You have cited the example of the London Olympics, which is a separate issue which, if I may, I will come on to in a moment. I also do not understand how the Secretary of State for Scotland can sign off on the Scottish budget if he has not got the resources of the Executive behind him saying, "This is going to work," "That is not going to work," "This is needed." I am finding it difficult to understand how this can actually work in practice.

Mr Swinney: Let me make the distinction about where the Secretary of State for Scotland fits into this. The Secretary of State for Scotland fits into this in only two respects. Firstly, he has first call to decide how much of the Scottish Consolidated Fund he intends to utilise to fund the Scotland Office, and the Scotland Act provides for that, and he decides that and then it gets passed to the Scottish Government, and then we have responsibility for deploying that expenditure. The second aspect is that the Secretary of State for Scotland signs off the Statement of Funding Policy which is a set of rules. Indeed it is published and available through the Treasury information channels. He signs that off in agreement with the Chief Secretary to the Treasury, but it is about the rules that we have to operate under within the Scottish Government. I find that an absurd way of operating. To give you an example, one of the issues I was troubled by in the Statement of Funding Policy last year, when the Scotland Act was agreed by the United Kingdom Parliament, there was a mechanism within the original Statement for Funding Policy which dealt with the pattern of increases in council tax benefit which is of course paid by the United Kingdom Government. Essentially the mechanism was in place and it was designed to make sure that if council tax benefit rose disproportionately faster in Scotland than it did England there would be a claw-back from the Scottish budget to the UK Government. That was the mechanism that was in place and what happened over the years, if my memory serves me right, 2001 to 2004, was there was a payment from the United Kingdom Government to the Scottish Executive then because council tax benefit rose disproportionately slower in Scotland than it did in England, so the mechanism that was there to claw the money back actually resulted in a rebate coming from the UK Government to Scotland. This went on for a few years and the UK Government paid the money to the then Scottish Executive and then somewhere round about 2004 began to get a bit sticky about this payment. My predecessors agreed a one-off settlement which resulted in a payment of around about £50 million from the UK Government to the Scottish Executive in about 2005 and 2006, on condition of the agreement that the mechanism was suspended and it did not apply. If that mechanism had continued to apply we would be entitled to a rebate year on year on year because of the performance of relative council tax benefit. I inherited a suspended mechanism. I tried to reactivate that in terms of the Statement of Funding Policy and the Treasury amended the Statement of Funding Policy essentially to entrench the suspension of that mechanism, against my view, because obviously it was a financial benefit to Scotland to have that mechanism in place at that particular time. I accept that at some stage in the future it might not have been a benefit to us because the pattern of council tax expenditure could have shifted, but it was suspended, and I disagreed with that and I made that point to the Chief Secretary, I argued about it, I wrote, I spoke, but it was done and we do not have a mechanism. I use that to illustrate the frustration of how the arrangements can actually be deployed in practice. You then have a wider question—

Q169 *Chairman:* You did not get the real money and that is frustrating, but that is politics, is it not?
Mr Swinney: Yes, but there was a mechanism in place which was suspended because it was not producing the result that was originally envisaged for it to produce. If the mechanism was there that would have said to me this was a part of the funding arrangements.

Q170 *Chairman:* You had about five or six years' benefit out of it. I do not know the details.
Mr Swinney: That is a view, Lord Richard to take, but that is not a view I take. I happen to think that if there is an arrangement in place we should operate by it.

Q171 *Lord Forsyth of Drumlean:* You are talking about the Barnett Formula on a statutory basis?
Mr Swinney: What I do not think has happened, Lord Forsyth, is I do not think that the funding arrangements have caught up with the change in constitutional arrangements that have taken place in the United Kingdom. I think what happens currently is that the Treasury continues to deal with the Scottish Government as if it were a department of Whitehall, and I think the devolved arrangements change fundamentally the balance of responsibility

within the United Kingdom, and the idea that somehow if I disagreed with the Treasury about something, and, with the greatest of respect, Lord Forsyth knows there is no inference in what I am about to say, as a territorial Secretary of State in the old Scottish Office days, the Chief Secretary if he went to the Prime Minister could just say, "The Secretary of State for Scotland is not getting it, and that is it," that was the workings of the United Kingdom finances. I think the workings have changed in the nature of devolution because we are a distinctively elected legislator within Scotland but the aspirations that we may have for some of the routine operation of financial arrangements are handled in a fashion that Whitehall departments would experience, and I do not think that is particularly credible.

Q172 *Lord Forsyth of Drumlean:* On that point, you are quite wrong about the Chief Secretary being able to say, "You are not getting it." If the Chief Secretary said to the Secretary of State, "You are not getting it," the Secretary of State would take it to the Chancellor and if the Chancellor said no, the Secretary of State could take it to Cabinet, it was a Cabinet decision, and in our circumstances we would invariably deploy arguments like, "Mr Swinney and his colleagues will make hay," and usually we got our way, which is one of the reasons why convergence has not actually happened!
Mr Swinney: I am glad that we were so useful to you, Lord Forsyth. I did not quite know we were so influential but that has reassured me enormously this morning! My point though is that the Secretary of State for Scotland may have had that ability to argue that point. My reflection on the funding arrangements that currently exist is that when the Treasury says no it is essentially dealing with the Scottish Government as if it were a Whitehall department, and I do not think that is the right representation of the fact that there is now in Scotland and Wales and Northern Ireland an elected legislator which has specific entrenched responsibilities allocated to each institution through legislation passed by the United Kingdom Parliament.

Q173 *Lord Sewel:* I think we have got to recognise that in all devolved regimes, and I think also all federal regimes, there is an element of grant support to expenditure. No matter what other elements of funding are available, grant is a common feature of those regimes. What I am trying to do is get the essential difference between what was pre-devolution and post-devolution, and it does seem to me that the real distinctive thing is that pre-devolution you had the Barnett Formula, and if the Barnett Formula consequentials came up with an answer which the

Secretary of State did not feel was essential, they had another route through bypass, as Lord Forsyth has argued. Now to all intents and purposes you have the Barnett Formula, you have the consequentials, but that bypass opportunity effectively no longer exists, and if you have a problem in a particular area, say the Health Service national wage awards, you are told you have got to vire, or you can use the element of fiscal autonomy that you already have which is the Scottish variable rate which at the moment, until now, you have not felt the need to use. Is that the essential difference?

Mr Swinney: I suspect that probably does capture the essential difference, other than the fact that the United Kingdom Government still has the ability to bypass the Barnett Formula, as in the example I cited on prisons. I do not at all shirk the responsibility to vire within the overall pot of money that is allocated to us.

Q174 *Lord Sewel:* That is what it is about, is it not?

Mr Swinney: The foundation of the Barnett Formula is that essentially it creates a pot. It is the fundamental principle of the Scottish Government now, but there would also be the way in which The Scottish Office would have operated in the past, that there was an ability to not follow the spending patterns in England.

Q175 *Lord Sewel:* But the difference is now, is it not—

Mr Swinney: The fundamental distinction that I am making is that there is still the ability to bypass the Barnett Formula but that exists for the United Kingdom Government.

Q176 *Lord Sewel:* Whereas previously if the Barnett consequentials came up with an "unacceptable figure" there was the opportunity of, let us call it, positive bypassing through the Secretary of State and the Treasury, and ultimately the Prime Minister if need be. Now the only way in which you can compensate for the same sort of unacceptable outcome is to use the Scottish variable rate?

Mr Swinney: Yes, but the Scottish variable rate essentially reduces one's ability to spend money because of the ceiling of the departmental expenditure limit within which we have to operate, so I cannot use the Scottish variable rate tomorrow to raise an extra three pence in the pound in taxation, which would be of the order of about £1.2 billion, and be able to spend that because that would break the departmental expenditure limit set by the Treasury. I would have to reduce public expenditure programmes by £1.2 billion to ensure that money could be spent, so there is a real restriction and limitation in any sense on the effectiveness of the

Scottish variable rate if we wish to cut taxation in that respect.

Q177 *Lord Sewel:* I am not talking about cutting taxes, no, I am talking about compensating for a shortfall in the formula; you could use the variable rate to do that.

Mr Swinney: Yes.

Q178 *Lord Forsyth of Drumlean:* This cannot be right. Are you saying that if you were to levy the Tartan Tax you would put three pence on income tax—and I am not advocating this I hasten to add—which will bring in £1.2 billion, the Treasury would then reduce your budget by £1.2 billion?

Mr Swinney: No, I am talking about tax reduction. The answer I was giving to Lord Sewel was about tax reduction.

Q179 *Lord Forsyth of Drumlean:* But the question was not about tax reduction, the question was if you needed resources over and above the formula consequences, the Tartan Tax is the only mechanism?

Mr Swinney: Yes.

Q180 *Lord Forsyth of Drumlean:* Whereas before going along with a hard luck story to the Prime Minister was the mechanism; now the only mechanism is to actually increase income tax?

Mr Swinney: That is why we come to the view—and I have laboured this point a number of times already, Chairman—that the funding arrangements need to be changed to ensure that we have the ability to exercise greater financial responsibility, to take account of the fact that we have such limited devices for handling these issues.

Q181 *Chairman:* It does seem that your basic position now is that as far as Barnett is concerned you do not think Scotland has done as well out of it as it should do but it does not really matter because we want to move to an entirely different system of fiscal autonomy?

Mr Swinney: That is my position.

Q182 *Chairman:* So if I asked the question do you think the arrangement is fair for Scotland, presumably you say some of it is and some of it is not but that is not what we want; we want fiscal autonomy. If I ask whether there is any different way of operating the Barnett Formula, again we get the same answer.

Mr Swinney: The constitutional debate is moving on, Lord Richard.

Q183 *Chairman:* We are not a constitutional committee.

Mr Swinney: I appreciate that, but I am simply giving you an insight into the debate as to where we are just now and where the debate is moving in Scotland. There is a need for us to move to the position of exercising greater financial responsibility, and that is where the debate sits.

Q184 *Lord Sewel:* Do you see the grant element being a constant feature of the relationship?
Mr Swinney: No, not necessarily.

Q185 *Lord Sewel:* Can you name another devolved administration which is based on that?
Mr Swinney: There will be various funding arrangements around the world where there are, in some circumstances, administrations raising the overwhelming majority of taxation in their own locality and then remitting some of that expenditure to the unitary authority to pay for certain services.

Q186 *Lord Sewel:* Can you name a system which does not have either a central element of switching revenues around on the basis of relative need between the constituent parts or is based on grant coming from the centre?
Mr Swinney: I am not familiar with every regime around the world but there will be some.

Q187 *Lord Sewel:* But you have done the work on fiscal autonomy so surely you must have done some international comparisons?
Mr Swinney: There will be examples where the ability to exercise greater responsibility for finances is entrenched within the component parts of a unitary state.
Lord Forsyth of Drumlean: Just going back to the Chairman's question—
Chairman: Can I just say one thing: this Committee is here to look at the Barnett Formula, not to discuss the demand for fiscal autonomy by the Scottish National Party. Fascinating though that would be and as much as I would wish to examine Mr Swinney on his demand for fiscal autonomy, that is not what we are here to discuss.

Q188 *Lord Forsyth of Drumlean:* Just going back to your question, Chairman, and underscoring what Lord Richard has said, you are the Finance Minister of the Scottish Executive. Next year there is going to be a squeeze on public expenditure. Whoever wins the next general election there is going to be real tightening of public expenditure. This Committee is going to make recommendations about the operation of the Barnett Formula. I think it is unlikely that a new system is going to occur this side of a general election so, wearing your responsible hat as the Finance Minister, are you really saying that there are no changes or improvements or anxieties that you

have about Barnett that this Committee might like to look at, because from where I sit the combination of the constitutional change and the operation of Barnett has left you in a very disadvantaged position, some of which could be put right by amending the Barnett Formula. Just to sit there and say, "Actually we would rather have something else," is not going to get you through next year and the year after, and it seems to me that there are very substantial physical consequences for people who are depending on public services in Scotland.
Mr Swinney: First of all, the analysis that you apply, Lord Forsyth, is absolutely correct about the future of public expenditure. It is not just a 2010–11 problem. Certainly if one looks at the chart of real increases in public expenditure in Scotland, in the period since the establishment of the Scottish Parliament there has been very substantial and very positive growth in real terms in public expenditure in every single year since the establishment of the Parliament and, of course, significant increases in public expenditure in the rest of the United Kingdom. Over the forthcoming eight-year period I think we will probably see something which is, I do not know the extent to which it will be a direct reflection of that pattern of very substantial increase in expenditure, but it will certainly be very, very flat in terms of real terms increases in public expenditure, and I suspect there is every likelihood that there will be real terms reductions in public expenditure in the period that lies ahead. I think that looks pretty likely from the any scenario planning that I assess about the period that lies ahead, so, yes, we are moving into a fundamentally different financial climate, and the Scottish Government has to operate within that climate. As to how we do that, what would certainly make our life a great deal easier is if we had in place the procedures and the processes that would allow us to have a more meaningful discussion and debate about some of the financial challenges that we face with the Treasury, some of which are illustrated by the fact that on the Statement of Funding Policy we are not the signatories, and I think it would be a healthy development if we were to be signatories to the Statement of Funding Policy and that we were able to see with greater transparency the way in which elements of the Barnett Formula were applied. I have given a number of examples where we are not satisfied in our now 20 months' experience in office that the Barnett Formula has actually been applied in relation to decisions on public expenditure.

Q189 *Chairman:* Can I interrupt again to clarify for myself that you do not mind whether the Barnett Formula stays based at present or whether it is changed to something which is based upon assessment of needs, it is not something that particularly concerns you one way or the other because of your demand for fiscal autonomy? Is that fair?

Mr Swinney: I think that we should move from where we are today to a position of having fiscal autonomy; that is my position. If you are saying to me would I prefer to go from where we are just now to a needs-based formula, I think we are better to stay with where we are. What I would prefer to have in place is a regime that gave us a greater ability to influence the way in which the Barnett Formula was deployed. I have cited to Committee this morning a number of examples where the current arrangements have failed to deliver the type of—

Q190 *Chairman:* So you would rather have a Treasury determination of priorities than one based upon an assessment of the needs?

Mr Swinney: What I would want, as I have said a number of times already, is an arrangement whereby we can properly influence the application of the Barnett Formula rather than a view that is deployed to us by the Treasury without any real ability to say whether that is something we think is being deployed properly or improperly.

Q191 *Chairman:* Do you not think that an objective assessment of needs—and I know it is difficult to do but the Australians seem to do it—is a rather better way of distributing money?

Mr Swinney: The idea that somehow there is a simple approach to a needs-based formula—

Q192 *Chairman:* I did not say that—

Mr Swinney: With respect, my Lord, it was almost characterised as a simple and clear way of going about this. A needs-based exercise is an extremely difficult exercise to carry out and one that is subjected to, I suspect, even more subjectivity than I am concerned about the current Barnett Formula.

Q193 *Chairman:* Local authorities do it.

Mr Swinney: Yes they do and I suspect certain local authorities—

Q194 *Lord Sewel:* You use it for local authorities.

Mr Swinney: I know and some local authorities are as dissatisfied about the formula today as they probably were when Lord Forsyth was exercising that responsibility in the 1990s.

Q195 *Chairman:* How do you assess the needs of local authorities? Obviously it is subjectively in a sense.

Mr Swinney: It is done essentially by an assessment of around about 100 different indicators which are various illustrations as to need. Population drives the overwhelming majority of the local government distribution formula in Scotland but there will be other examples, from road length, to number of primary school pupils, to number of older people.

Q196 *Chairman:* But all based on need and how much the local authority needs to satisfy those demands?

Mr Swinney: After that, once you identify all of these different characteristics, you then have to apply a judgment about how much weighting you apply to every one of those factors, and that is where there is a massive amount of subjectivity in the way in which that is carried out. The other point is then what is the mechanism for arriving at that needs-based formula. I pose that as a very significant question, and based on my experience of the application of the current funding arrangements of United Kingdom anything that was a needs-base formula driven by the Treasury is one about which I would have profound reservations.

Q197 *Chairman:* But the needs-based formula for local authorities in Scotland is driven by the Scottish Executive.

Mr Swinney: No it is not, it is driven by an agreement between the Scottish Government and the Convention of Scottish Local Authorities.

Q198 *Lord Forsyth of Drumlean:* It is the same thing.

Mr Swinney: No sorry, Lord Forsyth, it is most definitely not the same thing.

Q199 *Lord Forsyth of Drumlean:* The Executive decides.

Mr Swinney: Ultimately, but we have got to have agreement, this is the crucial point, we must have agreement and consent with the Convention of Scottish Local Authorities. Please let me make one more comment. Going back to the point I was making about the Statement of Funding Policy, on the Statement of Funding Policy, on the application of all these issues in Scotland, my agreement is not required.

Q200 *Lord Forsyth of Drumlean:* I understand that and I take that point and I see the difficulty, but you said a few minutes ago that you would prefer a system which was based on you getting your relative share relative to population rather than one based on need. You also said earlier on when you were describing your approach to the housing benefit dispute with the Treasury, that it was your job to get the best deal for Scotland. Do you think that if you had a formula based on need that you would get less than based on population?

Mr Swinney: It depends what subjective judgments are made on what definition of need happened to be because one person's view of need can be dramatically different to another person's view of what need happens to be.

Q201 *Lord Forsyth of Drumlean:* We are not talking about one person's, we are talking about having some kind of objective measure of need. You said you would prefer the existing arrangement to one based on need. I am astonished by that because your overall position as an Executive and as a party has been that Scotland does not get its fair share of resources, and therefore if you believe that surely having some kind of objective assessment of need would be to the advantage of Scotland, and yet you have rejected that. Leaving aside how you actually determine need, as a matter of principle you appear to have said that you would prefer to have something that gave us a relative share relative to population rather than something which was an objective assessment of need. That is a pretty fundamental position to take.
Mr Swinney: There are two points in there. One is that you are advancing an argument, Lord Forsyth, which says that there is an objective way of calculating need and I think, in all honesty, the Committee has to reflect on the fact that it is not possible to do. Need is a very, very subjective assessment. The second point—

Q202 *Chairman:* It is not. I do not agree with that, I really do not agree.
Mr Swinney: Of course it is, Chairman.

Q203 *Chairman:* Different people have different views about what their needs are but they can all be pulled together; it can be done.
Mr Swinney: I think you answered your point in your own remark there: all sorts of people have got all sorts of different views about need; of course they have.

Q204 *Chairman:* But you do it with local authorities and they have all got their own views as to what they need and somebody pulls it together.
Mr Swinney: And we go through that process and we agree that with the Convention of Scottish Local Authorities. My point about the existing financial arrangements of the United Kingdom is two-fold in this respect. Firstly, the whole exercise of need, in my view, is an assessment which is very, very subjective. Secondly, the current arrangements are such that they would not give me a great deal of confidence as to how the current arrangements would arrive at that to be in the best interests of Scotland.

Q205 *Lord Sewel:* Density might be a better may of looking at things and that is moving towards need. It is possible to look at Scotland and say what is the mortality rate, what is the morbidity rate, what is the sparsity of population, what are the needs of

transport, all the things that you do by agreement— I accept the point about agreement—with local authorities. And it would be possible to do that and you would have certainty about your position, you would not have any of this business of that is in, this is out, or we do not like you this year so we are not going to do that. I find it very difficult to understand why you can be against that in principle. There may be practical reasons why it is difficult to achieve but why are you rejecting it on principle?
Mr Swinney: Because it fits into what I have argued to the Committee this morning which is that if we are moving from the Barnett Formula, which we know and we understand at the present time, although we have issues of concern about how it is currently being applied, let us move to a more robust form of financing, which is the argument about fiscal autonomy.

Q206 *Lord Sewel:* Is the problem, almost rephrasing Lord Forsyth's question, that you are fundamentally against need as a basis of allocating expenditure or is it that you do not have confidence basically in the Treasury doing it for you?
Mr Swinney: What I am saying to you is that I do not think we can view the calculation of need as purely and simply an objective technical exercise because I just do not think it is that, it is entirely a subjective process.

Q207 *Lord Sewel:* Sorry, did you say entirely a subjective process?
Mr Swinney: It is not entirely subjective.

Q208 *Lord Sewel:* You can run a series of regressions to identify expenditure drivers.
Mr Swinney: Entirely exaggerates the position; it is substantially a subjective exercise.
Chairman: I do not think Lord Sewel would accept that.

Q209 *Lord Sewel:* I do not accept that.
Mr Swinney: Then there is a question of how that would be deployed and how it would be applied, and we have significant concerns about the arrangements of the United Kingdom being able to do that.

Q210 *Lord Sewel:* You have clearly looked at the Commonwealth Grants Commission in Australia. What was your view of that?
Mr Swinney: It certainly has undertaken what appears to be a fairly robust piece of analysis. It is one that obviously we would look at in further detail, but I come back to the whole question of the exercise having that significant and substantial element of subjectivity about it.

Lord Sewel: At least we have gone down and now the subjectivity is down to the level of "significant" rather than "complete" or whatever it was.

Q211 *Lord Rowe-Beddoe:* Mr Swinney we are where we are at the moment, and I have listened and understand your dissatisfaction but, having said that, it is also clear that for the next however many years the Barnett Formula will be the way in which the Scottish Executive is funded to undertake its duties. If you could just stay with that for a moment and perhaps you could help us by giving us an opinion as to whether you consider one of the avowed intentions, in fact the avowed intention of the arithmetic of the Barnett Formula was to deliver convergence on English public spending over time. It does not appear to have occurred and you have an explanation as to why this may not be so.
Mr Swinney: The issue of convergence has been examined very extensively and I think one of the significant pieces of work on this was undertaken by Professor David Bell from Stirling University. I am sure the Committee is familiar with his work. Essentially the Barnett Formula would suggest that with increases in public expenditure there is the likelihood of convergence, and that was essentially designed to be the case, and at different stages the population factors have been updated to ensure that they remain current with experience. Over time the objective of the formula has been to deliver that convergence. One of the difficulties in assessing whether that is the case is to ensure that we have all of the full and appropriate data to be able to make a judgment about whether that has actually happened.

Q212 *Lord Rowe-Beddoe:* That leads on to the question about data. Do you think that in fact the data that is available on a territorial basis is both adequate and transparent?
Mr Swinney: I think there are some significant issues about that. In the course of 2006 two economists in Scotland, Dr Jim Cuthbert and Dr Margaret Cuthbert (Jim Cuthbert was the Chief Statistician at the Scottish Office for many years) undertook some work which examined the information that was contained in the PESA publication which gathers a large proportion of the data for disaggregating PESA Country and Regional Analysis data, which goes down to a lot of that information at a very detailed level. I do not have the details to hand about that, they highlighted a number of judgments that were applied in the presentation of the statistical information essentially where errors were being made about the allocations of expenditure as to where it was actually carried out, and that led to a large amount of discussion between officials in both the Treasury and the Scottish Government about how

that information and data could be improved to relate to that point.

Q213 *Lord Rowe-Beddoe:* Has anything occurred since the last 20 months that you have been elected here in the Scottish Executive that gives you any alarm or concern that the data is not adequate in your understanding of what is happening across the United Kingdom as a whole?
Mr Swinney: I think a lot of these issues relate to the vexed subject of defining what is identifiable and non-identifiable public expenditure. Identifiable public expenditure, by its nature, is identifiable public expenditure. What we have to be clear about is that that information is robust and that it is fulfilling its purpose. What the Cuthberts' analysis found was that some of the drivers of what we would consider to be identifiable public expenditure territorially was actually not correct, so those issues have been raised around about the PESA Country and Regional Analysis because that is obviously a big driver of identifiable public expenditure. Non-identifiable public expenditure is a very subjective process as to where that is actually spent and how it is spent, and that obviously is a major factor in the calculation in that respect.

Q214 *Chairman:* Can I come back to need for a second. We know that the Treasury produced in 1979 an assessment of the relative needs of the component parts of the United Kingdom. Have you seen that document?
Mr Swinney: I have not personally seen that.

Q215 *Chairman:* It is now available and I was wondering whether you had any comment to make on whether it is a good assessment of need?
Mr Swinney: I have not seen it.

Q216 *Chairman:* You have not seen the 1986 relative assessment of need?
Mr Swinney: I have not either.

Q217 *Chairman:* You have not had a more recent one than 1986, just to make sure you have not seen anything we have not seen, that is all.
Mr Swinney: I cannot say I have, unfortunately.
Chairman: Because there were three assessments of need by the Treasury after a great deal of work, and they are not perfect, but it seems to us, at any rate, they are a reasonable shy of producing the views on the relative needs of the component parts of the UK and that it can be done, and can even be done by the Treasury, but I am not advocating that.

Q218 *Lord Forsyth of Drumlean:* May I just ask what advice have you been given by your officials on the impact of a needs-based assessment of funding on Scotland?

Mr Swinney: I would characterise the advice as informing the contributions that I have made to the Committee today about the challenges that are associated with needs-based assessment.

Q219 *Lord Forsyth of Drumlean:* Can I tell you what advice I was given when I was Secretary of State. The advice I was given when I was Secretary of State is do everything you can to avoid a needs-based assessment being implemented by the Treasury because the Treasury believe that it will enable them to reduce Scotland's budget by between £2.5 and £4 billion. The officials did not think the Treasury's assessment was correct but I just wonder whether you had been given the same advice.

Mr Swinney: What I have said to you, Lord Forsyth, is that the advice I have had from my officials informs the contributions that I have made to the Committee.

Q220 *Lord Forsyth of Drumlean:* You have not really answered my question. Some of the officials are the same officials, and it may have changed because the baseline has changed and Scotland has changed, but I think we should be honest about this, at the root of this there was certainly in my day within the Scottish Office a belief that if Scotland was subject to a needs-based assessment of funding that that would result in a reduction in the budget. I would be surprised if you had not been given the same advice. The fact that you are avoiding question makes me think that perhaps you have.

Mr Swinney: I have given you the answer I have given you about what advice I have had. What I would say is that if you look at the information that is published publicly about public expenditure in Scotland, which tries to assess the issue that Lord Rowe-Beddoe is raising about the allocation of public expenditure, the most recent government expenditure and revenue in Scotland demonstrated the perspective of public expenditure in Scotland versus public expenditure in the rest of the United Kingdom, and it shows essentially the fundamental make-up of how that identifiable and non-identifiable expenditure comes together. That obviously relates to current patterns of public expenditure. It does not relate to a needs assessment but it relates to the current levels of public expenditure in Scotland.

Q221 *Lord Forsyth of Drumlean:* Just to pursue this, I do not buy the advice by the way, but the Chairman has referred to two exercises on a needs-based assessment both of which ran into the sand. The first one was done because the intention of the then Labour Government before 1979 was that they would bring in a Scottish Assembly and they were looking at how it could be funded and they concluded—obviously officials had concluded—that if we were going to have a Scottish Assembly and change the constitutional arrangements, you had to have something other than a straight population-based method of funding, and that is why that exercise was done. I was not a member of the Labour Government and so I do not know what happened, but my guess is that governments of all parties have thought that a needs-based assessment might actually result in Scotland being disadvantaged and therefore the thing has been buried. There has now been a fundamental constitutional change of the kind you describe, and you describe some of the difficulties. I am trying to get to the bottom of why you are so hostile to moving from a just straight arithmetic population-based system of the funding to needs. I am just wondering if your officials are telling you that that would disadvantage Scotland.

Mr Swinney: The reason why I am against it is because I want to move to a more robust framework. I am sorry if that is a frustrating line of argument but that is my line of argument and that is my political position.

Q222 *Lord Forsyth of Drumlean:* I understand that, but we have to actually look at where we are and you have described some of the problems and I am just pressing you on this.

Mr Swinney: Where we are, Lord Forsyth, and where I want to go in this debate is, I am pretty certain, a different place to where you want to go to on the constitutional debate.

Q223 *Lord Forsyth of Drumlean:* I am not talking about that. We are not talking about the constitutional debate.

Mr Swinney: I appreciate that the Committee has a narrow remit around about the Barnett Formula, but my perspective is that I want the argument on fiscal responsibility to go into a direction which allows us to exercise greater fiscal responsibility and flexibility than perhaps personally you might wish, Lord Forsyth, or which the Committee's remit allows it to consider, and that is the difference of view that we have.

Q224 *Chairman:* I understand that that is your answer. You do not like the way in which the Barnett Formula operates at present and you have given us examples of that. You are not prepared to go down the road which says let us have a needs assessment. Can you say that Barnett in those circumstances is operating fairly?

Mr Swinney: I have given you examples where Barnett is not operating fairly.

Q225 Chairman: Do you not think if you went down a needs assessment route you would produce a fairer result?

Mr Swinney: On the basis of the high level of subjectivity that I think is involved in a needs assessment and, secondly, by virtue of the fact that the arrangements that we experience in relation to some of these questions, that would suggest to me that our ability to influence the composition of a needs-based formula would be entirely dependent on persuading the Treasury of their willingness to do certain things. I am not persuaded of that.

Q226 Chairman: You have a long-term objective but in the meantime you do not like Barnett, you do not think it operates properly, and you do not want a needs assessment, you really do not mind if it produces fairer results as a result of that needs assessment; you would rather live with what you have got?

Mr Swinney: I have made that position very clear this morning. I would rather deal with what we have got before I move on to the preferred option which I have set out publicly this week in terms of the exercising of fiscal responsibility.

Q227 Lord Sewel: And you reject a needs-based approach despite the fact that you use it in relation to local government and it is a needs-based approach that is used in just about every other state which has a broadly similar relationship between a central state and a devolved assembly?

Mr Swinney: I have set out the direction of travel that I wish to go in relation to this.

Lord Sewel: We accept that is the direction of travel but it is in this period that you are going to have a grant-based system for a period of time and you are saying no to needs in a way which I find difficult—I think we all find difficult—to understand, given that it is a needs-based approach which underpins the relationship between you and local government and underpins the relationship in other regimes between the central government and devolved administrations and federal administrations elsewhere. I am not aware, you see, of any funding basis that depends purely on a population accrued/population-driven approach that the Barnett Formula is and that you say is your preferred option in the short term.

Q228 Chairman: It gives you that result but it is a result you do not like because you do not think it operates fairly?

Mr Swinney: My perspective on this is why put off undertaking the fundamental change in the financial arrangements by constructing some other formula for doing this? Why do we not just change the financial responsibility that we have? That is my fundamental point.

Q229 Lord Sewel: It is a very dangerous zero sum game because you are actually saying, "I do not want to change the existing situation because I want something called fiscal autonomy." If you do not get fiscal autonomy you really do not have an argument about changing the existing arrangements.

Mr Swinney: I would rather concentrate on the argument for getting fiscal autonomy, for which there is a growing consensus within Scotland that that is the right way that we should proceed.

Q230 Lord Sewel: That is very risky, is it not?

Mr Swinney: It is a representative position of a broadly held view in Scotland that we need to have greater fiscal autonomy.

Lord Sewel: In the intervening period on grant you have no view?

Q231 Chairman: We cannot argue fiscal autonomy so that the position is that until you get fiscal autonomy you have no real view on the arrangements?

Mr Swinney: I have set out in a number of responses issues that concern me about the current funding arrangements.

Q232 Lord Sewel: Let us go at it another way because I want to get your criticisms on the transparency of the formula. You seem to be saying that your real concern is what comes within the purview of the formula and what does not, what goes into the formula?

Mr Swinney: Yes.

Q233 Lord Sewel: Right, so that is the criticism there. You think that because population has specific numbers associated with it, which are objective numbers based on the number of people, then the transparency is all right on that and that scores high on transparency; is that right?

Mr Swinney: Yes.

Q234 Lord Sewel: And then if we go on to its effect on your policy agenda, it would seem to be that you are almost content that what the formula produces does give you sufficient scope to shape your policy agenda because you are able to shape your policy agenda, as you say, by viring within the total and you have never felt the need to use what fiscal autonomy you already have, so clearly you do have scope to address your policy agenda under the present arrangements?

Mr Swinney: We will have aspirations to do other things and take other initiatives, but, quite clearly, the money will not exist to do all the things that we want to do.

Q235 Lord Sewel: Because of how much you get?
Mr Swinney: Yes.

Q236 Lord Sewel: Of course you do have fiscal autonomy in any case and you do not use it.
Mr Swinney: We have one tax varying power, and certainly my view is that the Government has not argued for the use of that tax varying power and we do not intend to use that tax varying power because it is not just increasing tax to get more money, it is not the end of the argument, it is a much more complicated argument than that. What the arrangements currently allow us to do is to make a judgment about how we distribute pretty much without restriction within two pots of what is resource and what is capital. We can make those judgments. Whether that is sufficient, whether that is enough to allow us to satisfy our policy agenda is a fundamentally different question and that is where I make the argument for greater fiscal responsibility to allow us to be able to take different decisions that would allow us to affect the size of that cake, because we have essentially a fixed financial envelope, with the one exception that we could increase tax by three pence in the pound.

Q237 Lord Forsyth of Drumlean: What about Lord Rowe-Beddoe's point about convergence, because if the Formula is just operating on a population basis and you do not have the opportunity to go along to knock on the Chief Secretary's door and get a good response, which is probably exacerbated if you have different political regimes in power in different parts of the United Kingdom, the effect will be mathematically, because the baseline is higher, that there will be convergence between England and Scotland. The effect of continuing with a population-based system without any bells and whistles will be that Scotland's relative share of resources will go down and your budget is going to get squeezed. What Lord Sewel is arguing is do you not want to be in a position to say actually we do not want convergence because the need in Scotland is greater, and by rejecting the idea of need and by embracing this position, are there some tactics here? Do you see this as a way of testing the system to destruction so you get whatever else it is you want? From our point of view as a Committee we look at this and say there are some problems here, how can these problems be fixed in the short term, if you want to change the system that is fine, but where the Committee is finding it quite difficult to understand is why are you not flagging up this problem of convergence which Lord Rowe-Beddoe mentioned because you are in a squeeze here?
Mr Swinney: Because I have my agenda, Lord Forsyth, which is to advance on the argument of ensuring that Scotland has the proper equipment of financial responsibility.

Q238 Lord Forsyth of Drumlean: What about protecting public services?
Mr Swinney: That is precisely why I pursue the agenda I pursue—to ensure that Parliament has the ability to exercise that greater degree of fiscal responsibility and flexibility that I seek.

Q239 Chairman: We are up against the wall of fiscal autonomy. I am told that you need to be away by quarter past. Can I thank you very much for coming. We have had an illuminating and interesting morning. I am very grateful to you for the candour with which you have answered our questions.
Mr Swinney: Thank you.

Memorandum by Professor David King (Professor of Public Economics, University of Stirling)

The Committee's Call for Evidence makes many references to needs assessment. I hope this paper will help the Committee's discussions of those issues. Points 1–5 below relate to the Call for Evidence paragraph 1a, which asks whether the current disparities in public spending between the countries of the UK relate to need.

1. Currently, spending per head on public services in Scotland is about 20 per cent above that in England, and one cannot say definitively whether this difference is in excess of its relative needs, because there is no definitive way of estimating needs.

2. However, it is most unlikely that any plausible needs assessment formula would treat Scotland so generously. Over half the relevant public service spending is accounted for by local authorities, and around 2004 I applied to Scottish local authorities the very complicated formulae used by Westminster to estimate the spending needs of English local authorities. Table 1 gives some results: eg spending needs per head on local education services were £505 in Scotland, slightly *below* the £509 in England.

3. Table 1 shows that Scotland had higher needs for other service blocks: eg £84 per head as opposed to £75 for personal social services for children; £128 compared with £107 for personal social services for older people; and £44 compared with £40 for highway maintenance.

4. Overall, the English formulae suggested that Scotland's needs for local authority services were around 6 per cent higher than England's needs.

5. As noted in point 1, different formulae might give very different results. Holyrood also assesses the spending needs of its local authorities, and it gets very different figures for relative need. Assuming, purely for example, that the English formulae were right, then Figure 1 shows that the Scottish formulae errors in 2003–04 for education ranged from eight per cent in East Ayrshire to +19 per cent in Eilean Siar. Figure 2 shows that the Scottish formulae errors for personal social services in 2004–05 ranged from 23 per cent in Glasgow to +49 per cent in Orkney. Figure 3 shows that the Scottish formulae errors for highway maintenance in 2004–05 ranged from 41 per cent in Inverclyde to +239 per cent in Eilean Siar.

Points 6–7 below relate to the Call for Evidence paragraph 4m, which considers the appropriate factors to allow for when estimating spending needs.

6. Needs assessment should certainly allow for high spending needs in areas which need relatively more units of output per head to provide a given service level: eg areas with relatively high numbers of children need relatively more school places.

7. Some people argue that allowance should also be made for areas which face higher costs per unit of output: eg London has high wage costs and so needs to spend more to provide each school place; and Scotland's sparse population leads to many small primary schools which cost more per pupil. But the case for allowing for these costs can be contested. At present, London receives generous grants to help it pay the high wages of its public sector workers, but these high wages arise because London is a popular place to live, and so has high property prices. Arguably, its high grants just make it a better place to live, and so attract migrants who drive up property prices further; the result is that public sector wages have to rise again, so costs rise still further, leading to yet more grants.

Points 8–9 below relate to the Call for Evidence paragraph 4o which asks whether any needs assessment formulae should be based on a wide or small range of factors.

8. The formulae used for local authority spending in England, Scotland and Wales are very complex and allow for many factors, most of them being demographic, social or economic. Spending needs per head probably vary much less per head between the four countries of the UK than between local authorities, so in principle it might be possible to use simpler formula that focused on a few key factors.

9. Nevertheless, there are many factors that vary sharply even between the countries. Eg Table 1 shows that only 1 per cent of Scotland's schoolchildren come from low achieving ethnic groups, compared with 9 per cent in England; Scotland would get £88 per child for children living in flats, compared with £30 in England; and Scotland would get £88 per older adult to allow for those on low incomes, compared with £52 in England.

10. Anyone who undertook the needs assessments would face great pressure to allow for many factors like these, if they could be shown to be relevant. Each factor might have only a marginal effect, but each country would have an incentive to seek factors that would give it a marginal advantage.

11. Also, once any formula was announced, English regions could at once see whether the public spending they enjoyed was above or below that which the formula would allow, and in practice it might prove difficult not to apply the formula to them. But needs will vary greatly between regions within England, especially between London and other regions, and it may well require a complex formula to allow satisfactorily for this.

12. In short, the prospects of getting wide approval for a simple formula may be slim.

Points 13–19 below relate to the Call for Evidence paragraph 4p which asks who should carry out any needs-based assessment. I would tentatively suggest the following:

13. The formula should be devised by an autonomous body such as Australia's Commonwealth Grants Commission. If the central government devised it, there would be sure to be accusations of bias.

14. The body should update its assessments annually: large periodic assessments would lead to the same adjustment problems that arise with periodic property tax revaluations.

15. The body would need people with links to each UK country. Ideally, many would have links to more than one country, to lessen the tendency for those from single countries simply to argue their corner. There should also be some overseas representatives.

16. The body should include people with direct technical experience of needs assessment. It would be useful for technicians from each UK country to pool their experiences.

17. The body should be willing to consider some specific grants as well as general grants.

18. The body should try to make provisional announcements well ahead.

19. Ideally, some members of the body would serve for fairly long periods of time. Currently, it is often hard to find anyone who knows why a particular indicator is used in the local government formulae, because it was already allowed for before the current team members became involved.

Finally, if the Barnett formula is replaced by a needs assessment exercise, the transition from one to the other must be handled with great care. A major reason for the unpopularity of the poll tax stemmed from the very carelessly designed transitional safety net arrangements.

Table 1

RELATIVE SCOTTISH AND ENGLISH SPENDING NEEDS FOR SOME LOCAL AUTHORITY SERVICES, AS ASSESSED BY THE FORMULAE USED IN ENGLAND

	SCOTLAND	ENGLAND
LOCAL AUTHORITY EDUCATION SERVICES, 2003–04		
% of children from low achieving ethnic groups	1%	9%
% of children who depend on an IS/IBJSA claimant	21%	20%
% of children who depend on a WFTC/DPTC claimant	20%	19%
% of children in sparse wards	18%	14%
% of children in supersparse wards	13%	3%
% of 3–15 year olds in high cost groups	4%	4%
Local authority education services, needs per pupil	£3,419	£3,319
% of population who are pupils aged 3–15	16.0%	16.7%
Local authority education services, needs per head	£505	£509
PERSONAL SOCIAL SERVICES FOR CHILDREN 2004–05		
Basic sum per child	–£18	–£18
Sum per child for children living in flats	£88	£30
Sum per child for long-term ill children	£63	£60
Sum per child for children who depend on an IS/IBJSA claimant	£93	£92
Sum per child for children living in 1-adult homes	£140	£122
Sum per child for dense population	£7	£16
Sum per child based on factors affecting need for foster care	£13	£15
Sum per child for area cost adjustment	£4	£19
Personal social services for children, needs per child	£337	£391
Children as % of total population	21.5%	22.4%
Personal social services for children, needs per head	£84	£75
PERSONAL SOCIAL SERVICES FOR OLDER PEOPLE 2004–05		
Basic sum per older adult	–£288	–£288
Sum per older adult for adults aged 75–84	£116	£121
Sum per older adult for adults aged 85 +	£120	£126
Sum per older adult for renting pensioners	£137	£92
Sum per older adult for those who are long-term ill	£156	£152
Sum per older adult for those who are on IS/IBJSA	£109	£92
Sum per older adult for pensioners living alone	£111	£102
Sum per older adult for those 65 + on AA/DLA	£197	£167
Sum per older adult for those not in couples	£49	£47
Sum per older adult to allow for those on low incomes	£88	£52
Sum per older adult to allow for sparsity	£3	£1

	SCOTLAND	ENGLAND
Sum per older adult for area cost adjustment	£9	£29
Personal social services for older people, needs per older adult	£807	£692
Older adults as % of total population	*15.8%*	*15.5%*
Personal social services for older people, needs per head	£128	£107

LOCAL AUTHORITYHIGHWAY MAINTENANCE 2004–05

	SCOTLAND	ENGLAND
Sum per head for weighted road length	£6	£4
Sum per head for traffic flow	£20	£20
Sum per head for daytime population	£10	£12
Sum per head for winter maintenance	£7	£3
Sum per head for area cost adjustment	£1	£1
Local authority highway maintenance, needs per head	£44	£40

Figure 1

PERCENTAGE ERRORS IN LOCAL AUTHORITY EDUCATION NEEDS IN 2003–04, AS ASSESSED
BY THE SCOTTISH NEEDS ASSESSMENT FORMULA, IF RELATIVE NEEDS ARE ACCURATELY
MEASURED BY THE ENGLISH FORMULA

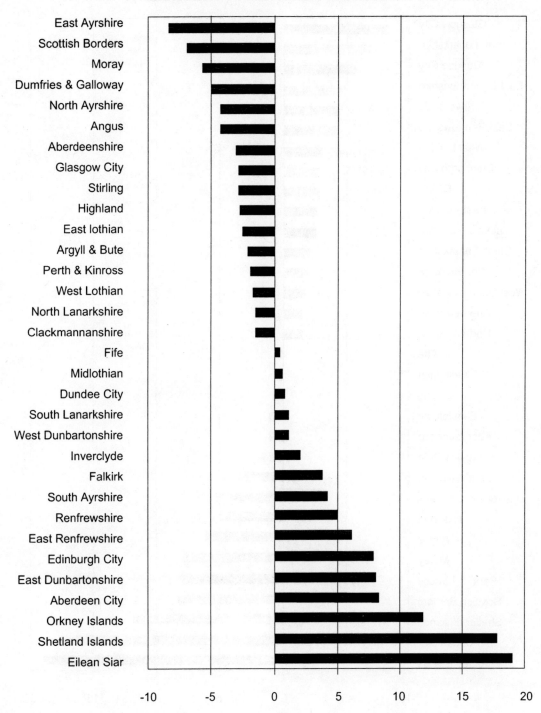

Source: D King, M Pashley and R Ball, 2004, "An English assessment of Scotland's education spending
needs", *Fiscal Studies* 25:4.

Figure 2

PERCENTAGE ERRORS IN LOCAL AUTHORITY PERSONAL SOCIAL SERVICES NEEDS IN
2004–05, AS ASSESSED BY THE SCOTTISH NEEDS ASSESSMENT FORMULA, IF RELATIVE
NEEDS ARE ACCURATELY MEASURED BY THE ENGLISH FORMULA.

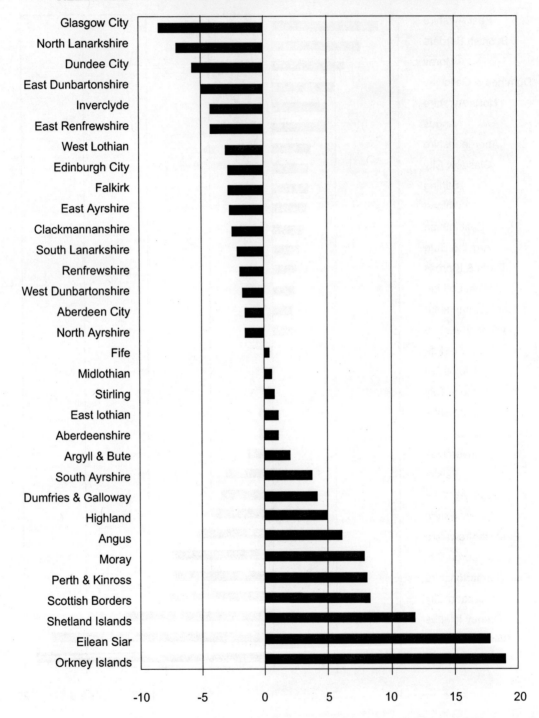

Source: D King, M Pashley and R Ball, 2007, "Scotland's social services spending needs: an English view,"
Government and Policy, 25:6.

Figure 3

PERCENTAGE ERRORS IN LOCAL AUTHORITY HIGHWAY MAINTENANCE NEEDS IN 2004–05,
AS ASSESSED BY THE SCOTTISH NEEDS ASSESSMENT FORMULA, IF RELATIVE NEEDS ARE
ACCURATELY MEASURED BY THE ENGLISH FORMULA.

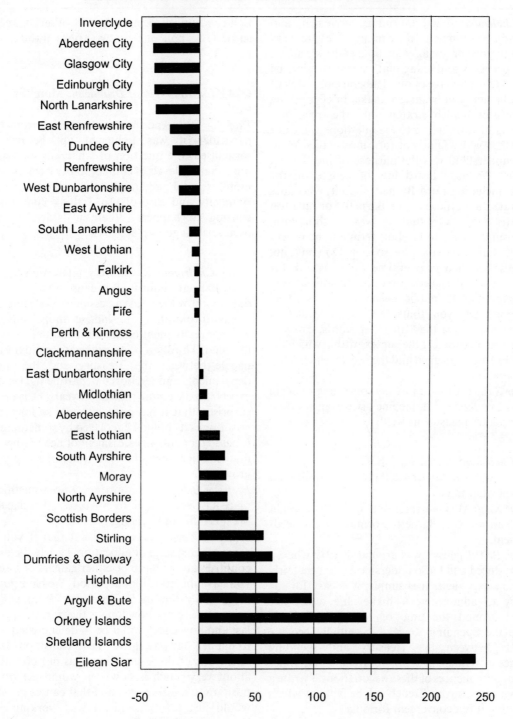

Source: D King, M Pashley and R Ball, 2007, "The environmental spending needs of Scotland's local authorities," *Local Government Studies*, 33:2.

Examination of Witnesses

Witnesses: PROFESSOR DAVID BELL, Professor of Economics, University of Stirling; PROFESSOR DAVID KING, Professor of Public Economics, University of Stirling; and PROFESSOR KIM SWALES, Professor and Head of Economics Department, University of Strathclyde, examined.

Q240 *Chairman:* Good morning, gentlemen, and thank you very much for coming. We are very grateful to you for giving your time and expertise. I think expertise is something that we will certainly be in need of at some stage of our deliberations. I do not know whether you want to make brief opening statements or launch straight into the questions. Shall we launch straight into the questions and can I start off then with a faintly historic look at this. What do you understand was the purpose of the Barnett Formula? We have heard lots of people on the purpose, including Lord Barnett himself, who does not elevate the purpose of the Barnett Formula too high. His view was that it was a short-term mechanism designed to be short term and he is very surprised that it went on quite so long. Do you think its purpose has changed over time? Do you think, for example, it was designed to reduce tensions arising from disparities in public spending per head of population? Do you think it has succeeded in resolving such disparities? In other words, can you give us a rounded look at the context within which the Barnett Formula emerged and the way in which it has been operating?
Professor Swales: Could I just say something to begin with. As I understand it, income tax was introduced as a temporary measure as well!

Q241 *Chairman:* And it was abolished at one time, was it not, and then came back. I do not know in what order you want to go.
Professor King: My main interest is in what you might do instead of the Barnett Formula with needs assessment.
Professor Bell: I guess I was around in 1979 when it was introduced and I also understood it to be a fairly temporary expedient. It is simple; it is easy for the Treasury to administer; it makes life much less complex around the time of Spending Reviews because the Spending Reviews essentially become bilaterals between the Treasury and spending ministries in Whitehall, Scotland, Ireland and Wales take the consequences of these negotiations. I wrote a paper with which Alan Trench will be familiar which implies that it is a convergent formula.

Q242 *Chairman:* I think we have the paper.
Professor Bell: And other people have argued similarly. There has been relatively little convergence through time. I guess, stepping back, that is an argument why it might really have been seen as a temporary expedient in so far as presumably it was understood at the time in the end to lead to convergence. Through time it has gradually been tightened up, it seems to me. Scotland managed, I suspect, to pull one or two tricks throughout the period.

Q243 *Lord Forsyth of Drumlean:* More than one or two!
Professor Bell: And then really starting from 1992 in particular it was tightened up, became more formalised, the question of what was in, what was out, what the levels of comparability were, were made more formal retaining the characteristics of simplicity and ease of use, I think convergence is starting to happen. Where it is leading is not necessarily a good place to be.

Q244 *Chairman:* It was very interesting talking to Lord Barnett about it all because he told us that he did not know the needs assessment was being carried out until told about it. And, secondly, convergence was not really mentioned and it certainly was not in his mind. Thirdly, it was designed to avoid the annual haggle between the Treasury and the spending departments and territorial departments. He did not expect it to last more than a few years, he is very, very surprised that it has gone on quite so long, and he now thinks it should be replaced by something which is based more on an assessment of need rather than a mathematical formula. It is rather like Topsy; it has grown.
Professor Bell: It is incumbency; once something is in place it is very difficult to move, so rather like income tax it is difficult to change.
Professor King: There is a point that if you found some other system of allocation, clearly the different countries are going to be either gainers or losers and you have this transitional period. We have got at the moment a rather *ad hoc* formula. We know how we have got here but how long is the transition going to last and how easily will it be to defend what is going to happen halfway through this transition? It seems to me one of the issues which has not been thought about very much is how you would get from one position to another one, and that causes problems. I would just mention this: I was working for the Department for the Environment when it introduced the poll tax—

Q245 *Chairman:* And you still bear the scars!
Professor King: Without wishing to defend it, if they had done the transition better it might have been rather less unpopular than it was. My lesson from that was that a lot of thought has to be given to transitional arrangements.

Professor Swales: As I understand it, it never has been stated as part of Government policy that there should be convergence. Although that might be implied by the mathematical formula, I do not think this has ever been stated as part of Government policy. A second thing is our take on this is that the Barnett Formula is just part of a bigger set of institutional arrangements, one of which is the fact that first when we had decentralised government from the Scottish Office and now in devolution you will have Scottish ministers who are arguing for the Scotland case, so that although you might have a formula which might appear to lead to convergence, then you have a one-way level of influence which is attempting to maintain the position of Scotland and maybe even the resources of Scotland. I disagree slightly with David about this. For Scotland there is a remarkable consistency in the Scottish expenditure per head over the UK expenditure per head over a long period of time. It is difficult to explain this except as being part of some kind of equilibrating system, I guess, where the formula gives you a baseline over the top of which you have special Scottish influence.

Q246 Lord Forsyth of Drumlean: Just on that point, when I was Secretary of State I cannot imagine how the system could have worked if it had just been based on the formula. The reason, as you say, that the advantage in terms of expenditure per head has been retained, which was inherent in the baseline at the time the formula was set up, is because we fixed it for that to happen, and there has been quite a lot of comment on that that this was for political reasons and, yes, there were some politics in it of course but also very practical reasons. For example, if you have a baseline which is 22 per cent, 23 per cent, 24 per cent higher on health, and if three-quarters of your expenditure goes on salaries, and if salary increases are negotiated nationally, then you are going to have a huge gap between the formula consequences of that pay increase and the bill you have got in the Health Service. In my day I would go along to the Chief Secretary and say, "You have got to give me the money," and if he said no I would go and see the Chancellor, and if he said no I would go and see the Prime Minister, and ultimately the Secretary of State could say, "If you do not give me this money I am sorry, I am off because this is not a workable position," and that is how it worked. What concerns me in the current position—and we have just been taking evidence from Mr Swinney—is that that mechanism, partly because you have different parties in power and partly because you have different constitutional arrangements, has gone, so now we just have a straight arithmetic means of determination. I have given the example of health but there are hundreds of other examples, for example housing capital, where all kinds of deals were done

and every year we had two or three months of absolutely bloody negotiations with the Treasury, so the notion that this simplified everything is wrong. It gave you a kind of starting position from which the negotiations happened. From what I see in the evidence we have heard that is absent now, and therefore the convergence which the Chairman is talking about will happen, in terms of the practical administration of government, I am amazed, and I think the only thing that has allowed this to continue has been the fact that there has been lots of money sloshing around and the budget is now twice what it was. However, we are now going to go into a period where that is going to go very much into reverse gear. To my mind, a mathematical way of determining expenditure, as opposed to one where there is some discussion about need, will result in convergence and will result in real injustices and difficulty. I do not know what you think about that?

Professor Bell: Your example is very interesting. David and I talked beforehand and we agreed that, if necessary, he would talk about local government and I would talk about health. What is happening now is exactly as you say. I wrote a short note on this where I point out the issue about the fact that of all of the major sectors that involve public servants in Scotland, health is the one where pay is agreed on a UK basis more than any other, more so than teachers for example. So Scotland has to fall behind whatever agreement is reached by the BMA, by the Colleges of Nursing, and so on. Health is also interesting because since devolution—and I communicated with John Aldridge about this—it is one area where there has been almost strict follow through on consequentials since devolution, so rather than second-guessing the amount of spending on health after a Spending Review has taken place, Scotland has applied effectively the Barnett consequentials to its health budget which are consequent on changes to the Department of Health's budget, so in a sense it is a pure application of the Barnett Formula. Other types of spending will have been affected by policy decisions that have been made by the Scottish Executive. It does look, when one compares the latest Comprehensive Spending Review, with 2002–03 when spending per head in Scotland would have been around 22 per cent above the UK average, as if spend per head will be under 10 per cent above the UK average by 2010–11, indicating fairly rapid convergence. There is no mechanism, as you say, to reflect the fact that standardised mortality rates, say, in Scotland are 16 per cent above the UK average. There is no mechanism so what would have to happen is that the Scottish Executive would have to allocate more money to health, which means less to other services

Q247 Lord Forsyth of Drumlean: So you think it is unhelpful?

Professor Bell: Well, you know much more about the bargaining position than I would. Clearly you can have bilaterals between Scotland and Westminster, that is one way of resolving it, and the other is to take the whole thing out of the political arena as they do in Australia and let some quango decide.

Q248 Lord Sewel: Could I just ask on the health thing, the credible expenditure driver that is the difference in standardised mortality rates, have you any evidence that there is awareness of that within the Executive at official and ministerial level?
Professor Bell: I do not particularly detect that the issue of the size of the health budget in Scotland has been prominent over the last year.

Q249 Lord Sewel: And the need basically to move away from a population-driven figure to a needs-driven figure for health, that has not been part of even an internal discourse?
Professor Bell: Not that I am aware of.
Lord Sewel: That is fascinating.

Q250 Lord Forsyth of Drumlean: Could I just press you on this because it seems to me to be fundamental. Because this Committee is not concerned with that, leaving aside all the kind of politics and the arguments about alternative methods of funding, we are where we are, and every year the Finance Minister in the Scottish Executive has got to find resources. If I could just press you on this. I do not believe for a moment that Barnett was introduced in order to achieve convergence. It is implicit that if you start with a higher baseline in Scotland which related to Scotland in the 1970s, that there will be convergence, and the constitutional changes mean that the kind of safety valves that were in place are no longer there, and therefore the effect will be, as you have pointed out—and I had not seen these numbers and they are very dramatic—that there is actually convergence taking place, and my question is: do you think that this is a harmful or a beneficial thing? I do not want to put words into your mouth, but if I were sat in John Swinney's seat I would be looking at local government, I would be looking at sparsity of population, I would be looking at what transport problems I had got, I would be looking at morbidity and mortality rates in the Health Service, and I would be wanting to make a case which was that the moving to convergence in a straight formulaic approach to this was actually going to damage public services and be unfair. When we talked to him earlier, he said that he was against any kind of needs-based system, which rather surprised me, and that he was content, albeit that he would rather have something completely different, to reside with where we were. I want to press you on whether you think that this convergence effect is fair and whether it is beneficial.

Professor Swales: One of the things is that the formula works in a very arbitrary way. I remember I was doing a seminar and trying to explain this to Israeli economists. I hardly got past the explanation when they said that this could not possibly happen. I was explaining what the impact would be of having this and they said, "No, it could not possibly happen." "This is what we have got." "It does not make sense," they said, "It seems to be an arbitrary mechanism." That is one of the things. Obviously the second one is if it is leading to convergence then we do not have convergence in expenditure per head in other English regions. We do not want equality in expenditure per head in other English regions, so you obviously would have to have concerns about it. If the mechanism were working just by itself in the way that David is suggesting it is now, which I think was a concern about when we moved to devolution, as soon as we move to devolution I think the whole mechanism had to be more transparent as well. Whereas before the Barnett Formula had always been extremely opaque, let us put it that way, as soon as it moved to becoming more transparent I am surprised that this convergence has not happened faster. Maybe it did not happen before because you had the same parties in Scotland and England.

Q251 Lord Forsyth of Drumlean: Because we stopped it.
Professor Swales: But obviously I think a system which automatically moved you towards equality with the UK would be one that we do not want. That would be my observation.

Q252 Lord Sewel: Is it fair to say that it only worked pre-devolution because you could do the type of formula bypass that Michael has talked about?
Professor Swales: Yes.

Q253 Lord Sewel: Now because you have got two different jurisdictions, the opportunity for positive formula bypass has virtually disappeared, and so it is a very unstable and potentially dangerous situation. Is that fair? There is nodding but we cannot get the nodding on the transcript.
Professor Swales: Yes.

Q254 Chairman: I am not sure there is nodding.
Professor Bell: In the absence of any other mechanism, yes.
Professor King: I was just going to come back to your question about why they are not pressing for needs assessment. Although you mentioned these problems like sparsity of population, there is a question of how much they push up the needs to spend in Scotland. Two or three years ago I did some research. A lot of the public services in Scotland are actually run by local authorities, and I asked myself this question:

suppose these local authorities' needs to spend were assessed on the horrendously complicated formula which Westminster uses to assess English local authorities' needs, how much higher would the needs of Scottish local authorities be? That was a question I started off with, with no notion of what the answer would be. The answer was, in terms of education, Scotland would have a lower need to spend fractionally than England per head, and if you looked at all local services taken together its needs to spend would be roughly 5 to 6 per cent above the English formulae. I am not saying the English formulae are right but nevertheless they seem to take account of an enormous amount of variables, including for example sparsity of population. It may be that Scotland thinks it is much better off with the present arrangement than it would be with needs assessment, but insofar as convergence may take place there could come a time when suddenly they decide that needs assessment would be a better deal than Barnett, but my suspicion is that that time has not arrived at the moment.

Q255 *Lord Forsyth of Drumlean:* I am not sure that is right. When I was Secretary of State the Treasury Secretary always wanted to move to a needs-based assessment and my officials at one stage told me that they thought the Treasury thought they could get £2.5 billion to £4 billion back if they moved to a needs assessment, and that I must at all costs resist this, which I did. But then we had a system whereby ultimately I could knock on the Prime Minister's door. John Swinney is not in that position and from the numbers that you have quoted we are moving towards convergence, and therefore I do not want to jump to any conclusions. In my mind, the way to fix this is to try and find some objective way not determined by politicians, or the Treasury for that matter, of doing the exercise which you do for local government and for health and transport and the rest, and which is seen to be fair, and which gives stability and certainty, but there does not seem to be much of an appetite for this.
Professor King: One of the problems is that I think Scotland would lose a lot of money if it went down that particular route. I would just mention one thing. You say that you want an objective assessment of needs and I do not think that is a feasible thing because different people can measure needs in different ways. I just mention another example of that. Having applied the English needs formula to Scotland's local authorities, you could see how the English formula regarded the relative needs of different Scottish local authorities. Scotland has an equally complicated formula for assessing the needs of local authorities, and there were marked differences between those two. For example, Glasgow would be getting 20 per cent more for

personal social services if they used the English formula than the Scottish formula. I thought there might be differences of 3, 4 or 5 per cent. On roads some authorities in Scotland are getting two or three times as much under the English formula as they get under the Scottish one. When you mention objective needs assessment, I have no reason to criticise the integrity of the people who do this at Holyrood or Westminster but they are very complicated formulae leading to extraordinarily different results.
Professor Bell: Can I just follow up on that. In health exactly the same thing happens. You have got this very simple allocation that is happening through the Barnett Formula where the consequentials are being taken through to Scotland. In England the Department of Health has the Advisory Committee on Resource Allocation which is continuously carrying out a needs assessment across health trusts in England. It has just published its sixth edition since 1997, which is 101 pages long. It is not really all that political, but it is highly complex because it is trying to take into account a multi-faceted set of health needs. In Scotland we have got the Arbuthnott Formula which is different from the English one, and but goes through exactly the same type of assessment. In between you have got this strangely simple mechanism, the Barnett Formula, which is determining the total amount that Scotland is getting. On David's point about objectivity, there is really a big question mark associated with what that might be, so you could argue that Scotland's decision to provide free personal care to the elderly is actually a decision to extend the boundaries of the NHS because it is free at the point of delivery. If free personal care is "needed", why should we accept an English view of what healthcare or a Westminster view of what healthcare comprises? Even if you could come to some agreement, there is an issue about information because personal care is not a category in England so there is no need to record what it is all about, so how could you bring it into a needs assessment in any meaningful way at the moment without doing an extensive statistical exercise. You are going to have to say these are the boundaries, a minimal set perhaps of services that the public sector will deliver, and base the needs assessment on those, and so some things in Wales like free prescriptions might be excluded.

Q256 *Lord Forsyth of Drumlean:* I think you are muddling two things, if I may say so. If you look at the needs of the population in terms of healthcare, leaving aside the whole issue of productivity of the NHS and how money is spent, I do not think we should get into the trap of thinking inputs is the same thing as outputs, but leaving that debate aside, I got a prescription the other day and I was astonished that it was only £5 because prescriptions had been cut, and it was a very welcome subsidy for me but I am not sure that I need it. That has got nothing whatever to do with the needs of healthcare. If you look at the overall population and you can take a view as to what kind of resource that might demand, you can equalise that between different parts of the United Kingdom, I would have thought. Then when they get the money, if they decide to spend that money in a particular way that is up to them, but the argument is whether you have a system that is fair. Are you saying that you just cannot devise such a system?

Professor King: Can I just take a very simple case where the only services involved were, say, police and primary schools. You might say to make life even simpler the only factor affecting the need for the police was the number of crimes and the only factor affecting the needs for primary schools was the number of children, but one area might say "we are not very interested in education, we want to spend most of our money on police" and another area might say "we are not very interested in police, we want to spend most of our money on education". Although you agree that what matters is the number of children and the number of crimes, it is the weight to attach to those factors which is still a matter of judgment. The UK Government might say we are not interested in crime, we are only interested in education, you have got a lot of crooks but we are not going to give you much money. They might say we are only interested in crime; we are not interested in education; we have huge needs for police expenditure so why are you not giving us the right amount of money?

Q257 *Chairman:* How do they do that with local authorities?

Professor King: They do not try and do that with local authorities. They say to local authorities we are going to determine what we think is a reasonable level of police services and primary education, we will give you an amount for that. If you happen to want to spend a lot more on police or a lot more on education, that is your tough luck if you have got a lot of crooks or a lot of children. You might say that that is a reasonable approach with local government because ultimately Westminster or Holyrood or whoever is in charge, but Holyrood might not say that was a reasonable approach if you were trying to sort things out between the different parts of the UK.

Q258 *Lord Sewel:* It has just struck me that the whole basis of devolution must be to allow different policy priorities to appear in different territories, but yet the funding relates back to an English profile. Does there come a time where the policy profile and therefore the spending profile is so different in the various territories that to source that expenditure from an English profile becomes virtually

meaningless because there is no connection between the two.

Professor Bell: I think that is quite possible. We do see drifting apart in the way that health is organised at the moment, and England could go towards more and more privatisation so that people are paying directly for healthcare. That could happen and it becomes less of a "public" service. That is true about schooling certainly in England already. Effectively what it reflects is differences in preferences across the different parts of the UK and it is therefore difficult, as David was saying, to get one set of weights associated with different public services that everyone is going to be happy with.

Professor King: If I can just qualify what I was saying, you could argue, "Well, you have got a lot of crooks, if you choose to devote a lot of expenditure to police we will give you a lot of money because you have got a high need for a service which you think is important. If you choose to devote little expenditure to the police we will give you less money." So you could make some adjustments. Having said the main factors are the number of primary school children and the number of crooks, you could subsequently change the amount you give in relation to those indicators on the basis of how much these recipients are actually spending on those functions. I am not saying it is easy but it would not be an impossible thing to do.

Lord Forsyth of Drumlean: I am not sure, Professor Bell, I understand what you are saying. Let us suppose that there is a change of Government in the south. Let us suppose that the Government decides that they are going to do away with the Health Service and they are going to introduce an insurance-based scheme. I think this is highly unlikely and I am not suggesting it but just to put a hypothetical case—
Chairman: It would be a good row!

Q259 *Lord Forsyth of Drumlean:* The formula consequences of health would disappear as far as Scotland was concerned in those circumstances. What would happen then? If you had a needs-based system which looks at the population overall and says that this is an appropriate amount of money, you do not have that problem, and where I am struggling with this set-up—and, as you know, I was not devolution's greatest fan, partly because I could not solve these particular problems—is they have set up this separate Parliament and separate Executive but they have not actually thought about the consequences in terms of the funding and Barnett. We have talked about convergence issues, and, yes, you can decide to have completely different policies north and south of the border, you can decide to have prescription charges or tuition fees or whatever, but it does not seem to be politically possible to do that in circumstances where you are just getting the numeric formula consequences. If we cannot have a needs-based system because it is too complicated, what are we going to do?

Professor Bell: An alternative is to go towards more accountability and therefore some more local taxation.

Lord Forsyth of Drumlean: We are not allowed to talk about that.

Q260 *Chairman:* That is all Mr Swinney spoke about!

Professor King: I am thinking about your question. Suppose it was decided that England would abolish the Health Service and have an insurance-based system, presumably they would say we want to cut income tax or value added tax because our public expenditure needs for health spending would be much lower, so they would cut those tax rates but there is no mechanism for them to cut those tax rates in England and not in Scotland. I am not quite sure what would happen in that case because the Scottish people would be saying we are paying much lower taxes, that is very nice, thank you very much because Westminster has cut these tax rates but we still want to have health as a public service. I think it would be very difficult to see how that would work.

Q261 *Chairman:* You could decide to spend it on something else without reducing taxation.

Professor King: Yes, okay, but I am trying to make it difficult!

Q262 *Lord Forsyth of Drumlean:* I was rather hoping you might answer the question! We are where we are.

Professor King: I think you reach the stage of saying you are going to run into problems if you have too much decentralisation without any decentralised revenue-raising arrangements. I know that is not part of your remit, but what could happen if Scotland were largely fiscally autonomous is they could say the English can cut their income tax and value added tax and have an insurance-based system; we are going to have higher income tax and higher VAT and a public system. If you are going to say that the tax arrangements have to be the same in each country, even though the spending arrangements could be totally different, then you hit insoluble problems.

Q263 *Lord Forsyth of Drumlean:* We are looking at the system as it is now where you have a Scottish Parliament and where the funding is on the basis of Barnett. I am putting to you a difficulty that arises from having a straight numeric formula and I am saying is the way round that difficulty to move to a needs-base system? Nobody is going to abolish the Health Service in England and I accept at the extremes there may be difficulties, but at the moment, broadly speaking, give or take one or two examples like care for the elderly, the systems are parallel. You started by saying that you were really an expert on needs. What is the argument that says that what the Scottish Parliament does for local government, which is to fund it on a needs-based system which I remember with great affection all the complexities, and the arguments with COSLA, and of course it will be controversial, but what is the argument against doing that in order to deal with the funding of the Scottish Executive, and is it possible to achieve such a thing? If it is not possible to achieve such a thing we can write it off, but what is the argument against doing it? It may not be perfect but would it not be better than what we have got now?

Professor King: To give a similar example I think it would be possible but there would never be complete agreement on the formulae. To go back to your earlier questions about an objective assessment of needs, there could be disagreements and when you consider the differences between the English and Scottish formulae these differences could be quite marked, but I think it would be possible to do it. Just going back to your Health Service question, the difference between using it for local government and using it in replacement of Barnett is that in local government the Scottish Parliament says to local authorities, "You are responsible for these services," and Westminster says to local authorities, "You are responsible for those services," but Holyrood at the margin would say, "We decide what services we as a Parliament in Scotland are going to be responsible for", and you would get difficulties. You mention at the margin free care for the elderly but if over time the differences between what Holyrood and Westminster felt ought to come within the public sector became quite different, I think you would have problems.

Q264 *Lord Forsyth of Drumlean:* We are not there.

Professor King: We are not there but that is because we started with complete equality, the opposite of Barnett, and differences could grow over time. I am just saying you could have problems if those differences grew and there was absolutely no revenue-raising capacity decentralised to help the different parts offset these.

Q265 *Lord Forsyth of Drumlean:* Is this not endemic in government? I think I set up this system that led to Arbuthnott, which is the way of funding health boards, and before that we had something else, I cannot remember what it was called, and there were endless arguments with Glasgow Health Board arguing that this did not take account of deprivation in the inner cities and that the weighting was wrong. Vast parts of my life have been spent in tedious meetings arguing about this and that is inevitable;

that is politics, that is what the thing is about. It was adjusted here and it was adjusted there and of course the politicians get involved and there is politics in this as well. I used the word objective, perhaps I should have said apolitical, something that avoided the, "Oh gosh, we have got to do more in this area because we have got five marginal seats" type of behaviour, which I am told does happen from time to time. The practicality was that you had to have some system. If we had allocated funding to Glasgow and Highland in the Health Service on the basis of some kind of population formula it would have been absolutely mad. So why does that not apply?

Professor King: I am just thinking with your Glasgow Health Board supposing they said, "In Glasgow we are not going to have any NHS dentists, it will be entirely private," would you still have been keen on giving them large systems of money because of the population deprivation where in your judgment they needed more money for dental services than, say, Lothian?

Q266 Lord Forsyth of Drumlean: The view I would have taken is if we have a formula which everybody agrees is fair how they run their health board, provided it is not going to result in huge deficiencies in the service, is up to them.

Professor King: So if they had wanted to spend less on dentists and more on—

Q267 Lord Forsyth of Drumlean: Absolutely. To give you a controversial example, if they wanted to spend less on direct provision of care and more on preventative care because they argued that that was what they should be doing, that would be up to them, and others may do a different thing. I thought that was the whole idea of a Scottish Executive. Whether it is a system of resources or whatever, we are just looking purely at the operation of the formula and we need some help as to how we can make it not perfect but better. The evidence we had from Mr Swinney was that we should leave be and leave it as it is because it is working perfectly well. I see a car crash looking at these numbers.

Professor Swales: Is not one problem here the asymmetric devolution problem? If it were the case that all the English regions were devolved so what you were doing was talking about a formula that allocated between all the regions of the UK, I think this would be a very difficult but much more straightforward process. What we have is one big region—England—which does not even want to be a region really, it wants to be the UK, it does not want its own Parliament, but whose views are going to dominate the allocation to these other three regions which have decided to devolve, who are voting for a different system than the English system. I think that is why some of these problems are more extreme.

These regions have actually taken a decision to be different from the rest of England. I am not saying it is insoluble or that this is not the best way to go, but that is an additional problem, I think, which would be less problematic if we had—

Q268 Chairman: There must be such a thing as objective needs surely? Coming back to dentists, it would seem to me if you were working out a formula as to how much money Glasgow was going to get in the health sphere you would make provision for dentists and if they do not spend it on dentists that would be a matter for them.

Professor Bell: It is some kind of minimal set because some people will always want to buy their own, to do better than what the public sector is willing to provide.

Q269 Lord Sewel: We have established a very nice context of concern and difficulty. Let us assume that there may well be some sort of change, and let us start from the initial building block. The initial building block is what criteria should be identified as being important in assessing what would be an appropriate funding system, what criteria should it fulfil, and to what extent does Barnett fulfil it, and to what extent can you devise a system that more closely meets the desirable criteria? What are they? That is your starter for 10!

Professor Bell: I think you have to have some broad consensus. Maybe we started in 1997 with broad UK agreement about what should constitute what we would call "merit goods", which are goods supplied to the public by the public sector because we feel it is appropriate or government feels it is appropriate, which might cover things like education and healthcare and so on. You could then identify a set of indicators associated with these. Then the standard argument would be what resource do you need to be put in place so that the provision at least of these services would be equalised across different parts of the country, which is the old standardised spending assessment argument. That is the one that effectively underlies the local government settlement in England, with adjustments for costs as well, implicitly, local government in Scotland, health in England, health in Scotland, so these mechanisms which are effectively needs assessments are running along in the background to all the political debate over Barnett that is taking place and are going along without a great deal of political controversy. Certainly there are disputes at the time but these mechanisms are not holding up the process of government to any great extent and the provision or supply of these services is not being put at risk because there are huge political arguments about the funding of the services.

Q270 *Lord Sewel:* Sorry, I do not quite understand what you are saying. What you are saying is that when you get to the level below the allocation to Scotland you have actually got mini needs assessments going on?
Professor Bell: Yes, sure, and the same is true in England.

Q271 *Lord Sewel:* So the obvious question is then why should you not have a needs assessment at the top level?
Professor Bell: It is not impossible. Other countries do it; Australia classically does it. I think it is the design of the mechanism that is crucial and how political it becomes. In Australia they have effectively taken it out of politics.

Q272 *Chairman:* We heard about that but what form of mechanism based on needs should it actually be? How would you do it?
Professor King: To make it apolitical I think you do need a body which is outside government. Notwithstanding anything I might have said or anything I might have said that could have been interpreted, I personally would support a needs-based allocation of funds between the four countries rather than Barnett. I would support that. I just think one has to be cautious in assuming that whoever designs the formula is going to get widespread support from everybody that they have got the formula correct. It is always going to be a matter of controversy, but clearly Barnett is a matter of controversy otherwise we would not be here today. I am in favour of this but I think it would need to be done by some impartial body.

Q273 *Chairman:* Do you know how the Australians produce their Commission?
Professor King: How they actually appoint them.

Q274 *Chairman:* They are appointed by the federal government?
Professor King: The Commonwealth government, yes I think so.

Q275 *Lord Sewel:* Are they required to consult?
Professor King: I have actually been to one of their meetings in which they listen to representatives from the different states arguing that the formula should be changed for such-and-such a reason. They debate this and they ask the other states, who always object to that reason because they will get a smaller share. I think it is a mechanism which if we were going to do a needs assessment in this country we would need to have a very close look at.

Q276 *Chairman:* What sort of people are on it?
Professor King: There are some academics which of course makes it more complicated!

Q277 *Chairman:* Some but not all.
Professor King: And some people from the different states. I think they have one or two non-Australians on it.

Q278 *Chairman:* Do they have the political parties represented or do they keep them out of it?
Professor King: I am not sure about that, no. I think if we were to do that in this country it would be a big advantage to have one or two people maybe from Australia and other countries that have done this just to give a slightly impartial air to it.
Professor Bell: And the relationship between that body and the Treasury I think would be very important, for the devolved bodies to have any confidence in it.

Q279 *Chairman:* Do you know what mandate this Commission has in Australia?
Professor King: The Commonwealth government decides it is going to allocate X billion Australian dollars between the states and this body has to decide how much of that is going to go to the different states, and they do that with a whole system called disabilities.

Q280 *Chairman:* States make submissions to them, do they?
Professor King: The states make submissions, yes, and of course it is an on-going process. It is revised every year or two about how these allocations are going to take place, so it is on-going submissions to this Commission.
Lord Sewel: It is going to cost more money than you are distributing.

Q281 *Chairman:* Would there be a transition?
Professor King: You would certainly have to have some transition.

Q282 *Lord Sewel:* The danger is that it is going to cost more money than you are distributing.
Professor King: No, I do not think so.

Q283 *Lord Rowe-Beddoe:* What is the size of the Commission and its staff? Do you have any idea?
Professor Bell: I think it is quite modest.
Professor King: The number of commissioners is 15 or 20 type thing and the staff is quite modest as well.

Q284 *Lord Forsyth of Drumlean:* Just for the sake of completeness, we talk about Barnett which is a population-driven one and we are now talking about a needs-based approach. Is there any other fair, equitable system around that is neither population nor needs, just for the sake of completeness?

Professor Bell: All of the others tend to involve a mix of taxation, it seems to me, all of the other systems that I know of.

Professor King: Who was it who suggested you should give it on an inverse of income?

Professor Bell: Ian McLean.

Professor King: He suggested that you should say that X is the poorest region so we will give it the most per head and do it on the basis of that. I think this is going to come unstuck because the area which gets the most is London which is simultaneously the richest. If you are asking for other alternatives, that is an alternative which has been suggested. I do not think even he accepts it any more.

Q285 Lord Rowe-Beddoe: What about social security spending per head, is that something that could be used?

Professor King: The trouble with that is that you could have an area with a hugely old population needing a lot of pensions but does not really need a lot of money for education, but your formula would be allocating a lot of money for education.

Q286 Lord Forsyth of Drumlean: All money goes to Largs! Just on this, I have a view which may be completely wrong but certainly when I was in the Scottish Office, as I have mentioned, needs assessment was considered a real threat. As convergence operates, and quite viciously given the absence of dialogue, there will come a point at which the Scottish Executive officials will start saying to their ministers, "We need a needs assessment."

Professor King: Exactly.

Q287 Lord Forsyth of Drumlean: I suspect that is what is behind the resistance. I do not think anybody really knows. Perhaps you have a view, but I do not think anybody really knows what the impact of a needs assessment will be now in Scotland and how that would affect the budget. If you want me to I can argue both sides of the argument. I have not got a clue what the outcome would be. Presumably to set up a body to do this work, which is unbelievably complex and difficult, and then to get some kind of agreement about the methodology, and then to find a means by which you resolve disputes between the Treasury, that seems to me to be quite a long job, years not months, and I think within a few short years we may come to the point where the penny drops in the Scottish Executive that they are disadvantaged. If there is a difference between what they would get on a needs basis and what they get now, it would be very difficult to say that is going to happen so you need to have some transitional arrangements to make it happen

over time. This is quite a long job; would you agree with that?

Professor King: Absolutely, as I have said earlier, the transitional arrangements are going to be crucial. It might be relatively simple in this case because we are talking about giving a large amount of money to each of the countries and at the moment the money is such-and-such and in the future it will be that, and one could have a taper.

Professor Bell: You could have a taper what matters is just how long you make it. A very quick taper gets you to the new system quite quickly but there are also a lot of political hurdles to jump.

Professor King: And if your share is going down you will have to sack a lot of people, which is difficult.

Lord Forsyth of Drumlean: If one was going to go down that route how would you set about making it happen?

Q288 Chairman: Where would you start. The decision has been taken politically that we move to a more objective needs assessment mechanism, where would you start? Would you start by assessing the needs or defining the needs?

Professor King: Can I suggest a possibility which you can knock down, you might say at the moment this area has 15 per cent of total expenditure, and under an objective needs assessment it will need only 12 per cent so we will give it 10 years to go from 15 to 12 per cent to reach its annual allocation.

Q289 Chairman: It is the objective needs assessment that I am interested in. How would you actually do that?

Professor King: I am assuming we set up this mysterious independent body and they do it.

Q290 Chairman: What is the progression? What is the principle? The Treasury did a big needs assessment in 1976?

Professor King: "Big" is possibly not quite right.

Q291 Chairman: It took three years.

Professor King: Yes, well!

Q292 Chairman: I accept that is not very big but assuming that a lot of work was done on it, it produced that needs assessment. There was another one in the mid-1980s, and I imagine there have been one or two since that we have not yet managed to get our hands on. Is that the type of needs assessment you start off with and you would work out on that basis what the needs of the four different components were?

Professor King: I think you raise an interesting point. I am saying an area is going to go from 15 per cent to 12 per cent but it would be several years before you knew whether it was going to go down to 12 or up to

17 per cent, and that would be quite a long process. One of the problems is that once you say this body has three years to decide whether it is going to be 12 per cent or 17 per cent, and then we are going to have a 10-year transition but during that transition the demographic will change, it is going to be a complicated business.

Professor Bell: I think you have also got to think how it fits within the current public spending system in the UK where you have got these Spending Reviews every couple of years that are looking three years ahead and how those would probably have to change, because essentially they are dialogues between Westminster and the spending departments in Westminster now. If need had changed drastically in one of the countries of the UK, that is not currently taken care of under the Barnett Formula, but presumably some kind of mechanism, some kind of interaction between the objective body that is handling the needs assessment and the Treasury would have to take place. There would have to be some kind of interaction to take account of that.

Q293 *Lord Forsyth of Drumlean:* I am not going to go down into the area of the merits of fiscal autonomy, but in practice will the sophistication of a needs assessment be dependent upon whether the territory had some additional form of fiscal autonomy? It could be broad brush if it had some other means, but if it was their only system of support, I would have suspected that it would have to be very, very finely sophisticated.

Professor Bell: I would tend to go along with that.

Professor King: It depends how significant this other support is. You could argue with local authorities in Britain that they have got the council tax, so if a needs assessment is not right they can raise the money they need on the council tax to make up any deficiencies in the assessment of their need. The council tax in some areas raises such a small proportion of revenue they might have to double it in order to make up the difference. If they had a local income tax and raised 70 per cent of their money, you could take your view rather more robustly than you would if it was only a small amount of revenue. I think it would depend how independent the fiscal means were.

Q294 *Chairman:* Professor Swales, you have been sitting there Buddha-like.

Professor Swales: I am agreeing with colleagues.

Professor Bell: You also have user charges, which for some services are quite important, so that is another lever you have got as well as the council tax, but together they still do not constitute a great deal of flexibility, so I tend to agree broadly that under the current system you would have to do a more detailed rather than a broad brush approach to it.

Chairman: Can I see where we have got to. I think we are all agreed that there are flaws in the Barnett system as it is. Secondly, I think we are all agreed that it would be possible and desirable to move to a different system which was based upon some kind of objective needs assessment. Thirdly, I think we all agree that in order to achieve that you have got to have some independent authority to work out the needs assessment and to actually allocate the cash. Fourthly, once you have allocated it, then the individual component countries of the UK should have a degree of flexibility in the way in which they operate it? Is that a fair resumé?

Lord Rowe-Beddoe: One thing, Chairman, is the timescale.

Lord Sewel: Transition and then constant review.

Chairman: Transitions are difficult.

Q295 *Lord Rowe-Beddoe:* Very difficult.

Professor Swales: One issue that might be raised here is if you went down this route, and if what was happening in England was different from the formula, then you would have regions in England which would be comparing themselves to Scotland with different allocations, with different spending. This happens at the moment but people are unclear about how the procedure occurs, but what you would have there, would it be the case that you would have English policy being driven by this body that is determining this because the English regions would be comparing themselves to what the devolved regions were getting? I think this is one of the issues of this asymmetric devolution. In actual fact, the regions which are devolved are different from English regions and, in a sense, having a formula which covers this is making them the same. I am not saying that is necessarily a problem but I think it is going to be a problem. You cannot have political decisions being taken by this apolitical body. This is one issue. Would it not mean that within England that would actually start to happen?

Q296 *Chairman:* It would help the regions of England which border Scotland but it would not help the regions of England that border Wales because it is exactly the opposite.

Professor Swales: Not even that. Let us say the South East had a certain set of characteristics, it would know from the needs assessment how much it would have got, but you could work out how much—

Q297 *Lord Sewel:* That would be an English argument, it would not be a comparator with Scotland, it would be an internal English argument.

Professor Swales: That is right but it would be the case that the UK has decided a set of criteria on which we should divide these needs but England has decided on some other criteria.

Q298 *Lord Sewel:* That is because public expenditure is not allocated to English regions, it takes place in English regions but it is not allocated.
Professor Swales: Yes, but it would be a political decision within England.
Professor King: Can I just develop this. Supposing there were this formula and Scotland got a certain amount of money, would not the different regions of Scotland start saying how much of that money would we get if it was allocated within Scotland to different parts of Scotland?

Q299 *Chairman:* How does it work now?
Professor King: There is not the formula. This is the advantage, the Scottish Government gets a certain amount of money but because it is based on the Barnett Formula, I do not think any of the regions of Scotland have said what they would have got.
Lord Forsyth of Drumlean: That is not right. Money has been poured into.

Q300 *Lord Sewel:* There are internal university allocations.
Professor King: All I am saying is if we just had a very simple formula that said it is going to be based entirely on income per head and the number of pensioners, some regions of Scotland would be saying they should get more than they do at the moment.

Q301 *Lord Forsyth of Drumlean:* Is it a bad thing? You have at the moment—and as a Committee we are not meant to be looking at this stuff but just to follow the argument without straying from our terms of reference—people in the north-east of England who argue that they are hard done by. I have no idea whether they are hard done by or not. There are people in the Midlands and elsewhere. If you set up a body, which is not by the way taking decisions about the overall budgets and allocation of resources, what they are doing is assessing what the relative need is, and if they produce some kind of unbelievably complicated formula which enables people in the North East or London to argue we are not getting enough or whatever, why is that a bad thing?
Professor Swales: The idea that somehow this is an objective measure, that somehow this body has decided how public expenditure should be divided up, because those needs will then determine what proportion of a certain amount of public expenditure goes to Scotland and these other areas. If you are saying that this is being done in some objective way you are presumably saying this is in some sense a non-political way.
Lord Forsyth of Drumlean: No, I am not. I am saying if Scotland ends up getting 11 per cent as opposed to 10 per cent of the total or Scotland gets 8 per cent and Wales gets a bit more or whatever, and England has

obviously got the largest share, I thought your argument was that by setting up this body, the English regions will start trying to apply this formula to argue that their share is not sufficient. If you break that down that will turn into the Department of Health or the CLG being asked why are they not doing the same. I can see that it is inconvenient but I do not see that it is a bad thing because it makes the whole thing more transparent, does it not?

Q302 *Lord Rowe-Beddoe:* I think it does because one of the great problems with this is that there is not perceived to be the transparency that there ought to be. What would you do, what Lord Forsyth has suggested there?
Professor Bell: Since devolution happened it seems to me that the argument of the postcode lottery has become a much, much more prevalent argument, and so people compare differences in provision of services, in different parts of UK and perhaps complain about the variation, but they do not have any understanding of why these might have arisen. They might have arisen to do with efficiency of delivery as well as amounts of expenditure allocated. The trouble with a very complex formula is that it is not very transparent. It is quite difficult to understand, but it seems—and I think David agrees with me—that it is necessary to have quite a complex formula because needs are complex.
Professor King: I am just thinking about these different regions of England saying "under the formula we would get more than we get at the moment." Of course an implication of that is that probably they will try to influence this independent needs assessment body, and that might be quite useful because until you mentioned that a minute ago I had always assumed this body is going to find the Scots, the Irish, the Welsh and the English coming along saying we think the formula should be tweaked in our benefit. We are then going to have people coming from the North East saying that there should be more for areas which are depressed and that have lost their ship-building industries, and they will come under a lot of pressure from other people which might make it easier to resist a sustained assault from one of the four constituent countries of the United Kingdom. I think it might be easier to run this body if they come under lots of pressure from lots of different people, rather than just four.

Q303 *Lord Rowe-Beddoe:* That is not the situation; the position is very clear we have heard about this asymmetric settlement, that is a fact, that is what exists, so we should not be moving that debate forward, in my opinion. What we are suggesting here, is that England should determine what it is going to do with the constituent parts of England that is England's opportunity rather than problem. At the moment all we can determine is what we can do for Scotland, Wales and Northern Ireland. I do not think we should be pushing this debate into what England does.

Professor King: I fully agree with that. What England is going to do should be entirely up to England. I am just saying that if the different regions of England start applying the formula to them and arguing that they are not getting their fair share, it is up to the English to handle that but they might in time also try to influence the formula. That is all I am saying.

Q304 *Lord Forsyth of Drumlean:* If constitutionally something happens whereby they are given the opportunity to influence.

Professor King: Supposing I am running Region X—

Q305 *Lord Sewel:* Nobody is running Region X, that is the point!

Professor King: I accept that but I am running a large authority in Region X. I could say under this formula the local authorities in this region would get, implicitly, more money than they get at the moment and I am going to put pressure on Westminster for that to happen. That is perfectly reasonable. However, I might also want to go and put pressure on this independent grants body because I could then say "if I pressurise them to change and tweak their formula, then my region would be entitled to even more money", and there would be a lot more pressure but also a lot more transparency. I am not in any way saying that is wrong. I am just saying it is one of the implications which is going to happen because there will be a lot more people working out what they would get. Just to take one example, this body when it is assessing needs might be concerned with the problems of island authorities, and it might say that Scotland has a lot more island authorities than England has, and that is one of the factors that affects Scotland's needs. However, the island authorities in Scotland might well be pushing for them to increase the allowance for island authorities and put pressure on Scotland to give them a larger share of the cake.

Q306 *Lord Sewel:* We have been talking about need but slipped into the difference in service provision, Professor Bell, is efficiency and there is also effectiveness. How do those criteria muddy the waters in terms of the basis of allocation?

Professor Bell: I think that is interesting in that one of the developments that I have witnessed and made a small contribution to (because I am interested in social care) has been the development of different policies in different parts of the UK, in Wales, Northern Ireland, Scotland and England, which are much more distinctive than they were pre-devolution. There has been quite an extensive dialogue between the different parts of the UK about issues like

efficiency, like effectiveness of service delivery and so on, which seem to me to be a very healthy outcome of devolution, with the ability to drive policies in different ways. Incidentally, here the asymmetric devolution issue is very important because Wales just does not have the powers to do what Scotland was able to do in respect of change.

Q307 *Lord Sewel:* Hopefully one would wish to reward efficiency and penalise inefficiency, so that is a real problem.

Professor Bell: That is a real problem with needs assessment.

Q308 *Chairman:* It is bad enough as it is.

Professor King: Is not the reward for efficiency better services though?

Chairman: One would have to deem it so.

Q309 *Lord Forsyth of Drumlean:* I am not sure I agree with you, Professor Bell, when you say it is a consequence of devolution that there was the ability to have differences in policy. We did not have a national curriculum in Scotland; we did not do all kinds of things. We did separate things, for example, in the Health Service where we had matching funding for hospices. I remember being beaten up by Virginia Bottomley for doing it because there was pressure on her to do the same. I do not think it is a consequence of devolution, but I think one of the difficulties—or perhaps you are meant to be answering the questions—do you not think one of the difficulties of not having something that everybody can point to and say this is a fair system of funding is that if you do innovate in ways which are attractive, if Herceptin is available in Scotland but not in England, or if your tuition fees are not up-front, or you do not pay prescription charges, or if you are elderly you will get care delivered by the Health Service, is that then creates enormous resentments which have a political effect which make the tweaking of the formula politically harder to achieve. You must be aware of this in the south. People like Simon Heffer and so on write articles that blow all my fuses, but there is undoubtedly a bandwagon being established, and it is very difficult to deal with that if you cannot say hang on a second, this body, which I do not think would be a ground-making body, would be a body which would assess need and make representations and would come to a conclusion about how the cake should be divided up. It would then be for Parliament and everyone else to say. Do you not think that having something that everybody can point to and say that is fair (we do not agree with every aspect of it) would take a lot of the heat out of this debate?

Professor Bell: It depends how damaging you think this debate is, it seems potentially to be very damaging, but the objective body would take some heat out of it certainly.

Q310 *Lord Forsyth of Drumlean:* If you are not a Unionist no doubt you see it as a wedge?
Professor Bell: There would still be differences whether caused by efficiency differences or by policy choices. I am not sure I agree with you that pre-devolution there was quite the latitude to change things that there has been post-devolution. It may be just a matter of degree. For example, the ability to change the free personal care thing was the ability to legislate on charging effectively.

Q311 *Lord Forsyth of Drumlean:* Which you could have done?
Professor Bell: Prior to—?
Lord Forsyth of Drumlean: Another quite radical example of differences is in the south they took the decision to close down all—and I have forgotten what the politically correct term is—what we used to call mental hospitals and transfer people into care in the community, where we took a decision in Scotland not to go down the same route with the same speed. That is another example of Barnett because we did not get the consequentials and we had to argue for that. There was freedom to do that. What of course was going on under the old system is that it had to be agreed collectively, so the Secretary of State, and, broadly speaking, you were given that. If you then had collective agreement you were able to argue on the funding. Where the change has occurred is that you do not have that opportunity to have a dialogue and if you have different parties there may be people who are determined to oppose it because it is not from their party. That is the negative side of it.

Q312 *Chairman:* Is an independent body not one of those things where you have got to end up in a situation where everybody is equally dissatisfied with its result, nobody is grossly dissatisfied but everybody is slightly dissatisfied so everybody can say, "We do not like it but . . . "? If you get to that stage it seems to me that you will make the most enormous progress.
Professor Bell: You will not eliminate the Simon Heffers but you may tone them down.

Q313 *Chairman:* You could try.
Professor King: There is another practical lesson. When I spent a year on secondment at the Department of the Environment, apart from introducing the poll tax Mrs Thatcher wanted the needs assessment formula simplified and argued that there were too many indicators in it. You have a group of people in a room acting like this. "How do we get rid of indicators, what happens if we take that one out, it does not make much difference, right we will get rid of that one. What happens if we take this one out?" It makes a lot of difference to three authorities, right, but could we help those three authorities if we attached more weight to this one? Without being unduly cynical, there was clearly an aim to reduce the number of indicators because that was what was being asked of us but simultaneously to change the allocation as little as possible. I suspect that this independent body would find some objective needs but within the margins of error they would try to change as little as possible from the current allocation.

Q314 *Chairman:* That is probably a good thing.
Professor King: It might be a good thing but this is just another aspect of the objectivity which would be at the margin, summed up as "let us try not to rock the boat too much".
Lord Forsyth of Drumlean: I am sure it was not the case with Mrs Thatcher! Generally speaking, where politicians wish to change the basis of the formula it is because they wish to see the money going to areas which are politically sensitive as far as they are concerned. That has been going on for years in local government, as you know.
Chairman: That is a bit too cynical! There are fairness arguments.

Q315 *Lord Forsyth of Drumlean:* No, but I am saying there is a tendency for politicians to want to change the formula because they feel, perhaps entirely rightly, that not enough is going to areas of the country where they may have very strong political representation and where they are under pressure from their colleagues.
Professor King: Or marginal constituencies.
Lord Forsyth of Drumlean: Indeed.
Chairman: I suspect that when we get to Cardiff what you will be told in Cardiff is that there is a basic unfairness in the way this has operated because the Welsh should have had more from the beginning. It is not a question of trying to get resources down into the politically sensitive areas.
Lord Rowe-Beddoe: They have done a very bad job of putting across public relations, it is totally misunderstood.
Chairman: People like Michael Forsyth ran rings round the Welsh Secretaries.

Q316 *Lord Forsyth of Drumlean:* That is the other aspect of the way it worked, is that when William Hague was Secretary of State, he and I would unofficially talk to each other to find out what lines the Treasury was taking to attack us and we would support each other and we operated as a pair.

Professor King: I would add that there certainly were occasions when it was suggested that the formula could be tweaked to help areas X, Y and Z, and although that is widely argued to happen, and I do not dispute that it does happen, there is a limit on that because how can you alter it to help areas X, Y and Z which you want to help when, if you give them more money you are going to hurt other areas, and do you want to hurt all other areas. It was always difficult to help the areas that you particularly wanted to help without either hurting some areas you did not particularly want to hurt and without helping some other areas you did not particularly want to help. Especially in England where there are lot more local authorities, it is harder to do that than it might have been in Scotland.

Q317 *Lord Sewel:* I want to ask a really very practical problem, if there is a move towards needs-based assessment, do we have the data?

Professor Bell: Well, I could quote health as an example and there are sets of indicators that you can get on disease from the Census on need. The complaint is that they are always out-of-date. In terms of health status, yes, there probably are data available. In terms of cost delivery, which may not be of particular interest to this body because they will concentrate on need per se, systems are quite different. The Department of Health and what is called the ISD Information System Division in Edinburgh produce completely different sets of health statistics for Scotland and England, and presumably the same is true in Wales. Local authorities similarly produce their own statistics and the ONS is not responsible for local authority statistics and health statistics in the same way, for example, that it is responsible for employment or unemployment statistics, so the areas of the public sector that we would really be looking at are not areas that are necessarily fully covered, although there would be indicators of need that probably could be broadly comparable, but not in great detail.

Q318 *Lord Sewel:* Are there any particular areas of difficulty?

Professor Bell: I would say social care is an example because the systems are different.

Professor King: There is a problem that you have issues where you might want to give more money to areas which have a lot of children with mental problems or learning difficulties, but who tells you how many such children there are? You cannot ask the local authorities because they say, "90 per cent of our children have these problems, we need a lot of money." Some of the things you want to take account of, you cannot actually get direct statistics on those and you have to use some proxy by saying there are more children with learning difficulties in areas with

a lot of unemployment, or something like that, so sometimes the data you want are data you cannot get and you can only estimate those things.

Q319 *Lord Forsyth of Drumlean:* I thought the Government was setting up a national database with every child in England?

Professor King: It could be but there are other issues such as older people needing care at home, who is going to decide who needs care at home? If it is up to the recipient countries they will decide all their older people need care at home.

Q320 *Lord Forsyth of Drumlean:* But that is to do with policy, or perhaps I am missing something.

Professor King: You asked a question about data and there are some data which are always going to be elliptical for that sort of reason.

Q321 *Lord Forsyth of Drumlean:* Professor Bell, you mention that social care because the systems are different. The systems are only different, as I understand it, that in Scotland there is free care available for elderly people because it is treated as being part of the Health Service not part of local government where it is means tested, but you can look at England and you can look at how many elderly people you have got and their needs, and you can look at Scotland. You can form a view on the relative resource requirement. If they decide in Scotland to make it free care and not have people making a contribution, that is down to them, that is a policy issue. The need arises from how many elderly people have you got who are not able to look after themselves in their own homes, surely? The data must be available for that?

Professor King: Who decides they are not able to look after themselves. That is the point.

Lord Forsyth of Drumlean: The answer is that there is an assessment of need made at an individual level. The fact that in Scotland when it is assessed that you do actually need care, either at home or in residential care, you do not get a bill for it does not alter, to my mind, the gathering of the data as to what the degree of need is. Am I missing something?

Q322 *Lord Sewel:* It may affect the classification.

Professor Bell: I could give you data on something called the attendance allowance across the whole of the United Kingdom, and if you looked at it you would see that the number of people per thousand receiving it is much higher in Wales than it is in other parts of the UK. Is that because there is a higher level of need or is it because the doctors, who are the gate keepers of this benefit, operate slightly differently in Wales than they do in other parts of the UK? We have to be assured, it seems to me, that there was a uniformity of assessment wherever we were trying to get some matrix on need, so there would have to be some assurance of that, it seems to me.

Q323 *Chairman:* I think that is absolutely true but I think the argument now about the quality of data is not going to help us in deciding what we ought to do about the Barnett formula. What is interesting to me is the degree of consensus there seems to be on both sides of this particular table.
Professor King: If I could just comment on that. If you took primary education, the most important factor is the number of primary school children you have got. There is no room for asking "is this a primary school child or not?". At the margin you could say that some primary school children need more money because they have got learning difficulties, and then it becomes has this child really got learning difficulties or not, and are they severe learning difficulties or not, but probably the percentage of the budget which is going to be dependent on these judgment aspects of data is going to be relatively small.

Q324 *Lord Sewel:* The only importance is whether that percentage is different in Scotland than in England.
Professor King: It depends who is assessing this. If the Scots take a much more robust view about learning difficulties, and the Welsh say anyone who has not got an IQ of 150 has got learning difficulties, then you have a problem,

Q325 *Lord Forsyth of Drumlean:* Given the sample size, it is highly likely that the proportion on some objective criteria of children with special needs in England will not be very different from Scotland or Wales. If there is a huge difference, then you might look behind that to find out what is going on to make that difference. Surely that is one of the tasks that that body would do?
Professor Bell: That is why you have 40 people rather than two.
Professor King: I accept that but if I just take one example from my local government study, one of the factors which is allowed for in assessing local authority needs on the spend on personal social services for older people is the number of people on low incomes and, surprising though this may seem, the allowance which would be given to Scotland is more than 50 per cent higher than what has been given to England, and one might well think between the countries there is not a lot of difference, but every now and then you get some indicators where there is a big difference. Another one is on the education one when English local authorities were given an allowance for children who come from what they politically correctly call low-achieving ethnic groups, and the proportion of children in England from those groups is something like nine per cent and in Scotland

it is 1 per cent, so every now and then you hit some indicator which is very significantly different, even between countries.

Q326 *Lord Forsyth of Drumlean:* But that is because they are different.
Professor King: That is because they are different, yes.

Q327 *Lord Rowe-Beddoe:* And you have confidence in them?
Professor King: In these numbers?

Q328 *Lord Rowe-Beddoe:* Yes.
Professor King: They are perfect! There are two sorts of comments. If I take people on low incomes, I have no doubt that is done on some fairly robust assessment of incomes, but that is meant to be a proxy for how much these people really need and whether they are measuring it in the right way for that. One would be less confident about that.

Q329 *Chairman:* Professor Bell, fairly early on in this discussion you gave some figures on convergence which I might say raised one or two eyebrows on this side. Could you perhaps put it on paper?
Professor Bell: Sure, I have got a picture here.

Q330 *Lord Rowe-Beddoe:* Could I just ask on data, which I have an interest in, there is a plethora of statistics created by government statistical services, whether they are in Scotland, or the ONS in England and Wales and so on. In all of that surely there must be something we can actually use as a sensible approach to needs requirements? After all, some of these are data are produced weekly, some monthly, some annually. We are about to spend a great deal of money on a Census. I just wonder if we have got the information we need if we only knew where to mine it?
Professor Bell: If you want to find out about the labour market there is a plethora of monthly statistics on each region of the United Kingdom that are published by the ONS, so all the stuff about unemployment and low incomes is included there. There are a few surveys which go into other areas, like health and care and so on, that tend to be annual, for which the sample sizes are big enough in the countries to be able to come to general conclusions, so I could say that in terms of recorded disability Scotland and England are pretty much the same but Wales is higher, so there is a set of statistics that I would be happy to list of the kinds of things that you might consider as a starting point, but there are some areas where in terms of what goes on, rather than the objective need, there are difficulties.
Professor King: Of course a lot of the indicators of need are demographic factors. There might be a really good Census every 10 years but in between them one

is relying very much on estimates which may turn out to be wrong.

Professor Bell: Of course there is a big issue in terms of need for England in particular which is migration, and the statistics here are fairly hopeless.

Chairman: Thank you all very much indeed for coming this morning. It has been a very good morning indeed. I have learned a great deal and I am delighted to see the degree of agreement there is. Thank you very much indeed.

FRIDAY 27 FEBRUARY 2009

Present	Forsyth of Drumlean, L	Rowe-Beddoe, L
	Richard, L (Chairman)	Sewel, L

Examination of Witness

Witness: MR DAVE MOXHAM, Deputy Secretary General, STUC, examined.

Q331 *Chairman:* Mr Moxham, thank you very much for coming, we are really grateful.
Mr Moxham: You are welcome.

Q332 *Chairman:* As you know, we have been set up by the House of Lords to have a look at the Barnett Formula and how it operates. Our terms of reference are fairly restrictive and I think you have seen them.
Mr Moxham: I have read them.

Q333 *Chairman:* So you know that we can look at the Barnett Formula but we cannot look at anything like fiscal autonomy.
Mr Moxham: I am glad of that; it takes up too much of my time already!

Q334 *Chairman:* If I may start with a slightly general question: do you think the Barnett Formula treats Scotland, Wales and Northern Ireland fairly?
Mr Moxham: It is a pretty broad question. I wonder if I could interrupt myself for a minute. Before I started I had intended to pass on the apologies of our General Secretary, Grahame Smith, who in normal circumstances would have wanted to give evidence himself but because of a previous commitment could not. I will then go on to talk about the STUC's position. We obviously recognise that the Barnett Formula, particularly in light of the evidence of Lord Barnett to this Committee, which I have read, was not created either to be long-lasting, or to be needs based, or indeed to provide convergence over a period of time. However, to some extent we believe, irrespective of whether that was the intention, that has been the effect of the duration of years in question. We recognise the fact that in 1979 a needs-based assessment was undertaken, although it appears that was entirely separately from the Barnett considerations, and certainly during the 1980s we would be of the view that the kind of differentials that the formula offered did reflect, relatively speaking, the relative needs of Scotland. We recognise that the convergence criteria such as they exist or do not exist have not been particularly transparent, and certainly it has not worked in the way that some people have described it. However, in broad terms over the piece over its 30-year period, we are generally content with it and generally content with the recognised need of providing public services in Scotland.

Q335 *Chairman:* On the whole Scotland have done quite well out of it?
Mr Moxham: We certainly would not be of the opinion that we have suffered as a consequence of it. The extent to which any extra advantage has been conferred is difficult to calculate, but our general view would be that particularly post-1979 when there was this clear separation, if you like, between provision of public services and the other forms of welfare transfers which continue to be devolved, mainly through the DWP budget. The DWP side of things would appear to show 108/109/110 per cent expenditure in Scotland and does not necessarily reflect the overall cost of providing the services which resulted from that need, and we would make reference to the National Health Service in particular in Scotland to give evidence.

Q336 *Lord Forsyth of Drumlean:* On that point about the Health Service, when I was Secretary of State I think the additional spending per head on health was about 23 or 24 per cent, and if the Barnett Formula had been allowed to operate purely on a share of population basis, given that health wages are negotiated nationally, and given that in the Health Service about three-quarters of its costs is actually wages, if you had Barnett operating purely on a share of population basis that would create an enormous gap in the funding for pay in Scotland.
Mr Moxham: Indeed.

Q337 *Lord Forsyth of Drumlean:* In those days the Secretary of State would go along to the Chief Secretary and say, "We are bombing here," and above him to the Chancellor or Prime Minister, and get the money. One of the things that is a bit surprising is that post-devolution there is no mechanism for doing that. Some people call it formula bypass, but actually it is a reflection of the fact that the baselines are very different, and that is how it operated before. We have heard this morning some evidence that indicates that that was never the intention, but people read that into it. Now the Barnett squeeze is operating so, wearing your TUC hat, are you not concerned that if this continues on a population basis rather than having some kind of needs element then the inevitable consequence will be very considerable pressure on areas like the Health Service and local government?

Mr Moxham: I think that is a very fair comment. In suggesting that the block grant governed by the Barnett Formula thus far has not done a bad job in assessing need, it should not necessarily be taken from that that we believe that the Barnett Formula should endure ad infinitum. Indeed, we have been relatively clear that, while we would not want to see any immediate change to the status quo without due consideration, a needs-based element to the funding of the Scottish government is absolutely vital. In relation to the funding particularly of the NHS, we have made some reference, although I would not claim to be an expert on it, to the various formulae that govern the disbursement of NMS funding across Scotland, and the Share and the Arbuthnott formulae which, as I am sure you know, are now being altered. What appears to be the case for us is that the type of redistribution that goes on in Scotland sits fairly well with the type of additional funding that the NHS is given in Scotland. By that I mean if you look at an indicator such as early morbidity, which is generally judged to be a reasonable indicator of overall health, if you take all local government areas in Scotland, nearly every one of them sits above the England and Wales average. If you then you look at how Share and Arbuthnott distributed the monies, that is on the basis of need and partially on the basis of geography, too. Those local authority areas which you could say were comparative with the UK for England and Wales in terms of early morbidity would appear to require that level of funding, and the additional funding was dispersed to areas of Glasgow and others based on their incredibly high levels of early morbidity. That is going beyond the question that you have asked but it gives you some background.

Q338 *Lord Forsyth of Drumlean:* It illustrates my point because I cannot remember what it is called now, but I remember wrestling with it prior to Arbuthnott (which I think was done in my time when I was responsible for health) and there you had an attempt to find some kind of needs-based way of distributing resources within Scotland between the various health authorities, so the problems that they have, for example, in Glasgow where they have higher morbidity rates and all kinds of different problems, is reflected in the overall distribution, but the amount at the top that Scotland gets for health is a straight percentage, relative to population, of the increase in England. It does not take any account of our higher morbidity rates or any other issues. One of the things that is slightly puzzling me is that you were like Francis of Assisi: "Lord, make me pure but not quite yet"! Is the reason that you do not want yet a needs-based system of the kind you have described internally in Scotland because you think that it would disadvantage Scotland?

Mr Moxham: I do not think that is the case. I think anybody who suggests that they have the answers to exactly what the needs-based redistribution would be has not done enough work to find out and they do not know how difficult it is. Maybe at the heart of this is our view that it clearly is not the formula but it is the original basis on which the formula was built, the population basis, which then saw the drop in Scottish population, which, if you like, has artificially placed Scotland in a situation today where we think that, particularly in relation to health, the type of settlement we receive matches need. However, I totally take on your point that were that to continue and were the differentials to narrow, that to do that and not test that against need at some point in the future would potentially disadvantage Scotland.

Q339 *Lord Forsyth of Drumlean:* Suppose we move into a period of inflation and constraints on public expenditure, then the effect of an inflation-matching pay rise in the Health Service on the Scottish budget would be enormous.
Mr Moxham: Indeed.

Q340 *Lord Forsyth of Drumlean:* The system has operated where there have been huge amounts of extra money sloshing into the system, and on health the formula consequentials have not been sufficient. We had evidence this morning from Mr Swinney and he said what they had got in health had not been sufficient to cover this and they had been able to vire from other areas, which you can do in a period where there is more availability of cash, but are you not concerned that as we enter into a period of restraint that the failure to actually make the case for some kind of needs-based approach and just relying on the population approach might do real damage to the Health Service?
Mr Moxham: Essentially I agree with you. Our position is that there needs to be a needs-based analysis at some time in the future for the UK as a whole. Our concern would be that that is done with due diligence over a reasonable period of time and that what we do not have is a rush away from Barnett onto a per capita basis which would be different but still done on that basis. We have no opposition whatsoever to a proper needs-based assessment of funding across the UK.

Q341 *Chairman:* We need a bit more than just an analysis of needs assessment. We need some kind of mechanism that actually distributes on the basis of need.
Mr Moxham: Indeed.

Q342 *Chairman:* Somehow it has got to be done that way?

Mr Moxham: Yes, and if we are assuming the current Scottish spread of spending, that is to say the provision of services essentially by the Scottish Parliament and the provision of welfare transfer by the UK Government, that system must take into account the cost of providing those services rather than simply be based on the economic indicators in terms of relative wealth.

Q343 *Lord Sewel:* I suppose the difficulty is how to get there, is it not?
Mr Moxham: Indeed.

Q344 *Lord Sewel:* Who would carry it out and over what period of time would we start introducing a needs-based assessment? Have you got any views on that?
Mr Moxham: I suppose you might consider this to be a defensive view, but I would reiterate our position which is not quickly, because we do not think it is something that could be easily undertaken and we would have concerns about it being undertaken outwith an overall assessment of funding across the UK, including within the English regions. We are quite aware of the comparisons that are made specifically between Scotland and the north of England, for instance, in terms of funding. We would want to see an assessment made in relation to the relative funding of all of the regions as well. I am certainly not going to suggest that any formula or any new mechanism would be easy. However, I suppose one of the advantages is to look at where the vast majority of Scottish spending is undertaken, which is essentially in the areas of health, education, care, and to some extent transport, and that provides it seems to me, a reasonable basis upon which to proceed. There are obviously other budget headings but, from memory, those would make up over 80 per cent of Scottish Government spending, so it seems to me the cost of providing those, taking into account geography, taking into account measures of health as opposed to simply measures of income, would be the very basic methodology that we would want to see followed.

Q345 *Lord Sewel:* One of the problems clearly is that everybody has got to have confidence in the system, have they not, and they have to feel that it is not being manipulated or that there has been cheating going on to satisfy any particular group or area? I suppose one of the advantages of Barnett is that at the margin it is a population-driven formula, so it is not open to that much abuse, where if you go to needs you always have a degree of, it has been put to us today, subjectivity on how you measure needs, how it is assessed. Do you see the need to set up some sort of independent body to carry out the assessment?

Mr Moxham: Our organisation has not specifically thought about how that would happen, although that seems to be a sensible suggestion. I suppose in broad terms one would look at the creation of a new baseline of need. It does not seem to me to be impossible that between that and possibly a reassessment of that, let us say on the basis of a Census or a decade-by-decade basis, that in between that time the formula would not operate on a population basis. It seems to be me the importance is to establish independently and effectively what the baseline should be.

Q346 *Lord Sewel:* To pay particular attention to the independent assessment of need. Then your view is that there would have to be a fairly long transition process if there were significant swings?
Mr Moxham: I think so. I am speaking entirely hypothetically. One might suggest, for instance, that the cost of providing education in Scotland per capita is not sustainable. Were we to pull 10 per cent funding from the Scottish education system it would collapse. I am not necessarily suggesting that. My educational colleagues would hang me up if I was suggesting that that was a fair settlement. However, it is possible to hypothesise that even in the case that unfairness were found, because education, justice and a range of other functions within Scotland have built up in a different way, that the withdrawal of a significant amount of funding from them would cause problems far beyond the proportion of the reduction that they might receive.

Q347 *Chairman:* Can I just go back to one thing you said to us a little while ago. You said that you want the assessment process to include an assessment of the English regions. Do you mean that? In other words, this assessment body that was going to look at expenditure between the four parts of the UK should actually get down to looking at expenditure between the north-east of England, the South West, the South East and Lancashire? If you did mean that, would you not have to do the same exercise with the Scottish regions? I think that is an enormous task.
Mr Moxham: I hear what you say but I think to some degree size matters. If you take any given region of England, you would find that in broad budgetary terms the type of sums of money we are talking about are similar. I am not specifically aware of how big the North East budget is but it is not of a completely different character to the Scottish or Welsh settlement.

Q348 *Chairman:* The North East does not have a specific budget.
Mr Moxham: It does not have a budget but it is possible using the same criteria as we use for judging spending in Scotland.

Q349 Chairman: You can get a rough ball-park figure?

Mr Moxham: You can give a rough ball-park figure. The role of the South East and the east of England essentially as exporters of productivity of or as transferers of income is obviously very well-established and has a very major effect upon the UK average when we are talking about the baseline figure of 100 per cent capita for funding. I forget the figures but I think the figures suggest that spending in the South East compared to GDP is something like 87 per cent. If we look across Europe and some of the big city regions of Europe, the pattern is quite similar. Interestingly enough, Catalonia, almost by a process of reversal, is a fairly large transferer of resources but similar patterns can be picked up if we look at the le de France and other areas. My point being without taking a view about the South East's and the East's position in relation to the rest of England, it is difficult to arrive at what a suitable baseline per capita figure is for funding on the basis of need.

Q350 Chairman: Surely you do not want Glasgow to be compared with London?

Mr Moxham: I do not want Glasgow to be compared with London but I am content for the north-east of England who, as you will be aware, are regularly compared to Scotland in terms of funding per capita for those services which can be compared, to be reassessed along with Scotland.

Q351 Chairman: It seems to me that what you are saying now is that the needs assessment process you are contemplating is infinitely wider and in effect it is assessing the needs of the four different parts of the UK and letting them decide where the money goes.

Mr Moxham: Essentially that is the case.

Q352 Chairman: You want a major one to look at all the regions of the United Kingdom, England, Scotland, Wales and Northern Ireland, and actually compare those regions and have needs assessment in relation to each of them?

Mr Moxham: Figures have been produced. I could not vouch for their absolute accuracy, but there is already a view abroad from the work that has been done on the relative funding of the English regions and clear comparisons have been made, in fact quite political comparisons have been made between that proportion of expenditure and those undertaken in Scotland. If you look at some of the key comparators between, for instance, the North East and Scotland, you find very similar levels of economic inactivity and levels of welfare transfer. Certainly if I were in the north-east of England I would be arguing that I want to be part of such as assessment.

Q353 Lord Forsyth of Drumlean: Is this not a different argument because I do not know the numbers now, I am out-of-date, but spending per head on health in the north-east of England will be considerably less than spending per head on health in Scotland.

Mr Moxham: Indeed.

Q354 Lord Forsyth of Drumlean: That is the political difficulty, but if you take spending on health in Scotland and you compare Glasgow to the north-east of Scotland, there will also be a differential.

Mr Moxham: Indeed.

Q355 Lord Forsyth of Drumlean: So are we not confusing two things here, which is really the Chairman's point?

Mr Moxham: I do not because I believe that the sums of money involved particularly the role of, as I say, the South and the East in essentially affecting the calculation of Scotland's baseline requires an examination of whether the settlement within England and the costing of delivery of services within England is fair as well.

Q356 Chairman: I do not follow that. I really do not follow that because it seems to me that what we need is a mechanism which is there in order to distribute resources between the four constituencies of the UK and that the way in which Scotland, for example, would then deal with its own money and its own people is a matter for the Scots, the same with the Welsh and Northern Irish and the English. Do we need to go further than that?

Mr Moxham: My view would be that it is important in terms of the integrity of the United Kingdom as a whole, and to ensure reasonably well-shared values of social citizenship, for want of a better term, that those in the various regions of England were able to say with some certainty that the criteria which were being applied to them were the same as the criteria which were being applied to the people of Scotland.

Q357 Lord Rowe-Beddoe: I was going to ask you is one of your concerns here the transparency of what is currently the system that allocates these funds?

Mr Moxham: I think there must be a problem with transparency when it is so little understood and so often misquoted. I suppose one of my concerns is that the most frequent comparison that those of us who attempt to defend levels of public spending in Scotland are forced to make is with the regions of England.

Q358 Lord Rowe-Beddoe: The thing about the regions of England is that they do not formally exist. We hear a lot and the press give us a lot about the North East. Can I ask you a slightly different question. Obviously you represent the trade union movement in Scotland. Do you find that this question is a question that concerns your membership, that you have discussions about it, or it is raised, as it were, during the year, or is it left to people in your position to be concerned about it?

Mr Moxham: I think it is fair to say that the discussion around the operation of the formula specifically has become more current and more widespread since the wider discussions prompted by Calman and the National Conversation about Scottish funding generally.

Q359 *Lord Rowe-Beddoe:* More of an awareness?

Mr Moxham: More of an awareness. I would say not necessarily a full understanding. I am also aware—and you will probably have guessed I am not Scots by birth—from my frequent visits to the South East of England that the level of discussion and debate there has increased quite significantly as well. Our annual Congress will hear 104 different motions later in April and there is not one on the Barnett Formula or the operation of it, so I would not try and pretend that it is an issue of enormous currency. However, I think the general funding relationships are of more interest and, in particular, people are beginning to hear the mood music of the discussion that is going round in some of the newspapers down south and beginning to become aware that it is an issue that we are going to have to discuss.

Q360 *Lord Rowe-Beddoe:* Can I just go back to this question of the regions in England which the Chairman has raised. I know this is outside our particular remit, but the whole question of the funding of these parts of England (if we do not call them regions for a moment) is a matter for England under this concept. We have a Barnett Formula. We are not entering into the political forum here and if it is accepted eventually to replace the Barnett Formula, it will be for the four constituents parts of the United Kingdom and Northern Ireland, to determine how they are going to allocate the grant. That is not satisfactory to you?

Mr Moxham: I believe that there would be enduring difficulties in relation to the "felt fair" of the system across England, which is after all the significant part in size of the United Kingdom, and I believe there is certainly the risk under that approach that we would not end up with felt fair across the regions of England and therefore the stability of any future settlement would potentially come into question.

Q361 *Lord Forsyth of Drumlean:* Why do you make that distinction between a future settlement and what we have now? I have now got the figures for what health spending is by region in England and the North East is actually one of the highest at £1,678 per

head. The Scottish figure is £1,771, which is higher than all the other regions of England and Wales by quite a considerable margin. There is a big variation between the parts of England from £1,402 in the South East to £1,417 in the South West, right up to the figure I have given you for the North East, so within the existing distribution, which we are not concerned with, in England you have a big variation between the regions but all of them are considerably less than Scotland. Do you think that reflects need?

Mr Moxham: It may well do but I would hesitate to say that it definitely does. It certainly reflects the increased cost of provision partially in relation to the geography, although I concede the North East would have some issues in relation to that, too, but we would need to then make a cross-comparison, in my view, with morbidity rates.

Q362 *Lord Forsyth of Drumlean:* I think the money is distributed by the Department of Health within England on the basis of a formula which takes account of need, which is why you get that distribution between them, and I have no doubt that people argue—which is not our concern—about what the North East gets, but the argument which I thought you were referring to is the one that says why does Scotland get £1,700 and why is the overall level of expenditure on health higher in Scotland. The fact that it is not actually possible to point to a kind of needs-based assessment makes it very much more difficult to justify that relative to the English regions. Is that not the political difficulty?

Mr Moxham: Yes, that is an accurate position.

Q363 *Lord Forsyth of Drumlean:* It is not so much about the distribution between the English regions as about the overall provision relative to England and Scotland?

Mr Moxham: Yes.

Q364 *Chairman:* It is also a perception, is it not, that unless you have got a needs-based assessment which people broadly accept as fair, you still get this argument going on between, say, the north-east of England and Scotland about their respective allocations?

Mr Moxham: Yes.

Q365 *Lord Sewel:* I think there is one thing we can agree on, if we do move to a needs assessment of the type that you are advocating, it will take a fairly long period of time, as you have said, to introduce. Are there any aspects of the Barnett Formula as it operates at the moment which cause you concern and worry and you would like to see changed in an intervening period?

Mr Moxham: We have not given specific thought to that. We are obviously aware that, in theory at least, over a period of contracting public expenditure, as we expect to happen now, that convergence would be slower. Taking into account the potential for rising inflation and wage costs to influence that, too, I think one of the clear problems that we have is that it is actually very difficult to predict where the formula will have us in five or ten years' time, and that is clearly a problem. I tend to think that any attempts to tinker would probably just produce further problems as opposed to clarifying the situation. To be honest, I would defer to people who have done more work on the operation of the mechanism itself rather than making specific suggestions.

Q366 *Lord Forsyth of Drumlean:* Is that another way of saying it is politically too difficult?
Mr Moxham: Yes, probably! I have yet to hear of anybody who has any confidence about what a future formula might look like.

Q367 *Chairman:* Well, thank you very much indeed. You have made your views very clear. I think a large chunk of it I find myself in agreement with.
Mr Moxham: It would be of some disappointment to me if I threw anything into the pot that was controversial. Thank you very much for listening to me.

Examination of Witness

Witness: MR RUCHIR SHAH, Head of Policy and Research Department, Scottish Council for Voluntary Organisations, examined.

Q368 *Chairman:* Mr Shah, thank you very much for coming. As I am sure you know, this Committee was set up by the House of Lords to look specifically at the operation of the Barnett Formula. Our terms of reference are fairly strictly drawn which means that we cannot look at fascinating but extraneous matters like fiscal autonomy for Scotland; we cannot look at the political systems anywhere in the UK; all we have got to look at is the Barnett Formula as it is, whether it has disadvantages or whether it has advantages and, if it has disadvantages, what we should do about it. On that basis can I ask you what you think about the Barnett Formula?
Mr Shah: I am representing the umbrella body for the voluntary sector in Scotland and what I can say is that there are certain factors which from the voluntary sector perspective would need to be in the discussions and would need to be for greater consideration. What I can do for you is give some sense of what those factors are. What I have tried to do is to relate it closely to the specific questions that you have asked because I realise it has to be within that. Having said that, by relating it to your specific questions, it will be only three questions that I am touching on in this, but I think they will be the ones that will be of most interest to you. Firstly, I can say something about the Scottish voluntary sector being quite highly geared towards the Scottish block grant. It is quite sensitive to the Scottish block grant and the way in which the block grant can fluctuate does have an up-front effect on the voluntary sector in Scotland. This is because the voluntary sector is in many cases funded on much shorter funding timescales than other sectors. It is probably just worth mentioning the other areas as well before going into detail on that. The second thing which I can probably say something on is that for the voluntary sector in Scotland (indeed for the whole of the UK) a formula

based on need rather than population may be more appropriate. I hope that will be useful. What I cannot do is say that we want to have a formula based on need, but I think it is a factor that needs to be considered. For the voluntary sector, social, environmental and cultural causes are the areas where needs-based distributions will work best rather than population-based, just because of the nature of the work that we do. The third area is really around the Barnett consequentials, which refers to your question five, and what I can say on that is that the Scottish block is not the only expenditure of interest to the voluntary sector which then attracts a Barnett consequential. There are a number of programmes which are designed within the English policy context which nevertheless have a Barnett consequential for Scotland's voluntary sector, and I can run through some of those as examples as well. How would you like me to proceed?

Q369 *Chairman:* I think you have got a piece of paper there. Why do you not read it to us?
Mr Shah: I only drafted it yesterday, I have to say. I will try and draw in and out from this as required. If you want to stop me at any point, please do. The first thing I mentioned was around how Scotland's voluntary sector is quite sensitive to the Scottish block grant and any fluctuations within that. Just to give you a sense of the Scottish voluntary sector, it is very similar to the UK voluntary sector in that 38 per cent of its income sources annually come from public sector funding sources, so it is not the entire sector.

Q370 *Chairman:* Is this Scotland?
Mr Shah: This is Scotland although the picture in the rest of the UK broadly matches that as well. Other sources of the sector's income base are also indirectly influenced by the scale of the block grant, the kind of

activities it carries out through trading, for example, the activities through voluntary income that comes from trusts and foundations and from general donations (ie the general public). These are not necessarily directly from the Scottish block grant but the scale of the public sector Scottish block grant in Scotland can indirectly influence it. That is the sense we get. The voluntary sector is therefore sensitive to any changes and it does mean that any changes to the Barnett system as such would need to be, I guess from the sector's perspective, phased in with due consideration slowly, gradually and with consideration of the immediate impact it could have on voluntary organisations. In Scotland the voluntary sector has quite an intricate infrastructure with a number of umbrella bodies and network bodies that support it. It is very intricate for a population of five million, I have to say. The umbrella bodies and sector infrastructure of the networks do get much of their core funding through the Scottish block grant.

Q371 *Lord Rowe-Beddoe:* Can I just ask, what is the total spend of the Scottish voluntary sector on an annual basis?
Mr Shah: We are looking at an annual income of £3.7 billion based on the latest figures.

Q372 *Lord Rowe-Beddoe:* That is income and I was asking about spend?
Mr Shah: What we have noticed is that the expenditure of the sector is kind of in-line with the income. It is not that far off because, as you can imagine, most of what the sector gets in goes straight back out again. There tends to be a narrow gap. In the latest estimates there was about £50 to £100 million less, so expenditure would be around £3.8 billion.

Q373 *Lord Forsyth of Drumlean:* How is that made up?
Mr Shah: How is the expenditure made up?

Q374 *Lord Forsyth of Drumlean:* £3.8 billion seems huge.
Mr Shah: Yes, 38 per cent directly through public sector funding sources, which includes grants, contracts, and a lot of public service delivery activity. Then you have a lot of social enterprise and trading activity, for example thrift shops on the streets, or engaging in providing services to other organisations or to members of the public, so a lot of income flows that way. Then you have some of the large housing associations which accounts for about £1.5 billion of income.
Lord Forsyth of Drumlean: Okay.

Q375 *Chairman:* Please go on.
Mr Shah: Because the infrastructure is quite elaborate and is quite heavily reliant on the block grant, it does suggest that the economies of scale that you might gain from the sector infrastructure, say for example south of the border, which is supporting a larger population because, okay, there may be 90 per cent of the population in parts of the UK and maybe 70 per cent in England, but there can be fewer umbrella bodies and fewer networks to manage that than you might need in Scotland because in Scotland those same networks and those same umbrella bodies and that same infrastructure has to deal with the Scottish Parliament as well. There are economies of scale gained which you will not find in Scotland because we are quite geared towards the Scottish block grant coming through the Scottish Government. That is a little bit more that should be said about the sensitivity of the voluntary sector to its funding. A lot of the funding sources do tend to be less than one year rather than multiple year as opposed to what you might find in other sectors. That is the nature of the way the sector is currently funded. The sector is trying to push for longer contracts, for example, but currently a lot of contracts tend to be one year or less, which means that any change to the Barnett Formula, or indeed to the Barnett system and the Scottish block will have quite immediate impacts on the sector. The second area which I was talking about is need versus population. What I was saying there was that a formula based on need might be more appropriate for the kind of work that the voluntary sector is involved in. Just to give you some context on this, the voluntary sector throughout the UK, and in Scotland, works in a diverse range of fields and the sector's client groups are often the "hardest to reach". The sector has very much set itself up to meet overwhelming need. There are a number of conceptual underpinnings for the differences in the budgetary spend in Scotland. Two of the most important are geography and deprivation. For us, geography is an obvious concern because providing services to small numbers of people living in large areas is much more expensive than providing similar services in smaller areas. I would like to draw your attention to Scotland's particularly large rural hinterland. Both our experience and evidence does suggest that the voluntary sector, in many ways, props up the rural infrastructure, so, for example, you will find voluntary organisations involved in things like community transport and other activities such as community energy and managing village halls. This is where a measure which is based on population really starts to get at odds with the kind of need that you have because of this large rural hinterland. Deprivation is also important for Scottish public spending as the proportion of households living in poverty as a percentage of the

population in Scotland (and, as you know, Glasgow is often cited as the major case in point here) tends to be much higher as a proportion of the overall population in Scotland than you might find in England. You do have pockets of extreme deprivation across England but as a proportion of overall population it is higher in Scotland and this is something the voluntary sector has to deal with here. The ease with which resources can be diverted is restricted by the relatively large number of deprived households against a comparatively smaller general population. Again, from a voluntary sector perspective, any formula based on need would be more beneficial to the client groups it works with as well as the kinds of activities and the kinds of geographies that it is dealing with. That is the second area which I was talking about. The third area which I mentioned was on the Barnett consequentials. This is where I mentioned that it is not just the Scottish block grant which is of interest to the voluntary sector; there are a number of other programmes which are usually designed within the English policy context because they are reserved programmes, which nevertheless attract a Barnett consequential for Scotland. One recent example that particularly affects us is the English Third Sector Action Plan which is a £42 million plan which was announced a few weeks ago. As part of this, £10 million has been allocated to the Department for Work and Pensions for specific volunteering programmes. This has a consequential for Scotland through Barnett, but the policy fit for that particular programme has been worked out for England and not for the policy fit in Scotland, so clearly there are issues where we would suggest there needs to be better alignment. Currently the programme is worked out with a particular context in mind and it then has to fit somehow in Scotland. This can have implications for how the voluntary sector can deal with the programmes in question. A second area you will be familiar with is the National Lottery. In Scotland, a lot of voluntary organisations have been concerned by the diversion of substantial funds of the National Lottery to the Olympics. The Lottery funding itself is based on a Barnett Plus Formula, which is based on Barnett but it has various adjustments made, to some extent on need. Scotland has experienced a cut of 70 per cent of its allocation by the Big Lottery Fund Scotland Committee.

Q376 *Lord Forsyth of Drumlean:* Sorry to interrupt you, perhaps I am out-of-date but I thought that Lottery funding was allocated by various arm's length committees. Are you saying there is a kind of rule that there should be a population share that goes to Scotland and they fit within that?

Mr Shah: Not at all. All I am saying is that I guess any kind of consideration of the Barnett Formula needs to be aware of how it is being used in programmes beyond the Scottish block grant. In this particular case the National Lottery and the way in which funding is provided to various organisations is indeed devolved to various committees. For example there is a Scotland Committee that makes those decisions. However, the amount of money that they can then allocate is affected by decisions taken centrally.

Q377 *Lord Forsyth of Drumlean:* Are you saying that the amount of money that is allocated to them is done on a population basis?
Mr Shah: That is our understanding. We have been told it is a Barnett Plus formula. It is not fully based on population. It starts off with the Barnett Formula and then there have been some adjustments made to it. I may not be an expert on this but the title I understand has been given to this is the Barnett Plus Formula.

Q378 *Lord Forsyth of Drumlean:* So if they spend £1 billion on the Dome Scotland gets £100 million?
Mr Shah: That is the kind of idea. With the Olympics it is the opposite way round. With the Olympics, if there is a cut, the cut also attracts Barnett consequentials.

Q379 *Lord Forsyth of Drumlean:* I am not getting this. Are you saying—and I do not know how it works—that if X is the amount which is available from all the various committees and ways of distributing the Lottery, that there is a Barnett consequential of X over 10, or whatever the share of population is, which goes to the Scottish Committee for allocation? I thought that is what you were saying. If that is the case, then presumably the money that is being spent on the Olympics is part of the overall pool? If you get the Barnett consequences of that, you have got it on the fact that they have spent it on the Olympics. Are you saying there is a third way of dealing with it, there is expenditure which is considered to be UK, which is top-sliced? Is that what happens?
Mr Shah: It is actually both, but the more important issue is the one you raised initially which is this 70 per cent cut which we have identified right across the board and affects parts of England just as it does parts of Scotland just as it does parts of Northern Ireland.

Q380 *Lord Forsyth of Drumlean:* That is top-sliced.
Mr Shah: In this case we can talk about it as top-sliced, so the question you would be asking me is what has this got to do with the Barnett Formula or the kind of inquiry that you are running. The point I

make relates to an earlier point I made which is about the policy fit. Those who are making decisions on the cuts are making those decisions in consultation with colleagues who are managing other resources which can balance out the impact of those cuts to some extent, whereas in Scotland where that cut appears in the National Lottery there is no corresponding balancing out happening in any of the third sector programmes that the Scottish Government is managing, so it is very much a policy fit issue that has been designed within the English policy context, and is not something designed necessarily within the Scottish context.

Q381 *Chairman:* The whole point of Lottery funding is that it was meant to be additional and therefore looking at it in terms of the Barnett consequences runs against the whole basis upon which it was set up.
Mr Shah: But that is the system that is used in order to allocate it per country.

Q382 *Chairman:* Why should the Scottish Executive not actually do the sort of balancing process that you say the English do?
Mr Shah: Ideally, they would, but the way the system works is that the decision is made very quickly, that is my understanding, and the design stage is something that you might want to look into. The programmes are announced and launched. The decision was made to take a cut for the Olympics but it was not necessarily made with the Scottish policy context in mind, and that is the issue to which I would like to draw your attention.

Q383 *Lord Forsyth of Drumlean:* Would it be possible for you to send us an idiot's guide, which will be very useful for me particularly?
Mr Shah: Absolutely. Of course this formula is not just used for the Big Lottery Fund which is the main good cause fund but also for the Heritage and Arts Lottery distributions as well, which are also based on Barnett Plus. Another similar area is around dormant bank accounts legislation.

Q384 *Chairman:* I am sorry, where does the money for the arts allocation actually come from, a pond in which the Barnett Plus formula is to be applied?
Mr Shah: This is the lottery sales.

Q385 *Chairman:* We are still doing Lottery.
Mr Shah: The Arts Lottery distribution is via a separate distributor from the Big Lottery Fund.

Q386 *Lord Rowe-Beddoe:* And heritage is a separate one so you have three.
Mr Shah: It is slightly complicated in Scotland because the Scottish Arts Council which manages the Lottery Fund also uses other funding which it gets through the Scottish block grant so it is all wrapped up and mixed up together.
Chairman: You want to simplify matters.

Q387 *Lord Rowe-Beddoe:* I think the point Mr Shah is making is that it has been significantly reduced as a result of the Olympics. Am I right?
Mr Shah: Absolutely, yes.
The third area to which I draw your attention to in terms of the Barnett consequentials is around dormant bank accounts legislation. You will recall that this is the idea that those bank accounts that have been lying fallow for many years should be used for some kind of good cause. The policy direction in which this is to be used is separate for England and Scotland. The decision on how that money should be used is devolved so Scottish ministers can direct the money, although there are other issues obviously with the banks at the moment. With the dormant bank accounts legislation, there is a population-based assumption at play which we would presume is based on a Barnett consequential. This is again another programme strand where the kind of levels, and the legislation to some extent, is taking into account the English policy context but it has a substantial Barnett consequential for Scotland. I guess our plea to you in terms of your review and your evidence consideration is to look at how any system that would replace or enhance the Barnett Formula can make sure that the particular policy devolution that we have can be aligned with the formula itself. Thus where the allocation is made, it can take into account the policy fit of the devolved nations as well as the policy fit at Westminster.

Q388 *Lord Forsyth of Drumlean:* How do you see that working?
Mr Shah: I am not entirely sure. It is something I just want to raise which others might not have raised.

Q389 *Lord Forsyth of Drumlean:* But I can see the difficulty with the top-slicing. I can even see the difficulty of saying we have got £X million, let us just give Scotland 10 per cent of that, rather than saying what are the needs in Scotland relative to other parts, but the overall volume of money that is allocated, how it is spent, is surely a matter for the devolved committees? The fact that the Scottish Executive is following some different policy or whatever is neither here nor there.
Mr Shah: It is, actually, because if you look within this system, the devolved nations do not have a say on the amount available for distribution. If it is distributed using the Barnett Formula and they are given a certain percentage, and this is how much you are going to get that is what they have to play with. They cannot comment on whether they need less or more of it, based on any other system.

Q390 *Lord Forsyth of Drumlean:* But the principle behind the Lottery funding—and I am now repeating myself—is based on additionality. It is not supposed to be spent on programmes which would otherwise be funded by government. It is meant to be used for purposes which are additional. How could you maintain that principle and devise a scheme that related to the policy decisions of the devolved administrations or Westminster?

Mr Shah: If we are going to be looking at this as additional funds, as you quite rightly pointed out, then there needs to be no duplication, but the problem is if the scope of the available funds, if the level of the available funds changes quite substantially, and there has also not been a policy fit to make sure there is no duplication with the policy areas that the Scottish Government might be involved in, then there may be an issue there. I think that is what I am trying to draw out.

Q391 *Chairman:* Give us specific examples where this has happened.

Mr Shah: The immediate example which I have already mentioned is the diversion to the Olympics which when we calculated it came to a 70 per cent cut in the first year. This was quite a shock to the system for the sector in Scotland and also, presumably, for the Scottish Government. For the voluntary sector it did mean that quite a considerable additional source of independent funding which is not tied specifically to a government priority was going to be drastically reduced, which meant that the sector would become much more reliant on those areas of specific and immediate government priority, if you see what I mean.

Q392 *Lord Forsyth of Drumlean:* But that is nothing to do with Barnett, that is to do with a decision taken by the Government to direct resources to the Olympics, which affects every part of the United Kingdom. I am very sympathetic to the problem but it is nothing to do with the distribution of resources within the United Kingdom under Barnett.

Mr Shah: The other example I gave is the £10 million of the English Third Sector Action Plan which had been passed on to the Department for Work and Pensions to look at specific volunteering programmes. It is these programmes, when they are decided, which attract a Barnett consequential, but the first time anyone actually hears about it in Scotland, from our knowledge, is when it has been announced. You have to then work out that any kind of new policy initiatives that have been introduced in Scotland have to then fit with this new, sudden increase or decrease in a certain area. I think the Lottery is not as good an example as the Department for Work and Pensions because the latter is a specific volunteering programme. Let us say, for example,

that the Scottish Government has seen a gap in partnership with voluntary organisations in Scotland with respect to volunteering programmes, so they put in place a major volunteering programme to start this year, going forward for the next three years, and the next day suddenly £10 million has been allocated to the Department for Work and Pensions for volunteering programmes which attracts a Barnett consequential in Scotland, clearly there is going to be duplication there.

Q393 *Lord Forsyth of Drumlean:* I understand that, but if the Department for Work and Pensions decided to spend £10 million under the Barnett consequentials, the Scottish Executive would then get £1 million. They do not have to spend that £1 million on any particular programme, they can spend it how they like, they have the ability to vire. They can get the Barnett consequences of a huge increase in spending in health but they can spend it on education or spend it on volunteers, so why is this a problem?

Mr Shah: I am not sure whether it would be the Scottish Government. I do not think it is a Scottish block grant issue for that particular programme. When this Barnett consequential was being worked out I think it was for DWP operations in Scotland rather than for the Scottish Government to deliver the programme for that particular issue.

Q394 *Lord Forsyth of Drumlean:* That is a separate point. That is the Department for Work and Pensions in carrying out their welfare functions deciding to implement the programme, but that is nothing to do with Barnett then, is it?

Mr Shah: It may not have anything to do with the Scottish block allocation for Barnett but it's derivation certainly uses the Barnett Formula.

Q395 *Lord Forsyth of Drumlean:* What you are complaining about is this is the Department for Work and Pensions not being sensitive to the Scottish dimension?

Mr Shah: I think so but they are using Barnett in their calculations, that is the issue.

Q396 *Chairman:* It is an odd insensitivity which results in all money going to the block grant?

Mr Shah: I guess, in a way.

Q397 *Chairman:* What you are saying is that Barnett is used as a kind of formula to do things which are nothing to do with Barnett?

Mr Shah: Which have nothing to do with the Scottish block grant, yes, and any system that you look at or review and revise may well have that kind of impact as well on these other programmes which have nothing to do with the Scottish block grant.

Q398 *Chairman:* How on earth can one avoid that? If the Scottish Government up here wants to treat the operation of the Barnett mechanism as some kind of iconic way of doing business and therefore they say we will apply that type of approach to something else, that is entirely for them.

Mr Shah: It is not the Scottish Government who would be applying it, this is DWP and the English Third Sector Action Plan that have that arrangement, so the Scottish Government are not in the picture there, if you like, in this particular case. Having said that, I guess if other programmes are using the Barnett Formula to allocate their own distributions or their operations in other countries, then if out of your review a new system is created which may be based on need more than population, Westminster Departments may well adopt that, and that may well have implications for these kind of activities and how they fit with policy in the devolved nations

Q399 *Lord Forsyth of Drumlean:* Is it your complaint that you only get a population share of these schemes run by Whitehall departments and you think that you should get more?

Mr Shah: I do not think it is about more or less, I think it is about policy fit.

Q400 *Lord Forsyth of Drumlean:* I am sorry, I am not grasping this. If it is the Department for Work and Pensions, how can there be a different policy in Scotland for the Department for Work and Pensions than England?

Mr Shah: It is about how their activities are fitting with the other programmes in the country. For example in Scotland, yes, the benefits system is reserved but clearly skills, education and other issues which have a direct relevance to any programmes that the DWP runs when it comes to benefits or volunteering in Scotland will have an impact on each other and will interplay quite considerably. I suppose that is where I am trying to focus on it.

Q401 *Lord Forsyth of Drumlean:* It is a slightly different area from what we are concerned about really. It is to do with Whitehall departments implementing programmes in Scotland and perhaps not being sensitive enough to the fact that there is a different approach.

Mr Shah: If we take a step back from that and just look at the Barnett Formula as an iconic formula that has been used not just for its original purpose, which is for the Scottish block grant, but all these other programmes as well—

Q402 *Lord Forsyth of Drumlean:* It is not an iconic formula. All it is is that you get your relative share of the population.

Mr Shah: Some of UK-level Government Departments expand on it and tweak it. For example, I mentioned Barnett Plus being used for the National Lottery.

Q403 *Chairman:* What is Barnett Plus?

Mr Shah: I do not fully understand it myself. This is something that is done behind closed doors but I think it tries to bring in an element of need into the population-based Barnett Formula.

Chairman: Our expert says nobody knows what it is but it exists.

Lord Forsyth of Drumlean: It sounds very interesting because Mr Shah says it attempts to bring in an element of need.

Q404 *Chairman:* That is coming from the Lottery as such, their contribution to Scotland, is it? Your complaint really is that the amount of money that is being distributed in Scotland is based only on the Barnett Plus population formula, and if we move away from that to some other formula based on need, we have got to make sure that that is administered sensitively as far as Scotland is concerned; is that right?

Mr Shah: I think so because the Scottish voluntary sector is highly sensitive not just to the Scottish block grant but to any funding sources. As I mentioned, this 70 per cent cut in the Lottery funds due to the Olympics has had a major effect on the voluntary sector in Scotland. You may well come up with a new formulation on how Scotland's Government gets its share of the funds, and that system may well then very quickly be adopted by other Department in operationalising programmes, whenever there is a kind of consequential for Scotland, and it would be good to be aware of that, yes.

Q405 *Chairman:* So it is the imitation of the principle behind the Barnett Formula that you are worried about?

Mr Shah: Indeed.

Q406 *Lord Rowe-Beddoe:* Did your sector have any warning about the 70 per cent cut?

Mr Shah: Of course yes, not from the DCMS I have to say, but a lot of people have been analysing this. My colleagues at the National Council for Voluntary Organisations have also been very much on this.

Q407 *Lord Rowe-Beddoe:* What I meant by warning was when did you know that you were going to have to find replacement funds somehow in order to carry out your programmes?

Mr Shah: We were on the case with the DCMS at as early a stage as we could and it really did depend on when they were able to pass on information to us. Obviously, a lot of this is intuitive understanding of other programmes taking place, like the Olympics and the threat that could have in terms of diversion of Lottery funding, and putting two and two together. It was then just a case of waiting or prompting DCMS to come out with a statement.

Q408 *Lord Forsyth of Drumlean:* Just returning to Barnett, you indicated that you would prefer to have a needs-based system rather than a population-based system.

Mr Shah: Not quite. I would not say that we would insist on a needs-based system. What I am saying is that the voluntary sector and the kind of areas it works in and the kind of client groups it works with would benefit financially more from a formula based on needs rather than on population. I think that is something the Committee should take into consideration.

Q409 *Lord Forsyth of Drumlean:* Are you concerned about the fact that because the baseline is higher in Scotland and that Barnett now post-devolution is being applied absolutely, and you cannot go and have a separate negotiation to take account of increases in the Health Service pay deal or teachers' pay, things of that kind, that the Barnett squeeze is now operating rather more savagely than in the past, and do you recognise that if left it will ultimately lead to convergence?

Mr Shah: To be honest with you, all of those aspects are very much masked by the effects of the overall squeeze on public finances right across the UK and how that translates into cuts.

Q410 *Lord Forsyth of Drumlean:* I must have missed that. When did that happen?

Mr Shah: It has been happening over the past five or six years.

Q411 *Lord Forsyth of Drumlean:* In terms of public finances?

Mr Shah: On the public sector funding that is available to the voluntary sector, which seems to tally with the overall finances of for example local authorities in Scotland with Scottish Government overall grants and so on. From a voluntary sector perspective, there seems to be quite a squeeze on public sector funding available for a whole range of areas which the voluntary sector is involved in. In Scotland, there has been a lot of disquiet about cuts made by various local authorities and a lot of that may or may not be a response to the current economic downturn. Some of it may well be in response to policy priorities. Certainly there is a tightening funding environment in the sector that we have seen in the past seven or so years, and that, I would suggest, masks any kind of changes, any kind of convergence that we might otherwise see in the environment.

Chairman: Thank you very much indeed. You have put down a marker which we have noted and we will consider. I am glad that I have understood it towards the end; I am not sure I understood it a bit earlier. Thank you very much.

Supplementary memorandum by the Scottish Council for Voluntary Organisations

MEMORANDUM FROM THE SCOTTISH COUNCIL FOR VOLUNTARY ORGANISATIONS SUPPLEMENTARY TO THE EVIDENCE GIVEN BY MR RUCHIR SHAH AT THE PUBLIC EVIDENCE SESSION OF THE COMMITTEE IN EDINBURGH ON FRIDAY 27 FEBRUARY 2009

INTRODUCTION

SCVO was grateful for the opportunity to present its evidence at the Committee's public session. There were a number of issues where SCVO thought members of the Committee might welcome clarification, explanation or expansion on the SCVO evidence. Should any further questions arise from consideration of the contents of this memorandum, we will be happy to try to answer these.

THE CONVERGENCE ISSUE

In Q409, Lord Forsyth asked about the so-called "Barnett squeeze" and the related issue of "convergence" between levels of need in Scotland compared to elsewhere in the UK. The Barnett formula was originally introduced in order to reflect the greater need for resources in Scotland to address persistent issues of multiple deprivation and poor health.

PAST VOLUNTARY SECTOR CONTRIBUTION TO CONVERGENCE

It may help if we look at these issues from the historic perspective of the voluntary sector. Many of the non-population elements that go into the Barnett formula are the focus for direct action by the voluntary sector. The sector's primary objective is to deliver public benefit. This involves working to return people to gainful and sustainable employment, supporting and rehabilitating those afflicted by bad health, disabling conditions, disease and addiction and funding major research programmes into such afflictions. The sector supports offender re-education and reintegration into society, helps keep communities safe through volunteering initiatives as diverse as Community and Neighbourhood Watch, acting as volunteer firemen and lifeboat personnel, improves the lives of children by direct help through fostering and adoption, through community based voluntary youth work and education. In more recent years, environmental activity has grown to include initiatives from community energy to local woodlands groups.

WIDTH AND DEPTH OF THE SECTOR'S CONTRIBUTION TO CONVERGENCE

The sector is active in every facet of national life. It contributes much of what it does at no cost to the public purse, the sort of intensive commitment to the resolution of the most intractable problems facing society, eg care of the terminally ill, those with high dependency health conditions, the need to build the national skills base. This all leads to small but measureable improvements in the well-being of society. These outcomes delivered by the sector at its own hand or working with its partners in local and national government and the private sector have achieved positive shifts over time. These collective efforts of all the parties in national life are reflected in progressive convergence in key indicators in health, employment, life expectancy, childhood mortality and income expectations with the wider UK population.

The gap between many of the individual elements of the Barnett formula in Scotland and England/UK has narrowed considerably.

REDUCING THE RESIDUUM—A FINAL PUSH TOWARDS CONVERGENCE?

A. *A hard challenge*

The challenge now for Scottish society, and the Scottish voluntary sector, is to reduce and eventually eliminate those factors which account for the remaining differentials, enshrined in the Barnett formula, between Scotland and the UK as a whole. By their very nature, the remaining problems are often the most difficult to resolve. The issues of multiple deprivation will need the holistic and integrated efforts of several voluntary organisations to secure better outcomes for society, eg in tackling persistent high rates of teenage pregnancy, in responding to the health and employment needs of households with so-called "chaotic lifestyles" as identified by the DWP.

B. *The need for joint research and intelligence to inform action*

Our efforts as the voluntary sector will continue to address and reduce the gaps in outcomes for individuals and whole communities, both as between Scotland and the rest of the UK and within Scotland itself. This will need agreement with Government and other partners on the outcomes to be prioritised and pursued. There are already excellent examples of the need to develop the intelligence from jointly funded research to identify and disseminate best practice, whether it be in cancer research, victim support, biodiversity management, numeracy and literacy or reducing addiction. Joint research into viable treatments for specific conditions can produce results that eliminate the impact those conditions have on deprivation outcomes as between Scotland and the rest of the UK, because such conditions are more common in Scotland (eg coronary heart disease). Here, altruistic voluntary giving by the Scottish general public to fund such research remains at a remarkable level internationally.

C. *Challenges to the rate of progress towards convergence of need*

An unrelenting smooth, virtuous curve of progress towards the achievement of full convergence cannot be assumed. The wider economic climate and technological change have a profound ability to check progress. The current recession may well prove to be the most significant check on progress towards convergence since the Barnett formula was first applied, on the basis of the pressures already being reported to SCVO by our member organisations. Convergence can be accelerated by new technologies (heart valves), exploitation of economic advantage (the oil industry) or new preventive drugs such as statins. Perversely, the closure of much of Scottish heavy industry has significantly reduced the previously markedly higher incidence of industrial injury and related household benefit dependency in Scotland, which will over time converge with the UK incidence of such morbidity.

Social factors can interrupt movement towards convergence. A good recent example is the sudden, sharp higher increase in smoking among women aged under 20 in Scotland, when compared to the rest of the UK. The unpredictability of such changes emphasises the need for careful monitoring to ensure that the needs based approach at the heart of the Barnett formula is fully informed by objective and trustworthy data.

D. *Policy changes and their impact*

Finally, and post-devolution, actual policy changes, or alterations in funding in the different national territories of the UK, can produce either more rapid or slower convergence of need, depending on the differential success of individual funding or best practice decisions, and the additionality secured. Consider the recent decisions on the most appropriate level of physical exercise per week to be provided for in schools curricula across the UK, or the differential investment in community as opposed to hospital based consultancy NHS services, the impact of out-sourcing or the ability to maintain sufficient numbers of highly trained, motivated and best paid teaching, nursing or care staff. Any differences in these supply side decisions between Scotland and the UK will impact on the pace of convergence. The most variable elements on the supply side will include the human intangibles—professionalism, quality, levels and application of training, diligence and the additionality secured from the interactive investment by all the parties (UK, Scottish, local government, public and private sector and private individuals) in their pursuit of public benefit.

We now turn to other questions raised by members of the Committee.

Q371 *et seq* SCVO would wish to point out the disproportionate importance of the income dimension for most Scottish charities, as so few, typically the largest, have significant reserves. The annual decision process on the operational percentage to be used to calculate the Barnett formula is of considerable importance to the sector. SCVO notes the slow progress in moving to full cost recovery in central and local government service delivery contracts with charitable and voluntary organisations.

Q383 and Q390 are perhaps best answered by a press release which SCVO prepared in 2008 on the impact of the Olympics in cutting Lottery funding in Scotland, and this is available from http://www.scvo.org.uk/scvo/TFNPR/ViewTFNPR.aspx?pr=8191. SCVO would wish to note that the scale of cuts in Lottery funding in Scotland arising from the unilateral funding decisions of the DCMS in respect of the London Olympics have produced a change in the type of outcomes as well as their amount.

Q386 SCVO would like to point out that there are in fact four (4) distributors involved in National Lottery funding. The highly successful small grants scheme, Awards for All, awards grants of up to £10,000, and is designed to help smaller charities and community based voluntary groups. Awards for All, continues to be able to approve over 75 per cent of applications for support. It has been of huge help in spreading the benefits of Lottery funding across Scotland.

Q390 For the distributors other than Awards for All, as funding availability falls very steeply, the issue for them becomes one of prioritisation within their overall fields of responsibility, with some areas being potentially and actually omitted completely from funding, rather than all applications competing equally for funding. If this has to be done, then SCVO would wish such decisions to be taken transparently by the distributors and publicised accordingly.

Q393 In the particular case of the Third Sector Action Plan published by the Office of the Third Sector in the Cabinet Office, there is no clear automaticity as suggested by Lord Forsyth. This is because the cash, while disbursed by the DWP, actually was originally part of the resources of the OTS and, had they been spent by that Department, could only have been spent in England. There is still uncertainty over whether such virement between Departments of State will then protect any such vired funds from a consequential liability for Barnett formula purposes. This position is made more complicated by the uncertainty over liability for a levy based on the Barnett formula when the expenditure is genuinely additional to voted total expenditure set out in the Finance Act for the Department concerned.

Q398 raises the important issue of the scope in future for participative budgeting. As a major player in service provision, innovation and development for large and expensive parts of the public services, the Scottish voluntary sector has had issues around the effectiveness of current budgetary processes, particularly in relation to planning forward activity. It has often been true that the position of charities at the national level has been simply overlooked—a good example being the decision to cut the base rate of tax from 22p to 20p in the 2007 Budget, without any appreciation of the impact on charitable income via Gift Aid, an error corrected by the introduction of Transitional Relief in the 2008 Budget, after campaigning by the sector. That one decision caused a potential loss of £10 million to the Scottish charitable sector. The required diversion of effort for senior finance staff in major UK and Scottish charities to secure the Transitional Relief Scheme was substantial, even with the active support on the issue from the Charity Tax Group.

Such unilateral action can have damaging impacts. There have been real problems involved where changes to provision have been made unilaterally by funding parties, causing real issues. However, what is of greater concern is where real, new additional financial resources are made available in either reserved or devolved areas and there is uncertainty about whether or not this new spending attracts a levy based on the Barnett formula. Sometimes we do not even discover the reasoning when a consequential is not generated. This issue is of equal concern to the growing problems caused by a lack of policy fit between the intentions of reserved and devolved Governments.

SCVO believes there should be a requirement placed on all statements made by way of Press Notice or to the Westminster Parliament that makes it plain whether and what are the Barnett formula implications for any additional expenditure generated in-year, when it is clearly in addition to resources approved by Parliament via the Finance Act of the year in question. While HMRC and the Treasury have held meetings with representatives of the charitable and voluntary sector on issues of mutual concern, SCVO believes it is essential for both parties to these discussions to continue to have the opportunity to discuss these existing sources of concern, how these might best be alleviated to save unnecessary bureaucracy and for there to be both transparency, consistency and compliance with agreed Guidance for Departments.

Q400 raised the important areas of hybridity and potentially cross-cutting types of spending. Included in this are policy areas such as skills and educational development and how these fit or not with the UK benefits system and how that is structured. As has been well evidenced in the debates on the Welfare Reform Bill currently before Parliament, it can be extremely difficult to "translate" spending intent when that intent is focussed on a policy architecture that is totally different in different parts of the country. An example would be current plans by DWP, contained in the Bill, to assume for spending purposes that all clients of the benefit system have a statutory right to child care, when, in fact, there is no such right in Scotland. This creates a really bad fit between DWP policies and those in place in Scotland. If the pound follows the statutory right, how can it then not follow those who do not have that right? How then is equality of treatment to be delivered, both for the benefit claimant and any dependent child(ren), ie the family or household unit? There cannot be an assumption that a level of resources already exists in a particular policy area, or that those resources will be ring fenced to contribute towards the realisation of another policy by another arm of government. Control of the spending power, once the Barnett formula has been triggered and received by the devolved Government, then lies with the Scottish Government, not DWP. The clear policy intent in the current Welfare Reform Bill breaches that convention by, in effect, demanding net new cash from the resources of the devolved government. The devolved Government should receive a properly considered Barnett formula derived amount to balance the policy assumptions. This need to balance assumptions is of course necessary in order to secure a policy fit that is consistent on reserved matters, but also fully recognises the legislative and policy position on devolved matters.

Q402 referred to variations of the Barnett formula deployed by Westminster Departments, and the particular case of the Barnett Plus version used by the National Lottery, approved by DCMS, as the Lottery's sponsor Department. Although the details have still to be announced, SCVO understands that there may be a variation on the Barnett formula which will be deployed in relation to the distribution of the proceeds from the Dormant Bank Accounts legislation (this was referred to in Mr Shah's response to Q387). SCVO is not aware of any coherent listing of such departmentally controlled variations, but believes publication of such a listing would certainly improve fiscal and financial transparency if these arrangements could be fully detailed by those Departments exercising reserved powers. They should be obliged to arrange for any changes to those variations to be publicised by appropriate means.

Q404 dealt with the sensitivity of the Scottish voluntary sector to funding decisions. The interplay of income from all sector funding sources is particularly important. There is evidence from past recessions that the level of public giving replaced temporary drops in the level of central or local government support for the sector, or when corporate giving is depressed, or when market circumstances depress the value of investments held by charitable Trusts and Foundations. What makes the current recessionary situation so threatening to the capacity and sustainability of the sector is that all these adverse circumstances have come together in something of a perfect storm. This has happened just at the point when the demand for the sector's services is exponentially increasing. It is in such circumstances that the Committee needs to consider how the Barnett formula can anticipate, then recognise and reflect the fact of reversal of the trend towards convergence.

Scottish Council for Voluntary Organisations

20 April 2009

WEDNESDAY 11 MARCH 2009

Present	Forsyth of Drumlean, L	Moser, L
	Hollis of Heigham, B	Richard, L (Chairman)
	Lang of Monkton, L	Rooker, L
	Mar and Kellie, E	Rowe-Beddoe, L

Memorandum by HM Treasury

This paper provides evidence by the Treasury to the House of Lords Select Committee on the Barnett formula. The paper describes how the Barnett formula works within the framework of the Government's devolved funding arrangements.

PUBLIC SPENDING: SETTING THE DEVOLVED ADMINISTRATIONS' BUDGETS IN EACH SPENDING REVIEW

United Kingdom Government funding for the devolved administrations' budgets is determined in spending reviews alongside United Kingdom Government departments and in accordance with the policies set out in the Statement of Funding Policy.

Aggregate public spending across the UK is set by the Government in the Budget preceding the spending review, within the Government's wider fiscal framework. The Government's fiscal framework is described in the Pre Budget Report published in November 2008 This aggregate public spending is then allocated to UK departments in the spending review and the population based Barnett formula is applied to changes in the departments' planned spending to determine changes to the devolved administrations' budgets.

The Barnett formula provides the devolved administrations with a population based share of changes in comparable spending of UK departments.

A worked example of the Barnett formula is set out below.

If, for example:

— the Government decides to increase the DEL budget of the Department of Innovation, Universities and Skills by £100 million; and

— the comparability percentage for that particular department for each devolved administration is 79 per cent (because that United Kingdom Government department carries out some expenditure at an all United Kingdom level); and

— the population proportions are 10.08 per cent for Scotland, 5.84 per cent for Wales and 3.43 per cent for Northern Ireland of England's population ;

then the following changes are added to each devolved administration's overall budget:

— for Scotland, £100 million (change in United Kingdom Government department's budget) x 79 per cent (comparability percentage) x 10.08 per cent (population proportion as a percentage of England's) giving a net change of 7.96 million;

— for Wales, £100 million (change in United Kingdom Government department's budget) x 79 per cent (comparability percentage) x 5.84 per cent (population proportion as a percentage of England's) giving a net change of £4.61 million; and

— for Northern Ireland, £100 million (change in United Kingdom Government department's budget) x 79 per cent (comparability percentage) x 3.43 per cent (population proportion as a percentage of England's) giving a change of £2.71 million. This amount is then abated by 2.5 per cent to reflect the fact the Northern Ireland Executive do not require funding to meet Value Added Tax costs incurred as these are refunded by HM Customs and Excise. The net change for Northern Ireland is therefore £2.64 million.

A similar calculation is applied to the changes in provision for all other UK Government departments in the spending review using the appropriate departmental comparability factors. The sum of the changes across all UK Government departments for the appropriate spending review year are added together to show the net aggregate (or total) change to the DEL budget of each devolved administration for that year.

Once the budgets of the devolved administrations are set it is for the devolved administrations to allocate their Departmental Expenditure Limit block budgets to devolved spending programmes in line with their own assessment of their priorities and needs.

As for UK Government Departments, the total budget of the Scottish Executive is composed of two separate categories of public expenditure. These are defined as Departmental Expenditure Limits (DEL), set over three years, and Annually Managed Expenditure (AME) updated in the Budget and PBR. DEL and AME together form Total Managed Expenditure (TME). In summary:

(i) Departmental Expenditure Limits (DELs) set firm, three-year spending limits. Changes in provision for the DEL for devolved administrations are determined through the Barnett Formula, details of which are set out in the Statement of Funding Policy.

(ii) Annually Managed Expenditure (AME) covers items which are not controlled through annual limits such as demand led spending and certain self-financed expenditure, whose provision is set by means of forecasts in the Budget and updated in the PBR. There are two main classifications of spend within AME: main departmental programmes in AME and other AME spending. Main Departmental programme spending covers policy-specific, ring-fenced items where provision is included within the Vote from the United Kingdom Parliament. Other AME spending includes locally financed expenditure, including any expenditure financed by the Scottish Variable Rate of Income Tax, not yet operated. The Treasury reviews the AME budget twice-annually, and forecasts are made for the three years ahead. The AME element of a devolved administration's budget is not determined by the Barnett formula and forecasts can therefore move up or down and the total budget moves up or down in line. AME expenditure cannot be recycled from one AME programme to another or recycled to increase the DEL.

DEL and AME budgets together comprise Total Managed Expenditure (TME). Once DEL and AME budgets are set, the United Kingdom Parliament then votes the necessary provision to the Scottish, Welsh and Northern Ireland Secretaries of State, and they, in turn, makes the block grants to the Scottish Executive, Welsh Assembly Government and Northern Ireland Executive as detailed in the Scotland, Wales and Northern Ireland Acts. The devolved administrations' budgets are not funded exclusively by grant from the United Kingdom Parliament. The budget is also funded from sources such as: funding financed by non-domestic rates; in Scotland, the Scottish Variable Rate of Income Tax if a decision is taken to use the tax-varying power; the European Commission; non cash items; and borrowing by local authorities for capital spending.

Any changes to the devolved administrations' DEL and AME budgets between spending reviews are determined according to the principles set out in the Statement of Funding Policy. For example the Treasury provides the devolved administrations' with the Barnett DEL consequentials of changes in provision announced for Government departments in the Budget and PBR.

In addition the Treasury monitors outturn spending against planned spending with the devolved administrations during each year, and underspends may be carried forward under the End Year Flexibility scheme, the drawdown of which is agreed with the Treasury.

The Statement of Funding Policy also sets out a dispute resolution procedure under which the devolved administrations may remit disputes to the Joint Ministerial Committee (JMC). In practice no disputes have been remitted to the JMC since devolution.

The Statement of Funding Policy is updated in each spending review in consultation with the devolved administrations. It includes updated details of the Barnett formula.

Estimates of identifiable public spending by country and region, including both devolved and reserved spending, are published annually in Public Expenditure Statistical Analyses. Details of the calculation of comparability factors are set out in Annex C of the Statement of Funding Policy.

CONCLUSION

The formula is updated in each spending review. The Treasury looks forward to seeing the Committee's report in due course.

March 2009

Supplementary memorandum by HM Treasury

INTRODUCTION

Q1. *What, in HM Treasury's view, are the chief merits and disadvantages of the Barnett formula as the basis for funding the Devolved Administrations (DAs)?*

A. The Barnett formula has pragmatic strengths such as being relatively simple, administratively efficient, involving little negotiation in spending reviews, transparent, providing stable and predictable funding, and allowing the devolved administrations to determine their own policies and priorities in allocating their block budgets. The devolved funding rules also embody important principles including:

— equity of treatment in the way public spending rules apply to the devolved administrations and England;

— pooling of taxes collected at UK level, and subsequent country public spending allocations being made on the basis of equal comparable spending per head increases through the Barnett formula; and

— a high degree of devolution of spending decisions ,while ensuring relatively little macroeconomic risk at the UK level and country level.

While we recognise that no system for allocating funding is perfect, the Barnett formula has stood the test of time well.

APPLICATION OF THE FORMULA IN PRACTICE

Q2. *It remains unclear how, in practice, the Barnett formula actually works—how changes in spending for England translate into changes in the block grants for the Scottish Parliament, National Assembly for Wales and Northern Ireland Assembly. Please show us how changes in spending for England (at the sub-programme level used in the Statement of Funding Policy) translated into changes in the block grants for Scotland, Wales and Northern Ireland, for the period from 2003–4 to 2007–8.*

Q3. *Please show how budgeted changes in spending at sub-programme level from 2007–8 over the period of the current spending review (ie to 2009–10) are expected to impact the block grants to the devolved administrations in Scotland, Wales and Northern Ireland. (The material submitted in response to this should also include planned changes arising from the 2007 and 2008 Budgets and the 2008 Pre Budget Review. We would appreciate a further update after the 2009 Budget.)*

A. The information sought by the Committee is available as follows. The evidence which the Treasury has already provided to the Committee explains how the Barnett formula works and provides a worked example. The devolved administrations are provided with unhypothecated block (rather than disaggregated by programme/sub programme) increases in spending reviews and these are published in spending review White Papers. The subsequent calculation of the block grants is set out in the territorial offices' departmental/annual reports. In year changes to the block grants are made through Supplementary Estimates which the territorial offices present to Parliament. The Scotland and Wales Offices' annual reports also provide details of in year spending changes to Departmental Expenditure Limits.

Q4. *The 2008 edition of the Public Expenditure Survey Analyses, table 9.2, provides a break-down of overall public spending by nation and region—but does not distinguish between spending by the devolved administrations and that of the UK Government. Please provide a version of that table, identifying spending between the different governments involved.*

A. Further information is provided in other tables of PESA. Table 9.11 of PESA shows spending by country, region and function. Table 9.17 of PESA identifies spending on services for Scotland, Wales and Northern Ireland, distinguishing devolved and reserved spending.

Q5. *What criteria does HM Treasury apply in determining whether spending is classed as "England" spending (so triggering consequential payments under the Formula) or as "UK" spending (so not leading to consequential payments)?*

A. For the purposes of the application of the Barnett formula public spending is divided into comparable and non comparable spending. Comparability is defined in the Statement of Funding Policy as the extent to which services delivered by UK Government departments correspond to services within the budgets of the devolved administrations. The devolution settlements and associated legislation determine the extent of devolution in

Scotland, Wales and Northern Ireland. Spending which is non comparable is that which is UK wide and for the benefit of the whole UK. The details of comparable and non comparable spending are published in Annex C of the Statement of Funding Policy.

Q6. *What criteria are used to determine whether it is appropriate to by-pass the Formula? Has the scope for "Formula by-pass" has changed since devolution? To what extent have measures such as EU Objective 1/Convergence Fund funding for Wales and Northern Ireland (PEACE II) cushioned the system from pressures caused by the failure of the Barnett Formula arrangements to provide funding on the basis of need? What will happen when these streams of additional funding come to an end?*

A. We assume that the term Formula by pass means increases in spending outside the Barnett determined increases in spending reviews. The Committee will be aware that when the Barnett formula was first introduced there were some programmes of spending such as industry and agriculture spending which were outside the Barnett block. However the Barnett formula currently applies to all changes in comparable DEL spending of UK Government departments in spending reviews and therefore the scope for by-passing the Formula is in that sense negligible, although it is possible for the Treasury to agree additions if appropriate. In year there is no automatic access to the Reserve and Reserve claims are assessed on a case-by-case basis as set out in the Statement of Funding Policy. The Barnett formula can be used to determine Reserve claims where appropriate. In practice Reserve claims are rare. Since 2005 spending financed by EU receipts is determined both for UK departments and devolved administrations by the amount of receipts (not by the Barnett formula). This approach applies to EU receipts generally not just Objective 1 and PEACE funding. When the stream of EU receipts ends the spending financed by those receipts ends too.

Q7. *Does the working of the Formula allow the Devolved Administrations sufficient scope to shape their own policy agendas?*

A. The Formula is used to calculate changes to the block DEL budgets. The devolved administrations have freedom to allocate the block budgets to reflect their own policies and priorities. Since devolution was introduced there has been considerable policy diversity across the UK.

Q8. *Recent Freedom of Information requests have confirmed that the Treasury or the Cabinet Office carried out a number of internal reviews of the relative needs of Scotland, Wales and Northern Ireland following the Needs Assessment exercise published in 1979. Please confirm exactly when each of these reviews was carried out, what the outcome of each exercise was, and what methodology was applied on each occasion.*

A. A formal interdepartmental needs assessment was carried out by the Treasury in consultation with interested departments in the 1970s and was published in 1979. Although the study was extensive it did not come to an agreed conclusion and it was not implemented. The Barnett formula was introduced at around this time. We are aware that in the period between 1980 and 1997 consideration was given to carrying out a new formal interdepartmental needs assessment, but no new one was agreed. We are also aware that in this period reference was made from time to time to the 1979 needs assessment methodology in public spending negotiations, but as far as we are aware no agreement on needs was reached. Since 1997 the Barnett formula has been regularly updated and published in the Statement of Funding Policy and this remains the Government's policy.

DATA QUALITY AND AVAILABILITY

Q9. *Does HM Treasury consider the data available about the territorial distribution of public spending across the UK to be adequate?*

A. Data on public spending is published annually in Public Expenditure Statistical Analyses. Over the years the Treasury has put considerable effort, with departments and devolved administrations, into ensuring extensive and good quality data in PESA. In addition the territorial offices publish a considerable amount of data in their annual reports and Estimates. Beyond that the devolved administrations produce extensive budget reports, accounts and Estimates for their own elected bodies.

NEED FOR REFORM/ALTERNATIVES TO THE EXISTING FORMULA

Q10. *If the Barnett Formula were to be replaced by a system more directly reflecting relative needs, costs of services or a combination of both, what factors should be considered as part of a needs assessment?*

A. Government policy on the devolved funding arrangements is set out in the Statement of Funding Policy. While the Barnett formula is regularly updated there are no plans to review the formula so the question of what factors should be considered as part of a needs assessment has not been assessed.

Q11. *What would be the implications of carrying out such a needs assessment? What resources, in personnel and otherwise, would HM Treasury think would be needed to carry out such an assessment?*

A. No assessment has been made of the resources which would be necessary to carry out a needs assessment for the reasons given above.

Q12. *Would it be appropriate for HM Treasury to do this, or should it be undertaken by an impartial body reporting to all four governments rather than a department of one of them?*

A. The devolved funding arrangements are part of the UK wide public spending framework for which the Treasury is responsible. However no assessment has been made of who should carry out a needs assessment for the reasons given above.

Q13. *Similarly, should HM Treasury continue to determine matters relating to the Barnett Formula such as the classification of spending as UK wide or England only or whether the Formula should be by-passed?*

A. As noted above the devolved funding arrangements are part of the UK wide public spending framework for which the Treasury is responsible. However the devolved administrations are consulted when the Statement of Funding Policy, which informs the Treasury's approach, is updated.

March 2009

Examination of Witnesses

Witnesses: Ms HELEN BAILEY, Director of the Public Services and Growth Directorate, Ms HELENE RADCLIFFE, Team Leader of the Devolved Countries Unit, and MR MARK PARKINSON, Devolution Branch Head in the Devolved Countries Unit, Her Majesty's Treasury, MR JIM GALLAGHER, Director General Devolution, Ministry of Justice/Cabinet Office, examined.

Q412 *Chairman:* Good afternoon and thank you for coming, and thank you for submitting some documents to us which we have read with interest, but I have to say with a certain disappointment which no doubt that will emerge in the course of the afternoon. I am sure you have all given evidence at these sessions before but I perhaps ought to remind you that evidence sessions are broadcast live on the internet and a full transcript is going to be taken. You will have an opportunity to make small corrections to the transcript but you will not be able to alter any of the sense of what you have said. I think perhaps I ought to make it clear right at the outset to you that you it is open to you supply the Committee with any additional evidence if there is some additional evidence you feel you ought to supply, and in return the Committee is in a position to ask you to supply additional evidence if we do not think that we have sufficient evidence. I wonder if you would be kind enough to introduce yourselves and tell us what you all do and then we can perhaps ask you questions.
Ms Bailey: Thank you very much for that introduction. This is actually the first time certainly that I have given evidence before a select committee so I am grateful for the advice you have given, Chairman.

We are very pleased to be here at the behest of Treasury ministers. We represent Her Majesty's Treasury, which is—and I think this is just worth saying in this context—a UK-wide government department concerned with fiscal policy and with public spending across the United Kingdom as well as with the wider economic matters which have featured recently in the public press. Our role is to answer questions on both the written evidence we have already supplied to you, to which you have alluded, and to attempt to deal with factual matters in relation to the operation of the Formula and in relation to the Treasury's work in that respect. Let me introduce my team. I have got on my right Helene Radcliffe, who is the Team Leader of the devolved administrations unit in the Treasury, and Mark Parkinson, who is an acknowledged expert on the operation of the Barnett Formula. I am Helen Bailey and I am a Director in the Public Services and Growth Directorate at Her Majesty's Treasury, and we look very forward very much to being able to assist you in any way we can this afternoon.
Mr Gallagher: I would like to introduce myself, Chairman. My name is Jim Gallagher and I am the Director General for Devolution in the Ministry of Justice and I work with Treasury colleagues.

Q413 *Chairman:* Thank you very much indeed. Perhaps I could ask the first question, which I hope is relatively clear. Does the Treasury think that the Barnett Formula treats all four parts of the UK fairly?

Ms Bailey: We think in the Treasury that the advantages of the Barnett Formula are that it gives an absolute increase in spending for every part of the United Kingdom which is the same when a spending decision is made by the UK Government. It has the merits of longevity, transparency and of familiarity.

Q414 *Chairman:* That was not quite what I asked you actually, with respect. Do you think it has the advantage of fairness?

Ms Bailey: In that it provides an absolute similar amount of money to each devolved administration, that speaks to its fairness. I think fairness is always a subjective issue and I think as officials we would wish to leave that there. It is perhaps worth saying that there is a dispute resolution mechanism built into the Formula, which can be triggered and which would take place in the form of a joint ministerial committee, and it may be significant to point out that that has never yet been triggered.

Q415 *Chairman:* I am sorry, I am trying to follow. Are you saying that you are not prepared to tell us whether the Treasury thinks that it is a fair formula, or are you saying that in your view it is a fair formula because it is clear, relatively simple and has operated for a long time?

Ms Bailey: I think we are saying, as you have just said, that it has the advantages of being clear and very well understood and it is fair in that it provides an absolute comparable level of increase in funding to each of the devolved administrations. Whether in any wider sense it was perceived to be fair or not I think is a matter for committees like yourselves to provide evidence to Government on.

Q416 *Chairman:* Well, not entirely because the Treasury has done these fairness exercises, has it not? You did one in the seventies and you did one in the eighties.

Ms Bailey: Indeed.

Q417 *Chairman:* You assessed the fairness, or otherwise, of the allocation of resources.

Ms Bailey: The work which was undertaken would inform the operation of the Formula in very different circumstances. Since the publication of the Funding Statement in 1999 we have kept the Formula under review at every Comprehensive Spending Review but we have not undertaken a needs assessment since then.

Q418 *Chairman:* You have not undertaken a needs assessment upon which there was agreement, but are you telling us that the Treasury has not undertaken any kinds of needs assessment between the four parts of the UK? Surely not? It must have done.

Ms Bailey: The Treasury looks at the way in which we apportion funding every time we do a Comprehensive Spending Review, so we did in 2004 and we did in 2007. We have not undertaken any wider full needs assessment.

Q419 *Chairman:* When you look at the allocation of spending between the four parts of the UK, does the fairness of the spending enter into the Treasury's calculations at all?

Ms Bailey: I think I would have to press you on what you meant by "fairness".

Q420 *Chairman:* I mean that on the whole people get the same amount of money for the same amount of services to deal with the same amount of problems. You have done it. You know what "fairness" is because you did an assessment of needs in the seventies and you did another one in the eighties, so there is nothing mysterious about bringing fairness into the equation, surely?

Ms Bailey: I think the bases on which we allocated money in the seventies and eighties and now are very different. The operations of the devolved administrations have been in place since 1999 and they themselves have considerable latitude to decide how to spend the money they get through the Formula on the services for people within their areas.

Q421 *Chairman:* So what is the difference? Why has it changed? If it is a different system of allocation now to what it was in the seventies and eighties, why? What is different?

Ms Bailey: Forgive me, I do not think I said that the system of allocation was different, but the circumstances in which we are operating that system are.

Q422 *Chairman:* All right. So what is the difference then?

Ms Bailey: The difference at the moment, the most obvious difference, is that we have the devolved administrations who have, as I say, considerable latitude themselves to decide how to apportion the funding they get in order to deal with their own perception of what is fair and reasonable within their own territories.

Q423 *Chairman:* Can I just ask you one final question, and then no doubt other people will want to join in. Do you think it will be possible to produce a system of allocation of resources between the four parts of the United Kingdom which is fairer than the one used at present?

Ms Bailey: I think in answering that question we would need to get some agreement about what constitutes "fairness", what constitutes "need", how those were measured and how that agreement was to be achieved. I am sure that were there such agreement it would be possible to come to an alternative system which dealt with it. At the moment the Treasury is not being asked to do that work and therefore we, as officials, have not addressed ourselves to that question.

Chairman: You have not done it unofficially? You may not have an agreement, as you did in the seventies, but surely—I mean, you do it for local authorities all the time.

Q424 *Baroness Hollis of Heigham:* Can I just come in on that? As far as I can see, your definition of "fairness" in response to the Chairman's question is that given the historic baseline, the Formula is fair because since then there have been proportionate increases in expenditure, which of course bedevils the question as to where you start from and where it has appropriately adjusted. I gather that you come from Islington. You would not accept that as a fair way of allocating local government expenditure, to take a snapshot back in 1979 and just do a percentage increase by virtue of population change with no other consideration subsequently, would you?

Ms Bailey: I am here to speak for Her Majesty's Treasury and not for any previous role, I hope, but I think it is fair to say that the way in which local government funding is distributed in England—it is different in the devolved administrations and this is the point you are hinting at, I think—is highly contested and I am sure that there would be many different views of what was fair in absolute terms as there are local authorities, and I suspect that also applies to devolved administrations. From the Treasury point of view, straightforwardly, we are not currently engaged in doing any work to say, "Is this fair?" in any absolute terms and we would require some ministerial or other steer as to what constituted "fair" in those terms.

Q425 *Lord Forsyth of Drumlean:* Just following up on the local government point, the formula which is used for allocating money to local government is highly complicated because it takes account, or tries to take account of some basis of need and that formula is always defended on the basis that it is fairer and that simply to allocate money on the basis of population but did not take account of sparsity of population, rurality, all these issues, would not be fair. How does the Treasury square having one view of allocating money for local government—and by

the way, the devolved administrations all see similar formulae to allocate the money—with taking the view that a simple population-based thing, which may be convenient? How do they square that difference in policy?

Ms Bailey: What we would say is that, as you say, the local government funding system is actually not a matter for the Treasury, so it is a matter for the Department of Communities and Local Government. At the level where it impacts on public spending, I am not denying that we have an interest in it, but it is not something that we ourselves administer. What we would say is that the devolved administrations have considerable latitude themselves to decide how to distribute the income they get from Government to local authorities. There is a range of functions with local authorities are responsible for—

Q426 *Lord Forsyth of Drumlean:* That is a red herring. I am asking you about the methodology and when you say the Treasury has no responsibility, the Treasury has an absolute responsibility for value for money, for making sure that resources are spent properly, and in the case of local government the money is distributed on the basis of some degree of need and the Treasury do intervene, and I have seen them do it, as to how the Formula is calculated because it has expenditure implications. So why is there this difference of view? That is the question, which you are not really addressing.

Ms Bailey: Forgive me, I did not say that the Treasury had no interest, I said that the Treasury did not administer the Formula. We do have an interest, and I entirely take your point that we have a responsibility for value for money and a responsibility for overall public spending. I take that point entirely. I think we have taken the view that the operation of the Barnett Formula in terms of the devolved administrations provides the framework within which they can make their own allocations to local government, but the functions of local government and the functions of the devolved administrations are not the same and that is the situation we are now in.

Q427 *Lord Forsyth of Drumlean:* Under the previous regime Lord Lang and I were Secretaries of State and we still had that freedom. This is not new. This is not an aspect of having a Scottish Parliament and, as I recall, the Treasury in my day was absolutely desperate to have a needs-based system, and in the Scottish Office we were doing everything we could to resist it because we thought we would lose out. So what has changed?

Ms Bailey: I am afraid I cannot comment because your knowledge is greater than mine.

Q428 *Chairman:* But you can comment, surely, on the general point which is being raised? How can the Government at one and the same time use a criterion of fairness in relation to one unit of government, local authority, and deny totally that fairness should come into the allocation of resources between the four parts of the UK? It is just inconsistent.

Mr Parkinson: The Barnett Formula is used to allocate a block of funding which comprises a number of different spending heads—health, education, local government, transport, and so on— and in England each of those has a different allocation formula, and some are not allocated by formula at all. As you say, each of the countries has got its own formula for allocating those as well. There is no single formula overarching all of those block headings, so it is a different problem from the problem of allocating one block of spending like health or local government. It is a multi-programme task.

Q429 *Lord Forsyth of Drumlean:* We are not talking about the additional amounts, which are population-based, we are talking about the baseline.

Mr Parkinson: Yes, but the problem, going back to 1979, is that at the end of the day there was no agreed methodology for allocating a multi-programme block of that kind where in each constituent country a different formula was used in each constituent part, so it is naturally complex. Local government is complex, but this is at a level of greater complexity because it is a multi-programme block.

Q430 *Lord Rooker:* Leaving aside the issue of fairness, what are the disadvantages of using the Barnett Formula as it currently exists?

Ms Bailey: I am conscious that you are one of three committees currently looking at the Barnett Formula and clearly there is some dissatisfaction, or there must be, in the way it operates. While many people have suggested that it could be better, we have yet to see a formula which commands the support of all the devolved administrations and the UK Government.

Q431 *Chairman:* Have you tried to get one?

Ms Bailey: I think at the moment the Treasury is in a position where we are listening to the outcome of this Committee, the outcome of the reviews that are taking place concurrently, and ministers will take a view on that basis.

Q432 *Lord Rooker:* Are there any disadvantages in operating the formula at the present time?

Mr Gallagher: Many people do see some disadvantages. The huge advantages that Helen has referred to and the essential advantage is that it gives adminstive simplicity and stability. The

disadvantage is that some people suggest, and the Chairman suggested, it is not easy to justify the outcomes, whether they are fair or not. Other people say that a disadvantage is that it does not provide fiscal accountability. Those are the disadvantages that various people mention.

Q433 *Lord Rooker:* Yes, I know. I am just asking, with respect, the Treasury. The fact is you were asked specifically in one of the written questions what were the merits and disadvantages. The second part of the question was completely ignored in your written answer. You did not list anything. Therefore, the assumption has to be you gave us all what you saw were positive issues, the merits, and there are not any disadvantages. That is how I read that. You point out the first one as being simple. I have to say, at the risk of bringing up the past, anything that is simple is unfair. The classic example, of course, is the Community Charge. Simplicity is unfair. I will ask you again, are there any disadvantages to the current operation of the Barnett Formula from the Treasury's point of view?

Ms Bailey: I think you will find in the situation where we have to face you as the officials who operate the Formula, not the people who gave rise to it, it is the formula that we have got and we have not been asked, other than by yourselves—I appreciate what you say about our answer to your question and I am sorry you feel as you do about it—to give an opinion collectively or personally on the merits and demerits of it but merely to operate it.

Baroness Hollis of Heigham: But it does not happen like that!

Q434 *Lord Lang of Monkton:* I do not know when the questions were sent to you from the Committee but we got your answers, in my case, yesterday and those answers are very sparse, very thin, and they refer to other documents which I have not had the opportunity to check, although from those who have checked up I understand the documents referred to do not in every case answer the questions asked. Just to follow up on Lord Rooker's point, the first question you were asked was, what are the chief merits and disadvantages, and you have given us no disadvantages. I think the point has been well made already that that is an inadequate situation. We expect you to come to the Committee ready to answer the questions we put to you. So far as the merits you refer to, they are all (as you call them) "pragmatic strengths", in other words they are administratively convenient to the Treasury, but what about the interests of the people of Scotland, Northern Ireland, Wales, and indeed England? What about the interests of the country? What about the considerations of need? You refer to it being relatively simple, administratively efficient and involving little negotiation. Is that a plus? Is that a good point in Spending Reviews? "Transparent"—well, that is highly controversial, which is one of the reasons our Committee is meeting—and "stable" and "predictable". Why no mention of economic efficiency? You know from reading our minutes, as I assume you have done, of previous meetings of this Committee that that is an issue we are touching on. Why no reference to economic efficiency?

Ms Bailey: I think we have done our best to confine our answers to you—and I apologise if you find them inadequate—to the comments we can make to the officials responsible for managing the system at the moment. We are in the disadvantageous position that we are not asked as officials to think about what sort of system would be ideal but to think about the practicalities, or otherwise, of operating the system at the moment. You have asked about whether or not simplicity—Lord Rooker asked that question—meant that it was fair. If we go back to a system prior to the Formula being in operation then, as my colleague has already said, there is a number of funding streams which are comprised within the devolved pot, all of which would be the subject of separate negotiation, the complexity of which could well have left the various departments in those days, the devolved administrations now, in a situation of considerable uncertainty as to their funding and as to their allocation. The advantage this has is that there is a degree of certainty and security about that and that is certainly in the interests of the wider efficiency and of the UK Government.

Q435 *Lord Lang of Monkton:* But you are the Treasury. You are not just responsible for the figures that are dished out, you are responsible for getting value for money for the taxpayer and that does not seem to concern you at all in what are substantial sums being dispersed?

Ms Bailey: Forgive me, it does concern us. We are also operating a system in this complex devolved world in which we now live where not only are we responsible for value for money for the UK taxpayer but we are responsible for devolving money to administrations which have their own accountability and have their own interests in getting value for money as well. So it is a complex and delicate situation in which we seek to operate that.

Q436 *Lord Lang of Monkton:* It is getting more complex and more delicate! Can I ask you about need? You do not mention need in your answer.

Ms Bailey: We are back, I think, to the conversation we were having just now. There was some element of need factored into the original baseline for the Formula. What the Formula does is to up-rate with

each change in spending the amount of money which passes through the devolved administrations. It does not seek to do a new needs analysis every time we pass the money across to the administrations.

Q437 *Lord Lang of Monkton:* I will not pursue that now because it has been touched upon under "fairness" to a large extent. I really wanted to ask you about convergence. Why is there no mention of convergence in your answer? Is that a merit or a disadvantage, or is it something that you are bound to?

Ms Radcliffe: In terms of convergence, the actual mechanics of how the Formula works, is that over time, other things being equal, we might expect to see some degree of convergence because of the way the Formula actually works.

Q438 *Lord Lang of Monkton:* Was it part of the purpose of the Formula to create convergence?

Ms Radcliffe: As I say, certainly if you look at the way the Formula actually operates—

Q439 *Lord Lang of Monkton:* Yes, I know that, you have just said that, but I am not asking you that. I am asking you, was it the purpose?

Ms Radcliffe: Was it an intention? I think the Formula was introduced quite a long time ago now. We are talking about roughly 30 years

Q440 *Lord Lang of Monkton:* Some of us were alive and some of us came into Parliament as it came into operation!

Ms Radcliffe: I think it is quite difficult, arguably, to distinguish between intention and purpose and exactly what that might have been at that time, but I think the key point in this is that if you actually look at the way in which the Formula operates then you would expect that over time it would deliver a certain amount of convergence.

Q441 *Lord Lang of Monkton:* Right. I think you are saying it is a convergent Formula. You are also saying, however, that it was not your intention. In that case, it should have been your intention that it should not be a convergent Formula, in which case why did you do nothing to amend it?

Ms Radcliffe: No, what I am saying simply is that the way the Formula works means that over time, other things being equal, because of the way it works mathematically you might expect to see a degree of convergence.

Q442 *Lord Lang of Monkton:* You have not said whether you regard that as a good thing or a bad thing.

Ms Radcliffe: It is just the mathematical properties—

Q443 *Lord Lang of Monkton:* You have no view on it?
Ms Radcliffe: No.

Q444 *Chairman:* You do know Lord Barnett's view of his Formula now, do you?
Ms Bailey: We have seen the evidence.
Ms Radcliffe: Yes.

Q445 *Chairman:* You have seen the evidence he gave to this Committee?
Ms Radcliffe: Yes.

Q446 *Chairman:* I do not think he is elevating it to quite the same extent the Treasury is. His view was that it was a short-term measure, that it is long overdue for reform, and indeed that it should be a needs-based assessment rather than the existing one. He says that convergence really did not enter into it at the time it was draw up, and indeed he told us that nobody told him that there was a needs assessment exercise going on in the Treasury for a period of four years. So somehow or other the operation of the Barnett Formula has been enervated from what was a short-term, I imagine fairly political measure, up into tablets of stone which, according to you, are un-amendable. It is the most extraordinary position.
Ms Bailey: Forgive me, Chairman, I do not think we have said they are un-amendable.

Q447 *Chairman:* You said you have got no views as to whether they should be amended.
Ms Bailey: We have no views as to whether they should be amended.
Chairman: You must have.

Q448 *Baroness Hollis of Heigham:* Forgive me, I was never an elevated Secretary of State but even at just a junior ministerial level within DWP our officials, directors, were expected to take on the responsibility of being guardians of particular benefits and when those benefits became misaligned from their original purpose or were producing perverse consequences they were expected, as part of their job at that level of seniority, to report back to the relevant minister, to ask the minister whether the minister would wish for a further review, and normally he would say yes. Are you saying that the role of the Treasury in this has been completely passive throughout, that it is handed down now and you have just got on with it and nobody has ever raised the question with ministers subsequently, "Oh, Minister, this is now no longer as fair as we thought it might have been. We need to review this"? That is the role of senior civil servants, to act as guardians of a particular formula or distribution and to bring it to the Minister's attention when they think it is perhaps becoming somewhat deformed. Has this never happened?
Ms Bailey: To be honest, I am relatively recently in the Treasury. I do not know whether it has ever happened. All I can tell you is that we are doing no work of that sort at the moment.
Mr Parkinson: The opportunity to change that, the main opportunity, was when devolution was introduced. That would have been a natural time to do it and ministers took a conscious decision that the Barnett block in the funding arrangements would be part of the Devolution Settlement and that was the basis on which the devolution referenda took place. Obviously at that stage ministers did take a conscious decision that that is what they wanted to do.

Q449 *Baroness Hollis of Heigham:* It is expected to be part of their ongoing, non-passive responsibility as guardians of public money.
Mr Parkinson: Obviously we keep spending under review and with every Spending Review ministers have an opportunity to update the Barnett Formula and ministers have the opportunity to change it more radically if they wish.
Ms Bailey: The Spending Review is the appropriate time to do that because we are looking ahead over three years' worth of public spending and inviting ministers to consider in the round what their priorities are and where they would wish to allocate that money. So indeed that opportunity is available. What we are saying is that it has not been taken.

Q450 *Lord Lang of Monkton:* But the convergence, I think we have established, is a fact of the Formula, even though it may be qualified and hard to pin down in some cases, and it is in large measure a consequence of the fact that the size of the Scottish block and some of the other blocks in the United Kingdom were larger per head of the population and therefore by applying the Barnett Formula to those larger blocks it created different results. At no time in your reviews of Government spending, whether annual, tri-annual or in what other form, have you contemplate whether or not that was fair, economically efficient or desirable in any way.
Ms Bailey: I am sorry to reiterate something we have already said, but I think what we are saying is that every time we undertake a review of public spending—and we are coming to the end of the CSR period we are currently in and we will have an opportunity to ask the question again—we ask ministers whether they think it would be appropriate to undertake that review.

11 March 2009   Ms Helen Bailey, Ms Helene Radcliffe, Mr Mark Parkinson
and Mr Jim Gallagher

Q451 Lord Lang of Monkton: But in your answer to the question—and I am still on question one here—you talk about "equity of treatment in the way public spending rules apply to the devolved administrations and England". It is hardly equity of treatment when there is this inherent imbalance at the very outset. You also talk about the basis of "equal comparable spending per head increases to the Barnett Formula". That, of course, disguises the fact that you were changing to a cash terms per head percentage, which of course is a smaller percentage per head and thus creates the convergence?
Ms Bailey: Indeed.

Q452 Lord Lang of Monkton: Do you not think these facts should be brought out more fully and how are they justified in terms of what you call "equity" or "equal comparable spending"?
Ms Bailey: I think what we are trying to say is that the property of the Formula and, as you say and as my colleague has already said, if all things were equal, there would be a degree of convergence in the Formula. What we are trying to achieve is the point I made right at the beginning, which is that there is an equal up-rating across the United Kingdom of spending in absolute terms, and I agree with your analysis that in percentage terms there is a difference and that leads, as you say, to a degree of convergence. That means that when we change spending in one part of the United Kingdom we change it in equivalent fashion across the United Kingdom. That is the equity of which we spoke.

Q453 Lord Forsyth of Drumlean: If you thought spending was three years ago per head, say in Scotland or Wales—I will not say "fair" but justified at that level and if the function of the Formula is to produce convergence, which means that the spending per head will be reduced in Scotland and Wales, how can you hold these two positions at the same time? Does it not create a doubt in your mind that if we are moving towards convergence, if we started from a position where there was an extra level of expenditure and we thought that that was a good use of taxpayers' money, surely we are going off the rails if we are moving towards convergence, and therefore we need to have some means of adjusting this Formula which takes account of some basis of need? Why do you not see that as a problem?
Ms Bailey: I think it is perhaps worth introducing into the conversation the fact that not all of the spending which takes place in the devolved administrations points to the social security spending, it is predicated by—

Q454 Lord Forsyth of Drumlean: That is a total red herring. Let us focus on this point. If it was right to have spending on health in Scotland at 23 per cent more per head than in England and if the function of the Formula will be to move towards convergence, given that they have higher mortality and morbidity rates than the rest at what point do you say, "Actually, we need to stop this mathematical machine and actually look at whether we are getting value for money and whether we meet the needs"?
Ms Radcliffe: There is quite a few issues there, but as you have said and as we have all agreed, in theory, given the way the Formula actually works you might expect to see a degree of convergence—

Q455 Lord Forsyth of Drumlean: It is not a theory, it is happening.
Ms Radcliffe: I think if you look at the PESA data there is limited evidence that it is happening, but I guess the point is, in answer to your question, that if over time ministers felt that convergence was happening too strongly it would be for them at that point to do something about it. The fact is that we have had this Formula in operation for a very, very long time and the PESA data showed, depending on what time period you are looking at, that it is actually quite difficult—
Chairman: Longevity is their argument, with respect.

Q456 Lord Moser: I find the whole convergence business quite confusing, including the Treasury's attitude. I think at the beginning some people said convergence was one of the aims, some people said it was almost accidental and some witnesses say, "Yes, it has happened," and some people say, "It hasn't really happened." Could I ask you a straight question on your opinions rather than on the facts? In your present Treasury view is convergence a good thing? Is this something you welcome? Is it something that worries you? Your views.
Ms Radcliffe: I think, as we have all recognised, it is simply just a mathematical proxy of the way the Formula works that you might expect to see some convergence over time. As to the extent to which that has actually happened, if you look at the PESA data it is quite difficult to draw firm conclusions about the trend. In policy terms there is no preset view or judgment over what time path convergence might or indeed should happen.

Q457 Lord Moser: Do you really mean that for all these years when the Treasury has been dealing with this you were sort of totally uninterested in whether they were converging or not converging? There must be a Treasury view because, as you say, it is meant to be the essence of the Formula and some people would say that if it is not happening then the Treasury should take steps to make it happen. There must be a Treasury view at least on whether you regard this as a desirable characteristic or not? It is a straightforward question.

Ms Bailey: I hate to disappoint you, but there is simply not a Treasury view in quite the way you have suggested there should be.

Q458 *Lord Moser:* I did not say it should be, but I would expect it. As a civil servant, I know the Treasury does have views occasionally! I am simply asking you to say how you regard the behaviour of the Formula.

Ms Bailey: I think we regard the behaviour of the Formula quite neutrally, which is one of the problems in answering your questions on it, and I think it is further complicated, given some of the examples we have heard around the table, by the fact that when the devolved administrations receive the money they themselves can choose how to apportion it between the various functions they spend it on, so it may be that they receive an up-rating in the funding because there is an up-rating expenditure on one element across the UK and decide in fact to spend it on something else themselves. Now, that is increasingly with devolution a matter for them rather than a matter for us, except in the manner which you have suggested to us. We have an overall concern for value for money in the quantum of public spending.

Q459 *Chairman:* I wonder if you could point out to me in the document in which you have answered our questions where there is expressed the view that the Treasury is neutral as to the operation of the Barnett Formula?

Ms Bailey: I do not think we have written that down, but that is the implication of what we have said.

Q460 *Chairman:* No, it is not, with respect. Look at the answer to question one. I do not want to go on about this or to cross-examine you as though it was the Old Bailey, but you start off by saying the Barnett Formula has pragmatic strengths. You say you know about its weaknesses but describe it as being "relatively simple" and "administratively efficient", *et cetera, et cetera.* There is not a word in there saying that the Treasury is neutral as to the way it operates.

Ms Bailey: Forgive me, when I answered Lord Moser's question he was asking me whether we thought convergence was a good thing and whether we had a view on that. When I expressed neutrality, it was neutrality as to whether or not that was a good thing. We have acknowledged that it is the property of the Formula and that it is likely to happen, all other things being equal, and there is a number of things which determine whether or not it will be convergent or not. What we have said here—

Q461 *Lord Moser:* It is not totally the property of the Formula. I do not think that is correct, with respect, because it has not actually happened quite as predicted. I speak as a statistician. I do not think it is a more dramatic characteristic of the Formula and that is why it is quite important. Supposing this Committee was so minded to have a new scheme. I wonder whether the Treasury would say, "Oh, that's good. That's really converging the scheme," or whether they would say, "Too bad, that's not going to be a converging scheme." I am simply trying to get you to express a view, the Treasury view, on convergence. You say you do not have one?

Ms Bailey: That is absolutely right, we do not have a view on convergence. We do have a view on the Formula and that is expressed in our answer to question one.

Q462 *Lord Rowe-Beddoe:* Am I correct in understanding that since the devolution of 1999 there has been no review of the Formula or working of the Formula in the Treasury? This is what I think you said.

Ms Bailey: There has been no major review of the Formula, but what we have also said is that with every Spending Review we keep under consideration the operation of that Formula and we have had Spending Reviews in 2004 and 2007, and probably previous to that, and at each of those we will have looked at the operation of the Formula. But the statement of funding policy which was published in 1999, and which has been most recently updated in 2007, absolutely governs the way in which the Formula operates and in which we operate it.

Q463 *Baroness Hollis of Heigham:* The implication of what you are saying seems to be that providing the Formula is simple to administer, the Treasury is neutral as to its outcome, given convergence?

Ms Bailey: Forgive me, I do not think I said that. The point on which I have expressed absolute neutrality, which is a matter for ministers rather than ourselves, is on whether or not convergence is a good thing and a desirable thing. We have expressed in our answers— and the Chairman has drawn our attention to this— the reasons why we think there are many merits to the operation of the Formula and that we would have wish to see any replacement to it operating with those merits and potentially others as ministers saw fit.

Q464 *Lord Rowe-Beddoe:* The implication, we have heard from Lord Barnett, was that this was a political fix brought in at the time a year or two before there were going to be major referenda in Wales and Scotland with regard to devolution. It did not happen at that time, but the fix was good enough to continue as it would take away potential arguments. I can quite understand why in 1999 nobody wanted to change it because that was a very delicate moment in political history, but I still cannot quite grasp why, as you say, every three years or so there is no conscious decision as to whether we are getting value for money and whether it is meeting the needs of the devolved administrations.

Mr Parkinson: The statement of funding policy is updated on each Spending Review. We publish a new statement of funding policy in each Spending Review and we update the Barnett Formula every three years, and that provides an opportunity for the devolved administrations, the territorial Secretaries of State and the Treasury ministers to review whether more fundamental changes are needed. Those opportunities arise in every Spending Review. Now, the devolved administrations themselves are not seeking major changes to the Barnett Formula. We know, of course, that the SNP would ultimately want fiscal autonomy, but for the time being it is not seeking to change the Barnett Formula itself, and the Formula has existed under Labour and Conservative administrations since 1980, so there is a broad consensus behind it. It is open to criticism and we have acknowledged in the evidence to you that no system is perfect, but the criticisms can be based on misconceptions. The main criticism in England is of a Scottish provision, but that is not a feature of the Barnett Formula. The Barnett Formula provides an equal spending per head increase. It is not a criticism of the Barnett Formula. The criticism in Scotland, Wales and Northern Ireland—and there is criticism—is about Barnett convergence, the Barnett squeeze, but that, as we have said, is a mathematical property of the Formula. The fundamental point is that it produces a sustained increase. Whether you live in Scotland, Wales, Northern Ireland or England, you have the same increase in comparable spending per head. There is a fundamental sense of fairness about that. There is disagreement. We are not saying that there is no disagreement and people have put forward alternatives based on needs, and so on, although there is no consensus as to how a needs-based formula would work, but there is that sort of broad consensus behind the Barnett Formula. But, as I say, every three years the devolved administrations can ask us for a fundamental review if they want. The Secretary of State can do so and the Treasury ministers can authorise that.

Q465 *Lord Forsyth of Drumlean:* Could I just ask Mr Parkinson, and perhaps Mr Gallagher may remember this from his previous existence, certainly when I was a Secretary of State in 1996 the Treasury did have a view on the Barnett Formula—and, by the way, when we talk about the Barnett Formula we are not just talking about the Formula allocation, we are talking about the whole method of distribution of funds to the devolved administrations. The Treasury did have a view and the Scottish Office (as it then was) had a view, and the Treasury's view was that it would like to move to a needs-based system for allocating resources to the devolved administrations. I do not know if you can recall that. Could the Treasury officials tell me—and if not this afternoon perhaps they could write to us—when did the Treasury cease to have that view?

Mr Parkinson: We are aware—and you are correct, we do not—that in the period between 1980 and 1997 the Treasury did from time to time use the needs assessment methodology to consider whether Scotland was over-provided and used the arguments in that needs assessment to consider the spending surveys in that time making the case as to whether adjustment should be made in the Scottish provision and we have released papers recently which confirm that was the case, but certainly since 1997 one of the big changes for devolution is that the funding principles are now completely transparent. They are published and there has been no consideration in Spending Reviews of the kinds of adjustments to the Scottish block which I think you are alluding to and we have published the Spending Reviews and we play it straight—

Q466 *Lord Forsyth of Drumlean:* My question is absolutely specific. Lord Moser put his finger on it. The Treasury does have views.

Mr Parkinson: The Treasury's view is set out in the statement of funding policy. We do not believe that Scotland is over-provided in that sense.

Lord Forsyth of Drumlean: I am not asking whether Scotland is over-provided. The question I was asking was when did the Treasury decide? The Treasury does have views, any minister knows that.

The Committee suspended from 5.01 pm to 5.13 pm for a division in the House.

Chairman: We will move on now to the Earl of Mar and Kellie.

Q467 *Earl of Mar and Kellie:* One of the features of devolution and the Barnett Formula is the issue of whether a form of spending is for England only or for the United Kingdom. It appears that the Treasury is the sole decision-maker on this?

Ms Bailey: The Treasury has responsibility for public spending across the UK and we published in the statement of funding formula the basis on which it is decided whether or not a matter is devolved or reserved, and depending on whether or not it is devolved or reserved then it is either subject to the

Formula or not. So our view is that that is reasonably transparent.

Q468 Earl of Mar and Kellie: There are two things which interest people in Scotland: whether the Olympics is UK or England only and whether Crossrail is. As I understand it, the Olympics is still regarded as a UK matter, but I think very recently it was decided that Crossrail had become an English matter in order to facilitate payment for a new bridge over the Forth at Queensferry. How did that latter come about? How was it suddenly possible under the Barnett Formula to find money for a new Forth bridge?
Ms Bailey: Let me first come to the Olympics. Our ministers believe the operation of the Olympics in 2012 will have benefits for regeneration across the United Kingdom and therefore the consequences apply accordingly. On the Forth Bridge, I wonder if one of my colleagues could assist?
Ms Radcliffe: As you say, there was a meeting recently where that was discussed and the various options as to how it might be funded were discussed, but those options very much sat within the statement of funding policy as was set out, so it was consistent with the existing system, the discussion.

Q469 Earl of Mar and Kellie: One of the things was that pretending that Crossrail was a UK matter meant that convergence could occur, but of course relenting on it and relenting on Crossrail being a UK matter and declaring it to be an England only matter has meant that any attempt at convergence has in fact been spoilt.
Mr Parkinson: No, Crossrail is a London project and is therefore an England only project, and that was the case in the Spending Review. What was announced recently was the quantum, the £500 million, which relates mainly to the next Spending Review period, but the decision to deem Crossrail as devolved, because it is a London project, was made in the last Spending Review.

Q470 Lord Forsyth of Drumlean: Perhaps another example which Mr Swinney gave us when he gave evidence was the Prison Service in England. As I understand it, the Prison Service is a devolved issue in Scotland, but on the extra money which was found for prisons which came from the contingency fund the Treasury decided there would be no Barnett consequences, according to Mr Swinney. So what you have just said, which is that where it is a devolved policy there will be the Formula consequences, did not apply in this case because it was argued it was coming from the contingency fund.

Mr Parkinson: The rules on spending from the reserve are slightly different. In the Spending Review the Barnett Formula is applied in a sort of reasonably automatic way as set out in the statement of funding policy. The statement of funding policy explains how there can be reserve claims and explains that there is no automatic access to the reserve. Reserve claims have to meet certain criteria which are essentially that the same circumstances exist in this case in Scotland as in England and that without the additional funding there would be unaffordable consequences for the devolved budget. The Treasury argued those conditions which are set out in the statement of funding policy were not met in this case. As I say, there are different rules for applying for reserve claims and the devolved administrations are consulted on those and the territorial ministers agree those rules and the Treasury applied them in this case. As you say, sometimes the interpretation of those rules is different north and south of the border, as it is in this case, but that was the rationale for the decision.

Q471 Chairman: Can I follow this up and just ask a more general question? What criteria does the Treasury operate when you have to decide whether something is UK or devolved?
Mr Parkinson: Broadly it derives from the devolution settlement. Either something is reserved or it is devolved, and that is set out in legislation. So that is not a Treasury decision, it is built into the law. There are occasional cases like the Olympics, where the Olympics is a UK-wide games and it clearly benefits the whole of the UK. It is the UK which bid for them and that was the argument for saying that the budget for the Olympics is UK-wide, which benefits the whole of the UK. The Scottish Executive took a different view and occasionally, as I say, there are issues of that kind but in 99 per cent of the cases it is a straight reflection of the devolution legislation.

Q472 Chairman: It is a decision taken by the Treasury, is it not?
Mr Parkinson: Devolution legislation is not taken by the Treasury.

Q473 Chairman: Of course it is not, but the way in which this operates, whether it is a UK matter or a devolved matter, that is a matter for you to decide?
Mr Parkinson: The public spending system is reserved, so ultimately it is the Government that decides the public spending framework, but the devolved administrations are consulted. This all derives from the comparability factors, which are published in the statement of funding policy and the devolved administrations are consulted in advance

and the territorial Secretaries of State agree those comparability factors.

Ms Bailey: What we are saying on the basis on which we operate matters set out in the statement of funding is there are occasions—I think we admitted that—where something arises which is outside the scope of the funding formula as we have published it and then ministers need to take a decision based on certain rules and in relation to the reserved, as Mr Parkinson has just outlined, there are other rules and circumstances.

Q474 *Lord Lang of Monkton:* How is the decision to treat the Olympics spending as a UK matter justified in terms of the construction that takes place? Nearly all of it is in the south of England. How much is there in Wales, Northern Ireland and Scotland, and in the after use of those facilities?

Mr Parkinson: Our argument is that the entire budget is necessary for the delivery of the Games. It was a UK bid, with the support of the devolved administrations, for the Games which is regeneration-based and it is not possible to split the budget up into regeneration activity, which is unrelated to the Games, so it is a single budget and therefore it has to be treated as a single budget. There is other spending which is related to the Games like Crossrail, which some in England would say it is wrong for Scotland to benefit from Crossrail, but we took the view that that was devolved spending for the benefit of London, and therefore Scotland should receive consequentials. But the argument fundamentally is that it is a single UK budget for the Olympics and it is not possible to split up one which is to deal with regeneration and the other to deal with the Games.

Q475 *Chairman:* But your decision on that is not challenged, though, is it?

Mr Parkinson: Yes, it is.

Ms Bailey: Yes.

Q476 *Chairman:* Who challenges it, how, and where?

Mr Parkinson: The devolved administrations can challenge it and there is a dispute resolution process set out in the statement of funding—

Q477 *Chairman:* This is a joint ministerial committee?

Mr Parkinson: Yes.

Ms Bailey: That is right, yes.

Q478 *Chairman:* That really has not got very far, has it?

Mr Parkinson: Well, it has never been used, but they have the choice to use it if they wish.

Q479 *Lord Moser:* Chairman, can I ask, at what level in the Treasury are these decisions made?

Ms Bailey: These decisions ultimately are made by ministers.

Q480 *Chairman:* I am reminded that when Glasgow bid for the Commonwealth Games in, I think, 2014 that was considered a wholly Scottish matter, whereas the Olympics has been considered a UK matter. Is there a sensible distinction between the two?

Ms Bailey: I think there was a decision of the UK Government to bid for the Olympic Games on the basis that it would have benefits across the United Kingdom and establish the facilities that would be of benefit to the whole of the United Kingdom. The Scottish Executive, as far as I understand it, made the decision about bidding for the games in Glasgow and therefore that sat within their remit and was a matter for them to decide.

Q481 *Chairman:* But there will be a UK team, presumably, at Glasgow, will there?

Mr Gallagher: No, there will be a Scottish team!

Q482 *Chairman:* There will be a Scottish team?

Mr Gallagher: Yes, absolutely. It is not a UK team, it is the Commonwealth Games!

Chairman: True! We can move on to question five, Lord Forsyth.

Q483 *Lord Forsyth of Drumlean:* I wonder if I could just ask you about what is characterised as "Formula bypass"? I know you have tried to deal with that in your answers to the questions which we put to you, but I am puzzled. We had an exchange earlier and we were talking about whether convergence is happening, depending on whether you look at the budgeted figures or the other figures and there is a debate, but one of the reasons why convergence has not happened, certainly under the pre-devolution regime, was that the Formula will determine what the resources made available for health, and so on and so forth, were and then the Scottish Office could decide to go from one programme to another and spend as they choose. For example, if there was a huge pay settlement in the Health Service, given that the Scottish baseline was 25 per cent higher in terms of expenditure per head and the Formula consequences might be around 10 per cent, there would be an enormous gap given that something like—I do not know what the figure is now, but 70, 75 per cent of the health budget was unpaid. Under the previous regime we were able to talk to colleagues in the Treasury and sort that and there would be an allocation made to take account of unusual circumstances of that kind. As I see the system operating now, there is no dialogue between the Scottish Executive and ministers and no opportunity for Formula bypass, so the effect of, for example, a large pay increase or a pay increase in the Health Service will be to squeeze other services. Is that fair, given that pay is negotiated nationally?

Ms Bailey: Given that health is a devolved matter, my understanding is not that the Scottish Executive has to accept the same pay increases for its staff as are negotiated by Westminster Government, but that the Health Service—

Mr Gallagher: It might be helpful to explain the constitutional background, Chairman. The Health Service is devolved, though Scottish ministers as a matter of policy have chosen to continue to opt into national negotiations for most, if not all, of the employees in the Health Service and that was the position pre-devolution as well, but Helen is right to say that as a matter of principle Scottish ministers could conclude now that they wish to withdraw from those national negotiations. They have not, as a matter of fact, done so.

Q484 *Lord Forsyth of Drumlean:* That may or may not be true and it would be controversial for them to do so, but it does not actually deal with my point. My point is that under the old pre-devolution system there was an opportunity, because there was a dialogue between ministers, that if there was an event—which might arise, actually, from the difference in the size of the baseline—to make an adjustment, and we did this. We did it on health. I can remember one particular pay settlement where we got extra money. We did it on housing and in other areas where there were differences in the baseline. As far as I can see, there is now no dialogue whatsoever going on of that kind and the Formula is being applied absolutely mathematically. That did not happen in the past. Is that a system which is actually workable and sustainable?

Ms Bailey: My colleagues will come in, but I think there are opportunities for that dialogue to take place, particularly around the spending reviews and around particular matters. We have already had the point about the Forth bridge for this, so there are individual dialogues for that specific matter. The Formula does not itself preclude that. The position is that in the absence of such a dialogue that applied to the Formula, it is possible for a dialogue to take place but it is normally the case that we would rely on the Formula itself.

Ms Radcliffe: Just to reinforce that, there are still opportunities for devolved administrations to raise specific issues with the Treasury and also it is possible, if everybody agrees it is necessary, for additions to be granted as well. An example of that is the increase in

funding that was given for stage one devolution in Northern Ireland.

Q485 *Lord Forsyth of Drumlean:* In your answers to the question which you gave us on this matter you say that the Barnett Formula currently applies to all changes in comparable DEL spending of UK government departments in spending reviews and therefore the scope for bypassing the Formula is in that sense negligible.

Ms Bailey: Indeed, although we do go on to say that it is possible for the Treasury to agree to additions if appropriate, which I think is the point which is made.

Q486 *Lord Forsyth of Drumlean:* Yes, but what I am saying is that the pre-devolution—and by the way, on your answer to question one where you present Barnett as being a happy, simple system, I can remember weeks of negotiations when we had the annual pay round arguing with Treasury ministers and officials and the rest. It was by no means simple and that process enabled the differences in the devolved areas, in this case what were then called the territorial areas, to be taken account of. It does not seem to me that that opportunity is there. You just simply have a mathematical formula and that must ultimately result in some inequities, particularly if you have administrations of different political colour?

Mr Gallagher: I wonder if I might be of some help on that? Long Lang asked earlier on, was the absence of the scope for negotiation a virtue or a vice in the application of the Barnett Formula, and of course what we have described as negotiation pre-devolution inside one government, ministers of the same party subject to the same collective responsibility. Post-devolution one of the advantages of a formulaic approach, whether it is this formula or another, is that it does not put ministers of one political colour, perhaps, in the devolved administration in the position of having to negotiate line by line their budget with a government which may well be of a different political colour. That is not, as Helen says, to say that it is completely impossible for some accommodation to be reached, even in relation to Scotland. I can think of one example where post-devolution some accommodation was reached in relation to funding and that was in relation to the Scottish Court in the Netherlands, which tried Mr Megrahi, which you will remember.

Q487 *Lord Forsyth of Drumlean:* What you describe as an advantage, I can see how it might be an administrative advantage, but from the point of view of people who are depending on the Health Service in Wales, Scotland or elsewhere, I do not see it as being an advantage, I see it as their resources actually being determined by a mathematical formula with no opportunity to say, "Don't you understand, we have this particular issue here and we have this particular need?" and the result will be that services will be squeezed. One response to that would be that if you had a system which was based on needs as opposed to mathematical formula, you would compensate for that?

Mr Gallagher: Another answer to that, I am afraid, is that of course it is not necessarily the case that a dialogue would produce more money. A dialogue might produce less money, so if you were thinking of the needs of particular users of the Health Service in Scotland the production of the budget by negotiation around the Formula might produce either more or less.

Q488 Lord Forsyth of Drumlean: But it would be transparent and it would be based on some objective criteria, not just some numbers?

Mr Gallagher: One advantage of the Barnett Formula, with respect, is that by comparison, for example, with the local government finance formula that we talked about earlier on it is a model of transparency!

Q489 Lord Rooker: On the issue of the devolved finance ministers, we understand, although I do not quite understand the background, that they meet regularly with the Chief Secretary a couple of times a year or so. When did that start and what is the purpose of the meetings?

Ms Bailey: The purpose of the meetings is to discuss financial matters of common interest and UK wide concerns, so the economic and fiscal situation of the whole of the UK can be discussed and we are due to have a meeting tomorrow at which I am sure ministers will wish to exchange views about the current economic situation.

Q490 Lord Rooker: When did the regularity of the meetings start?

Ms Bailey: I think it started immediately post-devolution.

Mr Parkinson: It was not quite immediately post-devolution, but it was about 2001. Fairly early on it was thought a good idea for finance ministers to meet collectively to discuss this, as Helen says.

Q491 Lord Rooker: Did it always cover the UK from the start in 2000–01?

Mr Parkinson: Yes, it used to happen every six months from about that time onwards.

Q492 Lord Rooker: With all four?

Mr Parkinson: With all four.

Q493 Lord Rooker: I am going to have to check my diaries, but I have to say that with the many jobs I have done between June 2005 and May 2006 I was the Northern Ireland Finance Minister and I do not recall attending or being invited to attend any meetings with the Treasury. Now, I was directly the minister, that is why I asked you when it started did it apply to all of the UK?

Ms Bailey: We can, if you like, check our records and check which meetings we have had within that time. If you were not invited, let me extend an apology on behalf of the Treasury retrospectively.

Q494 Lord Lang of Monkton: It would be interesting to know whether any decisions of any substance were taken at any of those meetings or whether it was just an exchange of views.

Mr Parkinson: It depends on the circumstances. As it happens, we have not had a meeting for some time. It will be the first one for some time. If we are doing spending reviews they can be of operational significance in the sense that there are issues to determine. At other times during the public expenditure cycle it is more a question of discussing issues of common interest, and obviously the economy is the top priority at the moment and so ministers will be talking about the economy tomorrow. So it is a mixture of operational issues and an exchange of views.

Q495 Lord Lang of Monkton: Have any issues been decided or policy change that relate to the Barnett Formula and the operation of it?

Mr Parkinson: In the run up to the Spending Review the Olympics was discussed, for example. You will not be surprised to hear that, but that is the sort of thing which is discussed.

Q496 Lord Rooker: Who represents England at this meeting?

Ms Bailey: The Chief Secretary of the Treasury on behalf of the UK Government.

Mr Parkinson: It is a meeting with the devolved administrations, it is not—

Q497 Lord Rooker: So nobody represents England because she is there as the UK minister?

Mr Parkinson: It is a devolved finance ministers' meeting.

Lord Rooker: The answer is nobody represents England. She is there as the UK Finance Minister, which is a similar arrangement we have with Brussels,

we devolve matters, and Defra is the England farming minister but I represented the UK. In other words, nobody is there actually representing England? There is Scotland, Wales, Northern Ireland and the Chief Secretaries of the Treasury. That is the position, is it not, nobody is representing England?
Chairman: I am sure it was Northern Ireland.

Q498 *Lord Rowe-Beddoe:* Something you have demonstrated that you do not particularly want to talk about is the question of a needs assessment-based distribution of funds to the devolved administrations, but if you were to talk about it do you think it would take a great deal of time to come to some sort of conclusion? Let us assume that you are brave enough to say that you would like to look at something which might be substituted for what we have.
Ms Bailey: We have already said—and I appreciate you do not find this hugely helpful—that you would need some determination of how we assess needs and what needs were prioritised. There are many different ways of doing this. Broadly you could start from the top-down UK Government looking down at GDP, and so on, or you could start from the bottom up and assess community by community what the differential needs were. Depending which method you chose, it would be more or less time consuming. You could do, in theory, a quick and dirty top-down exercise and say, "Right, this is the GDP per head of population or GVA of the population in a particular part of the United Kingdom and therefore the needs are greater." I do not know whether or not that would fit the bill, meet people's requirements or not. If you were to do a much more detailed bottom-up exercise, it would arguably take longer. So I think the things that are in place in order to judge the answer to your question are, do we have an agreed assessment of what the needs are, do we have an agreed view of how we are going to determine that, do we have an agreed view about whether or not we are going to buy the devolved administrations into that process or whether or not the UK Government is going to do it to them, and that will take some ministerial negotiation. Then the question I think you have notified us of is whether or not this should be done by the Treasury or whether we should get somebody else in to do it. I think that is entirely a matter for ministers, taking into account the questions I have posed to you and doubtless many others that I have not yet thought of.

Q499 *Lord Rowe-Beddoe:* I think we would perhaps all agree that it cannot be something which is a quick and dirty exercise because it has to satisfy the constituent parts of the United Kingdom and, to come back to the Chairman's opening statement, it has to be seen to be fair. So it is going to be, I would suggest, be quite a detailed exercise for it to fly. Could you give us some idea of how long a detailed exercise might be?
Ms Bailey: It is hugely difficult to do that without knowing what the component elements of such an exercise would be. I am not seeking to be unhelpful in any way at all, but depending on whether you wished to look at it by individual community, by geographical area or whether you wished to start from an income per head, whether you wished to look at, as I say, GBA per head of population—

Q500 *Lord Rowe-Beddoe:* But the Treasury would actually have to give the ideas as to what we should be doing?
Ms Bailey: Indeed, and there would be a considerable dialogue, I have no doubt, between officials, ministers and advisers, and there would be a dialogue with the devolved administrations. None of that has taken place, which is why I cannot answer your question in any more detail.

Q501 *Chairman:* I do not want to come back to where we started from, but could I just say that you did that exercise in the seventies. Why was it possible to do it in 1978 or 1979 but not possible to do it now?
Mr Parkinson: That is a benchmark. That study took about two years, just to give you an idea.

Q502 *Chairman:* Perhaps you ought to have a different way of asking?
Mr Parkinson: That was a particular study using a particular methodology, as Helen said. It is by no means obvious that we would use the same methodology again.

Q503 *Lord Rooker:* Even if it is being requested by the ministers? In the 1970s Joel Barnett did not even know about this going on and he was the Chief Secretary of the Treasury, so it was done without the minister asking for it to be done.
Ms Bailey: I have seen his evidence and I understand the point you are making. I do not know whether any other minister or ministers were involved in that decision, so I will not comment further, but an exercise of that sort –
Lord Rooker: I am sorry, it was a cheap question. I apologise for that.
Chairman: No, it was not cheap, I think it was rather expensive!

Q504 *Lord Lang of Monkton:* Were other government departments involved in the assessment?
Ms Bailey: Yes.

Q505 *Lord Lang of Monkton:* And they all agreed on the outcome?
Mr Parkinson: No, they did not reach an agreed outcome.

Q506 *Lord Lang of Monkton:* So you reached no conclusion?
Mr Parkinson: No.
Ms Bailey: No.

Q507 *Chairman:* Thank you very much. Two things, if I may. One is, you will have gathered there is a fair degree of unease, uncertainty and indeed disappointment at the views that are expressed, the ones you have given us today. So be it. There is a difference between us. There are various detailed questions on the figures which I do not think I am really qualified to put to you, but which Mr Trench, who is our special advisor, is qualified to put to you. I wonder whether you would be kind enough to talk to him about it? Secondly, it may well be that when we have had a good look at the transcript we may think that perhaps it would be helpful to the Committee if you were to come back and put your heads in the lion's den yet again, but on behalf of us all I think I can say thank you very much indeed. You have exposed certain problems and indeed expressed a clear attitude on the part of the Treasury, and for that we are grateful.
Ms Bailey: Can I thank you, Chairman, for those kind words. We would be more than delighted to talk to Mr Trench or any of your other advisers and take them through the detailed figures. We would be very happy to do that. I think I would just like to clarify some of what you call the difference between us. The Treasury's view, insofar as it has one, is set out in the statement of its funding policy and clearly the views of the Treasury are largely the views of our ministers, so we can help insofar as the practical operation at official level and we will happily do so and come back, as you so graciously put it, into the lion's den on any occasion you would wish in order to be able to do that. I apologise to you for the fact that we cannot go further than that brief.
Chairman: Thank you very much.

Further supplementary memorandum by HM Treasury

This supplementary evidence follows a request for further data by the Committee chairman at the hearing with Treasury officials on 11 March 2009.

What drives the Barnett formula and how are comparability factors calculated?

In arithmetic terms the Barnett formula is: change in spending of the UK Government department x comparability factor x population share.

The change in spending is the aggregate change in the UK department's DEL. For the purposes of the operation of the Barnett formula the Treasury does not need to know the sub-components of the change in the DEL other than the split of the DEL change between cash and non cash resource DEL and capital DEL. These figures are published in spending review White Papers.

It is also worth noting that for the operation of the Barnett formula it is not necessary for the Treasury to scrutinise the existing level of provision or baseline of the devolved administrations. The baseline level of provision ie in the year before the first year of the spending review is rolled forward over the spending review period and the Barnett consequentials are added to this baseline.

The departmental comparability factors are published in the Statement of Funding Policy and measure the extent to which the UK department's spending is comparable to devolved spending. An illustrative example is set out below:

— suppose the UK department has two programmes, one which covers the whole of the UK and costs £100 million and the other which covers just England and costs £50 million. The comparability factor is the weighted average of the two programmes ie $(100/150 \times 0) + (50/150 \times 1) = 0.33$ or 33 per cent.

Devolved and reserved public spending in Scotland, Wales and Northern Ireland over time

Data is published in table 9.17 of the Treasury's annual Public Expenditure Statistical Analyses on devolved and reserved public spending in Scotland, Wales and Northern Ireland. Data on past years from 2002–03 to 2006–07 (the latest available year) on a consistent basis is set out in the attached tables.

Changes is devolved spending between spending reviews

Information on changes in devolved spending between spending reviews is set out in the Scotland and Wales Offices' annual reports. The attached tables provide further disaggregation for the period covered by the last three spending reviews. In general most of the changes in spending comprise: agreed transfers between devolved administrations and departments; technical changes reflecting changes in the way public spending is classified; drawdown of End Year Flexibility underspends; and the Barnett consequentials of Budget and PBR changes in spending.

NORTHERN IRELAND - SR 2002

	2003-04 £m	2004-05 £m	2005-06 £m
SR 2002 settlement	**6,927.0**	**7,279.4**	**7,731.1**
Budgeting & classification changes	-57.5	-57.5	-57.5
Interdepartmental transfers	-3.3	-3.3	-3.2
Spending Policy:			
Pre Budget Report 2002 - Employer Training Pilots	3.6	0.0	0.0
Invest to Save Budget	0.4	0.2	0.1
TOTAL changes SR 2002 to PESA 2003	*-56.8*	*-60.6*	*-60.6*
PESA 2003 (tables 1.7 & 1.8)/ Main Estimates 2003-04	**6,870.2**	**7,218.9**	**7,670.5**
Budgeting & classification changes	-111.8	-107.2	-112.5
Interdepartmental transfers	-4.6	1.9	0.1
End Year Flexibility	434.3	0.0	0.0
Spending Policy:			
Budget 2003 - Futurebuilders	0.3	1.7	2.2
Budget 2003 - Parenting Fund	0.2	0.3	0.3
Budget 2003 - Capital Modernisation Fund	0.7	1.8	1.6
Budget 2003 - Landfill Tax Credit Scheme	2.8	3.1	3.1
Budget 2003 - SR 2002 corrections	1.2	1.8	2.4
Pre Budget Report 2003 - Local Authorities	0.0	12.7	2.7
Invest to Save Budget	0.0	0.1	0.1
TOTAL changes PESA 2003 to PESA 2004	*323.2*	*-83.9*	*-100.0*
PESA 2004 (tables 1.7 & 1.8)/ Main Estimates 2004-05	**7,193.5**	**7,135.0**	**7,570.5**

(for further changes to 2005-06, see CSR 2004 table)

	2003-04 £m	2004-05 £m
Budgeting & classification changes	0.0	40.8
Interdepartmental transfers	0.0	1.6
End Year Flexibility	0.0	340.7
Outturn adjustments	-412.0	-120.0
TOTAL changes PESA 2004 to PESA 2005	*-412.0*	*263.1*
PESA 2005 (tables 1.5 & 1.9)/ Main Estimates 2005-06	**6,781.5**	**7,398.1**

NORTHERN IRELAND - SR 2004

	2005-06 £m	2006-07 £m	2007-08 £m
SR 2004 settlement	**7,570.5**	**8,029.2**	**8,395.3**
Budgeting & classification changes	120.4	125.2	130.2
Interdepartmental transfers	-1.9	-7.9	-7.9
Spending Policy:			
Counter Terrorism	0.3	0.0	0.0
Pre Budget Report 2004 - Bookstart	0.3	0.3	0.3
Pre Budget Report 2004 - Early Education	0.0	0.3	0.3
Pre Budget Report 2004 - Employer Training Pilots	0.0	2.2	4.4
Pre Budget Report 2004 - Childcare	0.0	6.7	4.3
Pre Budget Report 2004 - Council Tax	4.2	0.0	0.0
Pre Budget Report 2004 - Landfill Tax	2.2	0.0	0.0
Pre Budget Report 2004 - Financial Inclusion Fund	0.5	1.1	1.7
Pre Budget Report 2004 - Learning Allowance	0.0	0.1	0.1
Pre Budget Report 2004 - Pathways to Work	0.0	1.7	1.9
Pre Budget Report 2004 - Admin of payments to pensioners	0.1	0.0	0.0
Budget 2005 - LAGBI	0.4	1.7	3.4
Budget 2005 - Russell Commission	0.3	0.8	2.2
Budget 2005 - Free Bus Travel	0.0	11.7	12.3
Budget 2005 - Education	0.0	8.3	10.4
Budget 2005 - Arts Council	0.0	0.2	0.2
Budget 2005 - Employer Training Pilots	1.3	0.0	0.0
Budget 2005 - Admin for Incapaity Benefit	0.0	0.0	0.0
Invest to Save	0.0	0.2	0.0
TOTAL changes SR 2004 to PESA 2005	*128.1*	*152.7*	*163.9*
PESA 2005 (tables 1.5 & 1.9)/ Main Estimates 2005-06	**7,698.6**	**8,181.9**	**8,559.1**
Budgeting & classification changes	-200.3	-122.4	-20.5
Interdepartmental transfers	-1.8	0.0	0.0
End Year Flexibility	273.6	0.0	0.0
Spending Policy:			
Pre Budget Report 2005 - Warm Front	0.7	4.2	3.1
Pre Budget Report 2005 - Holocaust Education Trust	0.0	0.1	0.0
Pre Budget Report 2005 - Education Exports	0.0	0.1	0.0
Pre Budget Report 2005 - Enterprise Education	0.0	0.1	0.0
Pre Budget Report 2005 - Youth Service Grant	0.0	0.9	0.2
Pre Budget Report 2005 - Carbon Trust Loans	0.0	0.5	0.7
Pre Budget Report 2005 - Employer Training Pilot	0.0	1.3	0.0
Pre Budget Report 2005 - Children's Document	0.0	0.9	0.0
Pre Budget Report 2005 - Financial Inclusion Fund	0.0	0.5	0.2
Budget 2006 - Education	0.0	7.3	12.1
Budget 2006 - Lone Parents	0.0	0.0	0.7
Budget 2006 - Grass Roots Sport	0.0	0.3	0.0
Budget 2006 - Education & Science	0.0	0.3	0.3
Budget 2006 - Further Education	0.0	0.0	1.6
Budget 2006 - Women in Work Comm	0.0	0.7	0.7
Budget 2006 - Energy Efficiency	0.0	0.2	0.0
Budget 2006 - Smart Metering	0.0	0.1	0.0
Budget 2006 - Football Foundation	0.0	0.0	0.0
Budget 2006 - Youth Opportunities Fund	0.0	0.1	0.0

Budget 2006 - Education & Exports	0.0	0.1	0.1
Budget 2006 - Youth Media	0.0	0.1	0.1
Budget 2006 - Workplace Nurseries	0.0	0.3	0.3
Budget 2006 - ICT in Education	0.0	0.2	0.2
Invest to Save	0.0	0.3	0.2
Outturn adjustments	66.0	0.0	0.0
TOTAL changes PESA 2005 to PESA 2006	*138.3*	*-104.1*	*0.0*
PESA 2006 (tables 1.5 & 1.10)/ Main Estimates 2006-07	**7,836.9**	**8,077.8**	**8,559.2**
Budgeting & classification changes	17.8	54.4	38.9
Interdepartmental transfers	0.0	-2.2	7.0
End Year Flexibility	0.0	70.0	0.0
Spending Policy:			
Pre Budget Report 2006 - Books for 11 year olds	0.0	0.0	0.1
Pre Budget Report 2006 - Secondary catch up	0.0	0.0	0.3
Pre Budget Report 2006 - Schools Standards Grant	0.0	0.0	4.3
Pre Budget Report 2006 - LBRO better regulation	0.0	0.0	0.1
Pre Budget Report 2006 - Gowers (trading standards)	0.0	0.0	0.1
Pre Budget Report 2006 - Retail enforecment pilot	0.0	0.0	0.1
Pre Budget Report 2006 - Warm Front	0.0	0.0	0.2
Pre Budget Report 2006 - Pensions data cleanse	0.0	0.0	0.2
Pre Budget Report 2006 - National In Work Credit	0.0	0.3	0.3
Budget 2007 - Mircrogeneration	0.0	0.0	0.7
Invest to Save	0.0	0.0	0.1
Outturn adjustments	-285.3	-162.2	0.0
TOTAL changes PESA 2006 to PESA 2007	*-267.5*	*-39.7*	*52.5*
PESA 2007 (tables 1.5 & 1.10)/ Main Estimates 2007-08	**7,569.4**	**8,038.1**	**8,611.6**
Budgeting & classification changes	72.9	70.7	85.8
Interdepartmental transfers	0.0	0.0	-11.1
End Year Flexibility	0.0	0.0	105.0
Spending Policy:			
Water Reform	0.0	0.0	100.0
Outturn adjustments	-7.8	-155.0	-247.0
TOTAL changes PESA 2007 to PESA 2008	*65.1*	*-84.3*	*32.7*
PESA 2008 (tables 1.5 & 1.10)/ Main Estimates 2008-09	**7,634.4**	**7,953.8**	**8,644.3**

Table 9.17 Identifiable expenditure on services for Scotland, Wales and Northern Ireland in 2002-03

All the data in this table are National Statistics

£ million

	1. General public services	of which: public and common services	of which: international services	of which: public sector debt interest	2. Defence	3. Public order and safety	4. Economic affairs	of which: enterprise and economic development	of which: science and technology	of which: employment policies	of which: agriculture, fisheries and forestry	of which: transport	5. Environment protection	6. Housing and community amenities	7. Health	8. Recreation, culture and religion	9. Education (includes training)	of which: education	of which: training	10. Social protection	EU transactions	Total
Scotland																						
Scottish Executive	432	432	-	-	2	684	1,599	491	29	1	546	532	119	1,123	6,656	125	1,854	1,711	143	278	-	12,873
Scotland Office	7	7	-	-	-	3	-	-	-	-	-	-	-	-	-	-	-	-	-	-	-	9
Scotland local authorities	333	333	-	-	3	952	685	110	-	-	17	558	390	141	-	551	3,486	3,481	4	3,132	-	9,673
Local government public corporations	-	-	-	-	-	-	-	-	-	-	-	-	-	-	-	-	-	-	-	-	-	-
UK government departments	52	37	16	-	0	-	901	170	140	252	18	321	159	0	34	85	27	17	10	10,033	-	11,292
Total identifiable expenditure in Scotland	824	808	16	-	6	1,639	3,185	771	169	252	580	1,412	668	1,264	6,691	761	5,367	5,209	158	13,444	-	33,848
Wales																						
National Assembly for Wales	189	189	-	-	-	13	1,038	478	-	-	281	279	69	41	3,454	76	1,058	1,010	48	104	-	6,042
Wales Office	3	3	-	-	-	-	-	-	-	-	-	-	-	-	-	-	-	-	-	-	-	3
Wales local authorities	207	207	-	-	2	613	340	60	-	-	4	276	220	245	-	260	1,841	1,823	18	1,505	-	5,234
Local government public corporations	-	-	-	-	-	-	-	-	-	-	-	-	-	-	-	-	-	-	-	-	-	-
UK government departments	34	25	9	-	0	439	649	258	40	116	8	227	15	2	14	128	36	30	7	6,427	-	7,744
Total identifiable expenditure in Wales	433	424	9	-	2	1,065	2,027	796	40	116	293	782	304	287	3,468	464	2,935	2,863	72	8,037	-	19,023
Northern Ireland																						
Northern Ireland Executive	288	288	-	-	-	57	1,169	287	35	202	350	296	30	507	2,038	74	2,032	2,024	8	4,410	-	10,605
Northern Ireland Office	68	68	-	-	-	1,022	-	-	-	-	-	-	-	-	-	-	-	-	-	-	-	1,090
Northern Ireland Court Service	-	-	-	-	-	95	-	-	-	-	-	-	-	-	-	-	-	-	-	-	-	95
Northern Ireland local authorities	-	-	-	-	-	-	8	8	-	-	-	-	102	88	31	178	-	-	-	-	-	406
UK government departments	11	6	5	-	-	1	56	12	27	1	3	13	7	0	7	28	7	6	1	305	-	421
Total identifiable expenditure in Northern Ireland	366	361	5	-	-	1,176	1,233	307	62	203	352	308	139	595	2,076	280	2,039	2,030	9	4,715	-	12,618

All the spending of the devolved administrations is identifiable except for spending by the Scottish Executive on Lockerbie

Table 9.17 Identifiable expenditure on services for Scotland, Wales and Northern Ireland in 2003-04

All the data in this table are National Statistics

£ million

	1. General public services	of which: public and common services	of which: international services	of which: public sector debt interest	2. Defence	3. Public order and safety	4. Economic affairs	of which: enterprise and economic development	of which: science and technology	of which: employment policies	of which: agriculture, fisheries and forestry	of which: transport	5. Environment protection	6. Housing and community amenities	7. Health	8. Recreation, culture and religion	9. Education (includes training)	of which: education	of which: training	10. Social protection	EU transactions	Total
Scotland																						
Scottish Executive	484	484	-	-	0	756	2,038	550	33	0	611	744	199	1,093	7,317	153	1,821	1,671	150	-9	-	13,850
Scotland Office	6	6	-	-	-	12															-	18
Scotland local authorities	349	349	-	-	3	1,051	746	119			20	607	412	155		610	3,818	3,811	7	3,234	-	10,379
Local government public corporations																						
UK government departments	60	42	17	-	0	0	848	149	146	294	17	242	180	0	43	107	40	27	12	10,954	-	12,231
Total identifiable expenditure in Scotland	898	881	17	-	3	1,820	3,632	918	179	294	649	1,592	791	1,247	7,360	870	5,678	5,509	169	14,179	-	36,478
Wales																						
National Assembly for Wales	219	219	-	-	-	30	1,057	484			296	276	86	-23	3,932	81	1,051	997	54	148	-	6,581
Wales Office	3	3	-	-	-																-	3
Wales local authorities	225	225	-	-	2	667	399	89			5	305	247	253		261	2,039	2,020	19	1,663	-	5,757
Local government public corporations																						
UK government departments	39	29	10	-	-	468	563	234	46	135	8	140	19	2	19	137	39	30	9	6,729	-	8,015
Total identifiable expenditure in Wales	485	476	10	-	2	1,166	2,019	807	46	135	310	722	352	233	3,951	480	3,129	3,047	82	8,540	-	20,356
Northern Ireland																						
Northern Ireland Executive	300	300	-	-	-	61	1,097	212	41	153	380	310	38	625	2,245	84	2,133	2,126	7	4,337	-	10,920
Northern Ireland Office	68	68	-	-	-	1,011															-	1,079
Northern Ireland Court Service						96																96
Northern Ireland local authorities							12	12					109	85	34	173						413
UK government departments	13	7	6	-	-	1	56	11	19	2	3	21	9	0	11	25	11	10	1	763	-	889
Total identifiable expenditure in Northern Ireland	380	375	6	-	-	1,169	1,164	235	60	155	383	332	155	710	2,291	283	2,144	2,136	8	5,100	-	13,396

All the spending of the devolved admistrations is identifiable except for spending by the Scottish Executive on Lockerbie

Table 9.17 Identifiable expenditure on services for Scotland, Wales and Northern Ireland in 2004-05

All the data in this table are National Statistics

£ million

	1. General public services	of which: public and common services	of which: international services	of which: public sector debt interest	2. Defence	3. Public order and safety	4. Economic affairs	of which: enterprise and economic development	of which: science and technology	of which: employment policies	of which: agriculture, fisheries and forestry	of which: transport	5. Environment protection	6. Housing and community amenities	7. Health	8. Recreation, culture and religion	9. Education (includes training)	of which: education	of which: training	10. Social protection	EU transactions	Total
Scotland																						
Scottish Executive	490	490	-	-	2	823	1,895	598	38	-	615	644	161	721	7,664	172	1,943	1,800	148	25	-	13,902
Scotland Office	6	6	-	-	-	8	-	-	-	-	-	-	-	-	-	-	-	-	-	-	-	14
Scotland local authorities	389	389	-	-	4	1,088	813	142	-	-	24	647	454	225	-	652	4,097	4,090	7	3,425	-	11,147
Local government public corporations	-	-	-	-	-	-	5	-	-	-	-	5	-	-	-	-	-	-	-	-	-	5
UK government departments	59	40	20	12	0	6	915	193	161	293	18	250	173	0	42	91	41	26	15	11,482	-	12,808
Total identifiable expenditure in Scotland	944	924	20	12	6	1,924	3,628	934	198	293	657	1,546	788	946	7,705	915	6,086	5,916	170	14,932	-	37,875
Wales																						
National Assembly for Wales	248	248	-	-	-	20	1,046	522	-	-	218	306	94	-5	4,236	84	1,127	1,069	57	162	-	7,012
Wales Office	4	4	-	-	-	-	-	-	-	-	-	-	-	-	-	-	-	-	-	-	-	4
Wales local authorities	212	212	-	-	2	674	446	109	-	-	7	330	273	268	-	317	2,162	2,142	19	1,780	-	6,133
Local government public corporations	-	-	-	-	-	-	2	-	-	-	-	2	-	-	-	-	-	-	-	-	-	2
UK government departments	43	31	12	-	0	516	553	189	51	134	8	170	14	3	18	145	53	42	11	7,056	-	8,401
Total identifiable expenditure in Wales	507	495	12	-	2	1,209	2,046	820	51	134	233	808	382	266	4,254	546	3,342	3,254	88	8,999	-	21,553
Northern Ireland																						
Northern Ireland Executive	227	227	-	-	-	73	1,161	227	51	172	399	312	69	694	2,438	81	2,206	2,201	5	4,628	-	11,577
Northern Ireland Office	57	57	-	-	-	1,044	-	-	-	-	-	-	-	-	-	-	-	-	-	-	-	1,101
Northern Ireland Court Service	-	-	-	-	-	116	-	-	-	-	-	-	-	-	-	-	-	-	-	-	-	116
Northern Ireland local authorities	-	-	-	-	-	-	14	14	-	-	-	-	112	90	35	191	-	-	-	-	-	443
UK government departments	14	8	7	-	-	1	62	21	19	1	3	19	2	0	11	27	12	10	2	821	-	949
Total identifiable expenditure in Northern Ireland	298	291	7	-	-	1,234	1,237	262	70	173	402	331	183	784	2,484	299	2,218	2,211	7	5,448	-	14,185

All the spending of the devolved administrations is identifiable except for spending by the Scottish Executive on Lockerbie

Table 9.17 Identifiable expenditure on services for Scotland, Wales and Northern Ireland in 2005-06

All the data in this table are National Statistics

£ million

	1. General public services	of which: public and common services	of which: international services	of which: public sector debt interest	2. Defence	3. Public order and safety	4. Economic affairs	of which: enterprise and economic development	of which: science and technology	of which: employment policies	of which: agriculture, fisheries and forestry	of which: transport	5. Environment protection	6. Housing and community amenities	7. Health	8. Recreation, culture and religion	9. Education (includes training)	of which: education	of which: training	10. Social protection	EU transactions	Total
Scotland																						
Scottish Executive	430	430	-	-	2	893	1,996	580	53	-	602	761	189	1,182	8,517	179	2,057	1,909	149	-4	-	15,441
Scotland Office	6	6	-	-	-	8	-	-	-	-	-	-	-	-	-	-	-	-	-	-	-	14
Scotland local authorities	593	593	-	-	4	1,150	955	167	-	-	22	765	491	217	-	678	4,405	4,396	10	3,649	-	12,141
Local government public corporations	-	-	-	-	-	-	6	-	-	-	-	6	-	-	-	-	-	-	-	-	-	6
UK government departments	73	51	22	-	-	9	973	228	184	307	17	237	505	0	48	109	49	30	18	11,782	-	13,547
Total identifiable expenditure in Scotland	**1,103**	**1,081**	**22**	**-**	**6**	**2,060**	**3,929**	**975**	**238**	**307**	**641**	**1,769**	**1,184**	**1,399**	**8,564**	**966**	**6,511**	**6,334**	**177**	**15,427**	**-**	**41,150**
Wales																						
National Assembly for Wales	265	265	-	-	-	20	1,163	508	-	-	355	301	104	196	4,552	90	1,158	1,102	55	201	-	7,750
Wales Office	4	4	-	-	-	-	-	-	-	-	-	-	-	-	-	-	-	-	-	-	-	4
Wales local authorities	287	287	-	-	3	721	502	108	-	-	3	392	300	274	-	325	2,282	2,257	25	1,902	-	6,596
Local government public corporations	-	-	-	-	-	-	3	-	-	-	-	3	-	-	-	-	-	-	-	-	-	3
UK government departments	58	46	13	-	-	530	587	212	67	150	8	149	14	3	21	148	66	56	9	7,248	-	8,675
Total identifiable expenditure in Wales	**615**	**602**	**13**	**-**	**3**	**1,272**	**2,255**	**828**	**67**	**150**	**365**	**844**	**418**	**473**	**4,572**	**564**	**3,506**	**3,416**	**90**	**9,351**	**-**	**23,027**
Northern Ireland																						
Northern Ireland Executive	299	299	-	-	-	76	1,293	209	51	166	532	335	80	773	2,614	94	2,246	2,243	3	4,701	-	12,176
Northern Ireland Office	53	53	-	-	-	1,121	-	-	-	-	-	-	-	-	-	-	-	-	-	-	-	1,174
Northern Ireland Court Service	-	-	-	-	-	116	-	-	-	-	-	-	-	-	-	-	-	-	-	-	-	116
Northern Ireland local authorities	-	-	-	-	-	-	12	12	-	-	-	-	125	101	38	206	-	-	-	-	-	483
UK government departments	17	10	7	-	-	1	61	21	19	0	3	18	4	0	12	32	13	12	2	863	-	1,005
Total identifiable expenditure in Northern Ireland	**369**	**362**	**7**	**-**	**-**	**1,314**	**1,367**	**243**	**70**	**166**	**535**	**353**	**209**	**874**	**2,664**	**332**	**2,259**	**2,254**	**5**	**5,565**	**-**	**14,954**

All the spending of the devolved admistrations is identifiable except for spending by the Scottish Executive on Lockerbie

Table 9.17 Identifiable expenditure on services for Scotland, Wales and Northern Ireland in 2006-07

All the data in this table are National Statistics

£ million

	1. General public services	of which: public and common services	of which: international services	of which: public sector debt interest	2. Defence	3. Public order and safety	4. Economic affairs	of which: enterprise and economic development	of which: science and technology	of which: employment policies	of which: agriculture, fisheries and forestry	of which: transport	5. Environment protection	6. Housing and community amenities	7. Health	8. Recreation, culture and religion	9. Education (includes training)	of which: education	of which: training	10. Social protection	EU transactions	Total
Scotland																						
Scottish Executive	460	460	-	-	3	896	2,893	632	23	-	628	1,610	171	1,397	9,027	204	2,424	2,279	145	43	-	17,518
Scotland Office (1)	6	6	-	-	-	1	-	-	-	-	-	-	-	-	-	-	-	-	-	-	-	7
Scotland Local Authorities	426	426	-	-	4	1,239	1,048	153	-	-	30	864	501	196	-	713	4,643	4,634	9	3,788	-	12,559
Local government public corporations	-	-	-	-	-	-	7	-	-	-	-	7	-	-	-	-	-	-	-	-	-	7
UK government departments	86	67	19	-	0	9	886	196	174	298	20	198	321	0	37	104	36	16	20	12,148	-	13,628
Total identifiable expenditure in Scotland	**978**	**958**	**19**	-	**7**	**2,145**	**4,834**	**981**	**197**	**298**	**678**	**2,679**	**994**	**1,593**	**9,064**	**1,021**	**7,103**	**6,929**	**175**	**15,979**	-	**43,718**
Wales																						
National Assembly for Wales	377	377	-	-	-	25	1,171	459	-	-	371	341	110	260	4,921	91	1,265	1,227	39	111	-	8,332
Wales Office (1)	4	4	-	-	-	-	-	-	-	-	-	-	-	-	-	-	-	-	-	-	-	4
Wales Local Authorities	225	225	-	-	3	747	522	105	-	-	5	412	332	281	-	358	2,398	2,369	30	2,029	-	6,897
Local government public corporations	-	-	-	-	-	-	3	-	-	-	-	3	-	-	-	-	-	-	-	-	-	3
UK government departments	55	44	11	-	0	547	562	201	52	150	9	150	131	4	13	159	58	48	10	7,471	-	9,000
Total identifiable expenditure in Wales	**661**	**650**	**11**	-	**3**	**1,319**	**2,259**	**765**	**52**	**150**	**385**	**906**	**574**	**546**	**4,935**	**608**	**3,721**	**3,643**	**78**	**9,611**	-	**24,237**
Northern Ireland																						
Northern Ireland Executive	346	346	-	-	-	82	1,206	193	44	147	447	374	86	775	2,866	102	2,382	2,380	2	4,944	-	12,789
Northern Ireland Office	67	67	-	-	-	1,153	-	-	-	-	-	-	-	-	-	-	-	-	-	1	-	1,221
Northern Ireland Court Service	-	-	-	-	-	122	-	-	-	-	-	-	-	-	-	-	-	-	-	-	-	122
Northern Ireland Local Authorities	-	-	-	-	-	-	15	15	-	-	-	-	140	98	39	172	-	-	-	-	-	464
UK government departments	22	15	7	-	0	1	73	32	19	0	3	19	2	0	6	37	8	6	2	913	-	1,062
Total identifiable expenditure in Northern Ireland	**435**	**428**	**7**	-	**0**	**1,358**	**1,294**	**241**	**63**	**147**	**451**	**393**	**228**	**874**	**2,911**	**311**	**2,390**	**2,386**	**4**	**5,858**	-	**15,658**

All the spending of the devolved administrations is identifiable except for spending by the Scottish Executive on Lockerbie.

(1) Scotland Office and Wales Office are no longer separate departments, but are now entities within the Ministry of Justice.

SCOTLAND - SR 2002

	2003-04 £m	2004-05 £m	2005-06 £m
SR 2002 settlement	**20,067.7**	**21,188.7**	**22,637.2**
Budgeting & classification changes	240.7	296.9	273.1
Interdepartmental transfers	10.5	9.8	9.8
Spending Policy:			
Aggregates Levy	3.0	3.0	3.0
Pre Budget Report 2002 - Employer Training Pilots	11.1	0.0	0.0
Budget 2003 - Futurebuilders	1.0	5.2	6.7
Budget 2003 - Parenting Fund	0.5	1.0	1.0
Budget 2003 - Capital Modernisation Fund	6.2	9.2	5.2
Budget 2003 - Landfill Tax Credit Scheme	8.6	9.4	9.4
Budget 2003 - SR 2002 corrections	0.3	0.5	1.1
Invest to Save Budget	1.5	0.7	0.3
TOTAL changes SR 2002 to PESA 2003	*283.5*	*335.6*	*309.6*
PESA 2003 (tables 1.7 & 1.8)/ Main Estimates 2003-04	**20,351.2**	**21,524.3**	**22,946.8**
Budgeting & classification changes	-18.3	-19.5	-19.5
Interdepartmental transfers	26.7	30.9	27.2
End Year Flexibility	392.1	0.0	0.0
Spending Policy:			
Council Tax/Rent rebate adjustment	40.4	0.0	0.0
Speed Cameras	9.3	0.0	0.0
Pre Budget Report 2003 - Local Authorities	0.0	34.9	0.2
Pre Budget Report 2003 - Employer Training Pilots	0.0	4.1	8.2
Additional ASLC provision	0.0	0.0	23.8
Invest to Save Budget	0.0	1.6	1.5
Outturn adjustments	-652.8	0.0	0.0
TOTAL changes PESA 2003 to PESA 2004	*-202.7*	*51.9*	*41.4*
PESA 2004 (tables 1.7 & 1.8)/ Main Estimates 2004-05	**20,148.5**	**21,576.3**	**22,988.1**

(for further changes to 2005-06, see CSR 2004 table)

Budgeting & classification changes	0.0	418.6
Interdepartmental transfers	0.0	11.5
End Year Flexibility	0.0	500.0
Spending Policy:		
Council Tax/Rent rebate adjustment	0.0	-84.6
Outturn adjustments	78.0	-500.0
TOTAL changes PESA 2004 to PESA 2005	*78.0*	*345.6*
PESA 2005 (tables 1.5 & 1.9)/ Main Estimates 2005-06	**20,226.5**	**21,921.9**

SCOTLAND - SR 2004

	2005-06 £m	2006-07 £m	2007-08 £m
SR 2004 settlement	**22,987.8**	**24,514.9**	**25,870.4**
Budgeting & classification changes	379.0	365.6	365.6
Interdepartmental transfers	-0.6	-0.7	-0.7
Spending Policy:			
Counter Terrorism	1.0	0.0	0.0
Pre Budget Report 2004 - Bookstart	0.9	0.9	0.9
Pre Budget Report 2004 - Early Education	0.0	1.0	1.0
Pre Budget Report 2004 - Employer Training Pilots	0.0	6.6	13.4
Pre Budget Report 2004 - Childcare	0.0	20.4	13.2
Pre Budget Report 2004 - Council Tax	12.7	0.0	0.0
Pre Budget Report 2004 - Landfill Tax	8.0	0.0	0.0
Pre Budget Report 2004 - Financial Inclusion Fund	0.2	1.6	3.1
Budget 2005 - Youth Crime	0.0	1.0	1.4
Budget 2005 - Regional Crime	0.0	1.0	1.0
Budget 2005 - LAGBI	1.1	5.3	10.4
Budget 2005 - Russell Commission	0.9	2.6	6.8
Budget 2005 - Free Bus Travel	0.0	35.7	37.5
Budget 2005 - Education	0.0	25.4	31.9
Budget 2005 - Arts Council	0.0	0.6	0.7
Budget 2005 - Employer Training Pilots	4.1	0.0	0.0
Council Tax/Rent rebate adjustment	-88.6	-88.6	-88.6
Invest to Save	0.0	1.6	0.0
TOTAL changes SR 2004 to PESA 2005	*318.5*	*379.9*	*397.6*
PESA 2005 (tables 1.5 & 1.9)/ Main Estimates 2005-06	**23,306.4**	**24,894.7**	**26,267.9**
Budgeting & classification changes	-185.8	-185.6	-151.9
Interdepartmental transfers	17.7	372.5	362.5
End Year Flexibility	190.0	0.0	0.0
Spending Policy:			
Pre Budget Report 2005 - Warm Front	0.0	12.7	10.6
Pre Budget Report 2005 - Holocaust Education Trust	0.0	0.2	0.2
Pre Budget Report 2005 - Education Exports	0.0	0.3	0.3
Pre Budget Report 2005 - Enterprise Education	0.0	0.2	0.0
Pre Budget Report 2005 - Youth Service Grant	0.0	2.7	2.7
Pre Budget Report 2005 - Carbon Trust Loans	0.0	1.5	2.0
Pre Budget Report 2005 - Employer Training Pilot	0.0	3.8	3.8
Pre Budget Report 2005 - Children's Document	0.0	2.7	2.7
Budget 2006 - Education	0.0	22.3	37.0
Budget 2006 - Neighbourhood Policing	0.0	8.4	0.0
Budget 2006 - Grass Roots Sport	0.0	0.8	0.1
Budget 2006 - Education & Science	0.0	0.9	0.9
Budget 2006 - Further Education	0.0	0.0	4.8
Budget 2006 - Women in Work Comm	0.0	2.0	2.0
Budget 2006 - Energy Efficiency	0.0	0.5	0.0
Budget 2006 - Smart Metering	0.0	0.4	0.1
Budget 2006 - Football Foundation	0.0	0.1	0.1
Budget 2006 - Youth Opportunities Fund	0.0	0.2	0.1
Budget 2006 - Education & Exports	0.0	0.2	0.2
Budget 2006 - Youth Media	0.0	0.3	0.3
Budget 2006 - Workplace Nurseries	0.0	0.8	0.8
Budget 2006 - ICT in Education	0.0	0.5	0.5

Invest to Save	1.1	2.0	1.8
Outturn adjustments	-94.0	0.0	0.0
TOTAL changes PESA 2005 to PESA 2006	*-71.0*	*250.6*	*281.7*
PESA 2006 (tables 1.5 & 1.10)/ Main Estimates 2006-07	**23,235.4**	**25,145.4**	**26,549.7**
Budgeting & classification changes	29.3	38.3	44.6
Interdepartmental transfers	0.0	3.8	8.3
End Year Flexibility	0.0	166.0	0.0
Spending Policy:			
Pre Budget Report 2006 - Books for 11 year olds	0.0	0.0	0.4
Pre Budget Report 2006 - Secondary catch up	0.0	0.0	1.0
Pre Budget Report 2006 - Schools Standards Grant	0.0	0.0	13.1
Pre Budget Report 2006 - LBRO better regulation	0.0	0.1	0.3
Pre Budget Report 2006 - Gowers (trading standards)	0.0	0.0	0.4
Pre Budget Report 2006 - Retail enforecment pilot	0.0	0.0	0.2
Pre Budget Report 2006 - Warm Front	0.0	0.0	0.6
Budget 2007 - Mircrogeneration	0.0	0.0	0.6
Speed Cameras	0.0	0.0	8.5
Council Tax/Rent rebate adjustment	0.0	57.0	0.0
Invest to Save	0.0	0.0	0.3
Outturn adjustments	-212.0	-142.2	0.0
TOTAL changes PESA 2006 to PESA 2007	*-182.7*	*123.0*	*78.3*
PESA 2007 (tables 1.5 & 1.10)/ Main Estimates 2007-08	**23,052.7**	**25,268.3**	**26,628.0**
Budgeting & classification changes	128.0	140.3	100.1
Interdepartmental transfers	0.6	0.5	44.6
End Year Flexibility	0.0	0.0	655.0
Outturn adjustments	0.0	-20.0	-42.1
TOTAL changes PESA 2007 to PESA 2008	*128.6*	*120.8*	*757.6*
PESA 2008 (tables 1.5 & 1.10)/ Main Estimates 2008-09	**23,181.3**	**25,389.2**	**27,385.6**

SCOTLAND - CSR 2007

	2008-09 £m	2009-10 £m	2010-11 £m
CSR 2007 settlement	**27,601.3**	**28,755.3**	**30,141.8**
Budgeting & classification changes	-40.0	-20.0	0.0
Interdepartmental transfers	1.4	1.4	1.4
Spending Policy:			
Budget 2008 - Child Poverty	0.7	2.1	4.2
Modernisation Fund (1)	5.0	0.9	0.3
Invest to Save Budget	1.0	0.3	0.0
TOTAL changes CSR 2007 to PESA 2008	*-31.9*	*-15.3*	*5.9*
PESA 2008 (tables 1.5 & 1.10)/ Main Estimates 2008-09	**27,569.4**	**28,740.0**	**30,147.7**
Budgeting & classification changes	17.0	11.0	5.0
Interdepartmental transfers	17.0	3.0	0.0
End Year Flexibility	300.0	0.0	0.0
Spending Policy:			
PBR 2008 - Citzens Advice Bureau	0.4	0.7	0.2
PBR 2008 - Warm Front	5.0	5.0	0.0
Modernisation Fund (2)	13.1	0.0	0.0
Adjustment to Health Capital	0.0	0.0	-128.6
Budget 2009 - Housing Package	0.0	33.7	11.6
Budget 2009 - Green Energy Package	0.0	21.8	5.7
Budget 2009 - Youth Employment Package	0.0	4.9	7.4
Budget 2009 - Employment Fund	0.0	0.0	0.0
Budget 2009 - Third Sector & Icelandic Banks	0.0	1.7	0.0
Budget 2009 - Capital for FE Colleges	0.0	16.9	0.0
Budget 2009 - VFM Savings	0.0	0.0	-391.7
Capital draw forward	53.2	294.5	-347.6
Total Changes PESA 2008 to date	*405.6*	*393.3*	*-838.0*
CURRENT POSITION	**27,975.1**	**29,133.3**	**29,309.8**

WALES - SR 2002

	2003-04 £m	2004-05 £m	2005-06 £m
SR 2002 settlement	**10,520.7**	**11,158.5**	**11,998.6**
Budgeting & classification changes	91.4	117.8	126.4
Interdepartmental transfers	-16.9	5.2	4.7
Spending Policy:			
Pre Budget Report 2002 - Employer Training Pilots	6.4	0.0	0.0
Budget 2003 - Futurebuilders	0.6	3.0	3.8
Budget 2003 - Parenting Fund	0.3	0.6	0.6
Budget 2003 - Landfill Tax Credit Scheme	4.9	5.4	5.4
Budget 2003 - SR 2002 corrections	0.2	0.3	0.6
Invest to Save Budget	0.6	0.3	0.1
TOTAL changes SR 2002 to PESA 2003	*87.5*	*132.6*	*141.7*
PESA 2003 (tables 1.7 & 1.8)/ Main Estimates 2003-04	**10,608.2**	**11,291.1**	**12,140.3**
Budgeting & classification changes	1.4	1.4	1.4
Interdepartmental transfers	0.3	-10.1	-6.4
End Year Flexibility	180.0	0.0	0.0
Spending Policy:			
ASLC Provision	0.0	0.0	7.5
Council Tax/Rent rebate adjustment	2.0	0.0	0.0
Pre Budget Report 2003 - Council Tax	0.0	20.0	0.0
Pre Budget Report 2003 - Employer Training Pilots	0.0	2.4	4.7
Invest to Save Budget	0.0	0.1	0.2
Outturn adjustments	-99.3	0.0	0.0
TOTAL changes PESA 2003 to PESA 2004	*84.4*	*13.8*	*7.4*
PESA 2004 (tables 1.7 & 1.8)/ Main Estimates 2004-05	**10,692.5**	**11,304.8**	**12,147.7**

(for further changes to 2005-06, see CSR 2004 table)

	2003-04 £m	2004-05 £m	
Budgeting & classification changes	0.0	121.0	
Interdepartmental transfers	6.0	19.1	
End Year Flexibility	0.0	286.0	
Spending Policy:			
Council Tax/Rent rebate adjustment	0.0	-23.6	
Outturn adjustments	-57.0	-153.0	
TOTAL changes PESA 2004 to PESA 2005	*-51.0*	*249.5*	
PESA 2005 (tables 1.5 & 1.9)/ Main Estimates 2005-06	**10,641.5**	**11,554.3**	

WALES - SR 2004

	2005-06 £m	2006-07 £m	2007-08 £m
SR 2004 settlement	**12,147.7**	**13,019.8**	**13,817.6**
Budgeting & classification changes	109.6	106.4	106.3
Interdepartmental transfers	-8.8	-1.1	0.6
Spending Policy:			
Council Tax/Rent rebate adjustment	-24.2	-24.2	-24.2
Pre Budget Report 2004 - Early Education	0.0	0.6	0.6
Pre Budget Report 2004 - Bookstart	0.5	0.5	0.5
Pre Budget Report 2004 - Employer Training Pilots	0.0	3.8	7.8
Pre Budget Report 2004 - Childcare	0.0	11.8	7.7
Pre Budget Report 2004 - Council Tax	7.4	0.0	0.0
Pre Budget Report 2004 - Landfill Tax	5.5	0.0	0.0
Counter Terrorism	1.2	0.0	0.0
Budget 2005 - LAGBI	0.6	3.1	6.0
Budget 2005 - Russell Commission	0.5	1.5	3.9
Budget 2005 - Free Bus Travel	0.0	20.6	21.6
Budget 2005 - Education	0.0	14.7	18.4
Budget 2005 - Arts Council	0.0	0.3	0.4
Budget 2005 - Employer Training Pilots	2.4	0.0	0.0
Invest to Save	0.0	0.3	0.0
TOTAL changes SR 2004 to PESA 2005	*94.6*	*138.3*	*149.6*
PESA 2005 (tables 1.5 & 1.9)/ Main Estimates 2005-06	**12242.3**	**13,158.1**	**13,967.2**
Budgeting & classification changes	-233.9	-233.9	-233.9
Interdepartmental transfers	149.8	132.6	134.2
End Year Flexibility	228.5	0.0	0.0
Spending Policy:			
Pre Budget Report 2005 - Holocaust Education Trust	0.0	0.1	0.1
Pre Budget Report 2005 - Education Exports	0.0	0.2	0.2
Pre Budget Report 2005 - Enterprise Education	0.0	0.1	0.0
Pre Budget Report 2005 - Youth Service Grant	0.0	1.6	1.6
Pre Budget Report 2005 - Carbon Trust Loans	0.0	0.9	1.2
Pre Budget Report 2005 - Warm Front	1.2	7.4	6.2
Pre Budget Report 2005 - NETP wage compensation	0.0	2.2	2.2
Pre Budget Report 2005 - Children's Document	0.0	1.6	1.6
Budget 2006 - Education	0.0	13.0	21.5
Budget 2006 - Grass Roots Sport	0.0	0.5	0.1
Budget 2006 - Education & Science	0.0	0.5	0.5
Budget 2006 - Further Education	0.0	0.0	2.8
Budget 2006 - Women in Work Comm	0.0	1.2	1.2
Budget 2006 - Energy Efficiency	0.0	0.3	0.0
Budget 2006 - Smart Metering	0.0	0.2	0.1
Budget 2006 - Football Foundation	0.0	0.1	0.1
Budget 2006 - Youth Opportunities Fund	0.0	0.1	0.0
Budget 2006 - Education & Exports	0.0	0.1	0.1
Budget 2006 - Youth Media	0.0	0.2	0.2
Budget 2006 - Workplace Nurseries	0.0	0.5	0.5
Budget 2006 - ICT in Education	0.0	0.3	0.3

Invest to Save Budget	0.6	1.1	0.9
Outturn adjustments	0.0	0.0	0.0
TOTAL changes PESA 2005 to PESA 2006	146.3	-69.3	-58.6
PESA 2006 (tables 1.5 & 1.10)/ Main Estimates 2006-07	12388.6	13,088.8	13,908.7
Budgeting & classification changes	21.9	30.2	29.1
Interdepartmental transfers	82.3	102.3	125.5
End Year Flexibility	0.0	98.5	0.0
Spending Policy:			
Pre Budget Report 2006 - Books for 11 year olds	0.0	0.0	0.2
Pre Budget Report 2006 - Secondary catch up	0.0	0.0	0.6
Pre Budget Report 2006 - Schools Standards Grant	0.0	0.0	7.6
Pre Budget Report 2006 - LBRO better regulation	0.0	0.1	0.2
Pre Budget Report 2006 - Gowers (trading standards)	0.0	0.0	0.2
Pre Budget Report 2006 - Retail enforecment pilot	0.0	0.0	0.1
Pre Budget Report 2006 - Warm Front	0.0	0.0	0.4
Budget 2007 - Mircrogeneration	0.0	0.0	0.4
Council Tax/Rent rebate adjustment	0.0	16.0	0.0
Invest to Save Budget	0.0	0.0	0.1
Outturn adjustments	-298.5	-106.9	0.0
TOTAL changes PESA 2006 to PESA 2007	-194.3	140.1	164.4
PESA 2007 (tables 1.5 & 1.10)/ Main Estimates 2007-08	12194.3	13,229.0	14,073.1
Interdepartmental transfers	0.5	0.4	1.4
Outturn adjustments	0.0	-211.6	-131.6
End Year Flexibility	0.0	0.0	90.0
TOTAL changes PESA 2007 to PESA 2008	0.5	-211.2	-40.2
PESA 2008 (tables 1.5 & 1.10)/ Main Estimates 2008-09	12194.7	13,017.7	14,032.9

WALES - CSR 2007

	2008-09 £m	2009-10 £m	2010-11 £m
CSR 2007 settlement	14,551.9	15,243.6	16,056.4
Interdepartmental transfers	1.7	1.7	1.7
Spending Policy:			
Budget 2008 - Child Poverty	0.4	1.2	2.4
Budget 2008 - Modernisation Funding	0.5	0.2	0.2
Invest to Save Budget	0.5	0.1	0.0
TOTAL changes CSR 2007 to PESA 2008	3.1	3.2	4.3
PESA 2008 (tables 1.5 & 1.10)/ Main Estimates 2008-09	14,555.0	15,246.8	16,060.7
Interdepartmental transfers	-15.0	-17.2	-18.8
End Year Flexibility	68.8	0.0	0.0
Spending Policy:			
EUSF funding for Flooding	0.2	0.0	0.0
Pre Budget Report 2008 - Warm Front	2.9	2.9	0.0
Adjustment to Health Capital	0.0	0.0	-74.5
Budget 2009 - Housing Package	0.0	19.5	6.7
Budget 2009 - Green Energy Package	0.0	12.6	3.3
Budget 2009 - Youth Employment Package	0.0	2.9	4.3
Budget 2009 - Employment Fund	0.0	0.0	0.0
Budget 2009 - Third Sector & Icelandic Banks	0.0	1.0	0.0
Budget 2009 - Capital for FE Colleges	0.0	9.8	0.0
Budget 2009 - VFM Savings	0.0	0.0	-215.8
Capital draw forward	28.2	0.0	-28.2
Total Changes PESA 2008 to date	85.1	31.5	-323.0
CURRENT POSITION	14,640.1	15,278.3	15,737.7

WEDNESDAY 18 MARCH 2009

Present	Forsyth of Drumlean, L	Richard, L (Chairman)
	Hollis of Heigham, B	Rooker, L
	Lawson of Blaby, L	Rowe-Beddoe, L
	Mar and Kellie, E	Sewel, L
	Moser, L	

Examination of Witnesses

Witnesses: RT HON LORD MACGREGOR OF PULHAM MARKET, a Member of the House and SIR BRIAN UNWIN, examined.

Q508 Chairman: Thank you very much for coming and giving us the opportunity to ask a few questions and to listen to what you have to say. The evidence sessions are broadcast live on the internet and a full transcript is going to be taken. You have the opportunity to make relatively small corrections to the transcript, but I do not think you can alter the sense of what was said. Can I also say that if you felt, after you had given evidence today, that you wanted to submit further written evidence we would be delighted to receive it if you felt certain areas had not been covered or not covered in sufficient depth. Perhaps I can start with a fairly general question. We are trying to get a real feel for how this thing actually worked and it would help us to know from both of you how rigorously was the Barnett Formula applied in funding the Scottish, Welsh Offices and Northern Ireland departments when you were at the Treasury. How much negotiation around the Formula took place and how important was that negotiation in making the machinery work? How much did this involve ongoing by-passes of the Formula, how much one-off additions to the territorial block grants and how much of that was pressure from the individual Secretaries of State? How did the Treasury deal with this when it happened?
Lord MacGregor of Pulham Market: Can I begin by saying it is interesting to be on the other side of the table for so many years in a different position. I would like to draw a distinction between the 1985–87 period when I was in the Treasury, which you do want to talk about and which this question is addressed to, where frankly these issues were comparatively minor in relation to the huge pressures I was facing on public expenditure at the time and the question of the Barnett Formula more generally. I have always been interested and had a view on it, although it has not been on the top of my mind in recent years. I would be happy to go into that as well if that would help. I have been trying to bring myself up-to-date by reading as much of the evidence as I could. On the question that you have asked, I think the answer is very little. The Barnett Formula as such was more or less a given. We did not attempt to deal with the issues

that were involved in the base line, the block. There were, of course, discussions about additional bids. There were discussions about what became later known as Formula by-pass issues and there were, therefore, some small additions, I recollect—it was a long time ago—but we did not actually get into the detail of challenging the block. That was left to the Secretary of State to dispose of as he wished and the Formula was applied.

Q509 Chairman: You did not get into how the Formula was made up, whether it should be changed or stay as it is, it was just a formula.
Lord MacGregor of Pulham Market: We did have a small issue in the report that Sir Brian Unwin did which was looking a bit at the Formula—and if you like I will go into that in some detail—but the basic position was we accepted the block and then there were discussions in negotiations between us on individual bids and so on, some issues about savings in other English areas and should they be reflected in additional expenditure for Scotland and that sort of thing but these were comparatively marginal. The other important point to take into account when you come to the Unwin Report was that I became Chief Secretary in September 1985, not a good time when the actual departmental negotiations were literally just about to begin, and found it very difficult to achieve the savings we were looking for in expenditure that time. Thereafter I raised certain issues right across the board, one of which was in relation to the Barnett Formula which we were going to look at in preparation for the 1986 Annual Expenditure Review and that is where the Unwin Report came in. In terms of actual negotiation with the Secretary of State for Scotland, it was as I have described.
Sir Brian Unwin: Can I, my Lord Chairman, just endorse what Lord MacGregor said and, first of all, say what a pleasure it is to be here myself. The last time I was in this committee corridor was before the Public Accounts Committee on many occasions, so this is a much more pleasant occasion. I was in the Cabinet Office, not the Treasury at the time; I was on

secondment from the Treasury. I was the Deputy Secretary, as they called it then, in the Cabinet Office in charge of the economic secretariat which was servicing all the economic business of the Cabinet and the economic committees of the Cabinet. My secretariat and I were called on to produce many interdepartmental reports and this was one of them. I have to be frank and say I had not thought of it since 1986 until it was raised again recently. May I make two points? Firstly, I very much agree with Lord MacGregor that the Barnett Formula was taken as given, as it were, and it was a convenient guide each year. We did not go back and renegotiate it and have a look at it. What it did was establish a formula that most people accepted although it only covered between a half and two-thirds of expenditure in the territories. It was the generally agreed basis for carrying forward the public expenditure projections although the Treasury did chip away at it from time to time. Secondly, if I may just add to what Lord MacGregor said, the 1985 public expenditure round was a particularly difficult one because the Treasury and the Chief Secretary were unable to reach agreement on many of the main spending programmes. The Prime Minister set up what was known as the Star Chamber, which was an ad hoc committee of senior ministers, chaired at the time by Lord President Lord Whitelaw and comprising a number of senior Secretaries of State who had either settled their departmental programme with the Treasury or had no major departmental responsibility, ministers with rather exotic titles like Lord Privy Seal and Chancellor of the Duchy of Lancaster and so on. I was in the Cabinet Office then and my job was to organise and run the Star Chamber under Lord Whitelaw. We did have particular difficulties with the Scottish Office that year. It was not the largest public programme by any means, in fact it was rather trivial in comparison with defence, housing and so on, but I do remember it was very difficult to reach agreement. I do actually remember being called to a meeting with the Prime Minister and the Lord President and being sent around to go and do a deal with the then Secretary of State for Scotland at the time, Sir Malcolm Rifkind. The genesis of the report I was asked to chair was partly to search for the truth, as always, but partly to see whether there were respectable arguments to make some adjustment in the Formula and possibly to reduce the allocation to Scotland. As you will have seen from the report, taking expenditure per capita on the block for England as 100, the Scots were around 126 so there was a very much larger proportionate share, for all sorts of reasons, going to Scotland than to England. That is the background to the report I was asked to produce.

Q510 *Chairman:* Was there a needs assessment of any kind?

Lord MacGregor of Pulham Market: Not at all. It was made very clear in the remit that it would not tackle the question of need. This was just one of several follow-ups to the 1985 round that we did with various departments, so the Scots were not unique, but this was one that we did want to tackle because we wanted to see if there were still further savings in the Scottish budget.

Sir Brian Unwin: Again, as the report makes clear, population was not one of the factors taken into account in producing the so-called Barnett Formula. In fact, our report went on to say that if you are looking for ways or reasons for changing it you could make use of population as well as possibly some other social or economic indicators.

Lord MacGregor of Pulham Market: It might be useful to go onto the report in due course but that is the background to why the Unwin Report was set up.

Q511 *Lord Forsyth of Drumlean:* When I was a minister in the Scottish Office, both as a junior minister and as the Secretary of State, I always had the impression that the view in the Treasury was that there was the need to have some kind of needs-based system for allocation, particularly as regards Scotland, because the feeling was that there was not adequate provision. Was that just paranoia on the part of some of our officials or was there a real cultural need? Looking at the history of this there has been a series of attempts to try and move towards some kind of needs-based assessment which have met a sudden death in a dark corridor for reasons which remain obscure.

Lord MacGregor of Pulham Market: When I was in the Treasury I was not aware, and I think Lord Barnett said the same, that the needs assessment was undertaken in the late 1970s. I have made clear already that when we were trying to see if there was scope for savings in Scotland through the Unwin Report, needs was excluded. I do not think at that stage, and I explained some of the reasons, that we were looking to tackle the block base line and the needs basis on which that was apparently drawn up. I have views about that which I can express later, but the answer to the question is that was not in the mind. What was in the mind was, as with every other departmental budget, where can we make savings.

Lord Lawson of Blaby: If I may, Lord MacGregor was Chief Secretary as the time I was Chancellor and I was very fortunate because I could not have had a better Chief Secretary as I could leave all this with total confidence to him, and with Sir Brian Unwin in charge of the Star Chamber that was in such capable hands that it really made my job very much less difficult than it would have been otherwise.

Baroness Hollis of Heigham: Why did you not sort it?

Q512 *Lord Lawson of Blaby:* The answer is, if I may, that if Lord MacGregor said that this was a relatively small issue compared with the much bigger issues he had to deal with, that was true in spades so far as I was concerned. If I may get back to the evidence we have just had, particularly the evidence of Sir Brian, he seems to get absolutely to the heart of this. The great curiosity in all this is that if you read, and I am sure our witnesses have read, the written evidence given by the Treasury they refer to it all the time as the population-based Barnett Formula. All the time it is the population-based Barnett Formula but, of course, on the population basis, which is attended to rigorously so far as the annual changes to the up-rating are concerned, there is no population-based base line and that is the extraordinary anomaly. Obviously population is not the only criterion; it is what you might call the first cut. There are other dimensions that have to be taken into account. It does seem anomalous, and this was the main burden of the Unwin Report, that whereas population is considered to be the most important basis for change, it is not considered to be of any importance at all for the base line. Obviously there are political reasons for this but it is a curious anomaly. It seems to me this is the heart of the problem and that is why Lord Barnett, when he gave evidence to us, was upset about what seemed to be the unfair treatment vis-a-vis Scotland and England. I wonder what was the reaction, either by Sir Brian or Lord MacGregor who was Chief Secretary at the time, to the report that Sir Brian made which actually did focus on this very point.
Sir Brian Unwin: My recollection, my Lord Chairman, is that no action was taken at all.

Q513 *Lord Lawson of Blaby:* Was any reason given?
Sir Brian Unwin: I simply do not recall. If I may say so, looking at the report again, and it is the first time I have read this since 1986, I am not particularly proud of it. It is a pretty thin report and looking at it now I would say we did not do a great deal more than go through the motions. What we did not tackle, and that was because I was not asked if not actually forbidden to do so, was to look at the needs basis. If we had done that it would have been a very much more profound exercise. If you do the whole thing thoroughly you would not only be taking account of needs but you would be looking at the quality of services, political preferences in the territories and so forth. This was a very quick and clean job which, in essence, said if you want to find some justification for making some changes, and quite honestly the best way of doing that would be just to make a one-off change in the base line, population is your best bet. Lord MacGregor, as Chief Secretary, may remember the follow-up but I do not actually remember any action being taken as a result of this report.

Lord MacGregor of Pulham Market: It was probably my decision if I remember rightly. I may be wrong but I will tell you why I think it was. It started from the point, and we must always come back to this, we had bigger fish to fry in the whole public expenditure rounds of much bigger sums. I had an instinctive feeling that at some stage the position in relation to the Scottish base line, as well as the Barnett Formula, had to be tackled but I did not really want to take it on that year for two reasons: one was that, as Lord Forsyth knows well and as Lord Lang knows, the Scots always had a very, very strong position politically. Lord Barnett said that governments are against change but actually it was not that, it was the political reaction. At that stage we were not prepared to open up this huge area from the political point of view. The second reason was that if you are going to go into a needs study you do not do it half-way through the Parliament. I think if you are going to do it, as it is such a big thing, it has to be done immediately in a new Parliament. It will take about two years for the study to be completed and then the follow-up action. I did not see there was going to be much political merit in tackling the whole base line in the Barnett Formula. Why did we not pursue the recommendations in the Unwin Report? If you actually look at the Unwin Report they had three recommendations. The first two were different variations of changes in the Formula whereby the territorial blocks were adjusted, and that was for the increase not the blocks themselves, on the basis of the existing Formula but in line with the population changes since 1979, which I think was what Michael Portillo acted on as Chief Secretary. If this had been in force in 1985 the saving in 1986–87 would have been £2 million, that was the change in the total for Scotland, and £2 million and £2 million in the next two years. That was just not worth entering into because it would very quickly have been absorbed in any additional changes in the Formula by-pass. In the other two the saving was £9 million which, again, is pretty small. There was a third and that was to adjust the base line once off to reflect the changes in population since 1979 so that was actually looking at the base line, but adjusting it once off. That would have produced a great debate about whether we were right to change the base line but even that would only have produced a reduction of £109 million going to Scotland, and in terms of all the other figures we were dealing with and the kind of issues we were arguing about off the Barnett Formula it was not worth it. That is why I say I think this period was a fairly minor one and the big issue is where we go now.
Sir Brian Unwin: In retrospect, I am surprised that we did not somehow latch onto the needs element in the rate support grant. There is a basis of calculation there used for the calculation of rate support grant and, looking back, I am not sure why we did not. We

had someone from the Department of the Environment on my group but we did not, for whatever reason, make use of that at the time perhaps because in my terms of reference I was asked or encouraged not to look at the needs element.

Q514 *Chairman:* There is no doubt that it is possible to do a proper needs assessment.
Sir Brian Unwin: I think it would be perfectly possible and would not take an enormous group.

Q515 *Chairman:* You could then work out the base line on the basis of that assessment.
Sir Brian Unwin: There would be a lot of political choices to address.

Q516 *Lord Moser:* On your former point, there had been a needs study in 1979 and we are talking about 1986. Was that suppressed? Were you not allowed to look at that? Were you not allowed, by your masters, to find out whether maybe it was worth going back to that?
Sir Brian Unwin: My recollection, and it is only my recollection because the copy of the report I have strikes out the introduction and I do not have my covering minutes to the Prime Minister, which no doubt repeated what I had been asked to do, is that I was probably discouraged from getting into the needs issue and so did not cover it.

Q517 *Lord Moser:* By the Treasury or somebody else?
Sir Brian Unwin: It was not the Treasury who asked for the report; it was asked for by the Prime Minister, I think, on behalf of the government.

Q518 *Lord Moser:* Who might have discouraged you?
Sir Brian Unwin: I simply do not know. It may have been that what the Prime Minister and ministers wanted was a pretty quick and clean report and to have gone into the needs element would have made it a much more complicated and lengthier exercise although it could have been done.
Lord MacGregor of Pulham Market: I think that is the answer, we were trying to find something for the 1986 public expenditure round. Looking at the whole of the needs basis would have been a massive task in a few months and we were looking for something that would have got quicker results. I repeat that I certainly did not know the Treasury had done a needs assessment in the late 1970s.

Q519 *Lord Rooker:* Thinking about the dates that we are talking about, 1985–86, this was raised with somebody else that came in front of us and I thought at the time you have to think of other things going on. Surely in 1985, in preparation for parliamentary year

1986 in terms of the atmosphere, particularly when you mentioned about the rate support grant, the legislation for the community charge for Scotland was actually right in front of us as parliamentarians. The legislation took place before the 1987 election so it was a real hot potato in 1985 as you go into 1986. Given the radical change, with the allegations that Scotland is being used as a test bed for this, if then someone starts an internal discussion about the Barnett Formula and chopping back in Scotland you can imagine closing that discussion down, and I am just thinking aloud. I am thinking of the other things going on at the time which would have caused the pressure. You do not go onto another debate when you already have this one; keep the Formula as it is, do not pursue the report that you used and do not open it up.
Lord MacGregor of Pulham Market: That may be part of it and it is difficult to reflect back on how many issues there were. Every week, sometimes almost every day, I came into the Treasury and there was a demand from somewhere for additional money as a result of EU decisions, European Court decisions and so on. I can remember on one occasion I had to negotiate very, very hard for a very quick period about some outcome of a thing called the Tin Council which was more than £400 million, so in relation to fighting those for £2 million that was just not worth it. I had hoped it would come up with more than it did.
Sir Brian Unwin: It is also true that in the context of the public expenditure round whether you did a bit more or less on Scotland, Wales or Northern Ireland was pretty irrelevant to the outcome of the whole exercise. The exercise was primarily about defence, health, housing, social security and so on. Important though the territorial issues were, they were not crucial to the conclusion of the public expenditure round.
Lord MacGregor of Pulham Market: Perhaps I can make one other point before we go onto other things. I am describing what happened exactly then but I have always been in support of Lord Barnett wanting to see a change in the Barnett Formula. I do very much agree that a needs assessment has to be the basis to see what the change should be. Although I did not tackle it ministerially then, I do strongly support it.

Q520 *Chairman:* What I find fascinating is clearly the base line, the block line, went on from year to year without any re-examination of what it should and should not be and no re-examination of needs either. The Barnett bit of it was really to do with changes in the existing expenditure round.
Lord MacGregor of Pulham Market: That is absolutely right. I have every sympathy with the point that Lord Barnett was making to you. I can remember 1978

very clearly. He was having a terrific problem with his Finance Bills because we had quite a powerful team on our side and these were the days when we went through the night. It was almost a full-time job in handling it. It was a tremendous pressure period and to get them off your back, in a public expenditure review, having to argue the minute details of the territorial departments was a great prize in the negotiations and so the Barnett Formula was created. Doing it on the basis of one year should not have meant that it lasted as a formula for 30 years. It was never conceived that way at all.

Q521 *Lord Lawson of Blaby:* Lord MacGregor mentioned, and it was also my recollection of that time, that as a government we were fighting battles on a number of fronts. We had to choose, and I am sure it was true with every government but it was certainly true with that government, which fronts we were going to fight because you cannot fight on every front at the same time because that would be stupid. The political battle on making an adjustment would have been a very considerable one and, therefore, you can say, even though objectively this does not stand up this arrangement, it is ludicrous, the battle would be such a big one that you choose battles where you are going to get a bigger return. The fact is that in the first instance, whether you have a needs assessment or whether you adjust on population because of the base line on population, it comes to much the same thing. The number one premise must be that needs are greater the greater the number of people. In the first cut, as you said, the population thing is the same as the needs and then you refine it further, of course. You say, "If we are going to do this we cannot do it straight away; we are going to have to phase it in over a number of years". If you phase it in over a number of years then the gain each year is relatively trivial and so you say, "We are not going to fight that battle. We are going to reserve our ammunition and our strength for fighting other battles" and that is, in fact, as I recall it, what happened.

Lord MacGregor of Pulham Market: I see that convergence has featured quite a bit in your discussions. I do not recall convergence ever being mentioned from the time I was there. The first time I was aware of the convergence argument was in Lord Lang's book which came out in 2002 and its pages on the Barnett Formula mentioned convergence. That was the first time I was aware there was a convergence.

Sir Brian Unwin: If I may just endorse what I think Lord Lawson was, in principle, saying, from the point of view of the public expenditure control troops fighting in the Treasury trenches, it was extremely convenient to have a formula which had automaticity each year however intellectually defective that might be. If the rest of Whitehall accepted it, it was convenient. You got that out of the way before you got on to the big stuff in the public expenditure battle.
Chairman: If you look at it now, clearly it was intellectually defective and for 30-odd years nobody has looked at the defects.

Q522 *Lord Lawson of Blaby:* We were aware of them but we had bigger fish to fry.
Lord MacGregor of Pulham Market: Several of us have advocated the fundamental assessment of the Barnett Formula in Parliament since. It has not been 30 years without it being challenged.

Q523 *Lord Smith of Clifton:* All these arguments about bigger fish to fry will always apply and, therefore, there will always be the convenience and opportunity across Parliament: let us leave it alone. Lord MacGregor said that he thought you should do this at the beginning of a Parliament and it would take two years. One of the questions I was asked to put was what would be the level of administrative resources. It seems to me the level of administrative resources would be disproportionate just to get an intellectually coherent formula; you might just as well carry on as before.
Lord MacGregor of Pulham Market: I do not agree with that.

Q524 *Lord Smith of Clifton:* I am not saying I agree with it. I am saying the argument would be persuasive at any one time.
Lord MacGregor of Pulham Market: Personally, I think the time has come to really look at it and it is up to your Committee to decide whether that is feasible and how it should be done. There are the grounds of equity and we all know those arguments. There are grounds that the base line was set in 1978 in totally different circumstances. We would probably have to look at the needs assessments in 1978 too, but it has carried on ever since and all of those arguments. The argument about convergence only makes a marginal difference. All of those arguments seem to be pointing to a need to look at a real needs assessment, and both in Scotland and England they do have it in local government in the way in which we distribute grants to local government. It is a big issue and that is why I think it needs to be tackled at the very beginning of Parliament.

Q525 *Lord Smith of Clifton:* What do you think would be the level of resources?
Lord MacGregor of Pulham Market: It depends how you intend to do it. It depends on what form of inquiry. You would have to have an independent inquiry of some sort, an independent task force, and not politicians, that would look dispassionately at the issues and the actual facts. I do not know how long that would take or how many resources.

Sir Brian Unwin: Probably the argument against it, as you imply, is the can of worms argument rather than the administrative effort and resources that would have to go into it. Even if you commissioned an external independent inquiry, it would not require all that much to do a decent job looking at needs and all the other factors, perhaps including tax although that takes you into another very controversial area.

Q526 *Baroness Hollis of Heigham:* I understand the comments made by Lord MacGregor and reinforced by Lord Lawson about bigger fish to fry and prioritisations. That would have a political judgment that we all sympathise with. What I do not understand however, and still do not, is the role of, if I may use a generic term, the Civil Service. In my limited junior experience, all the time benefits, forms of taxes and so on are kept under review. This is part of the guardian trustee role of the senior Civil Service, certainly for Grade 5 and elevated levels above. The fact that political masters may decide not to act on it is perfectly comprehensible given the situation. What puzzles me is the withdrawal from any apparent contemplation in a way that seems to me unprecedented from my experience, certainly on the benefits side. I would have expected every three to five years a senior civil servant, Grade 5 or above, to come along and say, "This benefit is now no longer adequate or fit for purpose. We believe we ought to review it. You may or may not find the recommendations acceptable, palatable, desirable or whatever but, minister, we will be failing in our duty as trustees and guardians of public monies if we did not go down that path." What baffles me is that failure of the Civil Service, particularly the Treasury, to act. I take Lord MacGregor's position and he might well have said "Go away. We are not going to do this" or it might go into the manifesto or what was thought appropriate. I do not understand the Nelsonian blind eye that the Treasury was knowingly engaged in. It seems to me really a dereliction of public duty.
Sir Brian Unwin: If I may answer as a former official, although I was not in the Treasury at the time but in the Cabinet Office, the Treasury's overriding duty was to control public expenditure in accordance with the economic policies of the government. In this case there was a formula which, though not perfect, and the report says there is no right answer, had been broadly accepted by Scotland, Wales, Northern Ireland and England as being an adequate one and was carried on from year to year with no particular challenge. I do not think there was any reason or incentive for either the Treasury or the Scottish, Welsh or Northern Ireland offices to seek to reopen the formula; it worked broadly.

Q527 *Baroness Hollis of Heigham:* I would have expected you to be evidence-based driven and clearly you were not. The fact that because politicians were not shouting about it then it was OK effectively, I am surprised at that.
Sir Brian Unwin: This review took place in 1986. The Formula was produced in 1978–79 so it was not all that long after the Formula was agreed and put on the table.

Q528 *Lord Forsyth of Drumlean:* The Formula was based on the base line and the issue was the base line. In my recollection, rather like Lord MacGregor, I was against a needs-based assessment when I was a minister because I believed that it would be disadvantageous to Scotland at that time. It was widely believed, mainly because people looked at the expenditure per head, which for example on health would have been about a quarter more, that Scotland was doing better particularly in respect to the English regions. Taking up your point about getting value for money for the taxpayer, every negotiation that I was involved with at the Treasury started from the proposition that Scotland was doing rather well and they were looking for ways to claw some of it back. Lady Hollis's question was why officials would not try and find a system which they could put to ministers which was fairer and which allocated public expenditure in a way which was more appropriate. I think one of the consequences of having that extra public expenditure was that value was not delivered because although we had 25 per cent more per head spent on health it is very hard to see that resulted in a Health Service that was 25 per cent better.
Lord MacGregor of Pulham Market: First of all, I slightly correct Lord Forsyth. I did not believe that a needs assessment should not be looked at. I believed that it should be; I just did not think it could be done at this moment in time.

Q529 *Lord Forsyth of Drumlean:* As a minister you took the view that what you thought should be done could not be done in your own office and I did the same.
Lord MacGregor of Pulham Market: I would have gone on later strongly to argue it should be looked at because I felt very strongly about what I thought were the inequities. One of the reasons why I suspect that the Scottish Office did not want to look at this was they knew, as you, Lord Forsyth, have brought out very clearly, there was a big benefit to Scotland calculated at somewhere between £1.5 billion and £4 billion. £1.5 billion and £4 billion is a very different figure from £2 million.

Q530 *Lord Moser:* It may be relevant to mention that we had evidence from the Treasury last week. The written evidence included a question, "What do you regard as the advantages and disadvantages of the Barnett Formula" and they could only think of advantages. I think it was the Chairman who asked what about disadvantages and they were rather lost to think of any. The present Treasury does not give me the feeling that they want to move on. Maybe there is something to be learnt from that.

Sir Brian Unwin: Although the Treasury always wants to come back on a departmental programme when it comes to the public expenditure round, there was no deep feeling, in my recollection, across Whitehall, either in the Treasury or in the territorial departments, that this formula was wildly out of kilter. All departments were happy to let the Formula roll over each year subject to some argy-bargy at the margins. As we see in the report, following the 1979 needs report the Treasury did actually cut the Scottish allocation down by over £200 million over that period. The report also shows that over the period between the establishment of the Formula and my report the increase in spending in Scotland, Wales and Northern Ireland moved very closely in line with the increase in spending in England. It was not perfect but I think everyone was reasonably satisfied that it was equitable and in the context of the annual public expenditure round it was a very convenient way of rolling the figures over.

Lord MacGregor of Pulham Market: I take a very different view from the officials. I do think it needs to be looked at. I think that basing expenditure rounds territorially today on a base line that was established in 1978 does not make any sense. I do actually think that it is inequitable or may be inequitable, I do not know. It looks as though it is inequitable with other parts of England and to England as a whole. We talk about Scotland being 126 if it is a 100 base for England, actually the eastern region of England, of which Lady Hollis and I are representatives, or I was, was 83 per cent. There was a huge disparity between eastern England and Scotland. Maybe that was justified but I do not think you can actually establish today whether it is justified without doing a needs assessment.

Sir Brian Unwin: I was only referring to the position in 1986 as compared to 1978 but, of course, since 1986 it has changed profoundly for all sorts of reasons.

Q531 Lord Forsyth of Drumlean: You, Sir Brian, keep focusing on the Formula which was supposed to produce convergence even though no-one noticed it.
Sir Brian Unwin: It was maintaining divergence.
Lord Forsyth of Drumlean: No, it was not.
Lord Lawson of Blaby: In practice it was.

Q532 Lord Forsyth of Drumlean: If the Formula provided for a 10 per cent increase, to make the numbers simple, and the base line on health was 25

per cent more, then the effect would be that it would produce convergence ultimately between what was spent per head in England and Scotland. Where it all went wrong of course was that the Scottish population was falling at the same time and the convergence effect was cancelled out by the population effect. There was no-one on either side of the border arguing about the Formula; what was being argued about was the base line. In those years we had phased discussions and every year the Treasury would try and do over the Scots, whether it was on council house receipts and how they treated on the capital programme, or the agricultural support programme or whatever, and there would be an endless negotiation. The premise behind that negotiation was: you are already doing very well on your base line. People were not arguing about the Formula, the 10 per cent, the additionality; it was the base line. I am with Lady Hollis on this. I do not have clear in my mind why nobody in the Treasury thought they should not be looking at the base line. To say that we were content with the Formula, of course you were content with the Formula because it was going to deliver ultimately if you dealt with population, convergence.

Lord MacGregor of Pulham Market: I take the view that convergence has not occurred even with the population aspect and, of course, Formula by-basses have made it even more difficult.

Lord Lawson of Blaby: This exposes most of the really important issues we have to deal with as a Committee. I would like to defend, if I may, Sir Brian Unwin and the Treasury from Lady Hollis's accusation of a dereliction of duty. That is a very serious suggestion indeed. The fact of the matter is that the Treasury's overriding duty was to maintain proper control of public expenditure. That was what the Treasury was doing and that was its priority. Going into a detailed needs assessment might have been somebody else's responsibility, I do not know, but certainly the Treasury's overriding responsibility was to have proper control over public expenditure, and indeed one might say that is something which is rather important today. In any case, I do not think you can accuse the Treasury of dereliction of duty. As for the question of convergence, it might be of some interest, and maybe academic advisers have done this, to do a simple statistical exercise of how many 100 years it would require to secure convergence under this absurd system. As to the question of the needs assessment or the population basis, what has happened particularly, which Sir Brian was saying, since 1986, which is almost a quarter of a century ago, the main thing that has happened and why this is a more serious matter now than it was then, and no doubt why this Committee exists, is that over the 23 years the divergence of the population of Scotland and the population of England has continued. It was alluded to in Sir Brian's report but of course it has got far, far worse since then and the difference is projected, if you look at the projections of population for the United Kingdom, to get even starker. Therefore, having a base line, unlike the annual increment, which does not reflect these changes at all is a much more serious matter now than it was in 1986 and likely to become even more so. Who is it who makes these projections for the government of population?

Lord Rooker: It is the National Statistics Office, formerly the Office of Population, Censuses and Surveys.

Lord Lawson of Blaby: If you look at their projections it is going to become even more absurd.

Q533 Lord Rooker: Going back to the time when you were dealing with the issue you talk about the Formula taken each year one with another and it was not worth looking at it. There was also another issue which I think Sir Brian touched on in the sense that the Formula only delivered half or two-thirds of the expenditure. We were given one of the Treasury documents, these comparability tables of each department's percentage of UK. Did you ever look at those? Were those ever altered? One thing I should have asked last week was whether they had been stable throughout the 30 years as different things have come and gone. Was that an issue that was dealt with?

Sir Brian Unwin: We certainly did. As the report brings out, we looked at three expenditure aggregates: the territorial blocks which were allocated to and under the responsibility of the Secretaries of State; the total expenditure in the territories under the control and responsibility of the Secretary of State; and total public expenditure. In the last category were things like defence, and so on, which were not allocated between the territories. We looked at all those aggregates and the broad conclusion was that over the fairly limited period we were looking at, 1978 to 1985–86, all these aggregates had moved in a broadly consistent fashion. In particular, spending in the three territories had moved in line with the general trend of expenditure in England. There was no dramatic divergence or lessons derived from that given the base line.

Q534 Baroness Hollis of Heigham: Simultaneously you, in conjunction with what was then still called the Department of the Environment, were making quite detailed adjustments to the RSGs going to local government within the regions on transitional periods over three years, and cushions and all the rest of it, so this was an exercise. When I was talking about dereliction of duty, I was not talking about bad faith but I am saying that I think there was a vacuum that should have been filled, in my judgment and in my view, by officials in the same way and analogous to what was going on within local government and regional expenditure. We expected this to happen. One of our difficulties in local government was we were always changing. There were always cushions, dampening, underpinning, caps, and so on, but this exercise was done, and done continuously, and continuously adjusted in the name of control of public expenditure, subset value for money, subset fairness, equity, *et cetera, et cetera.* In an attempt to meet the gap between needs and resources, however much that might be contested, sparsity versus density or whatever, we did this and that remains puzzling to me. Did the Treasury ever look at the regional heads, not necessarily the individual authority as that would be a matter for the Department of the Environment when I was involved in those negotiations? Did you ever look at the regional dispositions relating to your regional offices for similar activities?

Sir Brian Unwin: I cannot answer for the Treasury, Lady Hollis. I was in the position of, as it were, holding the ring in the Cabinet Office and chairing the group on which were representatives of the territorial departments, the Department of the Environment, the Treasury and so on and so forth. Whether or not during that time the Treasury were doing what you suggest, I do not know.

Lord MacGregor of Pulham Market: I am not aware of it. I certainly think that if I had sufficient time to get it done and was in a position to commission it I would want to do that because I think you are absolutely right. You put the subset of fairness and equity rather low down; I would put it higher up. We were always trying to do that based on need in local government, rates for grants and negotiations and so on, and the Scots were doing the same in the rate for grants negotiations. This would have been a bigger exercise but it has the same principles behind it. On the convergence point, when preparing for this I was struck by an argument on convergence on page 24 of the House of Commons research paper on the Barnett Formula which I would suggest you have a look at. It is a curious result, according to them, of convergence based on the amount per capita that actually the lowering of population in Scotland makes the convergence worse. It is well worth developing that argument too.

Q535 Lord Rooker: In some ways we have batted this around. Looking at the slot between 1978 and 1985–86 it is useful to know what we know about that but now we are in 2009. We are in a completely different situation now because we have got the regions, if I can call them that, Scotland and Wales, competing with England—and I will give one example in a moment—which did not happen before because the political control was different. That is what is different. I am not saying that is the reason for

opening it up but the fact is the English regions, the RDAs and that, effectively are not allowed to compete with each other. They are all doing their bit for each region in terms of competing, whereas there is an example I was unaware of until yesterday that the Welsh Assembly Government are offering a wage subsidy to manufacturing industry which Wales is not strong on so it does not cost very much. On the Hereford/Shropshire border in England you have got large manufacturing plants still and some of them have plants in Wales. Why have a plant in Welshpool and Telford when you can now go all to Welshpool and get a subsidy from the Welsh Government paid for by the excess. You have this competition across the border which did not occur. I am not arguing for total political change, although there is a Plaid Cymru-Labour coalition there and Scotland is clearly competing in lots of other ways. If we are going to have a reason to do this, if it is an independent body—we do not have Royal Commissions any more because they take so long— if you do something immediately at the beginning of a Parliament, a Royal Commission, it is 18 months at least and it reports and there is a debate. We are then back in the position we are in now coming towards the end of a Parliament when you have to take some action. I am not offering the best time but clearly enough people are looking at in now. The circumstances are completely different. The history is useful, but if we look at it now and assume for the foreseeable future the Scottish Government, the Northern Ireland Government and the Welsh Assembly Government and the Government here for England in Westminster will consist of different political parties which are by and large competing with each other, although you may get a couple the same, that is a completely different scenario from what we have assumed in the past. Devolution is the factor but devolution has brought about different competing parties using the money for competing across the borders within the UK. That is something I do not think was ever envisaged and that is the thing that is fundamentally different now. You could argue after 30 years is well worth a look at as to how the money gets divided up. If we go for a needs assessment in the sense of today's needs, we have to take out the competitive elements because they are building in these needs now. If we are not careful we are getting a false picture of what the needs in Scotland and Wales actually are based on what has been happening under devolution. Would you see major issues in assembling what the needs would be in the circumstances we are in now, not when you were in government? That is the key difference now.
Lord MacGregor of Pulham Market: Leaving aside questions of fiscal autonomy and all that sort of thing, which I know you are not allowed to look at, undoubtedly these sorts of issues will continue to

increase. We already have them in relation to Scotland with tuition fees and the rest which we are all very familiar with and yours is another example. I think these will increase. How you tackle it politically is an issue but I think it would illuminate all our thinking about it if we did have a proper needs assessment. That is the starting point.
Sir Brian Unwin: I think, if I may say so, if we had been asked to do a full examination formula and do a needs assessment in 1986 one of our guiding principles would have been equality of services throughout the United Kingdom. I am not sure that now applies for the reasons you were suggesting because with the devolved administrations there are different political priorities. There are different weights attached to the value of different services, so it would be a more complicated exercise now given the changed political situation.

Q536 *Lord Lawson of Blaby:* I said I would ask question three and you have confirmed there was no needs assessment done. This reinforces, in a sense, Lord Rooker's point. It always struck me when I was Chancellor that there was an element of make believe in all this where needs assessments were decided and calculated and this led to figures in the public expenditure White Paper for education and various other services which came under local government. People used to argue vigorously as to whether we had done the right thing in terms of too much or too little in education compared with other things. In fact, these figures in the White Paper bore only an accidental relationship to what was actually spent because local authorities, provided they fulfilled their legal statutory obligations, could use the money they got from the rateable grant for whatever they wanted. You were given this complicated needs assessment, so much for education, so much for local social services, and the public expenditure White Paper was just a make believe document apart from the totals which of course were very important. This has become even more so following devolution for the reasons Lord Rooker has pointed out. I am not saying we should not have a needs assessment at all but we need to be absolutely clear that what emerges from the needs assessment is most unlikely to be what happens on the ground. For example, there will not be an amount of money allocated for the Welsh Assembly to subsidise manufacturing across the border in Wales but that does not mean to say they cannot take it out of one pocket and put it in another. It is all a bit of make believe.
Lord MacGregor of Pulham Market: In terms of looking at the table in the White Paper, that may be so to some extent but I do not think it undermines the general principles because the two general principles are more devolution of decision taking down to the local level to distribute resources in accordance with

what they see as local need but a fairer way of distributing to the regions and to Scotland, Wales and Northern Ireland nationally. It is inevitable that if you base your distribution on needs in some regards, and that local authority decides to spend it somewhat differently, that will occur, but it is not necessary to say it is wrong.

Q537 *Lord Forsyth of Drumlean:* A third of the Scottish block was distributed to local government on a needs-based basis. The next largest slice was the Health Service, and the Health Service money was distributed—I cannot remember what it was called—on a very complicated needs-based formula to work out what the health boards got. In practice, although the money may have come as the base line plus the percentage increase that happened in England, when it was dished out and when the Secretary of State decided its priorities the bulk of it was actually distributed under a needs-based system. I just wanted to follow up on what Lord Rooker has said. My experience of the operation of the Barnett Formula was that you needed to have Formula by-pass to deal with particular exceptional circumstances that arose because the base line was higher. For example, if there was a nationally agreed pay settlement in the Health Service which was substantial the Formula consequences of that for Scotland, given the base line for Scotland was 25 per cent higher and given that three-quarters of the money went on pay, would have been far short of what was required to meet the pay bill. We knock on the Treasury door and say, "We are poor Scots. Can we please have an extra dollop of money?" We got that money in 1986–87. I think it was after you left. There were various adjustments made from time to time which is another reason why convergence has not happened.
Lord MacGregor of Pulham Market: Absolutely.

Q538 *Lord Forsyth of Drumlean:* Now we have devolution and what appears to be happening is there is no dialogue at all between the Scottish Executive and the British Government and they simply get the straight Formula consequences and ultimately that will lead to pressure on those budgets. Is there not an argument that you need to have a needs assessment in order to be able to defend what you are getting? There must come a point where what they think you are receiving will be not overgenerous but less than what is required in order to meet the needs. If you have not got some objective method of doing that, given that you have lost the ability of having one party in government and colleagues who do not want to embarrass each other and make it difficult, is there

not a requirement arising from the devolutionary situation, even if they pursue the same policies, to have some kind of system? The fact that they are pursuing different policies makes it even more important to draw the line at an early stage. That I think is the key question.
Lord MacGregor of Pulham Market: I agree with that conclusion. Could I say that it would not necessarily follow the consequences of pressure, with your Health Service for example, on the base line leading to the negotiations either side of the Formula. What could well happen, depending on the political strength and the position of the Secretary of State, is you would take the base line as a given and then argue in negotiations that of course the base line is there but he must have something extra because of the consequences of the National Health Service National Pay Agreement. That could lead to moving in the other direction, that the Formula by-pass gets bigger and bigger while the base line is still much higher than the financial average and is 126 against 100. It could work that way but I think we end up with the same conclusion.
Sir Brian Unwin: A key question, if I may just comment, is that whatever its defects the Barnett Formula, with some changes as we went along, was accepted over a long period as a reasonably fair and sensible base for the annual decisions on public expenditure. Perhaps the question for your Committee is whether there is a prospect of producing a substitute formula which is any fairer or more realistic or more acceptable in the more complicated circumstances of devolved government in the territories.

Q539 *Chairman:* You are absolutely right. One thing that is perfectly clear is the convenience of the Formula. Successive governments found it much easier just to let it run than to have a good look at it and decide how they wanted to finance the devolved administrations. It has not been done in any meaningful sense of the word. We had six questions on the paper and I think you have answered them all. Is there anything else you wish to add?
Lord MacGregor of Pulham Market: It is interesting that two former Chief Secretaries had to go along with the Formula for the reasons I have described with me and Lord Barnett described with him, but both of us did not like it and, in fact, think it needs to change.
Chairman: Can I thank you very much for coming? It has been a terribly helpful session. We have learnt a lot and had some enlightenment and are grateful to you for coming. Thank you very much indeed.

FRIDAY 20 MARCH 2009

Present	Mar and Kellie, E	Richard, L (Chairman)	
	Moser, L	Sewel, L	

Memorandum by Plaid Cymru

Plaid Cymru welcomes the establishment of the Lords Select Committee on the Barnett Formula.

SUMMARY

— Wales for much of the 20th century has experienced relative economic decline compared with the rest of the UK: this was principally a consequence of the decline in traditional industries such as coal, steel, agriculture and slate quarrying. Decline in these industries in Wales has accelerated since 1980, the year when the Barnett formula was introduced and used to determine changes in the block grant allocated to Wales. The formula, introduced only as a temporary measure, takes no account of the disproportionate impact that this decline has had on Wales compared with the rest of the UK and the current funding formula not only reflects the spending needs and priorities of England but seeks to converge identifiable funding per capita across the four countries of the UK irrespective of the differing and diverging needs.

— In designing a funding mechanism for funding the countries of the UK a set of principles needs to be established.

    — The funds available should be related not only to need but to remediation of disadvantage.

    — The Assembly Government should have some tax varying powers.

    — The Assembly Government should have borrowing powers.

    — The forum in which decisions are made regarding the allocation of funding to the four countries of the UK should be such that the governments of the devolved administrations have a key say in such decisions.

— The Barnett formula is both unfair and unsatisfactory and should be replaced. A detailed analysis of the strengths and weaknesses of the current formula is set out in Appendix 1 of this submission. It is estimated that Wales lost £778 million in 2006–07 due to the convergence effect of the Barnett Formula.

— A set of proposals designed to ameliorate the unfavourable treatment of Wales under the current formula and an approach to replacing it with a more satisfactory system involving the establishment of an independent funding commission is included in this submission.

This submission will: provide the background to the current position; propose the guiding principles for a fair and adequate funding mechanism; demonstrate the unsatisfactory nature of the current funding arrangements; and propose a set of measures to establish a more satisfactory approach.

INTRODUCTION

1. Plaid Cymru has a long record of opposition to the Barnett formula and welcomes the establishment by the House of Lords of a Select Committee on the Barnett Formula.

2. In economic terms Wales has long been a relatively poor country compared with other parts of the UK. The reasons for this are complex. Wales was slow to urbanise; was very dependent on an agricultural sector which suffered from a high proportion of poor quality, low productive land; and when industrialisation came it was concentrated initially on extractive industries with much of the added value being contributed elsewhere. Viewed from a UK perspective such specialisation may have made sense but it left Wales with an economy highly dependent on a few business sectors all of which suffered long term decline over much of the twentieth century (agriculture, coal, steel and slate quarrying). Although the Welsh Assembly Government is now making considerable efforts to strengthen and diversify the Welsh economy, most of the significant levers remain in the hands of Whitehall.

3. Thus Wales has the challenge of dealing with this legacy but during much of the last hundred years or more UK governments have regarded Wales as being on the periphery and have sought at best to ameliorate economic weakness rather than address the root causes. Since the implementation of the Barnett formula,

which takes no account of relative need, GVA per capita has declined from 88 per cent of the UK average in 1978 to 75 per cent in 2007.

4. The way successive UK governments view Wales is reflected in the way that devolved services are funded: in particular both the formulation and operation of the Barnett formula reflect the peripheral status of Wales. Changes to the block grant are a *consequence* of spending decisions made with respect to spending departments with responsibility for England. Indeed as is noted in the Treasury's Statement of Funding Policy "in the vast majority of cases, the United Kingdom departmental programme covers England only" (this is further demonstrated in the next paragraph) yet it is decisions made by such departments that drive changes to the funding of Wales.

5. Out of UK total managed expenditure (TME) in 2007–08 of £590 billion,[1] the UK Government was directly responsible for:

 — non-identifiable expenditure for the UK (£108 billion). This encompasses defence, interest on the national debt, cost of central government etc;

 — Social Security (£156 billion) which is a standard, needs related, UK wide set of programmes;

 — identifiable but non-devolved expenditure in Scotland, Wales and Northern Ireland (£3 billion); and

 — all public expenditure in England (£243 billion) excluding locally financed expenditure.

6. The devolved governments and local authorities of Scotland, Northern Ireland and Wales had responsibility for £60 billion of expenditure.

7. Thus essentially the UK Government is, from a financial viewpoint, responsible for all public expenditure associated with the UK *per se* (central government expenditure including social security) and for all public expenditure in England. In addition it is responsible, with the important exception of Social Protection, for a very small amount of spending on non-devolved, identifiable expenditure in the other three countries of the UK (£3 billion in 2007–08) which is less than 0.5 per cent of TME. The UK Government has a dual role: it is responsible for central expenditure and it is responsible for all non-local authority expenditure in England. This duality is the source of many of the difficulties associated with the allocation of funding for devolved services in the other three countries of the UK.

8. In addition the UK Government is responsible for fiscal policy ie setting and collecting all taxes and duties in the UK with the exception of council tax and business rates. A third financial role is that the UK Government is responsible for macroeconomic policy including the setting of overall public expenditure levels in the UK and determining the level of public sector indebtednesses.

9. The Welsh Assembly Government:

 (a) is responsible for public expenditure on devolved services in Wales;

 (b) has no fiscal powers;

 (c) has no control over the amount of funding it has at its disposal for public expenditure; and

 (d) has no long term borrowing powers.

10. Of total identifiable public expenditure of £24.2 billion in Wales in 2007–08, the Assembly Government and Welsh local authorities were responsible for £15.2 billion. The balance of identifiable public expenditure was Social Protection (£7.5 billion) and other programmes (£1.5 billion) which were controlled by Whitehall departments.[2]

GUIDING PRINCIPLES.

11. In reviewing the funding and financial arrangements for Wales we believe that certain principles should be agreed:

 (a) the funds available should be related not only to need but also to the remediation of disadvantage. Funding should be sufficient to enable the devolved administrations to address the underlying causes of any relative underperformance of the economy and its consequential social impact;

 (b) the Assembly Government should have tax varying powers;

 (c) the Assembly Government should have borrowing powers; and

 (d) the forum in which decisions are made regarding the allocation of funding to the UK and to its four member countries should be such that the governments of the devolved administrations have a key

[1] Pre Budget Report and Comprehensive Spending Review 2007. HM Treasury. Cm 7227.
[2] PESA 2008. HM Treasury HC489.

say in such decisions and the conflicted position of the UK government in its dual role as the government of the UK and of one of the four member countries of the UK should be recognised.

12. It is not sufficient to set funding levels in terms of relative need. It should be the objective of the UK Government to ensure that the devolved administrations have the financial means to address and materially reduce economic and social disparities between the member countries of the UK. The present funding arrangements appear, at best, designed to ameliorate the effects of economic and social disadvantage. It is noteworthy that in recent times the UK Government has to a marked extent abdicated to the EU its responsibility for the additional funding of disadvantaged areas. Even in the case of EU funding the UK Government sought initially not to pass on to Wales the EU Objective 1 funds but sought to treat these funds as part of Treasury receipts to be used for the benefit of the UK as a whole. The UK Government continues not to provide additional funding over and above the Barnett determined increase for the purpose of public sector match funding. As a result the Assembly Government has had to use the block grant to provide its share of the match funds for Objective 1 and successor Convergence Funding programme.

13. According to *Eurostat 2008 Statistical Handbook* the UK is the most regionally unequal country in the EU. In the case of the UK there is a factor of 3.9 between the two extreme values of regional GDP per capita. (The lowest values in the EU are in Sweden and Ireland where the factors are 1.6 and 1.5, respectively.) This outcome is indicative of the hitherto highly centralised nature of the UK state and of the failure of central government effectively to address the issue of regional disparities. The current Select Committee has excluded from its terms of reference the distribution of funds within the different regions of the UK. It should be noted that if identifiable public expenditure per capita were the same across the countries and regions of the UK then such expenditure in the case of England would increase by three per cent only and that the variation within England (ranging from 117 per cent of the UK average in London to 84 per cent in Eastern and South East England) is not a function of the Barnett Formula but of the distribution mechanisms employed within England. Thus concerns in parts of England regarding relative identifiable public expenditure compared with Scotland and Wales are often erroneously blamed on the Barnett Formula.

Pros and cons of the present formula-based approach to the distribution of public expenditure resources to the Welsh Assembly Government.

14. The strengths and weaknesses of the Barnett formula have been the subject of much analysis and comment and the balance of independent and academic opinion has long been unfavourable. No doubt the Select Committee will receive submissions drawing attention to weaknesses of the formula particularly from the point of view of its unfair and damaging impact on Wales over the last 30 years.

15. A summary of the strengths and weaknesses is set out here and covered in more detail in Appendix 1. It is in the context of the principles set out in paragraph 11 that the strengths and weaknesses of the formula are assessed.

16. In summary the weaknesses of the formula are:

    (a) the arbitrary setting of the baseline expenditures in 1978;

    (b) the inaccurate population ratios used to the detriment of Wales between 1980 and 1997;

    (c) the application of the formula is not subject to independent audit;

    (d) the formula is mechanistic rather than needs based;

    (e) it is an arbitrary convergence formula. In Appendix 1 we estimate that using 1999–2000 as the baseline year Wales lost £700 million in 2006–07 due to convergence;

    (f) there is a lack of transparency in its application particularly with respect to the determination of comparability factors and the resulting consequential changes to the block grant;

    (g) the formula is driven by the public expenditure priorities of England;

    (h) no account is taken of the massive structural changes that have taken place in Wales since 1978—changes which were proportionately far greater in Wales than in England; and

    (i) it is an outdated formula whose operation does not reflect devolution and the existence of the National Assembly.

17. It is claimed that the formula has certain strengths:

    (a) the formula reduces the need for negotiation with the Wales Office and the Assembly Government;

    (b) the formula leads to predictable outcomes; and

(c) the way the formula operates in practice offsets Wales's weak negotiating position.

18. As noted all these points are developed at greater length in Appendix 1 to this paper. It is our conclusion that the Barnett formula is unfair and inadequate and should be replaced.

Replacing Barnett

19. It is clear from the above and our detailed analysis set out in the Appendix 1 that Plaid Cymru considers the current funding formula both unfair and unsatisfactory. We advocate a number of steps to reform and then replace the current formula. The first three steps proposed here would be simple to implement but would not address the key weaknesses of the Barnett formula.

20. A useful first step, albeit a modest one, would be more clearly to identify within government reporting, expenditure by Whitehall departments which is for those services in England which in the case of the other three countries of the UK are devolved. This would enhance transparency and facilitate comparisons between the member countries of the UK. This would also reflect the recommendations of the Treasury-sponsored Allsopp Review.

21. A second step would be for the National Audit Office and the Wales Audit Office to review and report annually to Parliament and the National Assembly, respectively, on the operation of the Barnett formula. It is clear that many of the decisions made regarding the comparability factor of spending programmes are questionable and should be open to independent challenge (for examples see paragraph 6 of Appendix 1).

22. A third step would be to stop the Barnett squeeze by increasing the block grant to Wales by the same *percentage* as the corresponding increases in expenditure in England. In the absence of evidence to the contrary there is no justification for arbitrarily reducing relative identifiable public expenditure per capita on devolved services in Wales. Such a change would be a trivial modification to the current Barnett formula and would not increase total managed expenditure (TME) but would be a rebalancing of country allocations within the TME envelope.

23. A fourth, more significant step would be to apply the principle that relative funding of services in the four countries of the UK should be related to relative need as is the case for intra-country distribution of funding. Determination of relative need is of course a complex and potentially contentious subject. Given that expenditure on devolved public services is concentrated on health and education (approximately 70 per cent of the total) it should be possible to formulate an acceptable needs model. Assessment of need is a challenge not unique to the UK and the Select Committee should consider models employed in other countries with varying degrees of devolution. The additional funding needed to address remediation would be over and above the needs requirement.

24. Appendix 2 sets out relative identifiable public expenditure (IPE) *excluding* social protection, relative GVA and relative expenditure on social protection (SP) in the four countries of the UK (all on a per capita basis). As can be seen there is little correlation between IPE and SP in the cases of England, Wales and Northern Ireland. Whilst a case could be made for a correlation between IPE and the inverse of GVA there is no such pattern in practice. The position of Wales with low GVA and relatively high expenditure on social protection but a modestly higher identifiable public expenditure (excluding social protection) confirms the poor funding deal that Wales has received since the implementation of the Barnett Formula.

25. An independent standing commission should be established which would either determine or advise on the allocation of funds to the four countries of the UK. Such a commission should be at arms length from the UK Government in a similar way to the Monetary Policy Committee (MPC) of the Bank of England. The commission would:

— be given terms of reference unanimously agreed between the UK Prime Minister and the First Ministers of Wales, Scotland and Northern Ireland;

— be advised by experts;

— have an equal number of representatives drawn from each of the member countries of the UK;

— have a suitably qualified secretariat to support the work of the commission together with an appropriate budget;

— receive representations from interested parties;

— commission appropriate external work to support the commission in its task;

— as in the case of the MPC publish minutes of its meetings together with the evidence on which its recommendations are based; and

— schedule its deliberations to fit in with the Spending Review cycle of the UK Government.

26. Some may object that the allocation of public funds is a political matter that is too important to delegate to a commission. A similar view was taken by many when the MPC was established. At a minimum publication of the evidence gathered and considered by the commission, minutes of its deliberations and its recommendations would bring considerable pressure to bear on those charged with the allocation of funds to the four countries of the UK particularly if the recommendations of the commission were rejected.

CONCLUSION.

27. Plaid Cymru believes that the current funding arrangements for Wales are both unsatisfactory and unsustainable and should be replaced. Wales has suffered for far too long in terms of inadequate and unfair funding. The funding approach advocated in this paper would lead to a fairer allocation of funds.

APPENDIX 1

THE STRENGTHS AND WEAKNESSES OF THE BARNETT FORMULA

(1) It is in the context of the principles set out in paragraph 11 of our evidence that we will comment on the Barnett formula.

(2) The Barnett formula suffers from a number of significant weaknesses as a mechanism for allocating resources to Wales and should be replaced. The origins of the Barnett formula are well understood: the formula was intended as a short term expedient introduced in the late 1970s as a means of allocating certain monies related to expenditure on functions devolved to Scotland, Northern Ireland and Wales. Lord Barnett himself has on numerous occasions in the House of Lords drawn attention to the fact that the formula was intended to be a short term, stop-gap measure. In practice it has remained in place with little alteration for over 30 years.

WEAKNESSES OF THE BARNETT FORMULA.

(3) The Barnett formula has a number of weaknesses as well as one or two possible advantages. The first three weaknesses noted in this appendix (paragraphs 4 to 6) arise from faulty implementation whilst the remainder (paragraphs 7 to 14) are fundamental criticisms of the formula.

Arbitrary setting of base line expenditures in 1978

(4) Base line expenditures to which consequential increases were cumulatively added were themselves based on the expenditure patterns in existence prior to 1978: indeed in the case of Scotland allocations were partly related to the Goschen formula established in the late nineteenth century. Furthermore although the Treasury undertook a needs assessment exercise in the late 1970s the outcome was not used to alter the base line allocations used in the Barnett formula. This is in spite of the fact that the Treasury's assessment indicating that Wales was receiving less than its needs based share of funds and Scotland was receiving more.[3] The conclusion of the Treasury study was that identifiable expenditure on devolved services in Wales was 106 per cent of the corresponding level for England whilst the needs estimate was 109 per cent. This shortfall of 2.8 per cent was effectively locked into Barnett increases and has persisted for the last 30 years. An attempt was made by the Treasury in the early 1980s to resurrect the idea of a needs assessment in order to reduce the allocation of funds to Scotland and Northern Ireland (but not significantly to Wales) but was abandoned.

Inaccurate population ratios used from 1978 to 1997

(5) The population ratios used in the application of the Barnett formula did not accurately reflect the respective populations of the four countries of the UK and in practice favoured Scotland and disadvantaged Wales. The "consequentials" were allocated to England, Scotland and Wales in the proportion 85: 10: 5 whereas the actual population resident in the three countries would have suggested 85.3: 9.6: 5.1. Thus the initial distribution of funding when the Barnett formula was implemented and the population basis for allocating increases were flawed from the outset. The difference may appear small but the cumulative effect over the years prior to 1997 meant that annual increases for Wales were approximately 2 per cent lower than justified on a relative population basis. Until 1997 the population ratios were not, with one exception in 1992, adjusted to reflect changes in actual populations and this arguably further favoured Scotland, where the population was declining, and penalised Wales where the population was increasing broadly in line with that of England. (Between 1976 and 2008 the population of England grew by 11.0 per cent, Wales by 8.1 per cent and

---

[3] HM Treasury Needs Assessment 1979.

Scotland declined by 0.9 per cent). Population ratios have been adjusted annually since 1997 but the way that Wales lost out in the intervening period of almost 20 years has been locked in to the consequent baseline to which subsequent annual Barnett Formula increases have been added.

Application of the Formula is not subject to independent audit

(6) The application of the formula is not subject to independent audit despite there appearing to be instances of incorrect and inconsistent application of the formula. Examples of this range from relatively small areas of expenditure to more material ones and examples are set out in Appendix 3.

A mechanistic rather than needs based formula

(7) A central weakness of the formula is that it is a mechanistic formula based on relative population levels and does not take account of relative need except to the extent that such needs were reflected in the baseline expenditures in existence 30 years ago. (The authors of the Treasury needs assessment in 1979 were careful not to claim that the expenditure levels in existence then were related to need). There is significant evidence that relative needs have changed during the intervening period if measures such as relative GDP per capita or relative expenditure per capita on social protection are used as proxies for relative need. In the case of relative GVA per capita this has, in the case of Wales, declined from 88 per cent of the UK average in the late 1970s to 75 per cent in 2007 but this has had no influence on the Barnett formula determined increases to the block grant.

An arbitrary convergence formula

(8) Another objection to the formula is that it is a convergence formula: it is not passive. If the formula is applied rigorously, as it has been since 1997–8, then devolved, identifiable expenditure per capita will converge to the same level across the four countries of the UK. Expenditure *within* the four countries of the UK would not converge to a uniform level because different needs based formulae are used to allocate such intra-country monies. Changes to other identifiable public expenditure programmes and in particular Social Protection are not subject to the Barnett formula and do not therefore suffer such convergence.

(9) In the absence of needs assessment there is no cogent case for converging per capita public expenditure across the four countries of the UK. In the case of Wales the deterioration over the last 30 years in relative GVA per capita would suggest that identifiable expenditure should have been increased in relative terms.

(10) As has been noted the Barnett Formula has, with the exception of EU funding of Objective 1, been applied with rigour to Wales since 1998. To test whether or not convergence is happening in the case of Wales, data was analysed from the Treasury's Public Expenditure Statistical Analyses reports (PESA 2008, Table 9.4; PESA 2005 Table 8.4) which set out growth in total identifiable public expenditure per capita by country in *real* terms between 1999–2000 and 2006–07. Growth for England, Wales and Scotland was 33.03 per cent, 29.96 and 32.86 per cent, respectively. The lower growth in Wales cannot be attributed to expenditure on social protection which represents over 83 per cent of identifiable expenditure on *non-devolved* services (PESA 2008, Table 9.17) which remained constant in relative terms (~114 per cent of UK average) over the period. If identifiable public expenditure per capita in Wales had grown at the same rate as in England then it would have been £700 million higher in 2006–07 after allowing for the above Barnett EU funding (£128 million in 2006–07 compared with zero in 1999–2000). The impact of convergence on Wales will build up cumulatively if the Barnett Formula continues to be employed in determining changes to the block grant.

Lack of Transparency

(11) The absence of convergence in practice in the first 18 years of the formula is a perverse example of the lack of transparency in the operation of the formula. Students of the formula have found it extremely difficult to explain why the convergence inherent in the formula had not been noted in practice. This is particularly striking because for most of the period during which the formula has been in operation the changes in public expenditure used to determine changes in the block grant have been *nominal* changes which should have accelerated convergence. It is assumed that there have been many examples of the so-called by-passing of Barnett in the period 1979 to 1997 although academics and others struggle to find definitive evidence. It may be fair to surmise that the Barnett formula did not receive much government or public attention between 1979 and 1997 although recently released

papers from the then Scottish Office show that the Treasury attempted unsuccessfully in the early 1980s to reduce the block grant to Scotland and Northern Ireland but not, significantly, to Wales. It was thus possible for governments of the day to deviate from the formula without much public attention being paid to such practices.

(12) This lack of convergence was, of course, prior to the establishment of the Scottish Parliament and the National Assembly for Wales in 1999. It is also the case that in 1997 the incoming UK Government stated that it would apply the Barnett formula rigorously and this appears to be the case with a few, well documented exceptions. These include the provision of most of the EU sourced Objective 1 and Convergence funds to Wales being allocated over and above changes to the block grant determined by the Barnett formula. The UK Government also publishes a Statement of Funding Policy to coincide with each spending review and this casts additional light on the operation of the formula. However there appears to be no adequate means for challenging what appear often to be arbitrary decisions regarding comparability factors used in the formula (see Appendix 3).

(13) It is inevitable that many adjustments will be made to planned and actual expenditure over the life of the Spending Review cycle. These changes will have an impact on the Barnett consequentials but such changes are made by the Treasury and it appears that there are cases where that department is in practice "judge and jury" without reference to the Assembly Government (see paragraph 18 of this appendix for a material example).

A formula driven by the public expenditure priorities of England

(14) The Treasury remains the driving force and key influencer in all cases of budgets including public expenditure plans. The allocation of funds to the devolved administrations is a *consequence* of spending decisions agreed between the Treasury and the various departments of state in London. In particular, changes to expenditure on education and health *in England* represent approximately 70 per cent of the change to the block grant but in the case of Wales these programmes enjoy a high degree of devolution (100 per cent and 99.3 per cent, respectively). Thus spending decisions for England made by the Department of Children, Schools and Families and the Department of Health have a major influence on changes to the block grant to Wales despite the fact that policy-making in these portfolios is wholly devolved. The Assembly Government has minimal influence on policy making and, in particular, budgeting, by these Whitehall departments. Thus changes to the block grant are determined by departments of state which have little or no financial remit in the territories of the devolved parliaments and assemblies. Indeed with the exception of spending on social protection, there is a surprisingly small proportion of expenditure by UK government departments in Wales which have some responsibility for expenditure in Wales on non-devolved, identifiable expenditure. With the exception of social protection, £1.5 billion only out of total identifiable expenditure of £24.2 billion in 2007–08 corresponded to identifiable, non-devolved expenditure. To a large extent a number of UK departments of state are, from a financial viewpoint, departments for England only and yet changes to their budgets have a major impact on changes to the block grant directly impacting Wales and its citizens with little democratic input. Such a "rough and ready" approach may have made sense as a short term expedient but it is not a satisfactory basis for the longer term which in the case of the Barnett Formula has now been in force for 30 years.

A formula that takes no account of the massive structural changes in Wales since 1979

(15) Since the Barnett formula was introduced there have been massive structural changes in the Welsh economy such as the closure of the coal mining industry which employed 40,000 in 1979 and the run down of the steel industry where employment has declined from 51,800 in 1979 to approximately 10,000 today. Because these industries were concentrated in small areas of Wales they have had a devastating, knock-on social effect. These changes have proportionately been far greater in Wales than in England but the Barnett formula takes no account of this.

An outdated formula whose operation does not reflect devolution and the existence of the National Assembly

(16) The Barnett formula pre-dates the establishment of the National Assembly by 20 years but the approach remains the same and does not reflect the changes constitutional position of Wales. The Assembly Government has minimal influence on the funding of its activities and on the operation of the formula. The Joint Ministerial Committee has no formal role in the resolution of any disputes and the Secretary of State for Wales is in a weak negotiating position as a member of the UK cabinet which is dominated by the interests of England.

ADVANTAGES OF THE BARNETT FORMULA

(17) There are a number of arguments advanced in favour of the Barnett formula:

The formula reduces the need for negotiation with the Wales Office and the Assembly Government

(18) It is true that the formula reduces the need for the Treasury to negotiate with departments representing the devolved administrations. The counter argument is that there is a corresponding democratic deficit under the current arrangements. The Treasury is "judge and jury" in its own case with little scope in reality for challenge. If the Assembly Government and its members are to be empowered to represent the electorate of Wales they must be able to negotiate with the UK Government in such a crucial area as funding.

The block grant permits the Assembly Government to have a high level of spending discretion

(19) An advantage of a block grant (as distinct from the Barnett formula *per se*) is that once the size of the block grant is determined it is to a significant extent a matter for the Assembly Government as to how the money is spent. It is possible that a detailed needs assessment approach to determining the block grant could undermine that freedom.

The formula leads to predictable outcomes

(20) Defenders of the formula argue that outcomes on a year to year basis are predictable which facilitates the annual budget planning of the Assembly Government. Recent evidence tends to undermine this claim. In the run up to the 2007 Comprehensive Spending Review (CSR) the UK Government made a number of forward spending commitments in England including health and education. From those commitments it was possible to estimate the Barnett consequential for Wales for the three year CSR period: this indicated an average annual increase in real terms of approximately 2.7 per cent.[4] When the CSR was published this gave an annual increase of 2.4 per cent. However the baseline expenditure on which the growth was based had been reduced due to postponement of certain health expenditures in England during the prior spending period. As a result the year on year real increase in the block grant was 1.8 per cent. It was clear from the comments of the Assembly's Finance Minister that this was unexpected as well as unwelcome.

Operation of the formula offsets Wales's weak negotiating position

(21) Past evidence suggests that Wales has suffered compared with Scotland in the allocation of funds due to its weak negotiating position. One advantage of the current arrangement is that the Department of Children, Schools and Families and the Department of Health are powerful departments within Whitehall and Wales may indirectly benefit from such strength given the correlation between increases in spending in those departments and changes to the block grant. This may be true but it is hardly satisfactory that a democratically elected Assembly Government is not in a position to negotiate the funding settlement for Wales.

APPENDIX 2

IDENTIFIABLE PUBLIC EXPENDITURE (IPE)*: GVA PER CAPITA AND EXPENDITURE ON SOCIAL PROTECTION (SP) 2007-08.

(In all cases UK = 100)

	IPE	GVA	SP
UK	100	100	100
England	96	103	97
Wales	108	75	113
Scotland	123	96	109
Northern Ireland	125	81	126

* IPE excludes Social Protection expenditure and is a good approximation to expenditure on services which are, in the case of Wales, devolved...

Source: PESA 2008 and ONS Report 12 December 2008.

[4] Institute of Welsh Affairs, Agenda. Winter 2007.

APPENDIX 3

COMPARABILITY FACTORS

The Treasury's Statement of Funding Policy (last published in October 2007) contains a schedule of comparable programme objects with the corresponding comparability factors. The treatment of some of these raises questions as to whether or not they are applied correctly. The examples given here are of some that appear either to be incorrect or anomalous and are the more obvious ones. Many of the more material programme objects require disaggregating before a view can be taken as to whether or not the appropriate comparability factor has been applied. This is not possible using the information provided in the Statement of Funding Policy.

(1) The London Olympic Games. It was confirmed in Parliament in January 2009 that the overall public sector funding package for the London Olympics is £9.325 billion. £2.175 billion will be contributed from the National Lottery and central goverment will contribute £6.1 billion. It is expected that the expenditure will be overwhelmingly for the benefit of south east England and if this was recognised in the usual Barnett treatment Wales would receive consequential funding of just under £300 million. The UK Government has decided to treat the bulk of the spending as being for the benefit of the UK as a whole and Wales will receive £83 million only as a Barnett consequential. (Wales will lose approximately £100 million of lottery funds where Wales normally receives 6.5 per cent of UK allocations.)

(2) Cycling England has a comparability factor of zero which implies that the expenditure is incurred on behalf of the UK as a whole although it is an England only programme. (Following a Parliamentary Question regarding this subject the treatment was changed and the budget subsumed into another programme object with a comparability factor of 100 per cent.)

(3) Expenditure on the Royal Botanic Gardens, Kew has a comparability factor of zero which implies that such expenditure, although incurred in England, is for the benefit of the UK as a whole. This may well be the case but what of the Royal Botanic Gardens in Edinburgh and the National Botanic Gardens of Wales? Their role appears not to be recognised and any public funding of these has to be found from elsewhere within the Scottish and Welsh block grants. The way the Barnett Formula operates in practice is that expenditure incurred in the England may be either for England only or for the benefit of the UK as a whole but expenditure incurred in Wales can only be for the benefit of Wales and not for the UK as a whole. There is an asymmetric treatment of expenditure. In the case of the Royal Botanic Gardens, Kew in the 2004 Funding Policy statement the comparability factor was 100 per cent. What was the reason for the change and was the change challenged by the devolved administrations? If not, why not?

(4) The Channel Tunnel Rail Link and London & Continental Railways have comparability factors of zero but Crossrail has a comparability factor of 100 per cent. Presumably it is argued that the Channel Tunnel Rail link was for the benefit of the UK as a whole whereas Crossrail was for the benefit of England only. It is recognised that allocation of benefits in the case of transport networks such as roads and railways is challenging but the rationale behind the determination of comparability factors needs to be transparent and open to challenge.

(5) Nuclear Support for the former Soviet Union has a comparability factor of 100 per cent implying that the devolved administrations have comparable programmes. This treatment appears to be questionable.

(6) Grants to the Greater London Authority for Tourism has a comparability factor of zero which implies that such public expenditure is treated as being for the benefit of the UK as a whole.

March 2009

Memorandum by Professor James Foreman-Peck

1. This note first shows the spending pattern achieved under the current system of devolution financing. Consistent with the untrammelled operation of the Barnett Formula, Welsh public expenditure per head increased by a smaller proportion than English spending between 2002 and 2007. But Scotland, unlike Wales, obtained considerably more funding than predicted by a simplified application of the Barnett Formula. In the second section, an alternative rule is presented that maintains existing proportionate differentials in public spending between UK countries. This permits by comparison a calculation of the "Barnett Squeeze" on different assumptions. For Wales, taking 2002–03 as the baseline, the predicted "squeeze" on the 2007–08 budget was about £630 million, and compared with actual (planned) spending, it was around £860 million. The third section suggests a simple needs-based rule to replace Barnett. Household disposable

income is a more appropriate needs indicator than GVA per head (when both are adjusted for price differences between regions) because GVA measures production which is less related to need than is income. The rule takes as the needs standard variations with household income of UK state spending on benefits in kind. According to this approach a continuing "Barnett squeeze" is justified.

I. SPENDING PATTERNS UNDER THE BARNETT FORMULA

2. Under the Barnett Formula, once extra spending has been agreed by central government, it is divided between UK countries on the basis of population. Increases in English public spending in relevant categories ("comparable programmes") are matched by equal increases per head in devolved administration budgets. But since the devolved administrations spend more per head of their populations, their budgets are therefore augmented by smaller proportions than England's. Hence their expenditures per head tend to converge slowly to that of England (the "Barnett Squeeze").

3. Historically there was some "bypass" of Barnett Formula (and use of incorrect population factors). HM Treasury expected that the greater transparency introduced with the Devolution Settlement would reduce such anomalies—and certainly more information as to the operation of the Formula is now in the public domain.

4. The present exercise attempts to assess how much convergence of spending per head the operation of the formula has produced during the period 2002–03—2006–07 (and also to 2007–08, although only planned rather than outcome figures are available for the last date at present). This allows a calculation of (net) formula "bypass".

5. As a reasonable simplification, assume of total identifiable public spending on services at the country and region level, only "social protection" and "agriculture" are not devolved functions. Then the growth of such spending per head can be compared between England and the devolved administrations.

6. This calculation in Table 1 shows that public spending in Wales increased about as much as predicted by the Barnett Formula between 2002 and 2006. Despite Objective One funding, there was minimal net "bypass". Welsh "devolved" spending rose by a little more than 33 per cent, while comparable expenditure in England increased by over 38 per cent. With greater public spending per head, the Formula prescribes a smaller percentage rise in expenditure for Scotland than for Wales (about 31 per cent compared with 33 per cent). Yet Scotland, unlike Wales, appears to have "bypassed" the Formula, almost matching England's percentage increase in spending per head 2002–03—2006–07.

7. Between 2006–07 and 2007–08, planned spending was to rise by 8.6 per cent in England (Table 1). Allocating the implied sum of money per head to the devolved administrations according to the populations, should have given Wales a 7.5 per cent increase and Scotland 6.8 per cent. However Welsh "devolved" spending increased by 1.8 percentage points less than predicted by the Barnett Formula, while Scottish spending increased by one percentage point more.

8. These figures show that the "Barnett Squeeze" took less from Welsh spending than other budgetary influences between 2006–07 and 2007–08. For one way of calculating the squeeze is to compare the actual budget increment with how much money, say, Wales would receive if the percentage increase in budget was the same as England's under the Formula. But this approach would require a larger total UK budget. Calculating the "squeeze" within the existing budget requires an alternative budgetary rule against which the current Formula can be assessed.

TABLE 1

IDENTIFIABLE PUBLIC SPENDING ON SERVICES

	2002–03	2006–07	2007–08	2002–06 %	2002–07 %	2006–07 %
Wales						
"Devolved" per head (£)	3,662	4,802	5,051	31.1	37.9	5.2
"Devolved" (£ million)	10,693	14,241	15,049	33.2	40.7	5.7
"Barnett" predicted budget increase				32.9	42.9	7.5
Scotland						
"Devolved" per head (£)	3,922	5,289	5,676	34.8	44.7	7.3
"Devolved" (£ million)	19,824	27,061	29,168	36.5	47.1	7.8
"Barnett" predicted				30.6	40	6.8
N Ireland						

	2002–03	2006–07	2007–08	2002–06 %	2002–07 %	2006–07 %
"Devolved" per head (£)	4,497	5,368	5,684	19.4	26.4	5.9
"Devolved" (£ million)	7,751	9,349	10,008	20.6	29.1	7
"Barnett" predicted				26.7	34.9	6.7
England						
"Devolved" per head (£)	3,092	4,192	4,522	35.6	46.3	7.9
"Devolved" (£ million)	153,522	212,774	231,082	38.6	50.5	8.6
"Barnett" predicted budget increase				39.1	50.7	8.6

Notes: Calculated from HM Treasury PESA. Tables 10.1–10.4. "Devolved" = total identifiable spending—agriculture—social protection. "Barnett" predicted = increase over period* average population share.

II. BARNETT WITHOUT THE SQUEEZE.

9. The objective of allocating a given sum of money without the convergence property of the Barnett Formula is easily achieved. Calculate the total devolved categories of spending for England, as well as for the other administrations. Divide the total UK figure into the sum to be distributed. Then allocate to each administration a proportionate increase in their budgets equal to the resulting fraction. This ensures the continuation of existing disparities in proportionate terms. For any "comparable programme" a similar exercise can be undertaken.

10. As an illustration, suppose the increased money available is expected to be £15 billion and the current spend is £300 billion on "comparable programmes". Under Barnett the £15 billion is allocated according to population. For ease of calculation we assume in the planned expenditure period that England's population is 50 million, Wales three million, Scotland five million and Northern Ireland two million. Under Barnett England gets £(50/60)*15 billion = £12.5 billion and Wales gets £(3/60)*15 billion = £750 million. With "Barnett relaxed" each country receives (15/300=) 5 per cent. The corresponding number in sterling depends upon the country baseline. If England's baseline was £235 billion (£4,700 per head with no population growth according to these numbers) and Wales' £20 billion (£6,667 per head), England would receive (235*.05=)£11.75 billion, less than under Barnett, and Wales gets (20*.05=) £1 billion, more than under Barnett.

Table 2

BARNETT RELAXED AND THE SQUEEZE 2006–07

	% 2006–07	% point difference from UK % increase 2006–07 (8.3)	"Squeeze" 2006–07 £ million	% 2002–07	"Squeeze" 2002–07 (48.8% UK increase)
Wales					
Actual "devolved" increase	5.7	2.6	370	40.7	866
Barnett predicted increase	7.5	0.8	114	42.9	631
Scotland					
Actual "devolved" increase	7.8	0.5	135	47.1	337
Barnett predicted increase	6.8	1.5	406	40	1744
N Ireland					
Actual "devolved" increase	7	1.3	122	29.1	1527
Barnett predicted increase	6.7	1.6	150	34.9	1077
England					
Actual "devolved" increase	8.6	−0.3	−638	50.5	−2610

	% 2006–07	% point difference from UK % increase 2006–07 (8.3)	"Squeeze" 2006–07 £ million	% 2002–07	"Squeeze" 2002–07 (48.8% UK increase)
Barnett predicted increase	8.6	–0.3	–638	50.7	–2917

Note: The "Squeeze" columns do not sum to zero because of rounding errors.

11. Table 2 takes the figures for 2006–2007 and 2002–7 from Table 1 to calculate the difference the "relaxed formula" would have made to the allocation of 2007–08. Applying the "relaxed formula" for 2007–08 only, England loses 0.3 percentage points of the increase, amounting to almost £640 million. Wales gains £114 million compared with the Barnett formula and £370 million compared with the actual allocation. Scotland gains £406 million from removal of the "squeeze", but only £135 million more than planned.

12. The impact of the "squeeze" is cumulative. Had the "relaxed formula" been adopted in 2002, the effect in 2007–08 would have been much greater. A given percentage increase exercises a larger absolute effect the higher the base on which it is calculated. The earlier the base is raised (by adopting the "relaxed formula") the higher will be the base in any subsequent year. Table 2 shows that in 2007–08 England's allocation would have been £2.6–2.9 billion less, if the relaxed formula had been introduced in 2002, and Wales would have been better off by £0.5–0.8 billion. As with the one year exercise, the Barnett squeeze on Scotland is much more severe in theory than in practice. The opposite is the case for Wales.

III. NEEDS AND DEVOLUTION

13. The "Relaxed Barnett Formula" shares with Barnett the advantages of budgeting simplicity and ease of calculation. It also removes the apparently arbitrary convergence property of Barnett. But it embeds no less arbitrary differences in public spending per head of population between the countries of the United Kingdom. These differentials cannot readily be explained in terms of variations in "needs" between the countries. One reason is that there is no agreed measure of general public spending "needs".[5] GVA per head has been suggested as an aggregate regional indicator but GVA differences reflect divergent regional employment participation rates. Wales's rate was 55.4 per cent at the end of 2006 compared with the UK's 60 per cent. If Wales had achieved the UK rate it is reasonable to expect Welsh GVA per head to be 81 per cent of the UK average rather than 75 per cent.[6]

14. Household disposable income (standardised for household membership and including transfer payments) is not subject to this difficulty and is more obviously related to need than GVA, which concerns productivity and participation. Differences in regional costs of living should be factored into the needs indicator for an adequate comparison as well. Subject to these and other adjustments, it is possible to obtain a relationship between household income and utilization of public services for a cross-section of the UK population and apply this to a modified income index to obtain a public expenditure allocation model.

15. We use the approximation to "devolved" expenditure under Barnett across UK countries, because England is not subject to the Formula and the other countries do not have identical devolved spending powers. For present purposes we will assume that this measure of "devolved" spending is equivalent to "state benefits in kind"—of which health and education are the largest components. We can compare the equivalent benefit categories received by different income groups in the UK with the comparable benefit possibilities allocated to devolved administrations and English regions by average household income. If the Barnett Formula is working well, we should find similar relations between UK household receipt of state benefits in kind by income as between devolved spending and household income across regions.

---

[5] Particular needs indicators are more common but still controversial. Free school meals are sometimes used as an indicator of educational needs and the standardised mortality rate on occasion has been adopted for health needs.

[6] (GVA/Population.) = (GVA/worker).(workers/pop.). UK GVAP = 100, Wales GVAP = 75. (100/75) = [UK/WalesGVAper worker]*[0.60/0.554.]. Implied Welsh GVA per worker 81.2 per cent of UK. With UK employment rate Wales would achieve the same GVA per head.

Table 3

UK HOUSEHOLD INCOME AND STATE BENEFITS IN KIND

Household Income decile	1st	2nd	3rd	4th	5th
Equivalised disposable income £)	7,420	11,665	14,203	16,749	19,403
State benefits in kind (£)	8,003	6,951	6,495	6,324	5,774

Source: Economic and Labour Market Review, Vol 2 No 7 July 2008.

16. Populations of the devolved governments account for only about one sixth of the UK total, so atypical spending allocations to these countries will not significantly influence the total distribution in the present exercise. Table 3 shows the average state benefits in kind received by households by decile of disposable incomes in the UK. As incomes rise, state benefits utilised fall.

17. In table 4 and Appendix figure 1, which show the relation between household income by region and public spending, no such negative relationship is observed—once the lowest spending area (in figure 1 the bottom right), England, is excluded. The two highest areas of "devolved" public expenditure are Northern Ireland and Scotland. The lowest household income area is the North East region of England, which received higher public spending in 2007–08 than Wales. Consistent with the negative relation of Table 1, Wales has a greater household disposable income in 2006 than the North East. The anomalies by UK spending standards then are Northern Ireland and Scotland. These countries receive more in relation to household after-tax income in public spending than the rest of the UK. But Wales is slightly below a line connecting the North East and England as a whole, at least hinting that Wales, unlike Northern Ireland and Scotland, is receiving a slightly poorer deal than comparable English regions.

Table 4

GROSS VALUE-ADDED, HOUSEHOLD INCOME AND PUBLIC SPENDING

	GVA per head 2007	Gross Household Disposable Income 2006	"Devolved" public spending per head, 2007–08 planned
Wales	14,877	12,300	5,051
North East	15,688	11,800	5,425
N Ireland	16,170	12,000	5,684
Scotland	19,152	13,100	5,676
England	20,463	14,000	4,522

Source: ONS 12 Dec 2008 Regional, sub-regional and local gross value added; HM Treasury PESA Tables 9.10a and 9.10b.

Note: Definition of "devolved" as in Table 1.

18. Table 2 shows regional variations in the cost of living. Whereas prices excluding housing costs in Wales were about 4 per cent below the UK average, when housing costs are taken into account, the Welsh cost of living was 7–8 per cent lower than the UK average in 2004. How housing is taken into account in the needs indicator is therefore critical.

Table 5

PRICE INDICES IN 2004 RELATIVE TO THE UK (UK = 100)

	Excluding housing		Including housing	
	National weights	Regional Weights	National Weights	Regional Weights
Wales	96.5	95.8	93.1	92.1
Scotland	98.0	96.1	94.5	93.1
Northern Ireland	100.9	98.7	95.8	95.3
North East	96.1	94.9	94.2	93.0

*Source:*Wingfield, D. Fenwick, D. Smith, K. "Relative regional consumer price levels in 2004" *Economic Trends* 615 February 2005.

19. The bulk of devolved spending is on state benefits in kind. Figure 2 shows how these benefits vary with household disposable income. One description of the relation between income and benefits is that a one per cent rise in income is associated with 0.39 per cent fall in state benefits consumption (Table 3) A fair allocation would then be obtained from the proportionate deviation of devolved household disposable income from the UK average, adjusted for differences in costs of living.

Table 6

REGRESSION OF PROPORTIONAL RELATION BETWEEN HOUSEHOLD DISPOSABLE INCOME
AND BENEFITS IN KIND

Adjusted R Square	0.98
Observations	10

	Coefficients	*Standard Error*
Intercept	12.55	0.20
Disposable income	−0.39	0.02

20. In the case of Wales, household disposable income, now 11 per cent lower than the UK average, must be divided by 0.921 (Table 2) or 0.931 to correct for lower Welsh prices. Real income per head is then approximately 4 per cent lower than the UK average. Wales therefore requires 0.39*4 per cent = 1.6 per cent more spending per head or per household than the UK average, if the distribution of state benefits in kind in relation to income across the UK is taken as the standard.

21. According to this needs measure Welsh devolved spending per head should be reduced. Wales' identifiable state spending net of social protection and agriculture 2007–08 was £5,051 per head and the UK was £4,679. That is, Welsh state spending per head was 7.9 per cent greater than the UK average, compared with the 1.6 per cent warranted. For the other devolved administrations, the excess of budgets over those warranted by UK spending are far greater.

22. This aggregate approach to needs assessment has the advantage of relative simplicity, consistent with devolution. Devolved administrations themselves employ needs-based rules to allocate spending between health authorities and among local governments. They make the decision about the resources to allocate between spending departments. So for central government to employ a needs-based formula that explicitly takes into account health, education, transport and so on, would be second guessing the lower tier government. The weights assigned to the various indicators would reflect the central government's valuations not those of the devolved administrations.

23. A cost-based formula is unsatisfactory in removing incentives to control costs and to adjust provision according to circumstances. Scotland might have chosen a less expensive housing policy before devolution had it faced a less accommodating budget constraint. By contrast, a modified income approach provides encouragement for cost-containment and flexible cost-minimisation, at least in the short-run. If a devolved authority is less efficient than the UK average at providing public services, it will be less able to conceal the shortcoming by spending more on them.

24. While at first sight the Barnett squeeze appears arbitrary, the application of an aggregate needs indicator suggests it is a pragmatic solution to the excessive budgets granted to the devolved administrations.

APPENDIX

DATA FOR CALCULATING THE BARNETT REPLACEMENT

1. To calculate "devolved" spending, "social protection" is excluded from "regionally identifiable public spending", because most of this expenditure is not devolved. Agriculture is also excluded from "devolved" spending on similar grounds to "social protection". Most of the two categories are classified as Annually Managed Expenditure, rather than the Department Expenditure Limits expenditure, which broadly corresponds with the block grant to devolved governments (as well as with UK government departments' budgets).

"Spending that cannot reasonably be subject to firm multi-year limits is included in Annually Managed Expenditure (AME). ... It includes social security benefits, local authority self-financed expenditure, payments under the Common Agricultural Policy, net payments to EC institutions and debt interest." (http://www.hm-treasury.gov.uk/spend_sr00_repannexa.htm)

Aggregate Needs Indicators

2. GVA is available for 2007 (ONS First Release December 2008 *Regional, sub-regional and local gross value added)* whereas household income by region is only available for 2006 (ONS First Release May 2008 *Regional Disposable Household Income*). On the other hand, at first sight GVA is not such a good needs indicator as household income—because it includes the benefits in kind that we are trying to predict. These benefits are supplied at regional level and therefore their resource costs should be included in regional value added. Insofar as greater benefits are provided to lower income households, this redistributive effect of taxation should therefore tend to equalize GVA per head between regions with different household incomes. But, in the opposite direction, a region such as Wales with a low labour force participation will also have a low GVA per head. Household income on the other hand, which includes central government transfers designed to reduce interpersonal inequalities and "needs", will show less divergence from the national average.

3. The figures for Wales for these two sources show a marked divergence, with Wales 25 per cent below the UK average GVA per head in 2007 but only 11 per cent behind for household income in 2006. Although Welsh GVA grew more slowly than the UK average 2006–07, by 0.9 per cent, this is insufficient to account for the discrepancy when used to extrapolate the household income divergence.

4. Gross disposable household income is income after taxes and social contributions, property ownership and provision for future pension income. It includes pension income, income support[7] and imputed rent values—what owner-occupiers would have to pay for living in their homes if someone else owned them. Subtracted to get household incomes are "Other outgoings". These payments include those made by households to other sectors on interest (eg mortgages) and rent. So apparently the lower costs of property ownership in Wales are already taken into account with this measure.

5. The GVA measure (income approach) excludes transfer payments such as child benefit and the state retirement pension. It also includes an imputed value for rental incomes of owner-occupiers to cover the rental value of their properties. Regional estimates are calculated using estimates of average property prices by region. Higher property pries in SE England mean higher imputed rentals and therefore higher GVA and disposable income. But they also mean higher mortgage payments for those buying property, or higher actual rent outlays. GVA and disposable income should be deflated by the price index including housing costs in any needs index.

Estimates of UK State Benefits in Kind By Income Group

6. Data for the relation between state benefits and final income are from the official *Economic and Labour Market Review*, Vol 2 No 7 July 2008 "The effects of taxes and benefits on household income, 2006–07", Table 14 (Appendix 1). Average incomes, taxes and benefits by decile groups of all households, 2006–07. Figure 2 below shows the household deciles with a constant proportionate relation between the variables, and this is the basis of the calculation of Table 6 above. An equation relating benefits to the reciprocal of income fits the data slightly less well.

7. The largest spending items are health and education. How well does the ONS ELMR study estimate these items? Any survey-based estimate of, say, health spending utilisation will reflect not just "need" but the demand and supply responses as well. Higher income people may well be more articulate and accomplished at extracting the health benefits they require from the NHS. So if we could get actual health state benefits consumed by income group it would not necessarily tell us precisely what we want. The approach used in this survey (described below) is reasonable.

"Data are available on the average cost to the Exchequer of providing the various types of health care—hospital inpatient/outpatient care, GP consultations, dental services, etc. Each individual in the EFS is allocated a benefit from the National Health Service according to the estimated average use made of these various types of health service by people of the same age and sex, and according to the total cost of providing those services. The benefit from maternity services is assigned separately to those households containing children under the age of 12 months. No allowance is made for the use of private health care services."

---

[7]   http://www.statistics.gov.uk/articles/nojournal/Regional_Household_Income_article_March_2007.pdf

Figure 1

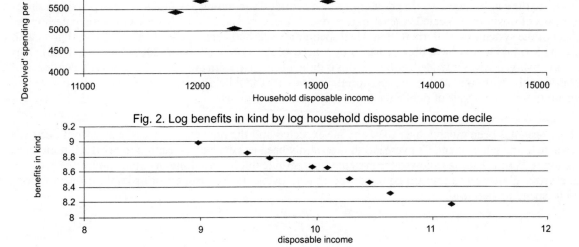

Fig. 1. Household income and public expenditure:
UK countries and North East Region

Fig. 2. Log benefits in kind by log household disposable income decile

March 2009

Memorandum by Dr Gillian Bristow, School of City & Regional Planning, Cardiff University

DEVELOPMENT OF THE FORMULA

1. *What do you understand was the purpose of the Barnett Formula was when it was first introduced, and has its purpose changed over time? Was it designed to reduce tensions arising from disparities in public spending per head of population? Has it succeeded in resolving such tensions?*

The Barnett Formula constitutes a temporary, political expedient which became permanent. In the run up to the devolution referendums for Scotland and Wales in 1979, the Treasury began to make plans for life after devolution and, specifically, the funding arrangements that would be required. The Barnett formula—named after the then Chief Secretary to the Treasury, Joel Barnett who formulated it—was the product of these plans. The Barnett formula was first used in relation to Scotland in 1978. Its origins are not well documented although it appears that it was introduced as a temporary expedient to determine how public expenditure should be allocated to Scotland in the context of preparations for devolution that subsequently did not occur (Treasury Committee, 1997). Indeed, Lord Barnett himself has subsequently stated that he did not expect the formula to last for more than a year, and certainly not for 30 (Barnett, 2000). However, the formula was extended to Wales in 1980 and has been used continuously, with some modification, ever since in public expenditure surveys.

The Barnett formula was designed to relate incremental changes in expenditure in Scotland, Wales and Northern Ireland to the expenditure margins which existed in 1978 between these countries and England. Baseline funding levels for Scotland, Wales and Northern Ireland were set at levels higher than in England to reflect the historic tendency for the territories with their particular economic and social conditions to receive higher per capita levels of funding than England. Thus the pre-existing pattern of territorial spending differences was built into the baseline.

APPLICATION OF THE FORMULA IN PRACTICE

2. *Do you consider that convergence in per capita levels of public spending on the English level was an intentional feature of the formula, or merely an incidental one? Do you think it is overall a beneficial or harmful feature of the working of the Formula?*

The Barnett formula was intended to provide a pragmatic way of allocating increases in spending to the territories in line with their population shares. Over time, initial expenditure advantages which were frozen into the base would depreciate as the base would come to constitute a smaller proportion of the block. The Treasury acknowledged in evidence to the Treasury Committee enquiry into the Barnett Formula in 1997 that one of the properties of the formula was that it would produce convergence in levels of public spending per head across the UK over time (all other things being equal) (House of Commons Treasury Committee, 1997). This was based on the assumption that the population-based increments would gradually predominate over the disparate inherited levels of public expenditure thereby effecting the so-called "Barnett squeeze". As such, the formula appears to have been designed to limit the financial commitments from England (the dominant UK state) to the smaller states (or to gradually reduce Scotland's spending advantage) and to provide a short-term means of obviating repeated cabinet battles over budgetary allocations. It was fully anticipated by the architect of the system, Lord Barnett, that when spending levels had converged sufficiently to be aligned with needs, the formula would have been replaced by a need-based system (Barnett, 2000; McLean, 2005). This suggests convergence was intended, although this is difficult to verify with any certainty. Convergence does not sit comfortably with the notion of territorial justice—that public spending levels should provide the opportunity for equal levels of public service provision across regions.

The long-term has been much longer than anyone expected and the predicted convergence has not occurred everywhere to the same extent. Convergence has certainly been less evident in relation to Scotland than it has in relation to Wales. This has allowed the system to perpetuate but has not fundamentally addressed growing disquiet from all quarters about the equity of the system, particularly in respect of its implications for levels of public spending per head.

NEED FOR REFORM/ALTERNATIVES TO THE EXISTING FORMULA

3. *What criteria do you consider to be important in assessing the success or otherwise of the present formula, and of any possible replacement to it? Would a fair or equitable allocation system necessarily be a needs-based system?*

Any funding system ought to be judged in relation to its ability to deliver territorial justice. This has long featured as a principle for guiding the spatial distribution of welfare services and the appropriate distribution of fiscal powers between different tiers of government, and has attracted renewed interest as a principle for guiding policy and underpinning inter-governmental financial relationships under devolution.

Traditionally, territorial justice has been understood as the principle that citizens should be provided with broadly equal levels of public services at a similar tax burden, irrespective of where they live, or to each according to the needs of the population of that area. Thus need here is specified very generally in relation to relative shares and not absolute levels of public service provision. This principle of equal social rights across the UK territory implicitly asserts that the UK is a unitary state with no sub-divisions subject to a different set of social rights. The onset of devolution changes things since it empowers autonomous regions and nations with the freedom to vary the provision of services to suit the demands of their own jurisdiction. As a consequence, territorial justice should now be defined in terms of equalising the capacity of decentralised governments to provide the same level of public service provision should they choose to do so.

Operationalising this principle in the particular context of UK devolution presents a considerable challenge since policy competencies are asymmetric among sub-central units, their sizes are not uniform and where social and economic needs are diverse and territorially concentrated. Any fair division procedure requires a prior agreement among the dividing players of their different entitlements or claims on collective resources. Entitlements may be couched in terms of proportionality, whether to units of measured need, to some notion of merit or desert, such as the inverse of Gross Domestic Product (GDP) per capita, or alternatively to the contribution made to financial resources. Needs assessments are commonly used in formal fiscal models but can prove problematic not least because in empirical terms, the identification of needs appears to be highly dependent upon the position of those making the identification. Thus, needs may be specified quite narrowly in relation to ensuring continued physical existence, or more broadly in relation to providing a broad range of opportunities. Allocations on the basis of merit are less common but may be invoked where there is some notion of providing a disproportionate benefit for some places which others are justly required to contribute to. The distribution of government resources on the basis of contributions is more familiar and well established in the UK welfare state through the insurance principle.

In other words, justice or equity does not necessarily require a needs-based system. It is not necessary to select one single overarching principle of equity or justice for guiding action. Indeed, it may well be more appropriate to use multiple notions of justice and equity and to prioritise them through ordering or trade-offs.

4. *To what extent are there tensions between allocating expenditure according to such criteria as need, efficiency and effectiveness? How would you suggest those tensions might be resolved?*

There is unlikely ever to be a perfectly rational, objective approach to allocating expenditure that will be entirely free from the primacy of politics or from potential conflicts and trade-offs with other factors such as policy choice or efficiency. In particular, there are likely to be tensions between the desire for policy autonomy over spending choices and the principle of equity. The key is thus finding the system that provides the most reasonable, acceptable working compromise. In the politically contentious arena of public expenditure allocations, agreement on an acceptable compromise will indeed be more important than the search for perfection and it is this somewhat pragmatic principle that should ultimately determine how the various questions surrounding the conduct of needs assessment are approached and indeed answered. Clearly the ability to reach such a compromise depends upon initial agreement among the different tiers of government that an objective of inter-regional equity is a desirable one to strive to achieve.

It follows that securing what is required is agreement around the principle that a sense of justice is essential to the legitimacy and cohesiveness of a devolved union state, and a sense of allegiance to and identification with a common set of beliefs and attitudes. A clear understanding of when territorial differences in per capita expenditure are just and when they are unjust or unacceptable, is critical to determining when and what sort of equalisation and constitutional structure is legitimate. In other words, we need to know the objective we are trying to satisfy through our territorial finance system, before we can re-design it accordingly.

5. *How effective would it be to use population or other proxy indicators of need, such as inverse GDP or perhaps social security spending per head, as alternatives to carrying out a detailed needs assessment? What would be the overall effect, in terms of the distribution of spending, of adopting those?*

A rigorous annual assessment of territorial equalisation and needs overseen by an independent body represents the best approach to achieving a more transparent, accountable and fair system of public expenditure allocation across the UK. As McLean and McMillan (2003) observe, there are various principles which could be applied to the design of the system to help ensure that it remains practicable:

— As with the present Barnett regime, the baseline level of expenditure per head could remain constant, and an independent territorial finance Commission could be established to recommend changes to the increment in grant to each territory. This would have the advantage of avoiding any unacceptable shocks;

— The apportionment to each territory should be unanimously agreed—the so-called "unanimity rule". This would give each region equal bargaining power—an equally credible threat, against the centre;

— If no unanimity can be reached by an agreed deadline, then the increase of grant to each territory should be calculated using a default or predetermined proxy for relative needs.

There are two possible default measures that could be adopted. The first is a poverty-based approach. This takes country social security expenditure per head as the guide to relative country need. MacKay and Williams (2005) argues that the case for a poverty-based measure is strengthened if one accepts the basic Rawlsian notion that a just society would have particular regard for the welfare of its most disadvantaged and vulnerable citizens. The poor have limited choice and their needs are thus greater. MacKay and Williams show that taking dependency levels (social security) as a measure of relative need, devolved spending per head should be roughly one-fifth higher in Wales and Northern Ireland than in England and more than one-tenth higher in Scotland than in England.

An alternative option is to use inverse GDP (or GVA) as a proxy for need (ie the increase in grant to each territory should be inversely proportional to its GDP). The problem with the social security option is that it itself derives from a government programme (albeit a non-devolved one). This risks circularity with elements of the same programme appearing on both sides of the regression equation. Furthermore, it may create perverse incentives for a region to become and remain "needy". The argument around the funding of Objective One in Wales represents a good example of the current perverse incentives that reside within the Barnett system. Wales gained from being "needy" and it will lose if and when West Wales and the Valleys cease to be needy.

The inverse GDP option has a number of advantages. It is transparent and less open to political manipulation. GDP per head is also not the direct result of government policy, although it is highly correlated with certain variables that governments must seek to improve such as health status and levels of human capital.

Furthermore, GDP per head has the added advantage of being measured by an independent non-partisan body—the Office of National Statistics. Finally, GDP per head would not create perverse incentives to be "needy". If a devolved administration improves it GDP per head, then income per head must rise by more than the grant per head would fall on an inverse GDP formula as government spending is less than 100 per cent of GDP.

6. *Assuming there is to be a mechanism for distributing financial resources from the UK Government to the Devolved Administrations, as the main source of revenue for the Devolved Administrations, do you think that a needs-based formula is the only real alternative to the current Formula? What other alternatives might there be?*

Equalisation payments from central government to regional governments based on needs are not the only way to achieve inter-regional equity. Central government can also employ a more active, redistributional regional policy, or utilise the territorial effects of national social security systems.

DATA QUALITY AND AVAILABILITY

7. *Are there still problems relating to the collection, quality or availability of data on the distribution of public spending and its effects? What issues are there on data about indicators of need and tax revenues?*

Positive steps have been taken to improve the transparency surrounding the calculation of the formula which was previously shrouded in mystery. In particular, in March 1999 the Treasury published a technical document outlining the categories of the devolved budgets over which there is scope for annual negotiation, and the role of the formula in determining changes in other elements of expenditure. In so doing, the comparability percentages and sub-programmes of spending to which they are applied were published for the first time. Since then, programme comparabilities have been updated at the start of each public spending review to reflect any changes in the policy responsibilities of the devolved administrations. Whilst the English spending programme figures to which the Barnett formula is applied remains opaque, it is understood that the devolved administrations are now provided with the Treasury's calculations of spending consequentials (ie the impact of changes in spending in England on the block grants) to enable them to establish firmly that they represent the full extent of the share of any new money that is announced. Data on inter-regional fiscal flows across the UK nations and regions is patchy (well-developed for Scotland, but poor elsewhere).

DECISION MAKING AND DISPUTE RESOLUTION

8. Most writers consider that procedural fairness and transparency are important aspects of any system of financing the devolved administration, and that this an area in which the present arrangements are defective. Do you agree? What information should be published or other processes adopted to improve procedural transparency?

Any fair division procedure should also satisfy the notion of procedural fairness and should thus be just in relation to its processes as well as its outcomes. Procedural fairness requires the existence of rules (formal or informal, explicit or implicit) which are consistently applied over space and time (Hay, 1995). In order to be sustainable, the mechanisms used to distribute public spending resources need to be transparent and fair in terms of both outcomes and the mechanics of their distribution.

There is mounting evidence to suggest that the Barnett formula provides a spurious sense of exactitude which belies a significant degree of discretion in its application. The consequence is that it is increasingly and widely perceived to be unfair. The increased incidence of formula bypass presents a case in point. The formula bypasses that occurred prior to devolution did so not because of pure political lobbying, but as an outcome of bureaucratic negotiations and wrangles. The Comprehensive Spending Reviews since 1997, which determine the budgets of the devolved administrations, however have produced political lobbying from the devolved governments in respect of specific, ad hoc funding demands or "needs" (as discussed above). These are addressed through bargaining procedures with no formal institutional arrangements for their presentation, assessment and resolution. With variable lobbying powers evident in the context of asymmetric devolution, the inevitable claim is that those better equipped to voice their demands have an unfair advantage (Bristow, 2001). A considerable degree of discretion also surrounds the classification of spending programmes by the Treasury and the decisions regarding which are deemed to be "English" programmes (for which there is a calculable Barnett consequential for the devolved block grants), and those which are deemed to be "UK spend" (ie which ostensibly benefits the whole of the UK and thus not subject to the Barnett formula and generative of additional spending for the devolved administrations). These decisions can have significant budgetary consequences for the devolved administrations however and provoke incendiary debate and reaction. Two recent examples highlight the growing dissatisfaction in Wales in this regard. The decision to regard spending on the 2012 London Olympics as "UK spend" has cost Wales an estimated £437 million in incremental spending to the Assembly budget (Shipton, 2007). Similarly, the decision to classify the spending by Cycling England as UK spend cost Wales a further £8 million when Cycling England was awarded an additional £140 million in government funding (Livingstone, 2008).

9. *How workable would be a UK Territorial Grants Board given that its Australian prototype, the Commonwealth Grants Commission, operates in a symmetrical, federal system of government, with substantive fiscal autonomy for the States? Can a Territorial Grants Board improve procedural fairness or provide a system which is deemed legitimate?*

The Australian experience provides some important less for the UK (Pickernell *et al*, 2008). It demonstrates:

— It is possible to develop an alternative to the Barnett formula.

— That any federal grant giving system opens up temptations by the grant giver to try to control where the grant is spent.

— A federal-state government arrangement can be particularly prone to attempting to direct where resources go if the federal government is responsible for substantial proportions of a state's expenditure through grants.

The choice in the UK is unlikely to be straightforwardly between a simple per capita Barnett-type system and an independent formula based system governed by a grants board. In practice, both these systems have some advantages and some disadvantages. The true choice is between sets of institutions for governing lobbying and deal making in determining budgets, and the openness of these arrangements. Most importantly of all, it is clear that while the formula design and system constructed around it may affect the form and nature of the politics of intergovernmental fiscal relations, they do not remove politics altogether. Any Commission-based system, however independent the committee calculating it and however sophisticated the estimates of need and cost relativities, is subject to lobbying.

More transparency and agreement in a Commission-based arrangement involving more co-operative solutions including agreed outcomes would, however, have the advantage of being based on partnership arrangements and would, in all likelihood, result in better outcomes. This would also obviate the need for "Barnett bypass" by making the governance arrangements transparent in areas likely to become increasingly contested. While it would also give some degree of leeway for the devolved administrations to pursue different policies, this would allow the UK government some "steer" over important areas of government expenditure, a solution perhaps more in keeping with the political realities of the UK's experience of devolution. Clearly there is no ideal technocratic solutions to the problem of allocating public expenditure, and whichever system is adopted, the power of politics will continue to prevail.

REFERENCES:

Barnett, J Lord (2000) "The Barnett formula: how a temporary expedient became permanent", *New Economy*, vol 7 (2), pp 69—71.

Bristow, G (2001) "Bypassing Barnett: the Comprehensive Spending Review and Public Expenditure in Wales", *Economic Affairs*, September 2001; pp 44–47.

Bristow, G. (2008) "All for one and one for all? Territorial solidarity and the UK's system of devolution finance". Paper presented to Seminar on Regional Economic Disparities, University of Edinburgh 10–11 April 2008.

Hay, AM (1995) "Concepts of equity, fairness and justice in geographical studies", *Transactions of the Institute of British Geographers*, vol 20, pp 500–508.

House of Commons Treasury Committee (1997) *The Barnett Formula*. Second Report of the Treasury Committee, House of Commons, Session 1997–98. London: The Stationery Office.

Livingstone, T (2008) "No cash for Wales—Barnett needs change", *Western Mail*, February 21, 2008; p 7.

MacKay R R and Williams J (2005) Thinking about Need: Public Spending on the Regions, *Regional Studies* vol. 39 (6), pp 815–828.

McLean I and McMillan A (2003) The Distribution of Public Expenditure across the UK Regions, *Fiscal Studies* vol 25 (1), pp 45–71.

McLean, I (2005) *The Fiscal Crisis of the United Kingdom*. Basingstoke: Palgrave.

McLean, I, Lodge, G and Schmuecker, K (2008) *Fair Shares? Barnett and the Politics of Public Expenditure*. Institute for Public Policy Research.

Pickernell, D, Bristow, G, Kay, A and Ryan, N (2008) "The Primacy of Politics: Intergovernmental Fiscal Relations in the UK and Australia", *Public Money and Management*, vol 28, no 2, pp 115—122.

Shipton, M (2007) "Shocking 'cost' to Wales of Olympics", *Western Mail*, October 6 1007; p 3.

March 2009

Examination of Witnesses

Witnesses: Dr Eurfyl ap Gwilym, Economic Adviser, Plaid Cymru, Professor James Foreman-Peck, Professor of Economics, Cardiff Business School, and Dr Gillian Bristow, Cardiff School of City and Regional Planning, examined.

Q540 Chairman: Thank you all for coming. You know what we are about. You have heard that we have this inquiry by the Select Committee of the House of Lords, and I think you have seen the terms of reference of the Committee, so you know what we can look at and what we are not supposed to look at. Can I say two housekeeping things? First of all, this is a public hearing. As I understand it, the BBC is taking a full sound video of the whole thing. Whether they use it or not, I do not know. A full transcript is obviously going to be taken. When the transcript is out, you will have an opportunity to look at it and see whether you want to make any alterations to it. If you want to make small alterations, fine; but if you want to change the sense of what it is you said, I am afraid, like *Hansard*, the answer will be "no". I wonder if I can ask you some basic questions to start us off! What do you understand was the object of the Barnett Formula? What was the object of the exercise when it was first introduced? Do you think its purpose has changed over time? It is a long time now since Joel Barnett—well, he did not introduce his formula—it was not even called a formula for about a decade, but it is one that now bears his name. Do you think it was designed to reduce tensions arising from disparities in public spending per head of population, or do you think that is the way it has developed, and do you think it has been successfully responding to any of those tensions?

Dr ap Gwilym: I imagine that the purpose is rather clear. Bear in mind the timing of this as well; it was in the run-up to the devolution referenda in 1979. There was already funding, with funds going to Wales, Scotland and Northern Ireland for devolved services. Clearly there needed to be some sort of funding mechanism. Why those three departments did not have bilateral negotiations with the Treasury the way other departments of state have, I am not clear. I assume one of the advantages to the Treasury was that there were three fewer sets of negotiations— remember the old days, the Star Chamber and all that—though that is speculation! I do not think it is reasonable, by the way, but it probably seemed reasonable from a London viewpoint that you said,

"Let us look at the changes in expenditure when planning our programmes in England, and in the case of those programmes where the spending on the programmes in Wales and Scotland is devolved, let us change those by the same amount as in England on a *per capita* basis." The interesting thing about that, of course, is that they did not do the obvious thing, which is that if spending is going up on a particular programme in England by X per cent, that you do the same for Wales and for Scotland. Instead of that, they said, "Let us take a monetary amount *per capita*"— and we will come, presumably, later on to the question of convergence, which is, to my mind, intrinsically built in to the way the Barnett Formula works. Nevertheless, it was a way of saying, "Right, we are going to spend so much extra on a programme in England and where it is devolved in those two countries, and we will take the lead from the change in England and that is how we will change the moneys coming to Wales and to Scotland." That was the purpose. I think the "reducing tensions" consideration, if it was there at all in those days, comes back to the next question you have got on your list, which is the convergence issue. I do not think it does reduce tensions because the key issue there, is that if you look at the disparity in identifiable public expenditure *per capita* within England, you have a very wide range within England, and that has nothing to do directly with Barnett at all. Barnett is designed to allocate moneys to three of the four countries of the United Kingdom and has nothing to do with intra-England allocations. Indeed, if you level the identifiable public expenditure *per capita* across the UK, England gets about 3 per cent more—that is all—so that would not sort out, for example, the north-east of England problem. If you look at the disparities, the IPPR report last year again, from Nuffield College, states that the huge additional spend is in London, where it is about 28 per cent above the UK average. Broadly, Barnett does what it says on the tin, as it were, which is to allocate these moneys in a fairly easy way, using a rather simple— people might argue crude—formula on a population basis. That is what it has done the whole time. We may come back, Chairman, to questions about convergence and why there has not been so much until the last decade, in a moment.

Dr Bristow: I would just echo that and say it is probably quite well acknowledged now that the Barnett Formula was a temporary, probably political expedient that became permanent. It is something that was designed principally, as Eurfyl said, in relation to the first proposals for devolution in the 1970s and used to determine how public expenditure should be allocated to Scotland principally, in the context for those preparations for devolution which subsequently did not occur. I think Lord Barnett himself has stated that he did not expect the formula to last as long as it has, but clearly it has been something that has worked. It has been practical and effective in that sense.

Q541 *Chairman:* He told us on a number of occasions that it was a convenient way of avoiding three different rows between parts of the UK and the centre; and the convergence as far as he was concerned did not enter into it at all. Interestingly, too, on convergence, we had giving evidence to us this week Lord MacGregor, who was Chief Secretary to the Treasury in the mid-eighties, and he said exactly the same thing; that convergence was not part of the exercise as far as certainly the ministers of the Treasury were concerned. Whether the civil servants of the Treasury took a slightly different view as to how this worked is another matter, but certainly as far as the ministers were concerned, two or three of them said it did not enter into their consciousness in the operation of the formula.

Professor Foreman-Peck: I do not have a great deal to add about the intentions of ministers, which were obviously opaque. One can infer what people intend from what they do, but this is a pretty risky strategy. Certainly on the basis of what you told us, civil servants are quite smart sometimes at getting policies through despite ministers, and that is certainly consistent with what I know in this case.

Q542 *Lord Sewel:* Jim Callaghan always said the real purpose of Barnett was to enable the Cabinet to have lunch! There might be an element of truth in that! Let us talk about convergence. It is a property of the Formula—there is no doubt about that—and we could have debates about whether ministers realised it or did not realise it. I am pretty sure that some people in the Treasury did realise it, because it sticks out straight away as soon as you look at it, that it has an inevitable convergence property, and you can almost leave it at that. The interesting point is, though, as I think was said earlier; if you look at Scotland the convergence has not taken place. There has been a series of Formula by-passes, partly a delay factor because of the Scottish falling population, which delays the impact from one comprehensive

spending review to the other, so you are always a bit behind; but, clearly, there were lots of wadges of public expenditure that were shifted to Scotland without going through the Formula—and I am afraid some of us were involved in those dirty deeds! It was basically national negotiated wage settlements that were the cause of major disruption in the progress in Scotland. That does not seem to have happened in Wales. Wales is almost the example of how the Barnett Formula is intended to operate where you do have a convergence effect. Any explanation for that divergent experience?

Dr ap Gwilym: I think it is quite fascinating, and we are going to come back later on maybe to talk about some data and information where you can have lots of distinguished academics, like these on my left, delving into this material for a lot of time, trying to work out what exactly happened. I take your point about national wage settlements and so on, the so-called Barnett by-pass, though sometimes I think Barnett by-pass is a convenient way of trying to explain away lack of convergence. Even in the case of Wales, there was not that much convergence until about 1997. Why I say 1997—bear in mind that soon after the Formula came into being, of course, there was a change of government at the UK level, and then the Conservatives had a long run until 1997. I get the impression—and it is only an impression—you will be better placed than myself to judge—that Barnett was often more honoured in the breach. Even in the case of Wales for a long period there was quite a skilful Secretary of State, Nicholas Edwards, Lord Crickhowell, who was quite influential and probably punched above his weight a little bit in Cabinet as well. Since 1999, though—first of all, bear in mind the incoming Labour Government did say, "We are going to use Barnett with some rigour." In the case of Wales there has only been one exception to my knowledge, which is the EU funding of Objective 1, and that effectively took the removal of the very first First Minister in Wales to achieve. However, if you look at the growth in total identifiable public expenditure in Wales—I say total not just the devolved, because again we have got problems with data—since 1999 it has grown in real terms by 2006–07 by 30 per cent, whereas England grew by 33 per cent and Scotland by 32.9 per cent; so Scotland is tracking England again but Wales has gone the other way. I think I put in my written evidence that in 2006–07, the last year for which we have reasonable public expenditure data, the shortfall for Wales was £700 million. If you take away the other elements of expenditure in Wales, you come back to the conclusion that it is due to the operation of the Barnett Formula, not necessarily only convergence of course, because there are substantial sums where the consequential (if I go to the jargon of Barnett) is zero, and where that money is spent of course—it might be spent in Wales, in

Scotland or in England, the theory being that it is for the benefit of the UK as a whole. I suspect most of that is spent in England, not on a population basis, but a disproportionate amount, just because the UK is a highly centralised state and many British spending programmes take place in the south-east of England. The £700 million has happened, and therefore we have experienced convergence in Wales since 1999; but I think that you can partly at least speculatively relate that to the incoming government saying, "we are going to use Barnett with rigour".

Q543 Lord Sewel: Is it also that actually getting round Barnett becomes more difficult in the context of devolution?
Dr ap Gwilym: I think that is a very good point, because it was much easier, to put it crudely, to do backroom deals in the old days, whereas I think it is more difficult now to do that. This, of course, does not explain Scotland, because Scotland has not experienced that reduction compared with England and Wales has. I think Northern Ireland has as well, by the way.
Professor Foreman-Peck: I think we can all agree—down here anyway we all agree that Wales has been squeezed and Scotland has not. We think that Wales has been squeezed because the Barnett Formula has been applied in Wales's case. We do not really understand what goes on in Scotland's case.

Q544 Lord Sewel: Mr Swinney, the nationalist Finance Minister in Scotland, is very much in favour of the Barnett Formula.
Dr ap Gwilym: I can well understand that he is!

Q545 Chairman: To be fair, he did not actually say that!
Dr ap Gwilym: I suspect—they always relate, if you ask them about it—"give us fiscal independence and then we can talk about Barnett", which is their way of addressing—or not addressing the question—

Q546 Chairman: Could not care less about Barnett; it did not really matter: fiscal autonomy was what they wanted.
Dr ap Gwilym: That is right. Scotland has—I hesitate to say this but it appears to have done rather well, going back to the Goshen Formula in the 1890s. I leave the Scots to argue their case. I do not feel obliged at all to defend them.
Dr Bristow: I would agree again with what was said. Wales has certainly experienced the Barnett squeeze since 1999 in particular because the Formula has been applied more rigidly. It is interesting in the case of the Barnett Plus Settlement that Wales secured, in as much as it shows how, with devolution, the whole issue around the settlements given to the devolved administrations becomes more transparent and has

become a bit more subject to political scrutiny and debate. That perhaps raises issues around how comfortably the Barnett Formula now sits and works within the system where we have devolved governments.

Q547 Lord Sewel: For the record, is convergence a good thing or a bad thing?
Dr ap Gwilym: It is a bad thing. It is very clear. In any sensible society—and I think James has done some work on this and maybe presented it in his evidence here—the amount of public expenditure a citizen makes use of, public services, is partly dependent on their own situation, whether they are young, old, poor, sick, healthy, in work or out of work. To the extent that it is unrealistic to expect to have a homogeneous distribution of those characteristics across the United Kingdom, you would not expect to have a level settlement of public expenditure *per capita*. Quite clearly, again, if you look at all the statistics, the UK is one of the most regionally unequal states within the European Union. It is most unequal in fact if you use measures such as GVA *per capita*. Therefore, you would expect logically that you have got some poorer regions which need a greater consumption of public services.
Professor Foreman-Peck: May I take issue with Dr ap Gwilym's contention of convergence not being a good thing? It is undoubtedly a good thing where Scotland and Northern Ireland are concerned. What the question begs is how we know what the appropriate devolved budget is for these authorities. That really seems to be the nub of the problem. There are two ways you can look at it, roughly. You can take an aggregate measure, because it is an aggregate budget; or you can try and get some more sophisticated needs analysis, paying particular attention to education and health. If you take an aggregate measure, which is what I favour, the obvious measure is disposable household income. This is not widely focused on, compared to GVA per head, but it is much more appropriate because income is a reflection of needs, in a way that gross value-added is not. The disparities between regions and devolved administrations are much less when you look at household disposable income; and they become even less when you divide through by regional prices. One of the reasons that Wales is such a pleasant place to live is that it is considerably cheaper to live than anywhere else in the UK, certainly once you have adjusted your budget or your spending pattern to take into account of what is cheaper here relative to elsewhere. If you take household disposable income, the gap, as last measured, is about 10 per cent in nominal terms between the UK average and Wales, maybe 11 per cent with a fair wind; but there is about a 7 per cent lower price level in Wales if you include housing—6–7

20 March 2009   Dr Eurfyl ap Gwilym, Professor James Foreman-Peck and Dr Gillian Bristow

per cent or 7–8 per cent. Once you have taken that into account the disposable income difference between Wales and the UK average is about 4 per cent. So if you take 4 per cent as the inequality level, it is not a great deal. That is why I submit that the inequities of the Barnett Formula are not that great for Wales. But when you apply this to Scotland and Northern Ireland and compare it to their receipts of public expenditure, they clearly do far better on this aggregate needs measure than England or Wales. For Northern Ireland and Scotland, it seems to me that if you have got to get some form of equity between England and Wales and these two administrations, convergence is a good idea.

Q548 Chairman: That is if you lump England and Wales together.
Professor Foreman-Peck: Wales is pretty close to England in a number of respects, but the critical one is in the level of public expenditure per head relative to income, and it is particularly close to the north-east of England in that respect—not perfectly close!
Dr Bristow: I do not think convergence sits comfortably with a notion of territorial justice or equity, which is an important principle. Public spending levels ought to be such that there is opportunity provided for the different regions to offer equal levels of public service provision if they wish. That is a fundamental principle.
Dr ap Gwilym: I do not want to get into too lengthy a discussion with my good friend James now—there will be another opportunity—but one thing is the provision of public services, but of course I do have a concern about things like gross value-added. One of the reasons why the cost of housing in Wales is on average lower than other parts of UK is because Wales is performing very weakly economically. The fact that relative GVA *per capita* is down to about 75 per cent of the UK average is indicative of this. Therefore, the danger is that you have Wales with a low cost of living, low housing, low incomes, and you say that they are not doing too badly overall. I must say that, having spent a lot of my career working in the City of London, I was very happy to pay high house prices in Central London, because that was a measure also of the high GVAs we were generating. I think gross household income and looking at the cost of delivering public services is a rather narrow view of looking at this. We would like to see Wales being in a position where it is going to generate more wealth for itself, which is why we talk about remediation of weakness, not just delivery of public services. That is quite a large field we could explore maybe some other time.

Q549 Chairman: If you want to produce a fair and equitable allocation system, to use a fairly neutral phrase, how do you do it? You would have to have

some kind of needs assessment involvement in it. I am not absolutely clear in my own mind as to precisely where it comes in and how it comes in, but to have one that is certainly divorced from any kind of assessment of what the needs of a particular country are seems to me to be very difficult to support.
Dr ap Gwilym: It is, and if you focus on spending—I think roughly 70 per cent of the block grant that comes to the Welsh Assembly Government is focused on education and health. Even if Wales pursued a somewhat different set of policies say from England or from Scotland, that will be the broad figure, so with slightly more than two-thirds being spent on education and health, one would hope one could come up with some measures in those areas of need and relative need. In fact, as you know, at various stages attempts have been made to do that. The Treasury did attempt this not just in the well-publicised case in about 1976–77 but we have seen from the Freedom of Information Act papers that came out last year that they had another shot at it in about 1984 and retired bruised from their confrontation with the Scottish Office. There are mechanisms for assessing needs. It is complex, and one needs to recognise that. That is the argument for having expert advice, but also having it done in a very transparent way, so that when people see these issues you can have an intelligent debate about them. At the moment what we have is essentially a very crude formula. The virtue of it is that it is quick and simple, but it has many drawbacks as well.
Professor Foreman-Peck: In my submission to the Committee I suggested a way of taking into account needs at the aggregate level by looking at the allocation or consumption of state benefits by income group across the United Kingdom. You can find that there is a very close inverse statistical relationship between income group and consumption of state benefits. That partly depends on the composition of the income group. But if you wanted a simple way of allocating money, you could just apply that inverse relationship that applies across income groups in the United Kingdom. You could apply that to the devolved administrations using average income groups of those administrations. That is the calculation that I did in my paper.

Q550 Lord Moser: I found your paper extremely interesting, as a statistician. Once we decide or are advised to go beyond the Barnett Formula towards needs assessment in a serious way, some people then picture an enormously complicated approach with hundreds of indicators. It can be done, as you know—and then there are weighting issues, *et cetera.* Obviously, it is rather off-putting. Some people favour getting it down to three or four indicators measuring maybe something very economic, something environmental, *et cetera,* and there are still some weighting problems but more manageable. Some people, including yourself in your paper, Professor Foreman-Peck, look for a proxy—not just population but, say, GNP, GVP inverse, or one of the papers we had suggested a poverty measurement. There are social security measurements. If I understand you right, you favour disposable household income. We have to think of the politics of all this and on the assumption that it is done by somebody other than the Treasury, because the Treasury probably would never do it. Could you talk a bit about the pros and cons of the multiple approach versus the proxy approach and your favoured examples for each? I would like to hear a little bit more why—I have not quite understood why in your paper disposable household income is superior to the conventional GNP measure. Any help on this would be appreciated.

Professor Foreman-Peck: To take the last point first, GVA per head is the critical indicator that many people favour. The reason why you get such wide discrepancies between regions in the UK is because participation rates vary very substantially. Wales has about a 4.5 per cent lower participation rate in the labour force than the UK average. That means, for various reasons, a smaller proportion of the population is working. GVA per head of population is not just a measure of productivity; you have to multiply participation in the work force times productivity of the work force to get GVA per head of population. That really is the critical issue.

Q551 *Lord Moser:* Could you do that?

Professor Foreman-Peck: Certainly you could do that, yes; you could control for whether people work or not. The second point is: what exactly has productivity got to do with what we are talking about here? Productivity is to do with industry and making things. Here, we are talking about, as I understand it, the equitable provision of public services. I would have thought most people would have said that those with low incomes are more likely to have unsatisfied needs than people with high income. That is the basis of my proposal to use household income as a needs indicator.

Q552 *Lord Moser:* Disposable household income.

Professor Foreman-Peck: Yes, after tax and after support. Arguably, the weakness of the numbers I come up with derive from the cross-UK consumption of state benefits in kind with income, because that is the only thing I could put my hands on at short notice. I think you can probably get a more precise indicator than that, given more time. I think social security is not a good aggregate index because that is already covered. In a sense, households receive social security, or social protection or family income supplement effectively from central government. It is

largely annually managed expenditure. So you would be counting the outlays twice in a sense. I am not convinced that that is a good idea. My objection—and it is not a particularly strong objection—I can see there are arguments for doing it, for looking at disaggregated measures of education and health and so on—is that when you devolve authority you allow authorities, administrations, to decide on how they are going to spend on education and health. So if you give them money based on your calculation of how much it is reasonable to spend on education and health, you are in a way double-guessing them. I did a little experiment in something that the IWA published a couple of years ago, called *Time to Deliver* where I compared health spending across regions and education spending and used standardised mortality ratios for health spending and free school meals for education spending; and you get very, very close fits. Wales looks fairly similar to the English regions in that respect. In fact it spends slightly less on education, especially about three or four years ago, and spends rather more on health. Scotland spends more on education and health than England on both those criteria.

Q553 *Lord Moser:* How would you feel about—Chairman, if I can go on for a moment—the other sort of approach, 4, 5 or 6 indicators, with suitable weighting? The weighting would probably vary between regions. Well, it would certainly vary between regions because of your 70 per cent that does not fit the other regions.

Professor Foreman-Peck: I have no fundamental objection to it. My understanding is that when you look at the way these formulas operate in practice, particularly in local government, they become areas for bargaining. There is a very strong pressure to increase the number of indicators and change the weights for special circumstances. In other words, it is a Pandora's Box and extremely boring as well! I favour simplicity on the grounds of sanity.

Q554 *Lord Moser:* On the assumption that Barnett is free of bargaining?

Professor Foreman-Peck: Barnett is not going to last for ever, and I think that a simple needs-based formula is better than a complicated needs-based formula.

Q555 *Chairman:* You could go half-way between the two, could you not? The suggestion Lord Moser is making is for four to six variables, which should not be too difficult to categorise, and on that basis you could arrive at a better assessment of needs and fairness than by just taking one.

Dr ap Gwilym: Without being facetious, I am not sure if you are familiar with the Lottery Fund, the way they allocate moneys. They have a formula that is related to GDP and to a deprivation index. I am not an expert on that at all, but it might be well worth a look at.

Q556 Lord Sewel: Should you put in the cost of providing services as factors? I have an interest here because I live north of the Highland line.
Professor Foreman-Peck: The cost of providing services is arguably determined by the system, and so if you have a formula that takes into account the cost of providing services, then it is likely to affect the cost of providing the services—and the cost-plus contracts in defence are the classic example. If you do want to take into account costs, you need to have something fairly sophisticated.

Q557 Lord Sewel: There is a problem, is there not, in, say, education provision in the Islands of Scotland? There is a cost driver there.
Professor Foreman-Peck: Yes, and this is why many people think that one of the indicators, which Lord Moser would favour, would be population density as a contributor.

Q558 Chairman: Except density has problems as well as advantages, does it not?
Dr Bristow: I would make two points. One is that there is never going to be a system that is perfect and entirely free of political bargaining, some degree of trade-offs and compromise, and that is the reality in a sense. Secondly the key then is finding a situation, or a settled compromise that minimises potential trade-offs and conflicts that might arise. What is critical is devising a system that is transparent and accountable; and we therefore have to understand what we are trying to achieve first and foremost and then design a needs-based system around that. It is important to have a debate about the key objectives you are trying to achieve, and then determine the indicators on the basis of that. There are a number of different options you might choose. One might be to have a fairly comprehensive annual rigorous assessment of needs undertaken, and therefore the desire that you try to achieve a unanimous verdict on the settlement as a result of that, and if you cannot reach some sort of unanimous settlement, then you go to a default option where you use simpler, cruder indicators as your default mechanism for allocated spending. That is certainly something others have suggested as a practical solution and way forward.

Q559 Earl of Mar and Kellie: I would like to ask about the absolute need for reform. From what I have seen and heard, the workings of the Barnett Formula are probably best demonstrated in Wales. I suspect they are distorted by other factors in Scotland and Northern Ireland. Therefore, I wonder whether a replacement will in fact ultimately be any better; and would any of these suggestions so far be fairer?
Dr ap Gwilym: I am not sure I would agree with you when you say "best works in Wales" because what do you mean by "best" and what are your criteria? As you appreciate, we would contend that it is very unfair to Wales, and therefore it does not work well for Wales; and therefore that is why we want it replaced. In my submission, I gave a whole series of criticisms of the Formula. One recognises of course that replacing it will be difficult and complex, but I think we need to replace it. The other issue is that whatever system we have, it needs to be open and transparent, and then you will have the debate. You will have disagreements but that is at the heart of democracy, that people debate and disagree and then try to reach a compromise. At the moment we do not get that. The other thing of course—I do not want to be party-political, but since 1999 when we have had the Assembly here in Wales, you have had the Government in London and the Government in Wales, even allowing for the couple of coalitions in Wales, being led by the same party. It might be somewhat different if you have a different party in London and in Cardiff; that might open up the differences a little bit more. At the moment you have not had a rigorous debate between those two organisations as far as I can see, about these issues. For obvious reasons, it is rather difficult, being of the same party. I suspect if you had a Conservative government in London and a Labour-led government in Wales there could be more friction, and hopefully out of that friction you might get a little bit more light on these mechanisms. I am afraid the whole working of the Formula is probably exemplified most clearly in Wales, and I think it exemplifies the weaknesses of the Barnett Formula as well.

Q560 Earl of Mar and Kellie: That was the point I was making; that it does need exemplifying. Do you believe that it is possible within the constitutional set-up of devolution, a relatively limited form of self-government, to have equitable or open discussion; and does devolution not imply that ultimately the Treasury will decide?
Dr ap Gwilym: The old saying is that power devolved is power retained, and that is a reality. Clearly, the Treasury is a very powerful player here, but that does not mean that one simply therefore gives up; one tries to shift the balance a little. I would say that opening up the discussion and being much more transparent about how the whole thing works and how funds are allocated would be a step in the right direction. It still would not be perfect. The other issue, as you know, a central one, is the way the Barnett Formula works is very much that the United Kingdom is a unitary state with some asymmetric devolution; and therefore

what drives the changes to the Barnett Formula overwhelmingly are decisions made about spending programmes for England. This is not being anti-English at all; it is just the reality: England is over 80 per cent of the UK's population, so that is the way it is. Therefore, what drives Barnett—the changes to the block grant are decisions made overwhelmingly by the UK/English Government for the spending needs of England; and then as a consequence, that indeed what it is called in the jargon, a "consequential", there are changes to the spending in Scotland and in Wales. One understands that reality, but I would say that we do need to move away from Barnett. It will not be easy. In my paper I described the potential process rather than the solution, if you like, so it sidesteps this whole issue, which Lord Moser quite correctly raised, about "what indicators do you have; three or four broad proxies or a huge number of detailed ones?" I confess I have sidestepped that question because I think that needs a lot more debate. Certainly, even using four or five more proxies, I would argue that it would almost certainly be better than using the current system, and having used the current system for thirty years the outcomes from the point of view of Wales are very unsatisfactory.

Q561 *Earl of Mar and Kellie:* Is there sufficient urgency?
Dr ap Gwilym: On whose behalf?

Q562 *Earl of Mar and Kellie:* My guess is that ultimately the Treasury will have to decide what they are going to allow as the criteria. Is there sufficient urgency yet for them to undertake this difficult task?
Dr ap Gwilym: I would say there should be, but I doubt if there is. The Treasury has somewhat larger issues probably on its mind at the moment. Therefore, it is not a good time in that sense—and of course it never is a good time. If you look back from about 2000 onwards, we enjoyed across the United Kingdom seven or eight years record growth in public expenditure, and therefore at that stage the pressures were less. Now we are reaching a period of course where there is going to be very little growth in public expenditure. The pressures will be greater, and of course on the Treasury there are far bigger pressures from elsewhere. The Treasury, I would imagine, is very content with the current system; it is simple and they basically work out the spending for England, and then you hit the calculator button and the consequentials come out for Wales. From their point of view, that is easy.

Q563 *Lord Sewel:* If public expenditure is severely under pressure, Barnett rides to your rescue.

Dr ap Gwilym: It could potentially ride to our rescue if you started getting negative nominal growth. I take your point. Even if it is going to be negative nominal growth, it is going to be at a very small level I think, even allowing for the dire state of the public finances.

Q564 *Chairman:* What is interesting from all the evidence we have heard and the papers that we have seen is that by and large nobody is prepared to say that the present Barnett Formula is an acceptable way of actually doing the job that it is supposed to. The only people who have gone anywhere near saying that is the Treasury, which for obvious reasons one would expect them to. There seems to be a general feeling that you should somehow or other introduce a needs assessment element into the way in which you allocate these resources. I assume, from everything the three of you have said, that you basically go along at least that far with this. The argument then becomes: what sort of needs assessment; how do you do it; what criteria do you take? Also, I suppose, you would want to say something about a transparency process by which the existing Formula is in fact being administered and on the reform to it. It seems clear that you cannot go on—I think somebody in London the other day described it to us as—it was not intellectually corrupt—intellectually defective. If it is intellectually defective, we have to try to see how we can do something about it.
Dr ap Gwilym: It is difficult. That is why I suggested these steps. Some are quite modest steps, and in the case of Wales, even such a radical one as "freeze the squeeze", if you like, so that rather than getting the same monetary increase *per capita* you get the same percentage increase. One of the objections to Barnett is that whilst it has no reflection of need, it is not a static formula, it is a dynamic one; it is a convergent formula that is used. It is not neutral, as it were; it is driving identifiable public expenditure on devolved services in Wales down compared to the average for the United Kingdom, year on year. Freezing the squeeze is one trivial thing to do and is an intermediate step. I do not think that is far enough, and that is why I suggest some further steps beyond that. I thought that was at least a modest first step.

Q565 *Lord Moser:* Do you think we are right, all of us, in thinking of the needs approaches as a total change from Barnett; or supposing we could agree on these two or three or four crucial indicators, could they be, in a multi-varied sort of way, included in the Barnett Formula population measurement? I have not thought this through, but what would be the objection to that?
Professor Foreman-Peck: In principle you could modify the Barnett Formula to do that. The problem is the baseline, and that is the way you would use those variables, to calculate the baseline. Then you

would go through a percentage increase from that baseline, once you have got the baseline.

Q566 Lord Moser: But not just on population!
Professor Foreman-Peck: No, you use the Formula to get the *per capita* allocation.

Q567 Lord Moser: So the Treasury could be fooled into thinking that we are keeping the Barnett Formula!
Dr Bristow: The other problem is that Barnett is a system that rests on linking spending allocations in Wales, Scotland and Northern Ireland to incremental changes in expenditure in England, and that is the fundamental issue that then would have to be addressed: how do you disentangle spending from England and what do you do about English regions?

Q568 Chairman: You have to look at the baseline. It seems to me that Barnett is used almost as a generic term for a block allocation as well as the method for dealing with variations in expenditure. It seems that if you are going to introduce fairness into the thing you have to look at the baseline as well as looking at the mechanism operation. I do not see how you can avoid that.
Dr ap Gwilym: I agree. Bear in mind that whilst the Treasury did a needs assessment in 1979, that did not change the baselines in 1979: whilst they did a needs assessment, they did not put that in as the baseline for Barnett nor adjust the existing pattern of spending. They did not adjust it. People often think they did but they did not. This goes back into deep history, if you like. When were the baselines established? They evolved over decades, prior to 1979.

Q569 Chairman: Presumably they were based on a baseline pre 1979 and pre needs assessment.
Dr ap Gwilym: That is right.

Q570 Chairman: Which, incidentally, the ministers of the day knew nothing about!
Dr ap Gwilym: Did they not?

Q571 Chairman: No.
Dr ap Gwilym: That is interesting.
Chairman: Joel Barnett said he did not know it was going on, did not know the results and was not told about it. It is the most extraordinary history that seems to be emerging. There we are!

Q572 Lord Sewel: I will say in passing that I do not think "freeze the squeeze" is a particularly romantic slogan!

Dr ap Gwilym: I am ready to take advice!

Q573 Lord Sewel: I just have a worry at the back of my head because years and years ago I used to be involved in local government taxation. There is almost a similar sort of argument: Barnett wrong; move to something called needs; leave it relatively undefined what is in the needs thing. That fits so easily with what happened with local government taxation. Property tax: wrong; move to something else; oh dear—even worse! The test is: moving away from Barnett is there an alternative to a needs-based assessment?
Professor Foreman-Peck: The simple one, which Eurfyl already mentioned, is just a percentage on where we are at the moment. I use the term "Barnett relaxed" which may be more saleable than "freeze the squeeze"—I do not know—but they are not the same. You accept the baseline from history and then just make sure it is embedded in the Treasury consciousness for ever.

Q574 Chairman: How do you determine who gets what percentage above the baseline?
Professor Foreman-Peck: When England increases spending the devolved administrations get the same percentage increase- I have a little calculation in my paper about how this would be done. I used illustrative numbers. This is on page 3. The problem is you have got to have a budget constraint. The Chancellor or somebody decides there is £15 billion available, and you keep the comparable programmes system so you know how much money is being spent on comparable programmes, and under Barnett you divide the £15 billion by population roughly speaking. Under the "relaxed Barnett" you divide £15 billion by the baseline spending, say £300 billion, so you get a percentage. Then you increase the budget allocations by that percentage. Under Barnett you have a lump sum, a numerical figure; under "relaxed Barnett" you look at the proportionate increase in comparable spending programmes.

Q575 Chairman: Are you in favour of relaxing Barnett?
Dr ap Gwilym: I do see that as a very inadequate early step because I think the fundamental objections are still there. The real difficulty of course is if the UK—I am not advocating this, by the way—were a federal state, then you would have a series of parties of roughly equal weight. The reality is of course that England has 50 million odd out of the 61 million population of the United Kingdom, and even more for GDP. I think we need to move beyond relaxing Barnett; we need to move beyond determining increases in public expenditure in the three other countries in the United Kingdom having that driven entirely by the needs of England. That is not

adequate either, in my view. Therefore, one needs to move to a system where you have—and this might sound a little naïve looking at the political and power realities—the three devolved administrations at least having a chance of debating and negotiation with the centre on the allocation of moneys. Otherwise, if we take relaxed Barnett, although I have said it is a modest step along the way—freeze the squeeze, relaxed Barnett—we still have the current baselines that are unsatisfactory. We still have the determination of spending priorities and total quantity in terms of the needs of England; and then we trail behind on the consequentials. To my mind that is really a slight improvement, but the danger there, thereby, by making that slight improvement is that that then stops any other further development for another thirty years.

Q576 Lord Sewel: If I understood you rightly, you are saying you want annual negotiation between the three or four elements.
Dr ap Gwilym: Either annual, or at the moment you have a spending review or comprehensive spending review every two to three years. Clearly, that is within UK parameters of total managed expenditure and so on.

Q577 Lord Sewel: Is that basically throwing the Formula out of the window?
Dr ap Gwilym: Yes.

Q578 Lord Sewel: So it is just hard negotiation across the table!
Dr ap Gwilym: No, I would not say that, because I have also said one would establish a commission to look into these matters. I do not want to push it too far, but like the Australian Commission where you have expert advice, and you have studies made in terms of needs, and you discuss the key indicators and which proxies we can use, rather than a whole gamut of too many parameters. That group advises the ministers, but you would then involve the finance ministers of the three devolved administrations.

Q579 Lord Sewel: It advises, it does not determine.
Dr ap Gwilym: No, it gives advice. Of course, if that advice is in the public domain, then the politicians, if they are accountable to the electorate, at least have to justify why they did not take that advice.

Q580 Lord Moser: Chairman, on this slightly more marginal point, but not really on the data quality/availability: as your papers have been extremely helpful in going into a great deal of statistical detail, is there anything we should be worrying about from a Wales point of view in terms of the data you are playing with both on the actual distribution of public expenditure, what comes to Wales, the effects thereof,

the tax revenues, and indeed the sort of data one might need for the sort of indicators that we are talking about? It would be helpful to know what you think we should be worrying about on data.
Professor Foreman-Peck: It is quite difficult to work out what is going on, or I find it difficult working out what is going on. It would be nice, and I think in the public interest—

Q581 Lord Moser: Can you expand the three words "what is going on"?
Professor Foreman-Peck: The calculations that I have done—and I have learnt a lot from Eurfyl in doing them—are based on the Treasury public expenditure statistical analysis that comes out every year. They do not correspond exactly, and it is very hard to make them correspond exactly with devolved budgets it would be helpful if it was possible to get, in the calculations we have done, equivalents to devolved budgets in England, so that we can see how comparable expenditure goes. For example, a difficulty we have in working out why Scotland has managed to by-pass the Formula seems to be a consequence of inadequate statistical data, and that may be the reason of course.
Lord Moser: Chairman, may I, across you, ask our expert adviser, who has made heroic attempts to solve this problem, his answer to what we have just heard, because you have tried in this table.

Q582 Chairman: I am told by our Specialist Adviser that we have been relying principally, so far, on PESA data and on such other data as we can obtain from the Treasury, which has recently, and without publicly—recently assisted the territorial offices in Scotland and Wales Offices in including some figures back into Scotland and Wales on this annual report. It is not exactly the sort of place one would normally look to find Treasury data about public expenditure across devolved parts of the UK, which, on a snapshot basis for the specific year that they cover go a bit further, and I would hope give some clearer idea about the relationship between UK Government spending and spending by the devolved administrations. Part of our concern generally remains, that the data we want are not published yet and remain unpublished in any one place, and the Treasury so far has not disclosed the sort of data we require.
Dr ap Gwilym: Chairman, it is interesting: recently I wanted to know what the block grant to Wales had been for each year since 1999–2000 for part of my exercise. I went to the back of the Wales Office annual reports, because they set out data for four or five years at a time. You do not have a full run of ten years, so I asked the statistical department of the civil service here, who were very helpful by the way, whether they had that time series, and they could not

produce it for me; so I still do not have a time series for something as elementary as the Welsh block grant from 1999–2000 up to the current year.

Q583 *Lord Moser:* That must be available. It simply must be available!

Dr ap Gwilym: All I can report back is my failure to get that information. The civil servants have been very helpful in other areas, I must say, so I am not being critical of them, but I was unable to get that information. In terms of PESA, something as elementary—you can sound a bit of a wonk on this, but if you look at table 9.17 it shows the expenditure in Scotland, in Wales and Northern Ireland, split down in the case of Wales by the Welsh Assembly Government expenditure, UK direct expenditure in Wales, things like social protection and local authority spending—it is very helpful. It would be rather helpful if one had the equivalent numbers for England. I am not sure why we cannot. You would have data for the four countries. Part of my thesis has often been that now we have got some devolution—a little bit like in the private sector where you have inter-firm comparisons, you could start having inter-country comparisons with the UK, even more if you look at policy differences and policy outcomes over a period of five or ten years. It is complex, I know. You might say that Scotland has done rather well with

that policy in that area; but that means you have a fuller set of data. In fairness to the Government, probably since 1997—though I stand to be corrected—they have produced the statement of funding policy and set out all the comparables in the back of that document. The only thing is that there I do wonder, because some of the factors are quite bizarre. One of the examples I gave you was that Wales enjoys a Barnett consequential for the money the United Kingdom Government pays towards decommissioning nuclear power stations in the Former Soviet Union. You think: "Why is Wales getting a Barnett consequential for that?" I am not wanting to turn away gifts, but there is a whole series of these, and those are more clear-cut ones. In the larger spending areas of course you are not sure. If those comparability factors are faulty—they appear to be faulty—are the other comparability factors fair and correct or not? We do not know.

Lord Moser: It may be very helpful—maybe it will be recorded—if we could know from Wales where your particular defects of data are felt. Maybe it will be covered in the record.

Chairman: Thank you very much indeed for coming. It has been very helpful. Part of the fascination about this particular Committee is that it is a learning process for those of us who are on it. I have to say you have advanced the learning process very considerably this morning. Thank you very much for coming.

FRIDAY 20 MARCH 2009

Present	Mar and Kellie, E	Richard, L (Chairman)
	Moser, L	Sewel, L

Memorandum by the Welsh Local Government Association

INTRODUCTION

1. The Welsh Local Government Association (WLGA) represents the 22 local authorities in Wales. The three national park authorities, the three fire and rescue authorities and four police authorities are associate members.

2. It seeks to provide representation to local authorities within an emerging policy framework that satisfies the key priorities of our members and delivers a broad range of services that add value to Welsh Local Government and the communities they serve.

3. The WLGA welcomes the opportunity to respond to Call for Evidence from the Select Committee on the Barnett Formula. This submission sets out the WLGA's views of the present formula and goes on to consider possible alternative funding mechanisms and the scope for the Welsh Assembly Government to have borrowing and tax varying powers.

THE EXISTING "BARNETT FORMULA"

4. The Barnett Formula was devised in the late 1970s as an adjustment mechanism, intended to adjust the historic expenditure baselines of Scotland, Wales and Northern Ireland in a manner which would ultimately achieve standard spending per head across the United Kingdom, ie achieve convergence.

5. Since devolution calls for a review of the Barnett Formula have grown stronger as questions have been raised about its validity as a means of distributing resources. With similar reviews being undertaken by the Holtham Commission in Wales and the Calman Commission in Scotland the House of Lords Select Committee is timely.

6. The existing formula appears relatively straight forward using population share and comparable functions as its drivers. In essence, when there is an addition to public expenditure in England on functions which have been devolved to Wales then there is a consequential addition to the allocation to the Welsh Assembly Government based on the ratio of Wales to England population. The allocation to the Welsh Assembly Government is therefore partly based on the historic allocation, fixed in 1979, plus population based changes made thereafter. Over time it was anticipated that the population based consequentials would grow to over-ride the historic allocation and convergence would increasingly be achieved.

THE BENEFITS OF BARNETT

7. There have been benefits to Wales from the application of the Barnett formula. The "automatic" nature of the consequential adjustment has provided the Welsh Assembly Government with relatively predictable and guaranteed increases in expenditure since 1999. The grant to the Welsh Assembly Government has remained very largely un-hypothecated and this has allowed the democratic politics of Wales to set and challenge public expenditure priorities. The formula has continued to provide a level of public expenditure in Wales on comparable functions which is higher than that in England, even if significantly lower than that in Scotland and Northern Ireland. Convergence has been slower than many would have expected. This is partly because population growth in Wales has been slower than that in England and because there have been occasional extra-Barnett allocations, eg the provision of additional public expenditure cover for European Structural Funds.

THE PROBLEMS WITH BARNETT

8. However, it is the view of the WLGA that the benefits gained from Barnett are now less significant than the anomalies it has created. In particular, the formula takes no account of the particular needs of Wales and there is no evidence available to justify the lower levels of comparable expenditure in Wales compared to that in Scotland and Northern Ireland. Another difficulty with the application of the Barnett formula which concerns the WLGA is its lack of public transparency and the apparently unchallenged ability of the Treasury to impose its own interpretations and amendments to the application of the formula (particularly between Spending

Reviews) in ways which are not open to public debate or challenge. For instance, we understand that the Treasury has determined that the local regeneration expenditures in south east England associated with the Olympics are not comparable expenditure so no consequential has been derived for the devolved administrations; there has been no public declaration, debate or challenge over this unilateral decision.

9. The Treasury's decision, in around 2003, to hypothecate the Welsh block into capital and revenue components is another example of a unilateral decision which has had a significant impact on public finances in Wales. Since 2003–04, the Welsh Assembly Government's settlement has been split into three fixed sub-limits for revenue, capital and non-cash (ie capital charges) all derived using the Barnett formula. Introducing these sub-limits with little or no flexibility to move between them has removed the discretion of devolved administrations to decide their own spending priorities within an overall block grant.

10. The policy intention of introducing a capital and non-cash limit was to improve the management of public sector assets and increase departmental accountability. While this may have worked in UK departments, the introduction of a capital limit using Barnett has not delivered the desired effect in Wales. Using Barnett to set a capital limit ignores significant historic differences in individual countries' asset bases (in terms of quantity, market value and quality) and the extent to which UK departments have used the Private Finance Initiative (PFI), compared to Wales. In Wales there is a multi-billion pound capital investment gap in public sector infrastructure (schools, housing, waste management and transport etc). One way forward would be to increase the revenue provision to local authorities in a manner that would allow them to extend their prudential borrowing to fund the necessary capital expenditure. The hypothecation of the block grant prevents this course of action. There is also a problem of inflexibility in financial management when inevitably some capital programmes do not fully utilize their allocation in a given financial year. Without the ability to switch such expenditure to revenue the allocation is returned to the Treasury and its future use may be restricted if the Treasury exerts controls over End-of-Year Flexibility.

11. The WLGA believes there is a need to formalize the arrangements between HM Treasury and the devolved administrations to ensure that decisions which affect funding allocations are transparent and are not taken without formal agreement from devolved governments. Such a move would ensure that the implications for devolved administrations of policies developed in Whitehall were fully understood before changes to funding arrangements could be made. This issue is discussed further in paragraph 18 below.

An Alternative Mechanism

12. The WLGA believes that an alternative distribution mechanism based on an open and transparent assessment of expenditure need would deliver more resources for public expenditure in Wales and, on that basis, supports the proposition that such an alternative mechanism should be developed and implemented. A needs based assessment would allocate above average resources to areas of greater deprivation, where the need for public services are greater, and to areas of sparse population where the cost of service delivery is higher. On both counts Wales would justify on a needs assessment above average expenditure levels to an extent that Barnett is currently not delivering and, given the intended convergence, will increasingly not deliver in the future

13. We have identified six key principles for any new mechanism:

1. The principle of Simplicity and Transparency;

2. The principle of Distribution according to Needs;

3. The principle of Non-Hypothecation;

4. The Principle of Independent Advice;

5. The principle of Fiscal Compensation; and

6. The principle of Flexible Financial Management.

The Principle of Simplicity and Transparency

14. Any replacement must be simple and transparent if it is to achieve the credibility that the current arrangements arguably lack. The public needs confidence that the future allocations are "fair" in outcome and in process. They need to be able to see the criteria that inform the allocations and need to be assured that the application of such criteria is not capable of any arbitrary manipulation.

The Principle of Distribution according to Need

15. In outline the assessment of expenditure need in any distribution formula has just three elements:

— The identification of the relevant population base for the expenditures being allocated;

— The identification of the relative need for the relevant public services and this will be driven by measures of relative deprivation;

— The identification of the relative costs of service delivery and this will be driven by measures of the relative sparsity of population.

16. Whilst there is conceptual simplicity in identifying just three elements, in practice the development of indicators and their weightings to give effect to these elements can lead to complexity and confusion. At this stage the best that can be said is that the indicators chosen should be relatively few in number, chosen and weighted in accordance with their broad effect on expenditure need. The alternative path of very detailed service based indicators leads to the sort of complexity that can bring these systems into disrepute and can lead, perhaps unintentionally, to a convergence of policies and priorities between the different devolved administrations.

The Principle of Non-Hypothecation

17. There is a danger that the UK Government would see the review of Barnett as an opportunity to introduce greater hypothecation of the grants available to devolved administrations, perhaps requiring that grants are made conditional on the pursuance of UK Government priorities. Such a move would be opposed by the WLGA which is convinced that the devolution of democratic political choice to devolved and local administrations is only made real when those administrations can set their own budgets. In supporting the Welsh Assembly Government on this principle Welsh local government would expect that the same principle is applied to the distribution of grants to Welsh local authorities.

The Principle of Independent Advice

18. In principle, the WLGA sees merit in the establishment of an independent organisation such as the Australian Commonwealth Grants Commission to advise on the process of equalisation between devolved administrations and regions. Ultimately the WLGA recognises that resource allocation is a matter for elected governments, but the availability of independent advice would require governments to explain their decisions and give reasons for the departures from the advice taken. This discipline on governments would mitigate against arbitrary or partial decision making. In the distributions to Welsh local government there have been occasions when independent reviews have been commissioned. Sometimes the advice has been accepted by the Welsh Assembly Government and Welsh local government, sometimes not; but the challenge provided by such advice has invariably been positive. An Australian style Grants Commission would provide this sort of advice on a standing basis and would ensure greater transparency of decision taking by governments.

The Principle of Fiscal Compensation

19. Should greater fiscal autonomy be given to devolved administrations through assigned taxation or tax varying competence then it must follow that the grant allocation to the devolved administration compensates for variation in the tax bases in each devolved administration. The grant distribution to local authorities is designed to achieve this. However in so far as total public expenditure in Wales relies on the contribution of the council tax and the Non Domestic Rate, the current Barnett formula is not designed to compensate for the relatively low tax base, driven by relative property values, in Wales. In this respect, and in respect of any further fiscal devolution, the grant distribution should provide for fiscal compensation.

The Principle of Flexible Financial Management

20. Local authorities have reasonable powers for flexible financial management in that they are able to borrow and hold reserves. The borrowing powers of local authorities were recently extended under the system of prudential borrowing which allows them to make a rational decision to commit future revenue, through borrowing, to finance capital projects in a manner that properly spreads the burden of funding long term assets to future service users.

21. The WLGA believes the Welsh Assembly Government should have similar financial flexibility to that of local authorities both in terms of borrowing powers and holding of reserves. Such a move would strengthen the financial responsibilities and accountability of the Welsh Assembly Government, which in turn should

improve the efficacy and efficiency of its financial planning and asset management. When combined with a needs based formula, these powers would enable the Welsh Assembly Government to enter into longer term financial commitments helping to address the country's infrastructure and revenue needs more effectively.

Issues for Further Consideration

22. Several academic commentators have remarked that public spending expenditure for a region and in a region are not the same thing at all. This is particularly important to Wales in the context of the high proportion of the population claiming welfare benefits which is non-devolved expenditure. What would be the implications, if any, for non-devolved expenditure should a replacement for the Barnett Formula be agreed? And how would this impact on the differentiation between the Welsh Assembly Government Departmental Expenditure Limit (DEL) which is subject to the Barnett formula and Annually Managed Expenditure (AME) which is not?

Conclusion

23. The WLGA believes that there are some clearly established and fundamental considerations that should inform the Select Committee's further work. These are covered in this paper. Equally, however, there are several key questions—also identified, but as yet unanswered which certainly bear further scrutiny to determine where the balance of advantage lies for Wales, but recognising that if a better model is to be found it will need to be acceptable to the other devolved administrations and take account of the fact that many in England believe that devolved administrations already receive in excess of their entitlement.

February 2009

Memorandum by the Chartered Institute of Public Finance & Accountancy (CIPFA)

1. Introduction

1.1 The interim report of the Commission on Scottish Devolution (Calman), sets out three main mechanisms used in funding systems: tax assignment, grant based systems and fiscal autonomy. At the moment, the system of devolved government across the UK relies on a grant based funding system. This approach has been consistent with the constitutional objective of the UK. The Barnett Formula has been the foundation for the grant based funding system. Given the choice of the grant based funding approach, any proposed changes need to be considered in terms of their impact on the constitutional objective.

1.2 As an accountancy Institute we believe that it is our role to help governments design funding systems but not to set out the constitutional objectives for which a funding system would support. We have recently submitted written and oral evidence to the Commission on Scottish Devolution (Calman) within which we restricted ourselves to answering those questions which relate to the funding mechanisms rather than considering the constitutional objectives which a funding system would support.

1.3 We have adopted the same approach in this response. As per the instructions accompanying the call for evidence, we have also restricted the length of our response.

Specific Comments

Question 1. *Application of the formula in practice*

(d) *What measure of flexibility do the devolved administrations presently enjoy in allocating funds, between various policy areas, between capital and current spending and for accounting purposes? Is there any need for reform in this area?*

Allocating Funds between policy areas

The allocation of public expenditure between the services under the control of the devolved administrations is for the devolved administrations to determine. Consistent with the arrangements for departments of the United Kingdom Government, the devolved administrations will normally be expected to accommodate additional pressures on their budgets, with access to the Reserve being considered in exceptional circumstances only. Unforeseen pressures should be catered for by offsetting savings and adjustments to plans.

Allocating funds between capital and current spending

As per the Statement of Funding Policy (October 2007) , the Scottish and Northern Ireland Executives and Welsh Assembly are free to allocate their capital and resources budgets, determined in spending reviews, to reflect their own priorities. They may also switch provision from resource DEL to capital DEL and in exceptional circumstances they may consider with the Treasury in year a switch from capital DEL to resource DEL.

Accounting Purposes

Financial reporting guidance in the UK public services is expressed as an interpretation of private sector guidance. This has the effect of facilitating comparability with the private sector and between public service sectors. Two different implementation approaches have been developed for different public services. Some sector regulators follow the Accounting Standards Board (ASB) process and develop Statements of Recommended Practice (SORPs). A different approach is taken in the central government, devolved administrations and health sectors: manuals are produced which interpret international financial reporting standards for the sectors, which are reviewed by a specially constituted group of government and other financial reporting stakeholders, the Financial Reporting Advisory Board (FRAB).

In the central government, health sector and the devolved administrations the requirements for financial reporting are set out directly in legislation, and responsibility for producing financial reporting guidance rests with the "relevant authority" under that legislation. The sectors have adopted a co-ordinated review process in order to produce consistent guidance: each of the "relevant authorities" is represented on the Financial Reporting Advisory Board (FRAB), together with an accounting academic, representatives from the national audit agencies, and ASB and CIPFA nominees. Under this unified approach a single government International Financial Reporting Manual (iFReM) provides guidance for central government in England and across the UK, and for devolved administrations in Scotland, Wales and Northern Ireland, while aligned guidance for health bodies is provided in NHS manuals and in an iFReM issued by Monitor, the regulator for NHS Foundation Trusts.

These processes seem to operate satisfactorily and we would not advocate significant changes.

Question 3. *Data Quality and Availability*

(j) *What body should undertake the collection and publication of such data*

The content of the existing Statement of Funding Policy, which stipulates the current financial arrangements between UK Government and the devolved administrations, and how it is applied, are matters for the UK Government. A case could be made for putting the maintenance, development and review of the Barnett Formula in the hands of an independent body like the Australian Commonwealth Grants Commission. This would of course require carefully prescribed terms of reference and statutory backing.

Although the Barnett Formula is in principle simple, it has not avoided a degree of controversy about its application, for example, in relation to Olympics spending or new spending on prisons in England. The Government in Scotland have exercised their right in terms of policies and spending priorities and these choices have received much media attention north and south of the border. The coverage of these choices has contributed to a mounting belief, emanating from a number of areas across England, that Scotland is getting a better deal under devolution than the rest of the United Kingdom.

Other countries, like Australia for example, have attempted to introduce an element of independent oversight to the system of grants based on a needs assessment. The funding allocated to states is based on an assessment undertaken by an independent body, the Commonwealth Grants Commission. The UK equivalent of this body would be a non departmental public body.

Question 4. *Need for reform/alternatives to the existing formula*

(k) *Do the advantages of the formula as presently constituted outweigh its disadvantages*

Listed below are the advantages and disadvantages we see in relation to the existing formula. These are considered through the lens of different facets of financial management.

ADVANTAGES
— Financial Planning: The devolved government's get a baseline budget which is essentially the budget from the previous spending review. A revised budget is calculated by adding or subtracting from the baseline an amount calculated using the Barnett Formula. This amount is a population share of the

change in comparable English spending programmes. This forms the new budget for future years. The inherited baseline is the largest single determinant of the budget. The combination of the baseline, Barnett and three year spending plans have the effect that the budget of the devolved governments are stable and substantially predictable;

— Financial Planning: The block grants (or assigned budgets) are contained within the devolved administrations' Departmental Expenditure Limits. Changes to these budgets are generally determined by the Barnett Formula. This helps to minimise the need for potentially protracted negotiations between Treasury Ministers, Secretaries of State and Ministers of the devolved administrations;

— Financial Planning: The block grant, which in part is determined by the Barnett Formula, is a non ring fenced grant and therefore offers greater overall autonomy to the devolved governments in terms of determining their own spending priorities;

— Financial Control: The current system imposes a firm financial discipline—devolved policy makers can only spend what they get except where over-spends are permitted by UK Government. End of year flexibility allows resources to be carried over from one year to the next (and into future spending review periods) but this is subject to HM Treasury restrictions.

DISADVANTAGES

— Financial Planning: The Scottish block is in part determined by changes in spending on equivalent programmes in England set by the UK Government and is not directly linked to the preferences of the devolved nations population nor their willingness to pay for the provision of services;

— Financial Planning : The formula is not related to need;

— Financial Planning: The formula does not reallocate existing expenditure, only changes made for that year (ie an uplift or decline on expenditure on the previous year. This is an incremental approach to budgeting which carries the inherent weakness of encouraging focus on changes at the margins rather than a challenging re-examination of the base budget;

— Financial Management: The formula delivers block grant to the devolved governments irrespective of the efficiency of the government or the performance of public bodies. Trade-offs between levels of spending and levels of taxation are obscure.

— Financial Management: The formula gives devolved policy makers no incentive or ability to retain a surplus achieved in good times (it would be returned to London) although it does prevent an emerging deficit in bad times (as devolved governments cannot issue debt);

— Application of the formula: There are transparency issues around what spending is actually subject to the formula. In most cases, it is easy to see what is and is not Barnett expenditure. But there are exceptions where the position is less than clear cut.

DEALING WITH LARGE SCALE INFRASTRUCTURE INVESTMENT NEEDS OF THE DEVOLVED GOVERNMENTS

The scale of investment required to fund a new Forth crossing is significant. If funded from within the current Scottish block grant, it would result in a huge volume of other priorities not being met. Where other parts of the Scottish public sector have needed to make similar significant capital investment and either do not have the power to borrow or have insufficient capacity to borrow, the route of funding has been the Private Finance Initiative (PFI). The PFI approach often meant that the underlying assets did not appear on the public sector balance sheet but instead were on the private sector balance sheet. This has been important as it has meant the associated debt was not viewed as government debt and therefore would not impact on the government's Sustainable Investment Rule. This did not mean that the capital investment was "free" to the public sector—instead, the public sector had a long term contractual commitment to repay a "rental" for the use of the asset.

Developments within the worldwide accounting profession, has seen a worldwide programme of convergence on internationally developed accounting standards. The UK is participating in this convergence programme. Significantly for PFI, the international accounting standards apply a different test to determining whether a privately funded "public" asset should sit on the public/private sector balance sheet. As a result, we face the prospect of many PFI assets coming onto the public sector asset.

In the context of the Forth Bridge, if the new crossing were financed through PFI, the adoption of IFRS would require the debt to be accounted for on the public sector balance sheet and this would count against the UK Government controls on borrowing and capital expenditure budgets and the (recently suspended) Sustainable Investment Rule.

The Scottish block grant is determined, in part, by the Barnett Formula which does not assess need and simply provides for a Scottish population share of the incremental awards to English spending departments—therefore no uplift will be provided within the Scottish block grant for the new crossing. It is useful to examine the treatment of the Olympic games—a significant financial investment which is viewed as having economic benefit for the whole country and therefore funding has been top sliced. A similar methodology may be required for other major infrastructure priorities and needs. In effect, there is a need for a state-wide co-ordination of government activity across the UK on capital investment.

(l) *Should the Barnett Formula be (a) retained in its current form, (b) amended or (c) replaced entirely*

There are a number of arguments for amendment and replacement of the formula:

AMENDMENT

— Greater clarity on Barnett consequentials—For example, recent proposals for police pensions will result in amendment to the calculations for pensions and for widows pension. There is debate about whether this spending should or should not count for Barnett purposes.

— Greater clarity on conditions around block grant—For example, the Scottish Governments recent proposals for a local income tax exposed a difference of opinion between the Scottish Government and UK Treasury on whether the council tax benefit element of the block grant (about £400 million) was ring fenced or not.

— Greater independence and transparency—In answering question 3j) we have suggested that responsibility for the maintenance, development and review of the Barnett Formula could be given to an independent body in order to encourage confidence in the formula. Such an approach would potentially bring greater transparency to the formula calculations.

— Provision for major infrastructure investment—large scale infrastructure in devolved administrations are not fully catered for in the current formula.

REPLACEMENT

— Reflecting Needs—the formula is not needs based. A needs assessment exercise was carried out for Scotland by the UK Treasury ahead of the planned devolution of 1979. If needs were to be re-addressed, then a new study would be required which would have to cover all the devolved nations and the English regions. However such a study would be a major undertaking and would be fraught with difficulties. For example, there would almost certainly be limitations to available data in some areas. Replacing the current formula with a needs based approach would likely involve significant transitional arrangements.

The Steele Commission[8] drew attention to the arrangements put in place when Australia introduced a major package of reform to its fiscal system in 1999. The changes came with a guarantee that each state would not be worse off during the transitional period than it would have been had the changes not been implemented. The transition period was approximately eight years and during this time states whose income fell below the guaranteed level were given non ring fenced grants to maintain overall revenue levels.

(m) *Should the Barnett formula be replaced by a system more adequately reflecting relative needs, costs of services or a combination of both.*

Hume Occasional paper No 80[9] sets out an interesting possible amendment: "one way to make the Barnett Formula work more effectively would be to recognise that it is a case of using one instrument to reach two targets. The targets are to provide the Scots with more money per head according to their needs ... while trying to preserve equity with the rest of the UK. This suggests keeping the base calculations as they are, but replacing the comparability percentage by a percentage calculated to reflect needs. These new percentages could be based on performance indicators as revealed needs and put in the public domain". Such an amendment would have the advantage of maintaining the stable platform but would start to factor in an assessment of need. However, such an approach might (over time) start to narrow policy choices as it would imply UK-wide agreement as the approach to, and cost of, addressing particular needs.

---

8 Moving to federalism—A New settlement for Scotland March 2006.
9 The David Hume Institute Options for Scotland's Future—the Economic Dimension November 2007.

Examination of Witnesses

Witnesses: MR PAUL GRIFFITHS, Welsh Local Government Association, MR IAN CARRUTHERS and MS MARIA JONES, Chartered Institute of Public Finance and Accountancy, Wales, examined.

Q584 Chairman: Thank you for coming. You know why we are in Cardiff and what we are taking, and I think you know our terms of reference, so you will know the extent of the inquiry we have been charged to make on behalf of the Lords. Can I say two or three housekeeping things before we start? Can I just remind you that evidence sessions are broadcast and a full transcript is going to be taken; but you will have the opportunity, if you want to, to make some corrections to the transcript. A bit like *Hansard*, you can correct the grammar but you cannot change the substance of what it is you might have said. Also, you may feel that when you have given your evidence this afternoon and when we have had our discussion on it that there is something additional you wish to add to it, so will you please feel free to send us a letter on it? Do you want to be treated collectively as the three, or different organisations?
Mr Carruthers: In a sense it depends how you want to direct your questions, because obviously both CIPFA and the WLGA have put in separate sets of evidence. It depends whether you want us to address similar questions.

Q585 Chairman: They are very similar questions actually. The most important single one from our point of view is: do you think the Barnett Formula treats Wales fairly? If you do not think it treats Wales fairly, why not—how come it does not?
Mr Carruthers: If I can start and give you an introduction to CIPFA as an organisation and then move on, CIPFA is the leading professional accountancy body focusing on public services, and is unique in that respect. As a professional member body for accountants we both train accountants and we are responsible for professional development and disciplinary matters. In particular, we comment on management and accounting for public money. In terms of today, obviously we are very interested in Barnett because we believe that good planning, financial management and governance are fundamental in terms of the management of public money. We are also an international body, and therefore we felt we had something to offer in terms of international experience in terms of the Committee's inquiry. Inevitably, in terms of the subject matter for this, it does have this strong political background, but in terms of offering our written evidence and in terms of the comments we will make today we are very much coming at that from being a professional body and a professional commentator. I have brought my colleague Maria Jones along with me. I am Director of Policy and Technical for the Institute; so in my comments I want to bring more of a national flavour to things. Maria leads on our activities in

Wales, and will then put, if you like, a Wales context onto things. In terms of addressing the question that you posed in terms of fairness, one of the things is that "fair" is different to different people. It is not an absolute concept, and particularly with regard to funding fairness is in the eye of the beneficiary, and that is very important. In terms of the way the Barnett Formula works, obviously it has three main components: the population base, the comparability element, and the spend element in England. It is obviously easy to be objective about the population element. Comparability is where we start to get into particular challenges in terms of the way that the Formula is built up, because it is built up bottom-up in terms of the way it operates. Looking at that individual programme object level that it is built up from, either it applies 100 per cent or it does not apply, in which case it is a zero. There must be a question as to whether that is true in all cases. The key issue that comes in there, in terms of comparability, is the fact that the Formula at the moment does not build in anything in respect of relative needs.

Q586 Chairman: Do you think it should?
Mr Carruthers: I think that is one of the issues as to where you come from in terms of what objectives you want out of the process because if you want equity, then perhaps needs is an objective; but if you want to look at it from a fiscal perspective, that would be something different. If you want equality of access, that would probably give you a different answer again, so it really depends on the objectives as to the answer you want. Clearly, in terms of need you have to look at the way in which you generate the data, the choice you make in terms of measures, the way you weight different measures and so on, so there are some issues there. Then, if you look at spend, the issue there is the fact that the Formula is very much based on patterns of spend in England. It is historic. Therefore, we are looking at a pattern that was there largely in the past. It is also generated—for example if you look on the capital side—very much by the distribution and condition of the asset base that was inherited in England, rather than being the asset base in Wales, and also what it is likely to be and what it is designed to be in the future.
Ms Jones: Good afternoon. I would just like to give you one or two examples really in terms of where we see that Barnett was not working in terms of Wales. One of them you will have heard about already, and it has been relayed to you at a number of the inquiries you have had so far, and it is in relation to the Olympics and the top-slicing of the allocation towards the Olympics. It is not the Olympics themselves but it is the regeneration aspect of the

Olympics that was in question at the time, and the lack of transparency in terms of determining that the Olympics were considered to be top-sliced from the overall moneys available before Barnett was applied to the remainder. The question for Wales then is in terms of its support for the Olympics, how the Welsh Assembly Government is intending to fund its regeneration projects that it chooses to implement as support for the UK Olympics bid.

Mr Griffiths: An equivalent introduction: I am here on behalf of the Welsh Local Government Association, which represents 22 local authorities in Wales. I have worked for the Welsh Local Government Association for 12 out of the last 19 years, concerned with distribution systems within Wales. I should point out that between 2000 and 2007 I worked as senior special adviser to the First Minister, and was therefore involved in distribution systems from the other perspective, and with relationships with the Treasury. I am here today in my WLGA role. The WLGA has not spent the last devolved decade deeply concerned about the Barnett Formula; it has been far more concerned about the best allocation and use of resources that come from that Formula within Wales. It is this inquiry and the Holtham inquiry that has led it to review its position. In the discussions we have had, I could best describe them as a discussion around a pragmatic balance of risk and what local government has been doing is considering the risk of not changing from Barnett and balancing that against the perceived risk of change. We have not been persuaded, as perhaps have some other participants in the debate, that there is a certain outcome through any change or from any new needs-based assessment; and there is unpredictability about that. Having said that, having reviewed the evidence and noted that the *per capita* advantage of relevant expenditure in Wales appears to have fallen from something like 13 or 14 per cent to something like 8 per cent, those figures are not hard—all the data is not available—there is that convergent trend, noting not only does that leave you in a worse position but it leaves you managing the rate of growth which is lower than in other parts of the United Kingdom and managing that lower rate of growth has its own problems. Taking those factors into consideration the WLGA has come to the view that the balance of risk for Wales would lie in exploring a needs-based assessment; but working in local government we are well aware of the difficulties and unpredictability around that. You may want to return to those points in questions. We are equally concerned about the absence of any independent evaluative mechanism in the operation of Barnett or any other system. Whether you have the existing one or a new one, there are judgments to be made. At the moment those judgments appear to be made wholly by the Treasury, which, if you like, is both a

competitive player in this process and a referee in the process; and it is a referee without a referee's panel. There does not seem to be any means whereby open challenge or explanation of the judgments can be made. The Olympics has been mentioned, but there is a range of other subjects that would benefit from a more open and transparent appraisal of the judgments that are being made. I would also make a case that just as local authorities have the flexibility of, for instance, the ability to hold a reserve, and the ability to borrow prudently and within rules, then we cannot see an explanation for why the devolved administrations cannot have equivalent powers as the local authorities they work with in that respect.

Q587 *Chairman:* Can I make one point? The WLGA submitted a piece of paper to us which was extremely helpful. You say in paragraph 12 of that statement: "WLGA believes that an alternative distribution mechanism based on an open and transparent assessment of expenditure need would deliver more resources for public expenditure in Wales and, on that basis, supports the proposition that such an alternative mechanism should be developed and implemented." That is your position. I got the impression you were a bit more tentative in expressing it today than perhaps—
Mr Griffiths: As soon as you read it out, I thought I was contradicting myself.

Q588 *Chairman:* There are shades—
Mr Griffiths: That paragraph represents the conclusion that has been come to on an assessment of that balance of risk. I do not think it was intended to contradict the fact that there is an unpredictability about that; but having looked at the risk of moving to something new, and having looked at the fact that we have 20 per cent less *per capita* wealth, having looked at the fact that our dispersal of our population is more sparsely populated than other parts of the United Kingdom, if most assessments of need use indicators of deprivation and population dispersal we would be well placed to gain advantage from the needs assessment, but as I say we also know there is an unpredictability about that.

Q589 *Chairman:* Can you help me a little more on this? You talk about balanced risks, risks for both sides. Can you spell them out briefly, what the risks are as you see them on each side of the argument?
Mr Griffiths: Pragmatically, our judgment is: what is going to provide more money for Wales? It may not seem to be the most idealistic position to take, but that is the one we are taking. The risk is that the Treasury will be in control of this process, and the Treasury will in the end conclude on the indicators that are to be chosen. On the indicators that we think are relevant and are used elsewhere, we think Wales

has a good case for equivalent or more expenditure from a needs assessment. But the risk is that for one reason or another the Treasury will choose other indicators, and that is what we have to judge.

Q590 Chairman: If the assessment were carried out by a body which is not the Treasury but was objective—I am not saying it would be easy to achieve this, but if it was—that would presumably deal with that particular issue.
Mr Griffiths: Yes, we believe it would lessen the risk.

Q591 Lord Sewel: You are being brutally frank, are you not? You are in it for the money!
Mr Griffiths: I would be surprised if anyone did it for anything else.

Q592 Lord Sewel: The trouble is that the two other devolved administrations might take completely the opposite view on that basis that Barnett—the Scots and the Northern Irish might well think that they stand to lose on the basis of a needs assessment. Is there any other argument you can advance rather than it gives you more money? I do accept that that is a perfectly legitimate and understandable argument, but try and convince me, as a Scot, why I should sign up to a needs assessment!
Mr Griffiths: Because the objective of public expenditure is to meet public need. An efficient allocation of public resources is one that responds to the differential positioning of that need in the United Kingdom or within your nation or wherever. If, on the evidence we have looked at, we believe that relative need in Wales is greater than elsewhere, and to an extent that is not currently covered by the allegations in the Barnett Formula, then it would be not just on the pragmatic conclusion of where we would gain, but on the criteria of efficiency and fairness that you would allocate resources to the areas of greater need.
Chairman: I think that was very precise!

Q593 Lord Sewel: Now we come on to the slightly more difficult bit. Okay, we have made the argument in favour in broad terms, in terms of equity and justice and to have a needs-based approach; how do we get there? Do we do an aggregate indicator like GVA or household disposable income, net household disposable income, or do we go for three or four variables covering the demographics, deprivation and the factors that affect cost of provision, or do we go right down to looking at the hundreds of individual drivers of need on a service-by-service basis?
Mr Griffiths: We have tussled with this, as you can imagine, within our own distribution formulas within Wales. Simplicity has its advantages. The disadvantage of going into micro service-based

assessments is that there would be those who would look at that mechanism and assume that service-based assessments you have made should be interpreted as hypothecations or targets for actual spend; so you have a dynamic, whether intended or not, where the various lobby groups—

Q594 Lord Sewel: It defeats the value of devolution.
Mr Griffiths: That is right. There are dangers to very detailed service-based allocations. No matter how often you say these are only calculating devices, the education community will say, "The assessment says we should have £4 billion and you have only given us £3.9 billion". There are risks there. On the other hand, I am not persuaded by Professor McLean's view that there can be a default position which uses GVA as a single measure of need to spend. It is simply an unproven hypothesis, that there is a direct correlation between GVA and what you need to spend on health of social services or education or whatever.

Q595 Lord Sewel: Do you think there is a single aggregate measure?
Mr Griffiths: Not a single one. My answer is that, as so often, you would have to find a balance which had simplicity as an objective but not the only objective. You should aim at as few indicators as is sensible, but you will need sufficient to capture the different variables involved. In terms of the Welsh Local Government settlement—do you want me to take you briefly through that? It is a reasonably standard one, as I look throughout the United Kingdom and other parts of the world. It is based primarily upon an assessment of the relative need to spend in each of the local authorities. There is then an assessment of the relevant tax base of each of those local authorities, and the grant is the difference between the notional taxable return and the relative assessed need to spend. We have a mixture. First of all, we do fall into the trap of making it service-based, not dozens of services but main services. I have learned from that, that it does lead you into the demand that the budget should follow the allocation so we have fallen into that trap, and others should be aware of it. But we have kept the indicators to a limited number. The other point you made is that the balance of them is about 70 per cent population and 24 per cent deprivation and 6 per cent population dispersal, so that is the broad bands there. If you looked at the deprivation indicators, you do find that they vary from service to service; so the ones that we use in schools or in education are selected and somewhat different to those that are chosen in social services. We have what I believe is a sophisticated approach to population dispersal which, interestingly, was not used in the Treasury assessment in the seventies, which I believe to have been—I have not seen it but I

am told about it—a fairly blunt division of the total area of the nation, divided by the number of people, in which case you tend to catch large areas of the country when nobody is there and not driving expenditure. What we do in our assessment is define viable settlements for service. It happens to be 7,500 people for a secondary school. We look at the proportion of people who live outside the viable settlement, and we build that into the calculation of the relative cost to spend there. The end result of that is a distribution which has been agreed formally by all the participants—this was agreed by local government and the Welsh Assembly Government at the beginning of the decade—and is then almost uniformly decried by everyone who suffers from it. I give the warning that no distribution formula is ever popular, and whenever it comes to results all the losers will line up to say, "it must be reformed", and all the winners are strangely silent. So if your quest is to find something that people will thank you for ever more, I suspect you will not get there. The other point I would make is that there is often a lot of concern on how you test whether you have the right indicators and you test the weightings you put on them. We use a mechanism which may not be available if you have only got four parts of the United Kingdom to deal with, and one of them a lot bigger than the others. What we do with 22 local authorities is statistically test whether the variable has had a correlation with expenditure patterns among the 22; and, if it has not, it is not used. We had an interesting debate only two or three years ago where we tested the social services expenditure against population dispersal and found no correlation. So we have a social services formula which has no indicator, no weighted indicator for population dispersal. Many in the rural areas were horrified. It must be the case that providing a service in small communities—needs assessment taking place over longer car journeys, increasing expenditure. However, the evidence was not there in the expenditure pattern, so we did not use it. That is the way we identified the right indicators and the weighting to put on them. I think that is a sophisticated approach and one relatively novel to Wales.

Q596 Chairman: Can I ask Mr Carruthers to comment on that!
Mr Carruthers: I think it is a very good example of the conundrum you face, which is: at what level do you set the indicators, and how detailed do you go? It is refreshing to hear that quite a lot of science has been put into it and the evidence base, because certainly one of the risks that we see in this process is that by going down in terms of levels of detail, what you do and substitute is a macro level judgment as to how you split expenditure with a series of micro level judgments, that is very much where we share the view

being put forward by WLGA. We included this in our submission, that we felt that an independent element was required in this process to give a view of what were the drivers and what were not the drivers. Due to the subjectivity and the fact that those that lose will be vocal and those that win will be quiet, you need that independent element. That operates both at an individual recipient level but also, as you have said, if Scotland wins out as opposed to Wales, then clearly that will skew the decision in a different way. If you had some kind of independent commission it will mean that different parts of the UK have to come together on a much more level basis and have an adult-to-adult discussion about how distribution should be done, the principles, rather than it descending into a haggling session, which happens behind closed doors at a fairly late stage in the process, as so often happens in the public expenditure process. I speak as somebody who used to work at the Treasury, and, albeit not directly involved, saw those negotiations happening and the fact that they tended to happen fairly late at night and fairly close to the deadline. You do need that independent element in the process in order to get that objective view as to what the right level to pitch it at will be, and it will vary from service to service.

Q597 Lord Moser: I really want to go back, if I may, to square one, because if the decision generally was to go back to the needs-based approach, there are no promises that it will help Wales or that it would be good for Wales or that it would harm Wales. I also respect your frankness in your basic criteria for wanting change. I have not understood from both organisations really whether intellectually, so to speak, you favour A versus B, the new approach versus Barnett. It is a very straightforward question. Irrespective of where it ends up for Wales or for anybody else, and on the needs thing, which we will talk more about no doubt, there are a thousand different ways of doing it, and I am not sure that I am totally convinced by the way you do it within your local authorities, but it is one way of judging whether a particular indicator makes sense or does not make sense. The basic question to me is: do you, like most of our witnesses, think that Barnett is so defective technically and intellectually, historically, that a change is indicated or are you not sure about that and therefore it is worth trying something else? I am not sure where you come in.
Mr Griffiths: The Welsh Local Government Association having considered your question and preparing evidence for this Committee has come to the conclusion that it would support a replacement of the current arrangements by a needs assessment; but it has come to that conclusion recognising some of the unpredictability of what the outcome of that may be. That is why I said that it has been based on a

balance of risk. That is the conclusion that it has come to. I have tried to give some intellectual justification for that. What I would say of course is that the current arrangement has an almost total absence of intellectual justification, based upon the historic base of 1979, added to by population-determined increments of spend in one particular country, and it is something that has survived on the basis presumably that we cannot agree an alternative, but it is not an arrangement that you could defend on an intellectual basis.

Q598 *Chairman:* It survived because it is convenient to the Treasury; to be brutal about it. It is terribly easy for them to administer. You do not have to do anything to the baseline, and if things get really hairy, you will then go outside the Formula and then in effect brave your way out of the problem. It seems to me the process by which this operates.
Mr Griffiths: I read the transcript of some of your earlier meetings on the experience of the pre-devolutionary times, where the by-pass route appeared to be used regularly to overcome specific difficulties. One of the features of post devolution is that you do not have a mechanism for providing such by-pass routes, so you are stuck with almost a rigidity of the basic Formula. The one example quoted in Wales of the by-pass was the additionality accorded to European Union support, but that was a very specific argument. Since then, I do not think the case has ever been made, let alone considered, for a by-pass. There is no mechanism to do that.

Q599 *Lord Sewel:* That is interesting. Certainly up until devolution Scotland was enormously successful in by-passing. I do not want to go into the reasons why. Wales did not seem to enjoy this great success, but now you could almost say that Wales was almost pure Barnett, and Scotland was a corrupted Barnett until devolution and now, as you say, the political institutional structure makes Barnett by-pass very difficult to deliver.
Mr Griffiths: I read with interest the illustrations you have heard of and felt somewhat jealous and aggrieved!
Ms Jones: I wanted to make a couple of points. Whatever distribution methodology is determined for the future, what is critically important is that the system has greater transparency, and there is an ability to have more independent monitoring and review within the process, as well as some procedures for adjudicating on disputes, because that is sadly lacking within the structure.
Mr Carruthers: It is more or less inevitable that within any disbursement system there will be disputes over what is right, and you see that wherever you go where you have a federal structure; there is always an issue about how, and on what basis, decisions are made.

Q600 *Chairman:* We will be taking evidence about the Australian system. Without getting into too great a detail, as I understand it according to the Australian independent commission, they produce their report and make recommendations, and there are then two days in which everybody complains that they are not getting enough and are being badly treated and it is unfair, and then they all go to sleep for the next 363 days until they produce the next one. That is something we could live with, as long as there is a basic satisfaction and understanding that the way in which the process takes place and the conclusions that are arrived at are reasonably objective and transparent.
Mr Carruthers: Yes. One of the advantages we see is that that is a debate that is had on a level playing-field between the federal government and the states and territories. Very clearly, the commission has terms of reference for particular pieces of work, so it is very clear what the objectives are. They are agreed up-front and, as you say, there is a short period of disagreement at the end, but it has been done on the basis that the clear set of objectives has been very well rehearsed and explained, and the public methodologies—

Q601 *Chairman:* It is clearly not being done by the federal government. That is the key to it, is it not?
Mr Carruthers: No. Formally the instructions are from the federal government, but they have to be agreed between various different states. You have that agreement up-front rather than from the position here that the devolved administrations have to argue at a very late stage with the Treasury when *de facto* the Treasury already knows the answer it wants.

Q602 *Chairman:* It is not the Treasury in Australia that determines the solution. That is the real point.
Mr Carruthers: That is right. That is why we see merits in that sort of system.

Q603 *Lord Sewel:* The slightly different view we have had in our evidence is that it ought to be done very similar to the Australian model—take the Treasury out because basically no-one trusts the Treasury, and get some quasi objective body to do it. The other is to set up some sort of commission that can give advice but then the final distribution being done across the negotiating table with the territorial authorities and the UK Government.
Mr Carruthers: I think if you go down that route, ostensibly there is more objectivity, but you have saddled yourself with extra process, and you still have the haggling that goes on at a later date. It seems to me that if you are clear about what you are trying to achieve and the methods up-front, then it takes away a lot of that scope for subjectivity. Frankly, if you are

better at putting your arguments, you get what you negotiate rather than what you feel you deserve.

Q604 *Chairman:* You want to take the smoke-filled room out of the process.
Mr Carruthers: Yes.

Q605 *Chairman:* You do not want the haggling, as they do in Brussels until the early hours of the morning.
Mr Carruthers: It comes back to what I said at the beginning; you need to be clear about the objectives of what you are trying to deliver. If what you are trying to deliver is an equitable solution, then you need to be very clear up-front what you are trying to achieve and how it is going to be achieved. You need objectivity and methodology and so on to get you there.
Mr Griffiths: I am equally suspicious of smoke-filled rooms of statisticians and accountants even. There is an important concept of political accountability, and resource allocation is at the heart of politics. I believe I can make a case that the ultimate responsibility for resource allocation needs to be made by a responsible politician, and if we are in the United Kingdom that would have to be the Chief Secretary or the Chancellor. The advantage to having an independent commission is that there will be independent advice, which, if the Treasury was not going to accept, it would have to provide very public explanations for why it was not going to accept it. There is a balance there.
Mr Carruthers: If I can add, there is a parallel for that in terms of the way that the financial reporting framework works across the public sector in the UK, which is the Financial Reporting Advisory Board, which reviews the guidance that is developed by the Treasury and the other relevant authorities. That reports to Parliament each year on the way in which the process has operated, and there have been a number of occasions where there was a potential for disagreement, particularly with the Treasury in the way that this operated, and on those occasions the Treasury has backed down because it has not wanted to press that nuclear button of publicly disagreeing with that advisory board.

Q606 *Lord Sewel:* The point about the dangers when you are doing these assessments going down to a service-by-service level—and the danger there being identified is a quasi hypothecation. Is there not another argument that as a result of devolution—indeed one of the objectives of devolution was to have Scottish solutions for Scottish problems with Scottish priorities, and the same with Wales—that the pattern of provision, the profile, will over time diverge significantly from England in Wales and Scotland; and if the reference is always back to an English profile, then that comes so detached as to be quite misleading?
Mr Griffiths: I agree, and that is why we have pointed out the danger of having a service-based set of assessments and indicators.

Q607 *Chairman:* What indicators would you like to have? I know your paper says you would like a few, and if there were too many of them I totally understand, but what sort of indicators?
Mr Griffiths: If I was re-designing the Welsh Local Government distribution, then instead of doing what we do at the moment, testing the salience of our deprivation indicators and population dispersal indicators, service by service, I would like us to test them against a basket of services so that we can conclude with indicators which have been tested for their relevance but not reaching conclusions on the assessed need to spend for primary schools or roads or whatever. That is not what we are doing at the moment, and in that sense I am suggesting something novel, but it does not seem to me to be methodologically impossible. It looks as though I have confused everyone!

Q608 *Chairman:* You have confused me a bit, but that may be my fault not yours. Try again more simply.
Mr Griffiths: The proposition that the proportion of your population which is in receipt of benefit, defined as "in poverty" is a driver of spend; then, rather than test the significance of that in terms of what you should spend on education or social services or health, test it against the basket of services. It is driving that basket, and you can come with an indicator that is tested, but not on a service basis. That may prevent you ending up with service-based assessments.

Q609 *Lord Sewel:* So you would do it on—say on deprivation, you would have the measure there of people in receipt of benefit, and you would test it against what?
Mr Griffiths: Against patterns of expenditure which you can find within the United Kingdom, to see whether those expenditure patterns have been correlated with that particular indicator; so has your range of care services, social services, health, education or whatever, been influenced by that indicator?

Q610 *Lord Moser:* I do not fully follow. It would be helpful to have this on paper. I do not think it is set out in detail. This is your way of choosing the indicators.

Mr Griffiths: Yes.

Q611 Lord Moser: Having chosen the indicators, would I be correct in assuming that the same indicators in your system would be used for every one of the devolved areas, though with different weights, in the sense that if one of the indicators is saying "health", that might have more weight in Wales than Scotland. It might—I am not saying it does. Could the weights differ between areas, though the indicators must be uniform?
Mr Griffiths: Certainly in our local government distribution, having tested the salience of the indicator we applied equally to all parts of Wales—

Q612 Lord Moser: The same weights.
Mr Griffiths: The same weights, yes. I would have to think through—

Q613 Lord Moser: Me too.
Mr Griffiths: —the case of doing the alternative.

Q614 Lord Moser: I was just trying to think of a way in which uniform sets of indicators would be acceptable for all the devolved areas, though they are actually of different importance and therefore one could cope with different weights. I thought you might be doing that, but you are not doing that within Wales.
Mr Griffiths: We apply a common set of indicators.

Q615 Lord Moser: And a common set of weights.
Mr Griffiths: I am trying to think this through. We have, for instance, a service concerned with sea fisheries, and various local authorities have no coast.

Q616 Lord Moser: That would be a good example of what we are talking about.
Mr Griffiths: they get no allocation for sea fisheries because one of the indicators is the length of coastline. That is zero, and whatever you multiply it with, it ends up as zero.
Lord Moser: If it is zero, it is easy, but if it is small it is not so easy. Maybe we could have a bit more background to this! It is interesting.

Q617 Earl of Mar and Kellie: During the course of the evidence I have been quite impressed by the purity of the Barnett Formula and how it has worked out even with convergence and everything in Wales. The only thing that does interest me is that I believe the cost of living in Wales is slightly lower. That strikes me as being quite a good thing. If there is a re-booting of the amount of public money allocated to Wales, would that compromise the cost of living?
Mr Griffiths: If I have taken the point you make correctly, my answer would be that I actually agree with the modelling done by Professor McLean where

he modified his GVA model to take account of differential housing costs. That is the one cost-of-living cost that varies. Our energy prices and food prices and everything else are pretty much the same. The thing that does vary is house prices and housing costs, so if you were using income levels as an indicator, it would seem to me that you would compensate that with some indicator for relative house prices.

Q618 Lord Sewel: I am totally ignorant—are labour costs any different?
Mr Griffiths: They are different in the sense that our incomes are on average about 20 per cent lower than the UK average, but I would argue that—

Q619 Lord Sewel: That may be a cost driver because the composition of the labour market will be different.
Mr Griffiths: Yes, but our composition is different, and sometimes in similar trades our incomes are lower. I do not think labour costs translate into costs of living. They may translate to some extent in cost of delivery, but given that public services are highly unionised with England and Wales' bargaining machinery, the end result is that you are better off as a public servant in Wales than in other parts of the United Kingdom.

Q620 Earl of Mar and Kellie: If we are to persuade the Treasury to alter the way they do things, it strikes me there are two things that we could do. One is that we invite them to have an independent commission advising them on a year-by-year basis as to how much to distribute round the three countries; or alternatively—and the one I suspect that is more likely—to go along with this they might do one needs assessment of this type and then revert to the Barnett Formula for a few years. Do you think that the latter could be helpful—is in fact a re-jigging of an alteration of the baseline and a fresh start, which I think the Treasury would probably like because they have only got to do it once? Could that be helpful?
Mr Carruthers: I think you would come up against the fact that if you try and move the baseline, then those that will gain will support that change, and those that will lose will not support it. It seems to me undeniable that if you want to change the methodology, you have got to have a good look at the alternative range of indicators, and needs, I think, has to be one of those that you would want to look at. Then you are going to have to look at the way in which you might balance it. I think the Treasury would probably agree if it is not going to require them to transfer any more resources than they already have to, but it seems to me that inevitably you would have to have some form of transition process, which indeed is the experience in Australia; that you have to

put more resources into the system during the transition period in order to get people to buy into that process. I think it is almost inevitable that to move people from where they are to where you want them to be, there has to be some kind of transition process. That may well be difficult to achieve in times when public expenditure is under intense and increasing pressure, as it will be over the next few years.

Q621 *Earl of Mar and Kellie:* What I am really getting at is that, since I believe it will be easier to persuade the Treasury to do this once as opposed to doing it every year, if that is going for a one-off and then re-starting the Barnett Formula—would that be at all helpful or would that be just a waste of time?
Mr Griffiths: I wonder if what you are suggesting is almost the norm in these needs-based systems, that you set up a needs-based assessment and you then inevitably have a long period of transition in implementing it. The only adjustments you make annually to that needs-based assessment is any input of fresh data, which is likely to be population data—so it looks a bit like Barnett. What I believe most of them do, and what we do in Welsh Local Government, is have a long-term planned cycle of reviewing the framework, bit by bit and indicator by indicator. You do not re-evaluate the whole thing each year. If that is what happens elsewhere, it is not so different from your proposition that you end up with a bit of a big bang with a transitional taper, and then population adjustments subject to a long cycle of review.

Q622 *Lord Moser:* We all talk about possibly replacing Barnett by something else, and the something else we describe in terms of different indicators: can you think of a way—I have not—of expanding Barnett into a Barnett type 2 formula which includes additional indicators, which goes beyond just population but includes a few of the others you have talked about. It becomes more sophisticated. I do not know whether one can think along those lines—I am just asking.
Ms Jones: In our submission to the Committee there was one suggestion in that vein, which was basically looking at the comparable percentage increase year on year, basically looking at the marginal increase year on year, which at the beginning might not disrupt the baseline, but it might be an occasion where consideration was given in a different format to how the comparable percentage was allocated. Over a period of time that would then overtake the baseline and re-establish over time that complete baseline as a new Formula-based allocation or a needs-based allocation. One of the issues there is that it might appear to be too prescriptive in terms of the need to spend in different areas, and it may compromise the ability to continue within the devolved environment, with the ability to determine the local policy priorities.
Mr Griffiths: I would like to think through what you have said and have a chance to come back.
Chairman: Could you give a piece of paper setting out the thoughts when you have them? That would be helpful. Can I thank the three of you very much for coming this afternoon. We have had a fascinating session. As I said to somebody else, from the point of view of people on this side of the table, this commission is in some ways a great learning process, and you have helped us in that learning process. Thank you very much.

Supplementary Memorandum by the Welsh Local Government Assocation

This note covers three issues:

1. How a relative needs based assessment could build upon the existing mechanisms for allocating resources to Devolved Administrations;

2. A summary of how needs based indicators are selected and weighted in the Welsh Local Government Distribution Formula;

3. A further illustration of the need for independent advice on allocative judgements

1. *How a relative needs based assessment could build upon the existing mechanisms for allocating resources to Devolved Administrations*

1.1 At the Select Committee's meeting on 20 March 2009 the discussion in which I participated concluded with Lord Moser's question of whether a needs based assessment of expenditure need could be utilised to provide a complement to the existing population based increment of allocation. I said that I would reflect on that question.

1.2 Given that any introduction of a needs based assessment would undoubtedly have a transitional process to diminish any turbulence in the allocations, I suggest that such a transition could perhaps best be achieved by using a needs based assessment as a complement to the existing Barnett calculation.

1.3 If we assume that agreement could be reached on the factors and weightings to be used in the assessment of relative expenditure need, taken together they could be used to calculate a "Composite Indicator of Relative Expenditure Need". So if some part of the United Kingdom was judged to have a need to spend on comparable expenditures which was 15 per cent above the UK average it would have a Composite Indicator of 1.15. In parallel there could be a calculation existing relative expenditure so that if the same part of the UK was spending 8 per cent above the UK on comparable expenditures then its indicator of existing relative expenditure would be 1.08.

1.4 The existing Barnet calculation of any change in the allocation to a Devolved Administration is:

Change to UK	Relevant	Relevant
Department's	X comparability	X population
Programme	percentage	proportion

1.5 It would be possible to amend the existing calculation in the following way to take account of relative expenditure need and relative expenditure by using the following calculation:

Change to UK	Relevant	Relevant
Department's	X comparability	X population
Programme	percentage	proportion

$$X \left(\frac{\text{Composite Indicator of relative expenditure need}}{\text{Indicator of existing relative expenditure}} \right)^3$$

1.6 The advantage of the above calculation is that it will achieve over time a convergence of actual relative expenditure with the assessment of relative expenditure need whereas the Barnet formula on its own is designed to converge on uniform per capita expenditure. The rate of convergence would be a matter of judgement and can be varied by the factor applied to the last part of the calculation. It is estimated that the suggested factor of three would achieve almost complete convergence with a relative needs assessment over a 10 year period if total expenditure growth in cash terms continued at its present rate.

1.7 In illustrating the impact of the above amendment to the Barnet calculation it is possible to consider the circumstances of the Welsh Assembly Government. The allocation to the Welsh Assembly Government for 2009–10 is £14.986 billion. It is currently projected to grow using the Barnett calculation to £15.389 billion in 2010–11—a rate of growth of 2.6 per cent.

1.8 If we assume that through some, yet to be developed, formula it was judged that the Welsh Assembly Government had a need to spend which was 15 per cent above the UK average then the composite indicator of relative expenditure need would be 1.15—this is an assumption for the purpose of illustration; it is not a prediction of how Wales would fair in any needs assessment. Let us assume that the indicator of existing relative expenditure was 1.08. The effect of these assumptions applied to the amended formula would be to increase the growth in WAG expenditure by around £80 million in 2010–11; increasing the annual rate of growth for 2010–11 to 3.2 per cent. By such an annual increase there would be almost full convergence of Wales' assessed relative need to spend and its actual spend over a 10 year period.

1.9 There could of course be periodic re-assessments of the relative expenditure need and these could be reflected in the annual calculation using the above amended formula. Significantly by implementing such reassessments through this formula their impact is dampened and achieved over a period of time.

2. *A summary of how needs based indicators are selected and weighted in the Welsh Local Government Distribution Formula*

2.1 In developing the Welsh local government distribution formula the aim generally has been that any indicator included in the formula should be subject to a statistical test of the extent to which existing expenditure patterns within Welsh local government correlate with the incidence of that indicator. If the correlation cannot be found the indicator is not included. The strength of the correlation informs the weighting that is given to that indicator. The advantage of this methodology is that it allows the expenditure priorities of all relevant organisations to inform the selection and weighting of indicators.

2.2 One problem of this method is that currently indicators are tested with reference to specific service expenditures and the end result of the exercise is that expenditures are hypothesised for each service in each local authority. This has led to demands by Welsh Assembly committees and various lobby groups that the hypothesised expenditures should be regarded as a target expenditure, thus undermining local budgetary choice.

2.3 In considering a UK needs assessment, it ought instead be possible to test the significance of any potential indicator, and thereupon calculate its appropriate weighting, by testing the correlation of a basket of service expenditure patterns against the incidence of that indicator. That basket could perhaps be as wide as the whole of comparable expenditure or it could be a limited number of groupings of services. In testing a basket of expenditure patterns against potential needs indicators the danger of hypothesised expenditures being seen as expenditure targets is diminished.

3. *A further illustration of the need for independent advice on allocative judgements*

3.1 All the issues of contention regarding the application of the current distribution formula appear to emanate from contestable definitions of comparable expenditure. This would equally be the subject of contestable judgment if a relative needs assessment was incorporated into the allocations and this adds to the case for an independent body to advise on the process.

3.2 Much reference has been made to the issue of expenditure on the Olympics. The Treasury view is that it is not possible to disentangle the element of the expenditure which is in support of an event which benefits the whole of the UK and that element which is primarily related to the regeneration of east London which would be comparable expenditure. However, whenever those responsible for the Olympics programme are asked to explain and justify the total expenditure they give specific figures on the proportion of total expenditure which is primarily related to regeneration.

3.3 The repeated reference to the Olympics should not lead to the view that this is a unique issue. For the sake of further illustration, attention is drawn to the complex issue of Housing Revenue Accounts (HRA). Since 1989 in England and Wales central government has set out a notional HRA account for each local authority which provides council housing. The notional account provides notional figures for rents and for allowable expenditure. Where rents are assumed to exceed expenditure, as in all of Welsh local housing authorities, the excess amount is then used for public expenditure purposes other than the provision of council houses. Until 2002 it was used to part-finance rent rebates, ie it financed a non-devolved welfare benefit purpose. Since 2002 the notional surplus has been received by the Treasury for its general public expenditure purposes. Since 1989 the "surplus" generated by local housing authorities in Wales, and lost to public expenditure in Wales, has averaged around £100 million a year.

3.4 In 1989 the legislation regarding Housing Revenue Accounts was not applied to Scotland. If Wales had been treated on a par with Scotland since 1989, there would have been around £2 billion extra public expenditure in Wales over the past two decades.

3.5 In 2001 the ODPM introduced a new element of allowable expenditure for the HRAs in England, called a Major Repairs Allowance. The effect of this was to reduce the "surpluses" generated by local housing authorities in England and therefore the amount received by the Treasury. The Treasury judged that this was a policy change and not a change in comparable expenditure in England and provided no consequential adjustment for Wales . Since that date Welsh local housing authorities have been required to provide each year the same historic level of funds to the Treasury, adjusted only in the cases of stock transfer. If, since 2001, Welsh local housing authorities had been treated on the same basis as English local housing authorities it is estimated that there would have been around £1 billion extra public expenditure in Wales over the past decade.

3.6 Attention is drawn to this illustration to show how the unchallengeable judgment of the Treasury on what is and what is not comparable expenditure can over time have very significant effects on the allocation of public expenditure across the United Kingdom. The existence of an independent advisory commission on inter-governmental allocations would have allowed an independent appraisal of such important exercises of judgment.

April 2009

Memorandum by the Wales Council for Voluntary Action

1. WCVA represents the interests of voluntary organisations, community groups and volunteers in Wales. It has over 2,600 members, and is in contact with many more groups through national and regional networks.

2. Its mission is to strengthen voluntary and community action at the heart of a civil society in Wales that:

— Is inclusive and offers equality of opportunity;

— empowers people to participate and fosters community leadership;

— encourages and promotes the independence of voluntary action;

— celebrates and reflects linguistic and cultural diversity and choice; and

— engages in genuine partnership with other sectors on a "who does what best" basis.

3. WCVA has consulted widely with the third sector throughout the process of devolution and recognises its role in promoting the interests of the sector in this process. We have been actively engaged in debates around the role of the National Assembly for Wales and its relationship with the sector from the original proposal to establish the Assembly, through the Richard Commission, the implementation of the Government of Wales Act 2006, and most recently the work of the All-Wales Convention established to explain to the Welsh public about the powers currently available to the National Assembly for Wales and assess the implications of moving towards full law making powers.

4. The third sector is broad and diverse and makes a major contribution to the economic, cultural, social and environmental life of Wales. Third sector organisations can provide valuable evidence of how government policies are affecting Welsh citizens, facilitate often marginalised voices to be heard, and contribute to the delivery of public services. Effective governance depends on government working with the sector and ensuring that its mechanisms for doing so are as transparent and effective as possible.

5. WCVA does not claim to be familiar with the internal workings of government finance. Our perspective is primarily a lay view from outside government. Our evidence is not technical, but is informed by the way in which a wide range of third sector organisations and networks experience government finance policies and arrangements.

6. In discussing the Barnett formula with third sector organisations, there are three main issues that have been raised.

7. Firstly, there is the question of whether any formula (either the current Barnett formula, or a potential alternative arrangement) is applied in a transparent manner that is clearly understood by organisations with an interest in government funding.

8. Secondly, there is of course the question of whether the existing formula fairly meets the distinctive needs of Wales, particularly with reference to levels of social need, and to providing services in sparsely populated areas.

9. Thirdly, there are occasions when the Barnett Formula is used as a basis for the negotiations regarding the division of non devolved funding or as a benchmark against which to measure the "fairness" of any allocations. The fact that the formula is not related to need or cost of service provision means that these allocations may disadvantage Wales compared to the rest of the UK.

10. The current formula is in fact relatively straightforward, using population share and comparable functions as the basis of the calculation. Its application leads to a stable, predictable and automatic increase in the funds available to the Assembly Government.

11. However, there is no doubt that many organisations are confused by the Barnett formula. Although there are reasonably clear explanations of how it works available, these are not well known or understood.

12. There are a number of questions that arise from the current arrangements.

13. As far as we understand, the formula is only applied to new expenditure. We are unable to comment on whether the historic settlement that pre-dates the application of the Barnett formula provided a fair allocation across the UK, but this is clearly a key consideration in determining the fairness of the current arrangements.

14. We also understand that the trigger is the commitment of new funding in England, providing a "catch-up" mechanism for the devolved administrations. Whilst it is right that UK government decisions for initiatives in England should lead to a commensurate increase in Wales, we are not clear about how the Assembly Government might seek additional Treasury resources, over and above the existing settlement, for initiatives in Wales that may not be desired in other parts of the UK.

15. Our members are regularly confused by the way in which the formula applies (or does not apply) to individual spending decisions and announcements. Spending announcements are frequently silent on whether a particular initiative is England only and funded from within existing English budgets (and therefore with no consequential for Wales); or whether there is new funding for which there is a consequential for Wales.

16. It is important that there is both transparency and debate about the way in which the Treasury applies the formula. As an example, we gather that the Treasury has determined that the additional local regeneration expenditure in south east England associated with the Olympics—which we had understood were to benefit the UK as a whole—does not lead to consequential funding for the devolved administrations. We are not aware of a formal mechanism for the devolved administrations to debate or challenge this decision.

17. Whilst the formula does provide more predictable funding levels, it takes no account of the particular needs of Wales. We are not aware of any evidence that supports the case for lower levels of comparable expenditure in Wales compared to that in Scotland and Northern Ireland. The very fact that two-thirds of Wales qualifies for European Convergence funding demonstrates the case for higher levels of expenditure.

18. The Barnett formula was not intended as a permanent arrangement, and the progress of devolution has inevitably focused attention on the formula. We do agree that it is timely for a review to be undertaken.

19. We are not in a position to suggest specific alternatives; but we do believe that it is important to investigate the following:

— Will a formula based on a combination of population, need and costs of service delivery would lead to a fairer allocation of resources?

— Will a formula that is implemented in an open and transparent way improve the confidence of the public, and third sector organisations?

20. An assessment of need could take account of:

— The relevant population base in relation to the expenditure being allocated;

— The need for services, reflecting relative social deprivation factors;

— The cost of delivering services, taking account of rurality and population sparsity.

21. This approach could target higher levels of funding at areas of greater deprivation, where there is a greater need for public services is greater, and to low population density rural areas where service delivery is more costly. We would expect Wales to warrant above average expenditure levels on both counts.

22. This approach could also be considered as a basis for the negotiations regarding the division of non devolved UK funding or as a benchmark against which to measure the "fairness" of any allocations. For example, the government is allocating Unclaimed Assets according to the Barnett formula so that the four countries of the UK will receive a population-based share of the assets available on a UK-wide basis. Again, an alternative to consider is a formula based on population, needs and service cost for such calculations.

23. Finally, the future application of any formula—either the existing Barnett formula or a new mechanism, will need to be easily understood and transparent in order the address the problems identified with the current arrangements. The government's partners, including the third sector, and the electorate, need to have confidence in the system.

24. We believe that formal arrangements between the Treasury and the devolved administrations should be introduced to ensure that decisions which affect funding allocations are transparent and are not taken without formal agreement from devolved governments. These arrangements could:

— Ensure that the implications for devolved administrations of policies developed in Whitehall were fully understood.

— Enable dialogue and agreement between devolved administrations and the Treasury before changes to funding arrangements are made.

— Require announcements about expenditure to be made simultaneously for England, Northern Ireland, Scotland and Wales, giving a greater sense of coherence and equity rather than the "catch-up" confusion that presently often exists.

— Enable third sector organisations to have an opportunity to comment to their government on the implications of spending proposals.

19 March 2009

Memorandum by Cymru Yfory—Tomorrow's Wales

1. A MECHANISM NOT FIT FOR PURPOSE

1.1 Cymru Yfory regards the current method of allocating funding to the devolved governments via the Barnett formula as not fit for purpose in a context where devolved parliaments/assemblies have now established themselves as key institutions within the wider UK governmental structure.

1.2 It seems clear that Wales suffers significant disadvantage as a result of the way in which the formula works and this is a matter of concern for us, particularly in view of the extremely tight public expenditure framework that will result from the current financial and economic crisis. However we are also aware of wider concerns. Bell and Christie are certainly not alone in their criticism: "The funding mechanism has been roundly condemned by all shades of public opinion… Unless this issue can be satisfactorily resolved, the tension caused by the perceived unfairness of the system of allocating resources between the constituent parts of the UK <u>will</u> <u>undermine the legitimacy of devolution</u>" (our underlining). Lord Barnett's characterisation of his own formula as "terribly unfair" is well known.

1.3 Gillian Bristow points out that Barnett "is an inherited legacy of the finance arrangements that existed pre-devolution and which operated within the era of territorial arrangements". When it was devised in 1978 in readiness for the devolution arrangements then being planned the intention was for it to be a temporary arrangement. According to Bristow, it was "an historical and temporary expedient which became permanent".

1.4 The assessment of need carried out at that time, according to Alan Trench, "showed that significantly greater amounts of spending would be justified for all three territories than for England—but that amount would be less than what Scotland and Northern Ireland already received". It is recognised that the reason those two territories enjoyed a higher level of spending than that provided for Wales was that they, unlike Wales, posed a potential threat to the union and, in any case, had administrative devolution for far longer.

1.5 The disparity was retained in the Barnett formula to avoid shocks and for reasons of political expediency. Thus Wales was disadvantaged in comparison with Scotland and Northern Ireland from the very outset. In addition, the Barnett formula, says Trench, was designed "to serve as a way of braking growth in Scottish spending" by incorporating a mechanism to bring about convergence in per capita spending levels in the four countries. Ironically, but perhaps not surprisingly, the resultant "Barnett squeeze" has probably punished Wales more than it has Scotland (McLean and McMillan).

1.6 When democratic devolution was introduced in 1999, a decision was taken behind closed doors, again for reasons of political expediency, to retain Barnett rather than consult on a new funding mechanism that would be appropriate for the new arrangements.

2. A Time for Reform

2.1 We have briefly rehearsed the Barnett story in order to illustrate the way that the current arrangements have evolved in an ad hoc and politically expedient manner rather than being based on any logic or fundamental principles. Such a state of affairs is our view no longer acceptable. It is time for reform, and if there is to be reform, it should be sufficiently radical to tackle head-on the chronic dissatisfaction that exists in so many quarters, specifically in Wales, and which is certain to get worse rather than better.

3. The Deficiencies of the Current Arrangements

3.1 We now list some of the deficiencies, of both process and outcome, of the current arrangements.

(i) Convergence

Our view is that the formula should converge, not on a per capita population basis, but on need (see below 4.1). Eurfyl ap Gwilym claims that the "Barnett squeeze" arising from the existing convergence principle, cost Wales about £1 billion between 1999 and 2006. McLean, Lodge and Schmuecker state that identifiable public spending, which they say "provide[s] the most accurate picture possible of monies flowing through the Barnett formula", fell between 2002–03 and 2007–08 in Wales from 13 per cent to 8 per cent over the UK average, in Northern Ireland from 31 per cent to 21 per cent, and in Scotland not at all.

(ii) Failure to reflect changing circumstances

— Since 1978 the population of Scotland has fallen and that of Wales has risen but this change was not reflected in the allocation of funds until 1997, by which time the baseline for the calculation of increased funding had been adversely affected.

— Over the same period, as a result largely of the decline of heavy industry, which was dominant in the Welsh economy, GPD per capita has declined from 88 per cent of the UK average in 1979 to 77 per cent in 2007. This decline is what led to the EU recognising the West and Valleys, four-fifths of Welsh land area, as being in serious need, having less than 75 per cent of EU average GDP, and thus eligible for Objective 1 status under the Structural Funds. However the Barnett formula remained unaffected by all of this.

(iii) The Formula is not needs-based

Basing the allocation of funding, ever since the initial estimation of needs, on a population basis has been severely disadvantageous to Wales. Two recognised proxy indicators of need are poverty, as measured by social security spending, and average GDP. According to Mackay and Williams, if the first were used, devolved spending per head should be roughly 20 per cent higher in Wales and Northern Ireland and 10 per cent higher in Scotland than in England. In the case of the second (arguably a more objective measure), the devolved spending per head should be 27 per cent higher in Wales and Northern Ireland and 6 per cent higher in Scotland than in England.

McLean, Lodge and Schmuecker state that identifiable public spending ("the most accurate picture of monies flowing through the Barnett formula") are as follows: Northern Ireland 21 per cent over UK average; Scotland 21 per cent; Wales 8 per cent. The same authors consider the relationship between public expenditure and GVA. They state that England has a GVA per head two per cent over the UK average, Scotland 5 per cent below and Wales, lowest among the UK regions, at 23 per cent below. They then proceed to calculate that in 2006—07 London received 65 per cent more than it would if public expenditure were allocated on the basis of GVA per head, with Scotland receiving 11 per cent more, and Wales receiving 14 per cent less.

(iv) *Allocations are based on departmental spending levels in English departments*

This is inappropriate in a system where the devolved assemblies and parliament exist in their own right as representative bodies of their peoples. Bell and Christie found that "there is no country in the developed world other than the UK that allocates resources at a subnational level using a formula based on spending changes elsewhere, rather than allocating levels of spending in relation to assessed need."

(v) *The way in which decisions on allocations are made is often opaque*

— There is no independent audit of the process or of the decisions made.

— Determining what counts as spending for England and what is for the UK as a whole, and therefore may or may not carry a Barnett consequential, may be subjective and arbitrary, as for example with spending on the Olympics and rail infrastructure.

— The extent to which convergence has actually occurred and why, including the various Barnett bypasses engineered, has been extremely difficult to ascertain, even by experts in the field.

Such weaknesses arise from the fact that the Barnett formula has no statutory basis and the way it is applied depends very much on informal practice, conventions and goodwill. We would argue that this is not sufficiently robust in the quasi-federal system that now exists in the UK.

4. PRINCIPLES FOR A NEW SYSTEM

4.1 We have no doubt that a new system for allocating resources should be based on need. We recognise that determining need is a complex matter and that opinions concerning what factors should be included differ. However the task is achievable, as examples in numerous countries demonstrate. Among the elements to be considered would be: geographical factors such as rurality and population dispersal; age profile; health needs; and average GDP or social security spending as indicators of deprivation.

4.2 The way in which resources are allocated to nations and regions within an union state should reflect the principles of solidarity, mutual dependence and justice. Indeed the very stability of such a state may depend on the application of those principles. This is the philosophical underpinning for basing allocations on need, but it should also lead to a commitment to the elimination (or at least amelioration) of disadvantage as well as compensation for it. The formula should therefore include an element of funding for achieving economic and social cohesion across the UK.

4.3 This is linked with the way in which the UK Government deals with the European Union's Convergence Funds. The UK as an EU member state accepts the criterion of a needs-based approach in order to promote economic and social cohesion across the EU and as a counterbalance to the internal market. As a result a number of UK regions have at various times been allocated structural fund resources. We believe that the same strategic policy approach should apply within the UK, as we argue in 4.2 above. Specifically, resources allocated to regions of the UK by the EU should always be truly additional to existing budgets.

New ground was broken in UK Government policy in 2001 with the famous "Barnett +" allocation to Wales for the delivery of the Objective 1 programme in the West and the Valleys and this is very welcome. However the failure to provide any resources for match funding this programme has imposed a significant burden on the National Assembly. Among the effects (combined with the impact of the Barnett squeeze) has been the increasing funding gap in education between Wales and England, which is particularly acute in Further and Higher Education. In the spirit of cohesion enshrined in the EU Convergence programmes, funds allocated to Wales should include provision of match funding for those programmes.

4.4 The introduction of a needs based formula should in no way imperil the devolved governments' autonomy in making decisions on public spending. In discussing the introduction of an "equalisation formula" for funding allocations, McLean and McMillan say that this would mean "placing each territory in a position to offer the same mean level of service, should it choose to do so" (our underlining). The Welsh Assembly Government may decide for example that investing in appropriate economic development or in housing, or in environmental improvement, is an effective way of tackling long-term health problems. It should be entirely free to do so. Policy divergence is a major justification for devolved government, and one of its advantages is that the countries of the Union can learn from each others' achievements as well as, sometimes, their mistakes.

4.5 Transparency should be a key principle of the new system. This does not mean that the new allocations formula would be readily understandable by the public at large—indeed the degree of complexity necessary to achieve a just allocation would make this difficult. What it does mean is that the principles underlying decisions would be explicit and all the information publicly available.

4.6 The relationship between the countries of the UK in determining a new formula and in negotiating allocations should be established on the basis of equality. Currently the bargaining position of Wales is weak in comparison with Scotland and Northern Ireland and the position of all three weak in relation to the UK Treasury. This needs to be corrected.

5. THE NEW ARRANGEMENTS

5.1 We strongly support the proposal made by a number of experts, notably McLean and McMillan, and Bristow, that a new Territorial Grants Commission, on the lines of the Commonwealth Grants Commission of Australia, be set up. It would be established by Act of Parliament and would be independent in status, similar to that of the Electoral Commission.

5.2 We support the following suggestions by Bristow: "It should be a non-governmental public body staffed by non-partisan public servants (eg secondees from the devolved administrations and relevant government departments) plus relevant experts in the field of public finance (eg academics, other professionals). The members of the commission would be appointed on the basis of widespread consultation with the devolved administrations and regional representatives . . . The Commission should be charged with making an annual report on regional expenditure needs and the relevant equalisation process with this report being made to a joint ministerial council of the UK and regional governments."

5.3 The final decisions on funding allocations would have to be unanimous. Failing that, we agree with the suggestion of McLean and McMillan that the default would be the use of average GDP per head as the proxy indicator of need.

5.4 We accept that the move from Barnett to a new needs-based formula will not bring change in one fell swoop. Rather there would be, to use McLean and McMillan's term, a "convergence on need" which would take a number of years to be completed.

6. CONCLUSION

6.1 The current arrangements for funding devolved government are flawed and unsustainable. As devolved government becomes embedded in the UK system and as Wales looks forward to the granting of primary legislative powers to its National Assembly, now is the time for a radical overhaul. Whereas we believe that Wales would benefit from the changes that we advocate, we also believe that the UK as an union state would strengthen its credibility by adopting a system designed to meet collective interests and to promote cohesion, equity, stability and transparency.

BIBLIOGRAPHY

In drawing up our analysis and recommendations we have drawn heavily upon the work of experts in the field and we wish to acknowledge our indebtedness to them. The relevant works are listed here:

Eurfyl ap Gwilym: "Barnett Squeeze" *Agenda* Spring 2006

Gillian Bristow: "All for one and one for all? Territorial solidarity and the UK's system of devolution finance". Paper presented to Seminar on Regional Economic Disparities, University of Edinburgh 10–11 April 2008

Gillian Bristow: "Barnett Issues Paper: Report for Adam Price MP" (2006)

Gillian Bristow: "Bypassing Barnett: The Comprehensive Spending Review and Public Expenditure in Wales". *Economic Affairs* September 2001

R R Mackay and J Williams: "Thinking about Need: Public Spending on the Regions" *Regional Studies* Vol 39 2005

I McLean, G Lodge and K Schmuecker: *Fair Shares? Barnett and the Politics of Public Expenditure* IPPR 2008

Ian McLean and Alistair McMillan: "The Fiscal Crisis of the United Kingdom". Nuffield College Working Papers on Politics 2002

The following essays in particular from Alan Trench: *Devolution and Power in the United Kingdom* (Manchester University Press 2007).

David Bell and Alex Christie: "Funding Devolution: the Power of Money"

James Mitchell: "The United Kingdom as a state of unions; unity of government, equalising of political rights and diversity of institutions"

Alan Trench: "The politics of devolution finance and the power of the Treasury"

March 2009

Examination of Witnesses

Witnesses: MR PHIL JARROLD, Deputy Chief Executive, Wales Council for Voluntary Action, MR PETER PRICE and MR CYNOG DAFIS, Tomorrow's Wales, and MR JOHN OSMOND, Director, and MR GERAINT TALFAN DAVIES, Chairman, Institute for Welsh Affairs, examined.

Q623 Chairman: Can I thank you all very much for coming this afternoon. As you know, I think, what we are charged with doing by the House of Lords is looking at the Barnett Formula, how it operates and whether there should be an alternative to it. You have also seen the restrictions there are upon the scope of this inquiry: we cannot go very much outside of it to consider, for example, whether or not Scotland should have full remedy-raising powers. That is a little outside. Subject to that, we will be extremely interested in what you all have to say. Can I say from the start that the evidence sessions are being taken and broadcast, and will be live I think! A full transcription is obviously going to be made of them. If at the end you would like to alter the transcript, rather like Hansard you can correct the grammar but you cannot actually change what you said. Subject to that, gentlemen, I will start. I understand that you would all like to make an opening statement. Can we start with Mr Dafis?
Mr Dafis: (Mr Dafis spoke in Welsh) I am told that it is not possible for me to speak in Welsh, so I am hoping I might persuade you. A special resolution—

Q624 Chairman: Can I just say one thing about it? It is a point that, having been raised, is something that we would have to go back to the Committee in the Lords to make sure it is possible for all sorts of internal and rather foolish bureaucratic reasons. I will do that, and if therefore we get down to Wales again, I would ensure that there are proper interpretation facilities. I am afraid on this occasion I cannot do it.
Mr Dafis: In that case, can I thank you very much for the opportunity to give evidence. Tomorrow's Wales's submission is concerned with getting primary law-making powers for the Assembly, but we felt it right to give evidence on this matter for two reasons: first, we think that Wales suffers under the present arrangements; but also because we think it is relevant to the constitutional arrangements that exist. On the unfairness issue there are ample data, and I do not

need to bore you with too many of those, except that there is one set that is just worth mentioning. According to what we read from the academics, Wales gets something like £5,000 per head of identifiable public spending minus social support, whereas Scotland and Northern Ireland both get in the region of £5,600 per head, and that is a clear difference. We think that a formula that generates outcomes of that kind is clearly perverse and needs to be changed. Secondly, we think in relation to the constitutional matter that the method of determining allocation to the territories is now inappropriate in a system where devolved government is embedded, and in which we are moving towards some kind of federal system. It is already described as a "quasi federal system". Being that we are living in a union state, on what one set of academics described as "a state of unions", we think that in those circumstances it is right to argue that the allocation of resources should reflect the principle of cohesion. I am using terminology that the European Union uses, which implies that there should be a redistribution of resources to compensate for disadvantage, but also to try over time to correct disadvantage. That is a fundamental principle as far as we are concerned. That implies that we should allocate resources, first of all based on the principle of need, and certainly not have the allocation converged on English *per capita* spending levels; we cannot see that that is appropriate within the framework we are proposing. That brings us then to the mechanisms that we are proposing for the new system—and they are not in the least bit original, of course, they are culled from various academics, including Bristow and McLean and others particularly. We do think that the idea of an independent territorial grants commission of the kind they have in Australia and elsewhere is the right solution. Such a commission would in the first place devise a new formula based on need, and then it would negotiate the allocation of resources, I suppose on a three-yearly basis co-ordinating with the CSR but also according to what is necessary on an annual basis as well. That kind of commission, we believe, should be constituted and would operate on a basis of equality. We cannot pretend of course that the relationship between the territories and the centre will be an equal relationship but it should be based on the notion of equality. The decisions that it should take should be unanimous because currently one of the problems is that Wales finds itself in a very unequal position and a very unequal bargaining position, and has done so for a long period of time; and that needs to be corrected in the structure. Finally, the last point I want to make now is that it is crucial that the autonomy of the devolved administrations in spending decisions be guaranteed. It should not follow at all from the idea of a needs-based formula, which would allocate on the basis of needs perhaps in certain services areas, that that implies there should be any direction from the centre to the devolved administrations as to spend equivalent sums in those areas—not at all; that would be contrary to the principle and to the whole purpose of devolution. I mentioned in the paper the example of health. Health needs might very well be an indicator, and that might be catered for in a formula, but it should not follow that the Assembly—it would not be sensible if the Assembly were to be obliged to spend that health allocation on the NHS. It might decide to spend it on appropriate economic development or environmental improvement or housing, as a way of raising the quality of health in a place like Wales.

Mr Price: Perhaps I can add just one brief comment to what Cynog has said on behalf of Tomorrow's Wales. I noted the word "objective" coming up this morning and a little this afternoon from time to time, but it is not something that your Lordships have focused on greater, and it strikes me that that is the starting point. There are several objectives under discussion here with the word "needs" being applied to them. Really, what we are taking—Cynog referred to the European Union approach and it is very much along those lines. That approach is about how one narrows the gap of prosperity over time. That means that there is an objective being set if you go down the principal route that we would propose, to try and seek to narrow over time the levels of prosperity, the disparities in prosperity in the United Kingdom. It is difficult to achieve and impossible to achieve perfectly, but there should be some objective of that kind. That compares with, if you wanted to reflect needs as they stand at any given moment in time—you might choose less ambitious needs indicators. The ideal, we suggest, is that one should be going down that road of cohesion within the United Kingdom, and it is of the essence of a United Kingdom to approach it in that kind of way. All of that, of course, takes us away from the Barnett Formula, which appears to have only one merit, and that is that you do not need to agree upon any particular system to change it. Apart from that, the Barnett Formula, recognised as being really a very, very rough formula in the first place, now historic in its nature can only be described as one of these quaint curiosities which the United Kingdom has in various sectors; but given the nature of the United Kingdom as it is today, made up of the four nations, the Barnett Formula is wholly inappropriate and should not survive any longer.

Mr Jarrold: Just a word about WCVA: we are the umbrella body for the voluntary or third sector in Wales, and a major part of our work has been about the relationship between third sector organisations and government, both UK and devolved government. Certainly since the onset of devolution we have been very active in trying to raise awareness and build confidence and interest from our sector in government. Our perspective of today's debate is very much from outside government; we do not claim to be experts on the intricacies of government finance. However, we can share the perspective of other organisations that have an interest in government, including how it is financed. In talking about the Barnett Formula with our members, there are two main thrusts of their comments. First, there are concerns about the transparency, or lack of transparency of the current system and how it works; and second, of course, the question of whether the current arrangement fairly meets the needs of Wales. There are a number of issues that have concerned people. One is that clearly the Formula only applies to new expenditure, and that assumes that the pre-Barnett settlement is a fair settlement. I do not think we have the ability to comment on that, but that must be an important factor. The only trigger is the commitment of funding in England, so that puts Wales and the other devolved nations in a catch-up situation. Whilst it is right that new expenditure in England leads to a commensurate increase in the devolved nations, I am unclear about what the mechanisms might be for the devolved nations to propose additional expenditure out with the existing settlement that applies to their own needs. Our members are regularly confused, I think, by the way the Formula applies, or maybe does not apply, to individual announcements. Spending announcements are frequently silent on whether they apply to the devolved nations and whether or not there is any consequential. I do think that that lack of transparency creates problems for organisations that are trying to track these issues. For example when the expenditure on regeneration in south-east England was announced, the decision was taken that there was not Barnett consequential for that. We were not aware of any means of challenging that. It does seem to have been an arbitrary decision made by the Treasury. In terms of the process, we would like to see much clearer arrangements, whether it is the existing Formula or a new alternative formula which is much more on a basis of negotiation between all governments. We would like to see a formal way for devolved nations to negotiate around the implications of England expenditure for policy here. We would like to see simultaneous announcements that additional spend announced in England was hand-in-hand with the consequences for other nations, other than the amount of catch-up that we now have. Finally, on the question of fairness, we would echo many of the comments that have been made about the need for a formula that takes account of need. We cannot see any evidence for a case for Wales receiving significantly less funding than Scotland or Northern Ireland, and certainly in terms of levels of social need there is a case for higher levels. The Europe convergence funding programme is just one very graphic example of levels of need. We would echo the evidence of others, that we want to see investigation of a new formula which would take account not just of population, but the need for services and the cost of services in terms of population and sparsity.

Mr Davies: My colleague, John Osmond, and I represent the Institute of Welsh Affairs, which is a relatively small think-tank in UK terms, but unlike a lot of think-tanks in London, we have 1,200 individual members, about 130 corporate members, and branches across Wales; so I think we feel comfortable that we are in reasonable touch with opinion, not just here in Cardiff but elsewhere. There are only a few points that we wanted to make because I think you will find quite a lot of unanimity around this table on many of the issues you have raised. We do welcome the inquiry not only because we hope that it will be a prelude to some change but also it is a chance to make the debate rather more intelligent than would appear if you read coverage of public spending in Scotland and Wales in the press. It is often caricatured quite severely. That is a real problem because the public in Wales consume overwhelmingly media produced in London, so when they read about announcements, which as Phil Jarrold has mentioned are without any reference to consequentials, you get a very significant level of mis-information. Mis-information affects the public in Wales just as much as it affects the public in England. The other thing that popular coverage does not do is differentiate between the situations of Wales, Scotland and Northern Ireland; neither does it, on the whole, recognise that fiscal transfers or territorial allocations are commonplace in many developed countries. We would regard it as a hallmark of a civilised society. I certainly want to echo the points

made about the whole question of allocations within the UK being not simply about meeting people's immediate needs, but about producing some kind of economic convergence. That may be a "promised land", but it has to be a very real objective in these very unbalanced islands. Briefly, we certainly agree that the Barnett Formula as it stands needs reform. Population allocation is too crude and does not take our objective circumstances into account. I think that its very deficiencies, in a way, are purely a resentment towards spending in the devolved administrations, a resentment in England that is actually not warranted by the objective circumstances. The second point is that the notion, the concept, of basing the Formula on spending decisions in departments in another country, as it were, and within the UK within another administration, would strike most people as fairly bizarre. On the convergence factor, I know that *Tomorrow's Wales* has written about the convergence factor in its own paper. In the Institute we looked at this issue in a policy research project that we did before the last Assembly elections, and certainly it was our feeling then that our conclusion was that when you compare Wales with England's poorest region, the north-east of England, we are very similar in terms of our economic circumstances, but certainly we concluded that the comparison between Wales and the north-east provides the strongest objective case to, as you may say, freeze and squeeze solely for Wales and not necessarily for Northern Ireland or for Scotland. Since Wales, I gather, is now generating a GVA per head of rather less than the north-east of England, then equity would probably demand that the convergence factor be suspended in Wales's case. I would have thought that there is actually some urgency about this because Wales and the other devolved administrations, as with all government, are facing a very severe Treasury claw-back in 2010–11, as outlined in the pre-budget report. The prospect of, say, a decision to suspend the convergence factor coming after that started to kick in could lead to some really wasteful spending decisions. The convergence factor would certainly be one. The other issue, and the main issue, is that there is no way currently of ascertaining that the Formula is being applied fairly. I know that in one seminar on this issue I raised the question of who audits it. Certainly we know that the Wales Audit Office does not apply itself to the application of the Barnett Formula and neither does the Auditor General in the UK; so the Treasury remains judge and jury in its own cause—I suppose you might say subject to Cabinet. That is a real issue, and it is complicated by the fact that UK ministers do sometimes have difficulty in distinguishing clearly between their British and their English roles. I will give you one example, which cropped up when I was chairing the Arts Council for

Wales, when Gordon Brown was Chancellor of the Exchequer. He made an announcement of allocation of some £12 million to develop leadership and management skills in the cultural sector. The money was then given to the Arts Council for England, which thought that this was actually a dollop of money for England. The Skills Council got involved and the Skills Council was a UK body, and so thought differently; so there was a period of immense confusion for some months as to how and where that money should be allocated. That is all I wanted to say. We believe that the formula should be based on need and should avoid complexity, both in the interests of transparency and in order to prevent pressures to reduce the discretion of devolved governments. We do believe that the new formula has to be subject to not so much independent adjudication but having some independent statistical basis that is decided independently of government. There are plenty of bodies in this country that were set up to guarantee the independence of statistics. They could be used at the front end of the process. That is a slightly lightweight variation, I think, of the full territorial board that I know academics have proposed. That really summarises what we would like to convey.

Mr Osmond: I would like to add a broad political point to all of this. If you survey the territory of this discussion across academia, and by and large across the political landscape, certainly here in Wales, you find by now extraordinary consensus around these arguments. By and large people agree with the critique, a fairly trenchant critique as you will have heard, of the operation of the Barnett Formula. There is also across academia and the political world reasonable consensus about what ought to be done about it, which is broadly what we have just heard. Given, it seems to me, the really trenchant nature of the critique—parts of the way the system operates is quite outrageous in terms of what happens as a consequence, what is called the Barnett consequence—it is fair to ask: why has more fuss not been made about it? We have been trundling along with devolution now for a decade, ten years; and yet no real fuss of great consequence has been heard, it seems to me, above the parapet as it were. Why is that? It seems to me that there are two reasons why that is the case. The first and most important is that public expenditure in the devolved fields has been rising quite extensively over the last 10 years. The Barnett consequence, especially for health and education, has been going up. The overall block grant has risen quite substantially. In those circumstances, the administration, certainly here in Wales and almost certainly in Scotland, does not want to rock any boats. There has been the feeling in particular, "Do not open this can of worms because we are fearful about some results in terms of our relative autonomy in terms of making decisions within the block." There has also been a fear of any change that might end up as being worse, and cautious, risk-averse civil servants will have advised the minister, "better to leave well alone; we are doing all right". That would have been the tone. That is the main reason why I think there has not been a very big fuss. The second reason is that by and large, as you know, there has been the same administration running Wales and Scotland as the Labour administration in London, and any critique of the system seemed to be a critique of your colleagues. Both of these circumstances, we all know, are changing substantially. We all know about the coming expenditure cuts. The claw-back so far as Wales is concerned next year is £500 million. We all know that the administrations in Scotland and Wales are changing colour and not the same as those in London. It seems to me that unless we have the foresight now to engage, which I am very pleased you are doing in this sense, to pre-empt—we could be entering a period of very, very choppy waters indeed around bitter arguments around money because most divorce cases end up being around money, do they not? That is my final point.

Q625 *Lord Sewel:* On that cheery note I am going to jump in and just challenge John Osmond's basic thesis that there is an anti-Barnett consensus! There certainly has been in this room today, but let us go through the players individually. The Treasury is not anti-Barnett by any means. Scotland on the whole takes the view that it most likely does better under Barnett than it would under a needs-based assessment. Put it this way, it is either being moderately supportive of Barnett or keeping quiet! It would not take kindly, I think, to a move away. Northern Ireland, similarly, considers that it does relatively well out of Barnett and would not like a move. So who is against Barnett? Wales seems to be against Barnett because it feels that it is being treated badly. England might be against Barnett because it is fed up dishing out loads of money to Scotland, Wales and Northern Ireland, and it thinks that it is completely on the wrong end of the stick there. I am challenging you to come up with an argument that is at least attractive to the other territorial areas, if you move away from Barnett.

Mr Osmond: If I could add and respond very quickly, my point—I was not claiming a consensus in the Treasury—Heaven forfend! I was claiming consensus in Wales. Of course, the Scots do very well out of the current system and are unlikely to want to change, or if there is to be change it will have to be eased in gradually over many years. The Treasury does not want to have this argument every day of the month. It seems to me, from the Welsh perspective, across both academia and the political landscape there is the kind of consensus that I have described. It is not purely on the basis of "we are being done down", in that pure sense; it is arguably objectively the case.

Mr Dafis: The consensus exists, as far as I have been able to identify, in the academic community. Those who have carried out detailed studies of the topic, universally as far as I have been able to find out, have come to the conclusion that the current arrangements are completely unacceptable and no longer appropriate, if ever they were, but certainly not appropriate in the kind of emerging quasi federal system that we have got in the UK. I take the point of course that it would be very difficult indeed in the case of Scotland and Northern Ireland, but Scotland particularly, from what I read—it would make things politically difficult in Scotland. But if one looks at the whole issue of the union and the credibility of the union, it seems to me that over time, and looked at comprehensively, the best way to protect the union is by giving it intellectual coherence, and to base it on the principle of justice and the just disbursement of resources. That is a much more powerful way of arguing the case for the union.

Q626 *Lord Sewel:* Can I interrupt for a moment? We are going to protect the union in Scotland by telling Scotland it is going to receive less money!

Mr Dafis: I acknowledge there is a difficulty, a practical difficulty there, and we said in our paper of course that there should be a convergence on the basis of need, which means that we would move to this over time. If it is possible to raise one's view of things above immediate issues of political expediency, and if it is something that one would want to do to present a case for the maintenance of political union here, it seems to me that spelling out the way in which these countries belong together and therefore owe a debt of allegiance to each other, and therefore want to redistribute resources among each other for the general benefit, is a good way of doing it.

Mr Price: It seems to me that the context which John Osmond referred to of public expenditure being squeezed in the next few years is a context which we ought to think about on an England basis. The public in England are increasingly concerned at news that in Scotland they have the benefits of this, that or the other thing, which they do not have in England. English politicians are increasingly finding ways of riding on that particular bandwagon—suggestions of who should vote in the House of Commons, and suggestions even of an English parliament. These things are increasingly being under active debate. The West Lothian question is becoming a more active subject of debate. It seems to me that the way in which you defuse it, in which people in England

would be prepared to go along with differential expenditure, allowing more to Scotland, Wales and Northern Ireland, is if there was recognised to be a fair objective needs-based formula. If you have that kind of basis, it is seen as being fair. Put quite crudely, Scotland will not get away with it for much longer; and it can end up either with some crude cutting free of Barnett with huge political implications, or we can move now to something that is intellectually coherent, which is manifestly objective. People will complain about the detail whatever formula is devised and whatever principles you come up with; but if overall it is a sense that this is something objective and intended to be fair, then I think it has some quality of durability about it. If you look specifically at Wales, in the context of the squeeze on public expenditure in the next few years, if you add that to a sense that the whole Formula is unfair and has a mechanism inbuilt within it to increase the degree of that unfairness, the squeeze, then you have created a very deep schism for the future years if, as I rather suspect, we are going to have quite a number of years of very tight public expenditure real-terms cuts.

Q627 *Lord Moser:* Chairman, just picking up your approach, which I welcome, rather than what the outcome of the Formula is you mentioned four criteria on which it should be killed, so to speak. One is that it is not needs-based. That is not what we are talking about, so let us leave that on one side—it is not needs-based. The second point—though it was not in this order—was that it is not fair, and you have given examples of that. I would welcome more examples on the other two criteria that I wrote down; one that it is not objective—what was in your mind and how that works—and the other one was that it was not intellectually coherent, and I wondered what was in your mind on that. I do not disagree with either but I welcome your expansion of those words; that it is not objective and not intellectually coherent.

Mr Dafis: On the objectivity question first of all, the story of Barnett suggests that at its inception it was as much a matter of accommodating the needs of Scotland, and it was more about that particularly than about devising a system for the allocation of resources that would be fair. In that sense it was not objective. There were no criteria set out by which a new formula would be devised. Your esteemed Special Adviser, Alan Trench, in one of his articles, describes the way in which, when a needs-based assessment was made in the 1970s, civil servants came to the conclusion that there was indeed a case for higher levels of spending in Scotland, Wales and Northern Ireland, but that there was no case for the level of spending in Scotland that existed, and that is why the convergence mechanism was introduced, as a way of squeezing spending in Scotland so that it would come more into line. There has been the whole issue since then of course of Barnett by-passes, which are mysterious, which even the academics say they have been unable to clearly identify. In that sense, there has been a complete lack of objectivity.

Q628 *Lord Moser:* So just on that point, this is a reference to the Treasury doing what it wants to, when it wants to do it.
Mr Dafis: Yes.

Q629 *Lord Moser:* So we are looking for a needs-based system which by-passes subjectivity. It is difficult.
Mr Dafis: Everybody agrees, I think, that determining needs—the academics say it is a contested concept. It is not easy to do, but we do not for a moment question the need to make the attempt. The attempt should be made. On the question of complexity against simplicity, we would argue that it needs to be as complex as necessary in order to make it fair and in order to make it just, and no more than that. Objectivity in that sense seems to me to be crucial, and it is very, very important in order to establish a sense of justice. There is a very happy coincidence, it seems to us, at this moment, between the whole question of justice on the one hand and what would be good for Wales on the other hand. It is nice to be able to be advocating both of those things at the same time, but I am not sure we would be advocating the—
Mr Jarrold: Most of our members are charitable, and therefore they focus very much on the objectivity rather than the politics of this issue. That is the very clear message that we are getting, people's unease really about what appears to them to be an unfair and non-objective process. In terms of Treasury decisions it may be about subjectivity but it is certainly about the rather arbitrary approach without any apparent open negotiation or discussion. That puzzles people and does not help people's confidence in government.

Q630 *Lord Sewel:* Could that be resolved by having some form of independent review of what is now a totally enclosed Treasury exercise in deciding what is the English expenditure and what is UK expenditure? That is where the lack of transparency is, is it not? If that was sorted, would it remove a fair chunk of your reservations?
Mr Jarrold: I think you need both. You need a better way of assessing how to allocate expenditure and a much more open way of demonstrating how that is being done. That is why I said earlier that, whether with the existing Formula or a new formula, I still think across the UK there needs to be a much more

formal process for determining different amounts and different allocations.
Mr Osmond: Can I give you an example, which I had not thought of myself until the other day, but it concerns your House, the House of Lords, House of Commons, Westminster!

Q631 *Lord Sewel:* I thought you meant my own house, and I was a bit worried!
Mr Osmond: There is no Barnett consequential on your expenditure on Westminster. That is to say that the cost of running this place is taken out of our block. You may say that is obvious, but why should it be so? This is a new expenditure, consequent upon devolution, which was a change, I would have thought, for the benefit of the whole of the United Kingdom.

Q632 *Chairman:* I am not going to stand behind the bill for the Scottish Assembly! I can see a marginal argument which says the centre should support the devolved administrations but not to that extent.
Mr Osmond: I am talking about the costs of democracy in Britain. Part of it is here, and we are having to pay for that out of expenditure that otherwise we would spend on health, education and so on. It is not an insignificant amount—£48 million a year.

Q633 *Chairman:* The trouble with this whole Formula is that it was intended—you elevate it, frankly, far, far higher than it deserves. We talked to Joel Barnett and he gave evidence in front of us and was perfectly clear that it was a short-term formula that was designed to get arguments off the back of the Treasury as to what the various parts of the UK should have. He did not expect it to go on. It was not even called a formula for the first ten years of its existence. The Treasury was doing a huge assessments need. Nobody told Joel that they were doing it. Ministers did not know it was being done. The history is phenomenal. It is quite honestly staggering that we have still got a situation in which somehow we have got to work out a proper system of allocating resources from the centre to the devolved administrations. It seems to me that the main attack on the Barnett Formula is that longevity does not necessarily produce the right result; it keeps it going and it is easy for the Treasury and they sign it off automatically, and that is easy; but in terms of the way in which you want this country to have its resources allocated, it does not do the job. What we would be interested to know is that if you want to change it, or say you want to change it, I have to say to John that the only body that has given evidence in front of us that wants to keep the Barnett Formula as it is, is Her Majesty's Treasury, which one can understand. No-one else seems to want it. But if you want to change it and have a needs-based formula, please what criterion do you want to bring in to use when you assess those needs? Do you want a big one, in which case you spend two or three years going into it, as the Treasury did in the seventies; or a narrow one where you take three or four main indicators and look at those and say, "it is not 100 per cent objective but it is 95 per cent"; and, if so, what would you like those indicators to be?

Mr Dafis: I simply start by saying we do not feel qualified to offer an alternative formula. We do not feel qualified really to suggest what the criteria might necessarily be. We are saying that we need an objective process of determining that. That is why we suggest the establishment of this commission on territorial funding. Its initial task would be to carry out an assessment of need and, secondly, to devise a formula based on new criteria. That would be a starting point for that commission.

Q634 *Chairman:* People would still argue about it. Whatever they came up with, some people would perceive themselves as losers and some people would perceive themselves as winners.

Mr Dafis: That is the human condition.

Q635 *Chairman:* So the only effect of the independence is to remove the odium of that argument off the back of the government of the day. That seems to me to be a thoroughly admirable thing, but nevertheless the mere fact that it is independent does not necessarily mean it will be accepted.

Mr Osmond: It would, wouldn't it, because it would be fairer? It would be seen to be fairer than the current situation. Nothing is perfect in an imperfect world, but we can do better than this—that is all we are saying, I think.

Q636 *Chairman:* What variables do you want to take?

Mr Davies: I think one of the difficulties common to the three organisations this side of the table, three small charitable organisations, is trying to face up to something that has enormous technicality to it. I do not want to put words into the mouths of colleagues, but I have a slight nervousness about the law of unintended consequences. I have seen so many complex papers setting forward a formula. I certainly do not think that our organisation has the capacity to evaluate all those. Clearly, you can see some very simple areas between social security payments or some sparsity factor, the GVA and so on, and it is a question of getting the right combination of those things and choosing a spot on the spectrum between over simplicity on the one hand and over complexity on the other, and allowing this to work in a way that

people understand. I would dearly wish the Institute of Welsh Affairs had a team of economists to grapple with this, but I must leave that to the better-resourced people.

Mr Osmond: As you well know, we have the Holtham Commission working away as we speak, and the Chairman of the board appeared before you; and in Scotland they have the Calman Commission. These people are going to come up with the answers to the technical question. I think what you need to decide is whether you agree with the principle.

Q637 *Lord Moser:* I have already heard in this meeting one suggestion about the approach to the choice of indicators, which I have not heard before, which came from Mr Price. If I understood you rightly, at the beginning you urged us to look at needs-based, in terms of prosperity over time.

Mr Price: Yes.

Q638 *Lord Moser:* That is a new thought to me, and a very interesting one. Could you expand on it for a moment, because that is a different dimension to today's measurement, what most people would think of in terms of forecasting indicators? You seem to be urging, if anything, to look at prosperity or lack of prosperity over time—backwards. I am not sure what you meant.

Mr Price: What I meant by that is that you look at the disparities at the time and that you set as a goal—this influences the factors you choose—to reduce those disparities. They obviously are not going to be reduced quickly, so I use the phrase "over time" so it is an objective that you seek to achieve by putting as at least one of the factors within, something weighted towards determining relative prosperity. That probably is GVA per head. I say it as somebody who is determined not to get involved in identifying precisely all the factors for exactly the same reasons as my colleagues: I am neither a statistician nor an economist. I am not equipped—

Q639 *Lord Moser:* You are lucky.

Mr Price: I am not equipped to know precisely what the consequences would be, and I fully appreciate the expertise in the room specifically on the statistics. May I just add also that in the course of the discussion we have talked about the objective, which I raised, and also we talked about the objective factors. It occurred to me once or twice that possibly some other word than "objective" is needed for the goal of what you are seeking to achieve, just simply to avoid that distinction. I think it is an important part of what is sought to be achieved, because if need is merely a reflection of in effect the services, the spend on services, that is a static sort of reflection. It may obviously change over time, but it does nothing about reducing the disparity, so it is a little more ambitious than merely talking about the need as a reflection of what services have to be provided at that time.

Q640 *Lord Moser:* That is a very important point. Thank you.

Mr Davies: It is a very interesting contrast, if I may say, on the word "convergence", which is used in the European context in order to try and bring people up to a common level. It seems to me that convergence in terms of the Barnett Formula is that it gives you precisely the opposite effect.

Mr Price: Exactly.

Mr Osmond: To be specific, as I understand it, when devolution began, for every £100 spend in England we were spending £125 in terms of the block, and that is now down to £114. If this goes on and we do not put a floor underneath it, our relative spending per head in Wales is going to fall below the poorest of the English regions, and I do not think that is tolerable.

Q641 *Lord Sewel:* Are we not here in the area of common cause, because the one thing I would have thought that all the territories do not want is convergence?

Mr Dafis: Convergence on the basis of *per capita*—

Q642 *Lord Sewel:* By strict Barnett, Wales has had most likely the purest Barnett application of all the territories. Post devolution the sorts of things done before devolution become much more difficult, so pure Barnett is likely to emerge as the basis upon which the territories are funded. I would have thought there would be common cause throughout the territories to avoid convergence!

Mr Dafis: We were asked some time ago about the indicators we would advocate. There was a discussion this morning, was there not, about whether as a fall-back or whether as an overall indicator, a proxy, you referred to GVA or to disposable household income. Professor Foreman-Peck was arguing that you should use disposable household income. If all you wanted to do was to devise a method of helping people who are disadvantaged to get an equivalent level of service, there is a case then for using disposable household income; but if you want to get to the root of the problem and bring about a radical change in the nature of the economy and society and the community in a place like Wales, then we would argue that GVA is a better way of doing that. If you look at the kinds of problems we have got in Wales that are identifiable and measurable, we have got serious health requirements; we have levels of economic inactivity with all the attendant difficulties that come with those: they are a consequence of

economic failure. In the South Wales valleys they are the consequence of economic collapse as a result of the collapse of coal and to some extent iron and steel. If you want to enable the people of those areas in those regions to improve their health and quality of their communities, then you have got to do something about the nature of the economy. That is the only way the valleys are going to pull themselves out of the difficulties that they are in—if their economy improves. That is why we say if you take GVA as an indicator or as a proxy, then you would be transferring resources in a way that would create a reasonable chance of tackling things at the root level; and that is a better way of doing it than constantly providing a subsidy in order to enable high levels of service need to be provided. That may be the difference between the Foreman-Peck approach and—

Q643 *Chairman:* I think that is probably outside our terms of reference. I regret it, but the way in which you revive the valleys I do not think is something that we can get into.

Mr Dafis: Can I not persuade you to regard that as an aspect of need?

Q644 *Chairman:* It is a good try!

Mr Jarrold: Peter Price's made an earlier comment about relative prosperity and relative health or relative educational attainment: if you wanted to take as part of our needs approach an approach that would generate the investment to create those improvements, what we would be looking for there is convergence in terms of attainment.

Mr Davies: It may be outside the terms of reference, but it is very, very germane to any sense of fairness. As somebody who spent a lot of my life working in Newcastle and the north-east of England, there is an element of that within England itself. I would argue that certainly since 1979 the notion of reducing these spatial disparities within the UK has not had a very high priority in the policies of government. That underlying fact, which takes you outside the question of identifiable public expenditure, is still a very real factor in people's perceptions of how these arguments are made.

Mr Osmond: By analogy—you have probably seen the operations in the EU and have experience of the Republic of Ireland—we all know that Ireland for many decades was a poor country, but partly as a consequence of EU subsidy in the form of Objective 1, it managed to reinvent the so-called Celtic Tiger. Then it began paying money back in as a net contributor to the EU, and that was partly a consequence of the operation of distribution of funds. I do not see why the same principles cannot apply to the way we operate distribution of funds within the UK.

Chairman: It is very interesting that we are charged with looking at the Barnett Formula and seeing the way it works and if it is not, what we are going to do about it!

Q645 *Lord Sewel:* I hope we do not return to Ireland . . . .

Mr Price: You have picked up my colleague Cynog's comments specifically about the regeneration of the South Wales valleys and we do not expect that you would make that an objective, but within the context of what you are looking at in examining a possible alternative to the Barnett Formula, you are clearly examining a needs-based formula of some description. What we are arguing for is much more than principle: that a goal of that formula, if it is to reflect fairness and need, is to reduce disparities for prosperity over time. We take that, as it were, as a factor that ought to be included in a good needs-based formula which looks to the future of the United Kingdom.

Mr Davies: I agree entirely with Peter there because you could take one example as proof of the fact that the current policy actually specifically excludes that from Barnett, and that was the question of the Olympic Games. Within a £9 billion budget there is a line within the budget of £2 billion for regeneration of East London, which is not included in the Barnett baseline. So that wider objective seems to be to be specifically excluded from the Barnett Formula, if you take that example.

Q646 *Chairman:* As I understand the Olympic example, what has happened there is that the Treasury suddenly decided that the regeneration bit should be a UK expenditure, which does not attract Barnett consequentials, as opposed to an English expenditure which would attract Barnett consequentials.

Mr Davies: Would that decision have been taken by an independent—

Chairman: No, of course not; it was taken by the Treasury behind closed doors without telling anybody what they were doing, as far as I can see. I am not here to defend the Treasury; on the contrary. In that part of the operation of the Barnett Formula there are very serious criticisms indeed that it may well be that this Committee at the end will wish to make. What I am concerned about is where we go from here. The message that I have from all of you is that we should move away from the existing formula to something based upon needs: precisely what sort of needs and how we define the needs, or what variables we use in order to assess the needs, I think all of you seem to say that that depends upon either the Calman Committee in Scotland or down here, or perhaps even with this Committee. We will do our best.

FRIDAY 27 MARCH 2009

Present	Mar and Kellie, E	Sewel, L
	Richard, L (Chairman)	

Letter from Mr Bruce Robinson, Head of the Northern Ireland Civil Service

Thank you for extending the invitation to submit evidence to your Select Committee. You will appreciate that the Barnett Formula and it's outworking is of great interest to the Northern Ireland Executive. I therefore welcome the opportunity to comment on the issues identified in the evidence call note. I have tried to follow the guidance instructions as closely as possible.

1. APPLICATION OF THE FORMULA IN PRACTICE:

When referring to "present disparities" in per capita public expenditure allocations across the UK countries I presume the Committee is referring to the Identifiable Public Expenditure (PE) per head data presented within HM Treasury's annual Public Expenditure and Statistical Analysis (PESA) publication. The trend data from this publication (table below) does suggest that spend per head is indeed higher in the Devolved Administrations but there are some concerns about how this table is compiled in terms of how expenditure is attributed to the regions. These concerns have existed for some considerable time. The extent of HM Treasury mis-allocation of expenditure to the devolved regions is considerable. An example of these anomalies was the inclusion of English and Welsh prison spend in Scottish estimated spend. These anomalies were acknowledged by HM Treasury under challenge from the Scottish Executive. The expenditure estimates for the devolved administrations were then subsequently revised downward.

It is also worth noting that the table highlights evidence of some degree of convergence in Northern Ireland with the UK average—presumably an outworking of the "Barnett Squeeze".

TOTAL IDENTIFIABLE EXPENDITURE PER HEAD INDEX: 2002–03 TO 2007–08 (UK = 100)

	2002–03	2003–04	2004–05	2005–06	2006–07	2007–08 (planned)
England	96	97	97	97	97	97
Scotland	117	116	113	115	117	118
Wales	114	112	110	111	112	110
Northern Ireland	130	126	125	124	123	126
UK	100	100	100	100	100	100

I would also make the important point that drawing conclusions from this table on whether a region is over or under-provided for in terms of public expenditure allocations is very risky and potentially misleading. The PESA data in no way reflects variations in regional needs. These needs reflect a range of factors such as demographic profiles (which influence spend in key service areas such as education and health), mortality, economic structure, peripherality etc. All these factors vary by region and determine the demand on public services.

The Barnett Formula process accounts for some 90.5 per cent of the Northern Ireland Executive budget. In terms of flexibility to allocate public expenditure, the Devolved Administrations have considerable autonomy. In the Northern Ireland case a Budget is approved by the Assembly which allocates money to spending areas according to the priorities defined in the Executive's Programme for Government. There are, unfortunately some constraints on flexibility imposed by HM Treasury such as the discretion to switch between current and capital definitions.

2. FORMULA BY-PASS AND THE BARNETT SQUEEZE:

Barnett convergence hastens during periods when public expenditure is growing above long term trend rates. It is therefore not surprising that there has been some degree of convergence over the last decade when the annual average growth rate of public expenditure was 7.6 per cent. The pace of convergence is ameliorated to some extend by receiving Exchequer funding outside of the Barnett process. This "bypass" was a common feature of Northern Ireland allocations when significant resources were received for various EU structural funds/PEACE programmes. The scale of these funds is now diminishing and so, therefore, is the influence of "bypass". One would also expect the pace of any convergence to slow over the coming years as the growth rate in UK public expenditure over the next few years is likely to fall below trend.

3. DATA QUALITY AND AVAILABILITY:

The HMT Statement of Funding Policy explains the mechanics of the Barnett Formula in a very transparent manner. There should not therefore be any misunderstanding about what it is trying to achieve over a long term time scale. Where confusion does exist is in understanding how HMT determines the extent of "comparability" in the tables annexed to the Statement of Funding Policy. These tables provide some insight into the degree to which English determined funding is replicated in the Devolved Administrations. The manner in which this data is presented and the inability to source the English expenditure attributions back to specific areas in Whitehall departments is a concern. There remains a concern that some of the comparability percentages are arbitrarily set. Clearly full transparency in the application of the Barnett Formula process requires better information on how the comparability percentages are derived.

One solution to this concern over how comparability is set would be for HMT to publish additional tables which explicitly link expenditure spending areas to clearly identifiable functions within the individual Whitehall departments. To ensure that the whole exercise was conducted in an objective manner, this task could be given to the Office of National Statistics (ONS) who have a statutory duty to remain independent in discharging such functions.

4. NEED FOR REFORM/ALTERNATIVES TO THE EXISTING FORMULA:

The Barnett Formula mechanism does bestow many advantages. It should give the Devolved Administrations greater certainty in terms of the quantum of resources that they have to incorporate within their budgets. It also has a degree of transparency of application (not withstanding the concerns over the comparability factors) and it reflects population variations.

There are however two major concerns over the application of Barnett. The first relates to the fact that the mechanism cannot account for regional variations in need. Issues such as demographic profiles, mortality rates, economic structures, peripherality etc all impose demands on public expenditure in the UK regions. In the Northern Ireland context, there are needs, particularly within the education and health sectors that cost considerably more to meet than the Barnett consequentials deliver.

The second concern about the Barnett Formula relates to the application process. HM Treasury arbitrarily determine the outcome without independent validation. This then allows HM Treasury to arguably abuse the Formula to ensure that bypass results in non-allocation to the Devolved Administrations. A recent notable example of this was the decision to exclude 2010 Olympics funding from the Barnett process.

On the specific issue of reforming or replacing Barnett, in the absence of an alternative process, I would suggest that the Formula process can undoubtedly be improved upon. Ensuring independent validation of its application (ie ONS) and creating some form of appeals procedure to allow a challenge to HM Treasury would be helpful.

The difficulty with any needs-based approach to determining public expenditure allocations between regions is reaching agreement on the actual definition of need and how it might be measured. The original HM Treasury Needs Assessment Model (NAS) contained a vast array of need indicators across many spending areas. These indicators then had weightings attached to determine relative priority within the NAS model but this determination was quite subjective in nature. Any future allocation model based on relative regional need will still have to overcome this qualitative allocation of weights.

If such as model is to be constructed, it is imperative that it is done so in a collaborative fashion with the full participation of the Devolved Administrations. Anything produced unilaterally by HM Treasury will be treated with healthy scepticism.

5. DECISION MAKING AND DISPUTE RESOLUTION:

I have already alluded to the rather arbitrary approach adopted by HM Treasury in allocating funds to the Devolved Administrations. There is often a lack of clarity in how funds are attributed to these regions. Furthermore, there is an increasing number of HM Treasury decisions on public expenditure that result in reducing the spending discretion of the Devolved Administrations either by imposing efficiency targets/cuts to baselines or tightening rules on issues such as resource/capital switching, access to end-year-flexibility (EYF) stocks accumulated etc. These all effectively reduce the spending power of the Devolved Administrations— thus undermining the principle of devolved governance.

There is also a concern about the manner in which HM Treasury impose alterations to expenditure allocations. There tends to be little in the way of advance consultation with the Devolved Administrations and even after public announcement, it is often very difficult to obtain a full understanding of what HM Treasury has actually done.

These concerns highlight the need for greater engagement between HM Treasury and the Devolved Administrations, at least at ministerial level, when amendments to financial allocations are proposed. Ideally there should be some form of formal mechanism established to allow for appeal/resolution. This mechanism could then be reflected within an amended Statement of Funding Policy document.

I trust the Select Committee will find this submission helpful in their deliberations.

17 February 2009

Examination of Witnesses

Witnesses: MR LEO O'REILLY, Permanent Secretary, Department of Finance and Personnel, MR RICHARD PENGELLY, Public Spending Director, and MR MIKE BRENNAN, NICS Chief Economist and Head of Strategic Policy Division, Department of Finance, examined.

Q647 *Chairman:* Gentlemen, can I thank you very much for coming. As you know, this is a Committee set up specifically by the House of Lords to look at the Barnett Formula, how it works, what it does, what its prospects are, whether it should continue, whether it should be replaced by something else and, if so, what. There are certain things we are not entitled to look at. I imagine you have seen our mandate. We are not allowed to look, for example, at the breakdown of cash inside England by regions of England. We are not allowed to look at revenue raising issues, so we cannot express a view as to what should happen about, say, the demand for fiscal autonomy in Scotland. Indeed, it is a fairly narrowly focused inquiry looking at Barnett, how it came into existence and whether it works. I am very grateful to you for coming to assist us in that task.
Mr O'Reilly: You are presumably going round all the regions of the Devolved Administrations?

Q648 *Chairman:* Yes. We have been to Scotland and Wales.
Mr Pengelly: Saved the best until last!

Q649 *Lord Sewel:* The missing bit of this is the authentic voice of Middle England.
Mr O'Reilly: Thank you very much for the invitation to attend. Obviously the Barnett Formula is something that we operate, as those who operate basically the central finance part of the Department of Finance in Northern Ireland, and are aware of on a fairly frequent and if on not a daily basis, certainly a monthly basis. At the times of Spending Reviews, et cetera, it comes into focus. It is also something which I know is part of the issues you want to raise with us, and is quite topical because of the discussions around it, which are the financial arrangements that surround the devolution of policing and justice. That, again, has refocused some interest in Northern Ireland on how the Barnett Formula operates and how it might operate in respect of policing and justice. Just by way of a general overview, to give a

potted overview of our perspective of the Formula, although I know you want to come back in some detail on it, generally speaking we believe that the Barnett Formula as it operates and has operated generally has been a fair and effective way of dealing with the tricky issue of how you allocate resources to devolved regions in a single state. Some of the difficulties that have been attributed to it reflect in some respects the fact of the significant imbalance in the size of the four regions of the UK, if I can call it that, where 85 per cent of the population is around England and 15 per cent in devolved administrations and, indeed, in the case of Northern Ireland roughly 3.0 per cent of the population. Any arrangement that operates has to take account of that very skewed distribution of population, and hence resources, around the regions of the UK. From our perspective, the Formula generally has operated effectively. The principal advantages, as we see them, are first of all that in a sense it takes immediate politics, if I can call it that, out of the negotiations on financial allocations to each of the devolved administrations. For example, particularly now that we have a devolved administration in Northern Ireland where local ministers obviously want to set their own priorities, the Formula, by allocating a global sum of money and leaving it to the devolved administration to decide how that money is spent, very much gives them a sense of much greater control over what is happening locally. It also takes away the enormous difficulty that would no doubt be in place if we had to negotiate with the Treasury about allocations of sums of money for different issues on an ongoing basis, which to some extent would cut across the devolution of political responsibility because inevitably the Treasury, Treasury officials, Treasury ministers, would take a view as to how money should be spent locally and that would cut across the devolved settlement in that sense. In a sense, it also bestows transparency. One of the positive things that have happened with the Formula since devolution has been the fact that the Treasury now publishes its statement of funding policy for the devolved administrations, so the detail is there and it is openly available. To some extent, I think that has helped remove some of the misunderstanding and mystique around the Formula. We have just a couple of difficulties as we see them, and we can come back to them later. First of all, the way the Formula is operated is while on the surface it appears straightforward, at times we have concerns as to the way the Treasury decide what is and is not falling within the scope of the Formula and what is and is not English expenditure as distinct from UK-wide expenditure. To some extent we are entirely dependent on the Treasury telling us what our comparable adjustments in expenditure are.

Q650 *Chairman:* Do they consult you at all?
Mr O'Reilly: In a sense it is a one-way flow of information.

Q651 *Chairman:* Do they consult you on this issue or not?
Mr O'Reilly: Sometimes, but often not. Often it is very much presented as a fait accompli. I will finish my introductory remarks now and then we can come back to these points. Certainly within the recent years there have been occasions, most particularly in the 2004 Spending Review, when the Treasury suddenly and with no warning introduced significant changes to the way the Formula operated in terms of the capacity of the devolved administrations to switch between capital and resource and also the arrangements for EYF, which locally meant that, for example, we simply had to set aside the budget we had planned for the following three years and do a new one. That obviously caused difficulties here. Those difficulties were lessened to some extent because at that time we had direct rule, but I can imagine that if we had had a devolved administration at that time it would have caused major difficulties locally. We feel the fundamentals of the Formula operate effectively. It is not ideal, but it is difficult to work up in your mind an ideal situation that would have no difficulties whatsoever. Our concerns in general terms are around how it is operated on a day-to-day and year-to-year basis and some of the transparency issues involved in it. Thank you.

Q652 *Chairman:* Thank you very much indeed. When we took evidence from Lord Barnett he was really quite firm about it. He said it was his intention when he did it in the 1970s—it was not even called the Barnett Formula for another ten years, I think it was Sir Leo Pliatsky who actually did it—that it was intended to be temporary to get over some political difficulties, to remove the argument between the devolved administrations, although of course they were not devolved then, but, if you like, the territories

and the Treasury over many years and it was a simple Formula that could be applied and was only to be applied to variations in the expenditure and not to be applied to the block. In his opinion it had outlived its usefulness, its day had passed and he thought that a Formula that was based virtually entirely on population was not reasonable and he wanted needs assessments to be pushed more into the equation. From your experience of Barnett, do you still think it is a useful and effective way of actually distributing money from the centre to the devolved administrations?
Mr O'Reilly: Yes. I will ask my colleagues to come in on that one in a moment. One of the things about the Formula is that it does not distribute the total of the funding to the devolved administrations; it deals with the marginal adjustments in funding to the devolved administrations. I suspect part of the reason for its longevity is the fact that its foundation was when the distribution of resources that were in place in 1977/78 were relatively favourable to the devolved administrations and that has allowed the Formula to continue in place and deal with subsequent adjustments at the margins. The other obvious point is the Formula only deals with part of public expenditure within the devolved administrations and in our case, if you add up our total DEL and AME, just over half of that is accounted for by the Barnett Formula, so a great deal of public expenditure happens and is distributed by other means.

Q653 *Chairman:* Can I ask you about negotiations over the block. How do you do that with the Treasury?
Mr O'Reilly: I will pass to my colleague, Richard, who does most of that.
Mr Pengelly: In terms of negotiation, the position has been changing over the last number of years. The Treasury has adopted a policy for the devolved administrations to try and get as much funding as possible channeled through the Barnett Formula rather than have what was lovingly referred to as a "Barnett bypass". Effectively, in terms of the Spending Review, the initial point is the Treasury will agree the baseline, so that is your starting point, which is effectively the conclusion from the previous Spending Review. They will produce a list of the comparability factors, and that is for all the Whitehall Departments. They will break the individual spend to a low level of analysis and for each of those units of analysis indicate whether it is a UK-wide programme or an England only programme. They send that to us and there is a dialogue. There is a particular issue around the Olympics, which we might come on to, which is a specific and thorny problem. That aside, to be fair to the Treasury, the debate around whether programmes are comparable or not has not in my time, going back

ten years, ever been a particularly problematic debate. In terms of the sub-programme, it is largely an objective issue. There are programmes solely covering England, and those which extend beyond England. There has been nothing like the Olympics before, frankly. We agree that and that gives the comparability factors. The population percentages are derived from ONS as a statement of fact and put into a spreadsheet and when the Chancellor announces the national spending review outcome it becomes a mathematical exercise. We obviously check and double-check the amounts because, being accountants, that is what we do. If I go back to previous Spending Reviews, for example the 1997 and 1999 CSRs, there were elements outwith the Barnett Formula where there was discussion. Peace funding was always outside and there was a discussion about the levels of that and there were some issues on agriculture around modulation matched funding. Those areas have been diminishing and we are now at the stage where off the top of my head I cannot think of anything where there is active discussion with the Treasury, it is all Barnett-based and formulaic. The negotiation, as such, happens around the statement of funding policy and that is where the difficulties are as opposed to the quantum of any specific item of funding that flows through Barnett.

Q654 *Chairman:* A lot of the evidence that we have heard has, in effect, concentrated on having some kind of needs assessment fed into the way in which the Formula is applied. As far as the Formula is concerned it only applies to variations, I understand that, but if you are going to look at the baseline, the block, do you not think that some kind of needs assessment should be part of the process?
Mr Pengelly: Mike can say more about the detail, but in terms of the starting point you have got to go back to go forward. The debate is about Barnett or not—to me the first stage in that is the debate about formulaic funding as against a negotiated outcome. In a sense that is about choosing objectivity over subjectivity. The view is objectivity and formulaic funding is better. If you make that choice but when you get into it if you introduce a needs factor you are reintroducing subjectivity because there can be no absolute statement of needs, it goes into the relativities. Maybe Mike could say more about that.
Mr Brennan: As Richard and Leo have said, the totality of the Northern Ireland block is a given, so Barnett really is amendments at the margins depending as you come to each Spending Review. It is a marginal adjustment mechanism. The main benefit of Barnett is the transparency in that we have the published statement of funding policy and you can look at the consequences at the back and see exactly how comparable you are to various Whitehall

departments. The minute you start to introduce the concept of a needs assessment you face two difficulties. The first one is do you want to do a needs assessment on the totality of the block allocation or do you want to take the baseline as a given and construct a mechanism based on needs assessment going forward. As Richard said, any one of those approaches is a highly subjective exercise and you would lose the transparency of the Barnett system. You then get into second order considerations and problems about how would you police a needs assessment, for example, and would there be a need for an independent arbiter. Those are second and third order considerations that come out of needs assessment.

Q655 *Chairman:* Very important ones.
Mr Brennan: Yes.

Q656 *Chairman:* Clearly it would have to be looked at. I get the impression, and I may be quite wrong about this, that on the whole you are satisfied with your block allocation and, therefore, you do not really need to look at Barnett because Barnett is there as a sort of mathematical formula which you can apply to variations up or down and that is enough. Is that right?
Mr Pengelly: We are trying to completely differentiate the size of the block as against the approach to determining the size of the block. In terms of needs, we have talked about the flaws because you are introducing subjectivity and the difficulty of determining needs. There is no question that there are issues of deprivation, geographic issues, peripherality issues, where Northern Ireland has higher need and, therefore, in our view it could make a coherent case for additional funding. The problem is, in terms of the mechanism to do that, that is not in the Barnett Formula. The other option is to set aside the Barnett Formula and have a subjective discussion with the Treasury. At any point in time, let alone in the current economic situation, you are entering the unknown. I would not say that our views on Barnett equate precisely to a view that we have an adequate block, there are issues in terms of the level of public expenditure in Northern Ireland.

Q657 *Chairman:* I am sure nobody would say they have an adequate block, but my impression is that on the whole you are not dissatisfied with the block and that Barnett, therefore, is a peripheral issue and you do not want to change the way in which the block is allocated except you want it to be a bit more transparent. Is that fair or not?
Mr O'Reilly: The absolute size of the block is not ultimately a Barnett issue, it goes back to the start of Barnett. In a sense that is a separate issue as to what should be the basic size of the block and how much

money should be allocated to each of the regions. If you wanted to look at that, Barnett as a formula cannot address that issue.

Chairman: I would agree with that, but it does not seem to me that you can look at this thing without looking at the baseline as well.

Q658 *Lord Sewel:* You are keen to avoid subjectivity, and I can understand that, and you say Barnett is the means of avoiding subjectivity, but, as you say, if you trace it back to its origins, that initial block, that is the historic accumulation of subjective judgments, is it not?

Mr O'Reilly: Yes.

Mr Pengelly: It is, but the other point I would make is that the block at a point in time was the basis on which the devolved administrations were established and they were aware of that in the context of the needs issues for Northern Ireland. To change that now means you reintroduce a subjectivity that in effect has been managed out of the system because of the transparency of the position at the establishment of the devolved administrations.

Q659 *Lord Sewel:* Yes and no. Yes, the year-to-year adjustment with minor reservations is non-subjective because it is a formulaic judgment. You could say the Treasury is making subjective judgments on what it decides on England and the UK, that is a subjective judgement, but certainly the application of the population is objective. That is the incremental bit. The historic substance is purely the project of subjective negotiations.

Mr O'Reilly: We did some local needs and effectiveness work back in 2001 and we will explain how that exercise went.

Mr Brennan: I take your point entirely about the totality of the block having been set in a subjective fashion some time in the dark, distant past. The difficulty we have in terms of trying to form a view on the needs assessment is that it has been so long since we have seen the Treasury's view of what a needs assessment might look like, they have not published anything, so we struggle to find where we might be in that counterfactual world. In 2001 when the new devolved administration came in we tried to do some preliminary work on using the old Treasury NAS model to try and form some—

Q660 *Chairman:* That is the 1976–79 model?

Mr Brennan: The 1979 model. We tried to form a view as to where Northern Ireland might be in today's world if we were forced to implement and police a NAS model. Over many, many months we laboured with economists and statisticians to first of all populate the model with the statistics and the indictors and we came to the conclusion that looking across programmes which covered 70 per cent of the

Northern Ireland DEL, at that point in time need in Northern Ireland was about 25 per cent above parity with England. We had not realised that the actual allocations that would come through in the Spending Review in 2002 would bring about very rapid convergence. That was a worrying position to find ourselves in, that the NAS model was saying, "Yes, you have a higher level of need but the actual provision you will get going forward for the three CSRs 1999–2002 will put you in a deficit".

Q661 *Chairman:* Was this based on the Treasury's needs assessment of the 1970s and did you take the same amount, the variables and the rest of it?

Mr Brennan: We looked at five particular areas: health and social care, schools, financial assistance to industry, training and vocational education and housing. Then we created one of our own, which was culture, arts and leisure. We took the Treasury model and then we added another sub-programme on, culture, arts and leisure. It covered 70 per cent of the total Northern Ireland DEL at that time, so it was quite comprehensive. As I say, we took a raft of indicators, many hundreds of indicators, in the Treasury 1979 model and we repopulated and updated the statistics within that model.

Mr O'Reilly: I am sure you know this, but any needs assessment is by definition ultimately a subjective exercise. A more recent exercise we did was in relation to some work we did following a report here by John Appleby of the King's Fund on the Health Service in Northern Ireland. We did some work following that up in terms of seeking to identify relative need in Northern Ireland compared to the rest of the UK. What came out of that very strongly was how big the differential was depended critically on how you treated deprivation and measures of deprivation as an indicator of health need. We found we got into this very complex debate as to the relationship between levels of deprivation and health need and whether deprivation is an absolute measure of health need or not. It brought back to me the non-objective nature of much of needs work and how do you measure needs in an objective way.

Q662 *Chairman:* We do for local authorities, do we not?

Mr O'Reilly: Yes.

Q663 *Chairman:* We do quite a detailed series of variables which people live with anyway.

Mr O'Reilly: Yes.

Q664 *Chairman:* I wonder, could we see your work in 2001?

Mr Brennan: There were two elements to the work that we were doing in 2001. The first one looked at the needs factors and the second one looked at the effectiveness of public service delivery. The public service delivery work is certainly published and we can make that available to you.

Q665 *Chairman:* Which one is published?
Mr Brennan: The effectiveness reports were published.

Q666 *Chairman:* Yes, but could we have a look at the needs assessment?
Mr O'Reilly: It was not published at the time.
Mr Brennan: The difficulty we had was just when we were about to publish we reverted back under direct rule and the Treasury requested that we did not publish it.

Q667 *Chairman:* A brick wall with the British constitution!
Mr O'Reilly: From memory, I am sure the work that was done more recently on the Health Service was published.
Mr Brennan: The Appleby work was all published and we can certainly send that to you as well.

Q668 *Chairman:* So we can have a look at the Appleby and effectiveness evaluations. As far as you are concerned you would not mind us looking at the needs but the Treasury say no, is that right?
Mr Brennan: Certainly the Treasury were aware of our research and where we were going.

Q669 *Lord Sewel:* The Treasury have a copy of it, do they?
Mr Brennan: Yes, they do.

Q670 *Chairman:* We will do a Freedom of Information request and see what we get. The Treasury put the block on it before the new devolved administration came in. The situation is now so different, do you think the Treasury block still applies?
Mr O'Reilly: It would fall into the category of papers of a previous administration for us at the moment.

Q671 *Chairman:* Okay. We will try.
Mr O'Reilly: We can ask the Treasury.
Mr Brennan: We can certainly register your interest in it with the Treasury and the fact that you would like to see a copy of it.

Q672 *Chairman:* Can we have a private look at it on the guarantee that it goes nowhere but to the Members of the Committee?
Mr O'Reilly: It is papers of a previous administration so it is not for us. We cannot give a definitive response.

Q673 *Chairman:* Who would we have to ask?
Mr O'Reilly: Possibly through the NIO at the moment.
Mr Pengelly: It was prepared under the direction of the Secretary of State in the NIO.

Q674 *Chairman:* So the Secretary of State for Northern Ireland would have the authority to release this?
Mr O'Reilly: Probably after consulting the Treasury.
Chairman: We are seeing him on Wednesday so we will ask him and see what he has to say about it.

Q675 *Earl of Mar and Kellie:* I think we have already mentioned the Olympics. What I would like to ask is whether the Northern Ireland Executive is concerned about the fact that it was the Treasury which got almost complete control of the scheme, particularly when it came to deciding a particular activity is an English one or a United Kingdom one. Does the Northern Ireland Executive see that as being fair and the way it should be?
Mr Pengelly: There are a number of issues. Despite what we said on Barnett, there are areas where some independence, some objective dispute resolution process at this level of detail would be good, and the Olympics is a classic example of that. Our Minister's position, and I think it is a position that we share with the Scots and the Welsh, is we do not question that there are significant elements of the Olympics which are being taken forward on a UK-wide basis and it is absolutely appropriate that Barnett should not apply to it, but there is in excess of a billion pounds of clear regeneration work and that regeneration is taking place in England only, therefore the Barnett Formula should apply. This was debated in many forms with the Chief Secretary of the Treasury and the Treasury view was that, while under the rules of Barnett when you disaggregate a spending programme into the sub-components and look at each sub-component and build up a weighted comparability factor, the Olympics was just one budget and it was either all in or all out.

Q676 *Earl of Mar and Kellie:* One budget which the Treasury was in control of?
Mr Pengelly: Absolutely.

Q677 *Earl of Mar and Kellie:* We heard in Wales that there had been a Barnett claw back over some English health spending which had an under-spend and led to some of the Welsh health Barnett money being clawed back. Has anything like that happened?
Mr Pengelly: We were in exactly the same position as the Welsh. Prior to the announcement of the 2007 Comprehensive Spending Review, the Treasury introduced a downward adjustment to the Department of Health baseline and Scotland, Wales

and Northern Ireland took a negative Barnett consequential for that. Again, in the Pre-Budget Report last November there was an adjustment for the Department of Health in 2010-11 which is the result of a downward adjustment. That is a slightly different issue from the Olympics because the Treasury position is that is a straightforward application of Barnett and when the health budget goes up we get Barnett consequentials.

Q678 *Earl of Mar and Kellie:* Was it a little unfair in Northern Ireland because of the fact that it related to the fact that in England they had not spent all of their health money which they had been allocated?
Mr Pengelly: I am not sure whether you are referring to the baseline issue back in the 2007 CSR or the recent PBR issue because they are two slightly different issues. In terms of the former, the Treasury were saying the Department of Health had a track record of under-spend, therefore looking forward into the future Spending Review they were going to make a downward adjustment to their baseline. As much as we could feel aggrieved by that, it does seem to sit within the conceptual framework for Barnett, as ultimately looking forward they were adjusting the long term spending plans. The recent one, which may be the one the Welsh have articulated, is essentially that the Treasury are anticipating that an under-spend will happen in 2010-11 and that that should be subject to Barnett. Our view is that it should just fall as an under-spend and end-year flexibility should apply for the Department of Health. If we under-spend we have end-year flexibility. They are different issues but it is extending the reach of the Barnett Formula because it happens to suit a position.

Q679 *Chairman:* The decision on the Olympics, how did you actually hear about that? Did somebody just ring you up and say, "This is going to happen", or did you get a letter saying, "This is the Treasury view as to what should happen"?
Mr Pengelly: From memory, and I would need to check, the nature of a Spending Review is that we are in almost daily dialogue with the Treasury and I think it was just mentioned in the course of one of those conversations.

Q680 *Chairman:* Were you consulted on it or just told?
Mr Pengelly: We were just told. I think the Treasury might suggest there was some consultation and what they would be referring to is in advance of the UK bid to host the Olympics there may have been a discussion at political level as to whether the devolved administrations would support the UK bid, and the answer was clearly yes. That was not a discussion about the Barnett Formula comparability factors. There was no discussion or dialogue about the comparability factors for the Olympics.

Q681 *Earl of Mar and Kellie:* How much money does it cost Northern Ireland, have you any idea?
Mr Pengelly: In excess of 100 million.
Chairman: Appreciable.

Q682 *Lord Sewel:* Consequentials have been applied.
Mr O'Reilly: Yes. Is that just to the regeneration element?
Mr Pengelly: We have not quantified it precisely because the debate was always on the fundamental principle because the principle is so flawed. If you could get past the principle you could either say that we get full Barnett consequentials on the regeneration element or we get a weighted comparability factor on the totality of the Olympics budget, which is the way Barnett normally applies to any Whitehall department, we get a reduced comparability on every allocation as opposed to full comparability on a particular element. We never entered that level of debate because the Treasury would not go past the high level point.

Q683 *Earl of Mar and Kellie:* Is the Olympics issue the biggest issue of this type or have there been other ones?
Mr Pengelly: The other one of a similar scale and political difficulty was that at the point of the establishment of the devolved administrations, Scotland, Wales and Northern Ireland had complete flexibility to move between current and capital allocations. However, in the 2004 Spending Review the Treasury reduced that to 3 per cent flexibility, and in their 2007 Comprehensive Spending Review they removed the 3 per cent flexibility. The numbers might be slightly different but they are on a par with each other in terms of their impact.

Q684 *Lord Sewel:* And the justification?
Mr Pengelly: The justification is that it is important to treat the devolved administrations like a Whitehall department.
Mr O'Reilly: The Treasury will say it has got to do with the Golden Rule but, in fact, if you look at the absolute numbers here there is nothing that the devolved administration could have done with this capital budget that would have affected the Golden Rule.
Mr Pengelly: In the dialogue with the Treasury we worked out that the exposure was something like 0.03 per cent of total public expenditure. Scotland, Wales and Northern Ireland in the previous Comprehensive Spending Reviews have not made any movements from capital to current, but on the assumption we exercised the maximum flexibility it would have been

0.03 per cent. Our position was that we did not necessarily want to make those moves but it was important to have that flexibility in a changing environment.

Q685 *Earl of Mar and Kellie:* Perhaps we can go on and ask about the prospective devolution of policing and justice. Is this expected to be a straightforward transfer of monies allocated presumably to the NIO to yourselves or is it going to be a new baseline? Is it going to be a planned Formula bypass?

Mr O'Reilly: There are two issues in response to that question and I will ask Richard to deal with the first one. The first set of issues deal with the question are the present budgets that are in place for policing and justice, primarily in the NIO but also in the Northern Ireland Courts Service, adequate. Once a settlement and decision is reached on how much money should transfer, the second issue is how will we then apply Barnett, if we do apply Barnett, to that baseline moving forward. We see those as two important aspects.

Mr Pengelly: In terms of the adequacy, we are locked in a process of dialogue with the two main organisations of the Northern Ireland Office, which will include policing and prisons, and the Northern Ireland Courts Service, and the big issue there is the Legal Aid budget. In terms of the dialogue we are having with them, at the moment the information we have is data they have given to us, we have not gone through it in detail and quality assured it, and they are telling us that over the remaining two years of the current Spending Review there are pressures totalling some £500 million above and beyond the level of funding that they have in place. That is against total funding for the same period in the region of about three billion, so some very, very significant issues there that are being presented to us to manage. There are big issues in policing. There is a hearing loss issue of former police officers who were not given adequate hearing protection for firearms training. At the time of the agreement on the CSR outcome for the Northern Ireland Office, it was expected to be an issue that might amount to a few million pounds at most, but it is now heading towards £100 million. There are issues around capital, a big issue around pension arrangements for police officers arising purely as a consequence of a decision by the Home Secretary, not a decision by the Northern Ireland Office. The other big issue we have in the Courts Service is the Legal Aid budget. Funding for Legal Aid is presented to us as an issue in the region of £60 million to £100 million and Treasury has acknowledged there is a problem there but we are still drilling into the detail of that. There are some very significant issues.

Mr O'Reilly: I was going to supplement that answer by saying there is also the question of how much money will transfer, but also out of the cake that exists at the moment how much needs to be held back to fund the future of NIO, as it is referred to, in other words the residual responsibilities that will remain with the NIO. A major issue that is being considered is how do you continue to fund the various inquiries that are in place or, indeed, may still be put into place in the future. The lesson from those is they have turned out to be quite expensive exercises. That is a fundamental issue which leads on to a related issue which is, as you may know, the mechanism for funding the Scotland Office and Wales Office is basically a top slice off the Barnett allocation to the Scottish Executive and the Welsh Assembly Government. We understand that while that does create some sense of friction between the Scottish Executive and the Treasury, by and large because the sums of money are relatively small, ie it is mainly maintaining the administrative offices in place for those two Offices, in the case of Northern Ireland the functions that will be retained and continue to be operated by NIO will be much more substantial, so there is an issue as to how those will be funded into the future. That is another aspect of the discussion that is continuing.

Q686 *Earl of Mar and Kellie:* The last thing I want to ask you is, is the future budget stable enough to become a new baseline or is there always going to be a need for a bit of a Formula bypass should the situation become less secure, for example?

Mr O'Reilly: Richard and Mike can come in on this. Unfortunately, within the last couple of weeks we have had an illustration where suddenly substantially new financial pressures can emerge because of a deterioration in the security situation. That is obviously an element of instability and the debate has been had around here as to what would have had happened if policing and justice had been devolved, say, a year ago to Northern Ireland. The point you have raised moves on to the second strand of this, which is what happens into the future. The context and background here is the Barnett Formula has not been applied to the NIO's policing and justice functions since 1998/99 because the Treasury acknowledged what they wanted to do was effectively bring down the scale of that expenditure moving into a period of stability whereas previously it would have been much higher in a period of instability. They openly acknowledged that what they wanted to do over those years was to bring that baseline figure down, which they have been doing. That is one issue. There is also a smaller issue around the fact that part of the expenditure that will transfer has never been subject to Barnett ever, namely the Courts Service expenditure. The basic question is do we put in place arrangements to reactivate Barnett in respect of policing and justice and, if so, what will be the detailed issues arising from that.

Q687 *Chairman:* I am sorry, I am getting a bit lost on this. If you are going to get policing and the Courts Service presumably you would want an alteration to the block?
Mr O'Reilly: The first issue is what size will the baseline be.

Q688 *Chairman:* That is what I am saying, you will have to alter the block and Barnett eventually, if need be, will apply but only on the same basis that it applies to anything else.
Mr O'Reilly: There are two options. You could decide not to apply Barnett to policing and justice.

Q689 *Chairman:* And do what?
Mr O'Reilly: Simply continue to operate on a negotiated basis with the Treasury. The downside of that is it would be inconsistent with the rest of the Northern Ireland block. However, I suppose the single biggest reason for considering that comes back to the previous question around the stability of this function and this budget.

Q690 *Chairman:* I can see Northern Ireland is a special case obviously, one accepts that, there are particular security problems that we do not have in the rest of the UK.
Mr O'Reilly: I think it is fair to say our view would be if the baseline figure was got right then the logical conclusion would be that Barnett should also be reinstated in respect of that tranche of block expenditure as well.

Q691 *Chairman:* So you are in negotiation with the Treasury about the baseline?
Mr O'Reilly: Yes. There are discussions continuing.
Mr Pengelly: We are locked in dialogue. Our main task at the moment is to try to understand the scale of the pressures.

Q692 *Chairman:* The pressures this end?
Mr Pengelly: No, the pressures in the area of policing and security because that fundamentally determines the way forward. If there are a number of unfunded pressures and if that transfers across and becomes part of the block, the only way the Executive could deal with those issues would be to divert funding that currently sits with, for example health and education and the range of other services for which they are responsible. If those pressures are not specifically funded, for that responsibility to devolve at the moment would have to be on the basis that there remains an open dialogue with the Treasury about additional security funding the way a Whitehall

department works. There are issues about when it comes within Barnett. In terms of total stability and being absolutely sure at the point of transfer that the services are adequately funded, that would make a very compelling case for a Barnett-based approach, but we are not there yet. We have recently initiated this process of dialogue to try and get to the bottom of that.

Q693 *Chairman:* I am sorry to be slightly pedantic about it, and it is a point you made very early on in this discussion, but you are using Barnett there as including the block, the block as well as variations in the block.
Mr Pengelly: Yes.

Q694 *Chairman:* When you say whether Barnett applies, you mean whether it applies to the baseline and whether it applies to the variations.
Mr Pengelly: Yes.
Mr O'Reilly: Barnett will only ever apply to the variations.

Q695 *Chairman:* Of course it does, except the way you are using the phrase "the Barnett Formula" would include negotiations about the size of the block.
Mr O'Reilly: We would see these negotiations about the size of the baseline for policing and justice to transfer as being a precursor to a decision on whether or not Barnett is reinstated.
Chairman: Okay. I think I understand that.

Q696 *Lord Sewel:* I want to talk about convergence and bypassing, but before I do that can I ask two questions. One is, is the population of Northern Ireland going up or going down?
Mr Brennan: As far as I can recollect it has been increasing in the last couple of years.

Q697 *Lord Sewel:* That has some consequences on squeeze. Secondly, in Wales there is quite a lively debate about the Barnett Formula and whether it should remain or go and in Scotland there is also quite a lively debate, not so much in the press but amongst the political class and the academics. Is there a debate in Northern Ireland about Barnett or is it something that is not really referred to?
Mr O'Reilly: I think it would be fair to say there is less of an overt political debate here about the issue. It is also a reflection simply of the fact that we recognise whatever happens to Barnett shall not be driven, shall we say, by Northern Ireland considerations, that Northern Ireland will deal with the consequences of whatever happens to Barnett because we are such a small proportion of the total, even of the 15 per cent of the total UK population affected by Barnett we are a relatively small proportion of that, so our concern

would be to highlight if and when such proposals as emerge for any change that we will want to engage on that.

Mr Brennan: On the issue of public understanding and awareness of Barnett, I think I would have to say that a lot of the public debate here about public expenditure allocations in Northern Ireland, for example, is quite ill-informed. The public do not readily appreciate the stricture that Parliament imposed on the devolved administrations in terms of you have a limited pot of money to use and at times you get this frustrating argument breaking out about going back to the Treasury to get more money. There is not a great awareness about how Barnett actually works on the ground here. On the issue of convergence, it is very difficult to say. You would think over the last ten years or so when there have been quite high levels of public expenditure across the four countries that the mathematic construction of the Barnett Formula would mean that there should be some convergence. The only proxy we have to try and get some insight into that is obviously the Treasury's public expenditure statistical analysis tables at the back where they have the territorial analysis and that shows, for example, the identifiable public expenditure in Northern Ireland has gone from 130 down to about 126 in the latest PESA publication. That suggests there has been some convergence over recent years and that does seem intuitively correct because public expenditure has been quite high.

Mr O'Reilly: There has been an intensive public debate, particularly just prior to devolution, on an area which I understand falls just outside your remit, which is the whole question of fiscal measures and tax autonomy. For example, there was a whole debate that happened in the period before devolution around comparable levels of corporation tax and the argument was put forward by some that corporation tax in Northern Ireland should be realigned with the levels in the Republic of Ireland to make us more competitive. That led into much wider interaction with the Treasury but also consideration of the European-wide dimensions of varying tax rates within particular countries.

Q698 *Lord Sewel:* Could we concentrate on convergence. The point was made, and you are absolutely right, that the Treasury wants to put more and more into the Formula and avoid the opportunity for bypass. I think that is inevitable in a fully devolved situation because you remove the opportunity for secretaries of state to sort things out, you just rely on a formula because a property of the Formula does mean that if it is applied in its pure way there is a dynamic towards convergence. You are also increasing in population, so that will add to a downward pressure on per head expenditure as well.

Why then do you want to stick with Barnett because you are going to have a significant squeeze?

Mr Brennan: I suppose the immediate response to that is we do not know what the counterfactual would be. It goes back to this question of if you decide not to go with Barnett and you go into the world of constructing some sort of needs-based system it would be very difficult to form a view on where Northern Ireland or, indeed, Scotland or Wales might be in terms of relative needs.

Q699 *Lord Sewel:* Do you accept that if you stick with Barnett and continue to have an increasing population you will face significant downward pressures on public expenditure?

Mr Brennan: The mathematics of Barnett suggest there will inevitably be what they call asymptotic convergence. That is inevitable.

Q700 *Lord Sewel:* Do politicians realise that?

Mr O'Reilly: I suppose the history of this has shown that over the 30 years of Barnett there has not been a major problem in the way the Formula has operated, so I suspect because of our historical experience we tend not to anticipate, perhaps incorrectly or unwisely, a major problem moving ahead around this issue for the foreseeable future.

Q701 *Lord Sewel:* That was because we were all at it doing bypassing as much as we could, was it not?

Mr O'Reilly: It is that combined with the pace and rate of increase in total public expenditure and now that we are entering a period where it is likely that public expenditure growth will be much lower than it has been over the last decade, say, then the convergence will lessen.

Mr Brennan: It acts as a dampener.

Mr Pengelly: Mike's point is very strong on the counterfactual position. Barnett in the last Spending Review delivered for the Northern Ireland Administration in the region of 1 per cent real terms growth per annum. If we compare that to the likely outcome from a subjective dialogue with the Treasury we could point to many Whitehall departments, which I suspect would be likely to present as compelling a case as we could for strong need, receiving flat cash or, indeed, cash reduction in terms of outcomes. It is trying to get a sense of what you are comparing it with. Barnett may not deliver as much as people want, but I suspect it delivers more than we would receive by another method.

Q702 *Chairman:* I still have problems with the application of a Formula which is based upon population ratios 30 years on from the time when it was first introduced.

Mr Brennan: Although the population ratios are updated now on an annual basis, that was not the case until ten years ago and that was a fundamental flaw. The Treasury agreed in 1997, I think, to use annual updated population shares.

Q703 Lord Sewel: The recalibration applies to the increment, it does not apply to the block. We are back to population increase again. If your population is increasing the block refers to a level of provision for a smaller population.

Mr Brennan: Yes.

Mr O'Reilly: Just reflecting on your comments there, part of the discussion we are having has to be constrained by your terms of reference but if you get into a more abstract discussion on these issues you inevitably draw yourself into issues of revenues and regional revenues and the issues that those raise because if you look at models of distributions to regions within other states in the world it is usual that there is an interaction between needs and local revenue raising or, as they talk about it, fiscal effort. In a sense, the UK system sets aside and takes as a given there is a national tax system and that influences how we approach these issues of dealing with expenditure levels in devolved administrations.

Q704 Chairman: Yes. I suppose if you had responsibility for social security expenditure you would do things rather differently. I think that is certainly true.

Mr O'Reilly: Inevitably.

Q705 Earl of Mar and Kellie: It is also interesting that when you were talking briefly about the possibility of varying corporation tax in Northern Ireland, that was not going to bring the Northern Ireland Executive any more money and it was not going to reduce it because that would have merely reduced the amount flowing to the Treasury, there would be no increase in income.

Mr Brennan: No, it would have cost both the Northern Ireland block and the UK Exchequer. There would have been a net cost to both.

Q706 Earl of Mar and Kellie: So if that had been implemented there might have been a claw back?

Mr Brennan: The implications of the distant, now infamous, *Azores* judgment would imply that the shortfall in revenue, in corporation tax, would have had to have been covered by the Northern Ireland devolved administration, but at a wider UK level there would have been a tax distortion as well in terms of shortfall in revenue through transfer pricing and also lower tax-take at a UK level. What Sir David Varney estimated was somewhere in the order of two billion over ten years.

Mr O'Reilly: Against that you have got to factor in that because of the market failure in our local economy there is a lot of public expenditure intervention, but with a different fiscal regime that market failure would reduce and, therefore, the need for public expenditure would reduce in terms of those issues.

Q707 Earl of Mar and Kellie: So there would be GVA. It becomes a very complicated way of working it out.

Mr O'Reilly: It does, yes.

Q708 Lord Sewel: There is another issue which is at the end of the day through the Barnett consequentials it is driven by an English pattern of expenditure. Is that not really incompatible with the concept of devolution because devolution is there to enable the territories to develop their own priorities, their own programmes, and over time it is clearly the case in Scotland that the profile of provision is diverging significantly from the profile of provision in England yet the expenditure reference is the English profile?

Mr O'Reilly: What you are saying is simply stating what is the truth, which is the variations in the Barnett Formula from one Spending Review to the next are determined by how the expenditure allocations work out in the Whitehall Spending Review negotiations. To take a simplistic example, we are always aware that if there was a very major push to increase defence expenditure substantially we would get no Barnett consequentials, therefore that would have a comparatively detrimental effect on us, whereas if there was a very major push to increase expenditure in the Health Service, because we have high Barnett comparability factors that would benefit us. In an absolute sense you are right, but then what other mechanisms do you have to lessen that distortion of basically being driven by Whitehall allocations. The main one is when there is money allocated to the devolved administrations via Barnett it is for the devolved administrations to decide how those sums are distributed amongst the various services for which the devolved administrations are responsible. Going back to the 2004 example, this is why the Treasury reintroduced the split between resource and capital and constrained the movement between those two control totals. It meant that, in effect, variations to our capital were being driven by what was the consequence of Whitehall departments' requirements for capital allocations and in a sense that accentuated the problem for us that you have highlighted.

Q709 Lord Sewel: This is a silly question in a way. In England, water is privatised and in Northern Ireland it is not. Do you get any money for the water?

Mr O'Reilly: No, we do not.

Mr Pengelly: I think that is a very important issue. The Treasury answer is that this reflects a policy choice by the devolved administration. Clearly, as regards the Barnett Formula, if things were in the private sector and outwith the public sector in England there is no public expenditure so there will never be a Barnett consequence and that is a very understandable and logical position. The Treasury view would be in essence that exacerbates the "Barnett squeeze" because you are having to divert money flowing from the Barnett Formula to services outwith, but there is an available solution to devolved administrations to deal with those issues, which takes us back towards the issue of revenue raising and I know you do not want to get into that. That service in the public sector as well as the private sector is funded by charging in England and Wales. If there is a policy choice by a devolved administration not to do that, the Treasury would not see that as an issue at all to do with the Barnett Formula, that is an issue purely about policy choices by a devolved administration.

Q710 *Lord Sewel:* What happens if the Health Service in England becomes an insurance-based service?

Mr O'Reilly: We would have an issue to consider.

Mr Pengelly: In many ways, certainly from the public perspective, notwithstanding devolution, there still is a National Health Service in the United Kingdom. The changes between England and the devolved administrations tend to be around the margins. Clearly a change of such fundamental significance as that would cause the health ministers in the devolved administrations to pause for thought if nothing else.

Lord Sewel: You certainly would not have any Barnett consequentials, would you?

Q711 *Chairman:* It does increase the block.

Mr O'Reilly: This line of questioning does get into something which I noticed you raised in the various questions that you might raise with us, which is the issue of the interaction. I know that national tax may not be outside the remit but local revenue raising capacity in terms of the council tax in Scotland and Wales and the rates system here obviously interacts with the overall capacity of a devolved administration to deliver services. That has a particular implication here because while council tax in Scotland and Wales, as I understand it, goes exclusively to support the local councils, in Northern Ireland part of our rates revenue is used to support the services funded by the Northern Ireland Executive and that simply reflects the historical fact that the Executive is responsible here for education provision and certain other services that in the rest of the UK the local government would have a key role

to play in in delivering the funding of those services. There is a further interaction around those issues locally.

Q712 *Chairman:* Can I come back to your papers in 2001-02. Did the Treasury, as far as you know, produce anything on their side of the argument?

Mr Brennan: No. We copied the Treasury into the work that we were doing as it evolved for comment but we got no formal critique back on the methodology we employed or the results that we produced.

Q713 *Chairman:* You did not gather that they were doing a needs assessment or something of that sort at that time?

Mr Brennan: No, not that I am aware of.

Q714 *Chairman:* So it was just Northern Ireland?

Mr Brennan: Yes.

Mr O'Reilly: It is fair to say that they were not enthusiastic about the fact that we were doing it, put it that way.

Q715 *Chairman:* I wonder why! Thank you very much, I think we have had a good run round the course and it is very interesting indeed. I have to tell you my experience so far with evidence is that on the whole some form of introduction of the needs assessment does seem to be fairly popular with many people we have talked to.

Mr O'Reilly: Our concern is with the complexity and subjectivity of such a needs assessment. I suppose I would say an essential requirement is that there would need to be some form of independent/objective oversight because our experience would indicate it could create difficulties for us if it was left exclusively to the Treasury to arbitrate.

Chairman: I think we would all agree with that.

Q716 *Lord Sewel:* If you could be absolutely copper-bottomed guaranteed that the needs assessment would be done by an independent, non-Treasury outfit, something like the Australian Commonwealth Grants Commission, would that change your view on needs assessment?

Mr Brennan: It would certainly mean that we would probably have less fear of what I call the Barnett consequential world that may exist out there. Basically we have got a great fear of the unknown.

Q717 *Chairman:* The other general point we have been hearing, particularly since we have been here, is you should not interfere with Barnett at the moment because Northern Ireland needs a period in which to let the devolved government bed in and the problems begin to resolve themselves rather more, but further down the road that might be a different proposition. Do you feel that?

Mr Brennan: This goes back to the earlier point I made about the level of understanding in the political class here about how Northern Ireland is funded. There is still a lot of education to be done out there in terms of where resources come from and how they are used. For example, if you were to impose a needs assessment model now the external shock that could bring to the decision-making process of the devolved administration could be very destabilising. Once you bestow credibility and there is greater understanding about how resources are allocated to Northern Ireland in that mature environment then you do have a debate.

Mr O'Reilly: There is a further interaction here with another major issue, which is the dependence of the Northern Ireland economy on public spending. It is an historical fact that we have an underdeveloped private sector, perhaps for obvious historical reasons, and people would say it is a clear objective of the Executive to build the size, coherence and strength of the private sector here but we would say that is going

to take a bit of time to allow that to happen and to reduce the scale of dependence in Northern Ireland, which I think most commentators accept is excessive dependence, on the public sector.

Chairman: That is a very long-term prospect.

Q718 *Lord Sewel:* So a "Barnett squeeze" would be economically attractive in that it would cease the crowding out of the private sector by the public sector, is that the sort of argument that you could make?

Mr Brennan: The key problem is the size of the private sector. It is not that the public sector in Northern Ireland is too large, it accounts for about two-thirds of regional GVA, but if you look at the public sector in Northern Ireland and compare it with Scotland, Wales or England in terms of the number of public sector employees or services provided it is very, very similar, it is that the private sector in Northern Ireland is far too small.

Mr O'Reilly: The problem is the overall size of the economy is too small here because you have an underdeveloped private sector.

Chairman: Thank you very much indeed.

Memorandum by Professor Colin Thain

RESPONSES TO SUGGESTED QUESTIONS FOR ACADEMIC WITNESSES IN NORTHERN IRELAND PRIOR TO THE EVIDENCE SESSION ON 27 MARCH 2009

DEVELOPMENT OF THE FORMULA

Q1. *What do you understand was the purpose of the Barnett Formula was when it was first introduced, and has its purpose changed over time? Was it designed to reduce tensions arising from disparities in public spending per head of population? Has it succeeded in resolving such tensions?*

ANSWER:

1. It is important to note that like so many developments in British public administration the Barnett formula evolved from rules and precedents going back well before the 1970s. There was a tradition of allocating resources to Scotland through the Goschen formula from 1891 giving Scotland 11/80th of British spending on comparable programmes, this continued long after population shifts meant this was generous to Scotland, and for education the formula remained in use until the end of the 1950s; in Northern Ireland from 1920 to 1938 special bilateral negotiations between the Treasury and the Northern Ireland Ministry of Finance enabled the Province to by-pass normal UK Department-HM Treasury discussions. By 1938 the two departments agreed the principle that Northern Ireland citizens should have parity of service provision with the rest of the UK. By 1942 it was recognised that this meant the province would require extra resources, and in 1950 a *de-facto* allocative arrangement based on local needs was established.[1] Although during the 1960s formula-based systems of allocation lapsed, the principle of using allocations agreed for English departments was the benchmark for discussions between the three territorial departments (the Welsh Office having been established in 1964). Moreover, the principle evolved that Secretaries of State (and the Northern Ireland Government, pre-direct rule) would have discretion in dividing the pot of resources and in practice block grant arrangements were in place. Thus some of the building blocks of what was to become immortalised as the Barnett Formula were already part of the non-statutory rules-of-the-game agreed between HM Treasury and its counterparts in Edinburgh, Belfast and Cardiff.

2. The immediate antecedents to the Barnett formula were the debates prior to the plans to devolve legislative and executive power to Scotland and Wales during the last years of the 1974–79 Labour Government. The Treasury led an inter-departmental review to try and establish an "objective" measure for needs for each part of the UK. The *Needs Assessment Study*[2] worked on the assumption that what each part of the UK received

in identifiable expenditure should ensure "broadly the same level of public services" and be "allocated according to their relative needs". The report was replete with caveats about the difficulty of deciding on needs and then measuring these objectively rather than subjectively. It concluded that in 1976–77 Scotland should receive per capita spending of 116, Wales 109 and Northern Ireland 131 on the basis of spending in England of 100. The reality was that Scotland received 123, Northern Ireland 136 and Wales 101—suggesting the baseline benefitted Scotland and Northern Ireland but not Wales. The Barnett formula then introduced in 1978 was based on a population balance between England, Scotland and Wales of 85, 10 and 5. Northern Ireland was treated differently with spending based Northern Ireland's share (2.75 per cent) of UK population, rather than a share of GB population used for the rest of the UK. The NIO was also ring-fenced outside the process with separate discussions between the Treasury and NIO on spending related to security, law and order and constitutional matters. A significant element of Barnett was that the territories received increments based on spending increases (or decreases) in comparable English functional programmes. It was therefore based on marginal changes in resources not the overall level. Once the increments were added up a block of resources was then created with a great deal of discretion given to the respective Secretaries of State to allocate down to local programmes. Barnett implied that the Treasury accepted that the levels of spending were roughly acceptable enough to justify a formula based on population rather than some more complex needs formula. Wales lost out in the setting of the baseline based on the historic accumulation of resources up to 1978. Thereafter the intention of the Treasury was that over a considerable time there would be convergence of expenditure toward population share. As spending continued to rise over time, there would be relative gains to England and Wales and losses to Scotland and Northern Ireland (cuts in spending levels would reverse this). The problem for both Scotland and Northern Ireland was that the formula was not revised until 1993–94, and the Conservative Government failed to cut spending thus ensuring the dynamic of the formula would produce convergence with English spending levels.

3. There is no evidence that the Barnett formula was anything other than a relatively short-term fix to potential problems created by devolution proposals which in the end failed to pass referenda in Scotland and Wales. It survived long after those initial circumstances passed into political history. That it survived was the result of inertia, the administrative *rationality* of the process, and some inherent flexibility in the rules of the game. It cannot be stressed enough how important it was to finance officials in Scotland and Wales (and by implication Northern Ireland) that the Treasury (a) left them alone to determine the value and effectiveness of particular programmes and (b) allowed their Secretaries of State to determine the allocation within a block grant between local departments and agencies, without recourse to the Treasury in Whitehall. English departments thus bore the brunt of Treasury scrutiny. This was rational for both the Treasury and the territories. In addition, for most of the period after 1978 the Territories could bid "outside the block" in exceptional circumstances. A careful balancing act was maintained with the territories seeking to extend comparability where appropriate and ask for more than the increments received, but not to press too hard so that the Treasury would then seek to open up territorial spending to greater scrutiny. For the Treasury it was administratively easier to devote scarce staff resources to scrutinising English departments than to delve into all spending in the UK. Thus a typically British solution evolved which just about worked, which maintained the closed world of administrative discretion based on uncodified and non-statutory rules.

APPLICATION OF THE FORMULA IN PRACTICE

Q2. *Do you consider that convergence in per capita levels of public spending on the English level was an intentional feature of the formula, or merely an incidental one? Do you think it is overall a beneficial or harmful feature of the working of the Formula?*

ANSWER:

4. As I note above, convergence was an intentional feature of the formula although the Treasury did not expect the formula to last as long as it has.[3] Given that more than 80 per cent of public spending is allocated to England, and that we still have what is in essence a unitary state (albeit with quasi-federal features), I would argue convergence in per capita levels of public spending is on balance a beneficial feature of the formula. Creating greater *equity* across the UK in terms of public policy outcomes should be the province of other public policies, many of which can be UK based and many determined according to local priorities and the operation of local politics, rather than the budgetary allocation system. The overall budgetary system needs to maintain a large element of convergence to ensure its acceptability to the majority of UK citizens. It is important to note that the current formula applies to DEL (departmental expenditure limits) or what might be called discretionary expenditure, rather than to AME (aggregate managed expenditure), which includes demand-led spending such as social security benefits and tax credits. Thus the total public spending allocation

system does include elements outside Barnett which in effect adjust spending to some elements of local needs (higher unemployment in Northern Ireland or higher working tax credits as a result of poorer income distribution).

NEED FOR REFORM/ALTERNATIVES TO THE EXISTING FORMULA

Q3. *What criteria do you consider to be important in assessing the success or otherwise of the present formula, and of any possible replacement to it? Would a fair or equitable allocation system necessarily be a needs-based system?*

ANSWER:

5. I would place a great deal of emphasis on the importance of the current formula in being *administratively* easy to apply, and the adjunct rules allowing a great deal of *discretion* to the territorial administrations in allocating resources to local priorities within the envelope of the block grant. If the Union is to survive it is important that the allocative mechanism used is in a rough and ready way based on population shares.

6. I would accept the tenor of the question that in practice there are many definitions of *fairness* when discussing budgetary policies. I am also sceptical that it is possible to arrive at a *needs based* allocation regarded as balanced and fair to all parts, regions and nations of the UK. As I note above, the division of spending into DEL and AME does allow spending based on needs to automatically feed through to deprived parts of the UK—assuming policies for ensuring take-up of benefits are applied equally across the UK.

Q4. *To what extent are there tensions between allocating expenditure according to such criteria as need, efficiency and effectiveness? How would you suggest those tensions might be resolved?*

ANSWER:

7. There clearly are tensions between the various criteria by which spending could be allocated. The current Barnett formula gives greater precedence to *efficiency* and *effectiveness* than to *needs-based* elements. I remain to be convinced that the way to deal with the political, social and economic inequalities in the UK is through wholesale changes to the Barnett formula. If the Union is to be maintained in more or less its current form, the onus should be on changing public policies, and changing the way in which those policies are delivered rather than through changes to the allocative mechanism. Greater emphasis on the demand (and by implication needs based) led element of spending outside the DEL process would be one way to help resolve tensions. If demand for social security payments rise differentially across regions, this is easier to "sell" as part of the social contract implied by the Union, than highly contentious debates about which parts of the UK have greater need.

Q5. *How effective would it be to use population or other proxy indicators of need, such as inverse GDP or perhaps social security spending per head, as alternatives to carrying out a detailed needs assessment? What would be the overall effect, in terms of the distribution of spending, of adopting those?*

ANSWER:

8. I can see many problems with using inverse GDP or social spending per head as proxy measures for need. GDP data is notoriously difficult to predict and is subject to considerable revision. Social security spending per head represents only one element of needs (and as I note above is already part of the non-Barnett element of public spending which acts as a social stabiliser). In Northern Ireland, for example there are needs which result from historic inequalities of opportunity in education and skills which would not be picked up through social security benefit indicators. The costs of separate schools and even health centres based on the sectarian divide cannot easily be calculated, but remain a significant element of any needs assessment for the Province (and could apply equally to parts of lowland Scotland) and other parts of the UK—the North East or North West of England—for example would not have particular elements of needs allowed for.

Q6. *Assuming there is to be a mechanism for distributing financial resources from the UK Government to the Devolved Administrations, as the main source of revenue for the Devolved Administrations, do you think that a needs-based formula is the only real alternative to the current Formula? What other alternatives might there be?*

ANSWER:

9. I would propose a Barnett-plus approach to reforming the current formula. Essentially the existing population based formula should be applied to comparable Departmental Spending, but a more explicit bidding process outside that allocation should be set up allowing the devolved administrations to bid for a *Reserve* of additional spending. This would be set as a proportion of total DEL and could also be open to the

regions of England (via the Ministers for the regions) to bid for specific additional resources seeking to address quantifiable social and economic need. The bids would be made on the basis of programmes to be funded for the three years of the Survey cycle (assuming there is another CSR in the near future). Allocations would be made on the basis of submission to the Treasury and final adjudication would be before a Cabinet Committee made up of senior non-departmental ministers. I would be open to persuasion that adjudication could be through the Australian model (in Q9) below or the Canadian model, rather than via a Cabinet Committee.

DATA QUALITY AND AVAILABILITY

Q7. *Are there still problems relating to the collection, quality or availability of data on the distribution of public spending and its effects? What issues are there on data about indicators of need and tax revenues?*

ANSWER:

10. We still have some way to go to have more reliable data on the distribution of spending and on need and tax revenues. The most pressing relate to assigning tax revenue where there is an HQ in one region for purely administrative purposes whilst there is a greater distribution of outlets in other parts of the UK—does this over-accentuate the dominance of London and the South East? How far can the administrative and HQ spending of UK departments be assigned more broadly when many departments (such as the Treasury and Cabinet Office) are effectively both English and UK departments?; how far should the MoD's central HQ spending be allocated outside London?. Much of this is the product of the failure by successive governments to move civil service jobs outside London. I am sure we could learn from comparative research on the way Canada, Australia or Germany arrive at data measures upon which to build fiscal transfer policies.

DECISION MAKING AND DISPUTE RESOLUTION

Q8. *Most writers consider that procedural fairness and transparency are important aspects of any system of financing the devolved administration, and that this an area in which the present arrangements are defective. Do you agree? What information should be published or other processes adopted to improve procedural transparency?*

ANSWER:

11. Transparency has been improved since the Treasury published the basic handbook on funding arrangements for the territories after each Comprehensive Spending Review.[4] Prior to 1999 researchers relied on occasional morsels from Parliamentary Written Statements or off-the record discussions with officials. It is now possible to track programmes and sub-programmes for English/UK Departments deemed comparable with spending in the territories, and read explanations about how different elements of spending are treated using the Barnett Formula. However, this only goes part of the way to opening up the process. It would greatly help if the Treasury published the actual increments distributed to the territories in the construction of each of the three block grants—it would then be possible to see how the territories had decided to allocate more or less than comparable spending in England. It would also enhance procedural transparency if details of bids outside the Barnett formula made by the territories were published, and outcomes agreed with the Treasury clearly outlined. The machinery for operating the concordats between Whitehall, Westminster and the Territories needs to be dusted off, oiled and given more regular outings, and minutes of meetings between Ministers published.

Q9. *How workable would be a UK Territorial Grants Board given that its Australian prototype, the Commonwealth Grants Commission, operates in a symmetrical, federal system of government, with substantive fiscal autonomy for the States? Can a Territorial Grants Board improve procedural fairness or provide a system which is deemed legitimate?*

ANSWER:

12. There is a need to debate comparative experiences and see what can be learnt by the UK. Although beyond the scope of the Committee's inquiry, there is a prior issue to be addressed—creating more explicit rules for our quasi-federal polity. If a Territorial Grants Board were to be created, we need to have clearer rules about representation (should English Regions through RDAs or regional assemblies be part of the process?), dispute adjudication, and whether a statutory framework should replace the "gentlemen's agreements" of the Concordats (as they so anachronistically define themselves). As so often in the analysis of apparently technical budgetary procedures, the real political issues which lie beneath are about constitutions, rules and procedural norms.

NOTES

[1] Discussed in Colin Thain and Maurice Wright, *The Treasury and Whitehall: The Planning and Control of Public Expenditure, 1976-1993* (Oxford: Oxford University Press, 1995), ch 14.

[2] HM Treasury, *Needs Assessment—Report*, Report of an interdepartmental study coordinated by HM Treasury on the Relative Public Expenditure Needs in England, Wales and Northern Ireland (London: HMSO, 1979).

[3] In recent discussions with Treasury officials as part of a current research project—the Treasury under New Labour (www.treasuryproject.org)—it was apparent that officials who deal with territorial expenditure are as surprised as outsiders that the system has survived more than 20 years. Lord Barnett is also on record as expressing surprise at the longevity of the formula to which his name was assigned.

[4] HM Treasury, *Funding the Scottish Parliament, National Assembly for Wales and Northern Ireland Assembly: Statement of Funding Policy*, 5th Edition (October 2007) [available from http://www.hm-treasury.gov.uk/d/pbr_csr07_funding591.pdf]

22 March 2009

Memorandum by Professor John Simpson

Please find below my written response to your questions in advance to your visit to Belfast on 27 March 2009.

DEVELOPMENT OF THE FORMULA

1. What do you understand was the purpose of the Barnett Formula was when it was first introduced, and has its purpose changed over time? Was it designed to reduce tensions arising from disparities in public spending per head of population? Has it succeeded in resolving such tensions?

The Barnett Formula was a useful expedient to reduce the need for detailed negotiations between the Treasury and each of the devolved administrations. Only as a secondary consequence was the convergence feature of significance. The expectation that it would significantly reduce disparities has now become a source of tension since the principle that equal spending per head would be a desirable outcome is likely to be challenged.

Northern Ireland is sometimes argued to have a very generous allocation of public spending as a result of the Barnett Formula. The apparently high per capita spending figures are distorted by the exceptional comparisons for spending on law and order, justice and policing. These services are still reserved to Westminster and even when devolved will merit a separate needs assessment outwith the annual Barnett adjustments.

APPLICATION OF THE FORMULA IN PRACTICE

2. Do you consider that convergence in per capita levels of public spending on the English level was an intentional feature of the formula, or merely an incidental one? Do you think it is overall a beneficial or harmful feature of the working of the Formula?

The ambiguity on the convergence objective lies between the direction of change (narrowing the gaps) and the final result (equal spending per head). The lack of clarity remains. Ideally an infrequent needs assessment (say every five years) should be followed by an allocation to each devolved administration based on need (possibly a figure such as 3.5 per cent for Northern Ireland) rather than a population ratio.

NEED FOR REFORM/ALTERNATIVES TO THE EXISTING FORMULA

3. What criteria do you consider to be important in assessing the success or otherwise of the present formula, and of any possible replacement to it? Would a fair or equitable allocation system necessarily be a needs-based system?

A critical assumption is that the intention is to give the devolved administrations a significant degree of choice in the deployment of resources. A needs based system should, therefore, avoid creating an expectation of direct parity in every service. That would transform devolution into only a form of administration. A composite needs indicator should suffice. This would mean that devolution allowed for (but did not necessarily mean) differences in outcomes.

4. *To what extent are there tensions between allocating expenditure according to such criteria as need, efficiency and effectiveness? How would you suggest those tensions might be resolved?*

The Barnett formula has the merit of having a justification based on historic trends and approximates to a needs based allocation. It leaves efficiency and effectiveness as issues for the devolved authorities. On a routine basis, this is an appropriate form of delegation.

5. *How effective would it be to use population or other proxy indicators of need, such as inverse GDP or perhaps social security spending per head, as alternatives to carrying out a detailed needs assessment? What would be the overall effect, in terms of the distribution of spending, of adopting those?*

Something akin to an inverse GVA per head indicator should be tested. A new formula would not necessarily change the distribution of spending.

6. *Assuming there is to be a mechanism for distributing financial resources from the UK Government to the Devolved Administrations, as the main source of revenue for the Devolved Administrations, do you think that a needs-based formula is the only real alternative to the current Formula? What other alternatives might there be?*

A population ratio weighted for some indicator of needs, or an assessed needs factor is possibly the best method of combining simplicity and devolution. However, this does not consider the merits or otherwise of a greater degree of devolution of fiscal charges. These options have been developed and challenged in the report by Sir David Varney.

Data Quality and Availability

7. *Are there still problems relating to the collection, quality or availability of data on the distribution of public spending and its effects? What issues are there on data about indicators of need and tax revenues?*

Yes. The present reporting and accounting systems do not demonstrate to people outside the official departments how the Barnett allocation is calculated. The outcome is accepted without detailed challenge. The accounting format for the complete devolved budget should also be made clearer in regular or annual publications.

Decision Making and Dispute Resolution

8. *Most writers consider that procedural fairness and transparency are important aspects of any system of financing the devolved administration, and that this an area in which the present arrangements are defective. Do you agree? What information should be published or other processes adopted to improve procedural transparency?*

See comments to question 7.

9. *How workable would be a UK Territorial Grants Board given that its Australian prototype, the Commonwealth Grants Commission, operates in a symmetrical, federal system of government, with substantive fiscal autonomy for the States? Can a Territorial Grants Board improve procedural fairness or provide a system which is deemed legitimate?*

A formal post-budget review (after the UK budget) with the devolved administrations to consider the implications for them would be useful to demonstrate the consequential linkages.

If devolution becomes more complex, with fiscal variables and/or different forms of access to capital funds, then the relationships would need to be formalised with guidelines on permitted discretionary variations.

March 2009

Examination of Witnesses

Witnesses: MR MICHAEL SMYTH, Head, Department of Economics, University of Ulster; PROFESSOR JOHN SIMPSON, Independent analyst, former economist at Queen's University Belfast; and PROFESSOR COLIN THAIN, University of Ulster, examined.

Q719 Chairman: Thank you very much for coming. It is good of you to give up this time to help us. We have been doing the rounds a bit; we have been to Scotland, Wales and obviously London. It helps us very much to get an academic feel for what the situation is in different regions of the UK. I wonder if I can start off by asking you how active an issue is the Barnett Formula here. What are the sorts of issues that people think about and talk about, if, indeed, they think and talk about anything?

Professor Thain: My take is that it is not a particularly active issue in Northern Ireland, although I think the general question of resourcing and funding is obviously something that concerns people. The actual Formula which your Committee is trying to focus in on as opposed to the broader questions of the powers of the Northern Ireland Assembly and Executive, revenue raising powers and so on, is an issue of some concern, but Barnett itself is too esoteric. Maybe that is less true in Scotland and perhaps less so in Wales. That would be my take.

Professor Simpson: Thank you very much for the invitation. For the people who talk about this subject with an amount of knowledge, the attitude to Barnett is leave it alone, it is fine. The attitude is it is serving Northern Ireland reasonably well. Suggestions that it should be revised are usually associated very quickly by the political people with the Treasury is going to try and trim down the level of finance in Northern Ireland. We have close on 4 per cent of national expenditure in the relevant areas for a population of 2.75 per cent or whatever it is. The Formula is generous. The only thing I would add is a very much smaller group who are aware of the Formula think of it as a block grant but there is very little awareness of what I call the convergence implication of the Formula. Those who read it say, "Yes, it is only 2.8" or whatever per cent "of the changes", so you are going from 4 per cent and must gradually be coming down. There is an awareness of that, a worry about it, but all the evidence is the convergence formula is not working, Northern Ireland has stayed at this per head basis near to 20–25 per cent higher than the UK average per head and it does not look as though it is going to shift. I will get all my points in on the first answer! The other point is in terms of understanding the way in which the Barnett Formula operates, there is no published statement each year saying, "Here is how we did the calculation", we all accept it on trust, and yet we know on the edges because of the specialist professional action of the senior civil servants you have just seen they are continuously arguing minor adjustments and the net effect is that a statement of the Formula and then a conclusion does

not fit the way that the Civil Service negotiates from here to the Treasury.

Q720 Chairman: Looking at the history for a moment, we had a fascinating session with Lord Barnett himself. Joel's view now is very simple: he says it was never intended to last, it was meant to be a very short-term political fix and the idea was you could get negotiations between the individual territories and the Treasury off the back of ministers. Good morning, thank you for coming.

Mr Smyth: Good morning. In mitigation, I had a macroeconomics class and, unfortunately, now with the state of higher education with modularised courses you cannot make it up in 12 weeks. They are the beneficiaries questionably.

Q721 Chairman: Thank you very much for coming. As I say, Joel Barnett's own view is that it was temporary, it was never intended to last, it was a political fix, it got him out of a corner of having arguments with the individual territories and did not want to go into a possible devolution exercise with the old type of negotiation hanging over his head. The Treasury at the time were doing a huge assessment of need, which we all know about, and he did not even know they were doing it. Nobody told him that the Treasury was doing an assessment of need. As far as convergence was concerned, it never entered anybody's vocabulary, it was not part of the exercise. That was confirmed when we had Lord MacGregor who was Chief Secretary of the Treasury in the 1980s. He gave evidence to us in the course of which he said exactly the same. He said, "Convergence never entered my mind, we never discussed it. If it is a mathematical fallout, well it is a mathematical fallout, unintentional".

Professor Thain: The difficulty is the political versus the official. Talking to Treasury officials in the 1980s, 1990s and now, they are well aware of the dynamics of the Formula, but whether they tell their ministers who do not want the flak of being told there is convergence, it is just going to happen the longer you leave it. The problem with people who look at Barnett is when Barnett was set up is it the same as Barnett now because there is the comparability exercise, as John said, adding bits on year-in year-out in negotiations gradually extending the web to cover a larger proportion of departmental expenditure and looking for proportionality of comparability, which has been done more and more in the last five years or so, so it is not just 100 per cent of a sub-programme, it is 40 per cent or 50 per cent. That sort of process has given it an administrative dynamic that has allowed

27 *March 2009*   Mr Michael Smyth, Professor John Simpson and Professor Colin Thain

the official side of the argument to say, "We are moving here, we are getting somewhere, negotiations have helped us get a little bit more" and that means we are not talking of the same beast maybe as we were in the late 1970s and even through the early part of the Conservative administration when they were trying to cut spending. The interesting dynamic of the Formula is if the Conservatives had been successful in cutting spending it would have reversed. We have not had many years where there have been the decrements as opposed to the increments coming to the devolved administration. Barnett is both a mechanism but also the block grant, plus a negotiating process, and as long as it has had that the Treasury and the officials across the various parts of the devolved administrations can see that there is movement, development, it is not a dead thing that has stayed the same.

Q722 Lord Sewel: We have got an interesting one here. When you have territorial departments before devolution it is absolutely clear that basically the secretaries of state are at it with the Treasury, they will be knocking on the door saying, "This is awful. We face electoral wipe-out in Scotland, give us a bit more money" and they can do that, that is a political fix, it is the nature of the game. Once you get to devolution where you do not have the same parties in power across the board then the dynamics completely change and the Treasury is now putting everything it can into the Formula, everything goes into the Formula, so the ability to do bypass is reduced and it was the bypassing, plus population loss, that stopped the convergence from taking place. Now we have got the likelihood that we will have purer Barnett. Wales' population is going up, your population is going up, and that affects the block impact because the block has been predicated on a lower population, so there is a significant squeeze in the process now and there is no clear way of seeing how you can avoid that. The response to that in Wales is to say, "Let's get out of Barnett as soon as we can", but the response in Northern Ireland seems, "We're not sure".
Professor Simpson: We have managed to hold a position that deep down we realise is actually quite generous.

Q723 Lord Sewel: But it is going to go, is it not?
Mr Smyth: Very slowly.

Q724 Chairman: I do not know about the politics of it.
Professor Simpson: We have a situation where we can manage with the present Barnett Formula to have our domestic rating at 50 per cent of the English level and we can afford to run our water service free of extra charges. That is a pretty good point of devolution.

Mr Smyth: We aspire also to imitate our neighbours to the south in terms of the transformation that is taking place there, but right at this moment in time it is the old Augustine thing, "Lord make me virtuous, but not yet". We are very content with the settlement that we have. We need time to bed down the institutions here and to take those kinds of radical policy decisions and Barnett helps that.

Q725 Chairman: That is a message we have heard.
Professor Thain: Have you also heard the message which maybe you got from the civil servants you talked to and it may be people like Iain McLean, who has done some absolutely fantastic work on his assessment of fiscal transfers and so on, most of which I would not disagree with. One of the things he does not make enough of is the fact that you do not have the Treasury walking all over your departmental spends, you do have devolution to the Ministry of Finance and Personnel and the equivalent in Scotland and Wales, and there is a sort of acceptance that they are going to do the Treasury's job for them rather than the Treasury sending in IMF-like teams of people to Northern Ireland to go over relatively small amounts of money in UK terms, but very significant.

Q726 Chairman: Well, that happens.
Professor Thain: But it is marginal, is it not? It is not the same as having the whole of the public spending regime in Northern Ireland looked at by the Treasury with a dedicated expenditure team saying, "Right, let's look at everything that's going on in Northern Ireland".

Q727 Chairman: What about the size of the block?
Professor Thain: The block itself, in a sense, is another reason why John mentioned earlier about people being happy with it here, the fact that you can move money around, except that which is ring-fenced in terms of social security and so on, within local political compromise to put more money into education or transport or whatever. There is enough scope there. In the 1980s, there was the whole waterfront development and urban regeneration, Belfast First, was paid for out of using the block imaginatively before we had the devolved administration. There is enough scope there to tinker and move around without having to justify it to the Treasury. That is worth its weight in gold as far as the discussions I have ever had with officials in the territories, not to have that and to have a kind of high level discussion with the Treasury but not a detailed one.
Professor Simpson: If we are going to have political institutions in Northern Ireland and Scotland—the Welsh have not gone so far—we do not want to turn them into a county council which administers

services and the standards are set elsewhere. Clearly the principle is you can have a bit of variation in your services, and we have a different administrative structure on health and social services and we have a very peculiar structure in terms of education and schools, but we are not doing it very efficiently at the moment. It is there and nobody in London would want to try and interfere. It is quite sensible in terms of administration to say, "That's your amount". I would not like to give the Health Service a predetermined sum. It is not a bad idea that a range of services in Northern Ireland have flexibility. Let me just make one other point. The block grant gives us a generous answer. Half of that generous answer comes from two sources. One is the social security budget, and the rates are not yet, and maybe never will be, determined locally, we accept UK rates, and if the block grants gives an extra couple of billion that accounts for £800 million of it. The other element that does not enter into a Northern Ireland institution as yet is the policing and law order budget which at the moment inflates the calculation of the block grant but not in a way that affects the Northern Ireland direct administration, it stays with the Northern Ireland Office, and that is creating about £200 million for the moment which is under very intensive scrutiny and argument as to what we do in terms of changing that budget in the years ahead. Half of what is causing the enlarged block grant will not be altered by saying to the Stormont administration, "We'll give you a lower ratio". A lot of what we are talking about, shrinking the Northern Ireland block grant, we exaggerate when we do not take account of the policing and social security budgets.

Q728 Lord Sewel: Is there a longer term problem over Barnett in the context of devolution because the justification for devolution is to have local priorities, local policies, distinctive policies in the territories, and yet when you trace back the funding it is driven through Barnett consequentials by the profile of the English public expenditure. As you get policy divergence there is a major lack of congruence there, is there not?

Professor Thain: I think you have put your finger absolutely on the problem. That is the crux. You mentioned earlier in your intervention about powerful secretaries of state, not devolved administrations with devolved aspirations to start making decisions locally, so you could argue Barnett worked better when you still had a unified unitary state without the quasi-federal structure that we now have. The further we move towards a proper federal structure, the more we are going to have to get into debates about a Canadian or Australian approach where basically you allow your states, as it were, to determine almost everything and have revenue

raising powers and then you have an equalising fund to try to more or less help the bits of the federation that are not doing so well, which I think is the tenor of some of your questions about an indexed GDP ratio and so on to try to help. We are not in that situation because we do not have a federal structure, we still have a unitary structure with elements of quasi-federalism grafted on that are becoming stronger maybe in Scotland, maybe a bit more in Wales, and, as Mike said, when Northern Ireland really beds down and the system has had a good period of time maybe we will have policies developing where people will start saying, "Why do we have to have an English style approach to this? Why can't we look at the Republic? Why can't we look at Sweden? Why can't we look at some other part of the world rather than look to England?"

Lord Sewel: It used to be called the arc of prosperity but we do not use that phrase any more!

Q729 Earl of Mar and Kellie: Can I ask whether there has been much policy divergence during the past ten years? It is certainly an issue in Scotland, but has it happened much here?

Professor Thain: I do not think it has happened here.

Professor Simpson: No, less here than in Scotland certainly.

Professor Thain: And Wales on the edges has started to develop in certain policy areas, mental health and so on. Northern Ireland is still learning to be a devolved administration.

Mr Smyth: From my perspective there has not even been a serious debate about policy priorities. When the first devolved administration in 1997 came around everybody agreed that the programme for government was boilerplate, it was there and ready to go to get the buy-in. The latest programme for government shows a little bit of policy debate but on water we fudged it, and we are fudging it on education. It is political immaturity that is still pretty strong here.

Q730 Chairman: It is all a very British mess, is it not?

Professor Thain: I say in my presentation to you that I actually like the British mess.

Q731 Chairman: There is a cosiness about it, a familiarity about it, I understand all that.

Professor Thain: It is not just the cosiness, and maybe that makes me sound more of an apologist, I like the inherent flexibility without excessive rules.

Q732 Chairman: You are saying the same thing as I did but put in a different way.

Professor Thain: A different style. It makes it more important that your officials and politicians are adept at arguing in the system that exists and that is about skills and style of approach and maybe Scotland has got the edge.

Professor Simpson: It only comes under real test and strain when there is not an annual plus increment to what we are doing. In a situation where your spend is increasing you can debate the allocation and it is not so serious, but if we faced two or three years when public sector spending in real terms was to be lower I suspect that the tension between the political process here and London would increase and the tension in terms of relationships with the Treasury would increase. Taking on the point that Mike was getting close towards, and I thought he was going to mention it, in the last 18 months we have had a debate about the possible fiscal variation of corporation tax. The principle behind that debate is fascinating. You know the Treasury put David Varney on to the job and he came up with a very predictable Treasury conclusion. If I had been working in the Treasury I would have come to that conclusion. The thought of Revenue and Customs operating without there being a political border for taxation was mind bending. If we move on and devolution gets to the stage of some form of fiscal discrimination then there will be, and there is, an interest in Northern Ireland that has been generated in the business community that will go for a tax system on the model that would satisfy the Azores principle, if I can use that example. The Azores managed to find a form of corporation tax in relation to Portugal where they are allowed to do various things because the Azores themselves set the rates and determine the revenue. That is not regarded as a State Aid, it is within their delegated authority. There is a tension here: would we like to have the fiscal authority for some things that would give greater freedom? If you just ask that people would say, "Oh, what a good idea", but if you ask "How would you use the freedom?" it is always on the basis of "We would charge less", there are very few people saying, "Well, we could put the rates up by a few pence in the pound so that we can do things at the moment we cannot do". That is not part of the agenda.

Professor Thain: Also you come across the problem of the subvention from the Treasury. If you allow Northern Ireland to have control over its tax revenue you have to subvent and what are you going to do about that, have a negotiation with the Treasury and the Treasury will quite happily say, "Okay, right, we'll forget about the subvention and then you can start having control over the whole of the waterfront", as it were.

Q733 *Lord Sewel:* The reality, at least into the medium term, is that on the bit of the argument we cannot have, which is about fiscal autonomy, whatever happens to that there will still remain a significant grant element. That is not going to disappear, there will be a significant grant element, and the argument is what sort of grant, is it not, so can we explore the needs approach? I thought your paper was quite interesting because the tone is you do not like needs, you like the population base, and then there is a bit where you actually list all of the distinctive needs that Northern Ireland has which would seem to me to open up the argument that it would be best met by some form of needs assessment.

Professor Thain: My problem is who decides on the needs. For example, I go back to Iain McLean's very good work. Why 60 per cent of income as a barrier to determine the level of need, why not 50, why not 70, why not 65? If you think of the problems there have been in England with the rate support grant, and as seasoned politicians in this room you will know the debates that we would have had with the different administration coming in saying, "let's give more to rural needs and less to urban needs because we're a conservative versus an urban labour administration", who will actually decide on the balance of the needs in the needs package? That is why I think the GDP figure which the European Union has used as a very good indicator to have with the Structural Funds is a good one, but it is fairly crude.

Q734 *Lord Sewel:* There is a problem about needs, which ones, what weights, everything like that, but at least that seems to be more easily related to expenditure need levels of public expenditure required than a formula which actually when you strip it all out and let it run comes to the conclusion that the per head of public expenditure in West Sussex should be the same as the per head of expenditure in West Belfast.

Professor Thain: Except it does not because the aggregate managed expenditure element of public expenditure allows for the fact that if we are going to have higher housing benefit, higher council tax, all of which are the real, crucial parts—

Q735 *Lord Sewel:* I accept that. Spending on education and health would be the same.

Professor Thain: Yes, and there are arguments to be had there. Northern Ireland has the problem of us wasting a lot of resources on a segregated education system and segregated health system.

Q736 *Lord Sewel:* Is that a need or a policy change?

Professor Simpson: The health system is not segregated.

Professor Thain: I do not know if you walk down the Ormeau Road and there is a spanking new health centre which is cheek by jowl with a more protestant health centre up the road and the degree to which the Alliance Party, for example, have calculated something like a billion pounds is spent in Northern

Ireland that is only on trying to duplicate not very efficiently services that are on the basis of quite understandable historic problems. I am not trying to minimise those.

Professor Simpson: The education point is valid.

Professor Thain: In fact, the expenditure in Northern Ireland on education and health, some of that has got to wind through historically to become a more normal pattern that is not based upon some of the questions of difference.

Q737 *Lord Sewel:* Would you accept in some of the areas covered by the Barnett Formula, not totally but for most of those services, the drivers are demographics, something to do with levels of deprivation and cost of service delivery, sparsity?

Professor Simpson: What about the cost of living?

Q738 *Lord Sewel:* That is a very difficult one, I know, because you are building an incentive for inefficiency, I appreciate that, but clearly it costs more to provide a primary school service in the Highlands and Islands of Scotland than it does in the leafy suburbs of Aberdeen.

Professor Thain: It is urban versus rural.

Q739 *Lord Sewel:* Going down those dimensions it seems to me that fits more rationally with levels of public expenditure that are required in those services in comparison with just a straight population driven approach.

Professor Thain: Except the straight population driven approach, I would argue, is easier to sell politically. In the end you have got to have an approach to distribution of resources that works politically. One of the problems I have with a lot of the debate that is going on about Barnett and fiscal transfers and so on is the degree to which English voters will see whatever is arrived at as being worth supporting as part of a contract of the union and is ignored often and put down to English voters not very happy with Scotland getting too much. That is a perception of the fact that Scotland is actually making waves rather than the fact that you can tell a voter, "Well, actually, resources are given to these parts of the United Kingdom on the basis of population and then there are policy divergences as a result of local decisions".

Q740 *Lord Sewel:* If you are going to say it is on population you have also got to attack the block, have you not?

Professor Simpson: At the moment we have a population plus formula. We have got 2.8 per cent of the population and 4 per cent of the spending. The Scots have got a slight plus in the same direction. The population in general do not understand that Barnett is not just on a per head basis. They do in the

northeast of England and particularly from the Newcastle area people say, "How come public spending in Northern Ireland is X per head and it's Y per head in Scotland and we in the northeast are neglected?"

Lord Sewel: I think the experts on the Barnett Formula are the people who live in the northeast of England actually.

Q741 *Chairman:* On a more general point, what I do not understand is this, and I am sure this is true: if the policies of the devolved administrations are going to increase substantially from the policies that we have seen by England and the Westminster Government, that divergence is going to increase. Unless you have a formula that is based upon need you cannot actually produce a structure within which it can operate. You cannot have an existing formula when they are going in opposite directions.

Professor Thain: I would argue the reverse, and maybe that makes me stick out like a sore thumb. This is beyond your remit, but unless we have a constitutional convention to look at this as a whole, and I think that is what has to happen, it is not just about Barnett, it is about revenue raising, it is about the mechanisms, the constitutional settlement, the powers of the various elements, the mechanism in London to adjudicate if there are problems, which you raise as an issue, and how do you set that up, these are big questions of the constitutional reconfiguration of the UK. We have got to do something about the English regions, very much so. To be fair to the Prescott drive to try to get regional assemblies, at least that was a mechanism where you had an identifiable element of the northeast, northwest, southwest or the Midlands, and at least you could give resources to that part of the country and then start talking about how you would divest those resources. We do not have that. That has got to be done before we have a fundamental reappraisal of Barnett in my view.

Q742 *Earl of Mar and Kellie:* Are you really saying that until there is a constitutional change, and that is Barnett is an easy formula for the Treasury to implement because it is the Treasury who are going to implement it, and various forms of needs assessment or, indeed, any other ideas there are for calculating how much should be transferred to the three devolved areas, it is not worth thinking about other ways of doing it until the Treasury give up the whip hand on this?

Professor Thain: I think you are opening a can of worms because why would English regions and English departments not start asking questions about, "We have got major need in a large part of the East Midlands, why can't we have . . . ."

Q743 Earl of Mar and Kellie: Have not the English departments already had that discussion as part of the triennial Spending Review?
Professor Thain: That work is done and it then transfers across to the regions.

Q744 Earl of Mar and Kellie: The English departments presumably have had their crack of the whip.
Professor Thain: I am saying if you remove Barnett and say, "Let's have needs assessment", you do not have those debates in England shaping the budgetary fallout and once that happens officials in departments in England can say, "Well, we've had the big debates, what is happening in Northern Ireland is marginally different from what we have done and what is happening in Scotland is different again, but it's not so far away from the fundamental unitary state having had the debates about 80 per cent-odd of public spending". My worry is the attack on the union will come from moving away from a population-based formula.

Q745 Earl of Mar and Kellie: Moving from a population base or moving from Treasury control?
Professor Thain: It depends if you regard the Treasury as the big, bad wolf always or as a department that never really got control of public spending until fairly recently. If you regard the Treasury as having an uphill struggle to try to keep the lid on public spending then weaken the Treasury.
Mr Smyth: I was with Colin all the way when he talked about looking at income and the expenditure side of this, but the fact remains statistically if you use GDP/GVA per head, devolution has not worked. Scotland has diverged from the UK average since 1995 and particularly sharply since 1997, Wales has diverged even further and we have flat lined at 80 per cent. My preference would be that in the UK we need to have a proper regional policy again and how that plays out I do not think necessitates further devolution but we need to have a regional policy. One of the things that has concerned me throughout all of this, and I know we are not supposed to talk about it here, is the unwritten assumption is if there is no fiscal autonomy in the devolved regions or no debate about reinstating regional policy, the Treasury is going to go on subventing places like Northern Ireland in perpetuity. I have to say, and John will agree with me, over the last 15 years, the so-called "nice years" of continuous growth and so on, the subvention has increased, it has not decreased, so it is mainly structural. It is the same in every other region. I have the statistics here and I will leave them with you. It is unambiguous. If we are serious about tackling fairness, and that is an issue that you have been dealing with in all the evidence I have seen, fairness means you look at all of the income and expenditure

side, but sadly the Treasury is prepared to go on subsidising economic failure in perpetuity. That is my take on all of this.

Q746 Earl of Mar and Kellie: We have the threat of convergence over public spending per head, but should we not be aiming at a different convergence, for example convergence on economics, that the Treasury enable each area to perform better so that you try to get the GDP per head equal?
Professor Simpson: That is very vulnerable to abuse. As I have listened to this discussion and the way it is evolving, one of the thoughts going through my head is how would you alter the structure of these allocations so as to put greater pressure on somewhere like Northern Ireland or Scotland to use its public resources more efficiently. By every comparison we end up showing by whatever margin in providing particular services we are less efficient than we should be. The system does not do anything to put pressure on that. If you fund us so that we have enough to close the economic gap from central funding, thank you very much, that makes life easier.

Q747 Chairman: Who would determine whether you are spending your money wisely or not? Do you really want somebody from outside to come and tell you?
Mr Smyth: We had it recently with the Appleby Review. The Appleby Review of Health compared a number of acute hospitals here with a number of acute hospitals in England as far as they could like-with-like and the productivity differences were shocking.
Professor Thain: I think the world is going to change come the next Comprehensive Spending Review if we have one, which we are not going to have in 2009, because public spending is going to be squeezed because the Chancellor has got a problem and it is getting bigger every time the Prime Minister globe trots because there is a pressure to put a bigger fiscal stimulus in that is going to create problems for public budgeting. The party is over, there will be a squeeze on public spending and it will come through in the Barnett Formula and then Northern Ireland is going to have to start asking real questions about how efficiently are we doing this, do we have too many officials doing this, do we have enough people upfront doing the service. As one of your colleagues once said to me, outdoor relief is a part of Northern Ireland's public sector.

Q748 Chairman: If the momentum comes from Northern Ireland that is fair enough. If Northern Ireland wants to decide what is efficient and what is not efficient, that seems to me to be entirely a matter for Northern Ireland. To have any outside body coming in trying to determine the competence or efficiency in any of the regions is very difficult indeed.

Professor Thain: I could not agree more. The pressure has to come in terms of local debates generated by concerns about improving the quality of service and maybe the comparative material that comes out is very useful sometimes. It is not always useful. The big debate in Northern Ireland is always to chastise the English education system and say, "We don't want to be like the English, do we?" and the comparison could be used rather crudely as a model for an English education system which I think does not exist any more because it is such a complex divergent monster now rather than a single "comprehensive" education system, but at least it is part of the debate to have that material and then for local politicians and pressure groups to start saying, "Why can't we do a bit better? Why can't we do it more like another part of the world?", and not necessarily the UK either but parts of the European Union.

Professor Simpson: My Lord Chairman, you are perfectly right, if the three of us were left you could rightly say, "You should be talking about the priorities and how you influence the local political system, but do not expect some group from London one way or another to solve that problem". That is accepted. We now have a system whereby Northern Ireland, in my book—the civil servants are not going to say this—is reasonably generously funded under the present arrangements.

Q749 *Chairman:* They did say that. I do not think they used the word "generous" but they said it. They were reasonably warm towards the application of the Formula.

Professor Simpson: As I said here I would criticise it internally to illustrate that we could have the debate, that we are not using our resources to bring our infrastructure up to modern standards as quickly as we could. We are using our flexibility to maintain an educational form of expenditure and we are using it also to maintain some other economic services. For example, we still have partial industrial derating here. If the European Commission eventually decide that this is not so small as to be ignored, they will say, "You are running an operating subsidy and should be rid of it". We should think that as well but there is the pressure from other disciplines. You could say, "Sort it out yourselves" and a bit more leverage from elsewhere would help.

Q750 *Chairman:* It seems to me that the present system is too crude, it is not sensitive enough and does not produce a sufficiently fair result from certainly my point of view looking at it, and for the life of me I do not see why you cannot have a system in which the allocation to the block is based upon a series of comparators and variables which take need much more into account than at the moment. I do not see why that should not be done and, therefore, when

Barnett comes to be applied it would be applied with a different mathematical formula than it is at the moment. What is wrong with that?

Professor Thain: Getting agreement on it is the problem. I still go back to my central worry that it depends on how far you think the union is important and how flexible you think the union is and if you think the union has got a degree of elasticity in it and can survive fiscal and economic change, and I am not so sure.

Q751 *Chairman:* It survives strongly if people perceive it as fair.

Professor Thain: Maybe so. I just worry that unless there is a proper constitutional settlement, fiddling around with Barnett is not necessarily going to have the—

Q752 *Chairman:* It is a bit more than fiddling around with Barnett.

Mr Smyth: I have looked at the Australian Commonwealth system and I know you have touched on the edges of it, but it is independent. It puts the onus on the devolved regions or countries to make the case. It also gets around the problem of lack of transparency of the data because the Treasury does obfuscate and does not release the data. This is the only part of the UK in which you have 100 per cent identifiable expenditure. It is a good thing in some ways but I think it is unfair as well. The only way to get round that is to have a transparent, independent, statutory commission.

Q753 *Chairman:* Do you think that could work in a system where you have got asymmetrical devolution? Do you think that makes any difference?

Mr Smyth: England is the problem.

Q754 *Chairman:* I would not disagree with that as a Welshman! I am thinking the way in which the powers have been devolved to the three devolved administrations is different and do you think that would make any difference to whether or not you could have an objective, impartial, transparent assessment?

Mr Smyth: Who speaks for England? In every other way that model would work.

Professor Thain: My argument in my paper, which maybe I did not develop enough, was to have a Barnett plus which is to have a kind of bidding process for additional spending on top of the allocation on the basis of need made by not just the devolved administrations but the Regional Development Agencies in England and whatever, the GLA, and in a sense the patchwork that England is in terms of identifiable political entities, ministers of the regions that have been drafted on recently.

27 March 2009   Mr Michael Smyth, Professor John Simpson and Professor Colin Thain

Q755 *Chairman:* There is not much difference between that and what I said, is there?
Professor Thain: The difference would be that you would stick to what would be easy to sell in terms of a population-based allocation, but then you would have an amount of proportionate DEL that you could bid for.

Q756 *Chairman:* That brings the bypasses under control.
Professor Thain: Yes, it increases the bypass, makes the bypass more transparent, and the bidding then puts the onus on the devolved administrations, the regions and the Treasury to be more open and persuasive in the case they make for the addition.

Q757 *Chairman:* You would leave the block as it is now?
Professor Thain: Yes.

Q758 *Lord Sewel:* I did not like that when I read it, quite honestly, just because of the political costs if you are going to get the territories and the regions bidding and I think you have said with a number of departmental ministers arbitrating.
Professor Thain: I did not develop it.

Q759 *Lord Sewel:* You would get accusations of favouritism, cronyism and deals, political sweeteners.
Professor Thain: That is the nature of budgetary politics. That is a reality. In the Australian and Canadian cases they still have political sweeteners, you still have the case of arguing with the federal Prime Minister in Canada to try and give them a bit more.
Chairman: But only for a couple of days. We did have evidence which in effect said they make their determination once a year, for about two or three days thereafter there is a row when everybody says it is unfair, then it calms down, continues, and the next year they make another decision and have two or three days of argument. That does not seem to me to be grossly unhelpful if that is the way you wish it to be done.

Q760 *Earl of Mar and Kellie:* It does seem to me that we could not have an Australian style of Territorial Grants Board here until there had been some form of devolution to England.
Professor Simpson: An English authority, yes.

Q761 *Earl of Mar and Kellie:* Which could come one of two ways, either England or a collection of nine regions, in which case the Australian model would not work for as long as England is directly administered by the United Kingdom Government.

Professor Thain: It is back to the constitutional settlement. It is back to creating a proper federal structure. Do we want to go there? Can we go there? Is there sufficient political will to actually uncover all that? Not just that, the problem is Richard Rose once said the problem with territorial allocation is it is functional, it is not territorial. It is the historic background of having functional administration of policy grafted on to territorial political structures, and until we move the boundaries of that we are not going to have a proper Australian-type system. You have then got to start asking questions about revenue raising and the independence of those regions to get on with their own thing rather than a kind of English steer with a marginal adjustment at the sides. Those are big questions which we need to address in the UK.

Q762 *Chairman:* I am happy to say they are way outside the remit of this Committee. Mr Smyth, you obviously had a good look at the Australian system.
Mr Smyth: Yes. It worked very well in Victoria, for example, in the aftermath of the fires. I looked at a couple of their annual reports in-depth and the sorts of arguments that are put are quite strong, well-supported, the evidence is there. The Australian public finances are completely transparent, at least as far as I could see. Under the Barnett Formula England is a pig and under an Australian-type system England would still be a pig. As I understand it, the Regional Development Agencies were a fallback position when Prescott did not get what he wanted. That is a framework. The research that I have seen on the performance of the Regional Development Agencies is that they are under-funded, but for what they get they do a very good job. That is a framework that you could develop to beyond simply industrial development. I do not think we have to have federalism in that sense. The more I read about this and the more we discuss this, the Barnett Formula is the least worst choice at the moment.
Professor Thain: Which is why it has stuck historically as well.
Professor Simpson: We are not having a discussion which would dictate the mood which says we are going to have a radical constitutional review of the whole of the United Kingdom, your remit will not take you that far. There are couple of illustrations. There is the illustration of can a workable form of fiscal discrimination be introduced. The other one that is there, and the Scots are making the point in their own way, is the Barnett Formula locks current and capital spending together, but capital spending has a different rationale. Now there is a need in Northern Ireland for a big catch-up in capital spending, much higher proportionately than the level of capital spending that would be in England. This is not in any sense acknowledged in the framework other than whether the Barnett Formula is going to

be generous enough to allow you to do a bit of that. The Scots recently made the point that there was an attempt to introduce permission for the Northern Ireland administration to be able to borrow capital. That has now been narrowed down by the Treasury, so it is only permission to borrow £100 million a year and that figure is capped. The Scots are making the point that as a legislature should they not have the right to borrow for their capital spending and take responsibility for it, but within the Barnett mechanism this opens up things that up until now have been closed.
Earl of Mar and Kellie: And no borrowing is specifically mentioned in the Scotland Act.

Q763 *Lord Sewel:* It is only borrowing to smooth.
Professor Thain: One of your Members would be able to tell you the story of the debate over the St Andrews' Agreement package that the Treasury were going to give to help Northern Ireland. One of the issues raised in 2002 and 2003 when Gordon Brown was Chancellor was you could use the regional rate to help pay back the Treasury for a long-term loan.
Professor Simpson: That was in the original deal, yes.
Professor Thain: And what is wrong with that?

Q764 *Chairman:* What is wrong with it is it is yet another example of pragmatism being pushed to the edge of distortion because a situation arises and you have a solution, another situation arises and you have another solution and they are all very rational in themselves but there is no structure, frankly, within which they are operating and I do not think that is good government. I think you have got to have a fairly clear line as to how you do these things.
Professor Thain: That comes back to the powers given to the three bits and the lack of the regional dimension in England having a proper rationale.

Q765 *Chairman:* I have always been opposed to the Welsh Assembly having tax raising powers for the very simple reason that the Scots got tax raising powers and have never used them but I think my countrymen would use them, and it is not a very good idea as far as Wales is concerned because I am not sure I have got sufficient confidence in the way in which they would spend the increased resources. In any case, frankly, the amount of money raised does not amount to a vast sum. I do not see how you can just do it on an ad hoc basis. If you have got a problem and somebody else has got a problem on something different, you fiddle a bit here and fiddle a bit there and in the Barnett bypass system quite a lot of money you get is down from the centre to the devolved authorities but in a really rather imprecise and ad hoc way and obviously it gives far too much power to the Treasury.

Professor Thain: We are learning to move from a unitary state to a quasi-federal.

Q766 *Chairman:* I do not want to move from a unitary state. What I want to do is to see that the devolved administrations within that unitary state are properly financed. I do not want to repeat myself but I do try to work out in my own mind why a needs assessment base for that distribution is so outrageous.
Professor Simpson: We are not arguing with you.

Q767 *Lord Sewel:* You said the Barnett Formula was the least worst choice.
Mr Smyth: Yes, for allocation changes. I do not disagree with the Chairman at all. In fact, I have dug out my old copy of the 1979 Needs Assessment Study and I remembered that after all the sophisticated analysis that went into that, at the very end they did a quick and dirty simplified assessment identifying more or less the same answer. Why there have been so few repeats of that exercise, I do not know.

Q768 *Chairman:* There was one in the 1980s. We saw one in the 1980s, I suspect there was something in the 1990s and certainly you tried to do something in 2001-02.
Professor Simpson: Yes.
Chairman: I do not know to what extent the Treasury were involved in any of that negotiation, but no doubt we will find out in due course.

Q769 *Lord Sewel:* Have you seen the Northern Irish 2001-02 attempt?
Mr Smyth: No. You have not either, John?
Professor Simpson: No.
Mr Smyth: It was closer to the cut down version, the Occam's Razor version than the full-blown one. Again, I would have thought with technology and better data you could do it a lot more cost-effectively now.

Q770 *Chairman:* The needs assessment?
Mr Smyth: Yes.

Q771 *Chairman:* Yes, I am sure you could. They do it for local authorities anyway.
Mr Smyth: The Barnett Formula is just to allocate the changes.

Q772 *Chairman:* If you are going to defend a system in which needs are excluded from—
Professor Thain: I do not argue with that. I think needs are going to be dealt with through other mechanisms. I go back to what Mike said earlier on about having a proper regional policy. There has got to be a regional policy for the whole of the United Kingdom, not just a regional policy for Northern

Ireland, although there are specific bits of Northern Ireland that would have a variation.

Q773 *Chairman:* How do you reconcile that with the idea of having a block grant which gives Northern Ireland a great deal of discretion in how it spends it?
Professor Thain: Because it is part of that compromise that gets the system to keep moving on.

Q774 *Chairman:* Who is going to decide what regional policy should be pursued in Northern Ireland?
Professor Thain: If we have a debate in England about regional policy, then Northern Ireland, Scotland and Wales get a consequential of the regional policy.

Q775 *Chairman:* So it is just the consequential?
Professor Thain: And also if Northern Ireland, Wales and Scotland participate in a proper debate about how we move regional policy on then that is a way of dealing with one of those elements of need which is about differential economic performance in inequalities of wealth. There are national mechanisms in the UK system—child tax credit, working tax credits, minimum wage—that then feed through to the regions of the United Kingdom.

Q776 *Chairman:* You cannot have variable minimum wages, can you?
Professor Thain: No, but we have a system and it does not have to be on the basis of Barnett to do all the work to deal with needs. That would be my argument. Policy debates then have to be in the specific areas.

Q777 *Lord Sewel:* Would you not accept that, say, social work expenditure is related to levels of deprivation? You need social work expenditure and the variations in social work expenditure must be related to something close to some measure of social breakdown of need or poverty.
Mr Smyth: It must be.

Q778 *Lord Sewel:* To do that you do a needs assessment.
Professor Simpson: It is not disciplined, it is guaranteed as a cash flow.

Q779 *Lord Sewel:* I missed the first bit.
Professor Simpson: Social security.

Q780 *Lord Sewel:* I am talking about social work.
Professor Thain: Then your argument is that England does not have social work problems that come through the social work allocation that then goes to Scotland, Wales and Northern Ireland.

Q781 *Lord Sewel:* England has some and it distributes its social work expenditure to local authorities on a needs-based formula, so why should the amount going to Scotland out of the UK bit not go on a needs-based formula?
Professor Thain: But it does via the rate support grant element of the Barnett Formula. If the debates are in England, the block figure in England, the consequential increases each year or in the three-year cycle of the Comprehensive Spending Review includes debates about putting more money into social work which you then give on the basis of need and then there is an increase in the budget for social work.

Q782 *Lord Sewel:* There is an increase in the budget for social work and you get a consequential of that, but that consequential is a population driven consequential, it is not a needs driven consequential.
Professor Thain: It is not related to pockets of particular need, absolutely not. My problem is how would you generate your formula so that would be acceptable to say social work needs in rural parts of Scotland or rural parts of Northern Ireland are more important than urban social work needs. How would you build a formula? It has been difficult enough with the rate support grant to come to an agreement about what figure is being given for that element of social need.

Q783 *Chairman:* Population cannot be a substitute for that surely?
Professor Thain: It is a proxy for the policy debates which you then have.

Q784 *Chairman:* It is a 35-year old proxy pretty well, is it not?
Professor Thain: It is not because it has moved on.

Q785 *Chairman:* The basis of the thing is.
Professor Thain: The upgrading of the population, Northern Ireland getting a larger proportion as its population rises, Scotland going down, admittedly it has not happened regularly enough for that to feed through to the Formula but a larger proportion of public spending that is going to be covered by the Formula, something like 90 per cent or so instead of something like 45 or 50 per cent when it first started, are all movements in the process. It is not a dead system that has kept the same, there are elements of dynamism.
Professor Simpson: I have no difficulty with the concept of the block grant being based on a needs formula which I hope would not be too complicated, not too many variables, but I am worried about the discussion that goes on to say we are going to try and assess need so we will end up knowing what the comparative need is for social workers, for doctors,

and the next step is you spend it without any discretion. For example, on the whole health and social services network we spend it differently. Put schools to one side for the moment. Part of the logic of what you are doing is leaving the regional authority, be it Northern Ireland or Scotland, with permission to play at the edges of that but they accept the basic principles of, say, a National Health Service. If Northern Ireland decided not to have a National Health Service then we would have trouble.
Chairman: I think we would, inside and outside Northern Ireland.

Q786 *Earl of Mar and Kellie:* Can I come back to the Australian model. Presumably the Australian Treasury gives a block grant to the Territorial Grants Board to divvy up amongst the states and territories, all of whom in theory have applied on the same basis.
Mr Smyth: Yes, on the recommendation of the Commission.

Q787 *Earl of Mar and Kellie:* Does this mean that the Commonwealth government decides how much is being put into the state and territorial activities, or do they say, "We would like so much, please send it to us"?
Mr Smyth: They make a series of reports. There are certainly annual reports under different headings to the Commission and then the Commission publishes its report and, as the Chairman said, there is always a big row and then it settles down. The states themselves have considerable discretion in how they use that money.

Q788 *Earl of Mar and Kellie:* The gross amount of money which is put to these activities is determined by the Commonwealth Treasury?
Mr Smyth: Yes.
Professor Thain: But it is a federal spend. It is like the US Federal Government giving money to the states. It is not the same as having what we have got.
Earl of Mar and Kellie: To a degree we are being encouraged to head towards the Australian system, but in actual fact it strikes me as being more different than I initially thought it was.

Q789 *Lord Sewel:* What is the best thing to read on the Australian system?
Mr Smyth: Their annual reports. They set out their desired outcomes and then their actual outcomes. Their annual reports are put in terms of, "Here's what we were instructed to do and here's our considered opinion" and they go through their decisions in detail each year.

Q790 *Lord Sewel:* Are there any articles on it at all?
Professor Thain: There is a very good serious by John Wanna of the National Australian University who has been working on budgetary policies.
Mr Smyth: I think the Institute of Fiscal Studies here did a study on the Canadian and Australian ones from about 2004-05 by Richard Blundell.

Q791 *Chairman:* How do they do it in Canada?
Mr Smyth: I know less about Canada but I think it is similar. It is an independent—

Q792 *Earl of Mar and Kellie:* No, it is not.
Mr Smyth: I thought it was independent oversight.
Professor Thain: It is a federal disbursement based on GDP variation between the territories and Quebec because there is an issue about the statistics you use. It is a variation from 100 per cent of GDP. So if a region is doing particularly badly it gets an increase in its federal disbursement. The Canadian model is one where it is based upon GDP.

Q793 *Chairman:* I think it is based upon tax revenues. Canadian equalisation is based on tax revenues.
Professor Thain: We may be talking about two separate things here.
Mr Smyth: The other advantage of the Australian model is it has the chairman and four members and, as far as I can determine, the membership changes at certain times. There seems to be no political connection between the membership of the Commission and any of the main parties.

Q794 *Chairman:* Any representatives of the individual states?
Mr Smyth: Three of them are from different states. The fourth one I could not determine. They are a mixture of former Treasury people and academics, or both.
Chairman: We will have to have a serious look at this because I am bound to say it is one of the mechanisms that seems to have attracted us as to whether this is one possible way of doing it.
Lord Sewel: We have been talking about that approach and I suppose we could ask the question would the data be available in the UK to do that sort of exercise?
Chairman: That is for the Treasury if the data is there.

Q795 *Lord Sewel:* I do not know whether the data is there.
Professor Thain: National statistics have improved.
Professor Simpson: It could be organised but I am not sure the political will is there to do it.
Mr Smyth: I am not sure about that. It changes so frequently. Their presentation changes suddenly and the only people who really know are a small number

of people in the Treasury and I think you would need to ask them.

Q796 *Lord Sewel:* Oh joy! Oh joy!

Professor Thain: Also I think there is an issue about national statistics in the UK and the quality and impartiality of them. Probably you should get Michael Scholar in front of you to ask him about the National Statistics Commission and see whether he thinks more work could be done to put pressure on to get an agreed set of statistics that we could all look at and say, "That is fair" and keep them consistent.

Mr Smyth: How would this sit within the increasing calls for an independent Monetary Policy Committee equivalent in terms of fiscal policy nationally? Could it be nested? If that ever came about, could you nest this underneath that?

Q797 *Lord Sewel:* I think a Fiscal Policy Committee is a big issue.

Professor Thain: Beyond the scope of the House of Lords!

Q798 *Lord Sewel:* It certainly is!

Professor Simpson: I cannot see any Chancellor of the Exchequer accepting that willingly.

Professor Thain: I think there is a strong feel for that.

Q799 *Chairman:* I may be wrong about this but I get the impression, or at least the beginning of a feeling, that this issue of how you sort out transfers between the centre and a lot of the administrations is an issue that people have got to start trying to settle.

Professor Thain: Yes.

Q800 *Chairman:* With the present situation you could argue for it, particularly a great ad hoc man like you, if there is a problem you move outside it and solve it, I understand all that, and politically that is very attractive, but I think there is a feeling as a country we have got to try and produce a structure and this Committee is a very small part of that.

Professor Simpson: You have been talking about a needs base and you may be aware the statisticians are actually reviewing the basis on which they calculate relative GVA by region in the United Kingdom, so if you are going to pronounce will you wait until they have got the revised figures. I understand it is at an early stage but the revision of GVA is going to make Northern Ireland's degree of poverty less.

Chairman: Well, gentlemen, we have had a good run round the course. Thank you very much indeed.

FRIDAY 27 MARCH 2009

Present   Mar and Kellie, E   Sewel, L
               Richard, L (Chairman)

Memorandum by the Northern Ireland Confederation for Health and Social Services

WRITTEN EVIDENCE

1. *Introduction*

1.1 The Northern Ireland Confederation for Health and Social Services is the voice of management in the integrated Health and Social Care system (HSC). Part of the UK-wide NHS Confederation, it is the only membership body for HSC organisations. At present, the membership includes all HSS Boards and HSC Trusts, the Central Services Agency and five of the smaller HSC bodies.

1.2 The Confederation welcomes the opportunity to comment on the House of Lords Select Committee Inquiry on the Barnett Formula. In developing this response, the Confederation has taken the views of its members and has drawn largely on secondary sources of information.

1.3 The Northern Ireland Confederation currently does not have the resources or capacity to respond in full or deal with all the questions outlined in the Select Committee's paper but we still felt it was important to respond and make our views on this important issue known. The evidence submitted remains within the Committee's terms of reference.

1.4 The Confederation would be happy to provide further clarification or expansion on any of the issues covered in this submission.

2. *The Barnett Formula*

2.1 Despite its apparent temporary use, the Barnett Formula is a mechanism that has been used by the UK government to apportion public expenditure changes to Northern Ireland, Scotland and Wales since 1979. The increase (or decrease) each year in public expenditure is distributed across the three countries according to their population at the time.

2.2 The Northern Ireland Confederation welcomes this Select Committee inquiry and is in favour of moving away from the Barnett Formula towards a system that reflects needs rather than simply population.

2.3 The case for change has gathered momentum across the UK. In particular, there are the *Calman Commission* in Scotland, which will produce its final report some time during this year, and the *Hothman Commission* in Wales. The Northern Ireland Confederation will closely follow developments and the outcome of the work of these Commissions as well the outcome of the Northern Ireland Executive's considerations of the implications of the potential reform of Barnett.

2.4 The alternative, reportedly favoured by both Commissions and the report *Fair Shares? Barnett and the politics of public expenditure* produced by the Institute for Public Policy research in July 2008, is to adopt a hybrid approach combining greater fiscal autonomy with the equity of a needs based grant.[1]

2.5 At this stage, the Confederation is not in a position to lend its support to any of the alternatives to Barnett as we have not had the opportunity to consider the options in detail. We however are clear in our support for a review of the Barnett Formula and have consistently recommended this.[2] The Barnett Formula takes no account of the higher levels of deprivation in Northern Ireland and hence is inequitable and outdated. It is purely a population based formula and therefore places Northern Ireland at a disadvantage trapping the region within an ongoing cycle of underinvestment. It is our opinion that deprivation levels in Northern Ireland are such that for the foreseeable future, investment here needs to exceed the levels of investment that applies to the rest of the UK.

2.6 The Northern Ireland Confederation is pleased that the debate on Barnett has been started. We recognise that finding an alternative will not be easy but we do believe that a major review of the Formula is essential to ensure equity of provision throughout the UK.

---

[1] Public Finance 21–27 November 2008 page 21.
[2] The Northern Ireland Confederation for Health and Social services: "A Research Paper on Funding for Health and Personal Social Services in Northern Ireland" (January 2002)

3. Application of the Formula in practice

3.1 Ultimately the Barnett Formula was designed to bring about equal spending per head in the four countries of the UK by slowly reducing differentials in spending between the four nations otherwise known as the "Barnett Squeeze".

3.2 One of the main outcomes of the Formula that has attracted criticism is the higher spending per head. The distribution of a per capita amount to Scotland, Wales and Northern Ireland higher than that allocated to England has led to calls for the formula to be reviewed. The relative differences are illustrated in the table below.

3.3 In 2007–08 identifiable public spending per head minus social protection and agriculture across the nations and regions was as follows

Nation/Region	£ per head	% deviation from UK average
Scotland	5676	+21
Wales	5050	+8
Northern Ireland	5684	+21
England	4523	-3
UK	4679	0
London	5985	+28
North East	4960	+6
North West	4927	+5
Yorks and Humber	4477	-4
West Midlands	4430	-5
East Midlands	4086	-13
South West	3947	-16
South East	3874	-17
East of England	3820	-18

Source: IPPR July 2008.

3.2 Over time, the use of Barnett will continue to reduce the percentage share of the overall public expenditure allocated to Northern Ireland. However, this population based formula is too simplistic as it does not take account of actual need. This may become a problem particularly when the convergence in the level of per capita public expenditure occurs. Issues may arise about differential expenditure needs throughout the UK eg the number of persons in the area requiring medical treatment, the number of elderly people requiring care, etc.[3] Such potential high public service demands could cause particular concern especially if combined with low incomes as is the case particularly in Northern Ireland, which has the lowest average earnings in the UK. We also have the lowest economic activity rate—71 per cent in work as compared with the UK average of 80 per cent.

3.3 Barnett does not give Northern Ireland the extra resources it needs to match the health and social care services that can be afforded in England. The Northern Ireland Confederation believes that the general standard of such services should be kept broadly in line throughout the UK. Accordingly, we need a system that makes proper allowance for the different needs of the four countries.

4. Northern Ireland has greater need

4.1 In August 2005, the *Independent Review of Health and Social Care Services* in Northern Ireland was published. The author, Professor John Appleby, concluded that it was necessary for Northern Ireland to spend approximately 7 per cent more than England in order for it to provide the same standard of care. The Appleby Report recommended an additional real-term investment of 4.3 per cent overall during the 2008–12 Comprehensive Spending Review period.

4.2 He described the Barnett Formula as a *"simplistic mechanism"* that did not take into account the differences in the need or health and social care expenditure between Northern Ireland and England.[4]

4.3 Updated figures from Department of Health, Social Services and Public Safety (DHSSPS) officials and Department of Finance (DFP) officials who considered the need identified by Appleby taking account of differences in age profile and deprivation levels and market force factors, show that the differential now stands at an estimated 14 to 15 per cent greater need in Northern Ireland compared to England.

---

[3] Northern Ireland Assembly Research and Library services Research Paper 12/01 A background paper on the Barnett Formula (September 2001)
[4] Independent Review of Health and Social care Services in Northern Ireland Professor John Appleby (August 2005)

4.4 The latest assessment of relative need is 10 per cent higher for National Health Service-type services, and up to 36 per cent higher for social services functions. To tackle that gap and match the 3.7 per cent growth rate in England, would mean that an additional £600 million to spend would be required by 2010–11. This is nothing to do with inefficiencies and waste as no matter how efficient we become in Northern Ireland, patients and clients here will not get the same standard of care as in England.

4.5 Consequently, there is a 25 per cent greater mental health need and funding is 25 per cent less than that in England—a clear differential. Northern Ireland spend on children is the lowest in the UK—we are 35 per cent behind England, and 44 per cent behind Scotland. The proportion of our population that is aged over 65 is growing at the fastest rate in the UK, and that means that need is growing quicker here than it is in other parts of the UK. Significant health and social care challenges remain to be addressed—much of which is a legacy of the "Troubles".

4.6 There are many examples of the gap in services here and the rest of the UK and this is not acceptable— waiting times are longer; if we had the same adoption rates as England another 50–60 children in care each year would be adopted; if we had the same rates of death 300 fewer people would die each year; and death rates from bowel cancer are 16 per cent higher than the average in the rest of the UK. We also are faced with considerable diseconomies of scale for a discrete region in health and social care—a typical Strategic Health Authority in England has a population of 7–10 million whereas Northern Ireland has had to provide the regional services for a population of about 1.7 million.

5. *Conclusion*

5.1 The Northern Ireland Confederation considers that as the Barnett Formula takes no account of the higher levels of deprivation in Northern Ireland, it is inequitable and outdated. The Barnett Formula never claimed to address issues around need and was a basic calculation on the basis of population. A new fairer way of funding taking account of Northern Ireland's actual needs is required.

5.2 Barnett places Northern Ireland at a disadvantage by trapping it within an ongoing cycle of underinvestment. Deprivation levels in Northern Ireland are such that investment here needs to exceed the levels of investment that applies to the rest of the UK for the foreseeable future.

5.3 Because Scotland, Wales and Northern Ireland have little influence over the size of their bloc grants, the Northern Ireland Executive is constrained in its ability to shape the policy agenda and this undermines devolution. For example, it is difficult for a devolved administration to increase public spending at a time when the UK government is cutting spending.

5.4 The Northern Ireland Confederation believes that the Barnett Formula has serious deficiencies and that an alternative should be found based on a more objective measure of relative need and a formula designed to produce equity in health and social care provision across the UK.

2 March 2009

Memorandum by Economic Research Institute of Northern Ireland

INTRODUCTION

1. The Barnett Formula is named after Joel Barnett (now Lord Barnett) who was Chief Secretary to the Treasury when it was introduced in 1978.[5] The use of a formula for allocating at least some expenditure among the territories (now called countries) of the UK goes back to 1888 when Chancellor George Goschen in preparation for Irish Home Rule introduced a set of proportions for allocating resources between England and Wales, Scotland and Ireland in the ratio of 80:11:9. This formula persisted in Scotland well into the 1950s whereas arrangements for Ireland went a different way with partition and devolved government in the North.

2. This short paper sets out the formalities of the Barnett Formula as they currently apply, with particular reference to Northern Ireland. It also gives some insight to how the formula has worked in practice. The detailed questions posed in the call for evidence are addressed in an annex.

---

[5] The formula was devised by Sir Leo Pliatsky and has always officially been known as the funding formula. The term "Barnett Formula" is attributable to Professor David Heald, a long time student of devolved finance in the UK.

THE BARNETT FORMULA BASICS

3. The most common misconception about the Barnett Formula is that it determines the total allocation of public expenditure to Scotland, Wales and Northern Ireland. This is not the case. The formula is a mechanism that adjusts the public expenditure allocations at the margins. Moreover, it applies only to parts of public expenditure. It does not, for instance, apply to demand-led expenditure such as social security benefits which are funded on a need or claimant basis.

4. The three key elements of the Formula are:

(a) changes in expenditure on services in England, England and Wales or Great Britain, depending on the coverage of the expenditure considered;

(b) the degree to which the English *et al* services have counterparts in the devolved administrations. This is called the "comparability proportions"; and

(c) each country's population as a proportion of the population of England, England and Wales or Great Britain depending on the coverage of the expenditure being considered.

The outcome of the formula is the product of (a), (b) and (c) and is know as the "consequential". This is the amount of additional spending made available to the devolved administrations.

EXAMPLE: Suppose expenditure on an English service increases by £100 million. The service is 100 per cent comparable in Northern Ireland and Northern Ireland's population relative to England is 3.4 per cent. Then Northern Ireland's consequential is £100m x 1.0 x 0.034 = £3.4 million.

As a rough rule of thumb a 1 per cent increase in a comparable service in England would provide enough extra resources to fund a $\frac{3}{4}$ per cent increase in Northern Ireland.

POPULATION PROPORTIONS

5. Population proportions are one of the more objective elements of the formula. There has been an erratic history of updating these percentages. Up until 1992 the mid-1976 population levels were used. In 1992 there was a one-off adjustment but from 1997 onwards the latest mid-year population estimates have been used. The failure to use up-to-date estimates was an advantage to Scotland where in the relevant period population proportion was actually declining. In the 2007 Spending Review the population proportions for Northern Ireland were 3.43 per cent relative to England, 3.24 per cent relative to England and Wales and 2.96 per cent relative to Great Britain.

COMPARABILITIES

6. Comparabilities are a key element of the formula and in some instances are open to considerable interpretation. Comparabilities are calculated as a weighted average of expenditures by the relevant Whitehall department. Up to CSR 2007 the basis of expenditures were the sub-programmes operated by the department. In CSR 2007 these were replaced by "programme objects". Comparability proportions for each devolved administration are estimated for each of these programme objectives and then a weighted average is constructed for the entire department using the baseline expenditures for each programmes objective in the year immediately preceding the CSR.

7. Two problems arise with this approach. First, a weighted average of a Whitehall department's expenditure may not be a good guide to actual expenditures in a devolved administration. Sometimes the latter will gain and sometimes lose from this procedure. This is known as "taking the rough with the smooth".

8. Second, where administrative arrangements for delivering services differ substantially, estimating a consequential can be problematic. The classic example is local authority delivery of services in England that are delivered by central government in Northern Ireland. In England these services are part financed by central government grants and part by the Council Tax and the authority's share of the uniform business rate. Calculating a consequential on the total spend would give Northern Ireland an advantage by relieving local ratepayers of having to make a contribution. On the other hand a consequential based on aggregate external finance (mainstream grants to local authorities in England) may fall well short of actual expenditure in Northern Ireland.

9. A further problem is "departmental unallocated provisions" or in simple terms the reserves UK departments are encouraged to create against unexpected expenditure demands. The convention is that consequentials for these provisions are calculated on the assumption that they mirror the weighted average comparability of the department. In principle this is fine so long as when these resources actually are spent they follow this pattern. Otherwise the reserve may or may not end up in areas where comparability is significantly higher or lower than the average.

THE "BARNETT SQUEEZE"

10. A mathematical feature of the Barnett Formula is that it should, other things being equal, tend over time to converge per capita spending on comparable services in the devolved administration towards the English per capita figure. This is known as the "Barnett Squeeze". The phenomenon arises because the formula gives Scotland, Wales and Northern Ireland additions equal in per capita terms to those in England (this is another way of saying these administrations get their population proportion relative to England of any increase). But it is generally the case that existing per capita expenditure on such services is greater than these marginal additions so that the average per capita spends will converge.

11. Theoretically the convergence phenomenon should be faster:

(a) the greater the initial per capita lead in the devolved administration; and

(b) the greater the increase in expenditure on comparable services in England.

Since the formula is entirely symmetric falls in English comparable expenditures should widen the per capital expenditure gap.

12. Empirical evidence for the "Barnett Squeeze" is limited partly for data reasons and partly because the convergence is likely to be slow, so that other changes to expenditure not dependent on the formula can cloud the issue. The usual data source used is "identifiable public expenditure" which is published in the annual Public Expenditure Statistical Analysis (PESA) which accompanies the Budget. Identifiable public expenditure is expenditure identified from administrative records as being in or on behalf of the devolved territory (country). Settling just what is identifiable expenditure in practice is an issue that at the margins provokes considerable debate, particularly in Scotland.[6] The current identifiable expenditure ratios for the devolved administration relative to the UK set at 100 are:

	2002–03	2007–08
England	96	97
Scotland	117	118
Wales	114	110
Northern Ireland	130	126

So over this period at least Northern Ireland and Wales appear to have been squeezed slightly but Scotland has extended its lead. However, not too much weight should be put on small movements over a short run of years particularly when classification changes and amendments to methodology are taking place.

BYPASSES

13. One reason why theoretical Barnett Squeezes do not materialise is that additional allocations are made to the devolved administration outside the working of the formula. These are commonly referred to as "bypasses".

14. Since the Treasury has invested heavily in the Barnett Formula they are generally resistant to bypassing it and significant departures are usually associated with either technically unavoidable changes or highly political issues. All the devolved administrations have benefited from bypasses at one time or another. Wales, for example, got over £200 million additional cover for Objective 1 EU Structure Funds programmes in the 1990s while Northern Ireland was given additional funding to support the privatisation of aircraft production and shipbuilding in the regions. Northern Ireland also secured additional funding to cover the series of Peace and Reconciliation Programmes launched by the EU in the mid 1990s and some costs associated with implementing the Good Friday Agreement.

15. In recent years the Treasury has tried hard to keep the devolved administration on a strict Barnett Formula diet and has largely succeeded. Despite announcements of new packages of support for devolution these usually turn out, on closer inspection, to be rescheduling of expenditure or movements in non-cash items in budgets.

---

[6] For example, J Cuthbert and M Cuthbert, "A Constructive Critique of the Treasury's Country and Regional Analysis of Public Expenditure", 2005, is an interesting example of the debate.

[7] Funding the Scottish Parliament, National Assembly for Wales and Northern Ireland Assembly: Statement of Funding Policy, October 2007, HM Treasury.

BARNETT AND THE FUNDING RULES

16. The Barnett Formula is the centre piece of the rules governing the funding of devolved administrations.[8] However, it is the interplay of the formula with these rules that gives the process texture and allows interesting possibilities to emerge.

17. Of particular interest is the rule that says "if the UK Government makes a general cut to the budgets of UK departments it is entitled to impose the same adjustments to the budgets of the devolved administrations".

18. Alternatively the reductions in UK departments could be fed through the Barnett Formula to give negative consequentials (reductions) to the devolved administrations.

19. An interesting combination is to apply across the board cuts to baselines including those in the devolved administrations and then give Barnett consequentials on any allocations restored to UK departments. Since the latter are based on population proportions while baseline proportions are usually higher this is an indirect way of cutting budgets for devolved administrations within the rules.

SETTING BASELINES: NEEDS ASSESSMENT

20. Baselines do not enter into the Barnett Formula except as weights in the calculation of the departmental weighted average for comparabilities. However, baselines are very important. As baselines stand at the moment they are historical constructs reflecting a myriad of past changes, including changes from previous applications of the Barnett Formula. A systematic revision of baselines requires some form of Needs Assessment.

21. The basic idea of a Needs Analysis is to start with a benchmark for expenditure in some policy area which in the UK is usually expenditure in England. This expenditure is then associated with a number of "objective factors" such as total population or population structure for those receiving the services and this gives an idea of the unit cost of the service "Objective" in this sense means factors that cannot readily be adjusted by policymakers. The pattern of objective factors in the devolved authorities is then compared to the same factors in England to give an idea of how much more or less it would take to deliver the same service as in England in the circumstances of the devolved administrations. Comparing this to actual expenditure shows whether the devolved administration is over or under provided for that service.

22. This is the barest outline of the technique and in practice Need Assessments are data heavy exercises fraught with difficulty in matching expenditure data and properly identify relevant factors. They work best where services are clearly linked to population such as in education or health programmes but are much less successful in areas such as economic programmes.[9]

23. The only official Needs Assessment in the UK was carried out in 1976 in preparation for devolution to Scotland. Only a summary report was published in 1979. Since devolution did not occur at that time this work faded from view, although there were periodic updates carried out internally by the Treasury. In 2001 the Northern Ireland Executive initiated a unilateral update of Needs Assessment but that work was abandoned when Direct Rule returned.

24. Needs Assessment is often presented as an alternative to the Barnett Formula but that can not be the case. The exercise is too resource-intensive to be repeated annually and there are concerns that as time goes on fundamental changes in the character of services in one area of the UK as opposed to another progressively render the needs assessment technique invalid.

25. Some commentators have argued that the approach adopted by the Commonwealth Grant Commission in Australia for allocating monies to the States could be adopted in the UK even though the constitutional situation is rather different. However, this again is an elaborate exercise and certainly not immune from political influence.

---

[8] Funding the Scottish Parliament, National Assembly for Wales and Northern Ireland Assembly: Statement of Funding Policy, October 2007, HM Treasury.

[9] See http://www.scotlandoffice.gov.uk/freedom-of-information/document.php?release=78&doc=179 ,for a description of the technique used for an update of the 1979 study for Scotland.

CONCLUSIONS

26. The Barnett Formula has been operating in its basic form for 30 years and has been incorporated into a comprehensive set of funding rules for the devolved administrations. It is a uniquely British approach to devolved financing with nothing similar elsewhere in the world.

27. Critics of the formula generally focus on two issues. The first is a fear that repeated use of the formula as the main means of adjusting devolved budgets will lead to steady convergence to English per capita expenditure on services. The other, which is basically the same point, is that using a formula that only takes account of population proportions is a poor way of capturing relative need.

28. One approach would be to replace the formula by one which was the reciprocal of the relative outputs of the devolved administration and the UK (or England). In Northern Ireland's case the relative output (GVA) ratio is 80 per cent so this formula would give Northern Ireland approximately 125 per cent of comparable spending the in the UK. Since regional productivity figures are notoriously unreliable this would not seem much of an advance.

29. Combining other factors with population in the formula raises the question of what these should be and what relative weight they should have. This in turn can lead down the path to what statisticians call an index number problem.

30. Convergence is an inherent characteristic of the formula but in practice has not been a critical issue. When devolution began some commentators feared that the new administrations would quickly run out of money as the formula took its toll. In fact the reverse could be argued, that the devolved administrations, at least initially, had rather too much money and made some unfortunate spending decisions as a result.

31. Another aspect of the formula is not its impact on the devolved administration but on England or at least the perception among some English commentators that it gives the devolved administrations too much. This, of course, is a misconception arising from confusing the baseline expenditure in the devolved administrations with changes in these baselines. Whether the devolved administrations have too much of a share of public expenditure or too little is not a question the Barnett Formula can answer.

32. Should the formula be abandoned or replaced with some other funding mechanism? That is essentially a political rather than a technical question but some points that need to be kept in mind are:

— The Barnett Formula does remove the need for detailed negotiations with the Treasury on the minutiae of budgets in Spending Reviews—a very big plus;

— It offers some protection to any existing expenditure advantage enjoyed by a devolved administration; and

— Its workings alongside the other funding rules are reasonably well understood so it offers a degree of stability that a replacement might take a long time to deliver.

Annex

RESPONSES TO QUESTIONS

1. *Application of the Formula in Practice*

   a. Are the present disparities in public expenditure per head of population between the countries of the UK a consequence of the Formula itself, the historic baseline or of other factors? To what extent are those disparities related to need?

   b. What effect does the Barnett Formula have in terms of equity and fairness across the UK as a whole?

   c. What effect does the Barnett Formula have on the aggregate control of public expenditure?

   d. What measure of flexibility do the Devolved Administrations (DAs) presently enjoy in allocating funds, between various policy areas, between capital and current spending, and for accounting purposes? Is there any need for reform in this area?

Response

   a. The current relativities between public expenditure per head in the countries of the United Kingdom are the result of decades of fiscal arrangements, including special deals and the outcome of successive rounds of applying the Barnett formula, and relative population growth between these countries. In Northern Ireland special factors such as the acceptance of the need to "make up leeway" in expenditure in areas such as road infrastructure in the 1960s and the effects of the "troubles" which spread far beyond security issues to loosen up funding from the Treasury all played a part.

b. The Barnett formula takes population as the effective measure of need but equity is not only an expenditure issue it also refers to tax effort so that shortfalls in the use of population as a guide to equitable treatment in expenditure have to be balanced with the cost to other regions in making good a shortfall of revenue in any country of the UK.

c. It reinforces control because the mechanism allows the Treasury to know exactly how much a given increase in comparable expenditure per head in England will cost in aggregate simply by using the comparabilities and relative populations for the rest of the UK to establish an overall control total.

d. The devolved administrations have total flexibility to allocate their Assigned Budget (the bit controlled by the Barnett formula) subject to the normal rules of the public expenditure regime which usually prevent veering from capital to resources (current). Changing this needs to balance the need for flexibility with the need for discipline in financial planning and the protection of capital spending which is always an easy target in the short term.

2. *Formula By-Pass and the Barnett Squeeze*

e. Has convergence of levels of public spending in Scotland, Wales and Northern Ireland based on the English level of spending happened and, if not, why?

f. To what extent did bypassing of the Formula occur before 1999? Has scope for such "Formula by-passes" changed? What have been the consequences of that change in scope?

Response

e. The evidence on convergence based on identifiable public expenditure figures is ambiguous and depends on the period examined (unfortunately changes in methodology for estimating identifiable public expenditure and sorting out the assigned budget elements for long periods, including times when this concept did not exist, makes this sort of analysis dubious). The chart below shows consistent figures but only over a five year period. The absence of strong convergence is noticeable.

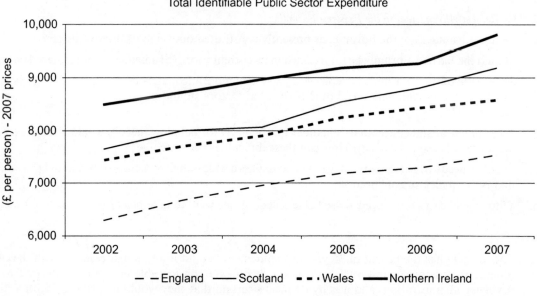

Total Identifiable Public Sector Expenditure

f. There has been extensive bypassing of the formula going back decades. As noted in the main text, Northern Ireland got money outside the formula for the EU Peace and Reconciliation Programmes from 1996 onwards as well as money for police and prisons reforms which went through the Northern Ireland Office, the benefit of which will, in due course, be inherited by the devolved administration. Wales got additional cover for Objective 1 receipts as a political arrangement. There were also deals done in Scotland and all of these are merely a sample.

Getting special deals from the Treasury has become more difficult and especially where these add to the baseline. Thus virtually all of the financial package given to the NI parties when devolution was restored after the St Andrew's agreement involved additions within a financial year and not a permanent baseline uplift.

3. *Data Quality and Availability*

g.   Are sufficient data available to enable a clear understanding of how public spending is distributed across the UK and to show the working of the Formula as set out in the Statement of Funding Policy?

h.   What additional data, or ways of presenting data, would be necessary to undertake a new needs assessment, or otherwise to reform the Formula?

i.   What additional data, or ways of presenting data, should be available to ensure that the Formula is transparent in its application?

j.   What body should undertake the collection and publication of such data?

Response

g.   In general there is sufficient information to estimate the distribution of public expenditure in the UK but it is scattered across many publications and is very difficult to interpret when the underlying institutions vary. Thus estimating expenditure on schools, for example, is virtually impossible to do on a consistent and accurate basis. Similarly housing expenditure is a nightmare to sort out. In the same way even though comparabilities and population figures are published in advance, working out whether the additions to the devolved countries are accurate is really only possible with inside knowledge.

h.   Needs Assessment is an enormously data heavy exercise and offers endless possibilities for argument. The 1979 Study was only a summary document and there are detailed individual programme studies behind it which were never published. A classic argument at that time which has never been resolved is, what is a good measure of health, mortality (which is fairly definite) or morbidity (which isn't). It is crucial to realise that the formula has nothing to do with needs assessment which is a periodic way of resetting the baseline whereas the formula is an ongoing way of adjusting it.

i./j.   It is an illusion to think that public expenditure and its presentation can be entirely divorced from politics. Spending Review documents, funding rules and statistical publications involving public expenditure are very carefully vetted.

4. *Need for Reform/Alternatives to the Existing Formula*

k.   Do the advantages of the Formula as presently constituted outweigh its disadvantages?

l.   Should the Barnett Formula be (a) retained in its current form, (b) amended or (c) replaced entirely?

m.   Should the Barnett Formula be replaced by a system more adequately reflecting relative needs, costs of services or a combination of both? If so, what factors should be considered as part of a needs assessment?

n.   What practical and conceptual difficulties (particularly for defining "need") would arise in carrying out a needs-based assessment? How can these difficulties be overcome?

o.   Should a needs-based assessment seek to encompass a wide-range of factors or be limited to a smaller number of indicators of "need"?

p.   Who should carry out a needs-based assessment, if one were to take place?

Response

k.   The formula has the benefit of 30 years of refinement behind it and it's interaction with the other funding rules is reasonably well understood. It offers a considerable degree of protection to the devolved administrations and it is by no means certain that they would be better off with a direct negotiation approach. There is no favourite alternative formula that has been thoroughly tested in the many situations that the Barnett formula has survived. In the absence of an alternative formula that all of the devolved administrations could unite behind they should weigh heavily the very great risks of direct negotiation with the Treasury which, after all, represents, in one sense, the 80 per cent of taxpayers that keep the rest afloat.

l.   If there is a workable formula that is fair to all who have a stake in financing the devolved administrations then it should certainly be adopted. None of the solutions presented by academics begin to approach this requirement.

m.   Practicalities have to be considered in this matter. It is not ideal that devolved administrations get their share of changes in a Spending Review on the basis of the average comparability of English departments but at least they get their allocations on the day of the Spending review announcement.

Would the devolved administrations be prepared to await the announcement of detailed allocations within English departments, which might be months behind the broad allocation to these departments' as a whole, before they knew the resources they had available? The preparation of estimates takes a long time and if the devolved administrations are dependant on the final distributions made by Whitehall Ministers amongst their comparable programme objectives to inform them of what their consequentials might be they would be a long way behind in their planning process.

n. The concept of "need" has to be anchored in criteria that are relatively immune to manipulation in the short term. That is why the "objective" factors used in traditional needs analysis tend to be population based such as the total population or its structure for various client groups such as school age children. Alternatively physical measures such as population density or even physical area might be used for some programmes. The more that one moves away from these relatively immutable factors the greater the difficulty in relation to need. Unemployment is a good example. What does this mean? Is it the administrative measure of claimants—Northern Ireland 38,000—or perhaps the Labour Force Survey definition—42,000—or perhaps economic inactivity in the population of working age—circa 100,000. The easier that a weighting factor like this can be manipulated by definition the less valid it is in a needs assessment. In addition it is a central assumption of needs assessment that throughout the UK administrations are striving to the same basic standard of public provision, the benchmark for which is provision in England. If that is in fact a deficient benchmark (as it might be in education, for instance) in what sense is the need being properly assessed. In 1979 when this technique was adopted it was at the cutting edge of methodology for a relatively homogeneous country. This may no longer be the case.

o. The larger the number of factors in any assessment of need the greater is the problem of assigning weights to these factors to come to an overall judgement. This is rich ground for argument. If a small number of factors are included that are closely correlated the result of a composite indicator is not much different than for a single indicator such as population proportions.

p. If this is going to be done then it cannot be a Treasury led exercise as in the past. Probably the best way forward would be a joint exercise by independent bodies from the various jurisdictions, such as the Institute for Fiscal Studies in London and research institutes or universities in the devolved countries. The funding should be borne jointly with a joint steering group drawn from officials in all of the countries involved.

5. *Decision-making and Dispute Resolution*

q. How effective, appropriate and fair are the processes and criteria by which HM Treasury determines matters relating to the Barnett Formula? In particular, is the way HM Treasury determines whether items of spending in England do or do not attract consequential payments under the Formula, and claims by the DAs on the UK Reserve, appropriate and fair?

r. Are the existing procedures for resolving disputes between HM Treasury Ministers, territorial Secretaries of State and the Devolved Administrations about funding issues adequate?

s. How could dispute resolution procedures be improved?

Response

q. On paper the procedures are very fair. Officials from the Treasury and the devolved administrations meet well in advance of the conclusion of the Spending Review and agree the necessary figure work regarding population proportions and degrees of comparability. Outside Spending Reviews the situation is less well structured and less transparent. Typically an initiative will be announced for England and when the DAs ask about their share the response will be that this is an existing allocation which is being re-brigaded and of course the DAs already have their consequentials. What is particularly annoying is when the Treasury announce at very short notice a change which though not strictly part of the formula nevertheless has implications for the DAs. The revisions made to certain UK departmental baselines just before the SR 2007 announcement is an example.

r. At the end of the day how negotiations between Ministers go depends on the force of the argument and the strength of the individuals. A DA with a good case and supported by a strong Secretary of State generally prevails over a Chief Secretary. However if the argument is weak and particularly if the Chancellor sees no merit in it the Treasury will usually carry the day. The current dispute between the DAs and the Treasury over bearing a share of additional resource releasing efficiency savings in UK departments (the Barnett formula working in reverse) should be instructive in this matter.

s.   Perhaps inserting a "no suprises" clause in the Funding Rules could help but this could be honoured more in spirit than practice.

February 2009

Examination of Witnesses

Witnesses: MR PATRICK MCCARTAN, Northern Ireland Confederation for Health and Social Services; and MR VICTOR HEWITT, Economic Research Institute of Northern Ireland, examined.

Q801 Chairman: Gentlemen, thank you very much indeed for coming this afternoon. As I am sure you know, we have been asked by the House of Lords as a Select Committee of the House to look into the operation of the Barnett Formula. I hope you have seen our terms of reference because you will see that they fairly focused and limited. We are not entitled to look at tax raising powers for any of the devolved administrations. We are not entitled to look at the division of monies among the English regions. Our function is to look at how Barnett operates and whether it should go on operating as it does. It is really quite an interesting conundrum as to what is the best way of getting money from the centre out to the three devolved administrations, particularly in a situation in which the three devolved administrations do not have symmetrical devolution, it is different in the three areas. What one wants to do is devise a system if one moves away from Barnett which produces sensible and effective allocation of resources and resources which, by and large, are fair. I wonder if I could ask you a general question to start off with, which is a very simple question to ask. Do you think the Barnett Formula treats Northern Ireland fairly and, if so, why, and, if not, why not?
Mr Hewitt: We must remember that the Formula is an adjustment mechanism, it is not a mechanism for setting a baseline, that has to be done by other means. Historically it takes the baseline and adds to it or potentially could subtract from it depending on what is happening across the world. It is a marginal adjustment mechanism simply based upon your relative population proportions and the comparability of your expenditure with expenditure essentially in England at this moment in time. It is a relatively simple conceptual formula. What it effectively does is to give each of the countries of the UK the same per capita increase in expenditure as is happening in England. That is effectively what it does each time it is applied. One of the consequences of that is if your baseline is proportionately bigger than your population proportion then there will be an effective squeeze upon the amount of money coming across because you are adding at the margins less than the proportion of the baseline. Is it fair? Well, we would need to look at not only the Formula itself because it only really applies to a proportion of the expenditure which goes on in the region and part of the expenditure in the region is outside the Formula altogether. Such things as social security and the annually managed expenditure money is done under an entirely separate mechanism, a sort of sale or return type mechanism. The Barnett Formula only tackles that bit which we call the assigned budget in the block, which is round about half of our total budget. Has it enormously disadvantaged or advantaged us? There has not been a sign that we have converged dramatically over time with the situation in England. There has been some movement, but quite often the relative figures are distorted because additional monies have come through other mechanisms, what Professor David Heald referred to as "bypass mechanisms". Money such as the funding of the EU Special Programme Bodies, the Peace and Reconciliation Funds, and in earlier times monies which were associated with the privatisation of Harland & Wolff and Shorts, all of these flowed into our block outside the Barnett mechanism and tended to push up the per capita lead. It is not just a matter of being fair but is it a mechanism which can be easily replaced by something which is as workable, that is the question which really needs to be addressed. It is okay in theory to devise all sorts of sophisticated mechanisms for allocating money out, but the practicalities are that on the day of a Spending Review the devolved administration would want to know how much they are going to get, and since Spending Reviews are not finished until the last minute there has to be a relatively straightforward mechanism for allowing them to calculate how much money is coming to them. That is a roundabout answer to your question. It is a complicated formula when other factors are taken into consideration. It is very simple in itself. By and large it has served us reasonably well. We cannot answer the issue of needs through the Formula and whether the amount of money we are getting is proportionate to our needs, that is a matter for needs assessment and perhaps we might talk about that later.

Q802 Chairman: Certainly it is true that the Formula narrowly applied only applies to the changes up and down, but it seems to be being used and understood and, indeed, applied now as to the block as well as the variations. Do you think the amount Northern Ireland gets for its baseline is a fair allocation?
Mr Hewitt: That is very difficult to say unless one were to carry out what is known as a needs assessment but, as in life, these things are never simple because there is not an absolutely agreed

methodology about how one should approach a needs assessment. As you are probably aware, the only published version of a needs assessment relates back to 1977 when devolution was first conceived for Scotland and not carried out at that time. A system was devised to estimate our relative need and that of Scotland and Wales relative to England, and I can go into the detail of that if you like. That has actually been updated annually but never publicly. The Treasury updates the needs assessment formula annually, or certainly it did well into the 1990s. They are less in favour of that methodology these days because they think the underlying structures for the UK have changed so much and different parts of the UK tend to have experiences different from London. For example, they will say that parts of England have a high influx of immigrants, and that is not quite the case for, say, Scotland or Wales, so that creates a particular need in England which is difficult to roll out to the others. The things which go into a needs assessment formula are supposed to be objective factors—population, the structure of your population, how many young people, how many old people and so forth—but inevitably there will be subjective things put into the mix as well. There are always arguments around the subjective things. What is the best indicator of ill-health, for example, is a classic one. Is it the standardised mortality ratio by the number of people who die, or is it some other measure of ill-health? That has always been a bone of contention when these things are looked at. Needs assessment is something which a lot of people talk about but very few people have ever experienced what a needs assessment is really like.

Q803 *Chairman:* But you say it cannot be done.
Mr Hewitt: It can be done.

Q804 *Chairman:* It does not have to be as complicated as it was in 1979.
Mr Hewitt: Once you start on these things it tends to become complicated.

Q805 *Chairman:* Only if you make it so surely. If you were to cut down the number of variables that you were going to take account of to four, five or six, I do not know, you would probably get 95 per cent fairness although you would not get 100 per cent.
Mr Hewitt: Possibly so. You will always have arguments from the other side that you have left out a very important dimension to the problem and there is the problem of what weight do you attach to these various things and there will be different views about the weight that should be attached to one factor as opposed to another. Once you get into those sorts of arguments you rapidly begin to think whether it was worth going down this route in the first place because you are not going to get agreement at the end of it.

Q806 *Chairman:* Have you looked at the Australian system?
Mr Hewitt: Yes, the Commonwealth Grants Commission. It is a pretty good example of the complications which arise in these circumstances but it is there for a different purpose than the allocation of public expenditure in the UK. It is there to essentially allocate out the proceeds of certain taxation among the states. It operates on a federal system. It is about horizontal equalisation, ie putting the various states on the same basis so that they can deliver services, but taking account of the amount of taxes which they actually raise. It does focus on a slightly different issue. We are a purely expenditure based system, taxation has no role other than through local government.

Q807 *Chairman:* But the needs assessment bit would be the same, would it not?
Mr Hewitt: Yes.

Q808 *Chairman:* In other words, if they assess need in Australia we can assess need here.
Mr Hewitt: Yes, indeed. Needs assessment is very simple in concept. The policies are broadly similar throughout the United Kingdom, so if it costs £100 to deliver some sort of service in England how much does it cost to deliver the same service in Scotland, Wales and Northern Ireland. That is the starting point for the whole thing. It then generates an index and typically Northern Ireland would come out at something like £125 through to £130 as opposed to an English spend of £100 in that context. The full-blown thing is an extremely data heavy exercise. The original one took three years essentially.

Q809 *Chairman:* Yes.
Mr Hewitt: Updates on these usually take at least 18 months.

Q810 *Chairman:* Do you know how long the Northern Ireland Government took to do its one in 2001?
Mr Hewitt: Since I was doing it, yes, 18 months. Of course, that was a unilateral thing, it was not done with the co-operation of the Treasury.

Q811 *Chairman:* But it was 18 months?
Mr Hewitt: Yes, about 18 months.

Q812 *Chairman:* If needs assessment could be done by an objective commission like the Australian Grants Commission, why should it not be applied to the UK?
Mr Hewitt: There is no logical reason why it should not. It would have to be done by something outside the Treasury.

Q813 *Chairman:* I think we would all agree with that.

Mr Hewitt: Because the devolved administrations will not accept that the Treasury is an honest broker in these matters, and rightly so. It cannot be done that often because we cannot really rely upon this to be an annual mechanism.

Q814 *Chairman:* They do it annually in Australia.

Mr Hewitt: Yes, they do, and it is a very large effort indeed. I was having a look at their website the other day and a very large effort goes into that. It is full of methodological pitfalls as you go along to calculate things on net or gross terms, you get different results on those sorts of things. How much of the block do you actually take into account? When it was done in the 1970s the law and order and protective services were effectively outside of it because of the extraordinary circumstances in Northern Ireland, so there will be judgments about things like that. It is certainly an interesting exercise but it is not a magic bullet in terms of guaranteeing that you are going to get more money from the Treasury at the end of the day.

Q815 *Chairman:* If there is a finite amount some will get more and some will get less. What we have really been concerned about is whether or not it could be feasible to have a needs assessment procedure along the lines of the Australian system which we could apply to the allocation of resources here in the UK. I think with all the qualifications you made about it you do think that is possible.

Mr Hewitt: Yes. The methodologies are relatively straight forward. The needs assessment system which we operated did not involve a lot of statistical work in the sense of doing estimations and stuff like that. It was certainly less complicated than the old standard spending assessments which operated in local government, which you might recall. It was never designed to be that, it was to take into account people's experience of how programmes worked, what was important in driving expenditure in a programme and so on. It is not quite as scientific as some of the work which is done in Australia. I think you will find the Australian system still produces results which are not universally welcomed by the participants.

Q816 *Chairman:* What we heard about it was it produces its report and then for about two or three days everybody says how unfair it is, but it gradually goes to another sleep for another 360 days until it produces another report and there is the same eruption. It is not a serious business but it is loud while it is going on.

Mr Hewitt: Even if you did this, what would you do in the intervening years? You would have adjusted the baseline and how are you going to continue to adjust the baseline outside that period. That is what the Formula is there to do, it is not there to set it but to adjust it.

Q817 *Chairman:* The Formula is not there to adjust the baseline.

Mr Hewitt: No.

Q818 *Chairman:* You would have to adjust the baseline

Mr Hewitt: Are you proposing to run the exercise every year?

Chairman: I should think so, yes. The Australians seem to do it and I do not see why we should not. I do not have violently strong views as to whether you do it every year, 18 months or two years but it has got to be done within a fairly narrow band of time. It has got to be able to stick to the length of time it is meant to be done for.

Q819 *Lord Sewel:* Can we look at convergence. I have seen some figures that indicate over recent years there has been some convergence in Northern Ireland. Obviously the weight of the past to prevent convergence was bypass and really bypass was not easy but at least it was a route that was accessible prior to devolution when we basically had the territorial ministers going to the Chief Secretary, and if that did not work going to the Chancellor and if that did not work trying the Prime Minister, and they were all ministers of the one government. Some were more successful than others, it has to be said. Then with devolution that system breaks down so the opportunity to bypass reduces. If you then have, if you like, more pure Barnett convergence is likely to kick in much more heavily. If your population is going up, which I understand the population in Northern Ireland is, then because your base is a product of a lower population you are also going to get a squeeze, yet people seem to be relatively content with Barnett whereas because of those factors if I was in Northern Ireland I would be pretty worried about that.

Mr Hewitt: The "Barnett squeeze" is primarily a mathematical phenomenon. The faster expenditure goes up in England, the faster the squeeze will be applied. In recent years we have been living through very rapid increases in public expenditure in the UK, certainly since 2000, therefore it is not surprising to see there has been some convergence. Of course, the absolute amounts of money which have been transferred through Barnett are very, very substantial. The second thing, as I emphasised before, is it only applies to part of the totality of public expenditure in the Province, the other half at least is coming through annually managed expenditure and the benefits system. There is also expenditure by UK departments actually in the Province, so the Ministry of Defence will be spending money in Northern Ireland which is not part of the block. Should we be worried about it? It has not really been a problem. I think David Heald put it quite well, that one of the great fears at the beginning of devolution was there was going to be too little money whereas in reality it appears that there has been rather too much money available to the devolved administrations. What is the evidence for that because that is a fairly harsh thing to say? If you actually look at the under-spends from the devolved administrations over the years, these have been very substantial and have not been diminishing very rapidly, so we are carrying forward from year-to-year substantial sums of money under-spent from the previous year. That does not suggest there is a vast shortage of money, but it may suggest there has been not very good estimating by departments.

Q820 *Lord Sewel:* Mr McCartan, would you like to comment?

Mr McCartan: I have to disagree from the other end, as it were, as a user or sufferer under the Barnett Formula in relation to health and social care. Health and social care accounts for 40 per cent plus of all public expenditure in Northern Ireland. It accounts for 70,000 employees, one in ten is employed in health and social care here, and is very much dependent on the allocation of public funds under Barnett. I can give you one or two examples of that. My own trust is Belfast Health and Social Care Trust and there are five other delivery organisations, including an ambulance trust. The Belfast HSC Trust has 20,000 employees, £1,100 million expenditure each year, which is 12.5 per cent of all public expenditure that comes through the Barnett Formula to Northern Ireland, together, the trust boards account for over £3 billion expenditure per year, but we are very substantially behind provision in England for health and social care, and the gap is growing. The only way it can be growing is because the overall cake that our Assembly has to distribute is not sufficient to provide us with enough to meet the gap, and when you are talking there about the squeeze, that squeeze is happening today and causing problems of reorganisation in our Health Service which are effectively restricting numbers of employees and our ability to address very specific need for the elderly, for the very young, the very vulnerable people in our society, people with mental health and learning difficulties, and of course acute care. Our acute care

is running at round about 10 per cent cent less funded than similar acute care in England. Our social care through our social care department is running at about 36 per cent less funded than similar social care provision in England. The reason for that is, of course, that we make bids, they go through our political system, and we now have 11 major departments all bidding and all saying they want more. We can measure the effect of that in that under the Comprehensive Spending Review period we are getting new money into health and social care, real new money, of 1.1 per cent. England is getting 4.3 per cent. We cannot address the need or close the gap with that method of funding, it is wrong and it does not work. We have four National Health Services in the UK, not one, and that is the position of the Confederation at national level. I am a trustee of the Confederation at national level, I do know the positions on the Scotland-England border and on the Wales-England border, and they are different. They are caused because of divergence in policies of the various devolved administrations. In our case, for our Minister, who happens to be a Unionist Minister, therefore one of the minority parties, to get more money he has to convince the other three major parties that his department deserves it and of course that is a horse trade from which we suffer, and are suffering increasingly. If Barnett was based on need, based on an assessment that actually reflects the differences in health and social care as well as other differences, then we would at least have a mechanism and a chance of trying to do things better than we are doing currently rather than seeing health and social care diverge. I am quite happy to talk about mortality rates and the differences between them here and in England, for example, where we are significantly worse off, and I can give you that hospital by hospital and area by area to show you. Those are real issues which we want to address and the current Barnett Formula and the "Barnett squeeze" is not allowing us to do that. Would the Government accept an argument that there should be some degree of equality of citizenship particularly in relation to something as essential as health and social care? If it does or if you think that it could then surely that should mean the Treasury should have a different approach to the way monies are disbursed than they currently are to devolved administrations. That is the sort of area where we are coming from.

Q821 *Lord Sewel:* I think we have got two things here. One, it is possible that health and social care in Northern Ireland has not had as much money allocated to it as England and Wales because Northern Irish ministers give it a lower priority. That is perfectly consistent with the idea of devolution.

The idea of devolution was clearly that the governments of the three territories should develop their own priorities and have their own policies, so the money comes to them in the pot and they decide in terms of their own local priorities where it should go. That is one thing. The other thing is that may be one of the reasons why your health and social care is not doing well or it could be that the pot is getting relatively smaller compared with the needs you have to address.

Mr McCartan: I have to say efficiency would be another issue. These issues were gone into in great detail in 2005 by Professor John Appleby and the Appleby report that was made to the DFP here, Department of Finance and Personnel, did address some of the efficiency issues and also the question of the gap in provision, the under-funding. It did make an argument for something like 7 per cent additional spend per head in relation to health and social care over a period of years to address the imbalance. You are right to say that is a matter for our devolved administration. They have not taken that matter up and some of what I am saying needs addressed could and should be addressed there, but it does not explain overall the whole question of both capital and recurrent expenditure and the effects of it on a regional basis in comparison with England or even Scotland or Wales. There is an under-capitalisation problem and an under-recurrent funding problem here. If you put yourself in the position of some of our health and social care organisations, what would you say about the Barnett Formula. Of course you would say it needs to be based on needs assessment. Those are not just health and social care needs, but needs assessment as a formula and a formula that can be devised on a UK-wide basis with appropriate indicators. My Lord Chairman raised the question of Australia and when I was there certainly I was aware of what was happening between the federal and the state and there are plenty of arguments, particularly in health, hospital and social care and how they are funded or not, but we do not enjoy those debates. We would love to be able to do that. Bear in mind that is where we come from. As representing the biggest part of government expenditure in Northern Ireland we want to be able to do more and better and that might mean the cake needs to grow.

Q822 Earl of Mar and Kellie: I was certainly interested by what you were saying about the four National Health Services that we have in the UK because we obviously do have four. I get the impression that in Northern Ireland you have done a needs assessment, you know what you want to measure, but what I would like to ask is have the other three National Health Services done that? Have they come up with the same criteria or something different because ultimately this is to be presented to

the Treasury and you have all got to be singing from the same hymn sheet?

Mr McCartan: I think the answer to that is no. I am aware of similar approaches and the fact that ministers now are starting to talk to each other between Cardiff, Belfast and Edinburgh, but not to the extent that they are making joint plans or provision. I think what each of those ministers would probably argue is there is a case for some divergence that you reflect local needs and local pressures, and that would be our experience. When it comes to what ought to be provided in overall terms, in macro terms as it were, for health and social care in each of the jurisdictions we would no doubt favour—I am not able to tell you there has been a decision on that—a common method of approach that allows us to plan on a proper basis to meet the need and to see some evening up, not totally but some, of provision in health and social care between the various jurisdictions. Why I say "not totally" is some services are reliant on a national approach. You need very specialist services in some areas of cancer care, transplant or others, and it is right that we should have one centre, for example, specialising in research-led approaches in those areas. It is the same in regions where you need a dynamic. The strategic health authorities in England have about ten million people to look after and as a result they can run proper paediatric services and a series of other major services, cancer services and so on. We have 1.7 million people. There is a diseconomy of scale that operates here right away. We have to provide regional services. The bulk of that falls on the trusts, by the way. That does work in a way which is counter to us being able to make the best provision. If we have to have our own cancer centre, for example, it is spread across 1.7 as distinct from the ten million that a similar centre would serve in the northwest. Those things work against us in a way. We are more than capable of managing to do all of that and work in a co-operative way with the rest of the United Kingdom, which we do, but not with the current method of funding. Coming from the Barnett Formula, which is being squeezed, into Northern Ireland, which then squeezes it again because it thinks, "Here's 40 per cent, we are not going to give 40 per cent to one minister", particularly if it is a minority minister, the effect of that, taken with the Appleby report which looked in detail at the differences in the cost and efficiencies, brings us to the view that we need to fundamentally adjust the method of funding devolved administrations. That has to be much more reflective of need. That is our position.

Q823 Earl of Mar and Kellie: Your colleagues from the other Health Services, who have presumably read the Appleby report, have they accepted it or rejected it, or said, "We will make one or two changes at the margin"?

Mr McCartan: The Appleby report is accepted on a national basis. John Appleby of the King's Fund does similar reports for the rest of the United Kingdom from time to time and his report is robust in that regard. It is not opposed, as it were, by other parts of the Health Service. It was accepted by the DFP here. It is the basis upon which a lot of our planning and commissioning has gone on. The problem is fundamentally under-provision.

Q824 *Chairman:* The message we have been getting from those people we have talked to here in Northern Ireland is on the whole they are reasonably satisfied with the way in which the present system operates, there is a feeling that the new government here deserves a period of calm and reflection to bed in before you have another great eruption in terms of how the monies are allocated to them and, therefore, for the time being many of the people we have talked to have said assessment based on need makes sense and is fairer, so at this stage they do not think this is the appropriate time to do it. Is that a fair summary of the position?

Mr Hewitt: The view will differ depending on the country. I should imagine that the Scots would run a mile.

Q825 *Chairman:* I was not talking about the Scots; I was talking about you.

Mr Hewitt: If you are going to have a funding system for the devolved administrations of the UK it would have to be a unanimously agreed funding system. If you are going to change it you do need the agreement of Scotland and Wales.

Q826 *Chairman:* Sorry, I was not making myself clear. What I was trying to do was sum up what the position here in Northern Ireland is.

Mr Hewitt: A lot of people do not really know very much about what we are talking about today, it is a relatively small circle of people who have operated in this area so they know the term "Barnett Formula" but not much beyond that. It is not really the Formula, it is the way the Formula interacts with all the other funding rules which apply to Northern Ireland. I give an example in my paper where the across the board cut approach can be mixed with the Barnett Formula to either advantage or disadvantage you. It is not just the formula itself, it is the wider funding rules. I listened with interest to the discussion on needs assessment. The Treasury will not accept any argument on needs assessment which is based upon a difference in policy. For example, they will not give Wales a penny because of the Welsh language. If you have a difference in policy that is down to you,

that is a subjective factor, and they will only give it on objective factors.

Q827 *Chairman:* The Welsh are bound to have a different policy on the Welsh language, I would have thought.

Mr Hewitt: The Treasury says the English taxpayer is not going to subsidise it.

Mr McCartan: Can we talk about tax for a moment because there are different methods of funding. There are local taxes and, of course, national taxation. When it comes to social care, this is a local authority matter in the UK as distinct from here where it is a central government matter. Of course, some scope for raising taxes through council taxes exists in Britain but not here, and that is a difference which does limit us. When it comes to needs assessment I think people in Northern Ireland would generally accept that we should be taxed on the same basis roughly across the board, no difference, provided it is distributed on a fair basis based on need. I am quite happy to see our council taxes go up and our water tax go up, provided it is part of doing something about the distribution of monies to try and get to this idea of equity of citizenship.

Q828 *Lord Sewel:* Could I just ask, is denominational schooling an expenditure need or a policy decision?

Mr Hewitt: That is a policy decision. If you want to maintain five school systems it is a matter for you. What they take into account is how many children of school age you have. They break it down into expenditure blocks, so there is expenditure on schools, primary schools, pre-primary schools, secondary schools, tertiary schools and so on, and the objective factor which goes into those is what size of population you are going to be serving in Northern Ireland as opposed to England. Running multiple school systems, deciding to keep the water system as a publicly funded operation, all of these are policy decisions taken by the devolved administration and the Treasury will say, quite rightly in many respects, "That is a matter for you. If you choose to do that, to provide free care for the elderly" as the Scots have done, "you are going to use your money for that, but you cannot come back to us and ask for additional money for other things if you have decided to do that".

Q829 *Lord Sewel:* So if in England, say, we moved to an insurance-based health system, what then?

Mr Hewitt: That would be a very fundamental change because the whole thing is based upon broadly similar policies being operated throughout the UK. Devolution does bring the spotlight on that as well as the extent to which a devolved administration can depart from what is happening in England without disturbing its funding.

Q830 *Lord Sewel:* That is one of the problems, is it not?

Mr Hewitt: Yes.

Q831 *Lord Sewel:* The theory of devolution must be that of the opportunity to develop local priorities, local policies, local solutions in terms of local need, yet when you trace the funding that enables that to happen you come back to English programmes. It is likely, and certainly happening in Scotland, you will get a greater degree of programme divergence, if you like, in Scotland from England, yet the funding is still tied back to an English programme. That is a strain in itself, is it not?

Mr Hewitt: Yes.

Mr McCartan: I do not disagree with you that there is this dilemma in devolution. There is still a legacy here that we like to have someone else to blame, which for 30 or 35 years was the mantra of every politician in Northern Ireland and now they have to come to terms with some decision-making. We are never very far away from that sort of system. Of course, we have the system of a land border with another EU country where there is an insurance-based two-tier system effectively of health and social care, which is not a good example. People in Northern Ireland would not want to go in that direction, that is very clear.

Mr Hewitt: There is an interesting situation which has developed out of our particular form of devolution. As you know, ministers hold their positions by virtue of a process called D'Hondt whereby the size of the party dictates whether they will hold a ministry.

Q832 *Lord Sewel:* We share very fond memories of D'Hondt.

Mr Hewitt: That, plus the consequence that there is no principal of collective responsibility within the Executive, means that you cannot really have a budget process except during Spending Review years when there is more money to be allocated. There is no mechanism for actually taking money out of departments in the intervening years. This is something which is slowly coming to light. The Minister of Finance is not a Chancellor of the Exchequer, the Chief Minister is not a Prime Minister and the Executive is not a Cabinet, so the Minister of Finance cannot come along and say, "Right, well I have decided our priorities require us to take X million pounds from the roads budget and put it into the health budget this year" unless the ministers involved actually agree to do that. They cannot be forced to do it. You can only really have proper budget allocations when additional money becomes available and this year, for example, we did not have a budget, we had a strategic stock take, nothing like

a budget at all. That is an interesting by-product of devolution itself.

Q833 *Chairman:* I have to say I have never heard that. How can you possibly run a government on that basis?

Mr Hewitt: That is a very interesting question.

Q834 *Chairman:* It is a question. Are you saying that you cannot have a coherent budget unless all the ministers agree to the proposals?

Mr Hewitt: Yes. There is a programme for government and a budget associated with it. It runs for three years and there is no mechanism for adjusting that except by agreement within those three years. They adjust within the year because a monitoring exercise goes on and some people who cannot spend the money during the year will surrender it in the hope that if in the future they need more money they will be able to bid it back. There is no actual budget process going on at the moment.

Q835 *Chairman:* I did not know that. You said a little earlier that the Treasury would not finance programmes which were not basic UK programmes. Is that an official statement from the Treasury or just your experience?

Mr Hewitt: Essentially it is the practice of the way the Formula works. The classic example of this for ourselves is water. Water and sewerage was privatised in England and Wales some considerable time ago, but it was retained within the government system in Northern Ireland. What that meant was there was no comparable public expenditure on water and sewerage in England, hence no consequential as they call it, no share of that was coming across to Northern Ireland to help fund a publicly owned system in Northern Ireland. We had the issue then that water could only be funded by taking money from other things effectively, including health, and there has been a very considerable debate about whether water charges should be introduced and they have decided not to for the moment. It is an interesting example where the Formula essentially carries across English policy, or the consequences of English policy.

Q836 *Chairman:* Consequences, yes, I understand that. You would not get the consequentials if it increased?

Mr Hewitt: That is right.

Q837 *Chairman:* How did you manage to finance water in the days before it was privatised in England?

Mr Hewitt: There were various mechanisms used for this, including an arrangement whereby we were able to offset some of the money that we brought in through the rates against the expenditure on water.

There was a process called an appropriation and aid process whereby rates money was treated as a receipt which could be offset against public expenditure, hence your gross expenditure could be bigger than your net expenditure.

Mr McCartan: The popular perception was that we paid for water through our rates and that perception is still retained by some.

Q838 *Lord Sewel:* But if something like that happens, yes you would lose the Barnett consequentials from the moment that the service was privatised, but in the base there would still be an historic accumulation of public expenditure.

Mr McCartan: True.

Q839 *Lord Sewel:* So if you had then privatised water there would have been a lot of money in the base that you could have used for something else.

Mr Hewitt: True.

Q840 *Chairman:* Why did you not?

Mr Hewitt: Why did we not privatise water?

Q841 *Chairman:* Yes.

Mr Hewitt: There was no appetite for it whatsoever in Northern Ireland.

Q842 *Lord Sewel:* That would have solved your Health Service problems, would it not? The services that the devolved parliaments and assemblies provide tend to be those services that can be seen as very sensitive to variation of need. If you look in terms of using the demographics, age structure of the population, ideas of deprivation and cost of service provision, although there is a big question mark there because you do not want to put an incentive for inefficiency, those three sorts of dimensions, and I appreciate there are all the subjective judgments on weights and which particular measures you would use, I see as being much more related to explaining and justifying expenditure rather than a pure population driven approach.

Mr Hewitt: If we look at the services which are provided through the Executive, the big battalions of spending are health and education. Essentially they are demographically driven. There should not be a huge variation in the unit cost of providing education for a primary schoolchild as opposed to a secondary schoolchild throughout the UK. There will be factors, such as sparsity, small schools in rural areas and so forth, that can be added into the mix, but basically it is a population driven factor. When you start to bring in many of these other things you tred into the policy dimension: should our curriculum differ from curricula elsewhere, and that is a policy decision to be taken; should the pay of teachers here be different from the pay of teachers elsewhere, again a policy decision. Once you break away from what they call the objective factors you start to undermine the whole idea of a needs assessment.

Q843 *Lord Sewel:* Talking to Mr McCartan about health, I only know Scotland and the Scottish health figures are appalling.

Mr McCartan: In terms of availability of treatments and services people here do expect the same standards from the National Health Service and same amount of care. We have problems because of financial constraints mainly in terms of the waiting lists and all of those other indicators that are largely caused by the under-funding that we have. The perception in the mind of every citizen is they are entitled to NHS services and care at the same level irrespective of what part of the United Kingdom. It is up to delivery organisations, like trusts, to try and provide that. That is increasingly difficult in the current methods of funding because expectation is rising so fast and we have the diseconomies of scale and the Barnett Formula squeeze.

Q844 *Chairman:* I fear we have run out of time. Thank you very much indeed for coming and for a fascinating discussion. I have learnt things that I did not know. We will now go away and digest them.

Mr McCartan: On behalf of the Confederation, can I say thank you for the work that you are doing and the attention you are giving to something that is of such vital interest to us.

Chairman: Thank you.

Examination of Witnesses

Witnesses: Mr Peter Bunting, Assistant General Secretary, ICTU; Mr John Corey, General Secretary, Northern Ireland Public Service; and Mr Seamus McAleavey, Northern Ireland Council for Voluntary Action, examined.

Q845 Chairman: Good afternoon. Gentlemen, thank you very much indeed for coming. You probably know what we are about and what we are doing here. We have been asked by the House of Lords to conduct an inquiry into the operation of the Barnett Formula. Our terms of reference are pretty limited and focused. We cannot look at the whole area of how you fund the devolved administrations. We cannot say whether Northern Ireland should or should not have tax raising powers. What we can do is look at the way in which money is allocated at present, see whether that works properly and, if it does not work properly, why does it not work properly, and what sort of alternatives there might be to doing it. Perhaps I can ask a general question to start off with and get your responses to it. Do you think that the Barnett Formula has treated Northern Ireland fairly, and, if so, why, or unfairly and, if so, why there too?
Mr Bunting: Our initial response to that is if we knew the answer we could give you a definite commitment one way or the other. I suppose in many senses that is the big conundrum. There are people in Northern Ireland, including ourselves, who are schizophrenic on that particular issue in that sometimes we believe it treats us fairly and sometimes we believe it treats us unfairly.

Q846 Chairman: That is only natural.
Mr Bunting: Greater minds than ours have attempted to answer that question as well. I will quote David Heald who said: "Although the Barnett Formula is now heavily criticised, these criticisms come from diametrically opposing viewpoints. The Formula is variously said to over-fund and to under-fund the devolved administrations". We could not come down in a definitive manner to answer that question. It is a Formula which has been in operation for over 30 years or so. Probably within the original answer to the question, does it treat us fairly or unfairly, there are difficulties as to how would you at some stage or other change that particular Formula. I know that is a question that follows. If we were clear on that we could give you a more definitive answer. It is problematic in many senses that in some cases because of the consequentials people may well argue that they did not follow on into Northern Ireland and people may well take a degree of umbrage at that, and at other times people say, "The Formula itself by the 'crude' definition based on population, is it fair, is it unfair?" and then you will have the whole area of a needs base as well. I know this is not very helpful to you in that sense but in many senses we believe that it has been a Formula which has been in operation for 30 years and, like every other formula and every

other criteria by which any funding is available, there are times when you are very happy with it and there are times when you are unhappy with it. You will always have competing variations as to funding and under-funding. It is very problematic to give you a definitive answer on that point. Some of my colleagues might join in in answering as well.
Mr McAleavey: I represent community and voluntary organisations in Northern Ireland and, like colleagues in the trade union movement, we have debated and discussed the Barnett Formula at times and how it has impacted in Northern Ireland. For most people obviously it is a strange thing, they are not quite sure how it really works. We do understand the notion, and you have been debating it, I suppose, about convergence, that if you apply the mathematics the Barnett Formula might lead to convergence in terms of UK spend, although like others we have seen how at times that does not seem to happen because of all the bypasses that take place with regard to Barnett. A lot of people are never quite sure what the actual funding relationship is. I suppose where we do think a formula or mechanism like this is a good idea is that it takes out what would be a very complex negotiation between the Treasury and a whole series of departments here in Northern Ireland and providing money by way of block makes devolution possible. We support the notion of the mechanism but how it is arrived at is the big question that is up for debate.
Mr Corey: I do not think I have a lot to add because I am from the same position as Peter from the trade union movement. You asked the question is it treating Northern Ireland fairly, but what is fair? Fair is a comparative question, so is it fair compared with what, does it treat Northern Ireland fairly in comparison with Wales, Scotland and England? We have no reason to say something else would have been fairer given the 30 years' experience of this. From what I read, that is not dissimilar from the view that was presented by our trade union colleagues in Scotland as well, that they could not say Barnett has been unfair to Scotland. Whether it should be maintained in this form is a more open point. If you are extending your fairness comparison to is it fair compared with an alternative formula, that gets you into a deeper area and presumably one that you are going to come to as to what are the alternatives to Barnett. As Seamus has said, we all recognise from a Northern Ireland perspective where people have to go and negotiate with Treasury for funding for Northern Ireland—that is the reality of life—if there is a relatively straightforward, simplistic formula that can short-circuit those negotiations or make them more automatic in terms of the response then that is a

fair arrangement to have. No matter what alternative you would create to Barnett, I know it is referred to as the Barnett Formula, you would have to create a formula that, as with the current one, still has to have some degree of simplicity for its application each year.

Q847 Chairman: I think that is a fair point. Lord Barnett came and gave evidence to us.
Mr Corey: We are aware of that.

Q848 Chairman: He made a very interesting set of remarks. He was very firm about this. He said it was only meant to be a short-term measure; it was designed to deal with a political problem at the time; it was designed to involve detailed negotiation between the Treasury on the one hand and what could have been the devolved governments on the other hand. He did not know anything about convergence. The Treasury at the time was doing a huge needs assessment in the 1970s and they did not even tell Joel Barnett that they were actually doing it, so he did not know about that needs assessment. His view was that it was now well past its sell-by date and needs to be replaced by something and his view is it has to be replaced by something which has a needs assessment element in it. He was not very specific about that, but he was quite specific that it has gone on far, far longer than it was ever intended to. Maybe that is just because it is a good Formula, it is simple, therefore, let us carry on with it.
Mr Corey: Maybe the mistake was giving it a name.

Q849 Earl of Mar and Kellie: Mr Bunting introduced the idea of the "Barnett follow-on". I think that was the phrase you used.
Mr Bunting: Sorry?

Q850 Earl of Mar and Kellie: You introduced the idea of the "Barnett follow-on". How aware are people, do you think, according to English spending, of, "We ought to have had such and such an increase in a particular service but, in fact, devolved government has spent the money differently so what we and a particular service thought we were going to get an increase on, we suddenly find that we have not"? Is that something people are aware of?
Mr Bunting: In various constituencies. One example of that would be the Trade Union Modernisation Fund and the trade union people said, "Oh, we'll go off to the Department of Employment and Learning and seek our Barnett share of the Trade Union Modernisation Fund", but when we went to the Department of Employment they said, "Well, we fund you on other issues, education and training, et cetera, and if you were to get more money out of this it's going to be decreased there, so the status quo prevails". In many senses people are aware, and I am

sure Seamus' constituents are as well. People will be aware but they will be aware of the simplistic notion that there is this automatic follow-on of an increase for England or there is money allocated to whatever, and one assumes automatically it will percolate directly across pro rata into Northern Ireland. In that sense I think there is a degree of confusion and probably a degree of ignorance. I spent last night reading some of this and it is a good thing to send you to sleep in many senses. It is not couched in a sense that many people, and particularly the constituents we represent, ordinary workers, would be tremendously aware of. Having said that, I suppose like many things in life, whatever the alternative may be, if there is an alternative, it has to be one that is open, transparent and simplistic. But, having said that, that is easier said than put into action. People will be aware of it in a very simplistic notion, that automatically there are going to be increases right across the board, but then you have to explain that does not actually happen, that even the devolved administration, although it gets direct grant, could spend it all on health or education to the detriment of something else and then you would have a public outcry, or whatever. That is probably the nitty-gritty that people are not really aware of.
Mr McAleavey: I come across that all of the time in that if you take it from the voluntary organisations' point of view, and we work with 1,000 member organisations in every sort of discipline, if there is a major announcement in England, as there have been over the years, about Government making a big investment in pre-school provision, and I would say SureStart was one, the amount of money would be talked about and there would be a consequential for Northern Ireland of X amount, I can guarantee you that all the children's organisations would think that is really good and that is going to happen here, but then when it does not it causes confusion. That is not a problem of the Barnett Formula. It seems to me fairly obvious that if we have devolution then local ministers have to have some control and discretion as to how they spend money. We could do with explaining that better to the public but we cannot expect that the public might be that interested at times until it personally affects them.

Q851 Earl of Mar and Kellie: So it would be more helpful if there was no reference to a Barnett consequential?
Mr McAleavey: It is always very helpful to me. If I know there is a Barnett consequential I am likely to know what extra money is coming into the Northern Ireland block and we think maybe it is worth pursuing for that activity. We have done that at times where we have said, "In England they are investing in whatever and we think it would be a good idea to do

that in Northern Ireland", but we have to argue the case with ministers.

Q852 *Earl of Mar and Kellie:* Is that an argument which actually works?
Mr McAleavey: Sometimes. Ministers will automatically respond, "You do understand that the money can be applied during direct rule by the secretary of state or now by the devolved ministers and it could be applied as they see the priorities", and certainly we accept that.

Q853 *Chairman:* Do you think that is right?
Mr McAleavey: I think so, yes, otherwise why devolution?

Q854 *Chairman:* I am not arguing it, I just wanted your view. I think it is right and inevitable.
Mr McAleavey: It will always cause confusion because, as I say, if you think there is a very good announcement that has been made in England then you would like to see that simply transfer across.
Mr Corey: I am not sure what the Committee has found in other devolved administrations, but if you did a poll in Northern Ireland a very large percentage of people would say, "Yes, I've heard of the Barnett Formula", no doubt about that. I do not know if it is like that in Scotland or Wales, but in Northern Ireland the term "Barnett Formula" is very familiar. That does not mean people understand how it works precisely and most people perceive that it determines the total public expenditure on the DEL side, as we would refer to it, when it does not do that. This is the point that Seamus made. The Barnett Formula now has to be considered in the context of devolved administration. Devolved administration in Northern Ireland is still finding its feet is a fair way to put it and that would not be the situation in Wales or Scotland. Any consideration of what you do or do not do about the Barnett Formula has a huge political dimension for all devolved administrations, but particularly for the Northern Ireland one. It goes back to the earlier question that if the Government of the UK announces, "We're going to give the highest priority to this head of expenditure" is there an expectation in Northern Ireland that will follow through, and the answer to that is yes, that is the expectation of people in Northern Ireland, but whether it does is another matter.

Q855 *Earl of Mar and Kellie:* So in some respects that is a perverse form of criticism of some degree of transparency, that it would be helpful if the increases were worked out not according to precise programmes but more on other vaguer, more objective factors.

Mr Corey: At the end of the day Barnett is a very simplistic objective factor, and that is the size of the population really, and to whatever degree it has been accepted or negotiated that this is comparable or not, so it is subjective to that extent. I think everyone agrees about the need for transparency, although to make Barnett transparent is no easy task. You probably have access to David Heald's report that he did a few years ago and that is probably the most extensive piece of work that I know of on Barnett with particular reference to Northern Ireland, and if anyone thinks that is transparent, it is transparent if you study it but, nevertheless, it illustrates how difficult it is to make this transparent to the public.

Q856 *Earl of Mar and Kellie:* I am interested in what for me is a new idea, that is the "Barnett disappointment". That was a factor I had not thought of before.
Mr Corey: It is not a phrase that has come to mind.

Q857 *Chairman:* I was not thinking of making it transparent to the public, I was thinking of making it transparent to the devolved governments. One thing that has emerged very clearly from all the evidence we have taken is the extraordinary extent to which the Treasury seems to take these decision on their own and then announce them.
Mr McAleavey: Absolutely.

Q858 *Chairman:* And then devolved governments have got no option.
Mr Bunting: Have no say in it, exactly.

Q859 *Chairman:* The Olympics is a very good example. As far as I can tell nobody was consulted about that in any detail, the Treasury took the decision and then told everybody that was what was going to happen, so no consequentials.
Mr McAleavey: It certainly seems clear to us that that big decision was taken, the Government decided, "We have got to back this and it will be expensive enough as it is, so no consequentials, keep it outside" and there you have got another bypass. Resource allocation is the most political thing that any government anywhere can do, it is what people are in politics for, and that is why you get all these swings and roundabouts and bypasses.

Q860 *Chairman:* You cannot run a system on the basis of ad hoc decisions dependent upon who thumped the table last, and that is the danger with the bypass, there is no coherent stream.
Mr McAleavey: I think the Treasury seem to have tried very hard in recent years to stop all bypass decisions with regard to Northern Ireland. That is our experience. When people talk about that "Barnett squeeze", we have seen it in Northern

Ireland in the last ten years in that there has been a significant drop in the per capita spend here on public expenditure over England. Scotland does not have the same, I am sure it is because there are various bypass deals, but certainly Northern Ireland has dropped from around 30 to 21, the increase in public expenditure working on the Treasury formula pushes it closer rather quicker. One of the things we worry about is if Lord Barnett did not think that there was a calculation for convergence, yet there so obviously appears to be in terms of the mathematical formula, somebody designed that in the Treasury.

Q861 *Chairman:* We do not deny that.

Mr McAleavey: You worry then if we move to assessment on need, how will the needs assessment be made, who will carry it out, and will you just make the figures suit the ones to where you want to get to. That becomes the worry.

Q862 *Lord Sewel:* You are quite right on "squeeze", and clearly there have been lots of bypasses in the past, and you are right to suggest that the more you go down the devolution route, the more the opportunity for bypass decreases. Also, it is important whether your population is increasing or decreasing. Your population is increasing, Scotland's is decreasing, so if your population is decreasing your base provides a very effective buffer to stop the "squeeze" squeezing. Let us go to alternatives. You mentioned needs assessment. The types of services that the devolved parliament and assemblies are responsible for, they are ones where need is a very sensitive, powerful driver of expenditure. I would have thought that in many of those areas you would be better off looking at issues like deprivation, cost of provision, including services, and the detailed make-up of the demographics as they affect the service, rather than just a straight population adjustment.

Mr Bunting: That is a fair comment. I suppose in many senses initially we would all be representing that our main ethos would be of social conscience and we would be in some way inclined to agree with that. We probably have the highest number of this, that or whatever, okay, the highest number of disabled people, especially with mental health needs, and probably the highest number of people deemed to be economically inactive, which is a wonderful phrase, but a lot of that came about through the manipulation of unemployment figures at one stage or other. This is where we have to be very careful. These are very subjective. The question is what do we mean by that because it varies from academic to academic and in the Joseph Rowntree Foundation's report on poverty and social exclusion in Northern Ireland, which we would maintain is quite high, but there again it could be comparable with other areas, for example in England, and I know we do not want

to go into that, but there is northeast England, northwest England, and huge levels of social deprivation right across the UK and Northern Ireland, much of it stemming in the valleys of south Wales from the demise of heavy engineering, which we experienced as well in Northern Ireland. The interesting point about unemployment, for example, was we had allegedly the lowest level of unemployment in 20 years in Northern Ireland last year, but since the global recession that has gone askew within a short period of nine months or whatever. There is an interesting development there. It also camouflages the fact that we still have over half a million people of working age being non-productive, whether it be students or whatever. How do you reconcile the economically inactive with a very low level of unemployment? It is an oxymoron in many senses. If you were doing this on needs it is very difficult from our perspective. The other point we would have to make is who is the determiner of deprivation and social need. That is very problematic for us. Having said that, if we could work out some form of combination would it be more beneficial to Northern Ireland, I do not know. The other issue in Northern Ireland from our perspective is that we are separated from GB by the ocean. We have a landlocked border with a country in many senses where their infrastructure 15, 20 years ago was less than ours—you knew when you entered into Northern Ireland by the quality of roads—but now we have the reverse, their infrastructure, their road network, is far superior to ours. We sit back and say, "Whilst we are competing with the regions within the United Kingdom and Northern Ireland, we are now competing with a far higher level of infrastructure in economic terms attracting economic development, et cetera. We need a dynamic economy to eliminate social deprivation, et cetera. I do not want to be of the begging bowl mentality because that is one thing I totally disagree with, but in relation to that those are objectives. In terms of criteria, where would you locate that land mass, that competition in economic terms, in infrastructural terms, and where do you go, because that is all rooted in attracting foreign direct investment, exports and all the rest of it. We have a problem with that. Whilst my heart would say it is a great way to go and I can throw all sorts of statistics at you, levels of mental health, disability, whatever, I have to say that is transient by its nature as well, very subjective and would it help Northern Ireland to get a fair shake, I do not know.

Q863 *Chairman:* Can I put this point to you. The Treasury did a very detailed needs assessment in the mid-1970s, 1977/78, and what they seem to have been doing over the last 30-odd years is updating that periodically and still using it not exactly as a base for the whole thing but as part of the calculations. If you

had a needs assessment drawn up by a wholly independent commission, nothing to do with the Government, you would have to take it out of the hands of the Treasury, I accept that—
Mr Bunting: I think we would all agree on that.

Q864 *Chairman:* So you take it out of the hands of the Treasury and you give it to an independent body and tell them to have a needs assessment, it need not be as detailed or as comprehensive as the one the Treasury did, which took about three years, but you could have five or six comparators, variables, and if they concentrated on those you would get 95 per cent fairness. You would never get 100 per cent fairness but you could get a very considerable degree that is fairer than the present system. That would take care of a fair number of your problems, would it not?
Mr Bunting: The other point that would have to be factored in there as well is the legacy of our own conflict.

Q865 *Chairman:* Yes, of course.
Mr Bunting: With the segregated society still there, is the conflict over, as witnessed two weeks ago, what is the future of it and where are we all going. If this formula came out and we examined it and said it had given us a degree of assurance, why not even if it went for a short period of time and then we could all stand back and review it.

Q866 *Chairman:* The Australians do it via a Commonwealth Grants Commission and review it on an annual basis.
Mr Bunting: Yes.

Q867 *Chairman:* They are independent of the state governments, independent of the federal government and they produce their assessment. I am told that what happens after that is for about two or three days everybody complains how unfair it is and, "They have forgotten this. We deserve more than X, Y or Z", but it then goes to sleep after that for another 360 days, then they produce the next assessment and you have another two or three day eruption and then it calms down again. I would not say it was an ideal system because there are obviously differences between the way in which they are structured in Australia and the UK and all the rest of it, but the principles behind that would seem to me at any rate to be something that clearly we should look at very, very seriously indeed.
Mr McAleavey: I think the reaction to the allocation, no matter what formula or method is used, is probably the same. I do not think there is anybody who would jump up and down and say, "The Barnett Formula is wonderful and does us really well", so everybody tends to say negative things no matter

what the formula may be. I would support a needs-based analysis because it seems that the only need in what is called the Barnett Formula that is recognised is population size, which is fairly objective but clearly very crude. I certainly would support a needs-based analysis. We used it here for small amounts of money in the first peace programme, we allocated money to district council areas by population with a weighting for deprivation and using the Noble indicators that were deprivation indicators here that the government had in Northern Ireland. I would support that type of thing. Where you get worried is how you arrive at what the needs are and are they different for Scotland, Wales and Northern Ireland. One of the issues in Northern Ireland is the economic one in that we do sit between the economies of the Republic of Ireland and England. For quite a while the Treasury lost 500 million a year in revenue in terms of diesel taxes because everybody bought their diesel south of the border because it was cheaper. The economic development that took place and the pain that has taken place has always had an impact on the development of our economy. Our economy is clearly under-developed with a heavy dependence on public expenditure and all of that. Is that going to be the same in Wales and Scotland? I am not so sure. I am wondering can the same indicators be used for all. The wider the indicators, the better they are at seeing need, but presumably it gets more and more complex and presumably the reason that the Treasury has stuck with Barnett for 30 years is that it has been relatively straightforward.

Q868 *Chairman:* It is easy. From the Treasury's point of view it is absolutely marvellous, they have not got to think too much about it and they apply mathematical formula and that is it.
Mr Bunting: They know exactly what the calculation is going to be for all of us.

Q869 *Chairman:* So from that point of view I can see that it is easy. The question is, is it sufficiently fair? I have doubts as to whether it is.
Mr Corey: I suppose you could almost argue that the Treasury's line saves public expenditure in that there is no money being wasted on complex formula. We represent working people and families in Northern Ireland, Seamus represents the voluntary and community sector, and our anxiety is not to see something which in time comes to be seen as having the result of less public expenditure being available in Northern Ireland. Everything is caveated by that.

Q870 *Chairman:* We understand that.
Mr Corey: The opening answer from Peter to the question "Has Barnett been fair" is we do not really know, in truth. I would make four points in addressing the needs issue. It comes back to

something you said, my Lord Chairman, a wee while ago about how the Treasury makes decisions, say on the Olympics, and nobody has a say in that. The first question is the Formula is about dividing up the cake and what size is the cake that is being divided up. At the moment the Treasury can make decisions about the overall size of the UK cake knowing that their decisions will have no impact on the devolved administrations in terms of their funding. It has an impact in the sense the cake has got smaller, but the Treasury can make decisions in terms of how it is going to spend money in the UK in the knowledge as to whether or not this is going to have a consequence for a devolved administration. If we were moving to a needs-based assessment, and that would be the needs of all regions of the UK and all devolved administrations, then the question would arise as to what is the cake that is going to be divided up in the needs-based assessment and is it the same cake that is there at the moment. Would it be the comparable services and functions formula that would be used or in some way would it be different. That is a question that occurs to me. The second point is in relation to the needs assessment itself you said could you have five or six comparables or variables. In moving to any needs assessment, all the commentators in everything we read say this is very complex, it is going to be subjective, it will not be wholly objective, and there will be all sorts of arguments as to what should or should not be in it. I think Seamus made the point, which is the third point I would make, is a needs-based assessment sufficient to accommodate any other inherent demographic or geographic differences between Northern Ireland as it sits—we are separated by water from the UK—which do not affect Wales or Scotland to the same extent or in the same way. Is needs-based assessment capable of addressing that. The other point would be to what extent can a needs-based assessment exclude politics in its application because, and I hasten to make it clear we are non-party political, we are a trade union without any political objects and we are not in any way linked politically, the reality is decisions about expenditure by the UK Government for Scotland has very different political implications than it does about expenditure for Northern Ireland in terms of the UK Government. To what extent can you create a needs-based formula and bring all the variables into play which would have no political influence or would be

objective as opposed to subjective. Those are the things we would be anxious to examine if someone was presenting an alternative by way of a needs-based assessment from a Northern Ireland perspective.

Mr Bunting: Just to add a caveat. Reading through Heald, I will read the quote again because you can understand our dilemma at times here. It says: "However, it is an illusion to think that a needs assessment automatically brings more resources". From an empirical researcher with data like that, that frightens me, worries me, concerns me.

Q871 *Lord Sewel:* There will be winners and losers.
Mr McAleavey: Inevitably.
Mr Bunting: We are not here to advocate that we be losers.

Q872 *Lord Sewel:* I think it is a little bit rich, quite honestly, to hear the argument, and you have not advanced it but we have heard it elsewhere, that because it is population-based it is objective and that contrasts with a dreadful, politically manipulatable, subjective needs assessment. Okay, the formula may be objective, but if you look at everything that is in the base from pre-1979 that was all subjective. If you look at the bypassing that went on right the way through, that was subjective. The total amount that is delivered through that process, a heck of a lot of it is subjective.

Mr Bunting: If you go back to what we have said about three or four times, we do not know if it is fair or unfair. It is unfair if we are in the very subjective position of others saying, "We're not going to advocate something in that sense", so denying people more public expenditure in Northern Ireland, and that is a problem for us. What happens will happen. No matter what it is in life, everything changes. Workplaces change, technology changes, terms and conditions of employment change, we all change. In essence, the Barnett Formula at some stage or other will be reviewed and everything has to evolve, nothing can stay static forever. That is life. What we would be attempting to do is get the best for Northern Ireland and you would not expect us to say anything else.

Chairman: I think you have made the Northern Ireland position very clear. Thank you very much indeed, it was kind of you to come.

WEDNESDAY 1 APRIL 2009

Present   Forsyth of Drumlean, L   Richard, L (Chairman)
               Hollis of Heigham, B   Rooker, L
               Lang of Monkton, L   Rowe-Beddoe, L
               Lawson of Blaby, L   Sewel, L
               Mar and Kellie, E   Trimble, L
               Moser, L

Examination of Witnesses

Witnesses: RT HON JIM MURPHY, a Member of the House of Commons, Secretary of State for Scotland, RT HON PAUL MURPHY, a Member of the House of Commons, Secretary of State for Wales, and the RT HON SHAUN WOODWARD, a Member of the House of Commons, Secretary of State for Northern Ireland, examined:

Q873 Chairman: Thank you very much for coming. You know what we are about and you know the limitations on our mandate and the extent of it. It is very important that we talk to the three Secretaries of State as to how they see it. I do not know whether each of you would like to make an opening statement or whether we can launch into the questions?
Mr Paul Murphy: Lord Chairman, we can launch straight in. We will all say the same thing anyway, I think.

Q874 Chairman: I have a general question to start off with and I would clearly like all three of you to answer it, if you would. What do you think are the chief merits and demerits of the existing formula as the basis for funding the Devolved Administrations? Do you think it is a sustainable basis for funding with Devolved Administrations in the long term? Do you think there have to be changes to the Formula? What effect do you think it has on equity and fairness across the UK as a whole and do you think it is a device which actually pulls the UK together or does it tend to drive it apart?
Mr Paul Murphy: I have lived with Lord Barnett's Formula for almost 30 years myself. When I talked to government a long time ago in Wales Lord Barnett had just started to implement his Formula and entering government a dozen years ago as Finance Minister in Northern Ireland, and then later as Secretary for Wales and Northern Ireland, it has been part of my life for a long time. Its longevity says something for it because it has been there for three decades and there have been a number of attempts to have a look at it and see whether it could be improved, or indeed completely replaced. All of those attempts, it seems to me, have come to nothing and I think that although inevitably any system will have difficulties and problems, my own view is that I think this one works reasonably well. I know there will be detailed questions about how it works during the course of this session, but as you are asking us, Lord Chairman, about the overall view of it, I see great

merits in it. I think that because the Devolved Administrations are able to spend the money that they get in what is effectively a block grant in a way they want is a good thing. I think it is good that they do not have to spend exactly the same way that it is spent in England. They may choose to do so but they do not have to and that is a good thing. I think its relative simplicity is good because any other system I guess would be more complex. I think it is reasonably fair with all four countries getting the same cash increase per head and I do think that to replace it would be more trouble than it is worth. Generally speaking, I cannot see any huge disadvantages but I do see pretty significant merits in it, even though it is not perfect. I suspect the reason why any system would not be perfect is that we do not have a federal system of government in our country, that our devolution system is an asymmetrical one with three different settlements being served by the same system of funding which, despite problems that may have occurred over the years, has stood the test of time.

Q875 Chairman: Do you know what Lord Barnett himself says about it?
Mr Paul Murphy: I do. He is my neighbour.

Q876 Chairman: He gave evidence here to us and he was really very specific and forthright about it and said it was a political decision to start the Formula in the first place. It did not even become the Barnett Formula until it had been around for ten years. It was designed to deal with the short term set of problems that they had with potentially Devolved Administrations but he thought it was way past its sell-by date and that there should be some question of some injection of the idea of need into the way in which the Devolved Administrations receive their money from the centre. Do you disagree with that?
Mr Paul Murphy: I disagree in the sense that I think he underestimated the success of his creation by those of us who have to administer it. Over 12 years on and off I have lived with this Formula and, although there

have been ups and downs, I cannot think of a better one. I suppose we will come later on to the detailed question of needs formula, but I think it has met the needs, certainly in terms of the country I represent around the Cabinet table. Obviously my colleagues will have to comment themselves on how they feel it meets the needs of Northern Ireland and of Scotland, but I do believe it has met those needs well. It has met them in the sense that, indeed, some English Members of Parliament and Members of the House of Lords doubtless would think it has met them too well, but then that is not my job. My job is to ensure we get the best possible deal for those territories and countries that we represent around the table, and certainly from the Devolved Administrations' point of view they have done pretty well out of the system.

Q877 *Chairman:* I do not think that is the view of the administration in Cardiff, if I may say so. We went to Cardiff and took some evidence down there. It was very difficult to find anybody saying an enthusiastic word for the existing Barnett Formula and the general feeling there seemed to be that a fairer system was capable of being developed and it would be more equitable were it to be introduced.
Mr Paul Murphy: As you know, the Welsh Assembly Government is having its own inquiry into how the Barnett Formula works. I have obviously met with the chairman of that inquiry and I meet on a regular basis with the First Minister and the Minister of Finance and of course there are issues which again we will come to later which are raised on a day by day basis. I am not yet convinced that there is a better one. I am not saying it is perfect but I do not think there is a better one and we must wait and see the evidence of that commission and see what they have to say. I am sure your Committee would find it of great use and interest. I think it has served us well.
Mr Jim Murphy: My namesake, the Secretary of State—and the irony is that the only one who is not a Murphy here is the one representing Northern Ireland, but that is maybe neither here nor there—has said that he has lived most of his political life under the Barnett Formula. I have lived most of my entire life under the Barnett Formula. The advantages are many of the ones Paul has already referred to but the relative transparency, the predictability, the stability that it offers alongside the three year spending review process—I think this terrible jargon that is in Anton Muscatelli's thoughtful report which talks about horizontal fiscal equalization; in other words, a degree of redistribution—I think that is a strength of the current arrangements and that is something that is referred to in Muscatelli's report. As we have already heard, it is not without its imperfections, but one of the strengths that the Muscatelli document refers to is, having looked at all of the other current articulated alternatives, it is certainly stronger than

those. Of course, it is something that the Calman Commission continues to look at and their work continues. It certainly offers those principles of transparency, stability, efficiency and on that basis it has considerable merit.

Q878 *Chairman:* Do you think it is fair?
Mr Jim Murphy: I believe so, yes.
Mr Woodward: I would endorse the comments made by my colleagues and really add that there is an expression of humility on the part of Lord Barnett in saying to some extent he is surprised that it lasted. The answer to that is it seems to me self-evident because actually nobody has produced anything better. The fact of the matter is that any system is going to produce unfairness. The question is whether or not you can actually produce a system which fundamentally and in a wholesale way removes the inconsistencies and the unfairness in the process. I do not think it has been a want of trying or a want of talking about it and a want of politicking about it; it has been the fact that nobody has produced anything. It may be that this awesome system responsibility that this Committee has taken on will actually produce that. I can certainly see that it is possible for the administration in Wales to make the argument that they do and I can see that the administration in some other part of the United Kingdom could make a similar argument, but in the end would we produce something which has as great an equitable value as this system has? That really leads me to say on the question of is it fair I can answer by saying yes I think it is reasonably fair. Does it, after all, through the Barnett squeeze actually work towards some kind of sense that one day we might have greater equality? Yes, it does, and it does it in an incredibly slow, tortuous and incremental way, which is perhaps quite a good thing in an English system, but fundamentally the question I would put on the table is "does it work?" At the moment it works. The only thing I would say is that before the wheel is reinvented, which I am sure it will be by this Committee, I only hope that what is put in its place, if that is the design of this Committee, will actually give whatever the inadequacies of Barnett, as great a fairness and as great a workability as this has, albeit, I am sure, it is perfectly possible for people in different parts of the Devolved Administrations to actually say it could be better.

Q879 *Lord Lang of Monkton:* The baseline for the Formula was not based on any assessment of need; it was based on an accident of history. Do you regard that as a fair long-term basis?
Mr Jim Murphy: It has borne the rigorous test of different political philosophies, change of governments and decades. It is a reflection of spend at that moment in time. On the basis that it is using

that baseline rather than a zero-based approach, then of course it is tied to that original baseline and events, priorities and profile at that time. I would argue that it starts from a reasonable basis. I can only speak in respect of Scotland of course. On the basis that it is a country with 10 per cent of the population, a third of the landmass, 800 islands, 8 per cent of Europe's coastline and public services are more expensive to deliver in Scotland and I think that is reflective of both what was happening in the 1970s, throughout the Eighties and today.

Q880 *Lord Lang of Monkton:* Do you see convergence happening in Scotland?
Mr Jim Murphy: With the drive theory of the Formula it is an in-built principle but the Government does not start on the basis of seeking to create convergence as a matter of policy but it is certainly part of the Formula, all other things being equal. Anton Muscatelli and his colleagues have reflected that as well.

Q881 *Lord Lang of Monkton:* We know that mathematically it should be happening but it does not seem to be happening in the way one expects. How do you explain that?
Mr Jim Murphy: It is the way in which inflation was treated up until 1992 in terms of the calculations. It was also a reflection of the way in which population shifts were not brought up to date and the fact that for a period it was eleven eightieths as opposed to eight eightieths in terms of population proportion, so it was the way in which some of the changes over previous history did not keep account of the trends in Scotland as part of the United Kingdom. It is population and taxation policy.

Q882 *Lord Lang of Monkton:* Could I ask your colleagues if they see convergence happening in their areas of responsibility and if they think it is a fair and good thing?
Mr Paul Murphy: It was not the policy of Lord Barnett but it will probably happen eventually as a by-product of the changes in spending and of course there are changes in population. Wales' population has risen since its introduction by a considerable number. I think it may eventually get that way but that was not the intention, nor is it now, as far as I can see, the intention of successive governments that there should be convergence but as a by-product of what has happened it may well be there eventually.

Q883 *Chairman:* It is convergence down, is it not, not a convergence up?
Mr Paul Murphy: Yes.

Q884 *Chairman:* Certainly so far as Wales is concerned, convergence insofar as it has taken place, Wales has lost money. That is right, is it not?
Mr Paul Murphy: But nevertheless, of course, on per head of population comparison with English regions. My colleagues elsewhere would not necessarily agree with that. The problem we have is that we will get people in Wales arguing the case that the Formula is not good enough for them and then you get people in England saying it is too good for them. It is quite a difficult one. English members have been asking me questions in the House of Commons for ten years on whether in fact they have been hard done by because of the Barnett Formula and then you go to Cardiff and they say we have been hard done by as well. I suspect that something in the middle is really what it has turned out to be.

Q885 *Lord Forsyth of Drumlean:* I am having some difficulty understanding what you are saying because, as Secretaries of State, you obviously fight for your corner and you want to get the best for the area you represent in Cabinet. The Secretary of State of Scotland has said that Scotland has got a third of the landmass and it has all kinds of additional demands upon it. The Secretary of State for Northern Ireland can make the case. All of you have higher baselines, higher expenditure per head than England. It is a mathematical certainty that the Barnett Formula will result in your budgets being reduced and eventually you will have the same expenditure per head as England. I am a little bit puzzled as to why you are happy with the situation. Under the previous pre-devolution arrangements which you will recall, the Secretaries of State would indulge in what is now called "Formula bypass", or ways of compensating for the effect. Assuming that the Formula works and that the population is correct, the effect of continuing with Barnett will be that there will be a reduction in the money made available. I would have thought that that could lead to unfairness. If Scotland had the same expenditure per head as England that would clearly be unfair and wrong and that is where Barnett is leading us. What do you expect to be done to avoid this happening?
Mr Woodward: We are now 30 years on since Barnett and we are a very long way away from convergence.

Q886 *Lord Forsyth of Drumlean:* That is because, to put it very crudely, the system was adjusted when we had one government governing the whole of the United Kingdom and ministers of the same party who were able to do so. You do not have that now. You have a situation where you have Devolved Administrations run by different political parties in some cases who are able to do their own thing and where the dialogue is limited. That is what has changed and that is why I am concerned that you do

not seem to see that this is going to result in an unfairness and a disadvantage in the long term to what used to be called the territorials by the Treasury.
Mr Woodward: It could do but let me give you a very good example about Northern Ireland. In Northern Ireland, because of the troubles, we have a situation whereby up until the beginning of this global recession we were in a situation in which something in the order of 72 per cent of the economy in Northern Ireland was in the public sector, 28 per cent in the private sector. One of the reasons there are all kinds of problems in Northern Ireland which therefore require all kinds of extra help, for which indeed the baseline needs figure actually assists with, is precisely because of that and as a legacy of the troubles. The difficulties we are facing at the moment affect this and as we come out of this recession the capacity for Northern Ireland to generate a very vibrant private sector is absolutely enormous and it will transform the needs of the economy in Northern Ireland at I dare say a far quicker rate than what happened in Scotland or Wales, for example, simply because they do not have only 28 per cent in the private sector. I put that on the table simply because I think the problem with all of these formulas are the danger is you think if we change this bit of the Formula we will get it right. The problem is there may be another bit of the Formula that is also going to change as well which is what really takes me back to saying I do not have a problem, Lord Forsyth, with you advocating whatever system you want, but as somebody who has to actually look after the interests of people in Northern Ireland do I believe at the moment that the system we currently have is inherently unfair, does not work, does not deliver for people across the public services? The answer is that I think that would be a wrong conclusion to reach.

Q887 *Lord Forsyth of Drumlean:* I was not advocating a system; I was just asking you how the changes that have been made as a result of devolution, if you stick with Barnett, would not result in Northern Ireland and the other territorials being disadvantaged?
Mr Woodward: Because I think other factors would actually change the economy in Northern Ireland more fundamentally than the Barnett Formula.
Mr Paul Murphy: There are examples too. On a couple of technical points, the spend per head is going up of course but at a slightly lower rate in Wales, but everywhere has had an increase in spend, it is just that the rate is lower; and secondly, budget and spend have to grow a lot for convergence to happen at all and so we are talking about very much in the longer term for that. In terms of Formula bypass, these have occurred, considerable ones in the Welsh context. When I was Secretary of State for Wales before, negotiating the Objective 1 funding for Wales, there

was an enormous bypass there amounting to I think £3 billion when it was matched by the Welsh Assembly Government so it does happen.
Mr Jim Murphy: In respect of my Lord Forsyth's point, it is a reasonable point to make which is this thing about the party political dynamic. None of us operate in a situation where our party has a monopoly of power and two out of three have no formal elected politicians in power in terms of party politics. That internal party dynamic, looking at it only in terms of Scotland, and I can only speak from my own experience over the few months I have been in this role, is that I try where possible to find common cause with a party that again philosophically I entirely disagree with, but there is a common effort to try and maximise the continuing benefits of the United Kingdom in terms of the support for Scotland. One example would be on this important project of the Forth Road Crossing where again a cross-party divide and with a lot of support from the Treasury there is a unique deal being put in place to ensure retention of efficiency savings to help fund that project. You may not call that a Formula bypass, but certainly it is a fiscal innovation which involves the Treasury essentially, myself and the Scottish Government under a separatist party. I just wanted to put that in terms of the point you made, Lord Forsyth, about the party political nature of it.

Q888 *Lord Sewel:* I think we are agreed that the Formula as such, and the way it treats the increment as a converging dynamic as a property, the question is why has it not happened? The answer to that is you have got a big base which is not based on population to begin with so you are always dealing with an increment upon an increment upon an increment, but the two factors that seem to have had the effect of delaying convergence are bypassing, which has happened less since devolution. I think that is the important thing. In the past pre-devolution bypassing was used to an extent to fund significant public sector wage settlements which were beyond the capacity of the Formula to absorb. I do not think that has happened since devolution and the fact that that has not happened and would be difficult to happen will make the convergence accelerate. Secondly, surely it is the importance of population, whether population is increasing or declining. If we look at the three countries there you have got two countries where the population is increasing and one country where it is decreasing. I think the reason why Scotland's convergence is much less than Northern Ireland and Wales is because its population continues to decrease. If that is a major factor I would have thought that it is worrying that one of the only ways in which you can keep the Scottish share up is for the Scottish population to continue to decrease.

Mr Jim Murphy: I do not think it is healthy for the UK as a whole, or Scotland specifically, to have those types of population shifts, a decline in population with the demographic trend within that decline. Since 1979 the Scottish population has reduced by 1 per cent where the English population has increased by 8 per cent. There are a clear set of trends there. The Scottish Executive (as was) and Scottish Government (as is now) have tried various measures alongside the Home Office to try and address that: the fresh talent initiative and others. Inside the Formula one of the difficulties was that up until—this is not a party political point but a statement of how the statistics and the Formula was updated—1997, the changes in population were not updated as regularly, but that is now happening more regularly.

Q889 *Lord Sewel:* That does not affect the base, does it? The population recalibration affects the increment but it does not affect the base.

Mr Jim Murphy: That is right.

Mr Paul Murphy: We have just mentioned again the Formula bypass issue which is important because the one that I touched upon with Lord Forsyth, which is the Objective 1 European funding for Wales in the 2000 spending review, was huge in its implications. When we found out that the Formula did not meet the situation that we qualified for 60 per cent of all the European Union Objective 1 funding for the entire United Kingdom. The Formula meant that we could only get 6 per cent of it. There were considerable long negotiations on it but eventually it was agreed, rightly, that Wales should benefit by a bypass to the Formula and it worked to the tune of a huge amount of money.

Q890 *Chairman:* I do not want to flog this but it really does seem to me that to argue that the Barnett Formula gets credibility because of the extent to which you avoid it by bypass does not seem to be a great commendation for the Formula itself.

Mr Paul Murphy: That was not the purpose of it. The purpose of my comment was nothing to do with that. My comment was about the issue of Formula bypass and that it is possible when you have an exceptional circumstance, which that was in fact, there were no considerable circumstances which were comparable to that in terms of the amount of money that actually came to Wales as a consequence of Objective 1 European funding. It has made an enormous difference to Wales but it would not have done if we had stuck to the Formula. The point was that the Formula is sufficiently flexible to take into account dramatic situations and anyone in Wales will tell you that, Lord Chairman.

Q891 *Lord Lawson of Blaby:* I ought to welcome the innate conservatism of our three witnesses. As Lord Sewel was saying earlier, the disparate trend, particularly in the Scottish population and the English population, has made the Scottish baseline somewhat anomalously high. I think that is acknowledged by the fact that more of you agree that there is some logic in convergence. I would like to ask two questions about convergence. First of all, there seems to be the view that convergence is all right provided it continues at the positively glacial pace which has occurred so far. My first question is do you think that there is perhaps the case for the process of convergence being slightly less glacial? Secondly, how far do you think convergence should ideally go? I am not saying how long it should take. At the end of the day where should we be?

Mr Jim Murphy: The point that the noble Lord makes on the baseline is that the population shift has not in and of itself affected Scotland's historic baseline. The baseline reflects what was happening at a particular point in relative recent history. What has happened is the increments or otherwise over time—

Q892 *Lord Lawson of Blaby:* If I may interrupt, that is not what happened, as has been pointed out. You get the same cash increase per head, that is catered for with the population changes. The point is that, as the Treasury has pointed out to us, but I think we always knew this and you certainly knew this, that there are very marked disparities between the various countries of the United Kingdom in planned total identifiable expenditure per head of population. That difference has been exacerbated by the difference in the population trends. That is the point.

Mr Jim Murphy: The public expenditure statistical analysis that the noble Lord is referring to is a mixture of reserved and devolved spend. It is a measurement of actual spend, not allocated spend, and it is more difficult to disaggregate the reserved fiscal footprint in respect of what the noble Lord mentions. You have the issues about social security dependency, the numbers of people on incapacity benefit and all of those other related issues. Scotland has, although there have been welcome reductions in the last couple of years, a dramatic and unacceptably high level of incapacity benefit dependency. On the point of the speed of glacial melt, the Government has not set out a timeline or a policy of when it would hope or expect to see convergence. As I said in answer to an earlier question, it is a theoretical part of the Formula that we have not set out a timeline as to when we would currently expect it to happen, or indeed when we would like to see it happen. It is not something that we have commented on publicly in terms of a timeline.

Mr Paul Murphy: There was never any policy intention for convergence to be a policy, full stop, and nor is there, as far as I am aware, any intention to recalibrate it so that it changes the rate at which it gets to that point. In terms of our responsibilities—Lord Forsyth quite rightly pointed them out—ours is to ensure that the Formula is the best for those countries we represent around the Cabinet table.

Q893 *Lord Lawson of Blaby:* I understand that but I would like you to look at it also as members of the Cabinet of the United Kingdom, not just fighting your own corners for your own people, which is thoroughly proper, but you are also members of the United Kingdom Cabinet and you look at things from a UK basis as well. From that basis do you think as fair-minded ministers—I would like to think that such a thing exists—that there is a case to be made for a degree of convergence and, if so, do you think the present glacial pace is good enough? How far do you think it should go? What should be the *terminus ad quem*?

Mr Woodward: The question posed is in danger of saying the convergence is an end in itself. Convergence is an end which we desire because what it may reflect about the conditions in which people live and the public services they enjoy, the wealth that they are able to create in the communities that they are in and this is a formula and a set of baselines on which the Formula is applied which tries, and has tried—whether it has succeeded or not is in other people's views, I happen to think it does work—but whether it has worked is a very important question. What is the point we are trying to achieve with convergence? The point you make is that it is glacial. Another word for 'glacial' might be 'evolutionary'. The real distinction here is to whether or not we actually have a pathway to convergence regardless, or whether it is a mathematical formula which reflects an aspiration to eliminate disparities in the system. Again, I come back to saying that I still have not seen anything on the table which at the moment could deliver something which would be significantly better than this. Perhaps this slightly pre-empts the question that Lord Lang posed right at the beginning. It is important to remember, which I am sure you have all done, what was there before 1979. Certainly what was there before 1979 was tortuous, unfair, involved line by line negotiation, was pretty opaque and did not much work. It seems to me that, despite the three years' work that was done on the baseline assessments between 1976 and 1979, the fact of the matter is a system was produced and, yes, it has been glacial, but I am not sure that it is any the worse because it has been glacial. I am not sure that it has been any the worse because it has been a mathematical formula rather than a pathway to convergence. At the end of the day I come back to

saying I find it quite difficult to see that there is a better system that would replace this, albeit that this perhaps is somewhat imperfect.

Q894 *Lord Rooker:* We had a difficulty with the Treasury that they could not give us a single disadvantage and you have not offered any except obviously in the round. The reason we are sitting, I suppose, is because of the pressures coming domestically from England and within the regions, which of course is not our remit, but the differences within those regions are part of the festering sore which then the Barnett Formula is tagged on. However, if it is so good and so satisfactory, and I am no expert on what I am about to say, how come the millions, indeed billions, of pounds of Lottery money are divided up between England, Scotland, Wales and Northern Ireland on a completely different formula that takes account of social deprivation, deals with environment, health, all the issues that devolved governments deal with? How come a different formula is used for that whereas you are saying there is nothing that anyone else can invent and leave the Barnett Formula alone because long-term the festering sore of discontent based on sometimes myths, I accept that, is still going to be there?

Mr Woodward: Can I just respond to the thought of it being so good and so satisfactory. To be fair, Lord Rooker, I do not think that is what we are saying. What we are saying is that it works. We are not saying it is the most sensational system that could possibly be devised and please keep your hands off it. That would be a caricature of what we are saying. What we are referring to is the fact that it works. I do think one of its strengths, for example, is that it is up to the Devolved Administration in Northern Ireland to decide how it wants to spend that money and, if it wants to, it can choose to allocate more money to one area rather than another and that not be decided here in Whitehall. I think that is a real merit of the system. Whatever is proposed to take its place, if your Lordships are so minded, I think it is very important that that is retained. That dimension of it is so good and so satisfactory. However, I do think if you want me to point to disparities here, part of the problem comes when you actually look at disparities within the Devolved Administrations themselves, and where you can begin to see quite big problems is potentially in how the Formula effectively applies itself in England. If you look at problems and indices to reflect poverty and deprivation in Wales or parts of Northern Ireland and you can readily find those in England, there are some very interesting questions to be asked around that. If you want to point to some of the problems I think you can begin to see difficulties that need to be addressed in that much more readily than we can between ourselves. I am sure we could make claims for what extra we would like if we wanted to between ourselves, but I do think in the area to which I have just pointed, particularly within England where you have these extraordinary disparities, I think there is some very interesting work to be done in that area.

Mr Paul Murphy: As far as the Welsh situation is concerned, where some of our English colleagues would consider that Wales is treated unfairly as a consequence of the Barnett Formula, the very fact that the Objective 1 funding was awarded to Wales was on the basis of an indication of need in most of Wales as well. The other point is, post devolution, the ability of the devolved assemblies and governments to be able to decide how to spend the money is also a complicating factor in the way that, say, the Lottery would decide to draw up how you give money to each of the countries. This block grant allows each of the individual Devolved Administrations to spend the money as they wish. At the end of the day they themselves work out how that money is distributed in order for deprivation to be met.

Q895 *Lord Trimble:* A point that has arisen from what Paul Murphy has said and what Shaun Woodward said, there are two different concepts here that we need to keep separate: one is a concept of a block grant. Nobody is talking about going back to the pre-1970s position where there was not a block grant. There is then the concept of the formula that is used to determine the block grant and that is the Barnett Formula. You could have a variety of different formulae that could be used to produce the block grant. I do not think anybody is calling the block grant concept into question but what they are saying is could there be better formula for working out the block grant? It is not necessary to go into an argument about the flexibility that there is in the block grant—nobody is challenging that—but it is a question of how you arrive at it.

Mr Woodward: Forgive me, but I think some people are challenging that. I am not suggesting that you are. I think the reason that some people are challenging it is precisely because of the baseline need that became the block grant that was the figure in 1979 to which a formula is applied, but for some people some of these disparities exist. For some people the argument is revisit the overall number to reflect baseline need and then whatever formula you come up with it would be different.

Q896 *Lord Trimble:* The question of the baseline is also a separate issue and we are best to keep these issues separate.

Mr Woodward: You would of course make the biggest difference, if you were so minded, to be addressing the baseline figure rather than the actual formula.

Chairman: We are.

Q897 *Lord Forsyth of Drumlean:* You keep talking about how there is no alternative.

Mr Woodward: I did not say there is no alternative.

Q898 *Lord Forsyth of Drumlean:* You said there is no obvious alternative. In each of your departments you allocate most of the block grant that you receive to local government and to health on the basis of a formula based on need, not on population. Is that not a contradiction?

Mr Woodward: I do not allocate them.

Q899 *Lord Forsyth of Drumlean:* The Devolved Administrations who get the money under the Barnett Formula then allocate that money to local government and to health and they use formulas which are based on assessments of need.

Mr Woodward: With respect, there is a big disparity in Northern Ireland.

Q900 *Lord Forsyth of Drumlean:* In the old days before we had devolution—I may be wrong about Northern Ireland—in Scotland and Wales the Secretary of State would allocate the money. It is now done through the parliaments or assemblies. The basis upon which that money is allocated is according to a formula which is actually about need and which is not based on a crude measure of population but based on a baseline that goes back to the Seventies. Is there not a contradiction there?

Mr Paul Murphy: Except, of course, that if we were to talk to local government in Wales, for example, their view, which I am not commenting one way or the other is right or wrong, would be that the formula that they use is itself something they could argue about. It is a difference of view about how in fact the formula is based; in other words, there is just as much an argument about the formula by which local authorities are funded in respective countries as there is about the Barnett Formula itself.

Q901 *Chairman:* It is not 30 years old, is it?

Mr Paul Murphy: No, but there was a formula, as you would know, Lord Chairman, which the territorials, when they had executive responsibility, did use and which was then inherited, so to speak, by the relevant governments in Wales, Northern Ireland and Scotland.

Mr Jim Murphy: I cannot really comment upon Lord Rooker's initial question as I do not know enough about the Lottery to know whether the Government spending should mirror the Lottery spending. Instinctively I do not think it sounds right. One of the first bills I served on in arriving here was about the allocation of Lottery funding. Lord Rooker asked about the current weaknesses in the system. I think the overarching weakness in Scotland—I make no comment about Northern Ireland or Wales—is the lack of accountability in relation to the politicians who spend the money and the lack of relationship between spending the money and raising the money. The Scottish Parliament has the variable rate of income tax but it has never been used, but this is something that the Prime Minister has commented on and Ken Calman and his commission are looking at.

Q902 *Lord Lawson of Blaby:* That is a very important point but unfortunately I think it is outside of our terms of reference.
Mr Jim Murphy: I was asked for an assessment of the weakness at the moment in terms of the architecture of spending powers in Scotland and I think for me that is the overarching weakness.

Q903 *Chairman:* From listening to the three of you, if you will forgive me for saying so, the picture is of contentment with the Barnett Formula despite the fact it is 30 years old, despite the fact that you have got flexibility by which you mean that you can go outside of the Formula if and when there is a major thing that you think needs funding and you cannot fit it into the existing baseline. With respect, it is a mess, is it not, however you look at it? There is very little logic attached to it. It is 30 years out of date.
Mr Paul Murphy: If it was that much of a mess there have been seven elections since 1979 and successive Conservative and Labour governments could have changed it if they came to the conclusion that there may have been problems with it, but it is a question of what you put in its place all the time.
Mr Jim Murphy: I am not the only Secretary of State for Scotland in the room, current or former.
Mr Woodward: I am sure they made strong arguments to reform the system at Cabinet.

Q904 *Chairman:* The great thing about the Barnett system is that it is politically easy. You do not have to go and haggle with the Devolved Administrations. There is a formula and you say we impose the formula and that is it. From your point of view I can see the advantages of it; from the point of view of the Devolved Administrations I am not so sure.
Mr Paul Murphy: I do not think it would be fair to say that there are not substantial negotiations on finance between the Treasury and the various Devolved Administrations because there are. There are, for example, very regular bilateral meetings between the Finance Ministers and the Treasury—the Chief Secretary mainly—but there are also quadrilateral meetings which are held two or three times a year of all Finance Ministers and the Treasury. I have been to a couple of them and I can assure the Committee that they are not walkovers; far from it. They are proper discussions and negotiations about aspects of the way in which the administrations

are funded and the flexibility, the points we touched on before, which are actually dealt with. I guess, Lord Chairman, you would be aware of the various disagreements that from time to time come up between the Devolved Administrations and the Government as to whether the Formula has been applied properly, which is a different thing again, and the disagreements on that. There are genuine negotiations and genuine results.

Q905 *Lord Moser:* I am genuinely trying to understand why what we are hearing from you is so totally different from almost everything else that we have heard in this Committee or read. Apart from the Treasury, which was also rather satisfied with the status quo for understandable reasons, everybody has criticised the Barnett Formula, including myself for all the reasons that we have already touched on. My puzzlement is more fundamental really. All our other witnesses have stressed the need for finding some way of relating spending to needs and that is something we are going to be struggling with. The Barnett Formula is extremely crude and simple. It is just a population formula; anybody can do that. We have been urged by everybody else who has spoken to us to be more subtle and to relate things more to what the different areas actually need. Why is it then that you do not take that line? I do not understand that.
Mr Paul Murphy: I think it depends on who you talk to. I cannot say that my postbag has been full for the last decade on whether the Barnett Formula works or does not work in Wales; in fact, for most people I talk to in Wales it would not be an issue for them. Obviously you have been very properly asking people who are experts in their field about specific views on these issues, probably some who think there should be a replacement of the Formula. I must say that in all the years that I have spent as a minister in Wales, and for that matter in Northern Ireland, this has not been a constant matter of complaint. There are areas undoubtedly where, as the years go by, you can see the process improving but the basis of it has not formed a great debate. The other thing is that the needs question is very important but that a great deal of the public spending per head upon the people of Wales, and for that matter Scotland and Northern Ireland as well, comes from the United Kingdom Government departments which look after benefits and pensions and so on and which take that need into account. There are deprivation needs, of course, with health and social services and other devolved areas, but there are other devolved areas in the arts and other functions of the Devolved Administrations which do not necessarily need to have a needs-based formula in the same way—of course it does not— then it is up to the individual Devolved Administration itself if it wants to spend more money on a sports stadium in Cardiff and at the same time

they want to build two more hospitals, that is for them to decide.

Q906 *Lord Moser:* The Barnett Formula is not all that important to you from the point of view of covering your national needs.
Mr Paul Murphy: As it happens it does cover it very well and that is the whole point. Why is it that week in, week out, I get complaints from English Members of Parliament that we are getting too much money in Wales? There must be something wrong somewhere.

Q907 *Baroness Hollis of Heigham:* We have the three Secretaries of State from the non-English territories. Were we to have a fourth Secretary of State here, a Secretary of State for England, do you think there would be quite such a common front? The point somebody made about the range of disparities within the English regions of course is because it is a zero sum gain. There is a hundred and if London has more for obvious reasons and the South West or East Anglia, which in some ways are poor like Scotland, get less because it is a zero sum gain around the English hundred, but I think most people are looking at the distribution between England and particularly Scotland—I think it is more marginal for Wales and for Northern Ireland on the one hand and on the other—which say that it is now the case that Scotland disproportionately benefits from an anachronistic formula which, as a result, produces head space for policies and nobody at all is challenging the block grant that I have heard in the weeks we have sat on this Committee that allows for development of policies with no fiscal capping because it is not fiscally accountable to the local electorate which result in real—I was going to say distress—concern in England which believes that this is the result of an unfair financial formula which is disproportionately benefiting Scotland. I think the other two jurisdictions are more balanced in that respect and that, as a result, this needs to be addressed. If any of you, I suggest, were in a spending department and allocating moneys of this size, you would not dream of doing so based on a population formula of 30 years ago and then compounding the interest on it. What you would actually do is expect to have a needs base, which we would hope would be broad, simple, transparent, accountable, but fair. The words you have used are you "cannot think of anything better", you think it works, it is easy to do and people know where they stand, but not one of you has actually prayed in aid the concept of fairness today, I think I am right in saying, that it is fairer. You have said it is better but "better" can be used as an administrative term, but none of you have said that it is actually "fair". Surely as a result of that you would agree that while it may suit you individually as Secretaries of State—we all respect the fact that you have to fight

your corners—that does not necessarily mean that it is the right, best and wise settlement for the UK.
Mr Jim Murphy: Lord Chairman, from your own very first question when I was asked earlier did I think it was fair and I gave quite a short answer and my answer was yes. I was asked is it fair and my answer was pretty direct and the record will show that.

Q908 *Baroness Hollis of Heigham:* Why is it fair?
Mr Jim Murphy: As I alluded to in my answer right at the beginning, it reflects in Scotland the specific challenges, the specific geography of Scotland in relation to, as I mentioned earlier, the size, a tenth of the population, about a third of the landmass, the additional cost of providing public services in that environment and that is the type of thing that the legacy of the 1970s in terms allowed.

Q909 *Baroness Hollis of Heigham:* The Formula was not based on that and the same factors apply in the South West and East Anglia. I do not see why you should regard that as a definition of fairness in terms of this Formula?
Mr Jim Murphy: It was based on a reflection of spend at a moment in time which reflected the cost of public services, a delivery in Scotland which would have reflected the geography and population.
Lord Sewel: The Formula deliberately does not do that. The Formula is population driven.

Q910 *Lord Rooker:* The baseline was a snapshot in time at that time reflecting the haggling that went on to pay for the inlets, the waterways, the roads, the bridges.
Mr Jim Murphy: The baseline was based on those circumstances at that moment in time. What has happened since of course has fluctuated around populations.

Q911 *Lord Rowe-Beddoe:* Moving on to another side of this, if—and we all agree it is clearly a very big "if"—having stated your position so clearly for the last 40 minutes you were to consider that the Formula should be replaced—if you could think that for a moment—do you think that it should be by a system that perhaps is more reflective of relative needs, the cost of services, or a combination of both?
Mr Paul Murphy: Speaking for Wales, and not for Scotland or Northern Ireland, the system that we have does reflect, generally speaking, the needs of the Welsh people and that the addition of the Objective 1 funding, the combination of those things has addressed a huge difficulty in bringing Wales into the 21st century in terms of training, in terms of entrepreneurship, everything you know about in terms of what has happened in Wales more than perhaps anybody. I think the combination of the

Barnett Formula and the Objective 1, the huge funding that we had, has actually met that need. It is something which has served us well to meet it and also that the policies of government in London also meet the other need with regard to the old age pensions and the other benefits that people get and which of course reflect more accurately people's needs.

Q912 *Earl of Mar and Kellie:* I would like to ask a question about the actual working of the Formula, and particularly that part of the Formula which is where it is decided whether spending is English or United Kingdom. I ask that question in the context that, after ten years of administrative, executive and legislative devolution we have clearly got in all three devolved areas an increasing policy divergence. We have taken evidence on the fact that it seems that the Treasury makes these decisions about whether it is English spending or not and hence whether there are Barnett consequentials, or whether it is a United Kingdom spend. Do you think that continues to be a reasonable way of doing it when the actual governmental programmes are getting substantially diverged?
Mr Woodward: It does not seem to me that it is a weakness that, after ten years, we have policy divergence. It seems to me to be a fundamental recognition of the strength of devolution which is that different devolved administrations could develop different policies at different speeds, but they decide what they allocate. An example that springs to mind that I remember when I was a junior minister five years ago first in Northern Ireland was when Martin McGuinness contacted me on behalf of a constituent who wanted to be prescribed Herceptin, which is the drug, as you may know, used to deal with breast cancer and it was not available. I think it mattered that I had the flexibility, although it was then a direct rule matter, to be able to do that. That did not apply in England. Whether it should or should not have applied in England is another issue, but I think it was a strength certainly in Northern Ireland that I was able to do that, so I do not see that it is a weakness that we have policy divergence. I also do not think that one, to be frank, wants the whole Barnett too accountable for policy divergence. It is an inherent principle in devolution itself. In relation to Barnett, it would be unfortunate if people were too quick to caricature what we are saying about it. We are not saying that it is the best; we are just saying that we have not seen anything that would work any better. If you can produce something that works better and is fairer, then who on earth in their right mind would possibly disagree with you? By the same token, I think it is unfortunate if our position is simply caricatured as there is one group of people who have been to see you who think it is the worst

possible thing on the planet and we have sat here and apparently said it is the best possible thing on the planet. What we are saying is we believe in our experience it works and the fact that there are other secretaries of state sitting in this room who have been in the positions that we have been in and did not seek to fundamentally change it and make a great deal of noise about it perhaps suggests that again in the priority of things it also was not something that desperately needed to be changed. I say that because what I am mindful of here is it seems to me that what Barnett essentially does strictly is to ensure that the increase in public spending per head is the same across the UK. That is what Barnett does. Lord Trimble shakes his head but there is quite reliable material I have got in support of that analysis.

Q913 *Chairman:* What material would that be?
Mr Woodward: House of Commons Library analysis, for example, of Barnett Formula issues.

Q914 *Chairman:* It is not internal documentation.
Mr Woodward: I do not have your internal documentation.

Q915 *Chairman:* No, yours.
Mr Woodward: No, this is publicly available House of Commons page 23.

Q916 *Lord Lang of Monkton:* You refer to the fact that there are other Secretaries of State in the room. Yes, there are, but we were Secretaries of State before devolution and we had other powers and abilities to involve ourselves in expenditure for Scotland by what is now called "bypass" and other such phrases. It was not just one big Objective 1 for Wales; it was a whole range over the things and amounted to many millions of pounds.
Mr Woodward: We, Lord Lang, in Northern Ireland, as you will also appreciate, had the experience of the yo-yo of being devolved, direct rule, devolved. There is some overall experience here. What I am saying is that it has managed to survive that too. I just keep coming back to the fact that I do think it is easy to tear this to pieces, bizarrely for a House of Lords to tear it to pieces because it has been there for 30 years.

Q917 *Lord Lang of Monkton:* We are not trying to do that. We are trying to establish some facts, information and attitudes. Presumably you are not reflecting the devolved assemblies' views on some of these matters. They must be rather unhappy about some elements of the Barnett Formula and the way it operates. Supposing they developed policies which diverge markedly from those of the United Kingdom Parliament, will the Formula work then to sustain those devolved policies?

Mr Paul Murphy: That is exactly why this Formula from that point of view is infinitely better than any that has already been suggested because what it does do is give the flexibility to the Devolved Administration to be able to spend their money in the way they want to spend it. If you ring-fence by implication, not by design, a needs formula which says you have to spend that much on health, that much on education, and this, that and the other, but if the Formula was publicly seen to be based upon a needs element which took into account how much you should spend on education and health, for example, then the chances are that all the pressure groups and the unions and people involved in health and education will say you should be spending exactly the same as they are spending in England on these things; in fact, it has happened. The way this now works is that the Devolved Administrations can decide for themselves if they have a policy divergence. Take free prescriptions, for example, in the health service in Wales. They are free for everybody. It is their choice at the end of the day.

Q918 *Lord Lang of Monkton:* Supposing the United Kingdom Government abandons a whole tranche of public expenditure and changes policy radically in an area where you do not want to change it in Wales, how are you going to fund it?

Mr Paul Murphy: I do not think we would find there would be such a huge change in policy. I cannot envisage a situation, for example, where the health service in England would be so dramatically changed that it would have a huge effect upon the Welsh health service; in other words, for the sake of argument you slash the health service budget by a third or a half in England and the consequential Barnett Formula for Wales goes by a half. I do not think that would happen, but you have to accept at the end of the day I suppose that the whole amount of the money that is allocated to the three countries comes from a British Government which has been elected on a mandate by the whole of Britain and our taxation is obviously the basis of a mandate in an election for everybody. In that case there has to obviously be an element of how that overall money is spent because of the general election result. It is a British Government that does it. I do not think they would be that dramatic. So far experience tells us that certainly in Welsh terms that they are very happy to be able to spend the money in the way they want to but without, for example, destroying the health service. There is no suggestion that that would happen. They still believe in it but would spend it in another way.

Q919 *Chairman:* Nobody is suggesting taking away the right of the Devolved Assemblies to spread the money.

Mr Paul Murphy: What I am suggesting is that this Formula is a better way of giving them that opportunity.

Chairman: What we are trying to put to you is that the way in which it gets the block to the Devolved Administrations that there is something wrong with that because it is 30 years old and it is only based on population. I am sorry to keep interrupting; I have been trying to restrain myself.

Q920 *Lord Rooker:* I agree entirely with what Shaun said about the drug. Policy diversion from devolution, that is what we expect. What we do not expect is competition. If it was thought by, let's say, the English that the Welsh, Scots and Northern Ireland got more unfairly and then used the extra bit for competition against them, they would be annoyed. The example I have got is this. As I understand it, the Welsh Assembly Government has given a subsidy to manufacturing industry causing mayhem with companies who have branches on the English side and the Welsh side of the border. Do they sack and close their factories in England and move to Wales to take advantage of that? This is not a devolved issue in the sense that subsidy to manufacturing industry does not figure on the list. The fact is they have got the money to do it. Because they have that extra money to do it that the regions have not got here, the RDA's in England do not compete with each other. It is set down in tablets of stone, I understand. They do not compete with each other with the various tranches of money they get. This is an example on the mainland where the border now is a problem and a policy divergence on an issue like that where it creates competition between the regions of England and in Wales cannot be acceptable.

Mr Paul Murphy: If those differences are as stark as that then I rather suspect the state aid rules would come in and tell us that that could not happen. Certainly there are different schemes and, Lord Rooker, if you want to let me know particularly what concerns you, we could look into it for you. There are different schemes in England and in Wales to help, particularly at this time of the downturn, companies which are in difficulty. My explanation for that is that there are different ways in which different governments decide to help. That is an inevitable consequence of the policy of devolution. If in fact there were regional governments throughout England, as some of us think there should be, then we would be perhaps in a better position. Wales would compete with Scotland, Scotland would compete with Northern Ireland and Northern Ireland certainly competes with the Republic of Ireland. I am afraid in a sense we have to live with that because that is the way we deal with it.

Chairman: We have a division.

The Committee suspended from 6.18 pm to 6.30 pm for a division in the House

Q921 *Earl of Mar and Kellie:* To finish off my question which was about how the actual process of decision about whether spending was United Kingdom or England, the one time when this definitely seems to have worked against Scotland, Northern Ireland and Wales would be over the regeneration aspect of the Olympics. We have been given evidence of the fact that the Treasury makes all these decisions but I wonder whether that is really the case. What was your part in the decision that there should be no Barnett consequential?
Mr Jim Murphy: I was dealing with the Lisbon Treaty in the House of Commons at the time which was much more straightforward.

Q922 *Chairman:* Do you know whether your predecessors were consulted?
Mr Woodward: I do not know.

Q923 *Chairman:* Would you expect them to have been consulted?
Mr Paul Murphy: If the Devolved Administrations had felt uneasy about the decision then most certainly they would have been discussing the issue with the ministers. That is my guess but I do not know.

Q924 *Chairman:* If you had been in that position would you expect to have been consulted before the decision was taken?
Mr Woodward: We cannot speak for our predecessors. That is relevant, Lord Richard, in relation to answering your question. What we can say of course is that this was discussed at Cabinet. The decision about the Olympics was discussed at Cabinet. There were Cabinet subcommittees and by implication Cabinet Members were involved in discussions about that. What none of us can possibly tell you is what any financial implications might have been from that and what discussions might have taken place. It would be risky for us to speculate.

Q925 *Chairman:* Can you tell me what was discussed in Cabinet? I do not want the details but just the subject?
Mr Woodward: You would have expected the Olympics to have been discussed at Cabinet.
Mr Jim Murphy: While it is not strictly the regeneration aspect, whether for example the associated investment in London around Crossrail with the approximately £500 million now confirmed as a Barnett consequential is something that since taking up this post I have been involved in discussion with the Treasury and the Scottish Finance Minister about. The read across from that number one

transport investment in London to the number one transport investment in Scotland would again be the Forth rail crossing.

Q926 *Chairman:* Are you getting anywhere with the discussions?
Mr Jim Murphy: Yes, it is now confirmed.

Q927 *Lord Forsyth of Drumlean:* What the Earl of Mar and Kellie was getting at was the arbitrary nature of the decision as to whether something is UK or English expenditure. Mr Jim Murphy, the Scottish Secretary, has had a victory in persuading somebody—presumably the Treasury—to treat the Crossrail expenditure part of it as being infrastructure and therefore having Barnett consequences in order to fund the second Forth Road Bridge crossing. The original position taken was that Crossrail was not expenditure which would have Barnett consequences. The point which the Earl of Mar and Kellie is making is is it not a great weakness in the system that somebody—we do not know who—in the Treasury will decide without any accountability what is UK and what is English expenditure and if there is accountability can we know what the criteria are for determining it?
Mr Jim Murphy: The way in which this is arranged of course is contained in the Statement of Funding which sets it out in a transparent way. Alongside the Statement of Funding there is also a disputes mechanism. As far as I am aware, but I stand to be corrected, none of the Devolved Administrations and none of the parties to that Statement of Funding have ever invoked that disputes mechanism. Not only is it there in the Statement of Funding, but there is an appeals procedure that has never been invoked.

Q928 *Lord Forsyth of Drumlean:* Why did it change on the funding of the Forth Road Bridge Crossing?
Mr Jim Murphy: A strong argument was made about the importance of the Forth Road Crossing, the way in which it was a strategic priority for Scotland and that that money should then read across on Barnett consequentials. This picks up on a number of points.

Q929 *Lord Forsyth of Drumlean:* When you say that a strong argument was made, what was the argument? Was the argument we are in great political difficulty here, we need the money, and somebody then decided there are Barnett consequentials, or was the argument about why it merited Barnett consequentials?
Mr Jim Murphy: There was an argument based on the merit of the individual case, based around the issue of the Statement of Funding made the argument in the context of the Statement of Funding that this was important and that there would be Barnett

consequentials. It was a detailed straightforward argument with the Treasury.

Q930 *Lord Forsyth of Drumlean:* I may be missing something but whether there are Barnett consequentials or not relates to whether or not this is English or UK expenditure, does it not?
Mr Jim Murphy: Yes.

Q931 *Lord Forsyth of Drumlean:* You must have had to argue that this was not UK expenditure but English expenditure in order to get it. It is nothing to do with the merits of the proposal.
Mr Jim Murphy: One never knows why one is successful in an argument with the Treasury. If one could make the precise argument and understand the most effective way of doing it, then you would use that argument on each and every occasion. I made the argument along with others, my colleague Des Browne as well, about the Barnett consequences on Crossrail and it is important in terms of that strategic infrastructure project that there is a read across in terms of Scotland as well.
Mr Paul Murphy: There are developments in terms of how disputes are looked at and hopefully resolved. They have grown up over the last number of years. There are three really: the first is the increasing use of bilateral meetings between the devolved finance ministers and the Chief Secretary to the Treasury on individual issues that affect the particular country. Secondly, quadrilateral finance meetings to which I referred earlier, but perhaps most significantly in the last year or so the Joint Ministerial Committee structure which has lain dormant for some time and has now been resurrected—it is my job to look after that side too—and a new Statement of Funding but also a new memorandum of understanding in the Joint Ministerial Committee which allows for distributes ultimately to go at the final point to the JMC to be discussed. Obviously it is best if they can deal with it earlier.

Q932 *Lord Trimble:* You have described how there are ways in which issues can be raised and to a certain extent resolved. We are dealing here with a situation where you have Devolved Administrations of a different political complexion than yourselves. Is it really then a hope that you should continue to play a role in these issues when we are dealing with different institutions and different parties? Is it appropriate that everything at the end of the day always comes back to the Treasury and the Treasury do things and you do not know what they are doing and you are not in a position to explain and there is not proper accountability, that there are not proper criteria? Would it not be better to have a more formal process here? We were given the example of the Grants Commission in Australia. There is a separate

commission which is not controlled by the Treasury there which handles these issues and does so by reference to clearly stated criteria rather than something that always comes back to some sort of star chamber-like proceedings.
Mr Paul Murphy: Australia has a federal system which covers the entire country and it is different when you have an asymmetrical system such as ours.

Q933 *Chairman:* Why does that make such a difference?
Mr Paul Murphy: I guess in Australia that it is based on their constitution.

Q934 *Lord Trimble:* It is a more recent development. Even if you go back to the very asymmetrical devolution of the Government of Ireland Act 1920, there was provision in it for a Joint Exchequer Board which would sit on and resolve these issues but for various reasons the board was never constituted and never met.
Mr Paul Murphy: I rather fancy that the Treasury might still have been as powerful in 1920 as it is in 2009.

Q935 *Lord Trimble:* That is the issue, is it not?
Mr Paul Murphy: Yes, but essentially because the British Government is funded by general taxation. Although in Scotland there is an option for some amount of taxation, there is none in Wales or really in Northern Ireland.

Q936 *Lord Trimble:* Is it not desirable to have some more transparent procedure because it is all very well to have this private proceedings with the Treasury virtually calling all the shots at a time when you had no significant difference in the political complexion of the regional administration and the centre. Now when there are political differences these are issues which are potentially difficult political issues and if there are not some clearly stated criteria, some clearly transparent procedure, are you not storing up trouble?
Mr Paul Murphy: There is a procedure there. The procedure which first of all allows for it to be resolved at the lowest possible base, either between officials and if it cannot be officials it is ministers between the two administrations and ultimately through the JMC machinery which has been revived and which has met on more than one occasion to deal with these issues with politicians from different political parties.

Q937 *Lord Trimble:* Is it not the case that JMC's are dominated by the London ministers?
Mr Paul Murphy: I would not say that to some of the members who come from the Devolved Administrations. They make their point very forcibly.

1 April 2009   Rt Hon Jim Murphy, Rt Hon Paul Murphy and Rt Hon Shaun Woodward

Mr Jim Murphy: This is an issue that Ken Calman and the Commission on the future of Scottish devolution is exercising some thought on. Initially this was not a piece of work that he had envisaged undertaking but the evidence took him in this direction of seeing what further could be done to enhance working relationships in addition to what Paul Murphy said and that is an important piece of work on which we will have some conclusions later this year.

Chairman: We have another division. Thank you very much for coming. You will appreciate that your views have not exactly met with universal approval.

WEDNESDAY 29 APRIL 2009

Present   Forsyth of Drumlean, L   Richard, L (Chairman)
            Hollis of Heigham, B   Rooker, L
            Lang of Monkton, L   Rowe-Beddoe, L
            Lawson of Blaby, L   Sewel, L
            Mar and Kellie, E   Smith of Clifton, L
            Moser, L

Memorandum by the Department of Health

REVENUE ALLOCATIONS TO PCTS

The Department of Health has used a weighted capitation formula since 1977–78 to determine target shares of available revenue resources between NHS areas. The underlying principle of the weighted capitation formula is to distribute resources based on the relative needs of each area to enable Primary Care Trusts (PCTs) to commission similar levels of healthcare for populations with similar healthcare needs. Since 1999 there has been a further objective of helping to reduce avoidable health inequalities.

The weighted capitation formula has informed the allocation of £164 billion to PCTs in 2009–10 and 2010–11. Under the formula, PCTs' target shares of the available resources are based on their share of the England population, weighted, to account for their populations' needs for healthcare services relative to that of other PCTs.

The development of the weighted capitation formula is continually overseen by the Advisory Committee on Resource Allocation (ACRA). ACRA is an independent committee that makes recommendations to Ministers on possible changes to the formula, prior to each round of revenue allocations to PCTs. ACRA's membership comprises, GPs, academics and NHS management.

Four elements are then used to set PCTs' actual allocations:

  (a) the target share;

  (b) the actual current allocation which PCTs receive;

  (c) the distances from target (DFTs)—the difference between (a) and (b); and

  (d) pace of change policy—which determines the level of increase which all PCTs get to deliver on national and local priorities and the level of extra resources to under target PCTs to move them closer to their target share. The pace of change policy is decided by Ministers for each allocations round.

PCTs have been given control over an increasing proportion of the NHS revenue budget and this is reflected in the weighted capitation formula, which has three components:

  (a) hospital and community health services (HCHS—by far the largest component, accounting for over 76 per cent of the formula);

  (b) prescribing (the drugs bill); and

  (c) primary medical services.

HCHS in turn has separate need formulas for acute services, maternity, mental health and HIV/AIDS.

Each of the components has adjustments for age, additional need and unavoidable costs with the exception of prescribing which has no adjustment for unavoidable costs. While these adjustments necessarily differ in detail for each component, they are based on the same common principles.

The Advisory Committee on Resource Allocation (ACRA) advises the Secretary of State for Health on the weighted capitation formula. ACRA is an independent expert body whose membership includes individuals with a wide range of expertise from within, and outside, the NHS. ACRA is supported by a Technical Advisory Group (TAG).

ACRA's most recent review, covering the main elements of the formula—the population base, the need adjustments and the MFF—is published in *Report of the Advisory Committee on Resource Allocation (December 2008)*.

Further information about actual allocations, recurrent baselines, DFTs and pace of change policies is available in the PCT Revenue Allocations Exposition Books, available at www.dh.gov.uk/allocations.

POPULATION

Health services are for people and the starting point and primary determinant of weighted capitation targets must therefore be the size of the populations for which PCTs are responsible.

The PCT responsible population for resource allocation purposes consists of:

  (a) the number of people permanently registered with the GP practices within each PCT area; and.

  (b) the number of residents within the boundaries of each PCT who are not permanently registered with any GP practice, but for whom the PCT has been defined as the responsible commissioner of health services to be funded by PCT revenue allocations. In practice, this group includes prisoners, armed forces and asylum seekers.

PCT responsible populations are based on Office for National Statistics (ONS) sub-national population projections (SNPPs) for 2009 and 2010, adjusted for patients resident in one PCT while registered with the GP practice of a neighbouring or other PCT.

NEED

Population is the starting point but the make-up of the population is also critical: people do not have identical needs for health care. A key difference is that need varies according to gender and age, and in particular, the very young and elderly, whose populations are not evenly distributed across the country, tend to make more use of health services than the rest of the population. The weighted capitation formula therefore takes into account the different age structures of local populations.

Even when differences due to age are accounted for, populations of the same age distribution display different levels of need. An additional need adjustment to reflect the relative need for health care over and above that accounted for by age is necessary.

Observing need directly has not proved possible to date. Instead, statistical modelling by academics has examined the relationship across small geographical areas between the utilisation of health services, socio-economic characteristics, health status and measures of the existing supply of health services. These models have been used to decide which characteristics to include in the formula as indicators of additional need, and with what relative weights.

Based on research published in *Combining Age Related and Additional Needs (CARAN) Report* (2007), ACRA recommended an acute formula which adjusts for age and additional need in one single stage. This one stage approach, however, was undertaken separately for each age group, thus allowing the relationship between age and additional need to vary between 18 different age bands.

CARAN also developed a separate formula for maternity services, where previously it had been combined with acute services, and a new formula for prescribing. The need formulas for mental health and for primary medical services (which reflects the GP contract) remain unchanged.

The new formulas capture need better than the previous formulas. However, as they are based on utilisation of health care, they capture the NHS's response to current patterns of health inequality. ACRA felt that they did not adequately address the objective of contributing to the reduction in avoidable health inequalities. ACRA therefore recommended a separate formula for health inequalities. This uses disability free life expectancy (DFLE), which is the number of years from birth a person is expected to live which are free from limiting long-term illness. It is applied by comparing every PCT's DFLE to a benchmark figure of 70 years.

It is not currently possible on a technical basis to determine the weighting for this health inequalities formula. Ministers decided to apply it to 15 per cent of 2009–10 and 2010–11 allocations (with the exception of mental health, which already includes an adjustment for unmet need, and HIV/AIDS).

UNAVOIDABLE COSTS

The weighted capitation formula has to take account of the fact that the cost of commissioning healthcare is not the same in every part of the country due to the impact of market forces on local costs. The market forces factor (MFF) is included in the weighted capitation formula to allow for these unavoidable geographical variations in costs. Under Payment by Results (PbR), a MFF is also paid to NHS providers.

The HCHS MFF consists of separate indices for staff, medical and dental, London weighting, buildings and land. The majority of HCHS spending is on staff.

The staff MFF is based on the General Labour Market based on the premise that the private sector sets the going rate for a job in a given area, even though NHS wages are determined nationally. If these wages are below the going rate in a given area, this leads to higher indirect costs in the form of a poorer quality workforce, recruitment and retention difficulties, increased reliance on bank and agency staff, and lower productivity.

Some of the differences are quite marked between neighbouring PCTs. These "cliff edges" are unlikely to represent accurately the true underlying differences in wages, not least near the borders of PCT areas, but instead are likely to reflect to some extent the effect of using a geography of administrative boundaries which are not self-contained labour markets. A smoothing technique was applied to remove artificial cliff edges.

The staff MFF is not applied to expenditure on medical and dental staff because their indirect costs do not vary differentially across the country as they do for other NHS staff. Instead, there is a separate index for medical and dental staff based on London weighting.

Each PCT's final MFF is a weighted average of the MFFs of the providers from which it commissions for acute activity, calculated using a purchaser provider matrix (PPM), and the PCTs' own MFFs for community programmes and maternity.

The primary medical services component of the formula also has separate MFFs for practice staff, buildings and land, and a GP pay MFF which is intended to compensate deprived PCTs which face greater GP recruitment and retention difficulties. The prescribing component does not have an MFF.

The emergency ambulance cost adjustment (EACA) within the HCHS component reflects the unavoidable cost variations of delivering emergency ambulance services in different areas.

SUPPLEMENTS TO THE FORMULA

There is one supplement to the formula. The ONS SNPPs that form the basis for calculating weighted capitation targets are based on past trends for births, deaths and migration, and do not take into account Government policy on expanding the housing supply in parts of the country. The Growth Area Growth Points adjustment therefore uses dwelling led population projections provided by the Department for Communities and Local Government (DCLG) which forecast the impact on population of additional housing for PCTs in the Growth Areas and Growth Points.

HEALTH INEQUALITIES

One of ACRAs objectives is to help to reduce avoidable health inequalities through resource allocation. ACRA concluded that it is not currently possible to ensure both equal access for equal need and help reduce health inequalities in a single formula. Therefore, it has recommended a separate formula based on differing levels of healthy life expectancy that shifts resources to those places with the worst health outcomes.

The health inequalities formula targets funds at places with the worst health outcomes, recognising that these areas require more funding than other areas to address the issue of health inequality.

The health inequalities formula is a transparent way of contributing towards the reduction in health inequalities through resource allocation, and highlights the commitment to tackling the issue of health inequality.

ACRA were unable to find any evidence to inform the proportion of allocations to apply the health inequalities formula to and left it to Ministerial decision. Ministers decided to target 15 per cent of spending at health inequalities to ensure the most deprived areas have the resources they need to tackle this issue.

ACRA is undertaking further work on how to address health inequalities through the resource allocation formula.

PACE OF CHANGE POLICY

PCT allocations are determined by pace of change policy—the level of increase given to all PCTs and the level of extra resources given to under target PCTs to move them closer to their weighted capitation targets. The government are commited to moving PCTs towards their target allocations as quickly as possible.

The pace of change policy for 2009–10 and 2010–11 ensures that:

  (a) average PCT growth is 5.5 per cent each year;

  (b) minimum growth is 5.2 per cent in 2009–10 and 5.1 per cent in 2010–11;

  (c) no PCT will be more than 6.2 per cent under target by the end of 2010–11; and

(d)   no PCT will move further under target as a result of above average population growth in 2010–11.

April 2009

Examination of Witnesses

Witnesses: MR DAVID FILLINGHAM, Chair of the Advisory Committee on Resource Allocation (ACRA), MS RHONA MACDONALD, Chair of the Technical Advisory Group (TAG), MR KEITH DERBYSHIRE, Senior Economic Adviser & Deputy Director-Financial Planning & Allocations, Department of Health, and DR STEPHEN LORRIMER, Deputy Director-Financial Planning & Allocations at the Department of Health, examined.

Q938 *Chairman:* Could I start by thanking you very much for coming. You know what this Committee is about, you know our mandate and we are very grateful that you are here to help us. Could I just deal with one or two housekeeping matters first? This is a public hearing. The public will be admitted to it, if any of them turn up! If they do not, it does not matter. The evidence sessions are broadcast live on the Internet. A full transcript will obviously be taken and you will have an opportunity to look at the transcript. We will send it to you very soon after you give evidence. If you want to correct some of it, that is fine. I think on the Hansard basis you can correct grammar but you cannot actually correct the substance. I think that is all I have got on housekeeping. Can I start by asking you in effect to make an opening statement? It would help us, I think, to hear from you how you do it, how it works and what the effect of it is, please.

Mr Fillingham: Okay. Good afternoon everybody. My name is David Fillingham. In my day job I am Chief Executive of the Royal Bolton Hospital, but I have also been Chair of ACRA, advising the committee on resource allocations since 2006. Perhaps my colleagues could introduce themselves as well, my Lord Chairman, and I will make an opening statement.

Ms MacDonald: I am Rhona MacDonald. I am Chief Executive of the Bath and North East Somerset PCT, but I am also the Chair of the Technical Advisory Group to ACRA and a Member of ACRA.

Mr Derbyshire: I am Keith Derbyshire, Senior Economic Adviser in the Department of Health and Deputy Director of Finance, and I sit on ACRA and TAG as well.

Dr Lorrimer: May name is Stephen Lorrimer. I am also a Deputy Director of Finance and I lead the team which is responsible for the operationalisation of the resource allocation process and also provide secretariat support to TAG and ACRA.

Mr Fillingham: If I could try and briefly explain who ACRA is and how we work—and apologies for the acronyms, the NHS does like its acronyms, being one itself—ACRA is the Advisory Committee on Resource Allocation. I will say a little about the funding formula and how the funding formula works. ACRA is an independent expert committee which overseas the development of the formula which is used to allocate resources to Primary Care Trusts in England. The Department of Health has actually used a funding formula for quite some considerable time. It was one of the first health systems to use a formula in this way and it has used it since 1977 to allocate resources to PCTs or to their predecessors. ACRA itself was established in 1997, so it has already got quite a pedigree, and it is made up of 27 members, and that is a combination of expert academics, namely statisticians, economists and geographers, and general practitioners, NHS managers (of whom Rhona and myself are two), Department of Health officials and experts, and then representatives from other government departments as well. Our role is to oversee the development of the formula and make recommendations to ministers. So, to be clear, although we are an independent advisory committee, ultimately it is for ministers to make decisions about funding levels and about pace of change, and I will say more about that in a moment. We have two objectives which have been set for us by the Secretary of State for Health in carrying out this work. The first is to make sure the funding formula ensures equal opportunity of access to healthcare for people who are at equal risk, and that is our definition of fairness or equity, I guess, and then secondly to contribute to the reduction in avoidable health inequalities. We try, through the funding formula and the allocation process, to achieve both of those objectives. The funding formula covers hospital and community health services, the drugs bill and primary medical services and by far the largest part of that, the biggest single component, is hospital and community services. ACRA, as I have said, has 27 members but we are supported by a technical advisory group, which actually Rhona MacDonald chairs, and that has a stronger make-up of expert academics, particularly statisticians and economists. Our work programme follows the Department of Health's allocation of resources to the NHS and since 2003/4 typically we have moved to see two or three year allocations of resources rather than single years, which means our work programme tends to span a two to three year period. Then following each allocation round we make recommendations to the Secretary of State based on his commission to us, and that involves us carrying out our own analytical work and research, particularly drawing on analysts within the Department of Health, but we also commission extensive external research from experts in the field. I said I would mention the pace of change, because I think it is important to say that ACRA does not determine the funding for any given PCT in any particular year, and that is because what we do is develop a formula which determines the target allocation for each PCT. The funding which a PCT gets is then a measure of the distance that PCT is from its target allocation. So PCTs have a historic position. We set a target and the pace of change policy is then determined by ministers and the way in which that worked in the last allocations round, for example, was that all PCTs got a reasonable uplift, a good settlement, but those which were further from their targets got a higher settlement and those which were some distance from their targets a slightly lower settlement. My colleagues from the Department of Health could explain that in more detail if you wish. Just to turn to the formula itself, there are four main stages to the way in which we develop the allocations formula. The first is the population count, so the starting point for the funding formula is the population for which the PCT is responsible. That is made up of those people in that area who are registered with general practitioners, who are on GP lists, together with people who live in the area but who are not actually registered with a GP, so that would include, for example, prisoners, the Armed Forces and asylum seekers, and the populations are based on ONS (Office of National Statistics) estimates of the sub-national population projections. That is the first thing we have to do, to count the population as accurately as we can, and I guess I was a little surprised, coming on to ACRA, at how difficult it is just to count the number of people and to do that accurately. Secondly, we then weight that population for the needs of that population and that is potentially a contentious process. Not all individuals have the same needs for healthcare. Need varies with gender, age and social circumstances. The very young or the very elderly in particular make greater use of the NHS. Even after age has been taken into account need is not uniform, so we do make a range of additional adjustments. That is something which has developed and evolved over the years I have described before into what is now quite a sophisticated approach based on research commissioned by ACRA, which examines the relationship between the utilisation of health services on the one hand and the socioeconomic characteristics of the population on the other. So we weight the population count to reflect the predicted demand for healthcare which we believe that population will need. The third thing we then add is a separate health inequalities formula. Because our

weighting of the population is based on what has happened in the past, based on existing utilisation, there is the risk that it does not account of un-met needs. There are the groups of the population who do not access health services early or do not access them at all, so we have developed a health inequalities formula to meet that second objective of reducing avoidable health inequalities. That is actually based on disability-free life expectancy, looking at a measure not only of how long people are expected to live but on how healthy they are during their lifetime. That formula was used for the first time in the last allocations round. We are quite unusual as a system in having a health inequalities component in our allocation formula for health services and in fact as part of our next work programme we have commissioned research to see how that can be developed further. The fourth and final element is an adjustment for the costs of providing healthcare, so the first three have been trying to estimate the demand from the population, the needs the population is going to have, but there is a final adjustment known as the "market forces factor" and that recognises that the costs of providing healthcare are different in different parts of the country. There is a number of elements to that—staff costs, London weighting and estates and land costs—but by far the biggest element is staff costs, even though the National Health Service has a national pay deal and national pay rates, the costs of recruiting and retaining staff are higher in higher cost (labour costs) parts of the country. In central London, for example, it is difficult to recruit staff and hospitals pay more in agency and overtime rates and the so pay costs are higher and the market forces factor has to reflect that. So based on those four elements our recommendations for the content of the capitation formula go to the Secretary of State for consideration. In 2009-10 allocations round our recommendations were accepted in full and have now been implemented for the financial years 2009-10 and 2010-2011. That is a very general introduction to who ACRA is, what we do and the way in which the funding formula is developed, and then where that is given effect to actually give allocations out to PCTs. We would be very happy to answer any questions on any aspect of that from the Committee.

Q939 *Lord Forsyth of Drumlean:* Having read the paper and listening to you, how do you avoid the problem of very efficient and good health authorities being punished for delivering? Perhaps they have more emphasis on preventative or other aspects, it could be anything. How do you avoid more money going to those people who do less well not as a result of what is inherent in their area but perhaps because of their own performance?

Mr Fillingham: I think that is exactly one of the problems which the weighted capitation formula is intended to address. If we go back before 1977 when the NHS had incremental budgets handed out to it, there was a risk that the people who used the money most efficiently would suffer. The idea of the weighted capitation formula is that it allocates money to a given population on the basis of that population's need, regardless of how that money is then used by the Primary Care Trust and the hospital within that area. So clearly for those health services which can get the best use out of that money, being the most efficient, they are going to get more healthcare per pound of taxpayers' money spent than a health system which is less efficient.

Q940 *Lord Forsyth of Drumlean:* I understand that, of course, but if you then further adjust that to deal with what you call "inequalities" does that not actually have an equal and opposite effect? Perhaps not an equal effect, but an opposite effect.
Mr Fillingham: I do not believe it does because the inequalities element of the formula is looking to address the fact that even though health services may be efficient, not everybody actually accesses them in an equal way. In areas of high deprivation it is often the case that people from the more deprived parts of the population do not get access to healthcare at all or access it less. Adding the health inequalities formula recognises that the capitation formula which is based on historic utilisation, may not be picking up all aspects and needs in the population.

Q941 *Lord Lang of Monkton:* I was going to ask about preventive medicine. Presumably in your four-part formula you weight the population count higher than everything else in expenditure on preventive medicine? Am I right or wrong?
Ms MacDonald: No. One of the challenges—and it relates to the last question—is that the formula until recently has been heavily influenced by utilisation, so most of the formula has related to data which is about the use of hospital and community services. It is a more recent development that we have actually looked at the impact of preventative services. I understand the point about if your preventative services were very good you might then have lower utilisation rates. Of course, if your preventative services are very good, your needs would be lower and the challenge is to actually be able to measure need. The spending on preventative services in the NHS is actually relatively small at the moment, but as part of the health needs adjustment that is the kind of thing we are looking at, what proportion of spend do you use the needs formula with, compared with the proportion of spend which you have for the utilisation? I think that is one of the challenges you

will face if looking at formulae for Barnett. It is about different spending streams and how you bring them together.

Q942 *Lord Lang of Monkton:* Could I just ask a supplementary? It really relates to Lord Forsyth's question. It sounds as though you are going to penalise success because the more efficient people are at using the funds given to them, the less they will receive in subsequent years. Is that the case?
Ms MacDonald: I think what would happen is that over time I cannot imagine a situation where we have mastered all health needs, so at the end of the day what you are trying to do is to get the most efficient system which responds entirely to needs. Because of the statistical techniques we use in modelling, we take out things like the supply effect, but it is true to say that everybody in the NHS is trying to reduce the use of hospitals and have more preventative measures. The pace at which people do that is different across the country, but the statistical modelling techniques enable us to deliver the averages. That is a terrible word to use and my colleagues might do better.
Mr Derbyshire: Can I come in there, because I understand what is behind the question. It is a question which goes back a long way in resource application formulae of a potential perverse incentive. The original allocation formula in the seventies was based on standardised mortality ratios in different parts of the country, so people said, rather cleverly, that if you were not very good at preventing death, if your death rate got higher, you would get a higher share of the total pot. Theoretically, that is a perverse incentive. It is very difficult to imagine that a health service would actually deliberately worsen the outcomes of the population to get more money. It just does not work like that.

Q943 *Lord Forsyth of Drumlean:* That is not the point. It is not that they would worsen their performance but that the most efficient are penalised for improving their performance?
Mr Derbyshire: They would get less money per capita if their population was healthier, that is correct, and if they are very good at improving the health of their population, you could say that they would be penalised by having less money in the future because they had a healthy population.
Ms MacDonald: Could I just add, I think also it is about the relative spend between something like the use of hospitals and preventative services. We spend far more on the use of hospitals, so the formula is weighted much more to utilisation than it is to preventative services. As people get better at improving preventative services, then more of the weighting moves to that formula. That does guard to some extent against the supposed perverse incentive,

so over time the weighting of individual elements of the formula do not stay the same. There is not one formula, there is a number of elements of the formula applied to different amounts of money.

Q944 *Lord Sewel:* Two questions, if I may. Firstly, in your paper you say: "It is not currently possible on a technical basis to determine the weighting for this health inequalities formula." Why? Ministers decided on 15 per cent. Why? The second question is, has anyone done any work along the lines that if the Scottish NHS was part of your system how that would affect allocation to Scotland?

Mr Fillingham: Perhaps I could make a couple of introductory comments on that and then I will ask my colleagues to comment. As far as the health inequalities formula goes, which is your first question, the research team last time they looked at the formula spent quite a lot of time to see whether or not we could incorporate a health inequality element within the utilisation formula and they felt that technically it was not feasible. Therefore, we developed this separate mechanism. We then looked at a range of ways in which we could provide objective evidence to say what the level of weighting should be, so we did consider, for example in relation to an earlier question, the amount of money which is currently spent on preventative services and should it relate to that. We also looked at the differentials in ill-health between different groups of the population. We concluded that this was a matter of judgment and that the evidence base was not strong enough to recommend to ministers a particular level, although I think ACRA did consider a range of possibilities and 15 per cent was within the range of possibilities we suggested would be appropriate, but the process of actually deciding on 15 per cent was subject to ministerial decisions.

Dr Lorrimer: The 15 per cent was a ministerial decision and it was based on looking at the way the various options, drawing on the ones which had been proposed by ACRA, distributed funds across PCTs. It was a matter of judgment rather than anything dramatically objective because there was this lack of evidence as to what the weighting should be, so ultimately it had to be a judgment for somebody and that fell to ministers. On the second point about whether we looked at whether or not we should apply this to Scotland, we have not. Firstly, we are an English department and so that would not be part of our normal remit. It is also not clear whether or not our formula would be appropriate for Scotland.

Q945 *Lord Sewel:* I appreciate that. I just wondered whether you were aware of any sort of sad academic who has done it? We have seen lots of sad academics who have done all sorts of various things.

Dr Lorrimer: I do not think I can think of any sad, or indeed interesting academics who have looked at trying to apply it for Scotland.

Mr Derbyshire: But they would if you paid them sufficient money!

Q946 *Lord Moser:* There are two parts of your paper which I find quite difficult to understand as a statistician. I have to admit that. There are two references where you shy away from trying to produce a formula and both of those struck me. I think they are unrelated. The first one relates to the first report combining age-related and additional needs. What you are saying is that you tried to get a formula which took account of the age composition of a population, not just the total numbers, and that is a very relevant point to us, but you shied away from it because for some reason you could not do it and you ended up in fact having a different formula for each age group, so you ended up with 18 formulae, if I understand that rightly. Maybe that is inevitable. Maybe we have to end up with 18 formulae. I hope not. The other one is the one which Lord Sewel has already asked you about and I did not understand your answer. When you were talking about health inequalities you said that you really wanted to find a formula but for some reason, which I think you have tried to explain but I did not understand it, it was impossible and therefore judgment was brought into the game and you ended up with 15 per cent. So two examples, which perhaps we should take very seriously, where you ended up saying, "No formula."

Mr Derbyshire: Yes. If I can try and understand that in the context of Barnett, which is obviously about having a formula which does a slightly different thing to what the NHS formula needs to do, the first thing to actually make quite clear is that we did not fail to take account of age in the formula, and formulae used to allocate resources to the NHS prior to this formula actually had four stages in the calculation of the weighted capitation. The first was to count the population and then adjust for age, because we know and have good quality data on the relationship between age for the average individuals and their needs for health services. Previous formulae had an adjustment for age and then had an additional adjustment for need over and above the age effect. What this formula does for the first time is to actually simultaneously estimate the effects of age and need together, which is why we consciously chose to have 18 different formulae for different age bands because the additional needs drivers for each age band are different. We have separate needs drivers for the 20-year-olds and the 50-year-olds. So we did not fail to take account of age, we just took account of age and need simultaneously.

Q947 *Lord Moser:* I think I understand your answer, but the whole point for us is that if one recognises something like the importance of age in the revised Barnett Formula, say, you talk about statistical modelling but it is not explained what you actually do. Is it not possible to get all that together by weighting?

Mr Derbyshire: It is by simple weighting, and previous health formulae in England and the health formulae used in Scotland, Wales and Northern Ireland do first of all adjust the population for age because demography plays a great part in the relative needs for healthcare. The second order is adjusting for relative need. All I am saying is that the current formula in England, which is regarded as an advance, estimates the age and need effects simultaneously.

Mr Fillingham: Perhaps, my Lord Chairman, I could give an example to explain that. The research has shown that there is a series of socioeconomic characteristics which impact upon the demand for healthcare, but they differ in differing age groups of the population. For example, if you look at young people not staying on in education, that has an impact upon the health needs of people in the 15—24 years age bracket. It does not impact upon the health needs of people in the 65 plus age bracket, whereas for pension credit claimants, for example, the opposite would be true. So what the new formula does is to look at the socioeconomic characteristics of the population in those particular age bands. That is what Keith means by combining age and need together.

Q948 *Lord Rowe-Beddoe:* In your opening statement you suggested that your recommendations from ACRA were, I think you said last time, accepted by the minister. I am not quoting directly. Can you give examples of where your recommendations in the last five years have not been accepted and what was the result?

Mr Fillingham: Certainly since I became Chair of ACRA, which is three years ago, our recommendations have been accepted in full but there may be earlier instances.

Dr Lorrimer: In preparation for this Committee we looked back through the records and we could not find any examples where a recommendation had been rejected.

Q949 *Lord Rowe-Beddoe:* I see. So your recommendations have been, as it were, taken up, the prescription taken?

Mr Fillingham: Yes.

Q950 *Chairman:* Except that there is a ministerial input, is there not? The 15 per cent, for example, was a figure the ministers produced, not you?

Mr Fillingham: There is certainly a ministerial input in a number of ways. The Secretary of State commissions our work programme and also sets the objectives for the Committee, so in the first instance there is a ministerial involvement there. There are occasionally some issues which we say are beyond the remit of ACRA or where we do not think there is the technical evidence and the weighting on the health inequalities formula was one of those, and of course the pace of change policy.

Q951 *Lord Sewel:* It is critical, is it not? That is the big one. The pace of change is the big one.

Mr Fillingham: Absolutely, because what we do is determine the target allocation. The actual allocation which is received is determined by the pace of change policy. I am conscious we did not answer your earlier question about the health inequalities formula. Just to be clear, there is a formula which determines on the basis of health inequalities, using disability, free life expectancy, what the differential is between different PCTs. For that there is a formula. The issue there is how you put that together with the needs formula to come to a bottom line. There is a number of options there. You could multiply them or you could add them together, and we recommended that they should be added together. The issue of judgment was the scale, the emphasis which you placed on health inequalities compared with the emphasis which you placed on the utilisation element.

Q952 *Chairman:* Could I just follow the 15 per cent for a second. I do not want to leave the 15 per cent sort of up in the air. As I understand it, you said to ministers, "Look, we can't really give you a precise figure," but the ministers said, "Well, we think 15 per cent is about right so that's what we're going to do"?

Mr Fillingham: In actual fact—and I think it is in our published report—we suggested, I think, four options, which were not having a health inequalities formula at all, 10 per cent, 15 per cent or 20 per cent, and there was a series of rationales for each of those, but there was not strong evidence to choose one or the other so we said we will not make recommendations, to which ministers then went for the 15 per cent. So it was not simply, "We can't make our minds up. What do you think, Secretary of State?" There was a range of options, but we did not recommend a single option.

Lord Forsyth of Drumlean: This is the same point. How do you ensure the integrity and acceptability of the system in those circumstances? I have to say that if I were the minister I would be running the numbers and seeing which marginal seats were affected, and things of that kind! Of course, it might not influence my judgment!

Chairman: That is why you are not the minister!

Q953 Lord Forsyth of Drumlean: But I would be tempted and people might think that I would be tempted. Surely the whole point of the system is that it should be objective?

Mr Fillingham: Absolutely, that is the point of the system and one of the key tests of ACRA is, is it felt to be fair by the NHS, and I think we were therefore pleased with this allocation round, but most of the commentary was suggesting that the recommendations we had made which were accepted by the Secretary of State were felt to be fair. Part of that is because we can point to an evidence base for those recommendations and people can see how that links back both to the need for healthcare and to health inequalities.

Q954 Lord Forsyth of Drumlean: But if you have a spread from nought to 20 per cent that is quite a wide margin for adjustment?

Ms MacDonald: Could I add something? I think in the papers one of the things we have made clear is that there is no such thing as the perfect formula. We have been doing this for a number of years and every year the aim is to be more refined and get it better. One of the things which have been missing from resource allocation has been any recognition—we have been so dependent upon utilisation we have not been able to pick up un-met needs, so nought would be an option which made no attempt to recognise that actually there were factors of need which were not addressed through utilisation of services. 20 per cent. What that does is to give you an idea of how much of the NHS budget would be focused on addressing inequalities, and that is not just about preventative services, that is about whether in a hospital people are treated equally, how you have to put special services into an acute hospital to manage people's learning difficulties. In giving the options to the Minister we were able to give him some ideas about the issues which the inequalities adjustment actually addresses, and we will do further work in order to improve it. I think the question was very much about should we take a step and how far should the step be? I think ACRA tried to produce enough evidence to say that there is definitely merit in taking a step towards inequalities. The service had long recognised that the formula was not as good as it should be, so we had to go somewhere. This is a journey and we have to keep pursuing it.

Q955 Lord Forsyth of Drumlean: That is very helpful. It is just that in the paper it says that in understanding from the ministerial decision how ministers decided to target the 15 per cent, they targeted it to ensure the most deprived areas have the resources they need, and that made me think they were looking at tables which showed that it was not

ten, 15, 20 per cent, which PCTs would benefit. What you are saying is that that was not the case?

Ms MacDonald: I do not know what the ministers saw. What I am saying is that in presenting the information to the ministers ACRA and TAG were able to look at the options we were offering and do some empirical checking about how that looked in relation to what we knew about deprivation. It was not a straightforward, "These are the ones that gain and these are the ones that don't gain." What you get are some interesting gainers and losers when you apply the formula. Then what you have to do is to look at that and say, "What does that say when we look at what we know about services and what we know from other formulae? What would that tell us? Does it feel fair?" So there is an element of ACRA and TAG exercising a "felt fair" judgment, but then recognising that actually we do not have the evidence. It would not be peer reviewable, so we have to give ministers a choice at that point. I have no idea and would not want to comment on what went through their minds when making the decision.

Q956 Lord Sewel: I am just making mischief! May I just ask Dr Lorrimer, you, in an aside, said you did not know whether the formula would be appropriate for Scotland. If you devised a formula which allocates resources according to criteria you set out, what on earth would be different about Scotland that would make it not appropriate to apply it there?

Dr Lorrimer: The first question would be, what would be the objectives and the policy context for the Scottish NHS as opposed to the NHS in England, and would those be different? For instance, ACRA has these two objectives of meeting need and also of addressing health inequalities. Those are set and commissioned by the Secretary of State. In Scotland would those necessarily be the same? I think you are right, that is probably a minor point. I think probably more significant from a practical point of view is that there will be two questions in my mind. One would be that some of the issues in Scotland are different in the sense that, for instance, the Scottish formula used at the moment includes a rurality correction which ACRA could find no evidence we needed in England, but it would be understandable why that might be more important in Scotland. The other question would be actually are the datasets which are available to us in England available in Scotland or not, and vice versa, are the datasets which are used in Scotland available in England? That would be the big practical barrier.

Q957 Lord Rooker: You said you used other formulae. With the local government system in England there is a point in time when the decisions are announced by ministers and there is actually an appeal window for local authorities. Is there any similar system operating within the Health Service?

Mr Fillingham: No, there is not a similar mechanism linked to the allocations round of the NHS.

Q958 *Lord Rooker:* So have you never been challenged by, let us say, a PCT which felt especially aggrieved about something? Is there a means of challenging it, and has that happened?

Mr Fillingham: Lots of people wish to draw their views to ACRA's attention. They write to us, they commission research papers, they seek to have various issues raised and presented, and we have listened to those, but we do not take on board lobbying because clearly our job is to try and use the best evidence which is available and the best expert advice available to come up with a formula that is as objective as possible. So there is not a formal appeals mechanism. Yes, it is true that clearly PCTs will have views on the process and their own position within the process and they raise issues and on occasions we have commissioned research to examine the issues they raise.

Q959 *Lord Rooker:* I appreciate that. I was thinking more of when the decisions are announced, if they are announced in principle. I do not quite know how it is done, but at that point. Obviously during the ongoing period of discussion people will always be bringing issues for you to look at. One other point is that there is an awful lot of money involved here in terms of the overall budget and the formulae. I do not know whether it is probably that there is nothing similar. Could I just ask you, you are all from the Health Department, does the Treasury take an interest in what you do?

Mr Fillingham: First of all, Rhona and I are from the National Health Service, not from the Department of Health. It is a small distinction, but important to those in the NHS. The Treasury reaches a settlement with the Department of Health. ACRA's role then is to determine how the money which is allocated to the NHS is allocated, so the Treasury does not have an active involvement with ACRA.

Q960 *Lord Rooker:* Do they show any interest in what you do is really what I am after?

Mr Derbyshire: Ten, 15 years ago there was interest from the Treasury side on how we allocated money and to make sure that the allocation delivered value for money on the ground, and also whether there were any lessons to be learned from the NHS formula compared with the local government formula. So they did the kind of thing you would expect the Treasury to do, to take a wider cross-government look at what we were doing, but there has been little interest in the last ten years, apparently because it is a

transparent process which effectively has got its own audit mechanism. Lots of academics pore over the work which has been done to actually check its validity.

Q961 *Lord Rooker:* One last question, which is probably completely out of order. In terms of formulae for allocating funds, have you looked at other formulae which are used for such a mechanism to assess whether or not what you are doing is right and fair and transparent, or whether there is anybody else within the country using formulae for other purposes? Have you ever assessed other formulae?

Mr Fillingham: Yes, indeed we have, and in fact as part of our research last time round we commissioned a review of international approaches to resource allocation in different health systems. There are essentially two types, systems which look at individual capitation, insurance-based system—the Netherlands is a good example of that and the Medicare system in the US is another example—and then systems which have an area capitation basis, a population basis such as ours. Many of those countries which have an area capitation-based approach have formulae which have similarities to that of the NHS, and indeed the Scottish formula what it is known as the Arbuthnott and the approach in Northern Ireland has a very similar approach. The Welsh formula is slightly different in that it is less based on the utilisation—this discussion we were having before—and much more firmly attempts to allocate on the basis of need. It is probably true to say that the English formula was one of the first to be developed on a weighted capitation basis and many of the other systems have emulated aspects of what we have done. We try and keep up to date with developments in other systems as part of ACRA's work.

Q962 *Lord Rooker:* You have not thought of adopting the Barnett Formula approach as a replacement for yours?

Mr Fillingham: It may be something which after this Committee hearing we will take away and consider.

Q963 *Lord Smith of Clifton:* I would like to ask you about turbulence. Presumably year on year there are slight incremental adjustments for most PCTs, but there have been reports of one or two PCTs, as a result of a surge in immigration, and so on, where there has been quite a change in population. Presumably those PCTs are outriders in terms of turbulence, they are more affected by this. Do you ever look back on this and the results of what has happened and do you identify, as it were, those PCTs which are most subjected to turbulence, because I can imagine, having served on a District Health

Authority (as it then was), that the kind of brake and accelerator effect makes it terribly difficult to take any medium term planning view?

Mr Fillingham: There are issues about turbulence in two ways, I guess, and I will let my colleagues comment on the technicalities. First of all, there clearly is an issue about population shifts and the formula does aim to account for that. We use quite sophisticated ONS projections and we also compensate for the growth areas and the Department for Communities and Local Government growth points are built into the population characteristics. There is clearly an issue as well that sometimes those different populations will have different demands for healthcare too, so we clearly attempt to take account of that. The other issue about turbulence is changes to PCT allocations year on year, and I think that is a very good practical recommendation, whatever the politics, for a pace of change policy because if we were to move every PCT immediately in the next target allocation the ones that would gain could not possibly spend all the money and the ones that were losing would be in serious difficulty, so having an element of stability makes sense from a PCT's point of view.

Dr Lorrimer: The only thing I would add is that immigration/migration generally is a big issue and particularly perhaps internal migration is a bigger issue for us in this work rather than perhaps international migration, but we are very actively involved with a project you may be aware of which ONS are leading to look to improve the migration statistics and the projections they produce and we are very hopeful that that will be a big help as we go forward.

Q964 *Lord Smith of Clifton:* Presumably the population projections are going to be even more volatile in a time of recession because you are likely to get greater movements of population both internally and within the EU? One can think of towns which have suddenly had a splurge of workers and then there is a change to the pound and they all disappeared. It is impossible to be that sensitive, but nevertheless they can be quite dramatic changes, one imagines, over a fairly short period of time?

Ms MacDonald: I do think, speaking as a PCT chief executive who has to manage the changes, the pace of change policy becomes really important and also remembering that our job is to manage the resources we have got. At the end of the day many PCTs are not at target, some are under, some are over, and there are all sorts of turbulence in the system. Our job is to manage, but I do think over the years the pace of change policy has been used sensibly because my own PCT, as a result of the last round of recommendations, has moved above target rather

more than I wanted. But in doing that, because the pace of change is relatively slow at the moment it has not given us a major problem. That allows us to look ahead, so now we are saying that over the next X years we know we now have to make that amount of saving.

Chairman: I want to come on to the pace of change policy in a minute.

Q965 *Lord Lang of Monkton:* As you know, we are looking at the Barnett Formula, which covers a whole range of expenditure far outside just the Health Service, but are there any aspects or principles you have identified in your work which underpin your conclusions which might carry over and apply on a wider basis, or is it so specialised as to have no value to that extent?

Mr Fillingham: I can comment on that, I guess, as a private citizen rather than as Chair of ACRA. I think the essence of the ACRA approach could be used to allocate funding to the devolved administrations. I think there are probably five essential elements. The first is being clear about objectives, so you do need to know on what basis you are allocating resources, but I think the model, secondly, of having an independent advisory committee of experts to advise on populations, on weightings, could be done. Thirdly, I think it is possible, and we have shown this, to allocate resources according to need rather than just to demand. Fourthly, then to develop a weighted capitation formula. I think all of those could apply to your work. Fifthly I think the other lesson from our work as well which is reflected in the debate we were just having, is about pace of change and about recognising the practical difficulties then of making changes to large elements of public sector funding. I think were the Committee to consider that, there are three sets of challenges probably which occur to me. The first straightforwardly would be administrative. It needs to be set up, it needs to be administered and you need to choose the right people to be on the advisory committee. There is a cost, although the cost of ACRA is relatively small actually, the overhead is not great, but the process and the governance arrangements, I guess, would be complicated in the Barnett case for establishing some kind of arrangement like that. Secondly, there will undoubtedly be technical difficulties because clearly you are talking about not just health but quite a wide range of public expenditure and there is a basic decision there about whether you try and drill down to quite a degree of granularity and develop a formula for each area of public spend which you then aggregate, or do you go for some form of proxy measure which determines need and demand for public services as a whole? There are also, I think, some technical challenges in data availability and also the way data is collected across the UK. The third set of challenges clearly are practical and political. Would there be support from the key stakeholders for this? How would you manage pace of change? So I think our conclusion would be that there are a number of things you could take from this approach which could be made to work, but there would be some significant challenges to be dealt with.

Q966 Lord Sewel: Moving upon that a little, your approach has been to make the formula more and more sophisticated, building up the formula. I tend to be in favour of building down and concentrating on a relatively small number of variables which explain most of the difference. Have you looked at it and said, "Do we actually need to go to this degree of sophistication? Don't we get 98 per cent of it by being a lot simpler?"
Mr Fillingham: I could almost imagine you have sat in on ACRA discussions actually, having put that question! It is a constant challenge. It is something which, as Chair of ACRA, is a constant balance because on the one hand our academic colleagues are often pushing for technical robustness and they are often in favour of quite complicated and sophisticated adjustments to the formula. We are always mindful of balancing that against comprehensibility and I think it is important that non-specialists can understand how we come to our conclusions and feel that they are fair. There is a tension between those two objectives which we try to manage and, yes, one of the statistical tests we do ask the researchers to apply is how much materiality, how much difference would this tweaking of the formula make. If it is not going to make a great material difference, then we may well not move ahead with that tweaking. There is a risk that with a Committee like this the formula becomes more and more sophisticated as you move forward.

Q967 Lord Moser: My question actually is on a very similar point. In your section on need there is a paragraph which comes close to what you have just been talking about. As I understand the thinking, you start with population, obviously, and you say, "That's too crude. We've got to look at age and gender. That's the next step." Then you say, "Well, that's still not quite enough. We must deal with need." Then you say that the paper says, "Observing need directly has not proved possible to date." I understand that, I think. So then you would turn to the statisticians --always dangerous!—and you say that statistical modelling is used and what you do there is you take small areas, as I understand it, and you collect lots and lots of data—I do not know whether it is real data or theoretical data—and what links with what, where are the correlations, and out

of that you choose one or two indicators actually to use for the process. Is that what you actually do? If so, I am left with the puzzle about these models, how you actually come to choose one or two indicators, which is what you say you do, I think. Is that right?
Mr Derbyshire: Yes, I think you are 90 per cent there in that we do look at the utilisation of health services by a small area and adjust it for relative supply, to try and identify legitimate needs drivers of different populations. So for the whole country of England we know what the hospital utilisation data is and where people live and we look at the utilisation by small areas, populations of 10,000, adjust it for relative supply, adjust it for age, and then try and explain the differences. So a ward in Hull might have a much higher utilisation of hospital services than a ward in Guildford and we look for legitimate explanations of that variation linked to mortality data, morbidity data and socioeconomic data, and we identify models which explain the variation in utilisation after adjusting for age and need which appear plausible, are relatively parsimonious and look intuitively correct. Then there is an element of judgment which is applied by ACRA and TAG over which models are the most legitimate for use in a resource allocation formula.

Q968 Lord Moser: You then end up with one or two indicators. It is a very interesting question which Lord Sewel just asked you really: can one end up with just one or two sort of proxy indicators for everything else?
Mr Derbyshire: Going back to the formula which was current in the 1990s, there were five indicators. I think in the current formula David is just telling me it is 12, but that is partly because we have got so many different age bands. One of the criteria we apply to formulae is simplicity.

Q969 Lord Moser: That is what we are looking for.
Mr Derbyshire: If simplicity is important, then you can certainly have simple models as an objective of the whole process. The original RAWP formula was very elegant and very simple. It had one variable, which was all age, all cause, mortality.

Q970 Lord Moser: It is twofold. First of all, simplicity, just so that it is not too complicated. Secondly, that everybody in the Health Service and people like me would actually understand what you are up to. Would you then just end up with a couple of indicators?
Mr Derbyshire: You possibly would. But there is perhaps a higher level decision than that, which is that we favour the empirical approach to identify a formula and that is where the process has got to over time. It needs to be justified empirically, but you

could say it is judgment actually. We could make a high level judgment that the ratio of needs for transportation or education, or health, varies according to this single index, whatever that might be, and have a judgmental formula. You would over time find it difficult to defend as people who were losing out from that formula began to do precisely the statistical analyses you indicate.

Q971 *Lord Moser:* That is why you turn to the statistical models, to make it more defensible?

Mr Derbyshire: The closer people get to target allocations, the more scrutiny the actual formula generates.

Ms MacDonald: Could I just add one point? We have talked a lot about the formula and the differential needs, but especially when we are talking about public expenditure the cost of meeting the objective is relevant. So at the end of the day what are you going to apply the formula to, and if you have got a simple needs formula but meeting health needs could be totally different costs from meeting education needs and from meeting transport needs. I think that is one of the questions. When David talked about the granularity you would want to consider you have to consider that actually it is not just about differential need, it is about what is the cost of meeting that need.

Q972 *Lord Forsyth of Drumlean:* May I just follow up on Lord Moser's point? If you abandon additional model complexity, what sort of spread does that give in the allocation? How much of a difference does it make? Is it just at the margin?

Mr Fillingham: If we are going for a straight population count, for example –

Q973 *Lord Forsyth of Drumlean:* Well, weighted population. If you did not go in for this model which adjusted, as has just been explained to us, and it was just a kind of crude approach and you did not have this additional layer of complexity, what difference does that make to the spread? I am sorry, I am back with the minister looking at the allocation. What kind of difference is there? Is it marginal or is it very significant?

Mr Fillingham: I will let my colleague come in as well, but in terms of the weighting my recollection when we looked at this is that if you just took a straight population count and did not weight for anything else, then the difference would be very considerable, so I think the biggest loser would be around 30 per cent and the biggest gainer 21 per cent. There is a range in between that, if you just went for age and gender and if you then added other needs. Keith, have we done those calculations?

Mr Derbyshire: Yes, we have done those calculations. Sticking with the range of 80—121 and the needs adjustment, then the complexity of the formula does not actually change that gradient.[1] The gradient is independent of the complexity of the formula or the number of variables in the formula. Certainly previous formulae which have had fewer variables and have had a similar needs gradient.

Lord Forsyth of Drumlean: I am sorry, I did not understand that answer.

Chairman: I think he is agreeing with you.

Q974 *Lord Forsyth of Drumlean:* Does that mean it does not make very much difference?

Mr Fillingham: I am not sure I understood it either, but essentially if you go back to the original RAWP (Resource Allocation Working Party—a predecessor to ACRA) formula which just used the one elegant mechanism of standardised mortality rates, the graph for the RAWP formula overall is not wildly dissimilar to the current graph of allocations, the 80, 120. However, the position of the particular PCTs on that graph might well change and the reason for getting to a more sophisticated formula is because people want to challenge the evidence and people employ their own statisticians and economists and do their own analyses. So although having more variables may not change the overall range of allocations, there is a greater level of confidence that you are getting it right for each PCT.

Q975 *Lord Forsyth of Drumlean:* I understand that, but my question is really just in terms of these PCTs. The ones who feel aggrieved will be the ones who asked for more complexity and the ones who are doing well will say, "This is a very good, fair and simple formula." I understand that. It is just the extent to which there is variation if you go for a simpler system, the degree of unfairness there is in it. It also strikes me—and I am sure I would not want your job as Chairman—if you start off with the formula it would be very difficult to change it because you will create winners and losers and the losers will complain. If one was going to find some kind of needs based system for allocating the Barnett funds you would probably want to make it as simple as you can, but at the same time recognise that people will come along and say, "We have worked out that if you add this complexity you will get X." What is in my mind is, how big is X going to be, based on your experience? The PCTs and the others will argue, of course, but it is the extent to which it is a problem.

---

[1] Gradient is shorthand for the range between high need and low need areas, eg, the most deprived PCT in England might have needs 21 per cent above the English average and the least deprived 20 per cent below the English average.

29 April 2009   Mr David Fillingham, Ms Rhona MacDonald, Mr Keith Derbyshire
and Dr Stephen Lorrimer

Mr Fillingham: Changes to the formula do take place based on further research commissioned by ACRA. For example, the previous formula—and I apologise for the acronyms—which was known as the AREA formula has now been superseded by the new formula which is known as CARAN, and the principal difference was this business at looking at each age band and identifying the characteristics of that age band and identified need linked to those. That has made quite a difference to the allocation. I think around 10 per cent is probably the kind of order of change that we might be seeing in the individual PCTs. So there was quite considerable change and you are right, of course, gainers are quite happy with that change. People who see themselves as losing out are less happy, but the issue is that there was a range of concerns raised, particularly by the academic community, about the previous formula. There have been developments in the statistical technique and in the availability of data since the previous formula was done, so it was right for us to update the formula and to recommend what we felt was now the best evidence based approach, even though that was going to create some winners and losers, because that new statistical modelling was available and because the new data was available. We needed to make those changes and to update the formula. The other issue, of course—and I am now going to mention pace of change—is that that alters the target allocation for the PCTs. The pace at which they get there is another matter. It may not hugely influence their actual allocation in a given year.
Chairman: Thank you very much.

Q976 Lord Lawson of Blaby: May I just ask one question? I have been much impressed by the conscientiousness and common sense with which you clearly operate the system with which you have been entrusted. As Mr Fillingham pointed out, he and Ms MacDonald, unlike the other two witnesses, have proper day jobs of a very responsible nature and I wondered how much of your time is taken in doing this. Also, Ms MacDonald mentioned, very importantly, how you have to look at the cost of these and she mentioned education as well as health. It occurred to me that the big difference is that in this country, unlike in France where they are both done on a national basis, education is for the most part a local authority responsibility in England and in other countries in the United Kingdom, whereas health is national. I wondered if you would care to tell us which of these two models you think works better.
Mr Fillingham: I will let Rhona think about that while I answer the first question. It is time consuming. It is also very interesting. It is quite different from the day job and trying to get consensus across such a diverse committee can be a challenge, but it is a very interesting challenge. We meet around five or six times a year. That tends to be less at the beginning of our programme and more towards the end, as we have got to consider the results of research, and they are full day meetings. I estimate I spend probably a day preparing for each meeting, reading papers and talking to officials, so probably somewhere in the order of ten to 12 days a year of my time, slightly more when I am invited to a Lords Committee!
Ms MacDonald: I spend a similar amount of time, but in relation to the education point, (a) when I mentioned education I was referring to the fact that Barnett would have to take account of different spending streams. Education per se does not feature in our world and I do not think I know enough about the difference between how education is allocated and how we do help to actually make informed judgments. I rather think that even with the local authority spend there is a national allocation process to local authorities which has an impact, so I do not think it is that different.

Q977 Lord Lawson of Blaby: There is a national allocation system and the local authorities take no notice of it, they just spend it as they wish. The public expenditure White Paper is an exercise in fiction, apart from the total!
Ms MacDonald: I understand, but I think that has also been a long debate in the NHS, in that we apply different formulae to different parts of the NHS spend. When it gets to a PCT, I can determine locally whether to spend it on acute services, community services or preventative services, so the same principle applies.
Chairman: Thank you very much indeed. I am bound to say, as far as I am concerned I found it extraordinarily helpful. I confess I did not understand the paper with perhaps the degree of clarity I should, but you have shone a light on it and I am very grateful. Thank you very much indeed.

WEDNESDAY 17 JUNE 2009

Present	Forsyth of Drumlean, L	Richard, L (Chairman)
	Hollis of Heigham, B	Rooker, L
	Lawson of Blaby, L	Rowe-Beddoe, L
	Mar and Kellie, E	Sewel, L
	Moser, L	Trimble, L

Examination of Witnesses

Witnesses: Mr Liam Byrne, a Member of the House of Commons, Chief Secretary to the Treasury; Mr Mark Parkinson, Devolution Branch Head in DCU; and Ms Helen Radcliffe, Team Leader in DCU, HM Treasury, examined.

Q978 Chairman: Chief Secretary, can I thank you very much for coming. I appreciate that you have not been in the post a long time, although there is a familiarity already, I think, with the Treasury, and no doubt the Barnett Formula will have crossed your desk at some point in the past. Thank you very much for coming and giving us this time. Can I just deal with one or two housekeeping matters? The evidence session will be broadcast live on the Internet. A full transcript will be taken and you will be sent a copy of the transcript and obviously you can correct it on Hansard terms, the grammar but not the content. If there are any issues which you have not been able to deal with or you want to deal with, then if you want to write to us we would be delighted to receive that. Do you want to say anything to start with?

Mr Byrne: Just very briefly, first to say thank you for allowing me to give evidence, I think a week later than scheduled. That has allowed me to spend a week and a half in the job before coming before you. I have brought with me Mark Parkinson and Helen Radcliffe, whom I think you have met before, and with your permission, Chairman, I might invite them to chip in when the limits of my technical knowledge are reached. Just to say by way of introduction, the Treasury is obviously a great supporter of devolution. We are also supporters of the principle that there should be a single tax policy for the UK which allows us to manage tax risks centrally and conduct spending reviews centrally. Obviously, in order to bridge those two principles, rules are needed. Our position is set out in the statement of funding policy. I am a great believer that pretty much every aspect of public administration can be improved upon, so as a new Chief Secretary I am very much looking forward to the Committee's recommendations. I know that we have provided a lot of evidence so far. I hope to add a little bit to that this afternoon and obviously if there is anything more we can do to help your inquiry we will do that.

Q979 Lord Lawson of Blaby: Thank you very much. Can I say one other thing before we start? The acoustics in this room are absolutely appalling, so if you could shout I would be grateful. Can I ask you to start off with one general point? What effect do you think the Barnett Formula has in terms of equity as between the devolved administrations across the UK as a whole? It is really a very simple point. Do you think it operates fairly—and I use the word "fairly" quite deliberately?

Mr Byrne: Is the Barnett Formula a formula which delivers a platonic, absolutely perfect semblance of fairness? I do not think it does. Does it deliver outcomes which are fair enough? Yes, I do think it does, because it acts at the margin, because it acts to share out increments. I think it does a good job at making sure that increases in public spending are shared fairly, but obviously what it does not do is disturb the baselines on which it builds, which date back to 1979/80. So there will be anomalies which appear when you step back and look at the distribution of public spending in the round, and no doubt we will go on to discuss different dimensions to that problem, but I think it is fair enough.

Q980 Chairman: As far as the increments are concerned?

Mr Byrne: Yes.

Q981 Chairman: I think that is a fairly automatic thing. There are problems with it, but it is a fairly automatic process, that bit of it, is it not?

Mr Byrne: Indeed.

Q982 Chairman: But it is the baseline point. Do you think the way in which the baseline has been calculated and the way it has been used in the last 30-odd years has produced a fair result?

Mr Byrne: The reason why I say "fair enough" is because, as I have dug into this question over the last week and a half, it strikes me that there would be at least three quite significant issues involved in getting into a process of really unpicking those baselines and building adjustments in a more radical way to those baselines into any new kind of formula. I think those problems, to me, feel like they fall under three headings. The first is obviously complexity. If you really wanted to get stuck into a ground up needs assessment then you have automatically got some pretty significant problems in coming up with a formula or different formulae which can operate across a whole range of public services, right the way across the UK. As I was thinking about it this morning, it just struck me that there is a fundamental tension involved here, which you have no doubt already seen, which is that on the one hand if you try to set out needs formulae which were capable of operating right the way across the UK that would be a standard thing, but the whole purpose of devolution is to give different nations more flexibility in defining what needs are important to them. So it struck me that you would immediately run into a fundamental tension which is involved in devolution and that formula would be complicated indeed. I began my short ministerial career as a social care minister and I remember how difficult some of these formulae are. They do involve different assessments of relative need. They involve matters of judgment about how much to weight the different kinds of need. They all involve floors, ceilings, dampenings, transitional arrangements; matters of judgment.

Q983 *Chairman:* In the seventies the Treasury did it?
Mr Byrne: Indeed. My point was going to be that it is a very complicated process. You run into a fundamental problem involved in the principle of devolution.

Q984 *Chairman:* Why does it have to be so complicated? Why does it have to take that time? Why can we not have a much simpler assessment of relative needs? I appreciate if you want to get into every issue, dot every 'i' and cross every 't' it will take a very long time, as indeed it did, it seems, in the seventies, but you could do it much quicker on an easier basis if you take out perhaps half a dozen or so comparators and use those?
Mr Byrne: Well, it is just an observation really. When you look at the way the Police Formula is distributed in Britain, if you look at the way health spending is distributed, the way local government spending is distributed, all no doubt started on the principle of administrative simplicity but all—and this is just an observation—have ended up in quite a complicated place. Again, all do involve matters of judgment about what factors, such as sparsity, you give different weight. My observation is that all involve different floors, ceilings, dampenings. There were just complexities involved in all of them. The second point I was going to make, my second difficulty, I suppose, is the question of consent because given the complexity which was involved in coming up with those formulae, I wonder whether you could come up with formulae—and it is an open question, I know—

with a UK-wide formula which was able to command the consent of political parties and politicians in different parts of the UK. If, of course, we could not, that immediately takes you into my third problem, which is about the cost of change, because if you came up with a new formula, that would inevitably involve, or one should at least plan for an outcome where you had different distributions of funding. You would then always almost certainly need transitional arrangements, which in themselves would be complicated. When you put all of that together, it just makes me think that the system becomes less predictable and from a good public administration point of view I think that three year budgets and the degree of predictability which we now have are good for good public administration because it gives frontline public service leaders, and indeed politicians, the ability to plan ahead a little more rigorously. If you had a situation of complexity which was contested, with complicated change arrangements, my suspicion would be that whatever the outcome was it would be more contested, it would be debated, it would be slower and harder to set up and, Heaven forbid, you may end up in a situation where you were not giving frontline public organisations their final settlement, definitive final word, all the 'i's dotted and 't's crossed, until some way into their financial year. As I say, it poses risks of predictability which I do not think would be good for public administration. It just struck me that those are the two sorts of things in the balance, which is why I came to the conclusion that it is probably fair enough.

Q985 *Chairman:* Do you think it has got any disadvantages?
Mr Byrne: Certainly, I think it has got some disadvantages.

Q986 *Chairman:* What do you see as the disadvantages?
Mr Byrne: I see three principal disadvantages. The first disadvantage is what I think is colloquially known as the "Barnett squeeze", which is that because of the higher baselines inherited, certainly in Scotland and elsewhere, when you have got these standard increments of new public money coming in, then proportionately those growth rates can appear lower in different nations. In theory, arithmetically that can produce a degree of convergence. When you look back over the last 20 years it does not appear to have produced much, but nonetheless it is a criticism which I know is well-rehearsed. Second—and this, I guess, is a criticism coming from a slightly different direction—if you did step back and look at what baldly are the different levels of public spending per region, why is it that that nation has got more than another nation, principally England? That, I think, is

another criticism which is well-made. The third criticism, which I think for me is the most important, is how precisely are we matching the delivery of resource with need? I think the current arrangements, as I say, do a reasonably good job of that but they do not allow us, when we discuss this level, at the level of the nation, to really answer the question with massive precision. For me those are two of the features which are well known. One is more, sort of, personal.

Q987 *Chairman:* But they could all be corrected, those three disadvantages?
Mr Byrne: I hope you are going to tell me that.

Q988 *Chairman:* It is a valid criticism, but it is a criticism which could actually be dealt with?
Mr Byrne: I hope so. That is genuinely why I look to the Committee's advice on this because, as I say, from my look at this over the great span of nine days I can see an argument which says, "This is fair enough. It does a pretty good job. There is a minefield of issues involved in moving away from it which produce new risks to good public administration," but if there is an alternative which is better, which is capable of commanding political consent, which can be delivered with satisfactory transitional arrangements which do not disturb too much the predictability which good public servants need in their finances, then I am all ears!
Chairman: You may be all eyes when we produce the report!

Q989 *Baroness Hollis of Heigham:* May I leapfrog, because this is actually a question I was going to raise? This is actually a point which you were making about the disadvantages associated with the risks of change, which in a way overlaps with a later question. I just want to press you on the outcomes. Your analogy of the local authorities and health authorities was absolutely right, but of course they are very small units and the smaller the geographical and population unit, the more precise you have to be in tailoring because they are very sensitive to the 500,000 here, the 500,000 there, and the bigger the unit, the less sensitive you need to be, the simpler the formula can be and the more there are conflicting pressures which even out the outcome. For example, Scotland will have higher morbidity rates amongst older people, Northern Ireland will have a higher number of younger children. They have different needs, but if you put them together against an English base they, so to speak, cancel each other out. Would you not, therefore, agree that a lot of your concerns and your analogies with local authorities, health authorities, police authorities, and so on, would not necessarily come into play provided (a) you could keep it simple, (b) the change was incremental, (c) the transitional arrangements were

sufficiently adequate, and (d) it showed a relatively clear correlation between, say, the rate of populations and some degree of other needs against outcomes?
Mr Byrne: That already sounds a complicated story to me. I am from Birmingham and we have a local authority in Birmingham which has got a population of a million –

Q990 *Baroness Hollis of Heigham:* It is the biggest in the country.
Mr Byrne: —total public spending is about £7 billion in Birmingham if you pull all the different agencies together, so I am not quite sure that I completely subscribe to the argument that all things even out if you deal with population units, like nations which are bigger. I think the list you have already given is long and I guess I would still just come back to one difficulty, which is that one of the principles of devolution was to give greater flexibility to different nations to prioritise need in different ways. For example—and this is a hypothetical example—it could be that in one nation people want to give much greater weight to the needs involved in sparsity, and that will be a political judgment. How could you, as the UK, if you like, say, "Well, that's all very interesting, but actually we're just going to have a standard set of needs and a standard weighting of needs and we are actually now going to override your political autonomy to adjust the prioritisation of those different needs in different ways"?

Q991 *Baroness Hollis of Heigham:* No, because we do that in local authorities now. We make an allocation of funds based on, say, the rate of population, but if Worthing decides to spend their monies for the over 75s on residential care and Bournemouth chooses to spend it on an ordinary alarm system, that is their determination of the best way to meet local need and how to assess it. So that happens now. You have a common basis of assessing need, but local authorities then have the power and the autonomy to determine how that resource, allocated by a standardised formula of need, is actually spent in their patch to meet local needs. I do not see any problem with that and I do not see why that would not apply under any system that we are proposing, perhaps, here.
Mr Byrne: If I may, let me just pursue this example of population density, because it is perfectly possible in this hypothetical world we are talking about for the Scottish Government to say, "Okay, you've got a formula for need there. We agree with a great deal of it, but actually we don't think you have given it anything like the right weight for population density," because, as you know, Scotland is the least densely populated part of the UK. How would you resolve this debate and this discussion about what weight to give to that particular need? I do not want

to flog this horse to death, but my point is that there will be different dimensions to any need assessment. You have got to make political judgments about what weight to give each one and the principle of devolution allows different politicians in different areas to assess needs differently and to weight needs differently. To then create a UK-wide needs assessment just appears to me to slightly reverse that and it is a conundrum which I do not offer an answer to. It is just an observation which struck me this morning.

Q992 *Lord Sewel:* Can I put to you that a fundamental weakness of the Barnett approach is to do with the baseline and the fact that population changes within the four territories have moved differentially over time, because most of the money that is in the baseline at the time that it went into the baseline went in through the population increment. The weakness is that over time, as the population shares have changed, the baseline has not changed to reflect the change in populations of the four countries, the four areas. So you get a situation where you are in one country, because of that, funding a population which is no longer there and in another country under-funding a population which has increased, and that seems to me to be fundamental weakness.
Mr Byrne: I think that is a fair point. Some figures I looked at for Scotland this morning make that point exactly, which is that if you look at the declining population of Scotland then that does mean that public spending per capita has gone up in part because of the declining population and that increase, because of the gearing, will not have been offset by slower rates of public spending growth as shared out by the Barnett Formula. So I agree that is a weakness and I guess I come back to this question about whether the weakness is so great that one should embark upon a new approach with all the risks associated with it, my sort of three 'C's, if you like, about complexity, consent and change. So when I look at it and I look at the outcomes which we have today, especially the outcomes which have already been published in PESA, and we will update the House again with new numbers tomorrow, you obviously do get some differences, so I agree that is one of the weaknesses. Again, I think you have got to make a careful judgment about how seriousness the weakness is, because if you look at some differences in some pretty basic dimensions, between, for example, Scotland and England, you can see that in terms of GDP per capita there has not actually been a huge convergence in GDP per capita rates between England and Scotland over the last twenty years. If you look at morbidity rates, life expectancy is still, unfortunately, quite substantially lower in Scotland than it is in England. Household income rates are not

converging rapidly either, so there do remain some differences in public spending per capita between Scotland and England, but there also appear to be some quite stark socioeconomic differences as well. So the conclusion I draw from that comes back to the first point I made really, which is that I think the formula as it exists at the moment is fair enough at this stage.

Q993 *Chairman:* "Fair enough" does not actually mean anything. In what respect is it fair and in what respect is it not fair? You have just answered a question about the different levels between England and Scotland, and look at the different levels, for example, between Northern Ireland, Wales and Scotland. Is that fair?
Mr Byrne: As I say, I think the Barnett Formula in and of itself does a pretty good, a pretty fair and equitable job of slicing up and distributing public sector spending growth.

Q994 *Chairman:* How is it a pretty good job? I understand that it is functional, of course it is. It is a quasi mathematical formula which is applied. It does not require anybody to do a great deal. You have got the figures and then you apply them, but how is that fair?
Mr Byrne: Because it is largely geared to the population and it does ensure that there are uplifts in per capita public spending growth across the UK.

Q995 *Chairman:* But you have just agreed with Lord Sewel that it did not.
Mr Byrne: No, my point actually was about baselines, which is that the thrust of this argument is that what the Barnett Formula does not do, the failure which you allege, is that it does not disturb the baselines inherited radically enough and we are all worried—you are worried and I am a bit concerned—about whether resources are matched tightly enough to need. The only kind of observation I was offering really was that if you go back to the inequalities which helped inform those baselines back in 1979–80—

Q996 *Lord Sewel:* It is only a small proportion of the baseline that is accounted for.
Mr Byrne: Yes, but the inequalities between the countries are still pretty stark, so GDP per capita is 7 per cent lower in Scotland than in England. If you look at mortality rates, they are 18 per cent higher in Scotland than in England. If you look at sparsity rates, Scotland has got the lowest population densities. So there remain some pretty profound and stark differences in inequalities. As I say, if you look at growth and wealth per head, those GDP per capita rates have not converged over the last 20 years. I am sorry to labour this, but that is a long way of saying

that many of the inequalities between Scotland, England and other parts of the UK which informed the baseline in 1979–80 are still with us and probably warrant different per capita rates of public spending.

Q997 *Lord Sewel:* In 1979–80 where were these inequalities in the baseline? Nobody did an exercise pre the application of the population increment to work out the funding between the different countries on the basis of some inequality of need.
Mr Byrne: Let me put to you this: if you look at the index of relative spending over time, if you look at 1977–78, if you take England at 100 per cent, Scotland would be at 128 per cent, Northern Ireland 141 per cent and Wales at 100 per cent. So in 1977–78 England would be 100, Northern Ireland 141, Wales 100 and Scotland 128. If you then looked at that same index of relative spending in 2007–08, England again is 100, Northern Ireland would be 130, Wales would be 113 and Scotland would be 122. Between Scotland and England there has been a degree of convergence, between Wales and England there has been a degree of divergence and between Northern Ireland and England there has been a degree of convergence, so I guess my argument is that there has not been a massive convergence between Scotland and England over that period, but nor has there been a wholesale closing of some of these gaps in equalities. Those gaps remain, I am afraid, a bit stark.

Q998 *Lord Forsyth of Drumlean:* I know you have just taken over your post, but I do not know if you have had a chance yet to read the *Calman Report*, which the Prime Minister welcomed with enthusiasm yesterday and which I understand the Government is committed to the proposals?
Mr Byrne: I have read a summary.

Q999 *Lord Forsyth of Drumlean:* I do not want to stray into the areas of tax raising powers, and so on, because they are not for this committee, but the *Calman Report* says, on p.111, where it is talking about the proportion of the block grant that is not raised by income tax, it says: "The block grant, as the means of financing most associated with equity, should continue to make up the remainder of the Scottish Parliament's budget, but it should be justified by need." It is on p.111, recommendation 3.4. Now, I do not want to get into the merits of the *Calman Report* but the question you were asked was whether it was fair or not, and *Calman* is resting on the point that it needs to be fair, and in order for it to be seen to be fair it has to be justified by need. You are justifying it by history and you are saying it is "fair enough", and "fair enough" seems to me to sound like, "It is administratively difficult for us to do this, therefore we just don't bother." My question is, what did the Prime Minister mean, and the Secretary of

State for Scotland, when he welcomed these proposals if the Government's position is not that the funding should be continued on a block basis but on the basis of some kind of justification by need?
Mr Byrne: If you look at the second sentence in 3.4 it says, "until such time as a proper assessment of relative spending across the UK is carried out the Barnett Formula should continue to be used as the basis for calculating the proportion of each block grant." What I do not want to rule out is the possibility of a more perfect formula. My only observation is that today, now, until your Committee reports, perhaps, there is big complexity –

Q1000 *Lord Forsyth of Drumlean:* I am sorry to interrupt you. I understand that point, but I am focusing on the Chairman's question, which is, is it fair, and *Calman* seems to be suggesting that no, it is not fair unless it is based on some assessment of need. I am just trying to get from you what the Government's position it. I appreciate that how you change it is a matter for us and for the Government, but the fundamental question is, are you satisfied with the system we have at the moment as being fair? This report is saying no, it needs to be changed. What is the Government's position? Is it in line with *Calman* or something else?
Mr Byrne: Firstly, we welcome *Calman*, welcome the principles set out, welcome the argument and welcome the recommendations. *Calman* makes some pretty astute and acute observations about the need for further work on taxes and the way that that will work in practice without setting up the wrong kinds of incentives, and we will carry on that work to puzzle through those questions. That is the position on *Calman*. The argument about the Barnett Formula versus proper needs assessment for me comes down to this: I think the Barnett Formula at the moment works pretty well. Is it my platonic ideal of equity and fairness? No, it is not. Have I seen the platonic ideal of equity and fairness? No, I have not, because what I do not want to do is to get trapped between false alternatives. At the moment there is not a choice between the Barnett Formula and another formula which is better; it is between Barnett and the kind of hypothetical, and that is where we are at the moment.

Q1001 *Lord Forsyth of Drumlean:* So you do not agree with recommendation 3.4, that it should be justified by need, the block grant? You do not agree with that?
Mr Byrne: I think it should be justified by need. I would agree with that, but my concern would remain that we would still need to devise a way of moving towards that position which we have not yet seen, which is why I come back to this observation I made at the beginning, which is that what we do not have

at the moment is perfection, incredible though that may seem.

Q1002 *Lord Lawson of Blaby:* I must say, I think you are making your task too difficult and I am surprised that the present Government will not undertake any reform until it has discovered the platonic ideal! I think that is rather too high a hurdle. If I may make another observation, because I have not got time to argue the case now, the three 'C's, which are your objections to making change where you cite the difficulty in finding the platonic ideal, which is not unique in this area, are four 'C's in fact, and I hope that in our report we will be able to demonstrate to you why that is so, which will be a fourth 'C', a great comfort to you! I would like to focus on the baseline question which has come up. You are aware that the Treasury gave us evidence—I will read it out in full if you like, but the summary is that they take no notice of the baseline or the existing level of provision, they are just concerned with the so-called Barnett consequentials and going forward. So it follows from that logically, does it not, that if the baseline is, for whatever reason, seriously wrong then since the baseline is so much larger than the consequentials then each year the settlement will be seriously wrong? If the baseline is seriously wrong and this is not looked at—and the Treasury officials in their evidence assured us that it is not; I can read it out, if you like, but that is the reassurance—then the settlement each year will also be seriously wrong?
Mr Byrne: I am sorry to be a bit thick, but I have not quite followed that argument.

Q1003 *Lord Lawson of Blaby:* The settlement is the baseline plus the consequentials, which you said steadily increase but I am not so sure you can count on that. I realise this is what you are grappling with at the moment, the overall public finances, and therefore I understand that you have not been able to devote too much of your attention to this. I fully understand that and I apologise for burdening you in this way, but it would have been discourteous to you if we had not invited you to come and talk to us about this. I will read it out. This is the Treasury evidence. "It is also worth noting for the operation of the Barnett Formula it is not necessary for the Treasury to scrutinise the existing level of provision or baseline of the devolved administrations. The baseline level of provision is in the year before the first year of the Spending Review and rolled forward over the Spending Review period and the Barnett consequentials are added to this baseline." Therefore, since you have a large baseline and relatively speaking small consequentials which you add on to get the settlement, this means that if the baseline is seriously wrong then each year's settlement is seriously wrong? Is it not so?

Mr Byrne: Not quite! Firstly, the increment and the Barnett Formula and the way it is devised is about sharing out equitably increases in public spending growth, but I think the more significant thing you say is that the baselines may be seriously wrong. I am not sure the evidence for that is clear-cut and it would be useful to get the Committee's observation on that. The reason I say it is not clear-cut is because of some of the facts and figures I have quoted earlier. There were differences in the distribution of public spending back in 1979/80 and there are differences now, but it is not clear that there has been a fundamental shift in inequalities which might actually point you to a need to fundamentally restructure some of those baselines.

Q1004 *Lord Lawson of Blaby:* I was just going to make one other observation, which is that there is one objection to change, which I think is the real objection to change, which you have not yet mentioned and that is the political difficulty of doing it, which is particularly likely to occur so far as Scotland is concerned. If you find the baseline is seriously wrong (to use my expression) and therefore because you want to get it right and because the Calman Commission and you have agreed that the baseline really should be based on need, the way you can ease the pain, as it were, is to have a transition period from the wrong baseline to the right one, which you may need to review, no doubt, every so often. How long a transition period would you think would be wise?
Mr Byrne: I did actually flag as one of my 'C's this problem of consent because I think one of the great risks, which you found looking at local government finance, is that there are big administrative and political risks associated with fundamentally restructuring some of these arrangements in a way which is contested. So given the complexities, with great respect to Baroness Hollis, which I think would be involved in coming up with this formula, I think it would be inevitable that the dimensions, the mechanics of that formula, would be contested. I think the result of that would be quite complicated change arrangements. When you look at the current local government funding formula, it is quite short, only 16 pages long. It is a sort of model of clarity from DCLG. It is full of floors, ceilings and dampening mechanisms. I remember being involved in some of those conversations myself three or four years ago and there are fine, delicate and difficult political judgments to be made in getting these transitional arrangements right, as you are all too familiar with. I just think that if you put all that together it really does create some quite big risks and that will damage predictability. It is not good for public administration.

Lord Lawson of Blaby: I am slightly surprised. You will recall that the Justice Committee of the House of Commons said, "The Barnett Formula is overdue for reform and lacks any basis in equity or logic." So I think it does seem to most people that there is a problem here. As I say, most of the difficulties you adumbrate I hope we will be able in our report to show are readily and easily overcome, and indeed in many cases it is like, having taken so long each year, you have to do things mid-year, but you say it may be contested. I am quite sure—certainly this is my experience as a Chancellor—with every Chief Secretary I have found that pretty well everything he proposes is contested by his colleagues!

Baroness Hollis of Heigham: Tell us more!

Q1005 *Lord Lawson of Blaby:* But that did not mean that decisions were not taken. That is the point. So I do come back to my question. You will listen, obviously, to the arguments, you will evaluate them very correctly and properly, and at the end of the day you will decide, I think sensibly, that an adjustment needs to be made. Then the question is, over how long a transitional period? How long a transitional period would you suggest, because obviously it cannot be overnight, but equally it would be a nonsense if it were too long because it would just prolong the pain? So what would you say?

Mr Byrne: Absolutely, and if you were sitting in my seat your advice to the Prime Minister, or if you were Chancellor, would be that you would choose a transitional period which took account of the greatness of the transitions involved. So I am afraid it is a hypothetical question and you would actually have to have a look at what kind of movements and money would be entailed.

Lord Lawson of Blaby: Thank you.

Q1006 *Chairman:* Can I ask you one further question on the baseline because it seemed to me that underlying what you were saying about the baseline in the Barnett Formula there is an assumption that the baseline is correct. What is that based on, because it is 30 years old?

Mr Byrne: My view is that looking at some admittedly quite basic matrix, I do not see a great convergence in equalities across the UK which implies that you should see some kind of much more marked convergence in the index of public spending. The Committee has got the secret needs assessment conducted by the Treasury in 1994, has it not?

Baroness Hollis of Heigham: 1984.

Q1007 *Chairman:* We have had a sniff at it!

Mr Byrne: Sorry, 1984.

Q1008 *Chairman:* Could I just say that if it is 1994 we would like to have it.

Mr Byrne: There are two, are there not? I think there is one that you had to FOI out of the Government in order to get it out, and there is another one which was last done in 1979/80. The only point I would make is that there was not a great deal of difference between the indices of needs assessment that was done then. Again, I quoted earlier some figures about the index of relative spending which showed that there had been a degree of convergence between Scotland and England over the last 25, nearly 30 years. So there has been a degree of convergence but the gaps remain. Is that a bad thing? Well, if you look at the differences in GDP per capita, if you look at the differences in life expectancy, if you look at the differences in household income, there also has not been a lot of convergence in those matrix either. That is my own, after a week and a half, personal view. I have not seen some great flash of insight which tells me that the differences in the baselines from 1979/80 absolutely demand –

Q1009 *Chairman:* Let me just give you a glimmer. You quote the 1984 assessment and you say there is not a big difference between 1984 and the one which was done in the 1970s, and that justifies a continuation of the baseline. I would just like to point out that between 1978 and 1984 is six years and between 1984 and 2009 is 25 years, so are we really going to base this whole thing on a set of calculations which were done 25 years ago?

Mr Byrne: That is why, cleverly, I did not rest my entire argument on that one data point! That is why I did pray in aid these other, I think, pretty important matrix like wealth per head, morbidity and household income. Because we have not seen such a fundamental convergence on those figures—I know you cannot read too much into it, but you have to look at those figures and say, "Well, based on those figures there is not overwhelming evidence for a fundamental restructuring of relative baseline differences."

Q1010 *Baroness Hollis of Heigham:* If you are right, what is the problem, because if you are right there will not be much change, and if you are wrong you certainly do need change?

Mr Byrne: I go back to my three 'C's. Those are my problems.

Q1011 *Lord Rooker:* I have to say, Liam, you deserve, I think, the Committee's respect given the fact that you have only been in the job a few days. You have clearly spent some time on this and we appreciate that, because that is obvious from the way you have answered the questions. I am desperately tying to think of a change what has occurred in the last 30-odd years since I have been in this place where everyone has been a gainer. There is not. The point is,

as we have discovered as we have looked at alternatives, the dog that is not barking—and you in one of your very early answers alluded to the figures—is Wales. The Welsh are the big losers. It was quite apparent to us. The Secretary of State (as was) did not quite appreciate how much they were losers under the status quo as it has gone on for 25, 30 years, and this is really more a question to ask you to go back and have a look at it because the status quo, as it drifts through the decades, is a festering sore now. The reason this Committee is sitting now is because it has been perceived that this issue is a festering sore between the nations of the United Kingdom. We have not quite got all the answers and we are not exactly clear what happened. We have got to look at it, and others have looked at it as well, but it is quite clear we are building up a huge problem for later on. In the meantime, because most of the discussion is UK v. Scotland, England v. Scotland, and Northern Ireland we almost park as a special case, significantly because of the nature of what has happened there in the last 20 years. I have no special knowledge of this, only what I have gleaned from this Committee, but the Welsh nation is the big loser of the status quo. It is amazing they are not up in arms about it, but they soon will be once various indices are published and various reports are published. This is the supreme difficulty, that while you say, broadly speaking it is fair enough –
Mr Byrne: Given the risks of change.

Q1012 *Lord Rooker:* Yes, given the risks of change, fair enough, but for how long? There is the six year gap and then the gap we are getting on to now is quite unsustainable, therefore—and I am just putting the bid in, I have no special axe on this, except that the figures we have seen in trying to get a simple formula, anything that is simple is unfair, it is too simple, I fully accept that, and you try and get it super-fair and you build in, as you have said, incredible complexity. We have got to try and find a way through that and we have got to look at some possibilities. Let me put this to you: it is just not fair and it is not good conduct of public administration to knowingly know that one of the nation states under the status quo is actually losing out, and it is getting worse each year, but it is the one that people do not talk about. That has got to be unacceptable and all I am saying is—because you have to spend a lot of time on this—this does need addressing by the Treasury and those policymakers you have got there.
Mr Byrne: Could I just make three points in response? On this question of dogs and barking—and again I just put this down by way of submitting evidence, as it were—if you look at the index of relative spending over time and contrast 1977–78 with 2007–08, in 1977–78 Wales and England were both at 100. These are two numbers which have

diverged now over the intervening period, so now Wales is at about 113 and England is at 100. So there has been a degree of divergence there. I just think that that is worth the Committee reflecting upon. The second point I would be fascinated to hear the Committee's observations on is that we are only talking about some dimensions of public spending in this debate, are we not? We are only talking about comparable spend and some of the most important public spending in the system is, of course, not allocated to local authorities or strategic health authorities, et cetera, it is allocated to individuals and it is called social security spend. So in the PESA estimates, which we will publish tomorrow to the House, I just think it would be useful for the Committee to opine on the fact that if you look at total public spending per capita in different regions you will get some quite interesting contrasts. So if you take last year's data, 2007/8 plans by country and region, put reserved and devolved spending together, London is at an index of 117, Scotland at an index of 118 and Wales is at 110. So when you consider all public spending you actually get different patterns of comparison between regions. This takes me to my third point on which I would also welcome the Committee's observations because I am intrigued by it. I have not got an answer to it and I do not fully understand it, I have not fully thought it through, but much of this question depends on how you draw your boundaries. If you were to look at public spending per capita in Hodge Hill, the fourth highest unemployment in the country, failed by a number of administrations in the city, I think it would be quite high and it would contrast, I think, with the Scottish average, the Welsh average, the Northern Ireland average and no doubt the English average. So I do not think we can entirely remove from this debate considerations on the question of what does the total spending picture look like per capita. Secondly, much will depend upon how you draw the boundary.

Q1013 *Lord Sewel:* You might be surprised we are on question three now, formula bypass—perhaps one of the reasons why there is not convergence. How does the Treasury decide whether it is appropriate to use a formula bypass, and to what extent has it happened since devolution?
Mr Byrne: Let me give you more on the examples since devolution. The pretty obvious examples we considered this morning, Scotland, G8 policing costs, Northern Ireland exceptional EU PEACE funding, Wales there have been increases to cover exceptional EU objective 1 funding decisions. The devolved administrations can bid to the reserve on an exceptional basis, but there are three tests, if you like: the spending does indeed have to be exceptional, it has to be unforeseen, and third, it cannot reasonably be "absorbed" (I think is the word) within existing

budgets. I think it would possibly help the Committee if I came up with some more examples of those exceptions since devolution

Q1014 Lord Sewel: I am sorry, I did not get the Scottish example.
Mr Byrne: The policing costs for G8, to keep everyone safe.

Q1015 Lord Sewel: I take it that has not gone into the baseline then?
Mr Byrne: Correct.

Q1016 Lord Sewel: Because the pre-devolution ones tended to go into the baseline because they were basically to help finance public sector wage settlements.
Mr Byrne: Yes, but I shall come up with a better and more comprehensive list.

Q1017 Lord Sewel: So effectively bypassing as a means of basically dealing with the problem of funding an unfundable wage settlement in the devolved areas is not a possibility?
Mr Byrne: Not really, because, as I say, you have got these three tests of exceptional, unforeseen and cannot reasonably be absorbed.

The Committee suspended from 5.00 pm to 5.15 pm for a division in the House

Q1018 Lord Trimble: Do you think that Parliament gives the devolved administrations sufficient scope for them to develop their own policy agendas?
Mr Byrne: I think so, because I think the arrangements allow the devolved administrations, if they want to, to depart in quite fundamental ways from policy positions adopted in England and elsewhere. The obvious example, which I am sure you have got already, is the policy of free care for the elderly in Scotland, funded out of the existing provision. I would be really interested in evidence from the Committee as to where more flexibility is needed.

Q1019 Lord Trimble: The example you gave does not strike me as actually being fundamental. While it is paying for that level of care in Scotland but is not available elsewhere, the sums involved were not huge. What would happen if there is a really fundamental divergence? Let us say, for example, the Government decided it wanted to change the basis on which the National Health Service was financed but the devolved administration wanted to keep to the old arrangements?
Mr Byrne: That is a very good example because you would then, I think, be in contravention of the NHS Act, clause 1.

Q1020 Lord Trimble: Assume the Government wanted to have a different basis?
Mr Byrne: I guess what I am saying is that I do not think the constraints necessarily would be financial because the dynamics of a block grant are to avoid any risks of hypothecation. As I say, the increments are bundled up, put in a block, moved over and the devolved administrations then have the flexibility to spend it as they see fit. I suspect the constraints on the kind of flexibility which you mentioned, for example, are in other aspects of legislation would be my working hypothesis.

Q1021 Lord Forsyth of Drumlean: We have an example. Water was privatised in England but not in Scotland, so the Barnett consequentials were lost in Scotland. With health obviously it would be a much bigger bundle?
Mr Byrne: Yes.

Q1022 Lord Trimble: Actually we preferred that we continued with water in the public sector, which led to significant under-investment because the money was no longer there and the scope for variation is actually very limited. My impression is that you can only vary policy where it does not cost a huge amount. Once it come to any significant amount of expenditure, then you have problems. That is why there has been so little variation, obviously.
Mr Byrne: I will have to reflect on that a bit further, but I think the constraints are not within the rules of how flexibly you can spend the block grant. There may be constraints which are imposed by the overall envelope which comes to different nations and there may be other constraints in legislation, but I should reflect on that a bit further.

Q1023 Lord Forsyth of Drumlean: When I was Secretary of State—Lord Sewel gave the example—we used to do deals. If there was a problem with, for example, a big pay rise in the Health Service and the formula consequentials were going to be less because our baseline was 25 per cent higher, there would be a big gap and I would go along to see the Chief Secretary and he would say "No," and then I would go and see the Chancellor, or whatever, and that is how the formula bypass operated. Now, of course, that you have different administrations and a different regime that kind of collegiate collective responsibility does not operate in that way and looking at what has happened since the Scottish Executive was established there has not been a lot of formula bypass. You gave some minor examples. Insofar as there have been disputes, they have related to English expenditure, which have been classified as English expenditure and not UK expenditure. There have been one or two issues, I think the Olympics, the prisons, and one or two other issues. So the question

I want to ask is, what are the criteria which the Treasury use to establish whether something is an expenditure which has not got formula consequences, i.e. is England only? It would be very helpful to have that, or even to have a note on it. The second part of the question is, why should the Treasury of all people be the sole arbiter in this matter because they are hardly impartial and without an interest? Is it not the Treasury's job to resist all expenditure of all kinds, in all circumstances?
Mr Byrne: Clearly the Treasury is the best judge of this question.
Lord Forsyth of Drumlean: Because?

Q1024 *Lord Lawson of Blaby:* No, that is absolutely right! It was a good answer!
Mr Byrne: I can do a note. I think there are basically three dimensions to this. The starting point is obviously the schedules to the Scotland, Wales and Northern Ireland Acts, which I read this morning. The schedules are very long and detail in great length exactly what are reserved matters and what are not, and what the Treasury does is basically take those schedules and translate them into budget lines, and those budget lines and, in essence, the comparability factors are then set out in the statements of funding policy. Those statements of funding policy are then consulted on with the devolved administrations. I think they have been pretty consensual, actually. I think people have tended to agree to quite a large extent on that sort of mapping between the schedules and the budget lines. Then the third dimension is obviously exceptions, as you have said, the Olympics. I think you are right to say that the controversies, such as they are, have centred on spending and projects in England. Two obvious examples are the Olympics, where the Treasury quite correctly said that that is a UK venture of benefit to the entirety of the UK. A different example would, for example, be Crossrail, which was judged to be much more of benefit to London and England and therefore did carry a series of Barnett consequentials with it.

Q1025 *Lord Forsyth of Drumlean:* But not initially? The initial line was that Crossrail, as I understand it, was not and there was this problem of funding the Forth Bridge and suddenly the Treasury decided that it was, which suggests that the Government –
Mr Byrne: It was clearly a finely-balanced decision!
Lord Forsyth of Drumlean: What was it balanced on?

Q1026 *Lord Rowe-Beddoe:* Chief Secretary, before I ask the question, in the absence of Lord Rooker I would like to place on record that I thought he should be recommended for appointment to the Order of the Red Dragon, First Class, for his intervention! I was greatly appreciative, and I know my Lord Chairman was, too. Let us talk about something which is really very speculative for you, I appreciate, but it is actually coming back to an interchange between you and Lord Lawson with regard to one of your 'C's, change, and how would one manage change. We understand that there is a six monthly meeting between the Chief Secretary and the three Finance Ministers of the devolved administrations. What do you think they do at that meeting and what do you intend to do?
Mr Byrne: I have not fitted one of these meetings in during the last week and a half, but my steering brief says that the last one was on 12 March and the last one focused on what I think is colloquially known within the Government as "fighting back against the global downturn", by which I think they mean the economy! Seriously, it centred on what measures can be conducted together to combat the recession. How do we make sure that the programmes for delivering counter-recessionary measures are delivered effectively because there are differences in delivery arrangements in different parts of the UK. They also centred on how we can improve value for money and how the Treasury's efficiency targets should be shared between different parts of the UK. So from that I take it that they will be pretty wide-ranging and it is my ambition to get one of these meetings in fairly quickly.

Q1027 *Lord Rowe-Beddoe:* You would obviously envisage that if you wanted to have a Barnett Formula discussion, this is the forum in which it could take place?
Mr Byrne: I think so. I think that would be a good forum. I am not sure what extent of agreement we would get out of it, but it would certainly be a good forum to start a discussion.

Q1028 *Lord Rowe-Beddoe:* Probably more than you would think at this stage, I would say?
Mr Byrne: With the Committee's report on the table we will all be better equipped to conduct it.

Q1029 *Lord Moser:* Chief Secretary, I think in your last post you were responsible for all government statistics. That is right, is it not?
Mr Byrne: Yes.

Q1030 *Lord Moser:* So I think it is quite appropriate that we end with this one. It is really just that a number of witnesses have expressed criticisms of one kind or another about the statistics bearing on the Barnett Formula and public expenditure generally. There are different kinds. Some of the complaints or some of the confusion is about how the Treasury works out the comparability factor. That is one thing. Some witnesses complained that it was extremely difficult to get data showing the spread of public expenditure across the UK, et cetera, so various points and I am sure at this time of day we do not want to go into details. I think what is important is whether the Committee might be in a position to say that the Treasury is improving the transparency of the operation of the Barnett Formula by publishing clearer and simpler statistics. You have made some progress in the last week or two, the Treasury has suddenly come up with more helpful data to us, so I think the basic issue for the Committee is whether, because so many witnesses have expressed frustration about the transparency of the operation, the way the formula works, we might be able in our report to say something positive about improving the data?

Mr Byrne: It would be enormously helpful to me personally to have the Committee's opinion on which data could really do with more clarity and more transparency. I guess I would urge the Committee to go beyond merely the elements in the Barnett Formula because, of course, they basically come down to what are the changes in DEL budgets, what are the ONS population figures, what are the comparability factors, and those data are pretty well set out in Spending Review White Papers and in the statement of funding policy and I have just got a sneaking suspicion that many of your witnesses will actually be interested in that basis, for sure, but actually they will be interested in some underlying factors as well, but it would be terrifically useful to have the Committee's advice on which is the real data that needs a better job done with it.

Q1031 *Lord Moser:* It may be, Chairman, if the Treasury has in mind any changes in the way it publishes data relating to the Barnett Formula perhaps we could have a note?

Mr Byrne: I would be very happy to do that. It may also be useful to either the Committee or the Committee's advisors to look at, I think it is either chapter 6 or chapter 9 of PESA published tomorrow, which obviously provides a complete comprehensive breakdown by region and by function.

Q1032 *Chairman:* Thank you very much indeed. There was one other matter I wanted to raise, if I might. I think the Treasury has offered to send us the 1994 assessment. If you could let us have a copy of that, we would be greatly obliged. It would be very helpful.

Ms Radcliffe: Yes, absolutely. You should have had it.

Q1033 *Chairman:* We do not seem to have had it, so if you could let us have it?

Mr Byrne: Yes, we will get it out of the basement!

Chairman: Can I thank you very much indeed for coming. It has been a very useful session and we have learnt a great deal. You have opened a few windows and closed others, but thank you very much indeed. You have been very helpful. You have been so generous of your time.

Written Evidence

Memorandum by the Alliance Party of Northern Ireland

The Alliance Party of Northern Ireland welcomes the opportunity to comment to the House of Lords Barnett Formula Select Committee in relation to its inquiry into the Barnett Formula. I further appreciated the opportunity to meet with some members of the committee recently in Belfast.

The Barnett Formula has generally worked well in this regard over the past few decades for Northern Ireland. The effects of the Barnett Squeeze have been minimal, and we accept that they have been offset to an extent by supplemental appropriations, such as the various rounds of Peace Funds. Policing and justice matters are not treated as an area of expenditure covered by the Barnett Formula at present, but this would change with the likely devolution of policing and justice responsibilities to the Northern Ireland Assembly in the near future. Northern Ireland benefits from other aspects of public expenditure, including the Annually Managed Expenditure that its processes, and from what can be regarded as truly national expenditures such as national defence.

From the perspective of Northern Ireland, our priority must be the provision of a formula that ensures that this region achieves a level of funding to address the needs of the population in a manner consistent with standards in the rest of the United Kingdom. This can be broken down into the two elements of first the underlying baseline, and second how variations in public expenditure are to be allocated.

The underlying needs analysis from which the Barnett Formula applies variations in public expenditure may well be historical in nature. However, in Northern Ireland, it is generally regarded as providing a fairly realistic reflection of the differing overall requirements for public expenditure here relevant to the rest of the United Kingdom. This may not be the same experience as the other devolved regions.

There are considerable differences in needs within Northern Ireland relative to the rest of the United Kingdom as a whole, arising from our lower level of economic activity, productivity, and incomes, different levels of health morbidity, a younger population, and a rural character. Many of these characteristics would be found in the other devolved regions and regions within England too. The problems in Northern Ireland have been accentuated by the social and economic legacy of violence, including problems of labour mobility, and deterrence of inward investment, both in terms of its level and quality.

Within Northern Ireland, there is a constant struggle to address public expenditure demands. As illustrated through PESA public expenditure surveys, in a considerable number of spending areas, the spending profile within Northern Ireland varies dramatically from the UK average in the respective areas, and also from 126 per cent overall variation in Northern Ireland as a whole from the overall UK average. For example, expenditure in areas such as law and order, criminal justice, education, economic support and agriculture is much higher, whereas in areas such as health and environmental protection is much lower.

Some of these distortions reflect local preferences and priorities, but others reflect a skewing as a consequence of communal divisions. Indeed, financially there is potentially a £1 billion cost incurred in Northern Ireland from managing a divided and segregated society, ranging from the direct costs of policing and security, to the indirect embedded costs of explicitly or implicitly providing separate goods, facilities and services to different parts of the community in Northern Ireland, in for instance education. There is a challenge for the devolved Executive to work to release such funds and to invest the proceeds for the benefit of the whole community. However addressing segregation alone is unlikely to address the significant needs differential with between Northern Ireland and the rest of the United Kingdom.

There would be a concern about the implications for a full needs assessment for all of the devolved regions due to the inherently subjective nature of any such exercise, and the potential consequences that could flow from different variations in underlying assumptions. There is no confidence that any alternative assessment would be any better in providing a baseline for the allocation of scarce resources to Northern Ireland.

Alliance also believes that a formula, such as the current population based Barnett formula or any successor based either on population or some other system, would be the best mechanism for dealing in upwards or downwards variations in public expenditure in the areas covered by system. Difficulties are essentially restricted to identifying what national expenditures can be regionalised through the Barnett Formula. Transparency issues are relegated to these types of issues on the margins.

While the alternative approach of regular negotiations between the devolved regions and the Treasury over the distribution of any variations in public expenditure at a national level may be superficially attractive. We appreciate that this is the model in some federal states internationally. However, the drawbacks of this process could be much greater lack of transparency, and difficulties in predictability and forward-planning.

A further problem lies in the very nature of devolution. The devolved Assemblies all have the discretion to make different decisions with respect to public expenditure in line with local assessments of priorities. If the process of allocating Barnett consequentials is subject to a process of negotiation, there may be an expectation from Treasury that the devolved regions would mirror the purposes of expenditure in England, otherwise the additional expenditure available would be reallocated.

The Alliance Party is currently playing an opposition role within the Northern Ireland Assembly. While we have many difficulties with the decisions and priorities of local Ministers and the Executive overall, we respect their right to take those decisions.

While we appreciate the restraints on terms of reference for this inquiry, the Alliance Party does feel compelled to make the point that our ambition is for Northern Ireland not to have the current needs differential with the rest of UK in the future. Northern Ireland's GVA is stubbornly stuck at around 80 per cent of the UK average, in line with other regions.

While there is a responsibility for the Government to address the needs differentials across the UK in terms of public expenditure allocations, there should be a parallel discussion as to why there are such variations across all the regions and what steps can be taken to close these gaps.

It seems that Government continues to view the UK economy in overall terms, protecting the dominance of London and the South-East of England, and a concentration of high productivity jobs and wealth creation, with little concern for regional balances. 9/12 UK regions are net recipients of fiscal subventions, with Northern Ireland the extreme case. This situation is neither economically nor environmentally sustainable.

At present, the Treasury does not envisage any meaningful GVA convergence between the Northern Ireland and the rest of the UK. This was reflected in the Treasury Commissioned Review of the Competitiveness of Northern Ireland (Varney II)—April 2008.The report argues that Northern Ireland can continue to receive its share from the overall success of the UK economy, through the Barnett Formula. This implies continued public sector dependency.

The Alliance Party does support the granting of greater tax-varying powers to the Northern Ireland Assembly, including the ability to vary corporation tax. Tax-varying powers would be additional to the Barnett Formula or any successor. Where the Northern Ireland Assembly wished to lower a tax, this would have to be funded out of its Block Grant allocation. Where it wished to raise a tax, this would provide supplemental income. At present, there is frustration at the inability of the Northern Ireland Assembly to make meaningful policy variations due to the absence of fiscal powers. We remain disappointed at the outcome of the Treasury's Review of Tax Policy in Northern Ireland (Varney I)—December 2007.

We hope that the House of Lords could return to these issues in the near future, and hope that the Committee feels that, within their existing terms of references, they are able to flag up matters such as overall UK regional policy and tax-varying powers can be explored.

The final matter we would wish to highlight are the financial arrangements surrounding the devolution of policing and justice responsibilities to Northern Ireland which we hope can be delivered later in 2009. The assumption is that the current NIO will be disassembled, and that the bulk of the current financial resources as allocated under the current Comprehensive Spending Review will transfer to the Northern Ireland Block. There are concerns regarding the transparency of this decoupling to ensure that the devolved responsibilities retain their appropriate share of resources. The bigger issue lies the with the pressures that have built up within the police service and other criminal justice agencies regarding legacy issues, ranging from personnel issues through to the potentially very expensive process of dealing with the past. It is important that the devolution of these very sensitive functions is not undermined by inherited financial problems. Accordingly, a supplemental appropriation to assist the process of devolution is essential. It is reasonable to say that Northern Ireland could handle the costs of policing a normal society in the future but it is not fair to burden it with the costs of policing the past.

In the medium term, policing and justice responsibilities will become part of the overall financial settlement provided to Northern Ireland within the next CSR, with variations thereafter handled through Barnett or some successor formula. However, there is a major challenge in finding the appropriate baseline for policing.

The Alliance Party has major concerns that any needs analysis across the United Kingdom would not sufficiently take into account the special circumstances and subtleties of Northern Ireland. These range from an inability to call on neighbouring police services to the ongoing threat from dissident Republicans. While the dissidents may be relatively few in number, they can be lethal as demonstrated in March 2009 with the deaths of two soldiers and one police officer in terrorist attacks. Northern Ireland is the only part of the United Kingdom where police officers are potential targets through simply being police officers. This reality impedes the normalisation of policing in a general sense, and specifically requires enhanced risk assessments for police officers in responding to calls for assistance, and creates a further pressure on scarce human resources and equipment. While consideration reform is possible within the current police service and other criminal justice agencies, these unfortunate realities provide major constraints. The danger is that once policing and justice matters are transferred, if the financial settlement or baseline is wrong, the Northern Ireland Executive will have to dip into other aspects of the Northern Ireland Block to meet security pressures.

23 April 2009

Memorandum by The Australian Commonwealth Grants Commission

ACHIEVING EQUALISATION

1. This document explains the role of the Commonwealth Grants Commission in the context of current federal financial arrangements, the principle of horizontal fiscal equalisation used in its work and how it is implemented.

ROLE OF THE COMMISSION

2. The Commission advises the Australian Government on the appropriate "per capita relativities" for distributing the GST among the States. The distribution is designed to provide all States with the same fiscal capacity to provide services to their populations—to achieve horizontal fiscal equalisation.

3. The GST revenue is important for State budgets. In 2007–08, it was $42 billion,[1] 57 per cent of the funds provided to the States by the Australian Government. The GST represented 33 per cent of State budget revenues, with the percentages for individual States varying from 25 per cent for Western Australia to 69 per cent for the Northern Territory.

4. Since 1988, the methods used to calculate the relativities have been reviewed approximately every five years. The last review was completed in 2004 and the next is due in 2010.

5. Between reviews, the relativities are updated annually to reflect changes over time in the circumstances of the States.

CURRENT COMMONWEALTH—STATE FINANCIAL ARRANGEMENTS

6. The arrangements for the payment of GST revenue to the States reflect the provisions of the Intergovernmental Agreement on Federal Financial Relations 2008 (IGA). That IGA superseded the IGA signed in June 1999. The Agreement says:

— all revenue from the GST, less the costs of collection, is to be "freely available for use by the States and Territories for any purpose";

— the GST will be distributed among the States on the basis of horizontal fiscal equalisation;

— the Commission is to calculate per capita relativities for this purpose; and

— the National specific purpose payments and most National Partnership payments provided by the Commonwealth to the States will be included in the Commission's calculation of relativities in recognition that they provide the States with budget support for providing standard State services.

7. The per capita relativities recommended by the Commission are considered by the Ministerial Council for Federal Financial Relations. The Australian Treasurer then makes a formal determination of how the GST revenues are to be shared.

THE PRINCIPLE

8. The principle of horizontal fiscal equalisation currently used by the Commission is:

State governments should receive funding from the Goods and Services Tax revenue such that, if each made the same effort to raise revenue from its own sources and operated at the same level of efficiency, each would have the capacity to provide services at the same standard.

9. The aim is for all States to have the same fiscal capacity to deliver services to their populations, after the distribution of the GST and taking into account their capacities to raise revenue from their own-sources.

---

[1] Commonwealth of Australia *Final Budget Outcome 2007–08.*

10. Equalisation does not result in some outcomes that are at times mistakenly attributed to it.

— It does not mean the same level of services is actually provided—the actual level delivered is a matter of policy for each State.

— It does not provide the capacity for equal services in all regions of the States. Equalisation reflects the policies of all States to provide different services to people living in different regions (such as urban and rural areas) and provides the capacity for equal services in comparable regions but for different levels of service between them.

— It does not penalise efficient States; nor reward inefficient ones. States are funded on the assumption that they can deliver services at the average observed level of efficiency. If a State is more efficient than the average, it retains the benefit. If it has below average efficiency it bears the cost.

11. Only differences that are beyond the control of individual States are taken into account in working out the GST each State needs. Each State's share is calculated on the assumption that it and all the other States apply average policies and practices in delivering services and that they all make the same effort to raise revenue.

12. With this approach, a State's own policies do not directly affect its share, although they do affect the average policies against which all States are benchmarked. States can and do make different efforts to raise revenue and have differing expense priorities, but these do not directly affect their share of GST revenue.

13. Precise equalisation may not be achieved in the year the assessed relativities are applied. Measuring State relative fiscal capacities requires reliable information on State finances and demographic and economic circumstances. Governments have decided fiscal capacities should be based on an average of the five most recent years (the relativities applied in 2009–10 are based on data for 2003–04 to 2007–08). Since State conditions are constantly changing, those average historical fiscal capacities may not be the same as those currently applying or those in the year the relativities are used to distribute the GST. Further, the five year averaging process, while providing greater certainty to State GST revenue, dampens relative changes in the observed fiscal capacities.

IMPLEMENTING EQUALISATION

14. Large amounts of information are required for the Commission to prepare its recommendations. That information includes details of State revenues and expenses, revenue bases, population and other factors affecting cost levels and service and infrastructure requirements, and State policies. It obtains that information from the historical record (called the assessment years).

15. The information is used to calculate how the GST available in the assessment year would have had to be distributed to give each State the same fiscal capacity, if all States had applied the same (average) policies. A set of relativities is then derived from the calculated GST distribution. Relativities from the most recent five years are then averaged to provide the recommended relativities.

16. This historical approach implies the average policies and the economic, social and demographic conditions in the historical years are a good guide to those in the application year.

The model

17. The GST each State requires to equalise its fiscal capacity in each historical year is determined by:

summing its assessed expenses for each service—assessed expenses for a service are the expenses the State would incur if it provided the average level of that service to its population;

subtracting its assessed revenues (including its actual revenues from Commonwealth payments for specific purposes)—assessed revenue for a State tax are the revenues it would raise if it applied the average tax policies to its revenue base; and

adding the average budget outcome—the difference between the per capita average expenses and revenues (including revenues from the Commonwealth) covered by the Commission's comparisons multiplied by the State's population.

Calculating average expenses and revenues

18. The starting point for the Commission's assessments is the average expenses incurred by States to provide services and the average revenues collected from their taxes and charges. These **financial averages** are the Australian average[2] per capita expenses and revenues. They are not the actual expenses and revenues of any individual State.

---

[2] In this report, Australian average refers to the all-State average. Australian Government and local government activities are not included. For a fuller explanation of terms used by the Commission, see Commission terminology, at the end of this report.

19. The figures for expenses are mainly derived from the Australian Bureau of Statistics Government Finance Statistics (GFS). The financial transactions in the operating statements of State general government sectors[3] are classified on a service (expense) or head-of-tax (revenue) basis. The financial average for each expense and revenue category is then derived by dividing the Australian total of State expenses or revenues by the Australian mean resident population.

20. The **adjusted budget** is the collection of all the expense and revenue categories the Commission examines.

Expense assessments

21. Expense assessments aim to measure the effects of each State's disabilities (which reflect their economic, geographic and demographic characteristics) on the average expenses.

22. **Disabilities** are circumstances beyond the control of individual States that require a State to spend more (or allow it to spend less) per capita than other States to provide the average level of service. Disabilities can be broadly classified into two types—use disabilities and cost disabilities.

— **Use disabilities** reflect differences between States in the use of services arising mainly from population characteristics. Use disabilities are assessed by identifying the users of the service, which may be the whole population, part of the population (for example, students for school services) or the number of businesses in an industry sector.

Next, the Commission looks to see if, across Australia, some groups in the population use the service more or less than others. For example, hospital services are used more intensively by some age groups and by Indigenous people and some welfare services are used more intensively by people on low incomes.

States are assessed to have a disability if the groups that make most use of a service are a larger proportion of their population than they are of the national population. Conversely, they have an advantage (negative disability) if the size of the group is smaller than the national average.

— **Cost disabilities** affect the cost per unit of service provided to particular groups of people or regions. For example, communication factors can increase the costs of providing services to people from non-English speaking backgrounds. In addition, higher costs might be incurred providing services in large cities or in remote areas. States with relatively larger populations in the groups that cost more (or living in regions that cost more) are assessed to have disabilities.

The prices of inputs used in providing State services may also vary for reasons beyond the control of individual States. For example, wage rates and office accommodation costs differ across the States and some States face diseconomies of small scale. However, higher costs arising from a decision by a State to provide a higher level of service do not constitute a disability.

23. In simplified terms, disabilities reflect the State's position relative to the average position—for example, a State's school enrolments under average policies as a proportion of its population relative to the aggregate enrolments as a proportion of aggregate population.

24. Each State's assessed expenses per capita for a service are determined by adjusting the average per capita expenses by its disabilities.

Revenue assessments

25. Revenue assessments aim to measure the revenue per capita each State would raise if it applied the Australian average tax rates to its tax bases—that is, if it made the average effort to raise revenue.

— Tax bases are generally measured using the value of transactions in each State that would be taxed under the average tax policy. For example, the tax base for stamp duty on conveyances is the value of property sold.

— Each State's assessed revenue for a tax is determined by applying the average effective rate of tax (the revenue all States actually collected from the tax divided by the aggregate tax base) to its tax base.

— A State has a revenue raising advantage if the per capita value of its tax base exceeds the national value—making the average tax effort yields above average per capita revenue.

---

[3] Some welfare housing public trading enterprises may also be included where the services are not delivered by the general government sector.

Some special cases

26. There are some cases where the Commission considers that:

— all differences in expenses or revenues are due to differences in State policies—no State has a disability; or

— there are disabilities but they cannot be adequately measured or we do not include them because they are not material.

27. In these cases, it assesses the revenue capacity or costs of providing services to be the same in all States using an equal per capita (EPC) assessment.

Bringing the assessments together

28. The individual assessments for each service and revenue are brought together to derive a State's GST requirement for each historical year using the model set out in paragraph 17.

29. A State's per capita relativity for each historical year is then derived by expressing its per capita GST requirement for the year as a ratio of the national average per capita GST distributed in the year.

30. This calculation is undertaken for each of five years in an inquiry.

31. An relativity below one indicates a State requires less than an equal per capita share of GST revenue; a relativity above one indicates it requires more than an equal per capita share. No State can have its relativity increased without one or more of the other States having theirs reduced.

March 2009

Memorandum by Madoc Batcup

I would like to make the following submission in respect of the Barnett Formula.

The main point that I would like to make is that the Barnett Formula is not the only way in which centrally aggregated funds are distributed between the different member countries of the United Kingdom based on a formula. The Big Lottery Fund also uses a formula to arrive at an appropriate apportionment. The formula is needs based, has been in existence since 1995, and has been reviewed on a number of occasions since then, but not altered. It is striking to note that the formula used by the Big Lottery Fund produces a radically different outcome, particularly for Wales, than the Barnett Formula, and the Big Lottery Fund have provided to me, under the Freedom of Information Act, information explaining the background to the formula, and the way in which it is calculated.. I attach the relevant correspondence.

The allocation between the four countries of the UK under the formula is as follows:

England	77.5 %
Scotland	11.5 %
Wales	6.5 %
Northern Ireland	4.5 %

The Big Lottery Fund arrives at this distribution by taking into account population, comparative levels of deprivation, measured by the level of social security benefits per capita, and comparative levels of available resources measured by GDP on the basis indicated in the correspondence.

It is interesting to note as well that there is considerable overlap between the general remit of the Big Lottery Fund and that of the devolved administrations. The formula was specifically adopted by the UK government in 1998 in the legislation relating to the New Opportunities Fund. The directions of the DCMS in 2005 to the New Opportunities Fund included the provision that:

1. The Fund shall, by 31 March 2008, commit funds to projects concerned or connected with health, education or the environment and intended to transform communities, regions or the nation as a whole pursuant to the initiative specified in the New Opportunities Fund (Specification of Initiative) Order 2005.

Health, education and the environment are some of the most important responsibilities of the devolved administrations, both in terms of policy priority and in terms of funding requirement.

It is therefore difficult to understand why the UK government should in the recent past regard it as perfectly possible to devise a simple needs based formula to allocate money across the United Kingdom in respect of expenditure in areas substantially parallel to those of the devolved administrations, but not feel capable of using the same approach instead of the Barnett formula. It is also notable that the Big Lottery Fund have had the formula reviewed on several occasions by independent reviewers, but felt that "there was no compelling case to change the existing arrangements.....We consider the formula satisfactory, and we do not have any current plans to review it."

The formula approach adopted by the Big Lottery Fund and its predecessors provides many of the administrative advantages of Barnett, while being considerably (and demonstrably) fairer. It has the additional advantage of being simple and transparent; it thereby achieves a balance between being simple and being fair. In addition the formula is tried and tested, relies on existing data series and has been specifically endorsed by the UK government as an appropriate method of calculating relative need between the different constituent parts of the United Kingdom in respect of areas of expenditure which parallel to a significant extent the major areas of expenditure of the devolved institutions.

I would therefore submit that there already exists an appropriate alternative to the Barnett formula which would be easy to implement, and by being objective would be easy to administer with few "grey areas"

Perhaps one of the few contentious areas which would remain (and it is difficult to see how this can be avoided whatever method is adopted) is the degree to which any part of UK government expenditure relates to UK expenditure, as opposed to eg English expenditure, and there will need to be discussions from time to time as to what percentage of comparability exists between the devolved institutions and the corresponding English Department. In the case of health spending, for example, nearly 100 per cent of spending is devolved, while in the case of Wales and the budget of the Department of Work and Pensions it is only about 6.5 per cent. The degree to which functions are devolved will inevitably have to be incorporated in the adoption of a Big Lottery style formula approach, in the same way as they are now under the Barnett formula.

I would suggest that the approach of the Big Lottery Fund represents a pragmatic alternative to the current system, and that it would be worthwhile for the Select Committee to investigate further the implications of using a similar approach to replace the Barnett formula.

March 2009

Memorandum by cebr ltd

INTRODUCTION

This short note is a response to the Select Committee's request for evidence. The response deals primarily with Questions 1a and 1b of the questions set out by the committee.

LEVELS OF PUBLIC EXPENDITURE AS A SHARE OF GVA

It is conventional to consider public expenditure in a region or country of the UK in relation to public expenditure per head. This is certainly an important indicator and should not be discarded. But the requirements for public expenditure and the cost of public expenditure are also influenced by the levels of prices and earnings in the different regions/countries and their levels of GDP or GVA.

The cost of providing equivalent levels of services will be affected by price and earnings differentials. This is an obvious point and does not need reinforcement. What is less obvious, but no less true, is that some of the requirements for services are affected by the levels of GDP/GVA. For example, transport projects are conventionally prioritised by the use of benefit/cost ratios. The relative benefit element of these ratios will largely be driven by relative GDP/GVA levels. Arguably some of the benefits of training, skills and education are also driven by the levels of regional prosperity.

It is conventional also to think of high levels of regional GDP/GVA per capita as an inverse proxy for the extent of social problems and hence as in some way justifying relatively low levels of public expenditure per head. But the evidence from the UK does not support this. The most glaring anomaly is that London has a regional GVA per capita of around 50 per cent above the UK average. Despite this, its regional unemployment level is one of the highest in the UK, 7.2 per cent compared to 6.3 per cent for the national average for the UK.[4] Moreover, the local area with the highest rate of unemployment in the UK, Tower Hamlets, is in London. Looking in detail at the extent of social problems on a wide range of measures shows that London despite its higher level of GDP/GVA has much higher levels of social deprivation and hence needs than other regions.

Since the evidence for the UK does not support the view that a high level of GDP/GVA per capital indicates a low requirement for public expenditure as a percentage of regional/country GVA it is worth examining the data for regional/country public expenditure as a percentage of regional/country GVA. The IMF points out

---

[4] Office for National Statistics, *"Labour Market Statistics, First Release"* (February 2009).

that "*International comparisons of public expenditure composition in relation to economic and social indicators can provide a useful basis for addressing imbalances in the use of public resources*".[5]

Cebr has for some years made this analysis, taking account of the regional data for public expenditure and the regional accounts and adjusting the data for consistency.

The results for total identifiable expenditure on services for UK regions and countries as a share of regional/country GVA are shown in Table 1. This forms part of cebr work carried out this year for *The Sunday Times*.[6] A graph of public expenditure per capita and GVA per capita for UK regions and countries is shown in Figure 1.

Table 1

	2003–04	2004–05	2005–06	2006–07
North East	50.7 %	51.2 %	52.3 %	50.8 %
North West	43.5 %	44.8 %	45.3 %	45.1 %
Yorkshire and Humberside	40.6 %	42.1 %	43.0 %	42.4 %
East Midlands	35.2 %	36.6 %	37.0 %	36.8 %
West Midlands	38.7 %	40.6 %	41.7 %	41.8 %
Eastern	28.5 %	29.5 %	30.2 %	30.2 %
London	28.8 %	28.8 %	29.2 %	28.5 %
South East	26.4 %	27.7 %	27.7 %	27.4 %
South West	34.9 %	36.1 %	36.3 %	35.9 %
Total England	33.8 %	34.8 %	35.3 %	34.9 %
Scotland	43.9 %	43.5 %	44.7 %	45.0 %
Wales	52.6 %	53.7 %	55.2 %	55.4 %
Northern Ireland	56.5 %	57.0 %	56.7 %	55.9 %
UK identifiable expenditure	35.8 %	36.7 %	37.3 %	36.9 %
Outside UK	44.0 %	45.4 %	38.8 %	39.0 %
Total identifiable expenditure	36.0 %	36.9 %	37.3 %	37.0 %

Figure 1

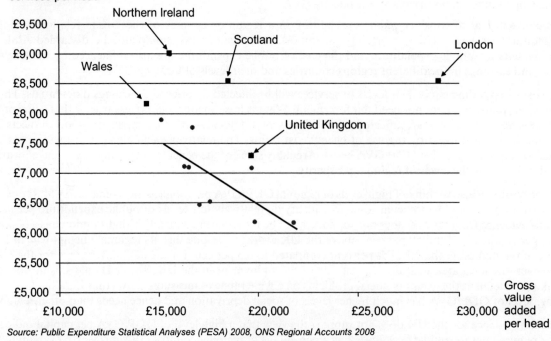

Source: Public Expenditure Statistical Analyses (PESA) 2008, ONS Regional Accounts 2008

---

[5] IMF Pamphlet 48 "*Unproductive Public Expenditures: A Pragmatic Approach To Policy Analysis Appendix: Patterns of Government Expenditure by Country Groups*".
[6] See The Sunday Times, 25 January 2009.

Included in the Annex to this evidence is the cebr Forecasting Eye Special from 11 March 2008. This document shows that public expenditure as a share of GDP has risen to an estimated 43.0 per cent of GDP in 2007–08. The Forecasting Eye Special also outlines our methodology for calculating public expenditure from total identifiable and non-identifiable expenditure from HM Treasury statistics.

IMPLICATIONS OF THE VARIATIONS IN REGIONAL PUBLIC EXPENDITURE AS A PERCENTAGE OF GVA

The unusually large variations in regional public expenditure as a percentage of GDP/GVA mean that in the higher income regions, many public services are disproportionately badly funded. This particularly affects unfairly those at the lower end of the income scale who are most dependent on public services.

The implications of the variation of the levels of regional public expenditure as a share of GDP/GVA are exaggerated in the UK by the existence of a progressive tax system that does not take account of local variations in the cost of living. As a result of the shape of the UK tax system, where the progressivity is concentrated at the lower end, the effects of this also particularly hit those at the lower end of the income scale in the higher income regions. They pay a higher effective rate of tax than those with equivalent real incomes in lower income regions.

Moreover, a further implication of the relatively high levels of public spending in relation to GVA in some regions/countries of the UK is that the private sector is crowded out. The large numbers of public sector jobs mean that employment patterns become distorted. Public sector pay in some regions is noticeably higher than in the private sector. It is no surprise that rates of business start ups in the regions/countries of the UK with levels of public spending as a share of GVA well above 50 per cent are very much lower than in the areas with much lower public spending. The tendency to look to the public sector to provide subsidised solutions to problems becomes built in.

Can the model of funding relatively high levels of public expenditure in relation to GVA in the North of England, Scotland, Wales and Northern Ireland be afforded in the future?

Cebr has generated a provisional analysis of the prospects for public finances that has underpinned the speech given by one of the co-authors (Douglas McWilliams) to the Associate Parliamentary Group on Wholesale Financial Markets & Services in the House of Commons on 11 February 2009. This analysis was reflected in the following section of the speech

> *"The calculations about fiscal transfers from the early 2000s indicated that London subsidised the rest of the UK by about £13 billion. My rough and ready estimate is that this rose to about £30 billion by 2007. This comes mainly from a mixture of corporation tax, national insurance contributions, income tax and VAT on spending raised on the relatively higher incomes and spending in London.*
>
> *I expect this to drop back to about £8 billion next year and to edge up to about £12 billion by 2013, and to continue to grow very slowly thereafter.*
>
> *What this means is that there is a shortfall of just under £20 billion (1.5 per cent) of GDP that will ultimately have to be made up. Now in a world where multi billion banking bailout packages seem to be announced almost monthly, this may seem like small beer. But unlike some of the other figures, which are often exaggerated and where the government has realistic hopes that it might eventually get most of its money back, this is a real shortfall.*
>
> *Can it be replaced? One option is higher tax rates, but very few studies are optimistic that this raises much more money. A second potential option is sustained high borrowing. But the bond markets would be most unlikely to accept it. The only alternative is for the regions with higher levels of public spending to cut their coats according to the cloth available. The high spending parts of the UK—Scotland, Wales, Northern Ireland, the North of England, the North West and Yorkshire and Humberside will need to cut their levels of public spending as a share of GDP by around 5 per cent of local GDP to offset the end of the subsidy from the rest of the country but mainly from London".*

IMPLICATIONS FOR THE BARNETT FORMULA

The Barnett Formula is designed to preserve in aspic the shares of public spending per capita for Scotland in particular.

Yet our analysis infers that public spending per capita in the parts of the UK where public spending is high will have to be reduced disproportionately; partly because it builds in unfairness, partly because it damages the private sector and entrepreneurship and particularly because the money to finance high public spending is unlikely to be available in the medium term.

There is therefore a need to change the Barnett formula to generate an outcome with a lower level of public spending in relation to the rest of the UK for the high public spending regions.

March 2009

Annex

How public money is spent in each region and country of the UK

The gap in public spending as a share of GDP across UK regions has been widening.

INTRODUCTION

Cebr has analysed in detail where public funds go, particularly in the context of the London economy, and we have had a number of projects which have required us to update this information.

We have repeated the analysis we conducted two years ago of public expenditure as a share of GDP for each region and country in the UK, updating the figures for financial year 2001–02 to 2005–06 and calculating new figures for 2006–07 and 2007–08—the last financial year. The new calculations are based on the latest issue of *Public Expenditure Statistical Analyses 2007* and incorporate the latest cebr regional forecasts.[7]

KEY POINTS

The analysis shows that public expenditure as a share of GDP in the UK has risen from 39.0 per cent of GDP in 2001–02 to an estimated 43.0 per cent in 2007–08.

This has happened at a time when the public spending share in most Continental countries has been falling. As a result the public spending share was higher in the UK than in Germany in 2007 for the first time since 1974.

Total UK public spending as a share of GDP is now forecast to stabilise—but if the economy remains weak the share could start to rise again.

Revised data suggests that the dispersion of public spending as a share of GDP between regions rose from 2001–02 to 2006–07.

Public spending as a share of GDP is rising fastest in the West Midlands, Wales and Yorkshire and Humberside. It is rising slowest in London.

How are the figures calculated?

This work is much easier now than 10 years ago because the government produces a little known report called *Public Expenditure Statistical Analyses*. In the past, cebr analysts have sweated over public expenditure line items looking at up to 4,000 different categories and then splitting them by various probable criteria such as population, local GDP and on other bases. Now the government makes its own split replicating much of the work that cebr analysts have carried out in the past, and this is published in these statistical analyses.

If you know how to interpret the information, it is a goldmine, telling you in great detail which regions and countries benefit from public spending and how this has changed. Not only does this show how total spending in the different regions and countries in the UK differs but also how the composition varies.

To understand the information properly and to make the comparisons that might normally be made on an international basis, it is best to scale the spending in each region by expressing it as a proportion of regional GDP. This is because regions vary by size and by cost of living. Crude comparisons of regions looking at spending per person can mislead because the cost of spending and the amount of economic activity that it is meant to support varies between region and country.

We have taken the figures showing the split of public spending by region and country straight from Table 9.1 of "*Public Expenditure Statistical Analyses 2007*".[8] This gives the regional and country split for the identifiable 83 per cent of "Total Managed Public Expenditure", which is one of the standard measures of total public spending. What is excluded is spending overseas and some types of public spending where it is conceptually difficult to allocate the spending by region or country including defence, debt interest and EU transactions.

In our estimates the figures for identifiable public spending are then scaled up for the non-identifiable items, assuming that they are split in relation to GDP. The logic of this is that allocating something like defence is perhaps most fairly done by allocating it against the economic activity that in some sense is being defended. This may be generous to the high spending areas, since they are likely to have contributed disproportionately to the build-up of debt interest and some benefit disproportionately from defence spending.

---

[7]   *cebr, the prospects service*, Regional Prospects, 14 January 2008.
[8]   Public expenditure statistical analyses 2007, HM Treasury, April 2007.

The estimates of public spending for 2007–08 are based on Table 9.15 of *Public Expenditure Statistical Analyses 2007*, which gives the data for spending for central government and for public corporations. To get a total for all public spending the figures are scaled up assuming that the ratio of spending by local authorities to spending by central government and public corporations for each region remains as in 2006–07.

We then divide these totals by workplace-based GDP from the official regionally disaggregated GDP data downloaded from the National Statistics website.[9] The regional data from National Statistics is for Gross Value Added (GVA), which is similar to GDP but because the figures are measured at basic prices rather than at market prices the totals are lower. Since public expenditure shares both in the UK and internationally are conventionally measured as a share of GDP, to make the data comparable with international data around the world we have scaled up the GVA data by the ratio of national GVA to GDP to provide estimates of regional GDP. The figures are updated using cebr's regional GVA forecasts and estimates to Q1 2008.[10]

All these adjustments are made to ensure that the shares of regional public spending in GDP are not exaggerated by the use of statistics that might otherwise be only partly comparable.

For the international comparisons, we have scaled the regional figures by the ratio of UK public spending shares on the total managed expenditure basis to the latest OECD estimate for UK public spending as a share of GDP. We have adjusted the figures for calendar years and have made an estimate of the 2006 position. These are compared with Eurostat or OECD data for the individual countries.

What do the results show?

Total spending in each UK region

There are four key messages emerging from the analysis for total spending in each region of the UK, which is shown in Table 1.

(1) The public expenditure share of GDP for the UK as a whole has risen significantly in the past six years. In 2001–02 the share was 39.0 per cent; in 2007–08 the share had risen to 43.0 per cent.

(2) Levels of public spending across the regions vary more than they did in 2001–02. In 2001–02, spending varied from 29.1 per cent of GDP in the South East to 58.1 per cent in Northern Ireland. In 2007–08 the range is from 34.1 per cent in the South East to 62.7 per cent in Northern Ireland. Over this period, the standard deviation of public spending as a share of GDP over the regions has risen from .086 to .089.

(3) The fastest growth in the public expenditure share from 2001–02 to 2007–08 has been in the West Midlands, Wales and the North West. The slowest growth in the public expenditure share has been in London, the East Midlands and the South West.

(4) The revised public spending data between 2006 and 2007 reduces the estimated public spending shares in many of the high spending regions (compare Table 1 and Table 2). The new figures look more plausible than the older figures.

(5) It remains the case that public spending as a share of GDP is higher than 50 per cent in all the three countries with devolved governments (Scotland, Wales and Northern Ireland) as well as in the North East and North West of England. By contrast, public spending is below 40 per cent in the South East of England, the East of England and in London.

INTERNATIONAL COMPARISONS

Figure 1 shows how the UK's position in public spending compares with that for Germany. It shows how rapidly the German share has fallen recently and how it is forecast by OECD to fall further. Indeed, the data indicates that for the first time since 1974, the public spending share in the UK has overtaken the German share.

Table 4 shows that this is not just a German phenomenon. For the euro zone as a whole, public spending shares have been falling since 2003 and are forecast by 2009 to be only slightly higher than in the UK.

---

9   National Statistics: Regional Gross Value Added, NUTS1 data tables, Table 1.1.
10 This may slightly exaggerate that growth in the divergence in public spending between regions because one would expect that in an environment where public spending is growing noticeably faster than GDP, that those regions with high shares of public spending might be likely to have faster than average GDP growth. However, the recent history has not in general supported this theoretical conclusion and so as a base assumption we have assumed GDP growth in line with that for the UK unless there is a good reason for assuming otherwise (in Scotland and London where we have more up-to-date estimates—though these show growth in GDP in both areas fairly close to the UK average).

Figure 1

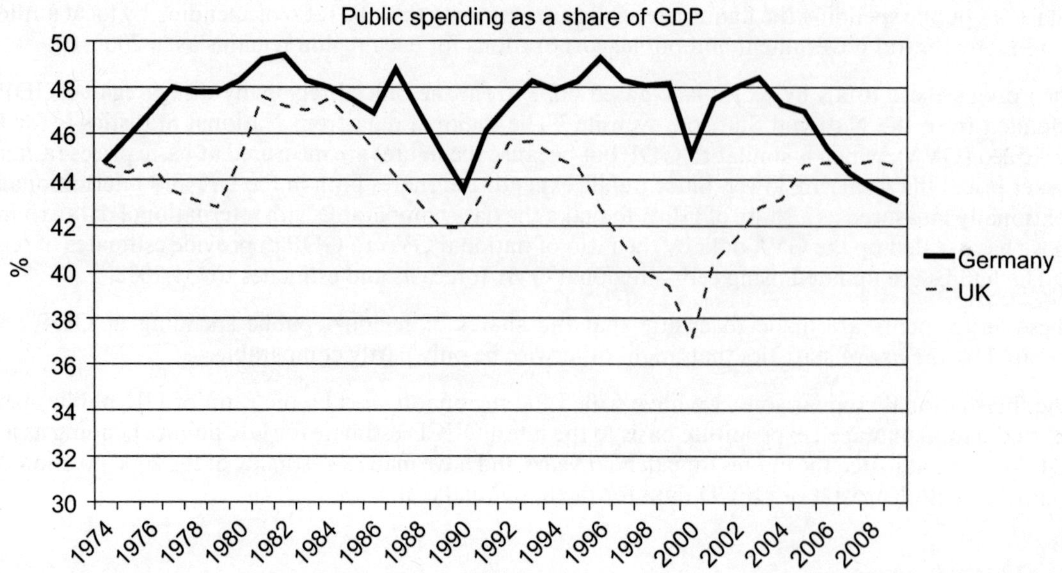

Public spending as a share of GDP

CONCLUSIONS

The analysis shows how great is the scale of divergence in public spending between region in the UK as a share of GDP.

It also shows that public spending as a share of GDP is rising in most regions in the UK as well as nationally.

To what extent this public expenditure can be afforded is a complex subject. cebr is on record as predicting that current UK spending plans will require tax rises if they are to be implemented.

However the links between public spending and taxation as shares of GDP and economic performance are complex. In general high public spending and taxation are bad for economic growth and low public spending and taxation are good for growth but there are plenty of exceptions to these rules.

We would reemphasise, however, our comment from two years that parts of the UK have become so dependent on public spending that it can crowd out private enterprise in these regions and countries. It is partly a chicken and egg situation—public spending in these regions is high because they are doing less well economically, but on the other hand a high public spending share can make a revival of the private sector difficult to achieve. And the latest data suggests that this problem is getting worse.

DOUGLAS McWILLIAMS, CHARLES DAVIS AND RICHARD SNOOK

cebr

Table 1

	Public spending as share of GDP by UK region						
	2001–02	*2002–03*	*2003–04*	*2004–05*	*2005–06*	*2006–07*	*2007–08*
North East	53.0%	54/0%	55.3%	55.6%	56.5%	56.8%	57.1%
North West	45.4%	46.7%	47.9%	48.9%	49.7%	50.0%	50.1%
Yorkshire and the Humber	43.3%	44.3%	44.9%	46.2%	47.0%	47.3%	47.0%
West Midlands	38.3%	38.7%	39.3%	40.5%	40.9%	41.6%	41.7%
East Midlands	40.4%	41.6%	42.9%	44.1%	45.0%	45.4%	45.9%
East Anglia	31.3%	32.7%	33.6%	34.4%	35.0%	35.2%	35.7%
London	34.0%	34.9%	36.2%	36.3%	37.3%	37.3%	37.0%
South East	29.8%	30.9%	31.8%	33.0%	33.1%	33.8%	34.1%
South West	38.6%	38.6%	39.6%	40.7%	41.2%	41.8%	42.1%

| | *Public spending as share of GDP by UK region* | | | | | | |
	2001–02	*2002–03*	*2003–04*	*2004–05*	*2005–06*	*2006–07*	*2007–08*
England	37.2%	38.1%	39.1%	40.0%	40.6%	41.0%	41.1%
Wales	52.3%	54.7%	55.3%	55.9%	56.9%	57.6%	57.4%
Scotland	46.3%	47.0%	48.2%	48.2%	49.9%	50.7%	50.3%
Northern Ireland	58.1%	59.7%	59.5%	60.1%	61.2%	63.5%	62.7%
UK	39.0%	40.0%	40.9%	41.7%	42.5%	42.9%	43.0%

Table 2

PUBLIC SPENDING AS SHARE OF GDP UK REGIONS/COUNTRIES FROM CEBR'S LAST REPORT ON THE SUBJECT IN MAY 2006

Total GDP (£ million)	*2001–02*	*2002–03*	*2003–04*	*2004–05*	*2005–06*
United Kingdom	38.9%	39.9%	41.0%	42.0%	43.0%
North East	56.4%	57.4%	58.0%	59.0%	61.5%
North West	47.8%	49.1%	50.1%	51.3%	52.6%
Yorkshire & the Humber	44.8%	45.2%	45.7%	47.2%	48.9%
East Midlands	39.1%	39.6%	40.7%	42.2%	43.6%
West Midlands	41.7%	42.6%	44.0%	45.4%	46.3%
East of England	34.5%	35.8%	36.8%	38.1%	38.5%
London	29.1%	30.3%	32.0%	33.3%	33.4%
South East	30.4%	31.3%	32.2%	33.9%	33.9%
South West	39.9%	39.6%	40.9%	42.3%	42.9%
England	37.5%	38.4%	39.5%	40.9%	41.5%
Wales	56.3%	58.8%	59.5%	60.3%	62.4%
Scotland	50.0%	50.4%	51.9%	52.0%	54.9%
Northern Ireland	65.2%	67.0%	66.6%	67.4%	71.3%

Table 3

STANDARD DEVIATION OF PUBLIC SPENDING AS A SHARE OF GDP BETWEEN UK REGIONS/COUNTRIES (LATEST DATA AS IN TABLE 1)

	2001–02	*2002–03*	*2003–04*	*2004–05*	*2005–06*	*2006–07*	*2007–08*
Standard deviation	0.08635	0.08896	0.08732	0.08567	0.08790	0.09139	0.08911

Table 4

INTERNATIONAL COMPARISON USING OECD DATA FOR PUBLIC SPENDING AS A SHARE OF GDP

	2001	*2002*	*2003*	*2004*	*2005*	*2006*	*2007*	*2008*	*2009*	*Change 2001–09*
OECD UK figure calendar year	40.4%	41.4%	42.8%	43.2%	44.6%	44.7%	44.6%	44.6%	44.6%	4.2%
OECD German figure calendar year	47.5%	48.0%	48.4%	47.3%	47.0%	45.4%	44.3%	44.3%	44.3%	−3.2%
OECD euro zone figure calendar year	47.3%	47.6%	48.1%	47.6%	47.5%	47.1%	46.4%	46.4%	46.4%	−0.9%

Letter from the City of London

This letter responds to the Committee's call for evidence as part of the inquiry into the Barnett Formula.

The City of London Corporation takes seriously its role in promoting the interests of London as an efficient and attractive place to do business and, while it is not in a position to respond to all areas of the inquiry, welcomes the opportunity to contribute to the Committee's deliberations.

The Corporation produces an annual publication "London's Place in the UK Economy" which highlights the importance of London to the nation's wellbeing. Central to this is the calculation of the net contribution of the London economy to UK public finances. In the most recent edition, published in October, new analysis for each region in the UK indicated that London continues to make a substantial net contribution to the Exchequer at a time when the national budget remains in large deficit. In 2006–07, the latest period for which figures are available, London provided some 17.5 per cent of public revenue based on residence and 18.5 per cent based on workplace. This places conservative estimates for London's net contribution to the UK economy at between £11.5 billion and £18.4 billion.[11] A high proportion of this comes from the financial services sector, which, according to a further recent study contributed an estimated 13.9 per cent of the total UK tax take in the financial year ending 31 March 2007.[12] Although these figures may appear a little dated and there is no doubt that the economy has changed dramatically since this snapshot was taken, they are the latest in a trend identified in previous editions of the annual report and illustrate a broad consensus among researchers that the capital is acting as a generator of resources for the country as a whole.

It is true that public spending per capita in London is significantly higher than the UK average but this partly reflects the unique nature of London as an urban environment, seat of government and the prime tourist destination for foreign visitors. On the other hand, when considered in terms of expenditure relative to wealth created, London receives considerably less than the UK average. In the period 2006–07, capital spending in London as a proportion of Gross Value Added was below the UK national average at 3.4 per cent. Redistribution of resources to other regions through the tax system is understandable, but Londoners continue to face a very high tax bill.

London is now expected, in a way that differs from other parts of the country, to contribute directly towards the funding of major infrastructure projects. Thus, the capital's council-tax payers must make an annual contribution towards the cost of the 2012 Olympic Games. Crossrail is largely to be paid for by London taxes and fares and many of the improvements to the capital's commuter rail system are being funded under an agreement with Whitehall that implies real long-term fare increases.

The City Corporation does not underestimate the impact of the current economic downturn on London's economy and it acknowledges the knock-on effect that this will have on the capital's contribution to the Government's total tax take. Research, commissioned by the City Corporation and conducted by PricewaterhouseCoopers (PwC), to estimate the cost of the losses made as a result of the downturn in relation to the financial services sector showed that a fall in profit before interest and tax of 20 per cent could reduce Government Corporation Tax receipts by £8.4 billion. Londoner's contribution through employment taxes is also forecast to decrease with job losses of 50,000 (around 5 per cent of the total number employed in the financial services sector) estimated as causing a Government tax take loss of approximately £1.3 billion.[13]

The importance of London's contribution to UK public finance is clear and, while it is right that London's successes should be to the benefit to the whole of the UK, it is also important that London too should benefit from its own success. London's success underpins and secures investment and jobs throughout the nation. While the City Corporation recognises that regulatory and cultural changes will need to be made to rectify the issues which have contributed to the current economic instability, it is important to remember that when the economy begins to recover it will still be London that will provide the growth necessary to rebuild the UK economy and that the financial services sector, whatever the regulatory architecture then prevailing, is bound to play a significant role.

3 March 2009

Memorandum by COSLA

INTRODUCTION

COSLA welcomes the opportunity to submit evidence to the Select Committee on the Barnett Formula. In presenting its submission COSLA has elected to present a view from a Scottish local government perspective and COSLA would like to acknowledge the assistance of local government officers in the preparation of its submission.

---

[11] London's Place in the Economy 2008–09", The London School of Economics and Political Science, published by the City of London Corporation, October 2008.
[12] Total Tax Contribution; PricewaterhouseCoopers LLP study of the UK Financial Services Sector for the City of London Corporation", PricewaterhouseCoopers LLP, 15 December 2008.
[13] ibid.

No consideration has been given to the issue of Scottish fiscal autonomy in this submission. This reflects the remit of the Select Committee request which specifically excludes such issues.

In its submission COSLA has considered the advantages and disadvantages of the Barnett Formula and has looked at an alternative to replace the current mechanism with a needs based assessment. Clearly there are many different permutations which can be considered, and the Select Committee will have received a great deal of expert evidence on this, however COSLA has chosen to focus on the needs based assessment as the most likely alternative. COSLA has chosen not to focus on detailed statistics, however the arguments presented are underpinned by a statistical analysis. Again the Select Committee will have received a great deal of evidence which can demonstrate the benefits or disadvantages of the current arrangements and any alternatives being proposed.

ADVANTAGES OF THE BARNETT FORMULA

The Barnett Formula currently preserves a higher per capita share in Scotland. Although there should be convergence over time, for the time being the per capita share continues to be higher. Any reduction in the relative share for Scotland would potentially have a significant impact on Scottish local government, given it has a one third share of the Scottish block, and therefore the current arrangement is considered to be an advantage.

The Formula ensures an automatic increase in funding for comparable increases in England and avoids negotiation with Westminster over increases in comparable spending in England. COSLA considers this to be generally an advantage in ensuring a fair allocation of resources across the UK.

Built in to the Formula is an assumption that devolved administrations are free to allocate resources within the overall block. The Formula simply determines an overall sum for the devolved administrations based on increases in comparable services in England. This is an important aspect as COSLA's preference is for resources to come to Scotland flexibly, given that the relationship between Local Government and the Scottish Government places flexibility and trust at its core. Any reduction in flexibility at the Scottish block level could have a knock on effect for flexibility in the resources coming to local government, which would be seen as a retrograde step.

The structure of the Formula *should* ensure the convergence over time of the relative per capita funding level in each devolved administration with that in England and, whilst this may suggest that Scotland may not be well served by indefinite use of the Formula, there is evidence to suggest that the Barnett squeeze has not affected Scotland over recent years and has had a greater impact on the other devolved administrations.

DISADVANTAGES OF THE BARNETT FORMULA

The Formula, which was introduced as a temporary measure pre-devolution, has no legal standing or democratic justification and may therefore be perceived as arbitrary and lacking robustness and may not reflect the post devolution landscape.

The Formula does not directly reflect public expenditure 'need' as the only factor it is considering is relative population and it is only looking at the margins rather than the whole of expenditure.

Whitehall defines which expenditure falls within the scope of the formula. There are no published rules or protocols that apply to this issue. It may also be the case that the decisions made on changes to expenditure in England may not be reflective of Scotland's expenditure needs.

Conversely there are areas which are excluded from the Formula which may have a relevance to the devolved administrations. For example no expenditure on the 2012 Olympics has been included within Barnett, however regeneration elements of this spend could be argued to fall within Barnett.

NEEDS ASSESSMENT AS A REPLACEMENT

The most likely alternative to the Barnett Formula would be a comprehensive needs based assessment covering the relative needs of the devolved administrations and England. This would not just focus on the changes arising from Barnett but would be a wholesale review of the relative needs across the UK. There is some merit in doing this, however if this assessment is not handled sensitively and fails to put the devolved administrations at the heart of the review, then this could simply be a means of channelling resources away from Scotland to the English regions.

The question of how much funding Scotland would receive under a needs-based assessment depends to a large extent on which needs are included and how these are measured. There are significant differences of perception about how to measure need for these purposes. For instance previous studies, such as that conducted by HM Treasury in 1979, included a range of factors that affect the demand for and cost of delivering public services, including: age, road lengths, crime levels, and housing, but they may not have recognised such factors as health needs and the cost of provision in rural areas.

The local government funding distributions for England are based on quite different ways of measuring need than is the case in Scotland and this suggests that, if a needs-based assessment is to replace the Barnett formula, it is vital that Scotland's needs are fully understood and represented in any review process to establish the relative needs of England and the devolved administrations.

In addition if funding were allocated on the basis of needs rather than the Barnett formula, this would not necessarily lead to a significant increase in England's funding. England gains a predominant share of "Barnett" public expenditure in the UK (81 per cent) as a result of its predominant share of the UK population (84 per cent). Even significant reductions in funding for the devolved administrations would produce gains that are insignificant on the scale of expenditure in England. The only way to effect a significant change in the level of funding for English regions is to alter the distribution of public expenditure within England, so the argument is not so much about the Barnett Formula itself but rather the distribution of resources across English regions.

COSLA believes that, when considering whether to replace the Barnett formula, the impact on the devolved administrations must be the paramount concern. If a needs-based assessment were to be introduced, it must make allowance for the much greater risks inherent in under-funding the need of the devolved administrations.

RETAINING THE BARNETT FORMULA

COSLA believes that retaining the formula has advantages which outweigh the disadvantages, the principal advantage being that the Formula provides a relatively straightforward mechanism for determining resources to the devolved administrations and ensures stability and flexibility for the Scottish block.

The Formula ensures that Scotland gets a fair share of increases in resources available for the UK as a whole and does not confer any special advantage to Scotland or the other devolved administrations and over time may indeed remove any apparent advantages due to the Barnett squeeze.

Whilst there is some evidence to suggest that the level of funding Scotland receives at present may exceed that arising from a needs-based assessment, nevertheless Scotland may lose out significantly over the shorter term if the Barnett formula were replaced by a needs-based assessment and this would be untenable.

Any impact on the overall resources available through the Scottish block will have a knock on impact on the resources available to Scottish local government. At a time when local government is facing unprecedented pressures on limited resources, COSLA would not wish to see a large-scale transfer of resources away from the Scottish block as this would lead to significant de-stabilisation, uncertainty and adverse impact on Scotland's communities.

As mentioned earlier in this submission, COSLA is arguing strongly for retention of the Barnett Formula as it stands and does not believe that Barnett is where the problem lies. The Select Committee needs to consider what the motives behind any change are and who is driving the change. If this is an argument about relative need for the English regions within the English block, then attention should be focussed on that issue and not on the devolved administrations' share of resources.

CONCLUSION

COSLA welcomes the opportunity to submit evidence to the Barnett Formula Select Committee. In presenting its submission COSLA has considered an alternative to the Barnett Formula based on a relative needs assessment for the devolved authorities, however COSLA has concluded that any such assessment would be highly disruptive to Scotland's communities and that any disparity does not in fact lie with the Barnett Formula. If the relative need within the English regions is the issue then this is where the focus of attention should lie. COSLA therefore strongly supports the retention of the Barnett Formula in order to preserve the stability and flexibility afforded by the current arrangements.

March 2009

Memorandum by the David Hume Institute

1. APPLICATION OF THE FORMULA IN PRACTICE

(a) *Are the present disparities in public expenditure per head of population between the countries of the UK a consequence of the Formula itself, the historic baseline or of other factors? To what extent are those disparities related to need?*

1. The disparities result from a number of factors one of which is the historic baseline. The first real attempt to introduce a "formula" to aid distribution of public funds throughout the UK occurred in 1888, when the then Chancellor of the Exchequer Viscount Goschen allocated probate duties to England, Scotland and Ireland according to the ratios 80, 11 and 9. (Wales was included as part of England.) This was largely based on the general contributions of each country to the Exchequer, albeit he was slightly more favourable to Ireland due to its higher level of poverty—a very early version of needs adjustment. The Scottish share co-incidentally corresponded, more or less, to its proportion of the total British population but, over time, as the number of Scots declined in proportion to the English population, Scotland's share became increasingly favourable. By the time the formula was abolished in 1959, it was extremely out of date, unsurprising given its longevity.

2. Between the abolition of the Goschen Formula and the introduction of the Barnett Formula in 1978, the levels of public spending in Scotland, Northern Ireland and Wales were established following annual negotiations between the relevant government departments. It has been suggested that Willie Ross, Labour Scottish Secretary to the Treasury (1964–70 and 1974–76) was particularly successful in procuring a good deal for Scotland in these negotiations, resulting in a relatively high budget for Scotland. This is important since this strong starting point has had implications for funding over the past thirty years.

3. However, the operation of the Formula (at least until 1999) also led to higher per capita spending in Scotland. The formula is driven by population shares. Thus, if the population of Scotland (or Wales) is falling (or rising less quickly) than that of England, then per capita spending in Scotland (or Wales) will rise relative to that in England. This was indeed the case for some time for Scotland, as the Scottish population fell relative to that south of the border each year from 1976, resulting in Scotland receiving a higher share of public sector funding growth than its population justified. However, in 1992, the ratios were revised within the formula, to reflect data from the 1991 Census of Population and later Alistair Darling as Chief Secretary to the Treasury announced in what is now known as "the Darling declaration" that, as of 1999, the population data used in the Barnett Formula would be revised on an annual basis to take population changes into account.

4. Other factors are also relevant. For example, annual uplifts were made by the Treasury to account for inflation whilst other "one-off" payments were made by the Treasury which by-passed the formula, for example, large pay increases for the public sector. Also, payments made, outside the Barnett formula have also added to total identifiable funding. These ad-hoc arrangements may have made a particularly large contribution as the former Scottish Secretary Ian Lang describes succinctly in his autobiography:

"The real scope for protecting Scottish interests lay in the side deals and the special ad hoc negotiations that stood outside of the corral of the 'block and formula'. I calculated after two years as Secretary of State that the Barnett Formula had reduced the Scottish Office budget by £17 million, whilst separate deals with the Treasury had increased it by £340 million. The very existence of the Barnett Formula, far from inhibiting me, enabled me to concentrate on special deals to augment our resources".[14]

5. Regarding the needs element, it has long been argued that Scotland has higher "needs" than most parts of the UK. Most of the relevant factors can be summarised under two broad headings. First there is a greater need for public services in Scotland due to greater deprivation, historically higher unemployment/lower economic activity, lower income per head, poor health record, a greater public ownership of housing stock, etc. Second the cost of delivery of public services in Scotland is higher than in England due to population sparsity and insularity and the associated education and transport issues. An additional point is a need for extra public spending because of the water industry remaining in public ownership. It can be argued that all these factors give rise to a need for a higher per capita spend in order to deliver the same level of public services or to reach equality on some "needs-adjusted" basis for levels of service.

[14] Professor J Ross Harper CBE & Iain Stewart, November 2007, Paying Our Way—Should Scotland Raise it's Own Taxes in "The Scottish Constitution in Search of a New Settlement," Policy Institute.

6. There will always be questions as to whether these justifications stand up to rigorous assessment. For example, if people choose to live in the Scottish islands is this not because of a perceived higher quality of life? If so would they not be prepared to trade off this high quality of life for either a lower level of public services or higher costs of provision? Or would that be inequitable? Is the continuation of a public water sector—a choice made in Scotland—a justification for extra spend? If the costs are higher could not it be argued "so be it—it was Scotland's decision"?

7. A needs assessment exercise was carried out for Scotland by the Treasury ahead of the planned devolution of 1979. It was fraught with difficulty, subject to major data limitations and inevitably involved highly subjective elements. It concluded that Scotland required 16 per cent higher spending per capita than England to achieve a needs-based parity, this is lower than the 21 per cent uplift Scotland receives at present. Even if the comparison were accepted for 1979, it cannot be taken to apply now, due to the number of years which have elapsed and the changes which have occurred in the Scottish economy since 1979. Thus, some of the higher spend does relate to need but the extent of this is unknown. It should also be made clear that there was no explicit needs element to the Barnett Formula (although it could be argued that since it started from a high level of public spending, this may, in fact, have reflected need).

(b) *What effect does the Barnett Formula have in terms of equity and fairness across the UK as a whole?*

8. It is a fact that Scotland has a higher level of per capita spending on public services than England and Wales (but lower than N. Ireland).[15] Identifiable per capita spending on services in 2006–07 in Scotland was £8,544 compared with £7,076 in England, £8,172 in Wales and £8,990 in Northern Ireland.[16] There is an increasing perception in England that Scotland has significantly better public service provision than in England and that English taxpayers are funding this through a net flow of funds from South to North. Various high profile Scottish Government initiatives such as abolition of tuition fees, free dental and eye check-ups, free care for the elderly (up to £210 per week) and the availability on the NHS in Scotland of a number of cancer drugs which are not prescribed in England have led to increasing resentment.[17] The list could go on and the blame has been placed on the Barnett Formula.

9. However, focussing on the spending data for England as a whole is potentially misleading when considering funding issues and particularly when making cross country comparisons. Figure 1 below shows per capita identifiable public expenditure on services in 2006–07 alongside real annual average growth from 2003–08 for the devolved nations, English regions and the UK as a whole. From this it is clear that there is not a uniform spread of spending across the English regions. Further, the identifiable spending in London was higher than that for Scotland in 2006–07 (the latest year for data on actual spend rather than planned expenditure) at £8,550 per head. Similarly, real annual average growth in per capita spending has been higher than that for Scotland at 3.9 per cent over the past five years. However, other English regions have fared considerably less well. At the other end of the scale are the Eastern and South East regions with per capita spending of £6,177 and £6,165 respectively. Annual average growth in the South East has not kept pace with the UK as a whole.

---

[15] Not all of the difference is driven by Barnett. Some of it is accounted for by UK Government identifiable expenditure in Scotland, eg social security.

[16] The source of this data is Public Expenditure Statistical Analyses (PESA) 2008, Chapter 9, Table 9.2. PESA has been used and not GERS to allow regional/country comparisons.

[17] The Sunday Times, March 9 2008, "English families spend thousands on public services that their Scottish equivalents receive for free".

Figure 1:

Identifiable public expenditure on services £/head and annual average growth 2003-08 (real terms*)

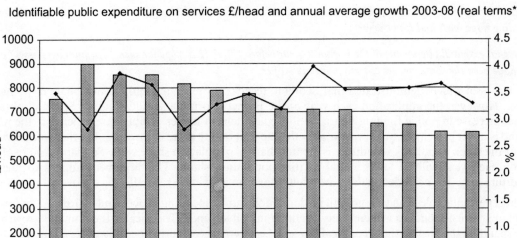

2006-07 prices

Source: Public Expenditure Statistical Analyses 2008

(c) *What effect does the Barnett Formula have on the aggregate control of public expenditure?*

(d) *What measure of flexibility do the Devolved Administrations (DAs) presently enjoy in allocating funds, between various policy areas, between capital and current spending, and for accounting purposes? Is there any need for reform in this area?*

10. Scotland is in a unique position regarding the balance between its control of public expenditure versus taxation (revenue) and micro versus macro decision making. Under the current devolved settlement, the Scottish Government has very little control over its macroeconomic environment or its fiscal decision making.[18] Decisions such as the appropriate level for interest rates or inflation targets are made for the UK as a whole by the Bank of England and the UK government (at which there is a representation of Scottish MPs), respectively.[19] On the fiscal front other than the, so far unused, "tartan tax", which allows the Scottish Government the scope to raise (or lower) income tax by up to 3p in the pound, decisions on all forms of taxation are, again, made by the UK government. Conversely, the Scottish Government has a remarkably high degree of control over microeconomic policies and spending decisions. In contrast, most other countries operate a variety of "central government controls" such as matching and specific grants, minimum standards, directives and ring-fenced expenditures. The "Block Grant" is handed over to the Scottish Government each year to spend as it sees fit. No other devolved nation operates under such mixed circumstances of high and low levels of control.

11. As a consequence questions have been raised over the stability of the current settlement, from both political and economic perspectives. It has also been argued that this lack of symmetry has had a negative impact on economic growth in Scotland.[20] Over recent years there has been increased debate and disquiet, on both sides of the border, over both the efficiency and equity of the current system.

---

[18] Of course it is the responsibility of the independent Central Bank to set interest rates without political interference. In this particular aspect it is no different than, for example, a country within the euro zone.

[19] The Scottish government can influence business rates. Also, local government in Scotland sets council taxes, influenced by the transfer from the Scottish government.

[20] MacDonald and Hallwood argue this point in "The case for Scottish fiscal autonomy", Fraser of Allander Quarterly Economic Commentary, October 2006.

2. FORMULA BY-PASS AND THE BARNETT SQUEEZE

(e) *Has convergence of levels of public spending in Scotland, Wales and Northern Ireland based on the English level of spending happened, and if not why?*

(f) *To what extent did bypassing of the Formula occur before 1999? Has scope for such "Formula by-passes" changed? What have been the consequences of that change in scope?*

12. It has been widely demonstrated that Scotland receives more than its population share of public sector funding. However, the application each year of the Barnett Formula should result in Scotland obtaining a nominal increase in public funding that is "only" equivalent to its per capita share. Therefore the result for Scotland is lower percentage year on year growth than that taking place in England. In other words Scotland's share of the stock of public expenditure is greater than its population share while Scotland's share of the net addition each year will be lower, equal to that population share. This argument applies to identifiable expenditure only. The non-identifiable part might change at a different rate, altering the overall rate of change.

13. Thus, percentage year on year growth in identifiable public spending in Scotland will always be lower than in England, whilst spending is increasing, resulting in convergence. The greater the nominal growth rate of public spending the greater the theoretical degree of convergence. (During periods of spending restraint and/or low inflation Scotland faces a slower rate of convergence. The reverse also applies) David Bell states succinctly in his 2001 paper "The Barnett Formula" that "the Barnett Formula actually narrows the gap between per capita spending in England and Scotland and therefore cannot be the cause of Scotland's higher spending levels".[21]

14. Neil Kay makes a related but slightly different point. He highlights that, in any one year, it is highly feasible that the operation of the Barnett Formula could result in a decline in real funding in Scotland, with a significant negative impact on services, whilst in England funding increases would match inflation. In 1998 he wrote:

> "For example, if public spending is increased by 4 per cent in England and Wales, the higher base for Scottish public spending levels means that Barnett translates this into a percentage increase in Scottish spending of around 3 per cent.....there are two problems with this situation. The first is inflation. Typically most public spending increases are to cope with the effects of rising prices. Suppose public spending is increased in England by 4 per cent to deal with an inflation rate of 4 per cent. The increase in public spending down south would just compensate for the effects of rising prices, but Barnett would convert the English settlements into a real decline of 1 per cent in the Scottish Block… The second problem is time. The difference between , say, a 3 per cent and a 4 per cent increase may be tolerable as a one-off, but the Barnett Formula implies a continuing squeeze on Scots public spending…."[22]

15. Ten years on from the Darling Declaration per capita public spending in Scotland remains considerably higher than that in England and there is no sign of convergence—yet. Table 1 highlights this clearly. It uses the 2008 PESA data on identifiable expenditure on services to show the annual growth rate (total and per head) in identifiable public spending in each of the home countries. This is shown in real terms, ie taking inflation into account, to remove the effects of inflation as discussed by Kay. The table shows that, in real terms, annual average growth in total identifiable expenditure on services in Scotland grew by 4 per cent in Scotland and 4.2 per cent in England over the period 2002–08 whilst, in per capita terms, the increases were 3.7 per cent and 3.6 per cent in Scotland and England respectively. Thus, depending upon definition, there has been either very little convergence or none at all. In any individual year, England may have received a considerably larger percentage increase but this has been redressed in following years.

[21] Professor David Bell, January 2001, The Barnett Formula, Department of Economics, University of Stirling
[22] Professor Neil Kay, December 1998, "The Scottish Parliament and the Barnett Formula", in FAI Quarterly Economic Commentary, Vol. 24, No 1,

Table 1

GROWTH RATES 2002–08 (PLANS) IN TOTAL IDENTIFIABLE PUBLIC EXPENDITURE ON
SERVICES IN REAL TERMS* (%)

	Scotland	England	Wales	N.Ireland
2003–04	4.7	6.5	4.0	3.2
2004–05	1.0	4.5	3.0	3.0
2005–06	6.4	4.1	4.6	3.2
2006–07	3.4	1.8	2.4	1.9
2007–08 (plans)	4.5	3.9	2.2	6.7
Total annual average growth rate 2002–08	4.0	4.2	3.2	3.6
Total annual average growth rate in per capita terms 2003–08	3.7	3.6	2.8	2.8
Actual per capita funding 2006–07	£8,544	£7,076	£8,172	£8,990

Source: Public Expenditure Statistical Analyses 2008, Table 9.4

— 2006–07 prices

The reasons for the lack of convergence are many:

— There was no adjustment for population for many years—as detailed in the answer to question 1 (a) above.

— Annual uplifts were made by the Treasury to account for inflation.

— Other "one-off" payments were made by the Treasury which by-passed the formula, for example, large pay increases for the public sector.

— Payments made, outside of the Barnett formula have also added to total identifiable funding. These ad-hoc arrangements may have made a particularly large contribution.

16. There was much scope to bypass the formula before 1999 and this clearly happened. Since then, a number of avenues to bypass the formula have been closed but there is clearly still no sign of convergence.

3. DATA QUALITY AND AVAILABILITY

(g) *Are sufficient data available to enable a clear understanding of how public spending is distributed across the UK, and to show the working of the Formula as set out in the Statement of Funding Policy?*

17. The charts and graphs used throughout this response highlight that there is sufficient data available to enable a clear understanding of how public expenditure is distributed across the UK and to establish how money is allocated as a result of the working of the Formula. However, there is a lack of transparency, including difficulties in deciding how expenditure and receipts are categorised and assigned. The Barnett formula is a relatively straightforward calculation. However, it does not account for all public spending and there are several cases where spending is seen to be exceptional and outside the Barnett formula. See answer 5 for more on this.

4. NEED FOR REFORM/ALTERNATIVES TO THE EXISTING FORMULA

(k) *Do the advantages of the Formula as presently constituted outweigh its disadvantages?*

18. There are advantages to the Barnett Formula:

— It provides a relatively stable and predictable source of funding.

— It avoids political bargaining from dominating annual spending rounds across the UK.

— It is meant to be simple and transparent.

— The alternatives (eg a need assessment exercise) could be very complex.

However, it could be argued that the disadvantages far outweigh these advantages:

1. There is a lack of transparency, including difficulties in deciding how expenditure and receipts are categorised and assigned. As highlighted above, the Barnett formula is a relatively straightforward calculation. However, it does not account for all public spending and there are several cases where spending is seen to be exceptional and outside the Barnett formula.

2. There are calls, generally from England, for equity in per capita funding across the UK (or at least a bit more equity than exists at present).

3. In Scotland it has been perceived by some that applying Barnett will tend to create convergence in per capita public sector funding across the nations and that this will be to the detriment of Scottish public services and, indeed the economy of Scotland.

4. As demonstrated below comparison of England as a whole with the other nations disguises a wide variation between the English regions. This applies to both spend per head and "needs".

5. It is argued that Scotland has higher "needs" for public expenditure than England, that Barnett does not take this into account and that any drive to convergence may be equitable but is not necessarily "fair".

(m) *Should the Barnett Formula be replaced by a system more adequately reflecting relative needs, cost of services or a combination of both? If so what factors should be considered as part of a needs assessment?*

(n) *What practical and conceptual difficulties (particularly for defining "need") would arise in carrying out a needs-based assessment? How can these difficulties be overcome?*

19. The debate on public funding covers equity issues as well as efficiency matters. As highlighted in the answer to question 1a, it has long been argued that Scotland has higher "needs" than most parts of the UK. Most of the relevant factors can be summarised under two broad headings. First there is a greater need for public services in Scotland due to greater deprivation, historically higher unemployment/lower economic activity, lower income per head, poor health record, a greater public ownership of housing stock, etc. Second the cost of delivery of public services in Scotland is higher than in England due to population sparsity and insularity and the associated education and transport issues. An additional point is a need for extra public spending because of the water industry remaining in public ownership. It can be argued that all these factors give rise to a need for a higher per capita spend in order to deliver the same level of public services or to reach equality on some "needs-adjusted" basis for levels of service.

20. There will always be questions as to whether these justifications stand up to rigorous assessment. For example, if people choose to live in the Scottish islands is this not because of a perceived higher quality of life? If so would they not be prepared to trade off this high quality of life for either a lower level of public services or higher costs of provision? Or would that be inequitable? Is the continuation of a public water sector—a choice made in Scotland—a justification for extra spend? If the costs are higher could not it be argued "so be it—it was Scotland's decision"? This is not the place to go into these issues in any depth or with due rigour; rather a time to point out that there are contentious issues even in determining what a needs-based assessment might imply. Further, even when you accept this "higher need" argument, it still requires a weighting and an assessment of how need should relate to expenditure.

21. There are two even more difficult questions to be posed. First, if funding should contain a needs element, then what is the true level of Scottish need? Second, is the current per capita funding level (ie the excess over the English level) sufficient to meet this needs-based differential?

22. Given the discrepancies in funding across the English regions, a needs assessment exercise just for Scotland would probably be deemed inadequate. The current system is not perceived as "fair" given that there are areas in the North of England, Cornwall (and indeed Wales) which may be seen as having greater need than Scotland, but where public funding on a per capita basis is lower.

23. A needs assessment exercise was carried out for Scotland by the Treasury ahead of the planned devolution of 1979. It was fraught with difficulty, subject to major data limitations and inevitably involved subjective elements. It concluded that Scotland required 16 per cent higher spending per capita than England to achieve a needs-based parity, lower than the 21 per cent uplift Scotland receives at present.[23] Even if the comparison were accepted for 1979, it cannot be taken to apply now, due to the number of years which have elapsed and the changes which have occurred in the Scottish economy since 1979.

24. Consequently if needs issues were to be re-addressed, then a new study would be required—and probably one covering all the nations and all the English regions. Many commentators have indicated that the exercise is too difficult to repeat, with potentially too many different outcomes depending on the value judgements of those undertaking the research, to permit the exercise to be seen by interested parties as objective and fair. It would take a brave set of statisticians to take on such a task.

---

[23] In "Options for Scotland's Future—the Economic Dimension", Andrew Hughes-Hallet contends that due to lower incomes and other factors discussed in his chapter, the true excess is probably about zero.

5. DECISION MAKING AND DISPUTE RESOLUTION

(q) *How effective, appropriate and fair are the processes and criteria by which HM Treasury determines matters relating to the Barnett Formula? In particular, is the way HM Treasury determines whether items of spending in England do or do not attract consequential payments under the Formula, and claims by the DAs on the UK Reserve, appropriate and fair?*

25. Although the Barnett formula itself is transparent there is an issue around what spending is actually subject to the formula. Most expenditure falls into a particular category and it is relatively easy to see what is and is not Barnett expenditure. However, instances arise where this is not so clear cut, leading to tension between the UK government and the devolved nations. Decisions as to whether an item of expenditure falls within Barnett will generally be for the Treasury to determine. Examples of this are numerous eg expenditure on the Channel Tunnel and the £1.2bn uplift in spending on prisons in England and Wales following the Carter Review. This spending was classified as outside of the Barnett formula therefore there was no consequential uplift in spending in Scotland and Wales. The 2012 Olympic Games is a more recent dispute. The funding of the games is being seen to benefit the UK as a whole and is being funded from the UK reserve. However, the devolved nations are arguing that the regeneration elements of this spending should be subject to Barnett consequentials.

26. There are other cases where the formula has been by-passed to benefit the devolved nations eg the Treasury's decision to provide match funding to allow Wales to obtain Objective 1 funding from the EU. Whilst this allows the UK government flexibility to provide funds in exceptional circumstances, the lack of transparency can cause issues between devolved nations and the UK government. Clearly, this requires to be addressed.

David Hume Institute

25 February 2009

Memorandum by the East of England Development Agency and East of England Regional Assembly

SUMMARY

— While English regions are not subject to the Barnett formula, at least not directly, they do experience many of the same drawbacks associated with that convention.

— English regions do not receive block grants from the national exchequer in the same way that the devolved administrations do. England is treated as a single block under current funding arrangements but the resulting pattern of expenditure has been, and continues to be one of large regional differences.

— A move to a needs-based system of allocation for the UK would be beneficial to the East of England, particularly in terms of tackling localised deprivation. In the current economic circumstances, a needs-based approach would strengthen the operation of fiscal stabilisers in the UK.

— Clarity on which items should not be covered by the Barnett Formula would strengthen the prioritisation of economically-valuable projects in general and better align regional and national investment priorities.

— Transport, skills and innovation all demonstrate the consequences of the discrepancies in patterns of expenditure and how a change in the system of allocations might work.

— A change of this nature would in turn have an impact on the efficiency of England and the UK's economy as a whole

The East of England Development Agency and the East of England Regional Assembly welcome the opportunity to submit evidence to the Committee's inquiry into the Barnett Formula. We recognise the remit of the Committee and its focus on the system of allocating block grants from the UK exchequer to the devolved administrations of Scotland, Wales and Northern Ireland. We hope the Committee will, nonetheless, wish to consider this evidence pertaining to issues around funding systems more generally in the UK.

THE EAST OF ENGLAND DEVELOPMENT AGENCY AND THE EAST OF ENGLAND REGIONAL ASSEMBLY

2. England's nine Regional Development Agencies (RDAs) were established in 1999 as Non-Departmental Public Bodies reporting to the Department for Business, Enterprise and Regulatory Reform. The RDAs were tasked with improving the economic performance of the English regions and reducing the gap in economic growth rates between regions. The East of England Development Agency (EEDA) takes the lead in addressing

key economic issues in the East of England such as innovation, business competitiveness, skills, transport and growth. EEDA's main roles in driving improvement in the region's economic performance are those of:

— strategic navigator—leading partners in delivering shared economic objectives;

— strategic influencer and expert—mobilising partners with greater resources and contributing expertise and discretionary funding to address particular economic failures; and

— commissioner—using scarce resources to commission projects or programmes at the right spatial level.

This includes a strategic leadership role in the region in formulating the Regional Economic Strategy (RES) on behalf of partners in the region. The RES assesses the region's strengths and weaknesses and the major trends that will affect businesses and communities over the next 20 years. It sets out an ambitious long-term vision for the region's economy, how we can get there and who will make it happen, underpinned by a comprehensive evidence base. The RES is owned by the region and shapes the work of a range of organisations and their priorities for investment. EEDA is business-driven, championing the business perspective in public decision-making in the region and ensuring that the climate for business success continues to flourish in the East of England.

3. The East of England Regional Assembly (EERA) is a partnership body bringing together elected councillors from the region's 54 councils and representatives from the private, voluntary and community sectors. The overall purpose of EERA is to promote the social, economic and environmental well-being of the region. The Assembly:

— is the voluntary regional chamber in the East of England;

— advises Government on regional planning, housing and transport issues, including priorities for public spending;

— scrutinises the work of EEDA;

— provides services to local government such as training, consultancy and advice as the regional employers association; and

— hosts the regional improvement and efficiency partnership "Improvement East" for local and fire authorities.

This includes responsibility for developing the draft East of England Plan—the Regional Spatial Strategy for the East of England.

4. EEDA and EERA are, therefore, well-placed to provide an insight into the impact of public funding levels on the East of England.

5. The East of England will not be able to achieve its ambitions for sustainable economic development without the support of government. This is particularly important for the East of England because the public funding levels for this region are amongst the very lowest, despite being one of only three regions which are net contributors to the exchequer.

How does the Barnett Formula relate to funding differentials across English regions and the East of England in particular?

6. English regions do not receive block grants from the national exchequer in the same way that the devolved administrations of Scotland, Wales and Northern Ireland do. With the exception of regional agencies such as RDAs, the major units for allocation of funds within England are local authorities and Primary Care Trusts (PCTs)—EEDA's budget last year was less than 0.5 per cent of public spending in this region. England is treated as a single block under current funding arrangements but the resulting pattern of expenditure has been, and continues to be one of large regional differences. A recent analysis by IPPR showed that these remain even if the estimates are adjusted for differences in need and spending on social protection.

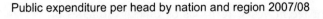

Public expenditure per head by nation and region 2007/08

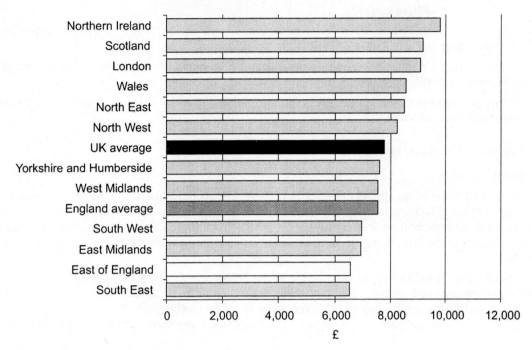

7. In 2007–08 the East of England received levels of public expenditure per head that were 13 per cent below the England average, and 16 per cent below the UK average. The chart below shows the size of these differences by broad policy area.

Public expenditure per head by function 2007/08

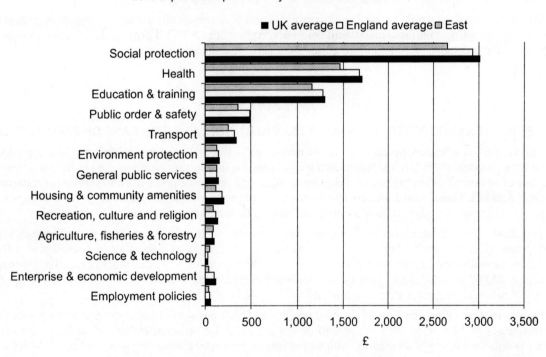

8. Though English regions are not subject to the Barnett Formula—at least not directly—they do experience many of the same drawbacks associated with that convention:

— England's public spending differential with the rest of the UK is carried over to the regions.

— English regions with above average population growth are likely to be disadvantaged in that accurate estimates of population by local authority or PCT are available only with the release of Census data every 10 years. In recent years, revisions to official estimates of England's population between censuses have all been upwards.

— The cost of service delivery differs between regions due to differences in wages, living costs, transport infrastructure and population density.

— Differences in need are often regional in character. For example, transport and higher-education have strong cross-jurisdictional externalities.

— Convergence of per capita public spending across England is not happening, even though transfers are not adjusted for need

Which reforms could benefit the East of England and the UK as a whole?

Needs-based allocation

9. The move to a needs-based system of allocation for the UK would be beneficial to the East of England, particularly in terms of tackling localised deprivation when the major units of allocation are local authorities and PCTs. In the current economic circumstances, a needs-based approach would strengthen the operation of fiscal stabilisers in the UK, as monies aimed at supporting enterprise, for example, would follow welfare payments.

10. A pre-condition would be to overcome technical challenges around establishing reliable proxies of need and differences in costs and ensuring these are closely monitored. The Local Economic Assessment duty on upper-tier authorities (to be introduced in 2010) could be flexed for this purpose: the statutory partners to that process cover the whole spectrum of non-defence spending bodies, including local authorities and the NHS.

Clarity on which items should not be covered by the Barnett Formula

11. Funding decisions around major policy interventions in England are influenced by their potential effect on overall UK public spending through the Barnett Formula. There are no statutory or publicly-available guidelines covering the definition of "national significance". As a case-by-case consideration, policy areas that are characterised by large capital outlays of national significance are vulnerable to distortions—spatial allocations that do not maximise economic efficiency for the UK as a whole.

12. Statutory guidelines would strengthen the prioritisation of economically-valuable projects in general and better align regional and national investment priorities. Appendices A and B provide details around how this might work for transport, skills and innovation in the East of England.

2 March 2009

APPENDIX A

PUBLIC EXPENDITURE ON INNOVATION AND SKILLS IN THE EAST OF ENGLAND

13. Innovation—the "successful exploitation of new ideas"—is a key productivity driver and is regarded as crucial to the success of the UK's economy as a whole. Innovation requires highly-skilled individuals who can make use of advanced technologies to develop innovative new products, processes and services in response to customer demand. These innovations create new markets, generate comparative advantage for companies and increase productivity through more efficient use of labour, land and capital.

14. The East of England makes a significant contribution to the UK's innovative and research and development (R&D) activity. The region contains the major facilities of a number of top 50 global R&D companies as well as the Cambridge technology cluster, which together represent more than 1,400 companies employing 43,000 people, along with other "knowledge-generating" technology, health and life sciences clusters of national and international importance.

15. By way of illustration, the East of England accounted for 27 per cent of R&D expenditure performed by UK businesses and attracted over 19 per cent of venture capital investment in the UK in 2007. Innovative activity is also the highest of all regions, with 69 per cent of businesses being "innovation active" in 2004–06.

16. Together with London and the South East, the Greater South East is Europe's only credible challenger with the critical mass to rival the major US economies and emerging mega-regions in Asia, accounting for 56 per cent of private sector R&D investment in UK businesses and attracting 68 per cent of venture capital investment in the UK.

17. However, the long-term competitiveness of the East of England is not guaranteed. As highlighted in the East of England "Innovation Baseline Study" (2009), the skills of the existing workforce and skills development capacity within the East of England presents a challenge for the region's—and hence the UK's—

innovation performance. Despite relatively good GCSE attainment, the skills profile of the region is weak. The proportion of graduates within the region is lower than the national average and over a third of residents have low or no qualifications. The capacity to develop high-level skills is lower in comparison to other regions, with East of England currently providing only 60 per cent of the UK average number of undergraduate places. The region falls even further behind on workforce qualifications and training.

18. The Government's "Innovation Nation" Strategy stresses that innovation performance and skills are inextricably linked. A more highly-skilled and expert workforce is more likely to generate new ideas and introduce and adapt to new technology and organisational change. Hence, in order to succeed, the UK needs to make use of the talents of all people and break down the barriers that prevent people realising their full potential.

INVESTMENT IN SKILLS IN THE EAST OF ENGLAND

19. Despite the East of England's poor skills performance and lower than average levels of improvement over the past five years, public sector investment in education and training in the region has remained fairly static as a percentage of the total (10.0 per cent of all investment in England in 2007–08, up slightly from 9.8 per cent in 2002–03 and in comparison to the region's share of England's population of around 11 per cent). The East of England has also received the lowest or second lowest level of education funding per head of population than any other English region in each year from 2002–03 to 2007–08.

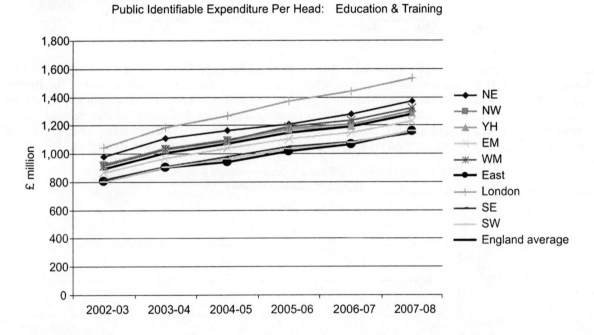

Public Identifiable Expenditure Per Head: Education & Training

20. Looking at funding available to the region from individual agencies, the Learning and Skills Council (LSC) and the Higher Education Funding Council (HEFCE) are currently the core funders of post-16 further and higher education in the East of England

21. In 2007–08, funding available from the LSC to be spent in the East of England on improving the skills of young people and adults through further education was the lowest per head of population and lowest per person without a level 2 qualification (equivalent to five high-grade GCSEs) of the English regions. The LSC itself makes decisions about regional allocations. It bases this on a wide range of factors including overall learner numbers and the contribution that each region can make to specific programmes and priorities.

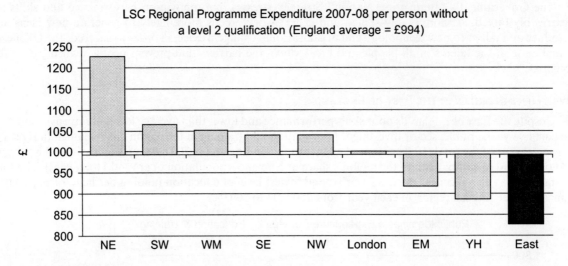

LSC Regional Programme Expenditure 2007-08 per person without a level 2 qualification (England average = £994)

22. The same is true of HEFCE's higher education teaching and research budget which, in 2008–09, was the lowest per head of population and per person without a level 4 (degree level) qualification of the English regions. HEFCE uses formulae to determine how most of its funding is allocated between higher education institutions. These take into account certain factors for each institution, including the number and type of students, the subjects taught and the amount and quality of research undertaken there. The low level of funding in the East of England reflects the low number of higher education places in the region.

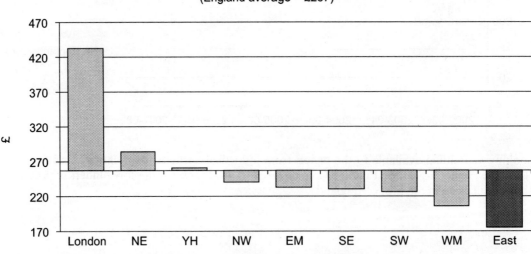

HEFCE Recurrent Grants 2008-09 per person without a level 4 qualification (England average = £257)

23. Recognising skills as a key priority for the region due to poorer than average performance and poorer than average levels of funding, the East of England has—where possible—re-prioritised some of its available funding to improve the region's skills base. For example, 5 per cent (£4.3 million) of funding from the European Social Fund (ESF) 2007–13 available for employment programmes was shifted to the ESF budget for skills—the maximum percentage available for re-allocation. However, this budget represents a very small proportion of available funding for skills in the region.

APPENDIX B

PUBLIC EXPENDITURE ON TRANSPORT IN THE EAST OF ENGLAND

24. The East of England has a distinctive role as the UK's gateway to global markets, and our major airports and ports are of growing national economic importance serving wide areas beyond the East of England region.

25. With Stansted and Luton airports, the East of England is a key region for passenger and freight transport by air. Between 1995 and 2005, the East of England experienced by far the fastest increase in air movements (183 per cent) and terminal passenger numbers (430 per cent) of the regions. Forecast growth in demand for aviation remains strong. The East of England also recorded a 152 per cent rise in freight lifted by air, second to the West Midlands. Stansted airport alone is the third-largest handler of airfreight in the UK behind Heathrow and East Midlands airports, with Luton airport also ranking sixth.

26. The East of England also contains a number of major ports, including Felixstowe and Harwich (both of which have significant expansion plans), Tilbury and the approved London Gateway Port Development at Shellhaven. The East of England's ports account for over half of UK container capacity and more than a fifth of UK port employment. With planned expansions at Felixstowe South, Bathside Bay and London Gateway, this will rise to over 70 per cent of the UK's container capacity.

27. However, there are significant constraints on access to and from the region's ports, particularly westwards from Felixstowe and Harwich to the East of England and the rest of the UK along the A14, as well as to London along the A12. There are also significant capacity constraints on the rail freight network, forcing freight onto already-constrained roads. This will increase as port capacities expand. Considerable transfer to the railway network will therefore be required to avoid increased freight congestion and minimise environmental impacts. This requires high levels of investment. The Felixstowe to Nuneaton rail improvements (both gauge and capacity) are widely considered to be a key port-related regional priority which will also bring wider national benefits.

28. Close links between the East of England's and London's economies also impact on the East of England's transport infrastructure. In 2007, workers living in the East of England produced over £9 billion of GVA in economies outside the region, particularly London. Hence around two-thirds of all rail trips in the East of England are being made to Central London. However, these links suffer the highest levels of overcrowding in the country, which will place constraints on the ability for further passenger growth—and growth of London's economy—in the absence of capacity improvements.

29. The UK Department for Transport is currently consulting on their "Delivering a Sustainable Transport System" approach to long term transport planning. The consultation document identifies 14 "strategic national corridors" (SNCs) critical to the economic success of the nation. These have been defined on the basis of connections to the UK's biggest conurbations (including London) and the country's major ports and airports. Of the 14 SNCs identified, seven fall within or pass through the East of England. This further demonstrates the importance of the East of England's transport networks to national economic prosperity.

INVESTMENT IN THE REGION'S TRANSPORT INFRASTRUCTURE

30. Despite the growing importance of the region's transport infrastructure to the UK economy, public sector investment has remained fairly static. In 2002–03, 8.4 per cent of public sector expenditure on transport was invested in the East of England (lower than the region's 10.9 per cent share of England's population). This rose to just 8.6 per cent of public transport investment in 2007–08 (compared to the region's 11.1 per cent share of England's population).

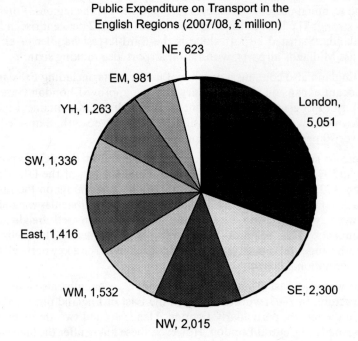

Public Expenditure on Transport in the English Regions (2007/08, £ million)

31. Significant funding deficits for transport in the East of England are therefore restricting the development of the region's transport infrastructure, with consequences for the region's and the UK's economy. The region must therefore divert attention to developing its own solutions by finding and agreeing new and innovative methods of funding, including different models for public/private funding and rolling infrastructure finds, such as a Regional Infrastructure Fund.

BENEFITS OF INCREASED INVESTMENT IN THE REGION'S TRANSPORT INFRASTRUCTURE

32. Congestion and overcrowding on the East of England's transport networks are costing the region's economy £514 million per annum (2003 prices). If all congestion could be eliminated and all travel was made at "free-flow" speeds (an ambitious and arguably unachievable target which would probably be uneconomic to implement), this rises to £986 million per annum.

33. These costs are not confined to the East of England's economy. Congestion and overcrowding in the East of England are costing the UK economy as a whole £721 million per annum, rising to £1,339 million per annum if congestion could be eliminated. Hence, around 27 per cent of the costs of congestion in the East of England are felt outside the region.

34. The costs outlined above only include those associated with journeys in the course of business. However, if all journeys are considered, including commuting journeys which clearly have a significant wider economic impact, these costs rise to £1,087 million and £2,197 million per annum respectively.

Benefits of Eliminating Congestion in the East of England in 2021

(GDP, £ million per annum, 2003 prices)

	East of England Economy	UK Economy	Percentage of total benefits outside the East of England
Conventional Benefits			
Business User Benefits	338	462	27%
Freight User Benefits	210	262	20%
Total Conventional Benefits	**548**	**724**	**24%**
Wider Benefits			
Agglomeration	339	493	31%
Imperfect Competition	55	72	24%
Labour Supply	45	50	10%
Total Wider Benefits	**438**	**615**	**29%**
Total Benefits	**986**	**1,339**	**27%**

Source: Adapted from the Transport Economic Evidence Study, Table 4.2

35. Congestion on transport links within and between the south of the region (Essex (including Thames Gateway) and Hertfordshire) and London has a particularly significant economic impact. With transport improvements on routes within and to London having the highest potential economic benefits in the UK, improvements in this corridor would yield high GDP benefits both for London and the south of the region. However, congestion and overcrowding on the transport networks in other locations and corridors in the East of England has also been shown to have a significant wider economic impact which if affecting national prosperity; these include Greater Norwich, the Haven Gateway, Greater Cambridge and Peterborough, and the Milton Keynes South Midlands Growth Area.

Memorandum by the Federal Trust for Education and Research

Please find below our response to the Call for Evidence from the House of Lords Select Committee on the Barnett Formula. We are grateful for the opportunity to put our views forward, even though the formal deadline has passed.

The Federal Trust is a think tank that studies the interactions between regional, national, European and global levels of government. At present we are engaged in a project considering the applicability of federal structures and principles to the UK constitution. We were pleased to learn that this committee is addressing an issue central to any such investigation: mechanisms for the central redistribution of funds, as at present determined to a considerable extent by the so-called "Barnett Formula".

We note that subjects specifically ruled out of the terms of reference of this inquiry include "The overall system of funding the Devolved Administrations – in particular the question of whether greater tax-raising powers should be accorded to the devolved administrations" and "Other political aspects of the devolution settlements".

However, the inquiry also proposes "to consider alternative mechanisms" to the Barnett Formula. We seek to address this issue, dealt with by Question 4 from the Call for Evidence – "Need for reform/Alternatives to the existing Formula"; and the first two sub-questions within it.

We believe that the Formula, as presently constituted, is a natural consequence of the present constitutional structure of the UK. The UK is a multinational, asymmetrical and highly centralised country. As a trade-off for their continued participation in a Union within which England is the dominant partner, a number of specific beneficial arrangements are afforded to the smaller nations, such as overrepresentation in terms of parliamentary seats relative to England. The Formula, which has in practice tended to preserve higher levels of per capita spending in the non-English UK nations, amounts to another such arrangement. While the UK remains a unitary state with centralised fiscal policy, the central redistribution of funds is always likely to be conceived primarily in terms of political concessions to particular nations within the UK.

The alternative, and in our view preferable, approach would be based on a clear distinction between the taxes raised in particular nations or regions; and the funds that were allocated to them from central resources according to some kind of needs-based formula. The ultimate outcome in terms of central redistribution of funds might not differ radically from present arrangements, but it is to be hoped it would be more possible to achieve a degree of public understanding and acceptance around it. However, the current unitary UK constitution does not permit such an approach. Within this system, however it is modified, the Formula is likely to bring with it similar problems such as resentment within England that it is subsidising other parts of the UK.

Do the advantages of the Formula as presently constituted outweigh its disadvantages?

The primary political goal of the Formula is to satisfy those nations within the UK that are in practice its beneficiaries that membership of the Union is advantageous to them; while not causing excessive resentment amongst the other nations (or rather, nation). So long as both these conditions are fulfilled by the formula, its advantages could be said to be outweighing its disadvantages. Inevitably, there will be those in both the smaller nations of the UK and in England who will be unhappy with the precise balance established by the Formula. Until now, both these minorities have been politically marginal, but there can be no guarantee that their marginality will continue indefinitely.

Should the Barnett Formula be (a) retained in its current form, (b) amended or (c) replaced entirely?

We believe that, while the status of the UK as a highly centralised, unitary state remains intact, there would little purpose in amending the Formula. Problems associated with the Formula are likely to remain roughly similar in nature while the current framework persists. For it to be "replaced entirely" in a meaningful way would involve alterations to the structural make-up of the UK.

March 2009

Memorandum by Professor David Heald

INTRODUCTION

(1) My evidence takes the form of direct answers to the questions on which the Committee asked for responses. The Committee's terms of reference, and the clarification of what is thereby excluded, have the effect of removing some of the questions and answers from their operational and political context. The meaning of the first and third "main areas" that are explicitly considered for exclusion is unclear; these could be interpreted in ways which would prevent the Committee from making a balanced assessment of the Barnett Formula.

(2) I have interpreted "Barnett Formula" in a broad way, as referring to the funding system as a whole and not just to the calculation of formula consequentials. The Barnett Formula is often criticised for what it does or does not do, without reference to its ranking against viable alternative methods of funding the UK Devolved Administrations. The Committee should distinguish those criticisms which are specific to the Barnett Formula from those which would apply to all block-grant funding mechanisms.

RESPONSES TO THE COMMITTEE'S QUESTIONS

(3) For readability, each question is reproduced before the answer. Answers appear in bold type. Some of these questions and sub-questions could be answered at great length, but the importance of brevity has been respected. Where amplification is clearly required, I provide references to my published work.

1. APPLICATION OF THE FORMULA IN PRACTICE

(a) *Are the present disparities in public expenditure per head of population between the countries of the UK a consequence of the Barnett Formula itself, the historic baseline or of other factors? To what extent are those disparities related to need?*

The terminology of "disparities" is loaded. Given the functional composition of UK identifiable public expenditure, and the economic and socio-demographic differences across the nations and regions of the United Kingdom, there is no reason to expect that each nation and region would have equal expenditure per head (ie a per capita index of 100 where UK = 100).[24] This point is reinforced by the analyses in *Public Expenditure: Statistical Analyses* of the regions of England; the choice of the unit of analysis is very important.

---

[24] Expecting all nations and regions to have an index of 100 (UK = 100) indicates that the only need indicator is population.

The key factors are clearly the pre-Formula baseline (determined about 30 years ago) and operational decisions about how the Formula is applied (eg population updating, changes in scope and formula by-pass).

It is impossible to answer the question as to whether differences in per capita indexes reflect differences in need. First, need would have to be operationally defined in relation to expenditure functions, and there would be value conflicts because the definition of need to spend involves political choices. Second, empirical evidence would have to be accumulated on relative need. Most needs assessments for public services are undertaken separately for England, Scotland, Wales and Northern Ireland, and institutional differences make read-across very difficult.

Neither the pre-devolution Secretaries of State, nor the Devolved Administrations themselves, have asked the UK Government to undertake a needs assessment. Given the convergence property of the Barnett Formula, this would seem to imply that (a) they privately regard the present funding relativities as reasonably generous, and/or (b) they regard the uncertainties attached to a needs assessment and its aftermath as something to be avoided.

(b) *What effect does the Barnett Formula have in terms of equity and fairness across the UK as a whole?*

A comprehensive answer to this question would be lengthy. This brief response draws attention to a number of important considerations:

— it is very difficult to confer operational meaning on equity and fairness, which in political conversation at least are near synonyms. There is a strong commitment to broadly equal treatment of citizens wherever in the United Kingdom they live. This is given practical expression by the centralised operation of the cash-benefit component of the UK welfare state and by many service-level equalisation formulae. The strength of this commitment—shared by most Western European states, but less so in the United States—is an important feature of UK political life. It necessarily involves large territorial shifts of resources, as reflected by large differences at the "regional" level between tax revenues and public expenditure;

— this generalised commitment to equity is complicated in the United Kingdom by its multinational character. England constitutes 85 per cent of the UK population; only 15 per cent of the population live in Scotland, Wales and Northern Ireland and that proportion seems likely to decline. This population imbalance raises a number of issues about the distribution of political power: do Scotland and Wales have equal status to England (as in the Six Nations Rugby Championship) or does England's huge population majority give it pre-eminence in terms of democratic authority? Federal systems of government—as in the United States—sometimes qualify majority rule by structuring voting systems and institutions in order to provide protections to smaller jurisdictions;

— majority opinion in Scotland, Wales and Northern Ireland favours a devolved system of government. Where there is genuine policy choice at the devolved level, that brings with it a conflict between interpersonal equity (each UK citizen faces the same treatment wherever they live)[25] and territorial equity (each political jurisdiction has the same fiscal capacity in relation to needs). Under territorial equity, each government would have the potential to meet UK standards/norms but devolved political decisions (eg the choice between education and health expenditure) mean that access by individuals to particular services may differ according to the political jurisdictions in which they live;

— it needs to be established whether judgements about equity are made solely with reference to the distribution of public expenditure, or whether the generation of tax revenues is also relevant. Higher tax revenues might flow from higher taxable capacity per head or from higher tax effort (eg on council tax). I make this point but do not develop it in light of the restrictions imposed by the Committee's terms of reference; and

— the establishment of this ad hoc Select Committee stemmed primarily, in my view, from the Barnett Formula being perceived in England as unfair to England and thereby lacking legitimacy. Paradoxically, some of the criticisms of the Barnett Formula as being unfair use as evidence the distribution of public expenditure across English regions. This distribution is generated by policy decisions within England, taken by UK ministers. Controversy has been stimulated by the way in which devolution has given higher profile in England to institutional and policy differences within the United Kingdom. In particular, certain Scottish policy initiatives (eg free personal care for the elderly, absence of higher education fees paid by students, free hospital parking, abolition of bridge tolls) is taken as evidence that Scotland is over-funded. In fact, such policies entail an opportunity cost, for

---

[25] There is no evidence that a centralised state is, in fact, capable of the uniform provision of service that is implied here.

example in terms of University funding. This sense of grievance in England has been made worse by the way in which the present UK Government closed down debate about the Barnett Formula, rather than either mounting a defence of the devolution financial settlement or debating alternatives.

(c) *What effect does the Barnett Formula have on the aggregate control of public expenditure?*

If it is accepted that the UK Treasury needs to control the aggregate of UK public expenditure, then the Barnett Formula assists that control. The Treasury negotiates directly with UK departments, knowing the size of formula consequentials that will be generated for Scotland, Wales and Northern Ireland by increases in "comparable programmes"[26] in England.

(d) *What measure of flexibility do the Devolved Administrations (DAs) presently enjoy in allocating funds, between various policy areas, between capital and current spending, and for accounting purposes? Is there any need for reform in this area?*

The great attraction of the Barnett Formula system to pre-devolution territorial Secretaries of State was that it gave them expenditure-switching discretion over the block. This was fed by formula consequentials, but— except for small amounts of expenditure, some connected with Europe—there was independent choice on how to allocate the increments and (over time and subject to obvious political constraints) the base.

This expenditure-switching discretion continued under devolution. However, there has been some subsequent erosion, particularly from Spending Review 2004; these changes occurred without any public announcement. At SR2004, the Treasury became more concerned about meeting the golden rule, and insisted on the distinction between Resource DEL and Capital DEL.[27] There are now two types of Resource DEL: near-cash and non-cash (covering depreciation and cost of capital charges). This partitions the Assigned Budget and qualifies the expenditure-switching power. These public expenditure control mechanisms affect the Devolved Administrations because it is possible to have the "wrong type of DEL" in both new formula consequentials and in stocks of End-Year Flexibility (EYF).[28]

These developments pose two threats to the devolved funding system:

(i)   restrictions on the fundibility of the Assigned Budget run counter to the principle that the Devolved Administration should have full expenditure-switching discretion; and

(ii)   these changes were made without either public announcement or justification, a situation that undermines transparency. The fact that this attracted minimal attention is perhaps attributable to the large volume of formula consequentials in SR2004 and to the Labour Party's role as UK Government and in all three Devolved Administrations.[29]

Although the Treasury's reasons for wishing to control the release of accumulated EYF to UK departments and Devolved Administrations are understandable given the large amounts now involved, the UK Government's control over such release gives them leverage over the Devolved Administrations that was not foreseen in 1999.

There are expected to be future changes in the UK public spending framework, as a result of the Treasury's "Clear Line of Sight" project.[30] This is likely to involve the abolition of cost of capital charges and of "non-cash". However, the Treasury will continue to be interested in the split between Resource DEL and Capital DEL as this affects compliance with UK and EU fiscal rules. In practice, the actual numbers relating to the Devolved Administrations may not be significant in relation to the fiscal aggregates, but the Devolved Administrations are deeply embedded in the UK public expenditure control system.

---

[26]   There are differences between Devolved Administrations in what is comparable and what is not, but that does not affect this point.
[27]   DEL stands for Departmental Expenditure Limit.
[28]   EYF stands for End-Year Flexibility and represents accumulated DEL underspends from earlier years, release of which to UK departments and the Devolved Administrations requires the agreement of the Treasury.
[29]   This issue arose while the Northern Ireland Assembly was suspended and decisions were taken by Direct Rule ministers in the Northern Ireland Office.
[30]   Treasury, *Alignment (Clear Line of Sight) Project*, Cm 7567, London, Stationery Office, 2009.

2. Formula By-pass and the Barnett Squeeze

(e) *Has convergence of levels of public spending in Scotland, Wales and Northern Ireland based on the English level of spending happened, and if not why?*

The mathematical properties of the Barnett Formula will, over time in the context of rising public expenditure, create a movement towards convergence on UK = 100, but there has never been a UK government commitment to arrive there. Full convergence would take place over a long period[31] and would only apply to that part of identifiable public expenditure that falls within the coverage of the Barnett Formula. There would not be convergence on UK = 100 of the indexes of per capita identifiable expenditure.

Inadequate data in the public domain mean that indexes that are calculated are only proxies for the correct aggregate. My own judgement is that, if appropriate data were available, it would provide evidence of some convergence—but not as much as expected. This judgement is heavily influenced by an analysis published in 2002 by Dr Andrew Goudie, Chief Economic Adviser to the Scottish Government.[32]

Although it is not possible to quantify the relative importance of factors that have inhibited convergence, several can be identified:

— in the case of Scotland, population relative to that of England has continued to fall and—even with updated population relatives for the calculation of formula consequentials—the per capita expenditure index is affected by the relative-to-England reduction in the denominator;

— not all public expenditure changes actually go through the formula; by-pass—if more favourable than formula consequentials—would operate against convergence;

— prior to 1992, there was some continuing up-rating for inflation for the horizon year coming into the Public Expenditure Survey period;[33] and

— there is a lot of noise in the data, arising from, *inter alia*, transfers of functions, changes in accounting conventions, and improvements in data collection.

If there were now to be a period of retrenchment of nominal-terms public expenditure in England that is assessed as comparable, then the mathematical properties of the Barnett Formula would—if not offset—lead to divergence rather than convergence.

(f) *To what extent did by-passing of the Formula occur before 1999? Has scope for such "Formula by-passes" changed? What have been the consequences of that change in scope?*

I wrote about formula by-pass in the pre-devolution period,[34] but it was only possible to describe—not quantify—examples. It is my understanding that, after 1992, the general tightening of public expenditure control limited opportunities for by-pass that was favourable to the territorial Secretaries of State.

Devolution in 1999 changed the Barnett Formula from a formula within a single government into an inter-governmental mechanism. With the publication of the funding rules (Statement of Funding Policy), which had never before been in the public domain, there was more transparency about processes but very limited transparency about relevant numbers.

There is a terminological problem about what constitutes by-pass. If this signifies anything that does not go through the Formula, then there has been positive by-pass to Wales (Objective 1 funding) and Northern Ireland (borrowing powers under the Regeneration and Reform Initiative).

By-pass was traditionally seen as beneficial to the territorial Secretaries of State, in the sense that they secured more funds than if the Formula had been strictly applied. Much of the discussion of formula by-pass originated in puzzlement about less-than-predicted convergence. However, there is no reason for this necessarily to be the case: for example, in-year allocations to UK departments for services in England out of the Reserve do not generate formula consequentials for the Devolved Administrations. Increases in expenditure in England might be structured in ways that avoid being categorised as comparable expenditure.

---

[31] More precisely, when the cumulative increments that have passed through the Formula have become extremely large in relation to the inherited expenditure base.

[32] A Goudie, "GERS and fiscal autonomy", *Scottish Affairs*, No 41, 2002, pp 56–85. Some updating has been done in successive issues of *Government Expenditure & Revenues in Scotland*.

[33] This important 1992 change to UK-wide practice, which passed a greater proportion of expenditure changes through the Barnett Formula, was not publicly announced until December 1997.

[34] D A Heald, "Territorial public expenditure in the United Kingdom", *Public Administration*, Vol 72(2), 1994, pp 147–75.

3. DATA QUALITY AND AVAILABILITY

(g) *Are sufficient data available to enable a clear understanding of how public spending is distributed across the UK, and to show the working of the Formula as set out in the Statement of Funding Policy?*

This constitutes two quite separate questions. On the first, the territorial data in *Public Expenditure: Statistical Analyses* are much improved, particularly with regard to the pattern of spending within England. However, there is no counterpart in Wales or Northern Ireland to *Government Expenditure & Revenues in Scotland*. In part this reflects the different nature of political debate from that in Scotland, and also the realisation that such an exercise would show the public finances of both Northern Ireland and Wales to be very weak.

On the second, detailed expositions of how the Formula operates in practice have not been published by the UK Government. For example, the generation of formula consequentials and the evolution of the Assigned Budgets have not been properly documented, with the gaps partially filled by academic analyses.[35] This has contributed to widespread misunderstanding of how the Formula works, and indirectly to the erosion of its legitimacy.

(h) *What additional data, or ways of presenting data, would be necessary to undertake a new needs assessment, or otherwise to reform the Formula?*

This is a massive question, to which my brief answers appear elsewhere in this memorandum of evidence.

(i) *What additional data, or ways of presenting data, should be available to ensure that the Formula is transparent in its application?*

Transparency in the application of the Formula, as it now operates, requires important changes, including the following:

— continuous updating of the published Statement of Funding Policy whenever there are changes (for example, in comparability percentages, populations and operating rules). At present the only updates are published at Spending Reviews, which are timed at the convenience of the UK Government, and information in the public domain lags practice;

— publication of time series of comparable spending in England, which requires three sets of tables because of differences in the scope of devolved expenditure in the three Devolved Administrations. This would bring into the public domain the three notional English blocks which generate formula consequences for the Devolved Administrations;

— automatic publication of "generation of formula consequentials" tables[36] whenever the Barnett Formula is applied; and

— automatic publication of the "chain-linking"[37] of one public expenditure announcement to the next, thereby identifying, *inter alia*, the effect of classification and accounting changes.

On a different but related point, updates of the 1979 Needs Assessment that have been prepared by the UK Government should be put in the public domain. These will not have direct policy relevance because circumstances have changed much since 1979: for example, there have been marked changes in the demographic composition of England. The main reason for urging publication now is that they are presently available only to the UK Government and not to the Devolved Administrations or the public. In addition, access to them might inform discussion about whether to have a future needs assessment and, if so, how to conduct it.

(j) *What body should undertake the collection and publication of such data?*

The answer depends on which data this question refers to. With regard to Question (h), the UK Parliament should establish an independent Territorial Exchequer Board as the Treasury does not have the credibility across the United Kingdom to undertake a needs assessment. The Devolved Administrations should have rights of nomination to this Board. If there is to be a needs assessment, it is unlikely that this can be done in a rough and ready way, and so that implies using Australia's Commonwealth Grants Commission as a model.

With regard to Question (i), this is a role that is best performed by the Treasury, in consultation with the Finance directorates of the Devolved Administrations. The additional information to be placed in the public domain is mostly generated, or could be generated, from existing databases held by the Treasury.

---

[35] See D A Heald and A McLeod, "The embeddedness of UK devolution finance within the public expenditure system", *Regional Studies*, Vol 39(4), pp 495–518. However, such academic analyses are one-offs and retrospective, therefore not meeting the transparency requirement of a timely and continuous flow of information.

[36] See Heald and McLeod, op cit, *Regional Studies*, 2005.

[37] See Heald and McLeod, op cit, *Regional Studies*, 2005.

4. Need for Reform/Alternatives to the Existing Formula

(k) *Do the advantages of the Formula as presently constituted outweigh its disadvantages?*

The answer depends on how this particular question is interpreted. Does it apply only to the generation of consequentials or to the funding system more generally (ie protected base, formula consequentials dependent on changes in England, and expenditure-switching discretion)? Moreover, advantages and disadvantages have to be evaluated in relation to credible alternative funding models.

A comprehensive answer would stray outside the terms of reference of the Committee. However, it is my view that, though some extension of taxation powers is desirable,[38] there are powerful factors in the United Kingdom that suggest that the Devolved Administrations will continue to be largely funded by grant from the UK Government. In such a context, it is essential to preserve the expenditure-switching discretion that has been a major feature of both pre-devolution and devolution.

(l) *Should the Barnett Formula be (a) retained in its current form, (b) amended or (c) replaced entirely?*

Option (a) has to be associated with greater transparency about the system, as this is a necessary feature now that it is intergovernmental rather than intra-governmental, and inter-party rather than intra-party. Retention is the default option if there is no agreement on alternatives.

Option (b) is not well-differentiated from (a) because the Barnett Formula system has clearly evolved through time.

Option (c) might be semantic—the name changes but the substance does not—or substantive. On the assumption that neither independence nor the reversal of devolution is being considered, that leaves two substantive funding arrangements:

— the conduct of a needs assessment which, after reporting and agreement, would require a formula mechanism to phase the movement of actual spending towards assessed spending need (on the assumption that sudden adjustment would be both disruptive to public services and politically destabilising); and

— a move to a system in which the spending of a Devolved Administration depends upon its own revenue generation and explicit equalisation payments. This is often described as "fiscal autonomy", but I would only accept that label if the Devolved Administration had control over tax rates (if not of bases) and extensive borrowing powers.

There has been discussion of modifying the Barnett Formula by using inverse GDP.[39] If this only applied to the increment, it would make relatively little difference to Scotland (whose per capita GDP is not far below UK = 100), but it would significantly benefit Wales and Northern Ireland. Alternatively, it seems to have been suggested that it could apply to the determination of Assigned Budgets. Given the scope of devolved functions, which exclude social security, there is no logic in treating per capita GDP as closely related to the overall need to spend of Devolved Administrations. Other factors are likely to be much more important: for example, socio-demographic characteristics and participation rates in publicly-provided education and health services.

I have briefly discussed in this response how the operation of the Barnett Formula could be improved. If it were to be "replaced entirely", the replacement scheme would have to be assessed carefully to establish whether it is consistent with the political objectives of devolution.

It is not an accident that the financial relationship between Scotland and the United Kingdom has been partly governed by formula (Goschen then Barnett) for about 100 of the last 120 years.[40] This is attributable to both ease of administration, particularly in the context of tight deadlines, and to the desire to minimise political conflict about expenditure that constitutes a small proportion of UK totals. In the context of Scotland's continuing membership of the United Kingdom, I would predict the continuation of a formula mechanism, whether or not that is called the Barnett Formula.

The viability of such formula mechanisms implicitly depends upon broad agreement across governments within the United Kingdom about the scope and size of the public sector. For example, a move in England to replace publicly-provided/funded provision by private provision would generate large negative formula

---

[38] I discuss this matter in my evidence to the Calman and Holtham Commissions.

[39] The inverse GDP proposal has been advanced by Professor Iain McLean of Nuffield College, Oxford; see I McLean and A McMillan, *Regional finance and GDP in Europe*, Memorandum submitted by Professor Iain McLean and Alistair McMillan, Treasury Committee Sub-Committee Minutes of Evidence, 3 July 2002, available at: http://www.parliament.the-stationery-office.com/pa/cm200102/cmselect/cmtreasy/1047/2070305.htm.

[40] D A Heald and A McLeod, "Scotland's fiscal relationships with England and the United Kingdom", in W Miller (ed), *Anglo-Scottish Relations, from 1900 to Devolution and Beyond*, Proceedings of the British Academy 128, Oxford, Oxford University Press, 2005, pp 95–112.

consequentials. Policy decisions about England have first-mover advantage: the resulting expenditure increases or decreases are then transmitted to the Devolved Administrations.

There is a further asymmetry. The funding rules require the devolved administrations to meet any additional costs imposed on the UK Government by their decisions. While there is some symmetry in that the UK government has to meet the additional costs for the Devolved Administrations of any of its decisions (provided they are not met by the operation of the Barnett formula), policy measures taken by Devolved Administrations that reduce the costs of UK departments do not lead to an increase in the Assigned Budget. This was the subject of dispute when Scotland adopted free personal care for the elderly in 2002 without gaining access to UK savings in attendance allowances.

(m) *Should the Barnett Formula be replaced by a system more adequately reflecting relative needs, costs of services or a combination of both? If so, what factors should be considered as part of a needs assessment?*

The wording of this question assumes that there is a current misalignment between actual spending in the four countries and the spending that would be validated by a needs assessment considering relative needs and costs of services. This might indeed be the case, but it is noticeable that criticism of the Barnett Formula in Scotland, Wales and Northern Ireland focuses on the "Barnett squeeze", usually portrayed as undesirable if not malign. In contrast, discussion in England usually focuses on alleged over-funding of Scotland and sometimes of Wales and Northern Ireland. However, comparisons of spending in Scotland, Wales and Northern Ireland with that in a specific English region have nothing directly to do with Barnett Formula, which affects the Scotland: England relative but not the within-England distribution.

Enumeration of factors relevant to a needs assessment is beyond the length of this written evidence. The contested issues are likely to be (a) the model of provision that is regarded as "standard" for costing purposes, and (b) the indicators that are considered valid causes of additional spending. There would be much rhetoric about neglecting genuine need and rewarding failure.

(n) *What practical and conceptual difficulties (particularly for defining "need") would arise in carrying out a needs-based assessment? How can these difficulties be overcome?*

There is sufficient UK evidence (eg distribution formulae for health and education) and international evidence (eg the work of the Commonwealth Grants Commission in Australia) to show that it is technically possible to produce quantitative indicators of the relative need to spend of particular jurisdictions. However, such exercises are time-consuming, data-hungry and expensive. They are, and always will be, politically controversial. Needs assessments are heavily driven by weighted population, which is an important characteristic given present controversies about measuring the size of the UK population in the context of high gross rates of emigration and (legal and illegal) immigration.

The major difficulties which would confront a UK-wide needs assessment include the following:

(i)   the needs assessment would take place in a context of contradictory expectations of final outcome (eg that the present relatives of Scotland and Northern Ireland would be shown to be justified by need; that Wales would be shown to be underfunded; and that England—and in particular certain regions of England—would be shown to be unfairly treated in relation to the Devolved Administrations, notably Scotland). This context would heavily politicise the environment within which the needs assessment took place;

(ii) the definition of need is, at least in part, values-specific, time-specific and location-specific. For example, the 1979 Needs Assessment[41] did not consider that the additional costs of bilingualism in Wales was a valid need indicator, a decision that now seems surprising. The need for spending on the elderly depends not only on longer life expectancies but also on changed attitudes about what is socially acceptable, and also the greater proportion of older voters. Prominent issues in a future needs assessment might be whether parallel denominational and non-denominational school systems are a need indicator or a policy choice, and whether English not being the home language is a need indicator for school education;

(iii) needs assessments usually take place in the context of a large number of jurisdictions, in which no one jurisdiction dominates the picture. With England constituting 85 per cent of the UK population (and likely to increase in future owing to demographic trends), any weighted average is much closer to England than to the Devolved Administrations. Where policies diverge, the issue would arise as to which policy should be costed: for example, the Scottish model of free personal care for the elderly or the English model. The calculated relative needs indexes might be quite sensitive to that choice. The Devolved Administrations would be fearful of a needs assessment becoming an extension of existing

---

[41] Treasury, *Needs Assessment Study: Report*, London, HM Treasury, 1979.

English funding models, thereby institutionalising policy leadership by UK departments with responsibilities for England. Such an extension would also have implications for England: some of the criticisms from English regions that the Barnett Formula is unfair to them appear to be rooted in discontent with the within-England formulae. To the extent that there is substance in periodic allegations that within-England formulae are manipulated for political reasons, extending such formulae to the Devolved Administrations would import irrelevant considerations into the assessment of their need-to-spend;

(iv) the "inherited base plus formula-based increment" model has protected the expenditure-switching discretion of the territorial Secretaries of State and of the Devolved Administrations. There is some public pressure for the Devolved Administrations to spend formula consequentials generated by changes in, for example, health expenditure in England on their own health programmes, but this is manageable and relates only to the increment. A needs assessment that explicitly stated how much a Devolved Administration "needed to spend" on individual programmes might strengthen sector-specific lobbies and pressurise conformity of actual spending with centrally-assessed need to spend; and

(v) before agreeing to participate in a needs assessment, the Devolved Administrations would be well advised to secure an agreement on the processes to be adopted in the case of assessed need to spend being calculated as less than actual spending. A sudden reduction in spending after a needs assessment would be seriously disruptive of service provision, and a sudden increase might be difficult to spend wisely. The adjustments—especially downward—would have to be phased over a number of years, probably by a formula.[42]

(o) *Should a needs-based assessment seek to encompass a wide-range of factors or be limited to a smaller number of indicators of "need"?*

If there is to be a needs assessment which then directly influences funding, it is difficult to envisage this not being a comprehensive exercise that encompasses a wide range of factors. Otherwise, there would be endless arguments about the hypothetical effects of excluded factors, including those used in distribution formulae within the devolved jurisdiction.

There is a different possible use of a needs assessment, one for which a more broad-brush approach might be acceptable. The purpose would be a pilot exercise to check on how needs relatives relate to existing expenditure relatives; for example, a Devolved Administration might believe that convergence has gone too far or the Treasury might believe that convergence has not gone far enough.

It is known from media reports and memoirs that the Treasury has, at various dates, updated the 1979 Needs Assessment, but nothing has ever been published. Two significant changes to the Formula have related to the population measure (the 1992 one-off updating of population relatives and the 1999 move to annual updating) and the several extensions of scope (expenditure previously outside the Formula has been brought within). The Committee might ask the Treasury to provide at least a summary of these updates to the 1979 Needs Assessment study, and what, if any, changes were subsequently made to the operation of the Formula.

(p) *Who should carry out a needs-based assessment, if one were to take place?*

The credibility and legitimacy of a needs assessment require that it be undertaken by an independent body. A Territorial Exchequer Board might have a governing body, on which the Devolved Administrations and the UK Government had representation, with the needs assessment undertaken by its operational arm. Results of a needs assessment undertaken by the UK Government would not be accepted, particularly if they led to a reduction in funding to one/all of the Devolved Administrations.

5. DECISION MAKING AND DISPUTE RESOLUTION

(q) *How effective, appropriate and fair are the processes and criteria by which HM Treasury determines matters relating to the Barnett Formula? In particular, is the way HM Treasury determines whether items of spending in England do or do not attract consequential payments under the Formula, and claims by the DAs on the UK Reserve, appropriate and fair?*

On the detail of comparability decisions and of claims on the UK Reserve, the Committee should seek evidence from the Devolved Administrations and the Treasury. However, two issues have reached the public domain:

— the Devolved Administrations have been dissatisfied with the classification of Olympics expenditure

[42] For an analysis of a modified Barnett Formula converging on a needs-weighted population index, instead of on UK = 100, see D A Heald and A McLeod, "Beyond Barnett? Funding devolution", in J Adams and P Robinson (eds), *Devolution in Practice: Public Policy Differences within the UK*, London, Institute for Public Policy Research, 2002, pp 147–75.

as non-comparable, even that expenditure openly declared to be motivated by the economic regeneration of East London; and

— because claims on the Reserve do not generate formula consequentials,[43] this affords a mechanism whereby some additional expenditure in England (eg on prisons) can be financed through a claim on the Reserve rather than as a programme increase triggering formula consequentials.

These examples confirm the importance of developing more formal rules that govern Treasury decisions on such operational matters, together with an appeals procedure. On 4 March 2009, the Scottish Government's Finance and Sustainable Growth Secretary (John Swinney) met the Chief Secretary to the Treasury (Yvette Cooper) and the Secretary of State for Scotland (James Murphy), in connection with the funding of the second Forth Road Bridge. The results of that meeting were loudly proclaimed by the UK Government as an "unprecedented package" for Scotland. In fact, there was little new in the announcement, other than the quantification of the formula consequentials from the London Crossrail project and announcements on access to End-Year Flexibility and retention of the proceeds of asset sales. The UK Government made it sound as if this was special funding for the second Forth Bridge, as well as promoting Public-Private Partnerships as a funding model.[44] This episode illustrated the unacceptable level of discretion currently held by the Treasury and the willingness of the UK Government to use this for partisan purposes.

(r) Are the existing procedures for resolving disputes between HM Treasury Ministers, territorial Secretaries of State and the Devolved Administrations about funding issues adequate?

I have no experience of these procedures. However, I would stress the importance of funding mechanisms being fully documented in the public domain. This is particularly important in the context of Devolved Administrations predominantly funded by grant from the UK Exchequer. There is the potential to discredit the funding mechanism without there being alternative mechanisms commanding sufficient support for successful implementation.

I mentioned above the Forth Bridge funding announcement on 4 March 2009. Another example is the fact that the Scottish Government reportedly does not yet know the size of the negative formula consequentials for 2010–11 arising from the £5 billion "value for money savings" in UK spending announced in November 2008's Pre-Budget 2008.[45] Although the figure of £500 million has been much quoted in the Scottish media, the actual number depends on the extent to which the UK expenditure reductions fall on comparable programmes. I would have expected at least a provisional figure for negative consequentials to have been notified by March 2009. This uncertainty hampers decision-making in the Devolved Administrations at a time when it is important to avoid unnecessarily aggravating the recession.

(s) *How could dispute resolution procedures be improved?*

I have no comment to make.

March 2009

Memorandum by The Independent Expert Group to the Commission on Scottish Devolution
[from Page 10 Paragraphs 5.7.1 to 5.7.2 of the Independent Expert Group's First Report]

1. CONSTITUTIONAL DESIGN AND FINANCING DEVOLUTION

1.1 Systems of financing sub national governments inevitably involve trade offs. The choices made between these trade offs require the philosophy (if there is one), or at least, the structure (as implied by the division of powers and the extent of their asymmetry) of the state to be established first. Finance is not the first link in a chain of constitutional design, but once the constitutional model is chosen, systems of territorial finance can

---

[43] This point is symmetrical in that access by the Devolved Administrations to the Reserve does not feedback to the UK departments responsible for programmes in England. However, it would appear that the main issue does relate to UK departments having access to the Reserve.

[44] Recourse to a Public-Private Partnership (PPP) would not resolve the budgetary problem faced by the Scottish Government in connection with Forth Road Bridge funding. From 2009–10, the UK Government and Devolved Administrations are moving from accounting on the basis of UK Generally Accepted Accounting Practice to International Financial Reporting Standards. This reflects the UK Government's commitment to use best private sector accounting practice. It is widely expected that almost all PPP projects not already on the public sector balance sheet will move on-balance sheet. Accordingly, a PPP-financed Forth Road Bridge would score against the Assigned Budget in the same way as would a publicly financed Bridge. As well as attacking the SNP Scottish Government's "ideological hostility to PPPs", the UK Government might have been signalling that more favourable treatment would be available if the PPP option were followed.

[45] Treasury, *Pre-Budget Report—Facing Global Challenges: Supporting People through Difficult Times*, Cm 7484, London, Stationery Office, November 2008, para 6.32 on p 122.

be considered which are likely to help the state to function in the way it is intended, and their properties can be considered, producing a balance sheet of strengths and weaknesses.

[from pages 20 to 23, paragraphs 1.3.1 to 1.9.2 of the Independent Expert Group's First Report]

2. RELATIVE LEVELS OF PUBLIC SPENDING IN THE UK

2.1 Scotland's budget is often perceived by observers in the rest of the UK as over allocating resources to Scotland, usually at the expense of the regions of England. Viewed from Scotland, the current SNP led administration portrayed the allocation from the most recent spending review in 2007 as "the worst settlement since devolution". Both of these positions merit some exploration.

2.2 Public spending per head in Scotland has exceeded that in England since around 1900, long predating devolution. The arrangements that preceded Barnett—the Goschen Proportion—derived from the 19th century and assigned Scotland £11 for every £80 assigned to England and Wales on particular programmes. This 11/80 derived from the relative populations when this arrangement was introduced in 1888, but by 1901, the Scottish population had dropped to below 11/80th of that of England and Wales. This decline continued through the 20th century—by 1976 the Scottish population was nearer 8/80th of that of England and Wales, although by the 1970's there were different political imperatives for maintaining high levels of public expenditure in Scotland. And by the 1970s, public spending per head in Scotland was over 20 per cent above that in England.

2.3 This history is important, for although the Barnett formula only applies to changes to the budget, the way the formula and inflation were treated through much of the 1980's and 1990's to some degree locked in the historical budget baseline from the 1970's, which in turn was perceived as being overgenerous. Indeed, in 1979, a needs assessment exercise undertaken by the Government of the day, determined that Scotland's public spending needs per capita for a range of services then managed by the Scottish Office, were around 16 per cent higher than for England, whilst actual spending levels were around 22 per cent higher.

3. CONVERGENCE OF PUBLIC EXPENDITURE LEVELS

3.1 Other things being equal, and in particular the relative populations, Barnett will lead to convergence of public spending per head between the constituent parts of the UK. Convergence should occur as the sum of the incremental changes becomes greater over time in comparison to the initial block grant of year zero (in fact 1979-80). Hence, the per capita spending on devolved policies will asymptotically equalise. So one would expect that the block grant to the former Scottish Office in 1979/80 which gave Scotland a 22% advantage over England would, through the passage of successive population based incremental increases, now lead to a block grant corresponding to per head spending on devolved issues to be nearer that in England.

3.2 There is no published data to support an exact analysis of convergence. There is no data published for public expenditure over time that identifies spending in England, or spending elsewhere in the UK, on those matters that are devolved to Scotland. The identification of UK Government spending on matters devolved to Scotland is further complicated by the asymmetry of devolution in the UK. Additionally, over time, new matters are devolved, most recently railways, which resulted in a transfer from the DfT budget to Scotland.

3.3 Further frustrating such analysis is that what published data there is relates to actual spending rather than allocations. Barnett convergence should apply to allocated budgets, but analysis over short timescales will mean the real world differences between allocations and actual spending (for example by planning enquiries halting infrastructure projects) necessarily exist. These will result in actual spending data potentially providing a distorted picture. Expenditure control rules implemented since 1997 mean that Government Departments can allow for these real world situations under the End Year Flexibility (EYF) arrangements. The significance of this is highlighted by the Scottish Executive having accrued £1.5Billion in EYF by 2007, compared to a Departmental Expenditure Limit of around £25Billion for that year.

3.4 But putting these difficulties aside, the best data there is (see chart below) does not show the sort of convergence of public spending levels that one might have expected, especially given the high growth of public expenditure at the beginning of this decade.

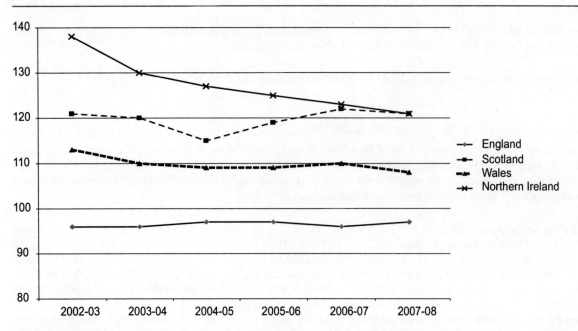

Chart: Index of identifiable public expenditure per head in the UK, excluding social protection and agriculture. UK = 100

3.5 Convergence has not happened for two reasons. Firstly, population factors were not updated very frequently until 1997, so Scotland's population decline relative to England would cause a degree of over allocation that will serve to work against convergence. Furthermore, the funding baseline of 1979, or the one created in each subsequent review, has not been adjusted downwards to reflect the relative reductions in Scotland's population. This will be significant, as Scotland's population has fallen by over 1 per cent since 1979 whilst that of England has grown by around 8 per cent. The second factor that has impeded convergence is that prior to 1992/3, inflation was allowed for in rolling forward the baselines of government departments, hence the Barnett convergence effect applied only to the real term expenditure growth (which was not substantial during this period). Since then, Barnett has been operated on a nominal cash basis—no separate addition is made for inflation and the overall change is determined by the formula.

3.6 Overall, it is not possible to conclusively rebut the grievance that Scotland continues to receive unduly high levels of public expenditure compared to the other countries and regions of the UK. There has been no new assessment of needs, and indeed assessing what constitutes need would be a controversial exercise in itself. For example, lower levels of life expectancy in Scotland might suggest a continuing need for higher levels of healthcare spending in Scotland than in England. However, what data there is does not show the sustained convergence in public spending one might expect to have occurred since Barnett began to be rigorously applied after 1997, which in turn suggests that some attributes of the original 1979 baseline may persist.

4. BARNETT SQUEEZE

4.1 But as stated above, some consider the exact opposite of this to be the case, and that Scotland is somehow hard done by Barnett. This prompts two observations.

4.2 Firstly, the term Barnett Squeeze is sometimes used to describe the arithmetical result of identical per head increases to public spending representing a greater percentage increase in per head spending in England than in Scotland. This arises because the English spending is from a lower per head base. The term "Barnett Squeeze" is therefore a presentational device to describe an intrinsic part of the operation of the formula.

5. WHEN SHOULD BARNETT APPLY?

5.1 A second criticism relates to the apparent uncertainty and sometimes, it is alleged, arbitrary nature of when spending has Barnett consequentials and when it does not. This has recently created tensions between the Devolved Administrations and the UK Government.

5.2 An example of this relates to the £1.2 Billion increase in spending on prisons in England and Wales in response to the Carter Review and pressure on prison places. This extra spending was taken from the UK reserve, outside of the Comprehensive Spending Review, meaning there was no Barnett consequential for Scotland. Further examples have been when spending has been deemed to be for the benefit of the UK as a whole, such as for the Channel Tunnel or for the 2012 London Olympics.

5.3 This criticism aside, one of the key attributes of the Barnett formula as currently applied is the ease with which it operates. It requires no complicated assessment of indicators, or even selection of indicators. Negotiations and disputes between the Devolved Administrations and the UK Government relate to the margins of the allocated budget rather than the greater part of its substance.

6. STRENGTHS AND WEAKNESSES

6.1 The key strengths of the Barnett formula are its operational simplicity, the stability of funding it provides to the Devolved Administrations and the clear reservation of managing economic and fiscal aggregates to the UK Government.

6.2 Starting with the baseline and using a population based formula to determine the changes to the budgets of the devolved administrations provides a streamlined process. Nearly any alternative is bound to be more complex and is likely to lead to protracted negotiations and/or incur additional administrative effort.

6.3 Barnett, allied to the UK Government's 3 year time horizon for spending plans, results in the Devolved Administrations having near total certainty over their assigned budget from year to year. They bear no revenue risk—that is borne by the UK Government.

6.4 Decisions over fiscal aggregates and stabilisation policy are entirely in the hands of central government, making policy coherence more readily achievable.

6.5 Perhaps the principal weakness of Barnett is that it creates a vertical fiscal imbalance:—the Scottish Parliament lacks financial accountability. This weakness also manifests itself in the Parliament having almost no control over the size of its budget. At present, the financial powers of the parliament relate almost entirely to spending decisions only. It has no powers to borrow for any purpose, nor does it have a tax base to borrow against. Furthermore, the absence of fiscal autonomy means that it is not able to exploit fiscal measures as policy instruments.

6.6 Part 1 of this [The Independent Expert Group's] report describes how a sub national government's revenue raising powers relate to its financial accountability with the links between spending and taxation more evident to the region's electorate. In other words, there is greater transparency of the trade-offs between the marginal benefit from extra services versus the extra costs of provision. At present the Scottish Parliament, SVR [the Scottish Parliament's Tax Varying Power or the Scottish Variable Rate] and local taxes aside, does not have such accountability. A different articulation of this argument is to note there is little political incentive to invoke policies to increase economic growth in Scotland because any increase in taxation revenue accrues to the UK Government.

6.7 Some commentators also assert that a vertical fiscal imbalance creates an incentive for governments to shift blame to one another and to shirk doing things that may be economically efficient but politically unpopular.

6.8 A related weakness of the current Barnett based system for financing the Devolved Administrations is that it is not enshrined in statute. Rather it is an accepted agreement between the Devolved Administrations and HM Treasury as set out in HM Treasury's "Statement of Funding Policy for the Devolved Administrations". So although this means that the operation of Barnett is very transparent and publicly accessible, changes do not require UK parliamentary approval or the agreement of the Devolved Administrations. This means that formula by-pass, parameter changes, and even changes in departmental baselines before applying the formula could be applied unilaterally by HM Treasury.

7. IMPACT ON EQUITY

7.1 The Scottish Parliament's budgetary allocation has no bearing on measured needs—therefore potentially creating a horizontal fiscal imbalance. The size of the original Barnett baseline in 1979 provided Scotland with a greater per capita expenditure than that in England. But Scotland now outperforms many areas of England—for example GVA/head in Scotland exceeds all the English regions outside of London, the East and the South East. This alone is not necessarily a good indicator of "need", but it does result in an increasing number of challenges to Scotland's budgetary allocation.

7.2 Although by its very nature, devolution means differing provision of public services will emerge in the longer run, these challenges are based on the assertion that some parts of the UK lose out, and it is therefore not possible to deliver similar levels of public services across the UK.

8. FISCAL CONSEQUENCES

8.1 As noted earlier, the Scottish Parliament—SVR and local taxation aside—has no tax raising powers. Nor can it increase its budget by borrowing as it has no tax base against which to borrow. But equally, as its revenues take the form of a block grant, it bears no revenue risk, so any need to borrow to compensate for lower than anticipated revenue streams is non existent.

8.2 This arrangement also means that the UK government is able to control fiscal and economic aggregates, with government debt centrally controlled. It also means that (again notwithstanding local taxation) that the tax base and rates are harmonised across the UK—there is no scope for tax competition between regions.

February 2009

Memorandum by the Local Government Association

SUMMARY

1. The Local Government Association is pleased to submit this memorandum, at the request of the Committee, to the House of Lords Select Committee on the Barnett Formula.

2. The evidence does not cover the formal view of the Association on the Barnett Formula. It does cover the following:

    (a) Make-up of relative needs formulae.

    (b) How relative needs fit into formula grant.

    (c) Development of the current formula grant system.

    (d) Updating and consulting on the formulae.

    (e) Key criticisms from local government of aspects of the formula grant system.

    (f) The case for an independent commission.

3. The key points made in the memorandum are:

    (a) Needs assessment is one part of a complex system—the effect of other parts of the system such as damping is crucial.

    (b) Although a variety of statistical techniques are used to calculate indicators, an important role is played by ministerial judgement.

    (c) The data used within formulae—notably population figures—has been criticised for not reflecting the current position faced by authorities.

    (d) The LGA would support an independent commission to oversee the grant settlement for local government.

NEEDS ASSESSMENTS IN THE FORMULA GRANT SYSTEM FOR DISTRIBUTING CENTRAL FINANCING TO ENGLISH LOCAL AUTHORITIES

4. The English formula grant system distributes £28.3 billion to local authorities in England in 2009–10. It is made up the following:

    (a) The "distributable amount" of National non-domestic rates (business rates)—£19.5 billion in 2009–10.

    (b) Revenue Support Grant—£4.5 billion in 2009–10.

    (c) The Police Grant—£4.3 billion in 2009–10.

5. Police Grant is distributed to Police Authorities. NNDR and RSG are distributed on the same basis:

    (a) a needs assessment (relative needs formulae—RNF) which is intended to reflect the relative costs of providing comparable services between different authorities. It takes account of characteristics such as population and social structure;

(b) a resources element (relative resources amount), which takes account of the different capacity of different areas to raise income from council tax due to the differing mix of properties. It is a negative amount as it represents assumed income for authorities;

(c) a central allocation which is the same per head for all authorities delivering the same services; and

(d) a floor damping block in order to give every authority a minimum grant increase. Grant increases to other authorities in the same class are scaled back to pay to bring all authorities up to the appropriate floor increase.

6. Thus needs assessments exist as one element in a complex system.

RELATIVE NEEDS FORMULAE

7. Relative Needs Formulae are set out in the Local Government Finance Report which is approved annually by the House of Commons.[46] In brief they consist of seven main service blocks, most of which are divided into sub-blocks (shown in brackets).

(a) Children's Services (Youth and Community services; Local Authority central education functions; Children's Social Care).[47]

(b) Adults Personal Social Services (Social Services for Older People; Social Services for Younger Adults).

(c) Police.

(d) Fire and Rescue.

(e) Highway Maintenance.

(f) Environmental, Protective and Cultural Services ("district" services; "county" services; fixed costs; flood defence; continuing Environment Agency Levies; Coast Protection).

(g) Capital Financing.

8. EPCS "district" and "county" services reflect the split between district and counties in two tier areas. "District" services include housing and council tax collection. "County" services include libraries and consumer protection. Unitary authorities such as metropolitan districts and London boroughs provide both sets of services.

9. Each of these blocks has a specific formula, which is set out in full in the Local Government Finance Report. In general they have the following format:

(a) An amount for the client group; for example the projected population aged 13–19 for youth services within the Children's Services Block.

(b) Top-ups for increased costs associated with particular characteristics of the population, such as deprivation, ethnicity and low income.

(c) A top-up for the increased costs of delivering services in sparse areas (in some of the blocks only).

(d) A top-up for higher input costs—mainly labour costs—in certain areas—known as the Area Cost Adjustment. This is expressed as a multiplicative factor. The labour costs element is based on the relative wages costs for relevant occupations in the local labour market, using a methodology recommended by a review commissioned by the government in 1996.[48]

10. The weights within relative needs formulae are set by a mixture of statistical analysis, mostly based on past spending or activity measures, and ministerial judgement. Annex 2 sets out briefly the position for each block/sub-block. An important source of data for indicators is the 2001 census.

11. The formula for Capital Financing is different to this—it is based on an estimate of historic debt, taking into account the annual supported borrowing allocations of the authority, on the basis of assuming a 4 per cent repayment of outstanding debt each year, and a pooled average rate of interest.

---

[46] The 2009–10 Local Government Finance Report is at http://www.local.communities.gov.uk/finance/0910/lgfr0910s/index.htm
[47] Note that this does not include schools' funding, which since 2006–07 has been done through a series of ring-fenced specific grants, principally the Dedicated Schools Grant.
[48] See technical guide on CLG website at http://www.local.communities.gov.uk/finance/0809/methaca.pdf

12. Each relative needs formula is scaled to a national control total; these are set out in Annex E of the Local Government Finance Report—the England total for all RNFs in 2009–10 is 0.7646. The scaling factors are in most cases close to unity—the weights of the coefficients are set to produce a result as close as possible to the predetermined control total and the final scaling factor is to ensure that they add up to 12 places of decimals.

13. The national control totals are indices—they do not represent amounts. The total of 0.7646 has no particular significance—it could as well be set to unity. According to CLG officials it was set to one during the phase of formula development before the 2006–07 settlement when schools' were still funded through formula grant.[49] The different service blocks have different weights within the total RNF—so for example in 2009–10 that for children's services is 0.1432 and that for adult personal social services is 0.2088—these are set by judgement.

RELATIVE NEEDS WITHIN FORMULA GRANT

14. Once calculated the Relative Needs formulae are split into a further series of elements reflecting which authorities are responsible for which services. These take account, for example, of the split in responsibilities between districts and counties in two tier areas.

15. These elements are as follows (with the service sub-blocks of which they are comprised in brackets):

(a) Upper tier (Children's Services, Adult Personal Social Services, Highway Maintenance, EPCS "county" services, continuing Environment Agency Levies).

(b) Police.

(c) Fire and rescue.

(d) EPCS "district" services.

(e) EPCS "mixed tier" services (fixed costs; flood defence; coast protection).

(f) Capital Financing.

16. For each of these elements the RNF is divided by total population so as to give RNF per head. From this is subtracted the minimum "threshold" RNF per head so to give an RNF per head above threshold.

17. The relevant RNF elements per head above threshold are aggregated to produce total RNF per head above threshold for each authority. This is then multiplied again by population and scaled to the total Needs Equalisation Amount—£17.519 billion in 2009–10.[50]

18. It can be seen therefore, that the Needs Equalisation Amount does not express total needs, rather relative needs.

19. A similar procedure is followed for the Relative Resources amount, which is negative, as it reflects capacity to raise income from council tax. The taxbase for each authority is divided by projected population to get taxbase per head. This is then split , again to reflect the different mix of service provision, into four. These weights are set by judgement.

(a) Upper Tier: (around 71 per cent of total taxbase in 2009–10).

(b) Lower Tier: (around 16 per cent of total taxbase in 2009–10).

(c) Police: (around 9 per cent of total taxbase in 2009–10).

(d) Fire and Rescue: (around 3 per cent of total taxbase in 2009–10).

20. Unitary authorities receive both the Upper and Lower Tier shares—or around 87 per cent of the total taxbase.

21. For each tier the taxbase per head is multiplied by the tier share. From this is subtracted the minimum "threshold" for each class of authority. The amounts below the threshold are then scaled to the total of relative resources amount,—£6.384 million in 2009–10.

22. The central allocation is made up of the sum of the elements below the needs threshold per head minus the sum of the elements above the resources threshold per head. Since these will be identical for all authorities responsible for the same services, it follows that the central allocation, per head, is identical for all authorities which deliver the same services.

---

[49] See http://www.statistics.gov.uk/events/gss2006/downloads/A1Sussex.doc p14

[50] The formula grant model for each authority for 2009–10 is on the DCLG website at http://www.local.communities.gov.uk/finance/0910/fgmodel0910.xls

23. Finally, a damping mechanism is applied to the sum of the relative needs, relative resources and central allocation (and police grant, for police authorities). For each authority class a minimum grant increase is set, when compared with the authority's allocation the previous year (adjusted for any functional changes to enable a like for like for like comparison). Authorities' increases above this minimum are scaled back by a constant percentage in order for the total damping effect to be zero for each class of authority. The minimum grant increases and scaling back percentages are, for each damping class in 2009–10 the following:

(a) Authorities with children's and adults service responsibilities (London boroughs, metropolitan districts, unitary authorities, counties); Floor: 1.75 per cent; scaling factor—73 per cent.

(b) Police authorities: Floor: 2.5 per cent; scaling factor—87 per cent.

(c) Fire authorities: Floor: 0.5 per cent; scaling factor—67 per cent.

(d) Shire districts: Floor 0.5 per cent; scaling factor—62 per cent.

24. The effect of the damping block is to override the needs and resources parts of the formulae. As the average increase per damping class is the same both before and after damping, the nearer the floor is set to the average increase the larger the scaling factor will be. So in 2007–08 for police authorities the average grant increase was 3.64 per cent. The floor was set at 3.6 per cent; meaning a scaling factor of—98 per cent. The result was virtually a flat rate grant increase for all police authorities in that year.

25. The box below shows how all these elements are put together to produce the formula grant for Bolton in 2009–10:

CALCULATION OF FORMULA GRANT FOR BOLTON IN 2009–10

Relative Needs

Bolton's Children's Services RNF is 0.0008023—or around 0.56 per cent of the total Children's Services RNF for England

This is added to other Upper Tier RNF elements to give an Upper Tier RNF for Bolton of 0.002608

This is divided by Bolton's projected mid-2009 population (266,293) to give an Upper Tier RNF per head[51] of 0.0097919

From this is subtracted the Upper Tier threshold (0.0059285—the Upper Tier RNF per head for Wokingham) to give an Upper Tier RNF per head above threshold for Bolton of 0.0038634

This is added to the RNF per head above threshold for Lower Tier, Mixed Tier and Capital Financing to give a Total RNF per head above threshold for Bolton of 0.0055754

This is multiplied back by population to give a Total RNF above threshold for Bolton of 0.001485

This is scaled to the England relative needs amount (£17,519 million) to give a Needs Equalisation Amount for Bolton of £94.237804million

Relative Resources

Bolton's projected council taxbase (Band D equivalents) in 2009 is 84,020

Expressed as taxbase per head this is 0.3155162

This is multiplied by the Lower Tier share (0.1618147) to give a Lower Tier Taxbase per head for Bolton of 0.0510552

From this is subtracted the Lower Tier resource threshold (0.0435316—the Lower Tier taxbase per head for Hull) to give a Lower Tier taxbase per head required to reach threshold for Bolton of 0.0075235

To this is added the Upper Tier taxbase per head to reach threshold—obtained through a similar procedure—to reach a Total taxbase per head required to reach threshold for Bolton of 0.0406216

This is then multiplied back by population to give a Total taxbase required to reach threshold for Bolton of 10,817

This is then scaled to the England relative resources amount (£ − 6,384 million) to give a Resources Equalisation Amount for Bolton of £ − 15.567996 million

Central Allocation

The total Needs Threshold per head for Bolton (and for all unitary authorities) is £498.79—this is the sum of all the needs element thresholds scaled to the total Needs Equalisation amount

From this is subtracted the Resources Threshold per head (£338.26) to give a net threshold per head of £160.53

This is multiplied by population and scaled to the total Central Allocation (£12,868 million) to give a Central Allocation for Bolton of £50.989027 million

Formula Grant before damping

Bolton's Formula Grant before damping—the sum of the Needs Equalisation Amount and the Central Allocation less the Resource Equalisation Amount is £129.658834 million

Effect of damping

Compared with Bolton's adjusted Formula Grant for 2008–09 (£119.572375 million) this would give Bolton a grant increase of £10.086459 million or 8.44 per cent

The amount of the increase above 1.75 per cent is scaled back by—72.92 per cent to give a final formula grant increase for Bolton of £4.257533 million or 3.56 per cent—a total Formula Grant of £123.829909 million

This is split between redistributed Business Rates (£100.608231 million) and Revenue Support Grant (£23.221678 million) pro-rata to national totals.

---

[51] Strictly speaking, RNF per million of population, but called RNF per head in CLG documentation

RELATIVE NEEDS FORMULAE COMPARED TO PREVIOUS SYSTEMS FOR ALLOCATING FORMULA GRANT

26. The internal structure of RNFs is not substantially different from the system of standard spending assessments (SSAs) which applied from 1990–91 to 2002–03 or from the system of formula spending shares (FSSs) which applied from 2003–04 to 2005–06. SSAs were a significant simplification of the system of Grant Related Expenditure Assessments which applied from 1981 to 1990 and which contained up to 40 separate service assessments. In SSAs the number of main service blocks was reduced to seven and many of the small services were grouped together in an Other Services Block—later renamed the Environmental, Protective and Cultural Services block. Formula Spending Shares introduced a clearer presentation of the basic per client amount and top-ups for the different service blocks and sub-blocks but maintained the same internal structure.

27. Both formula spending shares and standard spending assessments were expressed in cash terms—as the amount of spending which the government was prepared to support through grant. Formula Grant was derived as follows:

Formula Grant (before damping) = Formula spending share—(taxbase x assumed national council tax)

28. The new way of expressing formula grant has departed from any system of spending assessments and no longer contains an explicit figure for assumed national council tax. However the needs and resources blocks and the central allocation can be recast in the old form. Annex 1 shows this graphically.

Formula Changes and Consultation with Local Government

29. Since 2006–07, multi-year settlements have been announced in the November before the start of the period to which they relate; November 2005 for the 2006–07 and 2007–08 period and November 2007 for the period covering the years 2008–09, 2009–10 and 2010–11. Within multi-year settlements all data other than population and taxbase projections are frozen. The population projections are updated annually based on the most recent ONS subnational population projections for the year of the settlement (so the 2009–10 settlement uses 2009 projections, which are based on the five years of mid-year estimates to 2004 projected forward) and the taxbase projections updated by a similar methodology devised by CLG officials.

30. Between settlements there is a process of formula review carried out by CLG and other government departments in consultation with local government, through a body called the Settlement Working Group. CLG consults on a number of possible formula changes before they are implemented; the latest consultation, for the 2008–11 period, was in summer 2007. The multi-year settlements incorporate a number of these changes and in addition update data within the formulae—for example the latest available figures from the Annual Survey of Hours and Earnings for the Area Cost Adjustment.

VIEWS OF LOCAL GOVERNMENT ON THE FORMULA GRANT SYSTEM

31. It should be borne in mind that by its very nature the fairness of any distribution formula is bound to seen by authorities in the light of the way they perceive themselves to be treated. The following are some of the key criticisms:

(a) Amount of judgement used within the formula. Some of the key totals within formula grant are set by judgement rather than by formula. These include:

   (i) the total size of the needs and resources blocks and the central allocation;

   (ii) the tier shares in the relative resources block;

   (iii) the weight of the different service blocks relative to each other within relative needs formulae; and

   (iv) the "floors" and scaling factor used for damping.

(b) Effect of the damping block. The damping block can have the effect of cancelling out changes in the relative needs block. This has particularly become an issue in the case of supported borrowing (the capital financing sub-block) where authorities on the "floor" do not get any extra resources because of new supported borrowing, and authorities above the floor have this support scaled back.

(c) Lack of transparency and complexity. Although, as Annex 1 shows, the changes introduced in 2006–07 were purely presentational, they were widely seen as making the formula less transparent and easy to understand.

(d) Instability. Comparatively small changes within the formula can have significant effects. This includes changing the "threshold" authority within the different relative needs formulae which determines the split between the amount of the relative needs formula funded by the relative needs amount and that funded by the central allocation.

(e) Statistical techniques used in formulae. Using past expenditure to set weights through regression has been criticised on the grounds that it tends to give more weight to characteristics of authorities which spent more in the past. Multi-level modelling, as used in the Children's and Younger Adults blocks tries to get away from this as it concentrates on differences within authorities rather than differences between authorities but this has also been criticised for ignoring what are seen as real differences in need to spend between authorities.

(f) Population projections. Population is the most important variable within the needs formulae; it accounts for around 45 per cent of the total relative needs formula for all services.[52] ONS sub-national population projections have been criticised within local government for their backward looking nature—essentially they assume that past population growth trends continue. Thus they cannot predict growth such as new housing developments which do not conform to past trend growth. Population projections also omit short term migrants.

(g) Age of data used within formulae. Some of the data used in the formulae dates back to the 1980s. The 2001 census, now eight years old, is a crucial source of data. Some authorities argue that this data no longer represents the true situation.

(h) Influence of the relative resources block. It has been argued that changes in the relative resources block will have an influence before changes in the relative needs block. For example, new population growth may not come into the population figures for five to 10 years, whereas new houses—and hence new assumed income from council tax—will have a more immediate effect on the resources block.

32. However despite these criticisms local government prefers a formula basis for distributing grant rather than a bid-based system, such as was discussed in the Green Paper "Modernising Local Government Finance" in 2000.[53]

AN INDEPENDENT COMMISSION TO OVERSEE THE FINANCIAL SETTLEMENT FOR LOCAL GOVERNMENT

33. In our final evidence to the Lyons Inquiry, submitted in December 2006,[54] we made the case for an independent commission.

34. The purpose of an independent commission is seen as to depoliticise that which can be de-politicised. There are a number of precedents for this in banking and finance, for example the set up of giving the Bank of England control over the management of interest rates and the establishment of a light-touch regulator in the form of the Financial Services Authority.

35. The independent commission would not be involved in making political choices which should properly be down to ministers. Its role would be to provide independent evidence, evaluation and advice to central and local government. This would involve grant distribution and also provide the opportunity to devolve from Government a number of tasks which are currently carried out by government.

36. The key tasks of the Commission would be:

(a) Stewardship of the overall funding regime, including taking a view of the adequacy of resources for local government;

(b) Research and advice on grant distribution and equalisation mechanisms, ensuring that data and formulae were as up to date as possible, and co-ordinating formula reviews at regular intervals, This would include consideration of damping arrangements, consultation with local government and recommendations to ministers and the Central Local Partnership. It would take as its model the Australian Commonwealth Grants Commission (see Annex 3)

(c) Keeping data and taxbase valuations up to date; by commissioning contract work from the Valuation Office Agency, as necessary. This would include both council tax and business rate valuations.

(d) Regulation of a devolved fees and charges regime, and to investigate and advise on new charging proposals.

(e) Research on business rates; providing evidence for a guideline increase, which could be used as part of a relocalised regime. This could include evidence of GDP growth, council tax growth, and wider price inflation.

(f) Research and evidence on local government pay and prices, including for contracted services. It could commission and maintain an index of local government pay and prices, separate from the GDP

---

[52] Based on analysis in Society of County Treasurers—Standard Spending Indicators 2005/06—updated for service changes
[53] See http://www.local.communities.gov.uk/greenpap/index.htm—Part 3
[54] See http://www.lga.gov.uk/lga/aio/545958

deflator, which would command respect from both central and local government, and provide evidence for use in spending review work by both central and local government.

(g) Research and advice on new proposals for local government income.

37. Appointments to the Commission should be by an open national process.

April 2009

Annex 1

DERIVATION OF THE CURRENT FORMULA GRANT SYSTEM FROM THE OLD SYSTEM OF FORMULA SPENDING SHARES

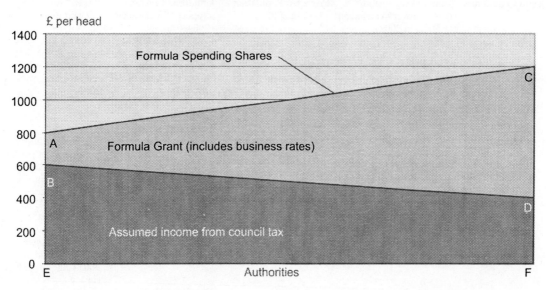

The figure above shows a simplified model of the grant system up to 2006–07, expressed on a per head basis, assuming all authorities deliver the same services. Formula spending shares (ACFE) reflect the differences in need per head. Assumed income from council tax (BDFE) reflect the differences in resources. Formula grant including redistributed business rates (before damping) (ACDB) is the difference between the two.

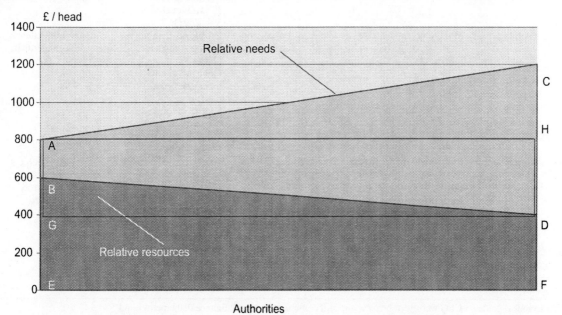

This figure shows the same simplified model under the post 2006–07 formula grant system. Formula grant before damping remains the same (ACDB). It is now made up of relative needs (ACH) plus the central allocation (AHDG) less relative resources (BDG). The central allocation (AHDG) is the difference between the amount below threshold for the relative needs block (AHFE) and that for the relative resources block (GDFE)

Annex 2

METHOD OF SETTING WEIGHTS IN RELATIVE NEEDS FORMULAE 2009–10

Block/Sub-Block	Method of setting weights	Basic client variable	Independent variables included in formula	Dependent variable used to set weights (if appropriate)
Youth and Community	Weighted regression (based on work carried out for DfES in 2002)	Projected Population 13–19 in 2009	Children of Income support/JSA claimants (2004–07) Low Achieving ethnic groups (2001)	Expenditure on relevant categories in 2002–03
LA Central Education Functions	Weighted regression (based on work carried out for DfES in 2002)	Pupils aged 3–18/Resident pupils aged 3–18	Children of Income support/JSA claimants (2004–07) Sparsity at ward level (2001) Fixed cost amount	Expenditure on relevant categories in 2002–03
Children's Social Care[55]	Multi-level model (2 stage regression) /top-up for fostering costs based on regression (based on work commissioned by DfES in 2005)	Projected population 0–17 in 2009	Children not in good health (2001 census) Children of Income support/JSA claimants (2004/07) Income support/JSA claimants aged 18–64 (2004/07) Children in black ethnic households (2001) People in ethnic group "other" and "mixed" (2001) Females 16–74 "looking after home/family" (2001) People with qualifications level 1/2 and level 3/4 (2001)	The cost of children's social services per head of total population aged 0 to 17 in 2003 in postcode districts in 141 local authority areas Unit cost of foster care estimated from the 2003 Children in Need survey
Younger Adults Social Care[56]	Multi-level model (based on work commissioned by DH in 2005)	Projected Population 18–64 in 2009	People on Disability Living Allowance (2004–07) Never worked/long term unemployed (2001) People in routine occupations (2001) Households with no family (2001)	Younger adult clients per 1,000 residents in each ward (2005)
Older People's Social Care[57]	Multi-level model (based on work commissioned by DH in 2005) Income from sales and charges estimated by regression on costs for 2005–06	Projected Population over 65 in 2009	Attendance allowance claimants 65 + (2004–07) Pensioner rented households (2001) One pensioner households (2001) Pension credit claimants (2004–05) Population over 90 (2009 projection)	Cost of older people's social service per person aged 65 and over in each ward (2005)

[55] See technical guide on CLG website at http://www.local.communities.gov.uk/finance/0809/methkid.pdf
[56] See technical guide on CLG website at http://www.local.communities.gov.uk/finance/0809/methpssa.pdf
[57] See technical guide on CLG website at http://www.local.communities.gov.uk/finance/0809/methpssa.pdf

Block/Sub-Block	Method of setting weights	Basic client variable	Independent variables included in formula	Dependent variable used to set weights (if appropriate)
Police	Regression based on activity analysis originally developed for Home Office in 1995; last updated in 2008—based on average of 2004–05 and 2005–06 data	Projected resident population in 2009	Daytime population (2009 projection) Number of bars Income Support/JSA claimants (2004–07) Single parent households (2001) Population density (2001) Long term unemployment (2001) Residents in routine or semi-routine occupations or never worked (2001) Student housing (2001) Residents in "hard pressed" areas (2001) Population sparsity at super output area (2001) Overcrowded households (2001) "Wealthy achievers" areas (2001) Terraced households (2001)	Number of recorded crimes of various categories (based on average of 2004–05 and 2005–06 data) Road traffic casualties Fear of crime measure Perception of disorder measure Number of calls for service (incidents)
Fire and Rescue	Regression based on expenditure to weight main formula risk index based on regression on number of fire calls Proportion for property and societal risk and community fire safety set by judgement	Projected resident population in 2009	Coastline Fire Risk index (Children of IS/JSA claimants (2004–05); Households without a couple with no children (2001); Rented accommodation (2001); School absences(2003–06); Areas with high proportions of elderly and flats (2001); Number of rooms per resident (2001)) High risk sites Property and Societal risk based on buildings information Community fire safety (number of pupils 5–10, areas "with need for fire safety education")	Net current expenditure over the period 1998–99 to 2000–01 Fire calls over period 1995/06—1999/2000 (used to weight risk index)
Highway Maintenance	Regression/ judgement	Weighted road lengths (2007)	Traffic flow (average 2004–06 Daytime population (2009 projection) Days with snow lying (1978–90) Predicted gritting days (1991–2001)	Expenditure per head (2003–04 to 2005–06)

Block/Sub-Block	Method of setting weights	Basic client variable	Independent variables included in formula	Dependent variable used to set weights (if appropriate)
EPCS "District" Services	Judgement	Projected Population in 2009	Density (2001) Sparsity (2001) Incapacity Benefit (2004–07) Income Support/JSA (2004–07) Older People on Income Support/JSA (2004–07) Unemployment claimants (2004–07) Country of birth of residents (2001) In-Commuters (2001) Day visitors (1988–91)	
EPCS "County" Services	Judgement	Projected Population in 2009	Density (2001) Incapacity Benefit (2004–07) Income Support/JSA (2004–07) Incapacity Benefit (2004–07) Unemployment claimants (2004–07) Country of birth of residents (2001) In-Commuters (2001) Day visitors (1988–91)	
Fixed costs	Judgement (based on work commissioned in 2002)	Fixed sum per authority		
Flood Defence	Past spending	Expenditure (2003–08)		
Continuing EA levies	Past spending	Environment Agency Levies (2007–08)		
Coast Protection	Past spending	Expenditure (2003–08)		

Annex 3

AUSTRALIAN COMMONWEALTH GRANTS COMMISSION[58]

The Commonwealth Grants Commission has operated in Australia since 1933. It is an advisory body that works according to terms of reference set by the federal government, after consultation with the states. It advises on per capita relativities for distributing, among the States and Territories (the States), the pool of general revenue assistance made available by the Australian Government. This covers both state services such as education and social care and health care. The general tax affected is the Goods and Services Tax, which is the main sales tax in Australia. In 2009–10 the total size of the GST pool is estimated to be around $A43 billion (around £21 billion).

References to the CGC are provided by the Minister for Finance and Administration; their content is usually decided in negotiations between the Commonwealth and the States, conducted largely through their Treasuries. While the resulting Commission reports are provided formally to the Commonwealth Government, they are made available to the States immediately thereafter. The relativities recommended in those reports are considered at the annual Treasurers' Conference. Thus the recommendations of the Commission are not acted upon until they receive political support.

The Commission works, in general, according to the principle of equalisation of needs and resources. On the needs side; expense assessments aim to measure the effects of each State's circumstances which affect spending. These can arise from population characteristics or the availability of private services. They also look at whether some ethnic groups (such as Native Australians) use services more intensely than other groups. On the resources side; income from other taxes such as mining and land taxes are taken into account, as well as specific grants (known as Special Purpose Payments) from the Australian government.

In 2009 the Commission issued a report on the relativities between states. This took into account changes in population, assessed need to spend and taxation income from other sources (such as mining income). These different relativities caused redistribution between the different states so that Queensland lost over $A380 million and New South Wales gained over $A600 million.

---
[58] See http://www.cgc.gov.au/

According to the Commission, the strong growth of the Western Australian and Queensland economies, fuelled by their mining sectors with flow on impacts on real estate markets and employment, was a main driver of these changes. This produced a continued strengthening of the relative capacity of Western Australia, and to a lesser extent Queensland, to raise revenue from their own sources, and led to a compensating redistribution of the pool away from them to other States, notably New South Wales and Victoria.

Although the Commission does not consider services provided by local government; in its equalisation of taxable capacity amongst the states it provides, as least theory the mechanism for them to contribute towards local government income. Therefore it could be said to have an indirect effect. In addition, some states have State Distribution Commissions which replicate the work of the national CGC at an intra-state level.

The CGC works on a five-year timescale for reviews; and the following review starts immediately the previous one is implemented. For example, the terms of reference for the review to be implemented in 2010 were sent to the Commission in 2005.

The CGC also has a role in looking at compensation for new burdens; it contributed a study to the Australian parliamentary report on new burdens for local government.

The CGC receive an annual grant from the government for its work; in the year ending 30 June 2008 this was $A8 million. However it had a 16 per cent underspend. It has 50 staff.

Memorandum from London Councils

1. London Councils welcomes the establishment of the House of Lords Barnett Formula Select Committee, and is pleased to provide this memorandum setting out our initial views on the formula and the need for its reform.

2. Due to the short timeframe for submissions, at this stage, we have not included substantive evidence about options for change.

3. We believe that the time is right for a fundamental review of the Barnett Formula. There is no harsher critic of the formula than Lord Barnett himself who stated in his evidence to the Committee on 28 January 2009 that it was only ever intended (in his mind) to be a short term and simplistic method of allocating public expenditure, but has now been in operation for more than 30 years.

4. As a mechanism for distributing funding across the UK it has led to a disproportionate allocation of resources from England to other parts of the UK and, in the view of London Councils, this has led to pressures on available resources for services in England, and a knock-on effect for London.

5. London Councils would welcome a fundamental review of the funding mechanism across the UK and believes that:

— the Barnett Formula should be abandoned (particularly in the light of flawed population statistics);

— resources should be allocated on a consistent needs based approach (ie consistent across regions, but also across funding departments), with rewards built in for effective and efficient use of them;

— the system should be sufficiently simple and transparent to foster understanding and trust; and

— there should be greater fiscal freedoms and flexibilities at local level to address local needs.

WHY LONDON COUNCILS BELIEVES THAT THE BARNETT FORMULA NEEDS TO BE REFORMED

6. The following sections set out our views on the reasons for reform.

Equity and fairness

7. The Barnett Formula *"does not directly reflect need beyond population".*[59] It is widely believed that population share alone is too blunt a measure to use to determine resources (particularly when it is accepted that the government's population statistics are fundamentally flawed as noted, for instance, by the House of Commons Treasury Committee which said *"Based on the evidence we have received, it is evident that there are substantial problems in generating accurate population estimates in some Local Authority area."*).[60]

8. Each area should be able to provide the same standard of public services, regardless of wealth or delivery costs for different services in different regions. Therefore, many critics point out that the idea that each region should achieve the same level of spending per head is misguided in itself. London Councils supports this position and would welcome the adoption of a needs based model underpinned by on a consistent approach

[59] Dominic Webb, The Barnett Formula, *Economic Policy and Statistics Section, House of Commons Library*, Research Paper 07/91, 14 December 2007, pp 10

[60] House of Commons Treasury Committee, Eleventh report of session 2007–08 (HC 183-1), para 71

across all funding departments and a system that is sufficiently simple and transparent to foster understanding and trust.

9. Many commentators have referred to the expected 'Barnett squeeze' that, in theory, would converge spending per head between, particularly, Scotland and the rest of the UK. However, it is widely accepted now that this squeeze has not happened and has instead, it is argued, overly disadvantaged Wales. In 2007-08 spending per head in Northern Ireland and Scotland was 21 per cent above the UK average; in Wales it was 8 per cent above, while in England it was 3 per cent below.[61]

10. There are two reasons for this lack of convergence; the first is the "all things being equal" assumption failing to account for a general fall in population in Scotland, and the second is the amount of funding allocated outside of the formula. Both have led to a failure of the "squeeze" effect and a continuation of an inequitable funding position for Scotland to the detriment of the rest of the UK.

11. The squeeze has also failed to operate at a time of unprecedented growth in spending on public services within England. Given that the squeeze is intended to operate at times of increased spending in England, and that spending is set to grow at a lower rate in the economic downturn, the Barnett formula will have even less squeeze, which therefore makes investigating its reform even more important.

The Barnett Formula is Arbitrary in Nature

12. The formula is not statutory and in theory could be revoked by the UK government. A parliamentary research paper has commented itself, *"The formula has no legal standing or democratic justification".*[62]

13. The process by which the Treasury decides whether spending is subject to the Barnett Formula can also seem arbitrary, with future decisions about what's in or out of the formula having the potential of being defined almost at a whim by future governments.

14. This lack of transparency, and the potentially arbitrary nature of the decision making process, reduces trust in the formula between the nations of the UK, especially where different political parties control different tiers of government. A tighter financial position, as is likely in the forthcoming Spending Review and Finance Settlements post 2011, can only exacerbate this problem.

Against the Spirit of Devolution and Economic Accountability

15. Since the Barnett Formula was first adopted local authorities in England have lost control of business rates and are subject to central government control around decisions about council tax. At the same time the devolved administrations have been given a very large measure of flexibility over both of these taxes (indeed Northern Ireland has retained its domestic rates system and Scotland has consulted on proposals to replace council tax with a local income tax), and Scotland has revenue raising ability (up to 3 per cent on income tax, known as the "Tartan Tax").

16. However, devolved administrations have little influence over the size of their block grant, potentially causing problems if a devolved administration wanted to increase spending at a time when a UK government was cutting spending in England. They would therefore be constrained in shaping their own policy agenda which could lead to conflict and undermine devolution.

17. A degree of fiscal autonomy has an important role to play in encouraging efficient spending. When regions depend on transfers of funding from government alone it is argued to encourage inefficient and profligate spending.[63] It has also been argued that the most effective form of political accountability is realised when the level of government that is responsible for spending public money is also responsible for raising that money.[64]

18. Nonetheless, even in this current system London has delivered, and is still delivering, efficiencies. Indeed, London authorities have exceeded their efficiency targets by over £100 million in 2008–09 and could do more with the opportunity for greater fiscal freedoms.

---

[61] In Scotland spending per head decreased between 2002–03 and 2004–05 from 21 per cent above the UK average to 15 per cent, but then it increased again sharply from 2004–05 onwards. Iain McLean et al, Fair Shares? Barnett and the politics of public expenditure, pp 16

[62] Timothy Edmonds, The Barnett Formula, *Economic Policy and Statistics Section, House of Commons Library,* Research Paper 01/108, 30 November 2001, pp 13

[63] Iain McLean *et al* Fair Shares? Barnett and the politics of public expenditure, pp 9

[64] However political accountability needs to be weighed against equity principles as poorer areas would raise lower amounts of tax and therefore transfers from richer regions would be necessary for principles of fairness in levels of public services.

CONCLUSION

19. In conclusion, London Councils welcomes this review of the Barnett Formula and the opportunity it presents to move away from a system that was devised some thirty years ago to one that is more suited to today's environment. We believe the new system should be needs based and sufficiently simple and transparent to foster understanding and trust. We believe that rewards for effective and efficient use of public funding should be built in, which we also believe would lead to issues of joining up across public services and resource allocation being addressed.

February 2009

Memorandum by Mr Russell Mellett

The following point form executive summary is based on the attached papers:

— *A Principles-based approach to the Barnett Formula*, The Political Quarterly, vol 80, no 1 (January–March), 2009.

— *The Importance of Raising your own Revenues*, forthcoming in Scottish Affairs, (likely May 2009).

NEED FOR REFORM/ALTERNATIVES TO THE EXISTING FORMULA

The Barnett determined block grant—paid annually by the UK government to each of the Devolved Administrations of Scotland, Wales and Northern Ireland—should be re-formulated, guided by the following principles: fiscal equity, accountability, transparency, and flexibility. The rationale for change is that the current arrangements make little policy sense and may not be sustainable in a changing political and economic context.

Fiscal equity is proposed as the overall policy anchor or framing principle for the block grant. The fiscal equity principle refers to equal treatment of equally placed taxpayers by government. This calculus spans the actions of all governments to which citizens pay tax and from which they receive public services. Fiscal equity implies that governments, taken together, provide reasonably comparable levels of public services at reasonably comparable levels of taxation. Or from the individual perspective, that citizens can access reasonably comparable levels of public goods at reasonably comparable levels of taxation. In practice, a block grant from UK government to the Devolved Administrations—anchored in fiscal equity—would enable similar outcomes across UK regions rather than guaranteeing these. So citizens can have access to reasonably comparable levels of public services at reasonably comparable levels of taxation, if their Governments (national, sub-national) make like choices over the range of public goods provided at any given level of tax. Actual outcomes can vary.

Expenditure responsibilities can and do vary between the governments of Scotland, Wales and Northern Ireland. For example, Northern Ireland has responsibility for welfare payments, whereas the UK government makes such payments directly in Wales and Scotland. On the revenue side, only Scotland currently has the power to vary the basic rate of income tax up or down by three pence on the pound. This small power to vary on the margin would not yield substantial revenues and there is little incentive for Scotland to bear the political cost of imposing the Tartan tax provided that the Barnett transfer is generous enough. Nevertheless, it can be argued that a permanent transfer of a meaningful level of revenue raising capacity from the UK government to each of Scotland, Wales and Northern Ireland would enhance the direct accountability of these governments to their citizens; and, together with changes in borrowing practices, provide reasonable fiscal and governance flexibility. Raising part of own revenues and insuring own borrowing could enhance responsive and responsible government for Scotland, Wales and Northern Ireland. To the extent that DA raise their own revenues or engage in own borrowing and the relevant facts are reported in the public accounts of each of these regional governments, transparency would improve. In any event, the block grant design should be flexible enough to accommodate changes in expenditure and revenue assignments between the UK government and the devolved governments, and to accommodate asymmetries in fiscal powers and practices between devolved governments.

DATA QUALITY AND AVAILABILITY

In general, data which support intergovernmental fiscal arrangements are contained in National Accounts, Public Accounts and in demographic surveys. Specific data requirements would, of course, vary with the specific measures used. It is most important that data are compiled on a consistent and comparable basis across regions. It is equally important that the statistical agency (the National Statistic Office, and regional counterparts) be professionally independent and be governed by a Statistics Act with respect to the confidentiality of data An example of international practice would be Statistics Canada's consolidated public accounts (federal, provincial, local) known as the Financial Management System (FMS), which, in turn, feeds into the System of National Accounts (SNA).

DECISION MAKING AND DISPUTE RESOLUTION: INSTITUTIONAL DEVELOPMENT

A key challenge in the UK grants context is to assemble basic fiscal and economic data within a common framework. An independent grants commission working with the statistical agencies of the UK and devolved governments could facilitate these data tasks. Independence of the data and calculation of disparities from the payments would allow the Chancellor of the Exchequer to decide on the final grant amounts on the basis of public advice from the grants commission. The chancellor must have the final say as (s)he is responsible to Parliament; however independence in the calculation and public advice would enhance public disclosure and would add to the appearance of fairness (in that the UK government did not manipulate the underlying data or calculations to get the required result). A possible model for a UK grants commission is the Commonwealth Grants Commission in Australia.

Overall, in addition to set examinations of fiscal arrangements by temporary bodies, UK fiscal relations could benefit from ongoing institutions which provide statistical support, the possibility of common revenue collection, and offer public advice on the payment of intergovernmental grants.

— The notion of statistic support via and independent national agency, and the idea of a Grant's commission have been broached above.

— Regarding own revenues: the basic idea is that own revenue raising by both the UK and regional governments (Scotland, Wales, Northern Ireland) is desirable from a governance perspective. The key to an effective system is to utilize a common tax collection agency and common definitions of what is taxed (common tax basis for say income or consumption). Such a possibility, whether immediate or not, should be part of the thinking about institutional development for UK intergovernmental finance.

CONCLUSION

To conclude, the policy principles and practice advocated above (and expanded upon in the attached papers) may be new to the UK, but are successfully and routinely applied in fiscal arrangements practice across a number of countries.[ii] The real issue for the UK is political will and time to develop the necessary data and formulae, not technical know-how.

ENDNOTES

[i] Heald and Macleod (2003) report that full application of the Scottish tax varying power, three pence on the pound was estimated by HM Treasury to be worth about 450 million pounds, or about 2.8 per cent of an estimated 16 billion pound budget in Scotland in 1997.

[ii] See, various examples in Ter Missian (1997)

References

Boadway, Robin and Paul Hobson, *Intergovernmental Fiscal Relations in Canada*, Canadian Tax Foundation, Toronto, 1993.

Gallagher, James and Daniel Hinze (2005), *Financing Options for Devolved Government in the UK, University of Glasgow, Department of Economics, discussion paper 2005–24*.

Heald, David and Alasdair Macleod (2003), *Revenue-raising by UK Devolved Administrations in the Context of an Expenditure-based Financing System*, Regional and Federal Studies, Vol 13, number 4, Winter 2003, pp 67–90.

Heald, David and Alasdair Macleod (2005), *Embeddedness of UK Devolution Finance within the Public Expenditure System*, Regional Studies Vol 39. 4 June 2005, pp 495–518.

Moore, Mick (1998), *Death Without Taxes* in The Democratic Developmental State Mark Robinson and Gordon White eds, Oxford University Press, Oxford UK, 1998.

Ter-Minassian, Teresa (1997), *Fiscal Federalism in Theory and Practice*, International Monetary Fund, Washington.

February 2009

Memorandum by the Parliament for Wales Campaign

SUMMARY

1. The problems with Barnett include convergence in funding when regional disparity dictates the opposite, that any original needs based data utilised or otherwise is dated, that several items of expenditure are not "Barnettised" when they should have been, that the update is on a population base which itself is debatable, that consequentials are decided unilaterally and there is no formal bilateral or multilateral agreement, that Wales doesn't receive its fair share of non "Barnettised" expenditure and the formula doesn't take this into account, that consequentials are dictated by the original need or lack of it which is that in England. That there is no mechanism for consequentials to operate in reverse. That the formula takes no account of the financial provisions of the Charters of Europe which we submit is the minimum level of acceptable financial autonomy. That there is no mechanism for the Assembly to increase its budget or to return non utilised expenditure to the people through lower taxes. That the settlement is demeaning in that the Assembly relies on an annual hand out from another Parliament. That there is no bonus incentive for the Assembly to improve economic performance in the formula. That most major and minor leavers of fiscal control all lie in London and that the principle of devolution and subsidiarity has not been applied to the Treasury.

2. We suggest that a UK Convergence fund based either on financial transfer or an allowance to a lower tax plateau similar to that in economic development zones is part of the funding mechanism.

3. That the convergence fund could operate in various ways including through a lower payment for non devolved UK services but also through the devolution of several taxes at a lower rate in a "tax subsidy".

4. The formula should take into account the lower than fair share of public expenditure that is non "Barnettised" at present.

5. We suggest that the Governments of Wales should have access to the cheapest forms of borrowing moneys as any other government have, and we suggest you publish a paper on borrowing powers.

6. If the principle of subsidiarity were applied then a raft of minor fiscal tools should be devolved.

7. We see no argument against hypothecating or assigning tax revenues to the devolved administrations.

8. A simpler system would include the allocation of taxes received in the devolved administration to that administration, together with a series of bilateral or multilateral agreements on the funding of non devolved functions whereby the devolved government returns finance to the UK government for services provided. We refer you to the operation of the Common Purse Agreement in the Isle of Man and other UK territories, it is not acceptable that offshore UK islands have substantially more financial autonomy that Wales or Scotland. Your committee appears stuck in the mindset of revamping a block grant formula as if Wales was a government department and decisions should still be made unilaterally. We argue that any new financial settlement should not rely on a handout from central government alone and that the fiscal tools to do the job are examined and devolved accordingly.

9. The Campaign would like you to include a financial bonus mechanism as part of a financial formula to reward economic growth.

10. We argue for not a static solution but a dynamic one generated by "Financial Competence Orders" or agreements.

11. There should be a joint standing committee of Ministers to oversee any solution.

EVIDENCE

LORDS

12. We are a cross party organisation representing people of all parties and none, and dedicated to achieving a fair and workable settlement for a Welsh Parliament. We would first like to congratulate you on your overdue review of the funding mechanism for the National regions. We firstly outline some of the ground rules on which we suggest a new fiscal settlement for devolution should be based and on which there should be wide agreement, rather than us defining a precise settlement on which there would be divergence of opinion.

PRINCIPLES OF A FINANCIAL SETTLEMENT

13. In the first instance we would like your Committee to take on board the basic principles we submit are the ground rules for a settlement. These are that the settlement is Transparent, Flexible in that it could vary its budget by a reasonable amount for unexpected expenditure, Fair, Accountable to the electors in Wales, and allowing a reasonable degree of financial Autonomy to the Assembly. We also strongly suggest that the ground rules take on board the principle of financial Subsidiarity and that the financial provisions of the Charters of

the Council of Europe be followed as providing a Legal Basis for a financial settlement. The European Charter of Local Self Government and the draft European Charter for Regional Democracy not only refer to the rule of subsidiarity between central government and the National regions, but also refer to a reasonable proportion of income not coming from a block grant system, as is the case in local government and a system that provides almost complete financial autonomy in the case of the GLA. Another guideline we suggest is Good Practice in the formulae for funding regional governments abroad, on which we suggest you commission research. Finally we strongly suggest that the new financial formula is seen as fair and not dissimilar to that to be implemented in other National regions and Crown Territories of the UK. It should take on board precedents set, so as not to appear unfair.

BARNETT AND THE PRESENT SETTLEMENT

14. We first refer you to work by PJ Williams on the Welsh Budget arguing in particular that inaccuracies in the present formula mask what could be presented as a fiscal balance in Wales, correlating government revenue with that spent in Wales. In particular he points to Wales receiving less than our fair share of UK research expenditure, identifying unidentifiable expenditure in non devolved functions and the lack of 'Barnettising' of London Transport and the Channel Tunnel expenditure, and no allowance for the larger number of elderly residents. The Calman Commission expert group at Heriot Watt University also point to similar inconsistencies in what should be included in the formula, whereas Scott refers to the log jam in the English NHS resulting in a consequential poor settlement in Scotland. We would like you to comment on these and to commission research to identify "non identifiable expenditure" and expenditure on non devolved functions as a useful starting point.

15. Historically we draw your attention to recent documents and press articles by the Institute of Public Policy Research—on the budget of the Welsh Office and now the Assembly which suggest that we have been underfunded by up to £2 billion. We invite you to confirm and to comment on this historic loss?

16. We would like you to calculate the amounts of moneys that should be due but have not been paid into the budget, such as the diversion of moneys for the Olympics together with the compensation for rural areas due to the Foot and Mouth epidemic stemming from a government laboratory from which we submit should have resulted in moneys from DEFRA to the Assembly Government, and other examples including those above and following.

17. Accordingly we would like you to look at the expenditure under Barnett and have we had our fair share? Has all the expenditure that should have been subjected to Barnett been allocated correctly? Should there not be a joint standing committee from the devolved administrations and the UK government overseeing any formula? We would like you also to look at areas which are either partly included in Barnett or partly not included eg has Wales received 5 per cent of rail expenditure or 5 per cent of government education research and other research moneys? In particular have rail projects such as Crossrail and Reading been "Barnettised"? Have we had our share for the social needs of a larger number of retired? We refer you to the work of Professor Cole, PJ Williams and others arguing that we haven't. We also refer you to Educationalists and others who point out that if we have had our fair share under the present formula than how come our education expenditure per child is less than that in England Some £150—200 per pupil—Secondary Heads Association Report 2005, and £355 less per pupil—National Assembly debate 2007. We suspect you haven't taken into account a probable lower local tax take amongst other reasons?

18. Would you confirm that any convergence as a policy or consequence of the present formula is perverse when from what we understand the GDP of Wales is diverging when the UK has been well documented and described as the most regionally divergent country in Europe. Surely a 'divergent' formula is needed to create a convergence of GDP or maybe any effect on GDP or employment isn't to be taken into account?

19. There should be a joint standing committee of Ministers to oversee any solution, as with Barnett there are many queries and suspicions surrounding what is and is not included in any formula. There is a need for greater transparency in any settlement.

A NEW SETTLEMENT

20. In the first instance we suggest that the financial provisions of the Local Government Charter of the Council of Europe are taken as the minimum level of acceptable financial autonomy. We are a cross party grouping who seek consensus on a new financial settlement and we suggest that the following is acceptable to a political consensus view.

21. We suggest that a UK Convergence fund is part of the funding mechanism. We ask you to bear in mind that by the time a new formula is implemented the next set of EC regional policies may see a reduction in finance to Wales.

22. That the convergence fund could operate in various ways including through a block top up grant and also through the devolution of one or more taxes at a lower rate in a "tax incentive".

23. Rather then a tax being devolved at the current UK rate it should be incorporated in an agreement at a suggested reduced rate to achieve convergence. eg Corporation Tax could be devolved as has been widely suggested by the business community and allowed by EC at reduced rates in Objective 1 areas. If it were also reduced in areas targeted for convergence in England this would mitigate against the argument of large scale uprooting of companies to the devolved National regions whilst still benefiting the Welsh economy.

24. We see no argument against hypothecating or assigning tax revenues to the devolved administrations as the first basic step to a settlement. Whilst this may show that revenues and expenditure do not match and will need to be added to by a block, the annual exercise in itself will create the need for better statistics and analysis for Wales to be produced.

25. The formula should take into account the lower than fair share of public expenditure that is non "Barnettised" at present. We refer you to Hansard on the recent debate on the Welsh police funding whereby "Barnettised" functions are funded on a population basis when need would dictate that they should receive more and the Police as a non devolved function in Wales received a needs based funding! Again we refer to the just the 0.2 per cent difference for the current year being equivalent to £2.2 million and 100 police officers less for Wales. Hansard, the blog of Adam Price M.P. and the implications of the comments of the chief constable for South Wales, Media Wales. Would the functions of the Home Office not be better off if they were devolved?

26. That a reverse consequential mechanism generated by a need in one or more on the devolved National regions is needed in the formula model. Does it make sense that a log jam in funding hospitals in England could reduce much needed budgets elsewhere of that an efficiency saving in the civil service largely in one of the most wealthy regions in the Europe has a consequential of up to £500 million less for the Assembly p.a. in one of the poorest in the teeth of a recession. An agreement similar to other UK territories could negate this problem.

27. The formula should reward the Assembly for good economic performance but not punitively penalise it in a downturn.

28. We do not see the need for a new collection system but we would like assurance that taxes from Wales are generally collected in Wales in order to safeguard administrative jobs and conform with the Welsh Language Act. We suggest that there is a need for a new financial/economic unit for Wales in conjunction with the new formula. This could be based at one of the soon to be vacant tax offices creating much needed employment.

29. The Campaign suggest a solution should both include fiscal levers devolved in an Act or agreement but allowing for others to be devolved for a purpose, as and when they are argued for. ie we argue not for a static solution but a dynamic one generated by "Financial Competence Orders" or agreements. Amendments to the formula itself should be by joint agreement, on a more formal basis than the current unilateral procedure.

30. We see the need for debate surrounding each financial competence and the reasoning behind each fiscal tool being devolved. The formula will therefore need to be flexible and with ground rules as to how new fiscal tools may be applied if they are either additions to the settlement or replacements. We envisage a block element gradually being diminished by this process.

31. Most people now accept that devolution is a dynamic process and not an event and our approach is consistent with the needs to create, amend and delete fiscal tools for economic and other reasons as events and reasons arise both fiscal tools alone or in conjunction with legal tools.

32. We suggest a fair settlement should be needs based and takes account of factors such as rurality, population, health problems due to an industrial past, tourism, and if the retired population is in proportion to UK demographics. Any needs based assessment from the time of Barnett is now out of date and we suggest that you commission a new one as a starting point.

33. We suggest that the cost of delivering statutory services is calculated, compared to other National regions and regions of England and an allowance built into the agreement.

34. The Campaign would like you to include a financial bonus mechanism as part of a financial settlement to reward economic growth. We suggest that the production of energy above either 5 per cent or the current base of production should also attract a bonus from central government. We suggest a financial mechanism is also devised so that Wales doesn't have higher energy costs if the 5 per cent or current base of production is exceeded. The needs, or block or top up of the formula could partly be reduced as well as the overall expenditure increased by hypothecating the take from tax, in particular on energy and water "exported" without the Assembly having powers devolved over taxes in this field. The reasoning behind this suggestion is fourfold in that it gives the National regional government an incentive to produce more energy and water supplies where there may be a reluctance or little incentive to do so. The Assembly would have a bonus in its

budget from any sudden increases in energy costs that it could utilise to promote green energy grants; It reduces the subsidy element of the revenue and starts to tackle the important misconceptions that Wales cannot pay its way and is heavily subsidised. It increases confidence in Wales in that it can pay its way and succeed economically. An economic unit has a role to play in these misconceptions introducing fairness an understanding of fair play into the system.

35. We would like you to look at other areas where the formula could usefully apply to revenue as well as expenditure and where bonuses could be built into the mechanism.

Borrowing Powers

36. The Campaign suggests that the Assembly have the power to issue bonds to finance capital projects.

37. We suggest that the Government of Wales should have access to the cheapest forms of borrowing moneys as any other government have, and we suggest you publish a paper on borrowing powers. We note the difficulties in utilising private funding mechanisms during the present economic turmoil and the political objections to utilising them. We suggest that Wales have the powers to borrow moneys on the capital markets and in doing so we suggest that it would need to have some tax varying powers as has the GLA to obtain creditworthiness and so obtain the lowest rates. We also note that devolving any taxes may necessitate temporary borrowing facilities probably from, or guaranteed by central government.

38. We would like you to look at the borrowing powers of the Assembly, Westminster, Northern Ireland and the GLA in proportion to the amount of public spend. In particular we would like you to make recommendations for the funding of major capital projects and alternatives to PFI and note those utilised for Crossrail?

39. We would like you to compare the amounts spent on capital projects in Wales in various fields with Scotland, England and London and include any recommendation in the settlement. Have we had our fair share of debt? With government borrowing fast approaching lunar proportions for how much is Wales responsible and for how much will we be penalised for years to come? Have we had our 5 per cent fair share and if not could we have it in borrowing powers to generate capital projects. Do you agree that increased borrowing powers could help lead Wales out of a predicted recession?

40. We would like you to look at the powers of the Assembly to acquire a stake in companies should they wish to do so and if this requires further powers in any finance bill.

41. We suggest that the formula needs to be flexible to take into account unexpected non budgeted expenditure such as we recall with the case of LG, or the match funding needed for some £100 million in additional funding from EC due to a fall in the value of the £, unpredictable increases in energy and fuel costs, or emergency loans to local councils.

42. We also suggest the need for temporary borrowing powers.

43. Similarly we would like you to comment on the situation where Wales apparently has a surplus where one Welsh Office Secretary of State saw fit to send moneys back to the Treasury and if this money is recoverable? You can confirm that moneys can now be carried over from one year to the next but the ability to pay back a surplus to the people through a lower tax or charge in the following year or to spend an amount deemed unnecessary is a glaring omission in the formula which we suggest you rectify.

General Comments and Points

45. We would like you to comment on the present financial powers of the Assembly and if they are being used in the best ways. eg the rate of business tax and if there is a tendency for the Assembly to raise moneys through the backdoor by decreasing local authority settlements or if this is not the case?

46. We would like you to look at the issue of match funding for Objective 1 and other EC moneys and if this should have been provided by central government and if so what the historic amount owed should be?

47. We would like yourselves, or the new economic unit we propose, to place a figure on projected growth in GDP if the settlement included all the moneys the Assembly should have received and with a revised needs-based settlement ie forecasts for convergence?

48. We would like you to put a figure on the increased tax take in Wales if additional moneys according to need and that not received as suggested above are included?

49. We would like you or the economic unit to put a figure on increased tax take and on economic growth if as we suggest functions, jobs and the finance for them, already transferred to Scotland such as the administration of the Police, Prisons and Courts are devolved to Wales?

TAX VARYING POWERS

50. The devolving and varying of a tax rate is the element of any formula that is likely to cause greatest debate and disagreement. While the Commission should include major taxes within its proposal we propose that an Enabling Act or agreement to be followed by Financial Competence Orders or further bilateral or multilateral agreements allowing for a proper debate and agreement on each fiscal tool to be devolved. Although your committee appears to concerned itself with a rehash of a unilateral hand out formula there is a need to look at all fiscal tools that could reasonably and practically be made available to the devolved administrations especially in the light of the current recession. A devolved settlement should include the devolution of fiscal tools that could reasonably and practically best be administered from the devolved administrations.

51. We suggest that you commission research on which tax rates or bases could reasonably be devolved to stimulate growth, reduce the carbon footprint or for other reasons and that the Economic Unit we propose continue this work.

52. We have noted reasoning and support for devolving a number of tax bases and rates including the following.

53. We do not suggest abolishing a grant element entirely but suggest that a variation in several taxes be allowed and devolved and added to by a grant based on means, together with a partial wealth transfer. The rate support grant to local councils operates in similar fashion utilising different taxes to that we suggest with a partial equalising of public expenditure between national regions of the UK. While the EC has a convergence fund, is it not time that the UK had similar?

54. If one of the smallest economic units is the village inn and the Assembly should have the fiscal tools to ensure that that village economic life continues, then it needs as many fiscal levers as possible over them eg to perhaps promote local beers or reduce taxes in times of economic crisis. Thus the devolution of tax on alcohol is a candidate but we suggest fiscal tools such as these are subject to bilateral agreement and in major cases could be subject to referenda. We strongly argue that the settlement should allow for fiscal devolution to take place. The alternative is fiscal autonomy.

55. Likewise the Tax on Tobacco. This could be utilised for the NHS.

Again we refer you to the Isle of Man Act, the Common Purse Agreement and the allocation of their various taxes. We also refer to the taxation and retention of the tax on the film industry in the IoM as an example of a fiscal tool that should be discussed in the context of Wales and economic development.

56. We have already suggested that fuel tax should be devolved within a band so as to allow a reduction in rural areas. If an average US state has over 100 fiscal leavers does it make any sense that the only action the National Assembly can take in a time of crisis is to raid its meagre reserves.

57. Of the major taxes, we detect support for the devolution of Corporation Tax. We suggest that if such a tax is devolved, it is devolved at a reduced rate with an Assembly ability to vary it upwards to the UK rate. The formula would need to compensate by calculating the norm of revenue to allow for the reduced rate in the likely area it is to be applied and any variation upwards would therefore increase the Assembly budget. Any major tax rate devolved should therefore be devolved at a reduced rate as a norm as part of a needs based convergence formula. The "tax raising" sceptre above the rate in England should therefore not arise. The economic activity rate in Wales is lower than England for various reasons and an allowance is needed in the settlement for this lower level together with policies to increase the rate.

58. We would like you to comment if there is a business case beneficial to the economy to devolve certain financial powers such as the rate of corporation tax in Objective 1 areas to generate a particular industry such as film and if such a policy is allowable under EC law.

59. The Assembly has also discussed measures to reduce the usage of plastic bags. It is somewhat bizarre that such bags could be banned in their entirety if the powers are given, but the lesser measure of just reducing their usage by taxing them by even 1p is not allowed under the current financial settlement and is we understand awaiting legislation for such a minor measure!

60. We wish the formula to offer sufficient flexibility for any fiscal tools to be taken up should a consensus emerge around them as circumstances dictate. We are arguing that a flexible process be created as well as a new settlement to create a devolved government fit for purpose

61. We suggest that a single tax solution suggested elsewhere may provide an inadequate flexibility of income. We note that at a time of crisis when the UK government is able to borrow and spend additional hundreds of £ billion that Wales and Scotland can only respond by utilising reserves of less than 1/2 per cent of budget.

62. The Campaign would like you to comment on the current economic downturn and if the Assembly has the fiscal tools required to manage it effectively.

PROCESS

63. We suggest that the new settlement allows for further fiscal devolution as stated above and we suggest that further financial powers could be devolved in a similar way to the enhancement of law making powers in that an enabling Act is followed by "Financial Competence Orders" or agreements with the Assembly outlining the specific reasoning for further financial powers.

64. That such Orders detail how the fiscal tool to be devolved (or abolished) should operate and if they are to replace another charge or tax, how the rate could be varied and if the block top up will compensate, increase or reduce as a result. The Order should also outline the reasoning why the fiscal tool is needed—as an economic stimulus or for behavioural change etc.

65. As we are suggesting a settlement based on laws and rights that National regions across Europe should possess, together with a fiscal process similar to the present process for devolving primary law, we do not see the need for a fourth referendum at this stage. If the proposal was for the Assembly to have complete fiscal autonomy that would not however be the case. We suggest that if the Assembly wished to replace the Council Tax with a local income tax through a "FCO" then this is the sort of issue that could be subjected to referenda rather than a complex formula. Referenda should be tools to consult on issues of large scale tax variation for a purpose, rather than the devolution of the tax itself.

66. There is little point in replacing Barnett with another formula which doesn't take into account the higher public spending outside Wales in non devolved budget headings. If we did we should name it after another part of London and the South East—"Stratford" or the "Berkshire" formula!

67. We submit that the National Assembly should be allowed to acquire similar financial powers to that of the UK Crown Dependencies an that the minimum acceptable level of financial autonomy is that outlined in the laws and Charters of Europe, to which the UK Government is a signatory.

67. Finally we submit that devolution is a process in itself and that including the new funding formula you will suggest and the further transfer of functions would enable Wales to have sufficient economic tools to lift itself out of recession and create economic growth.

REFERENCES

Steel Commission, Towards Fiscal Federalism. 2005. Scottish LibDems.

European Charter of Local Self Government, Council of Europe.

Draft European Charter of Regional Democracy. Council of Europe.

Estatut d'autonomia de Catalunya 2006.

The Future of Scottish Devolution within the Union. A First Report 2008. vol I & II.

Top 300 Business Manifesto, Business Wales, Media Wales. December 2008.

First evidence from the Independent Expert Group on the Commission on Scottish Devolution. 2008.

The Case for Replacing the Barnett Formula, Submission to the Treasury. Plaid Cymru 2002.

The Welsh Budget, P.J.Williams, Cyfres y Cynulliad 3, Y Lolfa.

Ross Mackay, *The Search for Balance*, Institute of Welsh Affairs 2001.

H.M. Treasury *Needs Assessment Study*—Report 1979.

Scott Argues for Loan Powers. Scotland on Sunday. 7.12.08

First Report, Scottish Council of Economic Advisers 2008.

Cynulliad i Genedl, Dewi Watkin Powell, Cyfres y Cynulliad 8, Y Lolfa.

"Wales Robbed of £2 billion a year". IPPR report July 2008.

"What is Wales Worth" Media Wales 24.6.08

"The Cost of being English" The Sunday Times. March 2008.

"Scotland—An Eye on its Own Tax System" Tax Adviser, Journal of the Chartered Institute of Taxation, November 2008.

H.M. Government evidence to the Commission on Scottish Devolution. Scotland Office. 2008.

An Economic Plan for Wales, P.J. Williams, D. Wigley, 1970.

A National Conversation, The Scottish Government

Wikipedia—*Barnett Formula*

Wikipedia—*the House of Keys*, Economy

Modifications to Taxation Strategy, Treasury Dept. House of Keys.

The Need for a Financial Commission, Adam Price M.P. address to the Parliament for Wales Campaign, National Eisteddfod, Abertawe 2006

Towards a New Constitutional Settlement, Smith Institute.

Lord Barnett, *House of Lords debate*, July 2008

Submission of the Parliament for Wales Campaign to the Scottish Governments consultation, Choosing Scotland's Future—a National Conversation.

The Barnett Formula, Research Note, Scottish Parliament, RN00/31 May 2000.

The Barnett Formula, House of Commons Library Research Paper 01/108, 30 Nov 2001.

An Independent Commission on Funding and Finance, National Assembly debate July 2007.

Irish and UK tax regimes, correspondence from the Republic of Ireland Treasury dept. to the Parliament for Wales Campaign.

What is Wales Worth, interview with Jane Hutt A.M. Business Minister 24 July 2007.

Cities Renaissance, Creating Local Leadership, Lord Heseltine's Cities Taskforce, 2007.

http://subsidiarity.cor.europa.eu

blog Adam Price M.P. 1/09

A Comparison of Funding in England and Wales, HEFCW 2003

Isle of Man Act, 1979

Kilbrandon Commission.

Common Purse Agreement, Isle of Man

Common Services Agreement, Isle of Man.

Alan Cairns A.M. National Assembly Debate on School Funding 5/12/07

Report of HEFCW by JM Consulting Sept 2006

Rees Review Progress report. National Assembly

Statement on Higher Education Funding—AUT Assistant General Secretary.

Report Secondary Heads Association (SHA) Guardian 17/3/05

Lord Barnett—evidence to your committee.

Statement by Barbara Wilding, Chief South Wales Police 17/2/09

Funding of the Police in Wales, Hansard 29/1/09

The Private Finance Initiative, House of Commons Library, research paper 01/117, 18 December 2007.

Brown: Scotland to get more Tax Powers, P. M. address to CBI Scotland, 5 September 2007.

Cymru'n Un—Joint Labour—Plaid Cymru manifesto for the National Assembly 2007.

Is there a future for Regional Government, House of Commons Communities and Local Government Committee, 2007.

The Financial Power of the Scottish Parliament, Scottish Parliament debate, 4 December 2003.

Guide to the Scottish Budget, SPICe briefing 07/33 13 June 2007.

Plaid Cymru views regarding the future of the EU Regional Policy

Devolution of Fuel Duty. Parliament for Wales—Media Wales

March 2009

Letter from Reform Scotland

Reform Scotland is an independent, non-party think tank that aims to set out a better way to deliver increased economic prosperity and more effective public services based on the traditional Scottish principles of limited government, diversity and personal responsibility. We welcome the opportunity to contribute to the House of Lords Select Committee's inquiry into the Barnett Formula although the main focus of the work we have done has been on how the financial relationship between Westminster and Holyrood might be improved.

Although I understand it is outside the remit of this inquiry, Reform Scotland's view is that the fundamental defect of the current devolution settlement is its lack of financial accountability. This stems from the fact that the vast bulk of its funding comes in the form of a block grant determined largely by the application of the so-called Barnett Formula.

Our principal objection is to the unbalanced nature of the existing financial relationship with its excessive reliance on a block grant rather than to the Barnett Formula *per se*. However, the Barnett Formula mechanism does mean that the Scottish Parliament's budget is determined neither by an assessment of need in Scotland nor by an assessment of what the Scottish electorate may be able and willing to contribute to the state in terms of taxation. Instead, the budget is largely determined by a formula that is based on the decisions taken about the level of public spending in the rest of the UK. This is a particular defect of the current arrangements and highlights the need for reform.

Our proposal is to scrap the Barnett Formula and the block grant system and enable both the UK and Scottish Governments to become responsible for raising the money they currently spend in Scotland. A copy of our report detailing our proposals is available from our website www.reformscotland.com

17 February 2009

Letter by Sustrans Cymru

I note from your terms of reference that you will be looking at the application of the Barnett Formula and assessing the effectiveness of the calculation mechanism. I thought it might therefore be useful to share our recent experience of how the formula is applied to Wales.

Sustrans Cymru is the Welsh arm of the UK's leading sustainable transport charity. We work on practical projects to allow people to travel in ways which improve their health and the environment.

We were instrumental in putting together a coalition of civil society organisations in Wales to call for the establishment of an independent commission, to look into the operation of the Barnett formula. We were joined by Wales' six leading education unions (NAHT Cymru, NUT Cymru, NASUWT, ATL, UCAC, and the ASCL), along with the British Medical Association (BMA Cymru Wales) and the Royal College of Nursing in Wales. We were therefore pleased when the Welsh Assembly Government established the Holtham Commission.

Since then we have become concerned about the application of the formula in the field of transport.

Spending on sustainable transport in England is channelled through a non-departmental body called Cycling England. As the name suggests, Cycling England does not operate in Wales. However in a letter to the *Western Mail* in December 2007 Eurfyl ap Gwilym, a board member of the Principality, revealed that spending by Cycling England is regarded by the Treasury as "UK spend".

Just as spending on Kew Gardens and on the London Olympics (even the transport and regeneration elements) is considered to be of benefit to the whole of the UK, so it seemed was money spent on sustainable transport schemes in England.

This was of particular concern to us as we had been having difficulty persuading the Welsh Assembly Government to fund schemes in Wales that are funded by Cycling England—even though WAG are keen to roll out such schemes.

In January 2008, the Department of Transport announced £140 million in funding for Cycling England. As walking and cycling is fully devolved, this spending should have resulted in a "consequential" increase for Wales. But if Eurfyl ap Gwylim was right, then this was not the case.

The Treasury in the 2007 Statement of Funding Policy published in October 2007 did show Cycling England as a separate spending programme, however, after Parliamentary Questions were tabled by Hywel Francis MP and Adam Price MP, this appears to have changed. The Treasury claimed that the Cycling England spend had been made part of the spending category "local transport". However, it is still unclear whether this results in a consequential.

After further investigation by Eurfyl ap Gwilym and Alan Trench of Edinburgh University, it emerged that the October 2007 Statement of Funding Policy, shows that the comparability percentage for Wales (and Scotland & Northern Ireland) on Cycling England spending is 0 per cent. Parliamentary Answers by Treasury Ministers implied that the Welsh block was getting a share of the Cycling England funding, but Statement of Funding suggests that the share is nil. That would suggest that even though the spending is comparable, the formula provides for no extra money.

It is unclear whether the block grant has now been increased to reflect the change in the treatment of Cycling England.

The facts are difficult to establish and as a result I am unclear about the true situation. I'd be very grateful therefore, if you were able to reflect on this example in your inquiry to establish clarity.

25 February 2009

Memorandum by the Society of County Treasurers

1. The Society of County Treasurers (SCT) comprises all Chief Financial Officers from the shire counties in English local government. Following the reorganisation of local government in 1997, the SCT expanded to include three shire unitary authorities that had similar vested interests in local government issues. Together, these authorities represent 48 per cent of the population of England and provide services across 87 per cent of its land area.

2. The Society would like to thank the Select Committee for this opportunity to submit evidence in relation to the Barnett Formula. This letter forms the Society's submission representing the combined views of the SCT membership.

NEED FOR REFORM

3. The Barnett System of allocating finance based on population was introduced in the run up to the planned devolution referendum in the late 1970s. The measure was only intended to be temporary until a more robust and permanent needs-based formula could be introduced. However, the methodology has been used for over 30 years to set public spending plans in the United Kingdom.

4. Its creator, Lord Barnett, himself pressed the Liaison Committee to establish an *ad hoc* select committee. Commenting on the continued use of the System, he told this Select Committee on 28 January 2009 "I do not consider it is successful. I do not think it is fair".

5. The Barnett System is advantageous to Scotland, Wales and Northern Ireland because not only are historic funding per capita levels above those of England locked in, but they also are free from Treasury scrutiny as they are free to allocate the funding as they see fit.

6. The Society believe a system that has no legal standing—it has never been brought before the House of Commons—nor democratic justification is in long-need of reform on a more robust basis.

CURRENT POPULATION FORMULA

7. At Spending Reviews HM Treasury, decides initial levels of spending, then any increase (or decrease) in public expenditure is distributed across the four nations, in proportion to their population. The formula determines the changes only when there are alterations to programmes that are comparable between England and the three devolved budgets. The amount added (or subtracted) also depends on the extent to which responsibilities "mirror" those in England. However, there is inevitably much discussion between departments as to what constitutes "comparable programmes".

8. A 1997 Treasury Committee on the Barnett Formula asserted that all Government expenditure should broadly reflect need. To this end, the Committee was disappointed that no Government in recent years had undertaken any evaluation of the Barnett Formula in relation to needs assessment.

9. The Society believe that in order for each area of the UK to provide the same standard of public services regardless of wealth or delivery costs for different services in different regions, a robust needs-based formula is required. This would of course be in line with the allocation mechanism used for local authorities in the United Kingdom. The currently implemented Barnett Formula does not directly reflect need beyond population resulting in a misguided idea that each region should achieve the same level of spending per head.

CONCERNS SURROUNDING OVER ALLOCATION IN SCOTLAND

10. The Formula does not determine the overall sizes of budgets (these are based on past allocations and decisions) instead the ratios apply only to the annual incremental expenditure. Therefore any perceived iniquity in the overall allocation is due to the historical levels of funding since these are by their very nature "locked-in" the system.

11. It is widely believed that reform of the Barnett Formula is long overdue as it over resources Scotland at the expense of other parts of the United Kingdom.

12. In his evidence to the Select Committee, Lord Barnett highlighted the diverging gap in expenditure per head between England and Scotland of £1,100 in 2002–03 to nearly £1,600 in 2007–08 (planned). This includes expenditure per head for Education, which has grown from a difference between England and Scotland of £170 per head in 2002–03 to £186 in 2007–08.[65] Divergence in expenditure per head between the two regions has been attributed to the divergence of population trends; an issue that the Barnett Formula has not taken into account.

13. A needs-quantifying exercise was last undertaken in the late 1970s when devolution was being considered under the repealed Scotland Act 1978 and the Wales Act 1978. Using data for 1977–78, the study found that to provide a standard level of service across the United Kingdom it would require spending differentials above England of 16 per cent in Scotland, 9 per cent in Wales and 31 per cent in Northern Ireland. At this time however, actual spending in Scotland was some 22 per cent higher than England, 6 per cent higher in Wales and 35 per cent higher in Northern Ireland. These figures are summarised in the following table.

Country	Using the Barnett Formula	Using the Needs Formula
	per capita spending above England	
Scotland	22%	16%
Wales	6%	9%
Northern Ireland	35%	31%

14. This would, if the research carried out in 1979 were still accurate, lead to immediate and substantial changes in provision for Wales, Scotland and Northern Ireland.

CONCLUSION

15. As part of the 2005 English Local Government Formula Review, the Government listed a number of aims for the resulting methodology, which the Society feels have relevance to the role of the Barnett Formula. These included:

— robust and fair; and

— for the purpose of a workable system, pragmatic.

16. Whilst there may be reasons for spending per head to be higher in Wales, Scotland and Northern Ireland, the SCT believe that allocating monies on a per capita basis is too crude a measure. Members support the option to replace the Barnett Formula with a full-scale needs assessment.

17. The Society agrees that whilst "fairness" is a difficult area in which to achieve consensus, there is growing concern over the divergence of expenditure per head in England and Scotland lending further support to the requirement for a needs-quantifying exercise.

18. The Society believes that, in order for each area of the United Kingdom to provide the same standard of public services regardless of wealth or delivery costs, a pragmatic needs-based formula is required.

The Society of County Treasurers looks forward to hearing the findings of the House of Lords Select Committee in the Barnett Formula.

5 March 2009

[65] *Source*: Public Expenditure Statistical Analyses 2008, HM Treasury.

Memorandum by the TaxPayers' Alliance

Are the present disparities in public expenditure per head of population between the countries of the UK a consequence of the Formula itself, the historic baseline or of other factors? To what extent are those disparities related to need?

1. The present disparities are in large part the consequence of the historic baseline.[66] In the case of Scotland, they resulted from the application of the so-called "Goschen proportions" introduced in 1888, which allocated Scotland a fixed proportion (13.75 per cent) of various public expenditures in England and Wales. That same proportion seems to have remained fixed for the best part of a century, even though Scotland's population share fell considerably through the period (by 1961 its population was only 11.2 per cent of that in England and Wales). Unsurprisingly, public expenditure per head in Scotland moved well ahead of England and Wales. In that sense, the disparity is an unfortunate historic legacy.

2. The persistence of the disparity over the last three decades reflects the failure of the Barnett Formula. When it was introduced in 1978, the Formula was supposedly going to reduce the disparity between Scotland and England. Yet the 2007–08 disparity of 28 per cent[67] disparity (identifiable spending excluding social protection) which was actually higher than the 22 per cent disparity the Treasury calculated for 1976–77.[68]

3. This disparity has not been driven by different needs, and there is no reason to think that it somehow reflects them. That point is underlined by the disparity between Scotland and some of the individual English regions. For example, Scotland gets 8 per cent higher per capita spending than North East England, but the latter has *per capita* income 15 per cent below Scotland.[69] The spending disparities in N Ireland and Wales have different historic origins, but there is similarly little reason to think they reflect differences in need.

What effect does the Barnett Formula have in terms of equity and fairness across the UK as a whole?

4. The Formula has failed to deliver the more equitable and fair allocation of spending originally envisaged. In particular, the promised "Barnett Squeeze" on higher spending in Scotland has not materialised. Over the last two decades (1985–86 to 2007–08), we calculate that higher spending in the three devolved territories relative to English spending levels has cost UK taxpayers a cumulative £200 billion:

— £102 billion in Scotland;

— £43 billion in Wales; and

— £57 billion in Northern Ireland.

5. In an era of devolved government, such spending gaps are impossible to justify to English taxpayers. They ask why they should subsidise higher Scottish, Welsh, and Irish spending? Why shouldn't those areas pay for their extra benefit themselves through higher local taxes? There is particular anger about the Scottish advantage because, whereas Northern Ireland's position is arguably justified on the basis of peace and reconstruction, there is no such case in Scotland.

6. On the question of fairness, it's also worth noting that Scotland's higher spending has not been funded by "Scotland's oil". Although this argument is often made, our calculations show that even ascribing 83 per cent of North Sea revenues to Scotland (the share currently claimed by the Scottish Government), oil would have funded the extra spending in only five of the last 23 years.[70]

What effect does the Barnett Formula have on the aggregate control of public expenditure?

7. On one level, the Barnett Formula ought to make the control of public spending easier. By providing the Westminster government with an automatic rule for allocating aggregate expenditure increases, it ought to reduce the scope for argument and spending creep. And as originally envisaged, it ought to squeeze spending in the devolved countries down to English levels. But in practice—as discussed below—the squeeze hasn't worked.

8. It is also doubtful that the Formula has contributed much to the control of aggregate spending. That's because Barnett is a key component in the UK's highly centralised system of taxation, which according to the OECD[71] is the most centralised tax system of any major developed economy in the world. In such a system, the recipients of public services are far removed from the taxpayers who finance them. Scotland's public

---

[66] For a fuller analysis of the issues and the background see TaxPayers' Alliance, Research Note 34—*Unequal Shares: The Barnett Formula*, 2008.
[67] HM Treasury, PESA 2008.
[68] HM Treasury, *Needs Assessment Study*—Report, 1979.
[69] Office for National Statistics, Gross Value Added at current basic prices by region.
[70] TPA Research Note 34—cited in 1.
[71] OECD: Fiscal Relations across Government Levels, 2003. Just 4 per cent of our taxes are both set and collected locally (and even this small proportion—essentially comprising Council Tax—is routinely subject to capping by Whitehall). And see the TPA Research Note 34, cited in 1.

spending premium is not financed directly and transparently by Scotland's taxpayers, but from a big central pot via the rather opaque operation of the Barnett formula.

9. Breaking the link between local service provision and accountability to local taxpayers ultimately makes public spending control more difficult. In the long-term, the key to effective control is efficiency and value for money, but under Barnett, local taxpayers have much less financial interest in ensuring local services deliver that.

Has convergence of levels of public spending in Scotland, Wales and Northern Ireland based on the English level of spending happened, and if not why?

10. In Scotland and Wales, published Treasury figures[72] point overwhelmingly to a lack of convergence. Between 1976–77 and 2007–08, the disparity between Scotland and England in identifiable spending per head (excluding social protection) actually increased (from 22 per cent[73] to 28 per cent).[74] And while there have been some changes in the scope and definition of the figures over the intervening period, the message is clear enough. In Wales, the figures show spending per head remaining in the range 10–20 per cent above English levels for the last two decades. Only in Northern Ireland do the published Treasury figures suggest some convergence, reflecting the peace process through the 1990s. But despite that, spending per head remains 30 per cent above the English level.

11. One reason that the Formula failed to deliver convergence is that its population ratio was frozen at its 1976 level, right up until 1992. In the intervening years, the Scottish population actually fell, so that the true ratio of Scotland's population to England's declined by more than one-half percentage point. And even though the Formula's population ratios are now updated annually, Scotland's population share has gone on falling, which reduces the speed at which the formula corrects Scotland's baseline advantage. Another reason is the so-called Formula by-pass, whereby certain additions to expenditure (eg some pay awards) have been allocated outside the Formula, to the advantage of the devolved governments. But this is not an area the TPA has researched in detail.

Do the advantages of the Formula as presently constituted outweigh its disadvantages?

12. No. The formula has failed to reduce the wide and unsupported disparities in spending.

Should the Barnett Formula be (a) retained in its current form, (b) amended or (c) replaced entirely?

13. The Formula should be replaced by a system that emphasises revenue rather than spending. The UK's public finance system is far too centralised, with for example, the devolved Scottish government relying on Whitehall for 86 per cent of its revenue.[75] In the long-term, we need a much greater degree of fiscal autonomy, with the devolved governments responsible for raising more of their own revenue. Replacing Barnett with a revenue sharing arrangement would be a first step in that direction.

Should the Barnett Formula be replaced by a system more adequately reflecting relative needs, costs of services or a combination of both? If so, what factors should be considered as part of a needs assessment?

14. Experience over many years with the local authority revenue support grant shows how difficult it is to agree an unambiguous definition of spending need. Even with the most sophisticated statistical techniques, the answers are often dependent on the prior definition of what constitutes need, and largely reflect the existing pattern of spending. While a revenue sharing arrangement would bring its own challenges, it would at least point us in the right long-term direction.

27 February 2009

---

[72] The Treasury now publishes annual estimates of identifiable spending in each of the devolved territories, as well as England. However, these were not published for the years prior to 1985–86. For summary of available data see Table 8.1 in Public Expenditure Statistical Analyses 2002–03, HM Treasury, May 2002.
[73] HM Treasury, *Needs Assessment Study*—Report, 1979.
[74] HM Treasury, PESA 2008.
[75] 2008–09 Spring Budget Revision, The Scottish Government, 2009.

Printed in the United Kingdom by The Stationery Office Limited
7/2009   429415   19585